MODEL ENGINEERING

General Editor, BERNARD E. JONES

WARNING

Remember that the materials and methods described here are from another era. Workers were less safety conscious then, and some methods may be downright dangerous. Be careful! Use good solid judgement in your work, and think ahead. Lindsay Publications Inc. has not tested these methods and materials and does not endorse them. Our job is merely to pass along to you information from another era. Safety is your responsibility.

MODEL ENGINEERING

A Guide to Model Workshop Practice

With Working Drawings of Engines,
Boilers, Rolling Stock, Cannon,
Electric Machines, etc. etc.

By

HENRY GREENLY

With 85 Photographs and
724 Line Drawings

CASSELL AND COMPANY, LTD
London, New York, Toronto and Melbourne

Model Engineering

by Henry Greenly

Originally published by
Cassell and Company Ltd
London, New York, Toronto & Melbourne
1915

Reprinted by
Lindsay Publications Inc
Bradley IL 60915

ISBN 1-55918-312-8

2004

1 2 3 4 5 6 7

EDITOR'S PREFACE

THIS book is the work of a thoroughly practical engineer possessing unequalled experience of model making, and it is addressed to the amateur desirous of learning how mechanical models, chiefly prime movers, operate and how they can be made in the home workshop. It fully describes the tool equipment necessary, shows how to use the tools and how to execute the numerous handcraft processes involved, and then enters into the details of steam, petrol and electric models; it shows the functions of the various parts, and explains, step by step, the actual amateur workshop methods of building them up, the reader being taken easily and gradually through the construction of every part and the assembling of the complete models, these including boilers, steam engines, internal-combustion engines, steam locomotives, electric locomotives, permanent ways, power hammers, cannon, etc., etc.

Almost the whole book is from the pen or drawing board of Mr. Henry Greenly, who has, however, at my suggestion, availed himself of a few illustrations and of a small amount of text contributed by other authors to "Work" (the penny weekly journal of Handicraft and Mechanics).

Particular attention is directed to the great number of working drawings of engines and other machines, details, accessory apparatus, etc., to be found in this book. The author has proceeded on the principle that the amateur's first need in seeking to understand any piece of mechanism is a good drawing of it. No similar book, if one exist, is so lavishly illustrated by actual drawings and photographs of the mechanisms described.

The model-engineering public, to whom the name of Henry Greenly is a household word, will appreciate a few notes on his career. He was apprenticed to a jeweller, in whose workshop he gained a knowledge of small tools and minor processes which was afterwards to stand him, as a model maker, in such good stead, and of which the early chapters of the present book are such an excellent reminder. But mechanical engineering was soon to claim him for her own, for he entered the Regent Street Polytechnic, London, as the winner of an L.C.C. scholarship which carried with it both practical and theoretical training. As a student, he assisted in the building of a quarter-full-size model locomotive, and on the completion of his Polytechnic course he went to the Metropolitan Railway works as locomotive, carriage and wagon draghtsman, being promoted, two years later, to be assistant to the surveyor and architect. His experience was now richly increased by an insight into land surveying, building, and civil engineering, knowledge to be applied in due course in the laying out and building of miniature railways in Great Britain and in parts of the Continent. Mr. Greenly is the designer of certain parts of models upon which the universal standard practice is now based; and the results of his helpful interest are to be traced in almost every department of model-engineering work. It is particularly gratifying to know that, although in the Pre-War days the bulk of the shop-built model engines sold in Great Britain had been "made in Germany," the greater part of them—whether British or German—had been designed by the author of this present work.

Mr. Greenly's instructions are extremely clear and readily understandable; but if, here and there, there is a point upon which a reader needs further enlightenment, all he need do is to state his case concisely to "Work," in whose columns (but *not* by post) its model-engineering adviser, Mr. Greenly, will cheerfully supply the required help.

B. E. J.

La Belle Sauvage,
London, E.C.

CONTENTS

MODEL ENGINEERING

CHAPTER I

THE EQUIPMENT OF A MODEL ENGINEER'S WORKSHOP

THE equipment of a model workshop after the manner common to most amateurs, that is, the gradual acquisition of the numerous tools required, must be considered from many points of view. Naturally, it depends somewhat on the size and situation of the workshop itself, and on the character of the work proposed to be done.

The Position of the Workshop. — Whether the workshop is to be inside or outside the house cannot always be determined by the fact that in an inside workshop the ravages of our damp atmosphere are not so apparent. The home mechanic is usually an evening worker. His labours may continue beyond the usual hours of the retirement of his nearer neighbours, and the tap, tap, tap of the hammer and the screech of the file do not always meet with their full appreciation. The model-maker is often banished to the attic, which particular room, if not especially prepared, is likely to be rather warm in summer and cold in winter, a state of things that can be improved at small expense by lining the rafters with thin match-boarding. Usually the question of light is a serious problem in the case of attic workshops. The reader should always choose an inside workshop, if the other circumstances mentioned are favourable.

In some houses there may be a conservatory that can be converted for the purpose; if it is on the northern side, it will not be too hot or too brilliantly lighted, and the prevalent rainy "south-westers" will not beat on its window-panes. The writer's workshop is of this type.

Planning a Workshop.—The space available for the workshop is shown on the plan (Fig. 2), and the photograph (Fig. 1) clearly depicts its equipment. The other part of the conservatory is used for horticultural purposes; but not in such a way as to produce the warm and humid atmosphere of the hothouse. Except for broken panes and a heavy rain after a prolonged drought, no trouble has been experienced in the matter of dampness. Tools are carefully greased if the shop has to be left for a prolonged period, and, of course, need a few minutes' cleaning before resuming work.

The space used is not more than 7 ft. 6 in. by 8 ft. 9 in., and it is so arranged that a friend can come in and assist without overcrowding.

Two vices are fitted, one heavy one and one light one, at the fitting or assembling bench. The lathe is between. The position for the large vice was, however, more or less settled by the presence of a good post. The forge is in the darkest corner, although with both top and side light no place is really dark. However, in choosing the position for a soldering and brazing hearth or forge, a dark situation is desirable, as, especially in the case of silver-soldering and brazing, a bright outside light would prevent the operator readily judging the heat of the work. This is a small but important matter.

Another point is the top shelving. This is not a board or plank shelf, which would be likely to accumulate small things, dust and other rubbish. It is made up of slats, thus compelling the worker to store his scrap metal, tubes, fittings, and other items dear to all model-makers in boxes, while large tools such as planes for woodworking, which are seldom used, may be placed on the shelves quite safely. In the spaces between the shelves hammers and the like are hung. Always avoid working on a bench littered with small tools. The tools get mislaid and their edges injured, which is impossible if the tools are put back in their proper places—a habit easily acquired. Of course, the accumulation of some of the tools on the bench is often unavoidable, and to accommodate them it is well to provide one or two small trays (lids of tin boxes) each fixed on a wooden or metal post fastened to the bench, so that the tray is 4 in. or 5 in. above the bench (see Fig. 3). On this tray may be

Fig. 1.—Interior of a model engineer's workshop

safely laid any small parts or screws which may be taken from or prepared for a model, clear of the tools lying on the bench.

Of course, if the space on the western side marked " not

usable " in Fig. 2 is represented by a wall, the lathe may be moved along and the bench extended to this wall. The heavy vice would then be placed at the right-hand end of the lathe, and still provide plenty of room for two workers,

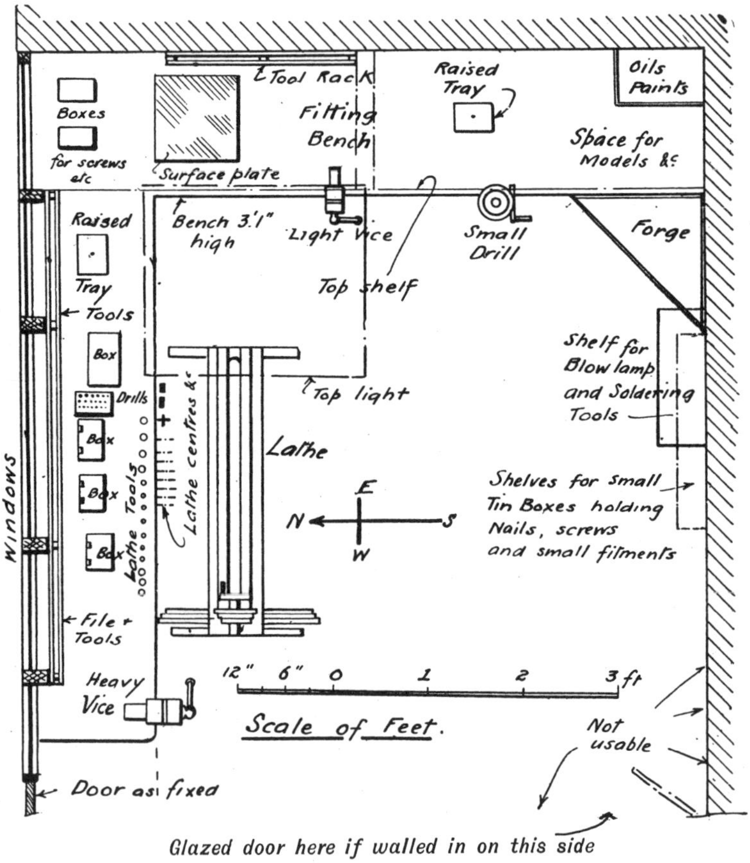

Fig. 2.—Plan of workshop

one of whom may be moving to and from the lathe as occasion may require. What would be the western wall may then be used for nails supporting lathe fitments, such as change wheels and faceplates, which the writer now hangs in front of the lathe on the mullions of the windows. In any case, the door is best placed at the south-westerly corner. This will enable the most use to be made of both wall space and floor area. The fitting bench being on the northern and eastern walls receives the best light. Of course, the writer has top light as well as the front windows. In arranging the windows, if they are not continuous and cover the whole wall, they should be placed near to the ends, so that there are no dark corners. A large window in front of the lathe and two others extending to within 6 in. of the end posts are to be recommended, together with a good top light over the eastern bench, if possible vertically in line with the light vice and the end of the lathe, as shown by the dotted lines in Fig. 2.

The Work Bench. — The arrangement of the work bench must depend on the construction of the shop. If the floor is of concrete, then the supporting posts of 3-in. by 3-in. section may be let into the ground without any further fixing, care always being taken to fix posts in positions where hammering is likely to take place. The remainder of the framing for the bench may be of 3-in. by 2-in. battens, the planking, which should be $1\frac{1}{4}$ in. or 1 in. thick in front and $\frac{3}{4}$ in. behind, being screwed or nailed on the top. Fig. 4 shows the arrangement of the bench behind the lathe in the writer's workshop. The outer longitudinal timber is placed on edge, and the cross-bearers flatwise, the latter being mortised and tenoned into the outer timber at one end, and supported on the wall at the other. On the top of the cross-bearers, inside the edge timber, a single 9-in. plank of $\frac{3}{4}$-in. deal should be fixed, the inside edge having a bead nailed to it to prevent tools and small fitments being pushed off on to the floor. Behind this bench is a long tool rack, made by nailing two 2-in. by 1-in. battens together, with a $\frac{5}{8}$-in. space between them, packing blocks or distance pieces being placed between the battens at frequent intervals. This rack is fitted to the cross-bearers; but experience has shown that it is not entirely satisfactory. Where tools have identical handles it is difficult to pick out in a moment the one required, it being necessary to lift the tool until the point is exposed. To get over this difficulty, the rack may be raised by making the back board 5 in. or 6 in. deep, as shown in Fig. 4.

Fig. 5 shows the plan of the timber frame for the bench, and provides for an extra post between the light vice and the hand drilling machine. This is an improvement which the writer finds necessary in his own shop, as a bench anvil is installed at this point. The bench behind the lathe should be a little higher than the fitting bench, and the outer timbers may therefore be easily carried across each other with a half lap joint.

When the workshop is inside the house (more especially upstairs), the post supporting the heavy vice should be at least 4 in. by 4 in., and to transmit the pressure over as large a number of joists as possible the bottom of the post should terminate in a balk of wood, say 3 in. by 6 in. section, laid flatwise and as long as can be conveniently fitted in the space available. Indeed, this timber might be continued under the back feet of the lathe standards, similar pieces being fitted under the front feet, as shown in Fig. 6. This will, of course, increase the height of the lathe; but in the case of the Drummond 3½-in. centre lathe more particularly, this will be found an advantage. If a layer of felt is placed between the 3-in. by 6-in. timbers and the floor, the noise which attends the use of the lathe and vice will be to a large extent deadened. In the case of the vice, the heavier post and the flat timber underneath it will absorb the blows of the hammer much more effectively.

The edge timber of the bench behind the lathe is used to hold lathe centres, tools, and other fitments which are constantly required in turning (see Fig. 2). For the centres and tailstock chucks and pads, holes are bored at an angle in the face of the 3-in. by 2-in. edge timber, as shown in Fig. 7, and similar vertical holes in the top to hold the lathe tools. For the spanners and chuck turnscrew, ordinary nails are driven into the face, as shown in Fig. 8. The latter arrangement has worked quite well with the spanners, but with the chuck turnscrew it has been found better to tie it to the lathe bed with a piece of string.

The use of the mullions of the window in front of the

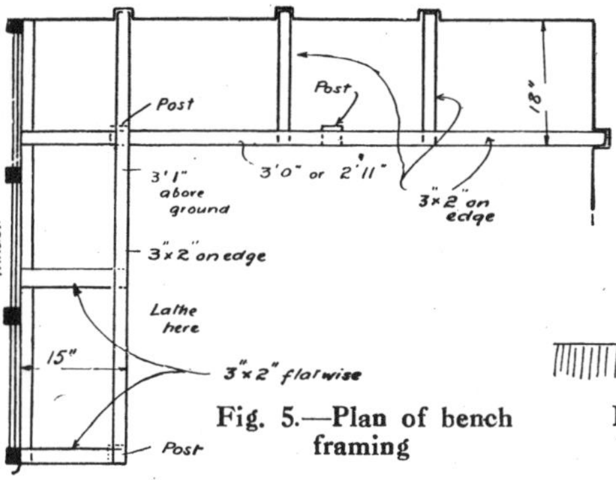

Fig. 5.—Plan of bench framing

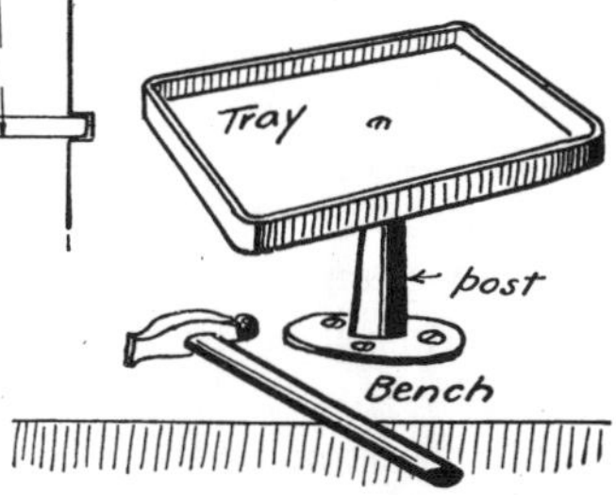

Fig. 3.—Raised tray to serve as rack for small pieces of work.

Fig. 8.—Method of hanging lathe spanners, etc.

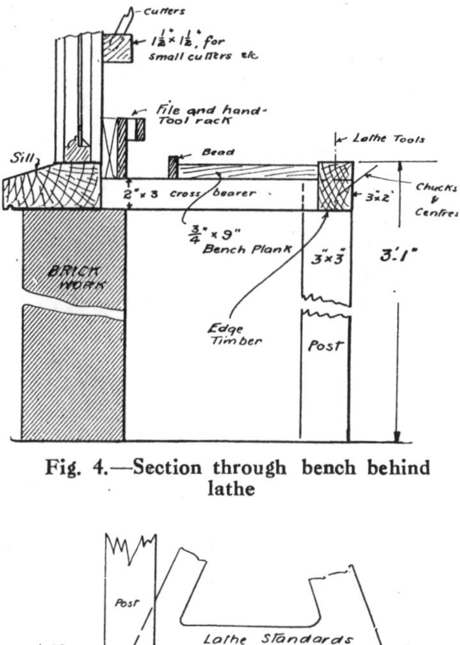

Fig. 4.—Section through bench behind lathe

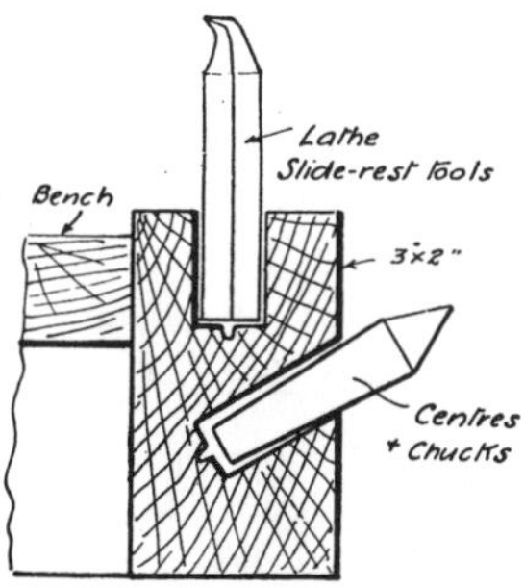

Fig. 7.—Section through edge timber of bench behind lathe

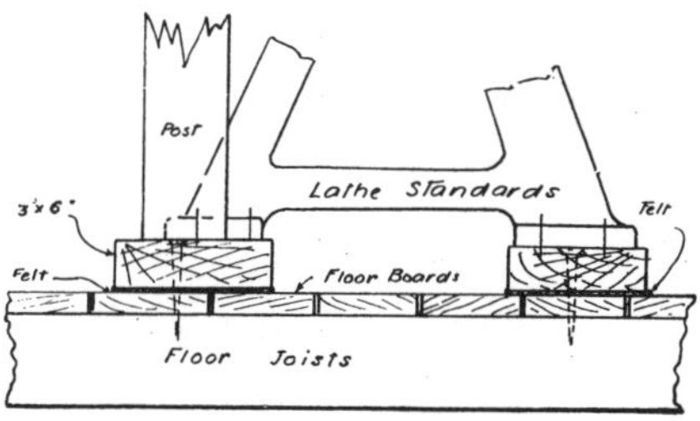

Fig. 6.—Blocks under lathe and vice posts for an upstairs workshop

lathe for hanging the change wheels has already been mentioned, but the window frame also provides for another fixture. A piece of $1\frac{1}{2}$-in. sq. hard wood, shown in the photograph (Fig. 1), is fixed across two mullions just above the tool rack. This is bored with inclined holes from the top, and holds reamers, broaches, and the small cutters used in a patent lathe tool-holder.

The section of the fitting bench is shown by Fig. 9. This is wider than the one behind the lathe, and also heavier, the front plank being $1\frac{1}{4}$ in. or 1 in. thick, and the one behind of $\frac{3}{4}$-in. wood, both being 9 in. wide. The tool rack, which holds only the shorter files and tools, is placed on the wall behind, well above the bench level. In arranging this rack, the back should be a thin piece of wood, say $\frac{1}{2}$ in. or $\frac{3}{8}$ in., about 6 in. deep, and on it two strips $1\frac{1}{4}$ in. deep by $\frac{3}{8}$ in. thick should be nailed, the back one being flat on the 6-in. piece, and the front strip planted on with suitable packing blocks at the end and centre, so as to leave a slot $\frac{1}{2}$ in. wide. The inside strip is used to keep the handle of the tools as far away from the wall as possible. If they are too near they are less easy to get hold of.

The top shelf is placed not less than 5 ft. 10 in. above the ground level—at any rate, it must be clear of the worker's forehead—and should be about 1 ft. 4 in. wide. So long as it is used for light articles, a single central bracket made up of 2-in. by $\frac{3}{4}$-in. stuff should suffice, with, of course, a fixing at each end. The slats of the shelf in the writer's shop are the same section, with $1\frac{1}{2}$-in. spaces between them. The wall behind the fitting bench may be used to hold larger tools, and also tube, rod, and strip material, and coils of wire, as illustrated in the photograph (Fig. 1). The white card shown on the wall in this picture is a table of screw threads and tapping sizes, which have been cut out of a workshop handbook and pasted on a stiff piece of strawboard. To preserve the card it should be sized and given a coat of best paper varnish.

Bench Fitments.—Tin boxes are used on the benches to hold small screwing tackle, strips of metal for packing up lathe-tools, faceplate dogs and bolts. These boxes will retain any oil that is sprinkled over the tools to prevent rust. A box is kept for odd and broken drills, the regular set of drills being kept point upwards in a block of wood drilled with holes for each drill. In purchasing drills, if the expense of a full set is to be avoided, it is best to obtain all the regular sizes by 32nds up to $\frac{5}{16}$ in. in diameter, and

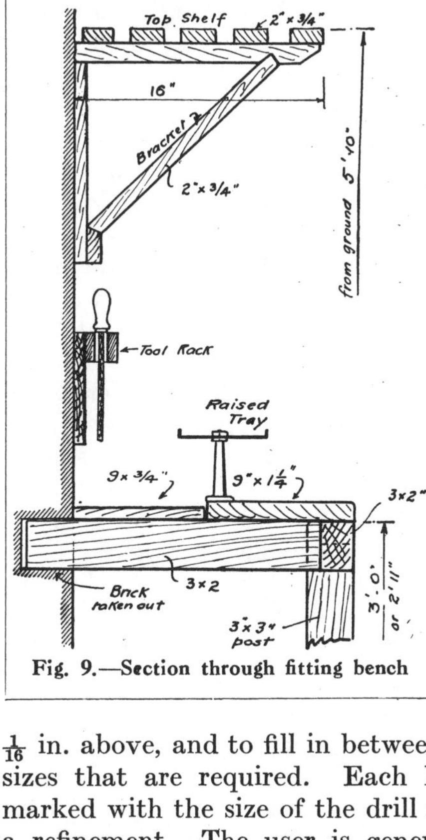

Fig. 9.—Section through fitting bench

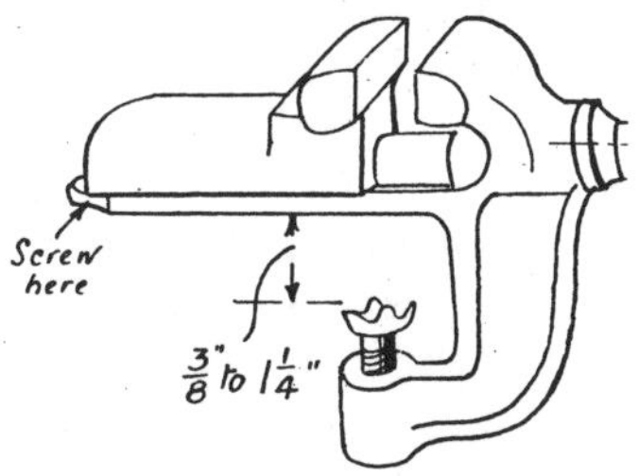

Fig. 10.—Table vice, fixed by turnscrew from underneath

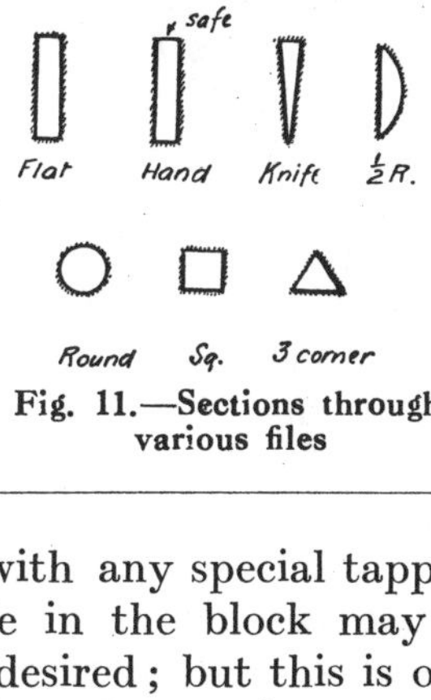

Fig. 11.—Sections through various files

$\frac{1}{16}$ in. above, and to fill in between with any special tapping sizes that are required. Each hole in the block may be marked with the size of the drill if desired; but this is only a refinement. The user is generally able to pick out the required drill without any such marking.

With regard to the surface plate, the writer finds that a piece of $\frac{5}{16}$-in. plate-glass serves his purpose quite efficiently. A very small iron plate of the proper type used by engineers is hardly any use for marking out, and a large one will be found a very expensive accessory. The accuracy of a sheet of really good plate-glass is all that a model-maker can desire.

Workshop Tools. — In addition to the lathe and its accessories, which will be dealt with later, the following is a list of the most desirable tools for a model-maker's workshop, arranged more or less in the order they may be acquired. There is no need to mention any particular dealer ; in the proprietary articles such as Morse and Standard companies' drills, Swedish blow-lamps, self-centre chucks, the quality is usually assured by the respective manufacturers' names and trade marks. However, to return to the list of tools. (1) vice, parallel type ; (2) files, general assortment ; (3) drills ; (4) hand drill (geared) ; (5) soldering-bit and kindred tools ; (6) screwdrivers ; (7) hack-saw ; (8) measuring tools ; (9) metal shears ; (10) pliers and hand vices ; (11) broaches ; (12) hammers ; (13) punches and chisels ; (14) screwing tackle ; (15) lathe with faceplate and centres ; (16) carriers and faceplate dogs ; (17) hand tools ; (18) slide-rest tools ; (19) self-centre chuck ; (20) chasers ; (21) accessories for the back headstock ; (22) blow-lamp or gas blowpipe and bellows ; (23) machine vice ; (24) shaper or planer and tools ; (25) drilling machine ; (26) milling appliances for lathe ; (27) special hand tools suitable for larger model work only and to particular branches.

The tools referred to under the first half of this list are really necessary to enable the amateur to make any sort of a beginning in model-engineering work, and as some of the headings involve several tools, an assortment more suited to immediate needs must be selected.

In the case of the vice, the heavier it is the better. A very small vice can be added as an extra accessory, this somewhat depending on the range of work to be done. There are many patterns of vices to be had. The old leg vice is still favoured by many ; but unless there is a lot of heavy hammering to be done in the vice, what is known as a "parallel" vice, with jaws at least 3 in. wide, will suit the amateur much better. The "Parkinson" firm make a very good range of plain, strong parallel vices (see Fig. 12) ; the name is well known in connection with the "instantaneous grip" vices, in which the operator has a trigger which releases the screw, and immediately extends the vice jaws to any required size within the capacity of the vice, the final grip being given by the hand lever in the usual way. These vices, however, cost over double that of the plain ones.

If it is not possible to instal even a plain parallel vice of the heavy type, there are several types of what are known as amateur bench or "table" vices on the market. These have parallel jaws, but have the disadvantage of being fixed to the work-bench by a turnscrew from underneath. Usually there is not more than from $\frac{3}{8}$-in. to $1\frac{1}{4}$-in. range in the screw (see Fig. 10), and if fitted to a bench similar to that described, the 2-in. by 3-in. edge timber must be notched down, and thereby weakened. In the writer's shop one of these vices is the light vice mentioned, and cutting down was found necessary. This is also one reason for fitting a vertical post near to this vice as already recommended. Only vices that have provision for a screw or screws into the top of the table or bench should be employed. The best position for one of these vices is really on the edge of a good, wide $1\frac{1}{4}$-in. plank bench.

Fig. 12.—Good type of parallel vice

Files.—These may be procured in innumerable patterns and sizes (see Fig. 11). English files, which are useful for all ordinary work, have three cuts—"bastard," "second-cut," and "smooth." Second-cut and smooth should be chosen for model work. The usual size is 8 in. or 9 in.; but, if desired, one or two 10-in. may be added. The shape most useful to the model-maker is the hand or "parallel" file, which has one "safe edge," that is, an edge without cutting teeth. Other shapes are the flat, in which the blade tapers to the end, and which is employed for ordinary filing. The pillar file, which is of oblong section, but with perfectly parallel sides both in width and thickness, is used for slotting. The half-round, round, square, and three-cornered files are useful shapes; but in model work may be (at first) restricted to the quality of file known as the "Swiss" file. There is a greater variety in the cuts of these files; in the hand file, in which, by the way, the blade does not taper in width, the cuts obtainable vary from No. 00 to No. 6, the finest; but No. 6 cut is the same in one length as in another. In English files, the "bastard" cut is quite different in a 14-in. file from what it is in a 6-in. The cut is coarser as the files get bigger.

As an amateur may find it difficult to make a suitable selection out of the many that offer themselves, the following list of useful sizes may be welcomed :—

Selection of Files for the Model-Maker

English Files

1 Flat..	.. 9	in.	.. Second-cut
1 Flat..	.. 9	in.	.. Smooth
1 Hand	.. 8	in.	.. Second-cut
1 Hand	.. 8	in.	.. Smooth
1 Hand	.. 7	in.	.. Second-cut
1 Half-round..	8	in.	.. Second-cut
1 Three-corner	7	in.	.. Second-cut

Swiss Files

1 Hand or pottance	6	in.	.. No. 1 cut
1 ,, ,,	6	in.	.. No. 4 cut
1 ,, ,,	6	in.	.. No. 6 cut
1 Half-round..	6	in.	.. No. 2 cut
1 Round	.. 6	in.	.. No. 2 cut
1 Round	.. 4½	in.	.. No. 3 cut
1 Square	.. 4½	in.	.. No. 3 cut
1 Three-cornered	4½	in.	.. No. 3 cut
1 Knife-edge..	6	in.	.. No. 3 cut

The "Dreadnought" files, a brand in which the teeth are cut like a milling cutter, are very good where aluminium, copper, or other similar soft metals have to be worked. They have the advantage that they do not clog.

Drills.—There are three main types of drills suited to model work. The first is the diamond-pointed drill (Fig. 13); in a general way this is very good, especially in very small sizes and where expense is an object. These drills are sold in sets, and are sometimes called jeweller's drills; and for a dozen of the smallest diameters are well worth the sixpence or eightpence they cost. Always buy round-shank drills. In larger sizes this type of drill is very useful, and is much employed by iron-workers. Where a special size is required it may be forged from round or square tool steel.

Twist drills are the most commonly used for nearly

Fig. 13.—Diamond-pointed drill

Fig. 17.—Home-made screwdriver

Fig. 14.—Parallel-shank twist drill

Fig. 15.—Taper-shank twist drill

Fig. 16.—Straight-fluted drill

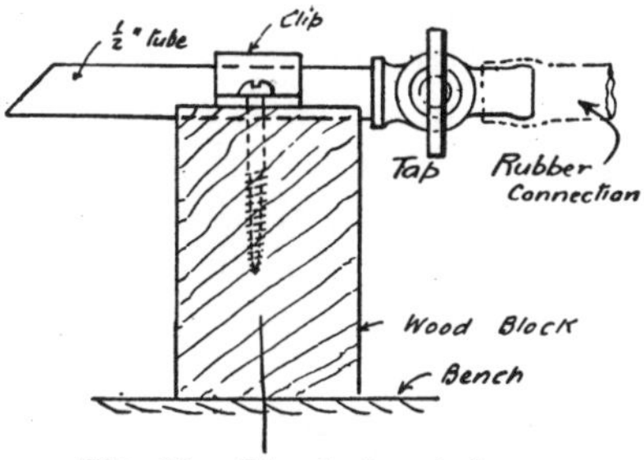

Fig. 22.—Simple bench burner

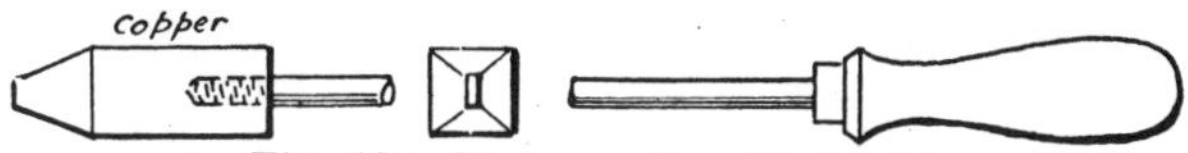

Fig. 18.—Home-made soldering-bit

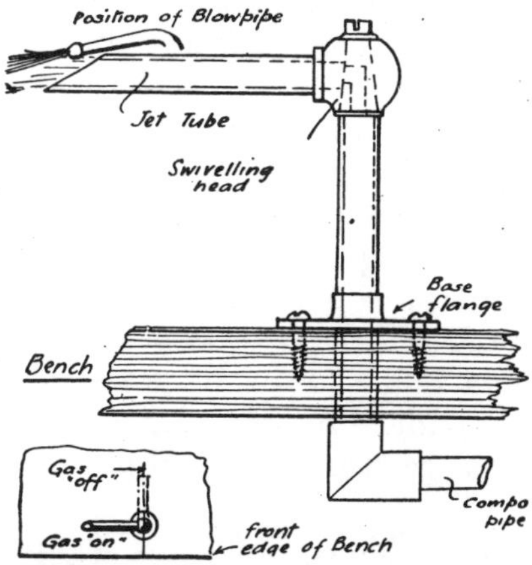

Fig. 21.—Swivelling bench soldering gas-burner

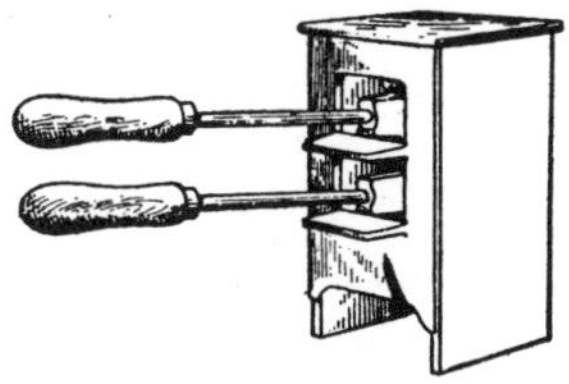

Fig. 20.—Gas-stove for heating soldering-bits

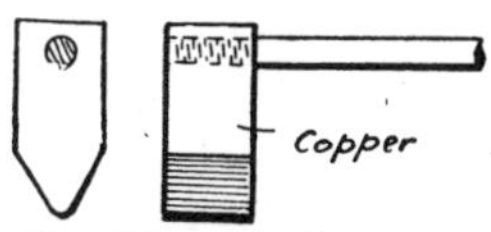

Fig. 19.—Hatchet-type soldering-bit

all purposes nowadays, and a suitable range for a model-maker is as follows :—$\frac{1}{16}$ in., $\frac{5}{64}$ in., $\frac{3}{32}$ in., $\frac{7}{64}$ in., $\frac{1}{8}$ in., $\frac{9}{64}$ in., $\frac{5}{32}$ in., $\frac{3}{16}$ in., $\frac{7}{32}$ in., $\frac{1}{4}$ in., $\frac{5}{16}$ in., $\frac{3}{8}$ in., with No. 56, No. 50, No. 40, No. 31, No. 17, No. 11, No. D, and No. N for the Whitworth tapping sizes, and possibly clearing sizes tabulated on page 22. For $\frac{3}{16}$ in. tapping size a $\frac{9}{64}$ in. drill is employed. These sizes are for Whitworth standard threads. The B.A. (British Association metrical) threads require a different range of drills. Lists are given in most tool catalogues.

Twist drills if used in brass—in plate and sheet stuff more particularly—will be found to " grab " the work, and therefore a variety known as the " straight-fluted " (*see* Fig. 16) are to be recommended. These do not grab like twist drills, but in deep holes they require more frequent withdrawal to clear the point from chippings and to prevent seizing. In drilling brass with either twist or straight-fluted drills, the drill should be withdrawn at every $\frac{1}{4}$ in. or $\frac{3}{16}$ in. of advance, otherwise the chippings will be compressed, and cause the drill to seize and break in the hole.

In purchasing twist and straight-fluted drills, especially in the smaller sizes, it should be remembered that the short variety, stocked by the best tool dealers, is less liable to break when used by inexperienced amateurs.

Hand drills are numerous in design, and are obtainable at various prices from 6d. each. The cheapest form is the Archimedean drill, which has a helical or screw shank, on which is a large nut. The movement of this nut up and down revolves the drill. Improved patterns have arrangements which prevent the drill turning in a backward direction on the up stroke ; or in the case of one sort, the drill cuts in both directions. However, if 4s. or more is to be expended, it is better to buy a " Millers Falls " type of geared hand drill, with a handle at the side. As a rule, the drills supplied with these hand drills are of no practical use except for wood.

Screwdrivers need little or no description ; for engineers' use the oval handle is most comfortable to use. For small work, jeweller's swivel-handle screwdrivers are very good tools to use. A handy form of screwdriver for model work is shown in Fig. 17. It may be made by fixing a wheel or other disc about $1\frac{1}{4}$ in. to $1\frac{1}{2}$ in. in diameter at the end of a piece of $\frac{1}{8}$-in. to $\frac{3}{16}$-in. silver-steel rod. The length of the rod may be from 6 in. to 8 in. Two sizes, $\frac{1}{8}$ in. by 6 in. and $\frac{3}{16}$ in. by 8 in., are recommended.

Soldering Accessories. — A soldering-bit (often miscalled an "iron") is an indispensable article to the model-maker, and is, of course, usable only for soft or tinman's solder, and on objects which require the heat to be applied locally. There are two patterns, both of which the model-maker is advised sooner or later to get; the straight type

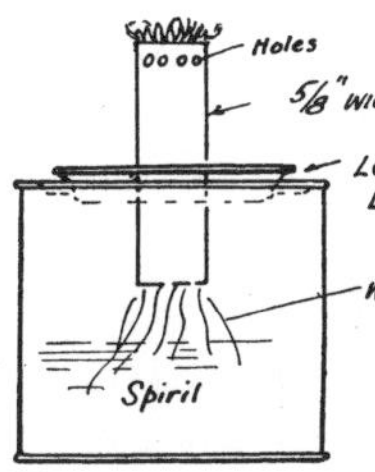

Fig. 23. — Home-made spirit lamp for soldering

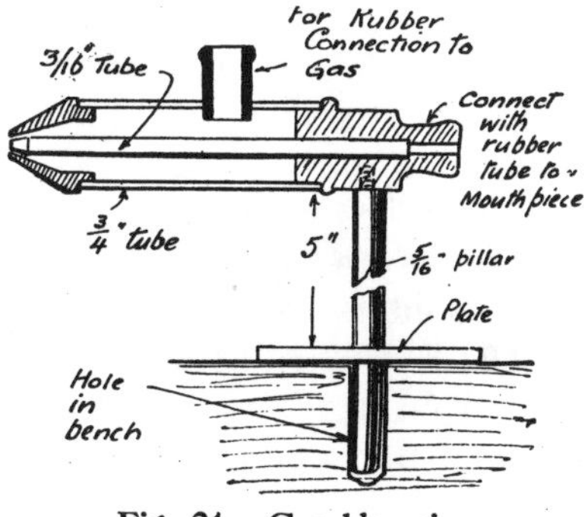

Fig. 24.—Gas blowpipe

(Fig. 18), of which not less than 8-oz. or 10-oz. size should be obtained, and the hatchet (Fig. 19), the 4-oz. or 6-oz. size of which will suffice if the larger straight copper bit is also obtained. Two bits are very useful in doing a large job, as the work can then be arranged to progress continuously; one bit is heating whilst the other is being used. Of course, a copper bit suitable for lighter work can be easily made if a piece of copper, say, $\frac{1}{2}$ in. by $\frac{1}{2}$ in. by $1\frac{1}{2}$ in. long, is obtained. It should be drilled and tapped for a piece of $\frac{3}{16}$-in. steel rod 12 in. long, either in the end or in the side, and a handle fitted at the other end.

A useful means for heating soldering-bits is a gas-stove (Fig. 20) arranged for two bits. Such a method has the advantage of keeping the soldering-bits clean, and also the heat may be easily regulated.

The mouth blowpipe is an inexpensive appliance that is most useful for both hard and soft soldering, and with either gas or a methylated-spirit flame. The best form of gas bracket is one having a horizontal swivelling arm, and screwed to the bench by a flange, as shown in Fig. 21. The swivelling head is also a cock, which shuts off the gas when the jet arm is pushed over at right angles to the edge of the bench, as indicated, and the gas is connected by an iron or compo pipe under the bench. A second gas tap should be arranged in the supply to regulate the amount of gas, and for reasons of safety. A simple device (see Fig. 22) may be made by any amateur, and connected to a rubber-pipe connecting head on the gas bracket supplying light to the bench and workshop. A methylated wick lamp may be easily made out of a small "self-opening" canister, as shown in Fig. 23. The holes near the top increase the efficiency of the flame.

Soft solders melt at temperatures between, say, 350° F. and 650° F. Hard solders require red heat, and are usually arranged to melt only just below the fusing point of the material being operated on.

For soft solder either the bit or blowpipe may be employed. On large sheet-metal work the bit is the handier, as the heat must be applied locally; for pipe, small fittings, and other work which can be held in the hand or pliers, the blowpipe is to be preferred, and the solder may then be applied in small $\frac{1}{8}$-in. or $\frac{3}{32}$-in. squares before the work is heated. This is more or less necessary, as both hands are occupied holding the work and operating the blowpipe.

A design of gas blowpipe which leaves one hand free is shown by Fig. 24. This enables the worker to apply the solder to the work (holding the end of a strip against it), after it has been brought to the melting heat of the solder. The blowpipe is arranged so that it can be held in the hand or dropped into a hole in the bench.

Soft solder requires either a zinc chloride, resin, or paste flux. Resin is the only safe flux which can be allowed on fine electric-wiring work, as, although it is not such a "ready" or quick-acting flux, it is not a corrosive, and will not subsequently detrimentally affect the work. There are several paste solders on the market, which have certain merits and are favoured by many model-makers. Zinc chloride, commonly called "killed spirits," is, however, a very good liquid flux. It may be bought in bottles under various names, but can be made at home quite easily. Obtain some commercial hydrochloric acid (muriatic acid), and place in a gallipot or old cup. Throw in zinc cuttings or chips, and put somewhere whence the noxious fumes the mixture emits can get away. When the action has ceased, and the acid will not combine with any more zinc, decant off into a clean bottle, add a small quantity of sal-ammoniac, and dilute the whole with about 50 per cent. of water. A short heavy bottle about 3 in. or 4 in. high is best for bench use, the flux being applied with a piece of wood, say a wooden meat-skewer: an open dish is sometimes used in place of a bottle. In any case, soldering and soldering tackle should be kept as far away from other work (and steel tools) as possible.

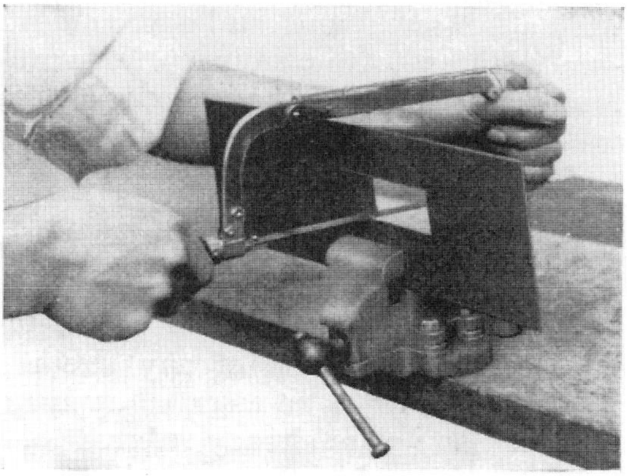

Fig. 25.—Side cutting with hack-saw

Hard soldering embraces operations known as brazing and silver-soldering respectively. Model-makers should reserve brazing for iron and steel objects, the solder being "brazing spelter," an alloy of copper (brass), which can be obtained in various degrees of fineness. The best form is brazing wire, as this is more easily applied. For copper, brass, and german silver, silver alloys are best used as solder. The flux for silver-soldering and brazing is borax.

Hack-Saws.—Item No. 7 in the list is hack-saws. A "Star" frame may be obtained from about 1s. 3d., but most extensible frames are dearer. The "Star" frame will take the blades in two directions, the position for side-cutting being shown in the photograph (Fig. 25) herewith. The 9-in. size is recommended, and also, for model-making, saws with twenty and eighteen teeth per inch. The advantage of the extensible frame is that broken saws may be used up; the fractured end of the saw may be softened in a flame, and a hole punched or drilled in it. For very fine work a fret-saw frame can be recommended, and thin blades—in addition to the ordinary fret-saws—can be used in a frame of this kind. Cheap bent-wire frames are obtainable, which will hold 6-in. fine saw blades $\frac{1}{4}$ in. by ·014 in. thick and with No. 30 pitch teeth.

Measuring Tools.—Measuring appliances should include inside and outside callipers, metal square, 4-in. or 6-in. rule, 12-in. rule, 3-in. centre punch, and, if much woodwork is done, a carpenter's wooden 2-ft. rule. For marking off model-engine work of any size a scribing block (*see* Fig. 90, page 52) is an essential appliance, coupled with the piece of plate-glass already referred to.

The 4-in. rule is a convenient size for the waistcoat pocket. Chesterman's No. 321D pattern in 4 in. and 6 in. gives spanner and tapping sizes for Whitworth screws on one edge, and $\frac{1}{32}$, $\frac{1}{64}$, and $\frac{1}{16}$ divisions of inches on the other. The handiest 12-in. rule is No. 378D, which has millimetre dimensions on one edge, and inches divided into $\frac{1}{16}$, $\frac{1}{32}$, and $\frac{1}{64}$ths on the other.

Callipers for model-makers need not be larger than $3\frac{1}{2}$ in. or 4 in., and good English-made callipers compare very favourably with those of American manufacture, although the latter are made with all kinds of convenient devices and useful attachments. If the model-maker has no dividers among his drawing instruments, then a pair may be added to the workshop equipment, should the occasion require them. Of course, both scribing block, complete set of callipers, squares, etc., are more useful to the worker who makes fairly large models and has a lathe. In such work the same methods of marking out and setting up adopted in real practice are employed. Indeed, the work is really engineering in miniature. To the other amateur, whose materials are scrap brass, tinplate, and steel rod, and whose tools comprise only a vice, hand drill, hammer, and a few files, such instruments are largely superfluous.

Centre Punches.—For general marking out and for centre-popping work preparatory to drilling, centre punches are required. These can be made from round tool steel, and for model work $\frac{5}{16}$-in. stuff should be big enough. Pieces $3\frac{1}{2}$ in. long should be cut off and shaped as shown in **Fig. 26.** The point should be $\frac{5}{32}$ in. or $\frac{1}{8}$ in. in diameter, and the angle

Fig. 26.—Centre punch

Fig. 27.—Hollow punch for driving round-headed pins

about 60°. The punch will require hardening by heating to a white-red heat and plunging in cold water. Then, for tempering, brighten the point and let down, heating the top until the point turns a dark straw colour. A larger size may be made out of $\frac{7}{16}$-in. or $\frac{3}{8}$-in. tool steel rod with a point $\frac{7}{32}$ in. or $\frac{3}{16}$ in. in diameter.

Automatic centre punches, while rather expensive, are extremely useful for marking out as well as for other purposes.

Hollow punches (Fig. 27) are useful for driving small round-headed pins (gimp pins) used in model railway permanent way and woodwork. To form the semicircular sinking in the end, first countersink with the point of a drill, and then place the end of the punch on a very small steel ball (as used in ball bearings) and give it a smart blow with a hammer. True up and finish the end off, and then harden and temper the punch past the dark straw to the blue colour. For instructions on hardening and tempering, *see* pages 77 and 78.

Screwing Tackle.—In the matter of screwing tackle the best is the cheapest in the long run. The old Lancashire screwplates and taps at about 1s. 6d. a set are to be avoided, the threads not being as a rule standard and the square taps not cutting easily or well. Good quality standard thread screwplates are obtainable, either in the B.A. or Whitworth threads, of the well-known "Reliable" series. The better screwing tackle costing a trifle more per set of three threads is to be recommended. It has circular spring dies which are separate and are adjustable, and the stock is provided

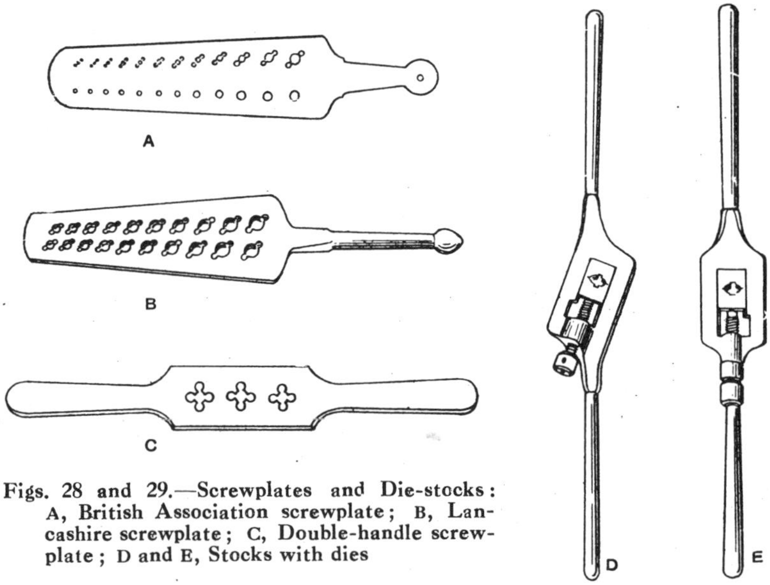

Figs. 28 and 29.—Screwplates and Die-stocks: A, British Association screwplate; B, Lancashire screwplate; C, Double-handle screwplate; D and E, Stocks with dies

with three set-screws. The centre one engages the split in the die, and if screwed up opens the die. The other screws tend to close it, and with the three screws a slightly different diameter is obtainable. It often occurs in model-making that either a tight or loose screw is required, and by this means the desired result may be accomplished. The most useful sizes are $\frac{1}{16}$ in., $\frac{3}{32}$ in., $\frac{1}{8}$ in., $\frac{5}{32}$ in., $\frac{3}{16}$ in., $\frac{7}{32}$ in. and $\frac{1}{4}$ in. Extra taps and dies are obtainable. The older type of adjustable stocks and dies is to be recommended for larger sizes, that is, above $\frac{1}{4}$ in.

The British Association thread is suitable for small model work, but, while screws, taps and dies are readily obtainable, small hexagonal-headed model engine studs, bolts and nuts are not, as far as the writer knows, supplied by model-dealers. The B.A. thread gives a stronger screw than the Whitworth, and is used exclusively for electrical instrument and similar work. It was primarily designed for small sizes ranging below a $\frac{1}{4}$-in. diameter. (Strictly speaking, the

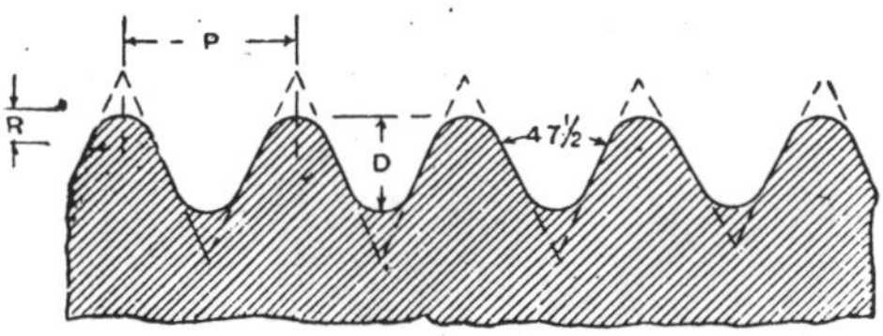

Fig. 30.—British Association thread

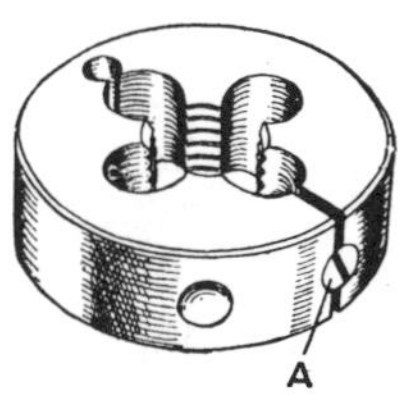

Fig. 32.—Adjustable die

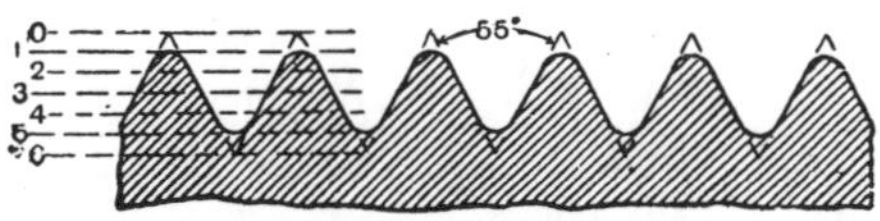

Fig. 31.—English standard, or Whitworth, thread

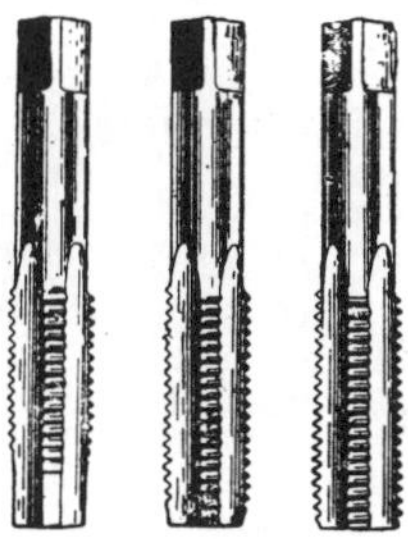

Fig. 33 Fig. 34 Fig. 35

Figs. 33 to 35.—Taper, second, and plug taps

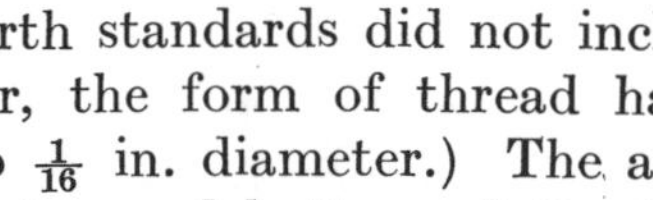

Fig. 35a.—Hand chasers for internal and external threads

Whitworth standards did not include diameters below $\frac{1}{4}$ in. However, the form of thread has now been standardised down to $\frac{1}{16}$ in. diameter.) The angle of the thread is $47\frac{1}{2}°$, and the top and bottom of the threads are rounded to the same radius as illustrated in Fig. 30. The English "Whitworth" threads (Fig. 31) have an angle of 55°, and one-sixth of the nominal height from 0 to 6 is rounded off. This rounding strengthens the bolt at the root of the thread and reduces the likelihood of damage to the thread. The tables give some particulars of the various sizes, pitches, and clearing and tapping drills required. The safe loads on such screws are calculated for steel at 4,000 lb. per sq. in.; for brass screws the values should be reduced by one-half.

Fig. 32 shows an adjustable die which, for use, is fixed in a hand wrench by means of pointed screws; these screws, also, close in the die when the threads become worn, the screw A being withdrawn slightly to allow of this being done.

"B.A." (British Association) Threads

No.	*Diameter in.*	*Approx. No. Threads per in.*	*Clearing drill*	*Tapping drill*	*Proportionate strength*
0	·236	25¼	No. B	No. 12	142 lb.
1	·209	28¼	No. 3	No. 19	110 lb.
2	·185	31⅓	No. 26	$\frac{3}{16}$ in.	85½ lb.
3	·161	34¾	No. 19	No. 30	63¾ lb.
4	·142	38½	No. 27	No. 34	48¾ lb.
5	·126	43	No. 30	No. 40	38½ lb.
6	·110	47¾	No. 34	No. 44	28½ lb.
7	·098	52¾	No. 39	No. 48	22½ lb.
8	·086	59	No. 43	No. 51	17 lb.
9	·075	65	No. 48	1½ mm.	12½ lb.
10	·067	72½	No. 50	No. 55	10 lb.
12	·051	90¾	No. 54	No. 60	5½ lb.

Note.—A good range of sizes for model work includes Nos. 0, 1, 2, 3, 5, 7, and 10. The drills required (where numbered) are standard Morse twist and straight flute drill sizes, which may be quoted in purchasing.

Small "Whitworth" Threads

Diameter in.	*Number of Threads per in.*	*Clearing drill*	*Tapping drill*	*Proportionate strength*
$\frac{1}{16}$ (·0625)	60	No. 52	No. 56	6½ lb.
$\frac{3}{32}$ (·093)	48	No. 41	No. 50	17¾ lb.
$\frac{1}{8}$ (·125)	40	No. 30	No. 40	34½ lb.
$\frac{5}{32}$ (·1562)	32	4 mm.	No. 31	53¾ lb.
$\frac{3}{16}$ (·1875)	24	No. 12	$\frac{9}{64}$ in.	71 lb.
$\frac{7}{32}$ (·218)	24	No. 2	No. 17	108 lb.
$\frac{1}{4}$ (·25)	20	6½ mm.	No. 11	138½ lb.
$\frac{5}{16}$ (·3125)	18	No. 0	No. D	229 lb.
$\frac{3}{8}$ (·375)	16	No. N	No. W	359 lb.

Note.—The $\frac{3}{16}$-in. size gives a comparatively weak screw, and by reducing the coarseness of the thread to 32 or 26 threads per in. greater strength is obtained. Indeed, for many purposes 40 threads per in. may be used for $\frac{1}{8}$ in. and $\frac{5}{32}$ in., 32 threads for $\frac{3}{16}$ in. and $\frac{7}{32}$ in., and 24 for $\frac{1}{4}$ in. The drills recommended are standard Morse numbers.

For pipes, tubes and boiler fittings a finer thread than either Whitworth or B.A. is required, since the Whitworth thread would in many cases cut through the entire thickness of the metal of a tube. The use of 40 threads for all diameters of $\frac{1}{4}$ in. and below is, therefore, to be recommended. Above $\frac{1}{4}$ in. and below $\frac{3}{8}$ in. diameter, 32 threads is used, while the "Brass" gas thread of 26 per in. is used for $\frac{3}{8}$ in. to $\frac{1}{2}$ in. inclusive. Many boiler fittings have threads as follow :—$\frac{3}{8}$ in., $\frac{5}{16}$ in., $\frac{1}{4}$ in. and $\frac{3}{16}$ in. diameter, 26 threads;

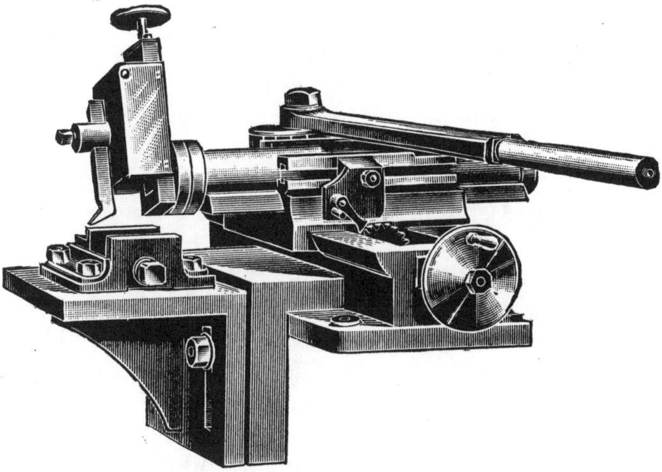

Fig. 36.—Excellent type of hand shaping-machine

$\frac{3}{16}$ in. diameter, 35 threads; $\frac{5}{32}$ in. and $\frac{1}{8}$ in., 40 threads. These sizes lead, however, to very coarse and clumsy fittings.

For screwing internal threads, taps are required, a set of three being shown by Figs. 33 to 35. They are used in the order given in the illustrations.

The safe loads in the tables show the nominal and comparative strengths of the screws and demonstrate the general superiority of the B.A. threads in the smaller sizes. The weakness of the $\frac{3}{16}$-in. Whitworth thread is also demonstrated. A screw of this diameter with 26 threads instead of 24 could be safely loaded to 76 lb., while with 32 threads the load could be 90 lb.

This portion of the table will be found of service in determining the number of screws required in a cylinder cover or other similar engine part subjected to pressure. If the cylinder is $1\frac{1}{8}$-in. bore (and therefore has 1 sq. in. area) it will have to resist a force of 100 lb. at a pressure of 100 lb. per sq. in. This means that at least 6 screws $\frac{3}{32}$ in. diameter (strength $17\frac{3}{4}$ lb.) would be required, viz. $6 \times 17\frac{3}{4} = 106\frac{1}{2}$ lb., which leaves a few pounds to spare. In any case a greater strength (say, 20 per cent. to 60 per cent.) than the tabulated figures show should be adopted. This is more especially necessary in small sizes to provide for corrosion, imperfect workmanship, and faulty materials.

A few hand chasers should be purchased, and some idea as to their uses will be found in subsequent chapters. Fig. 35A shows the internal and external types.

Shaping and Planing Machines.—In the production of flat surfaces the shaping and the planing machine, both of which appliances can be obtained in a hand-operated form, will be of great service to the amateur. The planing machine is suited to essentially model work, as the capacity of the machine is limited by the size of the table. The hand shaper is therefore to be preferred for all-round purposes, and, while cheaper for the weight and power of the machine, provides for key-way cutting and similar operations in fairly large work. Messrs. Leyland, Barlow and Co., of Manchester, make the excellent machine shown by Fig. 36. It has a hand or self-acting feed and swivelling spring tool box. The table may be fitted with a machine vice, as shown, and it is slotted so that other fitments to hold the work may be bolted to it.

Power for Model Engineering Workshops.—The addition of mechanical power to a model-maker's workshop gives the worker an immense advantage over those who are provided with foot- or hand-operated tools. A small electric motor of $\frac{1}{2}$ B.H.P., or a gas or petrol engine of similar output, is all that an amateur requires. In choosing either an electric motor or a gas engine the largest machine for the power (that is, a slow-running one) is advisable, as for personal comfort the least possible noise is desirable, a fast-

Fig. 37

Fig. 38

Figs. 37 and 38.—Exterior and interior of Mr. Paul Blankenberg's workshop

running machine being bound to make more noise. Of course, this entails a greater first cost, but the engine will last much longer. Should a steam engine be installed the same applies in a certain measure, but it must be remembered that a large low-speed steam engine is a very uneconomical machine. The best combination is therefore a large natural draught coal- or coke-fired boiler and a small but heavy quick-revolution engine of the enclosed kind.

A gas engine is an ideal engine for an amateur's purpose; but if gas is not available, then for powers less than 1 B.H.P. the petrol engine is advised. Paraffin engines of low powers are rather troublesome, and, although the fuel is cheaper, they do not show any saving over petrol engines. For a workshop a petrol engine with a wick carburettor will prove very economical. Electric ignition is strongly to be recommended, more especially as a small charging dynamo and accumulators are a useful adjunct to an electrical model-engineer's outfit. With a sufficiently large engine the shop may be illuminated at the same time, a low voltage (say, 8 to 10 volts) scheme being employed. This will reduce the number of cells required for the storage battery. A few large open cells will come out cheaper, comparatively, than a greater number of small-capacity cells, which would be required for an installation of high voltage.

An old acquaintance of the writer's, Mr. Paul Blankenberg, when residing in London, fitted up a very neat garden workshop with power drive. The engine used was the smallest size "Ideal" engine by Messrs. Hardy and Padmore, Ltd., of Worcester. The engine was placed in a small outbuilding, as shown in the builder's photographs, Figs. 37 and 38. The engine was made get-at-able by a door on the outside and another smaller glazed door connecting the engine house with the workshop. The engine could by this means be started up from the inside and while the noise was cut off its working could be readily observed from the inside. The water tank and silencer were placed outside, although from the point of view of the freezing of the cooling water the latter would perhaps have been better if arranged to be placed inside the outhouse.

CHAPTER II

The Lathe and its Fitments

Choice of Lathe.—The purchase of a lathe—the most important tool in a model-maker's workshop—is a matter which individual circumstances must determine. The price of an amateur's lathe may vary roughly between 30s. and £30. A fair lathe of light build with a single-speed mandrel can be obtained for 30s. to £2 10s. Cast-iron work,

Fig. 39.—Small pulley on treadle flywheel for single-geared lathe

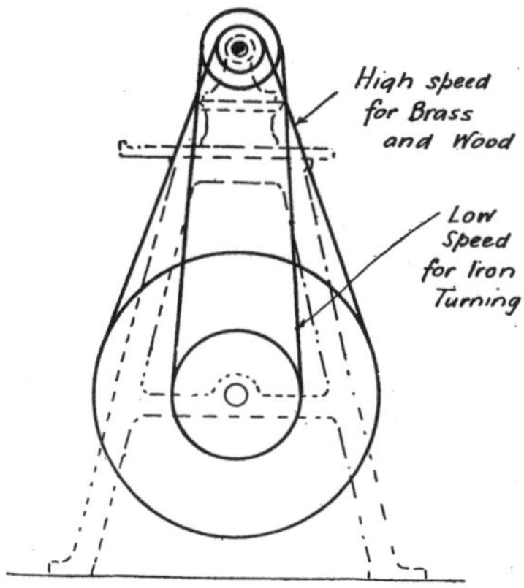

Fig. 40.—Pulleys required for high and low mandrel speeds of single-geared lathe

however, demands a back gear; and cylinder boring can be done, without undue labour and special tools, only by the aid of a slide-rest. For large model and small power work, a back gear and a slide-rest are indispensable; but for smaller work a single-speed lathe will be found quite suitable, especially when mainly brasswork is done. In some cases amateur model-makers have found a watchmaker's lathe quite satisfactory.

In any circumstances, the *best* lathe one can afford should be chosen, and the following points should be considered before purchase: (1) Hollow mandrel; (2) largest diameter of mandrel nose; (3) rigidity of bed; (4) ample dimensions of bearings of mandrel; (5) use of Morse taper loose centres for both back and poppet mandrel; (6) ample wearing surface on slides of bed and slide-rest (if any); (7) convenient and quick attachment and locking of various fitments; (8) heavy flywheel and easy-running foot gear.

If the amount to be expended does not allow of a back-geared lathe being considered, then a lathe with a very small diameter pulley on the flywheel is advised. This will be found necessary to enable the model-maker to turn cast- and wrought-iron and steel objects in the larger diameters. Figs. 39 and 40 show the arrangement. The belt should be in two parts, so that the smaller piece may be removed when working on the low-speed pulley.

Hollow Mandrel.—The model-maker works with so much rod and wire material that the use of a hollow mandrel is almost essential. Coupled with a good self-centre chuck, it largely eliminates the necessity of employing the back centre in most ordinary jobs. If, however, owing to the construction of the lathe a hollow mandrel is impossible, then the mandrel may be bored down as far as possible, the bore being (see Fig. 41) one-half the outside diameter of the screwed nose of the mandrel.

Chucks.—The type of three-jaw self-centring chuck well suited to the amateur's purpose is that known as the hand-lever scroll chuck (Fig. 42). If not supplemented by a drill chuck, the geared chuck (Fig. 43) should be chosen, as it has a sufficiently powerful grip for drills and smooth rods. Both of these chucks are made in sizes from 2 in. to 5 in. in diameter, and are made with two sizes of jaws. The inside jaws are employed for holding cylindrical work from the inside, as shown in Fig. 46, and to hold rods and other solid work from the outside (Fig. 44). Having three jaws, these chucks, of course, hold hexagonal objects perfectly, and are therefore useful in making nuts and screws. The outside jaws will carry large diameter work from the outside (Fig. 45), the steps in the jaws being so arranged

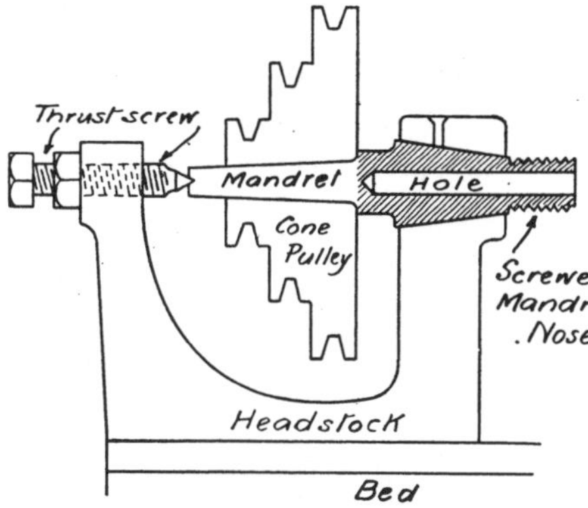

Fig. 41.—Headstock with bored mandrel

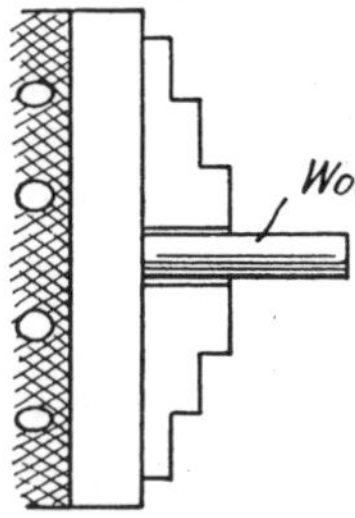

Fig. 44.—Rod held in hand-lever scroll chuck

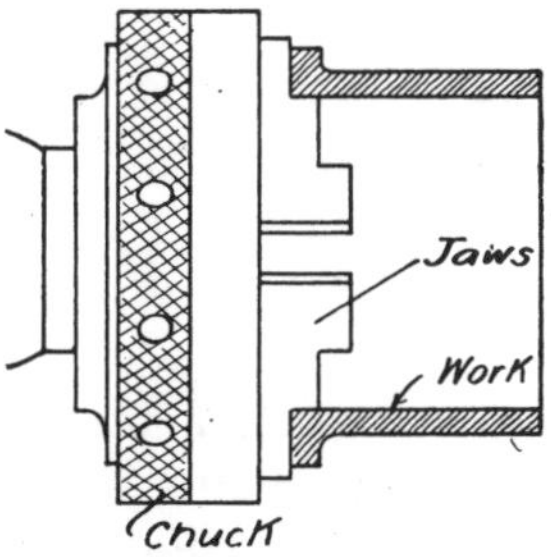

Fig. 46.—Cylinder held inside by hand-lever scroll chuck

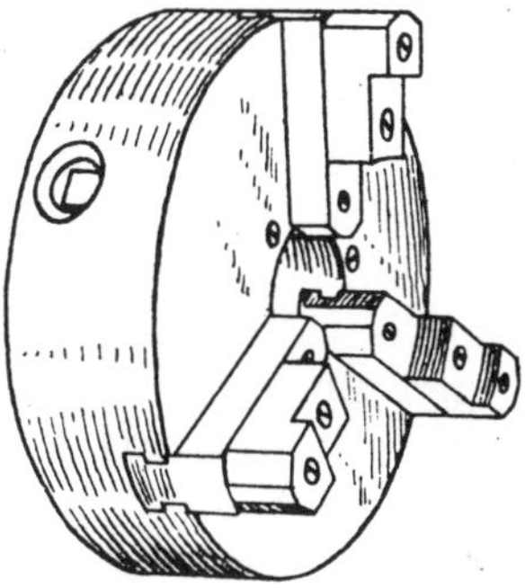
Fig. 43.—Geared scroll chuck

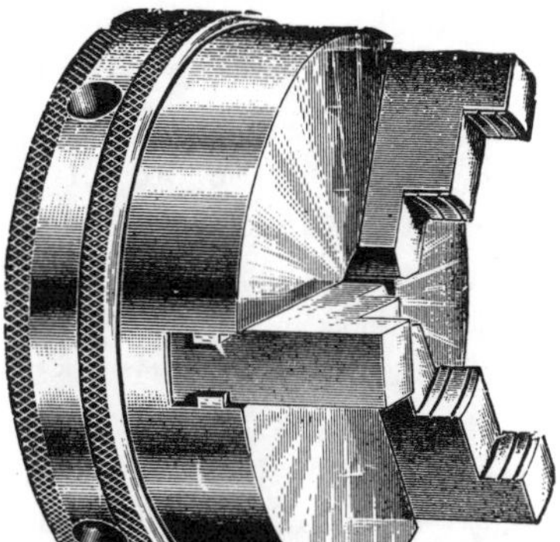
Fig. 42.—Three-jaw self-centring lever scroll chuck

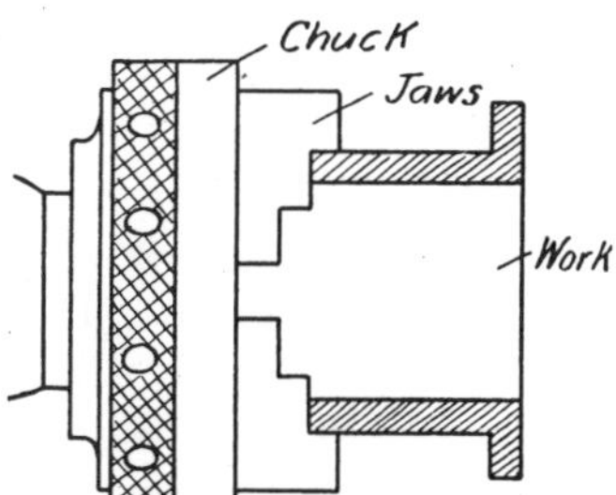

Fig. 45.—Cylinder held outside by hand-lever scroll chuck

that work of 25 per cent. larger diameter than the body of the chuck can be held comfortably. All the chucks hold work down to zero diameter in the centre of the jaws.

While a 2-in. diameter chuck may be used for drills, the writer cannot, even for the smallest lathe, recommend less than a 3-in. chuck. Small lever scroll chucks have little gripping power, and in any case should be used for work of lighter character.

Even when the geared scroll chuck (Fig. 43) is also fitted, the lever scroll variety is very good, especially with a permanent gap-bed lathe like the Drummond 3½-in. centre, as the depth is no greater in a 5-in. chuck than in 2 in. or 2½ in. This means that objects with a long sweep, like, say, a combined eccentric strap and rod casting, can be bored in the chuck, as the rod will clear the gap in the bed.

The smaller chucks, 2 in. and 2½ in., are generally fitted on a bush or arbor, which is in turn screwed to the nose of the lathe mandrel. The larger chucks must be attached to a special faceplate (*see* Fig. 47). This faceplate must be tapped for the lathe, and then turned up true whilst it is in position on the lathe mandrel. If no tap is available, the model-maker must get the screwing and rough facing of the plate done for him. When fitted, the face and edge of the faceplate should be turned up truly, so that it just fits in the recess formed in the back of the chuck. The plate may then be marked out for the holes for the set-screws which secure the chuck, and which are usually provided with it. Sometimes the chuck is found to be out of truth with the back. In such cases the back should be turned up with the chuck mounted by its own jaws on a mandrel running between the centres of the lathe.

The driver chuck may take either of the forms shown in Figs. 48 and 49. The first is simply a stud fixed in a small faceplate, the usual Morse taper centre being placed in the hole in the mandrel nose. Four holes are drilled and tapped at different radii, to enable the driving pin to engage large or small carriers of the type shown in Fig. 115, page 61. The older pattern (Fig. 49) carries its own centre. The live centre need not be hardened, but preferably is

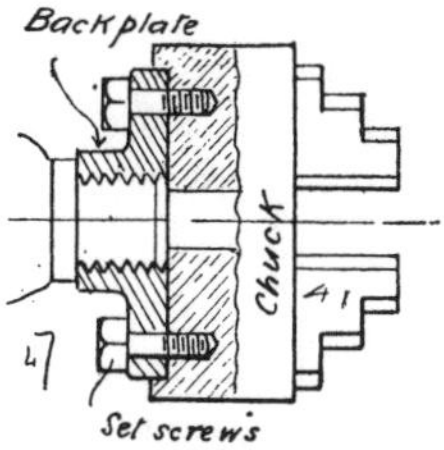

Fig. 47.—Scroll chuck attached to special face-plate

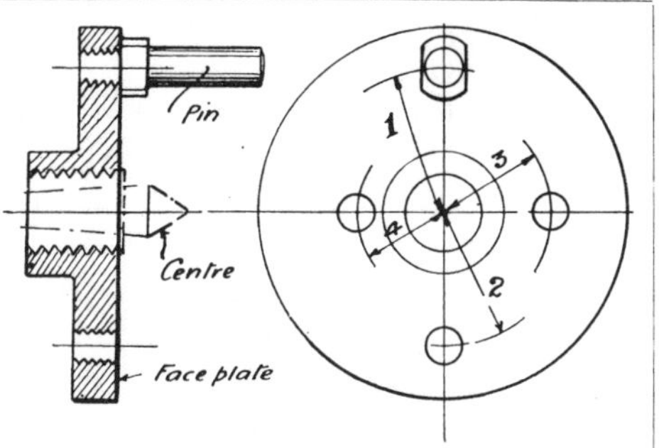

Fig. 48.—Simplest form of driver chuck

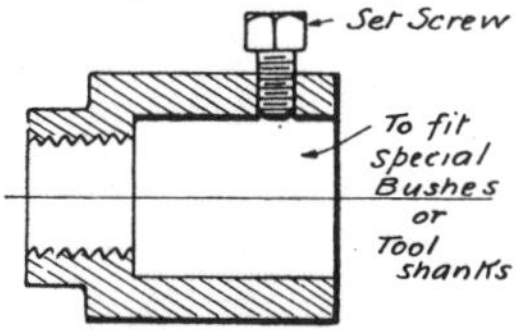

Fig. 50.—Master chuck

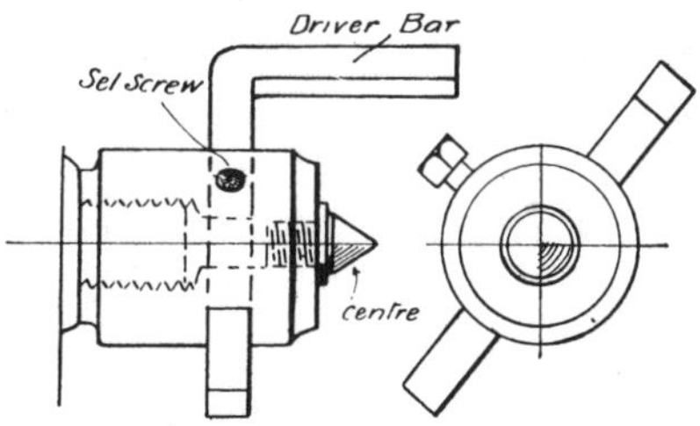

Fig. 49.—Old-pattern driver chuck with cranked driver

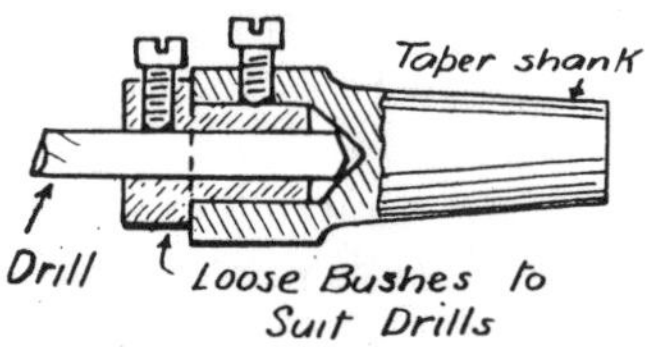

Fig. 53.—Taper-shank master chuck for drills

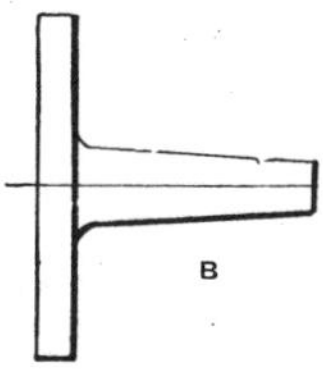

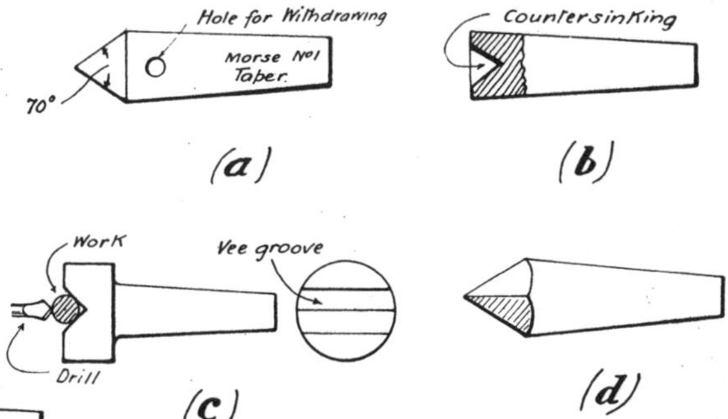

Fig. 51.—Four useful centres

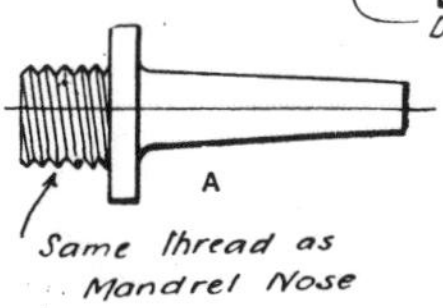

Fig. 54.—A, Screwed centre; B, Drilling pad

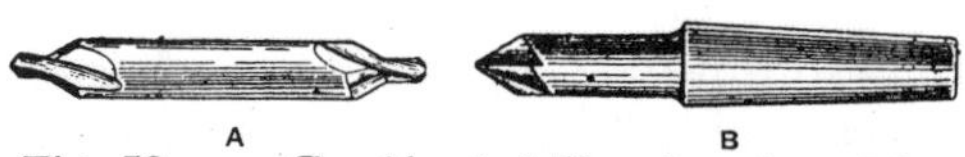

Fig. 52.—A, Combined drill and countersink; B, Centring cutter

made of tool steel. It should be trued up in position in the lathe, the driver bar being temporarily removed for the purpose. The position of the driver bar is adjustable by means of the set-screw.

The master chuck (Fig. 50) is similar to the bell or cup chuck, but smaller, and is machined all over, the hole being some standard dimension. In this chuck other wood or metal chucks may be fitted, or special tools may be designed with shanks of the standard internal size of the master chuck. The set-screw, of course, holds the smaller chucks and tools fitted into the master chuck.

Tailstock Centres. — Among the many fitments that may be made or purchased for the lathe, those that increase the capacity of the tailstock are not the least important. Fig. 51 shows four useful centres: (*a*) the point centre for parallel turning between centres—two are required, the one for the back poppet being hardened—(*b*) the hollow centre for carrying drills; (*c*) the "vee" pad centre for drilling round objects; (*d*) the square centre, which must be hardened and ground, for making and enlarging centre holes in work revolving on the mandrel. For ordinary centring, however, the "Slocombe" combined drill and countersink (A, Fig. 52) is now employed, and this tool may be held as an ordinary drill in the tailstock or back poppet of the lathe, or in a master chuck with a taper shank (Fig. 53). An improvement on the square centre is shown in Fig. 52 B. This may be used also for countersinking screw holes.

Large drills are centred at the back end, and may be held with the ordinary hardened point centre (*a*), Fig. 51. Small drills of less than $\frac{3}{8}$-in. diameter are usually pointed, and therefore call into requisition the hollow centre (*b*), Fig. 51.

Another type of centre is the screwed centre (A, Fig. 54). The nose of this should be screwed exactly the same as the mandrel nose. By the aid of this appliance chucks and other accessories usually fitted to the mandrel may be attached to the sliding poppet. A drilling pad used for holding up large flat objects against a drill running in the chuck is shown at B, Fig. 54.

Other Accessories.—Although the foregoing does not nearly exhaust the list of accessories which may be added to the model-maker's lathe, they embody all those essential to ordinary work. Where the lathe is required for gear-wheel cutting, milling, ornamental turning, and other more advanced work, what is known as "overhead gear" must be added to the lathe. Eccentric chucks, drilling and milling spindles, vertical slides, division plates, and other more or less expensive appliances used for such advanced work, are ordinarily much better purchased than made, and tool-makers' catalogues should be consulted to find out

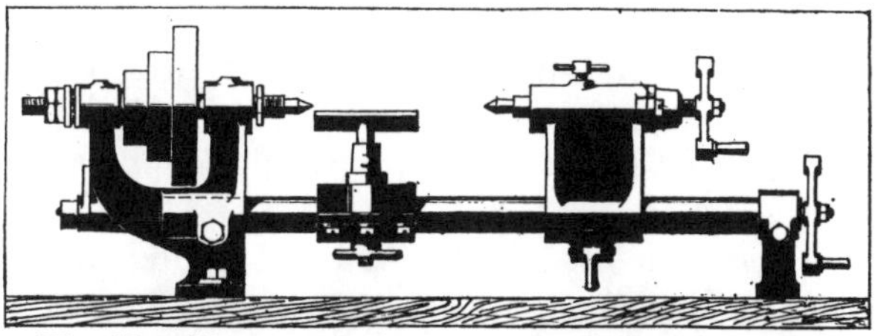

Fig. 55.—Home-made lathe with drawn-steel bed-bar

what is most suited to the work contemplated, and to the particular lathe in use.

A Home-made Lathe

The building of a lathe sufficiently strong and true for metal turning is a problem which many amateurs have attempted to solve. The accuracy of a lathe depends largely on the truth of the tool on which it is made, and this accuracy is again reflected in the work subsequently turned out. In the ordinary way the construction of even a small lathe involves the use of heavy and expensive machines such as planers and shapers. Of course, it is possible to make a lathe with a wooden bed and with the mandrel bearings simply drilled out, but such a tool would not satisfy the model-maker. Another idea is to use commercial angle iron for the bed-plate.

In the design shown by Fig. 55 (all the details being given by Figs. 56 to 65) the main feature of the construction is the use of drawn or turned steel shafting, a commercial material of very reasonable accuracy and finish. The various additions and final fitments of the lathe may be accomplished on the tool itself, once the basis of the work is finished. The lathe can be finally made up into a really respectable screw-cutting lathe by adding part by part as time goes on. At the outset, the boring table and leading screw need not be fitted. The only work that need be put out is the turning down of the mandrel and poppet bar to $\frac{1}{2}$ in. at each end, the casting of the cast-iron and brass portions, and the drilling of the $1\frac{1}{8}$-in. holes in the head-stock, back poppet, boring table and end supporting leg. The boring of the mandrel to make it into a "hollow mandrel lathe" may be left until the lathe is otherwise finished. Even the drilling of the cone pulley may be done on the lathe itself, a temporary or "jury" pulley being rigged up for the time being.

The whole scheme of the lathe depends on the use of commercial bright-drawn steel bar for the bed of the lathe. This material is cheap, and is very true both in diameter and in straightness. This fact is made use of to obtain an accurate lathe without recourse to planing. The materials, drilling, screws and bars for the plain lathe (without lead screw or boring table) are estimated to cost not more than 15s. to 17s.

The first thing is to prepare the patterns, which may be made by any amateur, as core-boxes can be dispensed with. The $1\frac{1}{8}$-in. holes may be bored out of the solid casting, the coreing of the holes for the white metal being left to the foundry to provide. As a rule, a foundry can supply all round cores. Should the three-step pulley-wheel be determined upon at the outset the pattern for this will be required to be sent to a wood-turner's. However, it is quite possible that some firm will adopt the suggestion of supplying the necessary castings and parts already drilled, and thus make it possible for the amateur to accomplish the work of building up the lathe with only the hand tools common to every home workshop.

Presuming that the rough castings have come to hand,

Fig. 56.—Front and end elevations (with headstock partly in section) of home-made lathe with drawn steel bed-bar

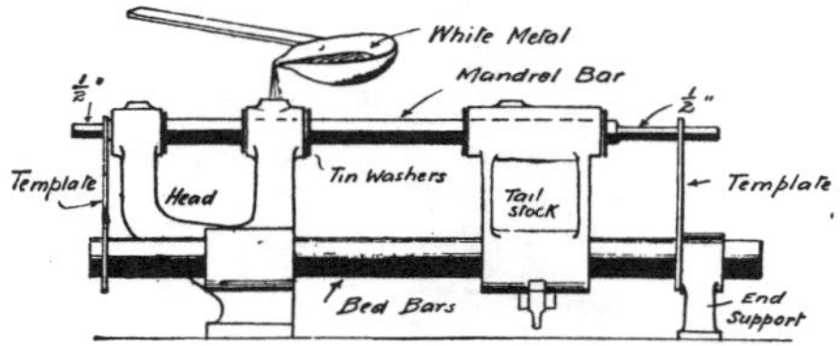

Fig. 57.—Running in the white-metal bearings

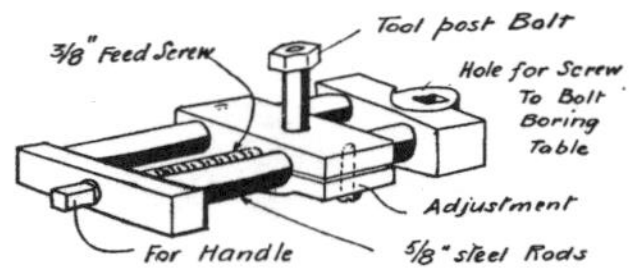

Fig. 58.—Bar slide-rest

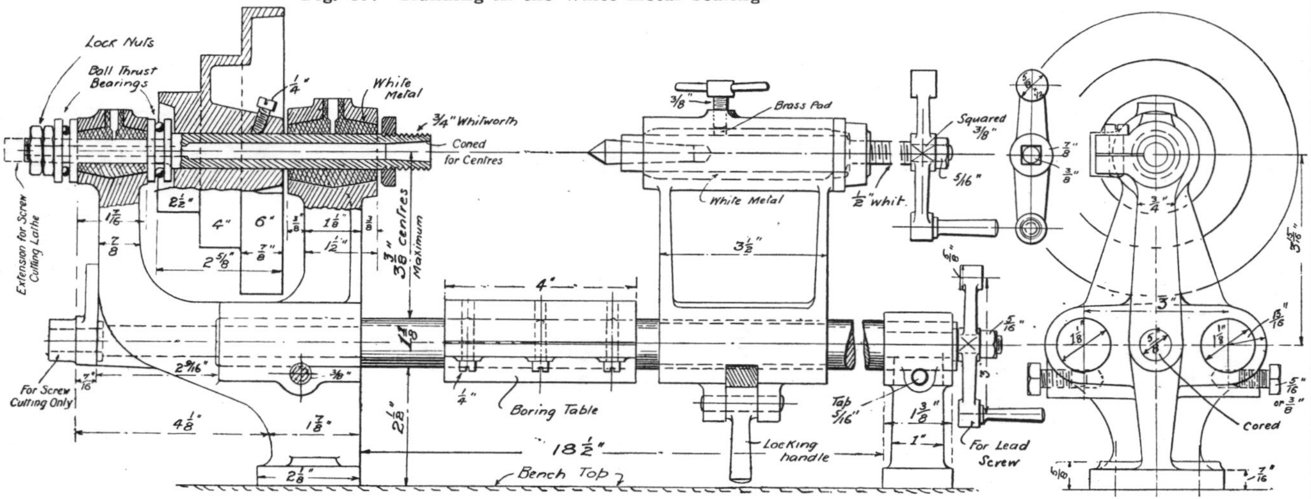

Fig. 56

extreme care and accuracy will be required in drilling the holes for the two shafts which form the bed of the lathe. These holes should be $1\frac{1}{8}$ in. to fit the shafting, and a trial hole may be required to be made in an odd piece of iron to test whether the drill in use will give a satisfactory result. The commercial bars should just go in the holes, so that the set-screw shown in the drawings of the headstock will securely tighten up the parts and yet allow them to be removed at any time without trouble.

The headstock should be tackled first, and when drilled this may be used to form a jig for drilling the second and all the other holes, a short piece of the bar being cut off for this purpose. The back foot or support for the bed of the lathe should be drilled next, and with the piece of rod inserted through the adjacent holes the second hole should be bored as shown in Fig. 59. Next comes the back poppet casting, and as the capacity of the average drilling machine and the length of the drill are not such as would take both the headstock and the back poppet superposed on the drilling table, the back support may be utilised for the purpose. The idea is to ensure that both the holes are equidistant, as on this the success of the lathe depends. This, with the turning of the mandrel bar down to $\frac{1}{2}$ in. diameter at each end, and the skimming up of its middle surface, is all the machining that need be given out. If a slide-rest is contemplated, then the boring table (Fig. 65) should be dealt with in a similar manner as the headstock and at the same time.

The main parts can then be threaded on the bed-bar, which should be cut into equal portions, and the holes for the set-screws securing the headstock and back foot drilled and tapped. Ordinary screws may be used, and when the lathe is finished and running these may be removed and turned down with taper points, so that they tend to thrust the bed-bars in an upward direction in tightening on them. The next process is to fit the mandrel and poppet to the head- and tailstock castings truly parallel with the bed. By the devices and processes to be described, no machining is required for this work. While the drilling of the two $1\frac{1}{8}$-in. holes is being accomplished, two templates should be prepared out of $\frac{1}{16}$-in. plate, as shown in Fig. 62. Three holes, two $1\frac{1}{8}$ in. diameter and one $\frac{1}{2}$ in. diameter, to correspond with the centre of the mandrel and the bed-bars, are required in these templates. These holes should be drilled while the plates are either riveted or clamped together, to ensure accuracy.

Pushing the bed-bars through the headstock, well beyond their proper position, as shown in Fig. 57, the templates should be erected on these bars, and the mandrel, which at the outset is in one piece with the back poppet, should be rigged up as shown in Fig. 57. Presuming that the templates are true, this will provide the required parallelism in the centre lines of the mandrel and bed-bars. Both the mandrel and poppet should be blackleaded very thinly, the blacklead being mixed with grease. When all is ready, the white metal should be heated up in a ladle and poured into the cored cavity between the several heads and the mandrel. The castings should be warmed up with a gas-jet preparatory to pouring, and washers of tin-plate (also blackleaded) should be clamped or bound up with wire against the open ends of the cavities. In the case of the back poppet a small ($\frac{3}{32}$-in.) vent hole should be drilled from the top into each end of the cavity to let out the air. The metal is poured in by the oil holes drilled in the headstock and by the clamp-screw hole in the tailstock. The small vent holes in the latter may be redrilled later on to serve as oil holes.

Before actually running the metal in, the tailstock lock should be fitted, so that the latter can be clamped to the bed-bars. This is a very simple yet efficient contrivance (see Fig. 59). A slot should be arranged in the pattern of the tailstock, and when cleaned out to size a piece of $\frac{1}{2}$-in. × $\frac{5}{8}$-in. steel bar with two circular recesses filed in it. In the jaws of the tailstock casting a small eccentric-headed handle made out of steel-bar is filed up and fitted in. The pivot pin is a small piece of $\frac{1}{4}$-in. steel rod. This eccentric handle forces up the bar and clamps the tailstock to the bed-bars.

When the white metal is cold, the mandrel may be removed and sawn in halves to form the mandrel and the sliding poppet. This is screwed $\frac{1}{2}$-in. Whitworth on the reduced diameter to fit a gun-metal cap tapped with the same thread. This cap is screwed on to the end of the backstock with two $\frac{1}{4}$-in. screws, and the end of the poppet is squared for the handle. The screw holes are marked out from those in the cap flange, with the cap in position on the tailstock feed-screw. The clamping screw is a $\frac{5}{16}$-in. set-screw with a hole through the head for a $\frac{3}{16}$-in. pin. To protect the poppet from damage a pad of brass rod is dropped into the bottom of the hole (see Fig. 56).

Progress having been made so far, the mandrel may be removed and, if there is any tendency to shake, the two bearings of the headstock may be slit with a hack-saw as shown in the drawings. In any case this had better be done, as it will enable the bearings to be adjusted for wear. To effect this adjustment screws are fitted into the lugs provided in the castings. Another idea would be to cut the slits before running in the white metal. The slits could be forced open slightly by pushing in a piece of plate or wood just before running the metal. This slip would then be removed, any white metal cleared out of the slit, and the tendency then would be for the head to grip the white metal independently of any pressure put on to the latter by the adjusting screws at the side.

The nose of the mandrel should be screwed with the dies $\frac{3}{4}$-in. Whitworth thread, and a standard steel lock-nut should be driven on tightly to the end of the thread. This lock-nut may be faced as soon as the tool-rest and driving mechanism are completed. The main bearing is a bearing only. The thrust and end adjustment of the mandrel are all arranged for at the outer bearing. Two commercial ball thrust bearings or collars for $\frac{1}{2}$-in. spindle are fitted on the reduced diameter of the mandrel. These are brought up to the inner and outer faces of the outer bearing of the headstock by double nuts, and where a screw-cutting lathe is considered as a final development of the lathe the mandrel should be left about $\frac{3}{4}$ in. longer than ordinarily required at the outer end. The thrust having been fitted, the pulley may be fixed on to the mandrel. With a reasonably true and clean

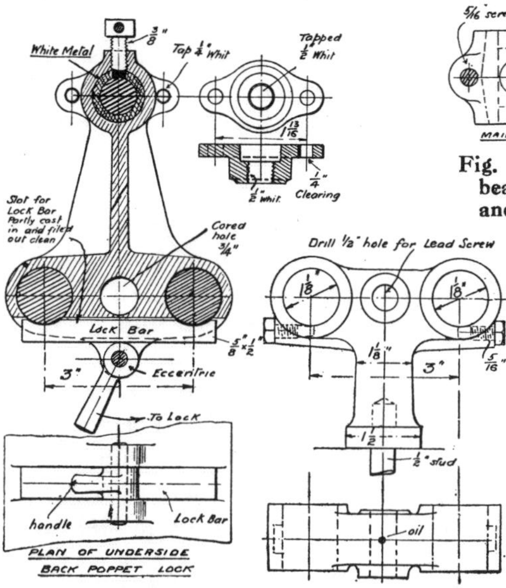

Fig. 59.—Details of tailstock and end support

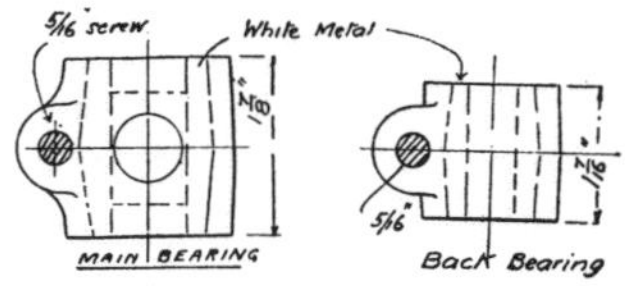

Fig. 61.—Plans of headstock bearings, showing cavity and the adjusting screws

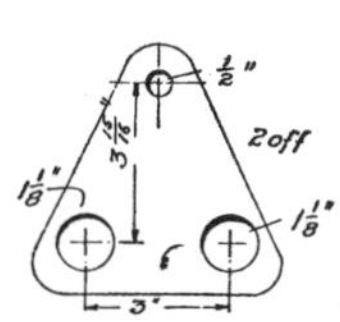

Fig. 62.—Template for setting up mandrel

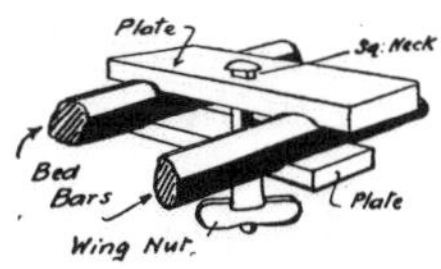

Fig. 60.—Bed for tee-rest

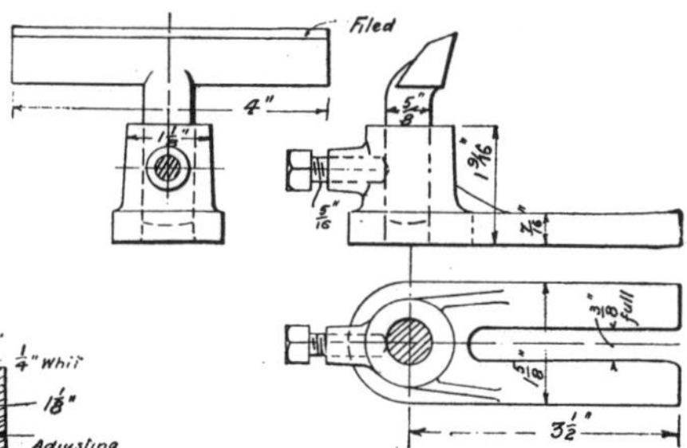

Fig. 64.—Details of tee-rest

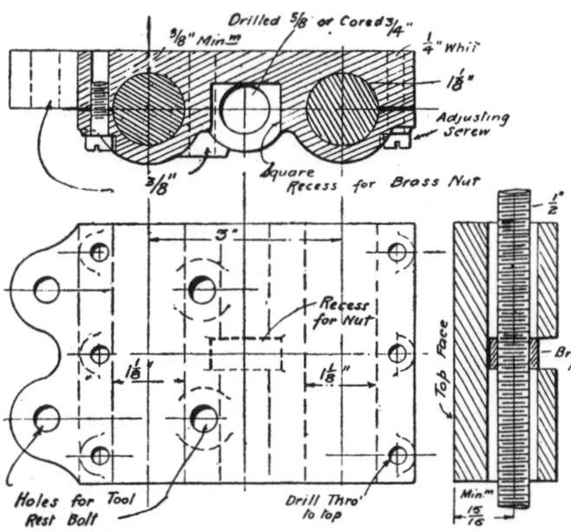

Fig. 65.—Details of boring table

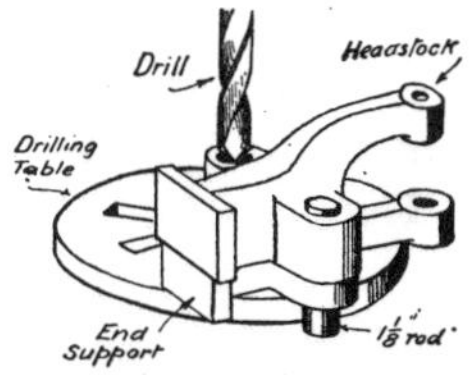

Fig. 63.—Drilling end support, using headstock as jig

casting this need only be bored, the belt faces being skimmed up one by one with a file after the lathe is fitted up. If the boring is to be done on the lathe itself, then a " jury " pulley made out of wood must be rigged up, as already mentioned, and a faceplate provided on which to bolt it. This job, however, is one which may be " done out " with the drilling for the bed-bars. By the time the lathe has reached this stage some sort of a driving mechanism must be provided. The making of a pattern and getting a wheel cast in iron is the proper method, but this will be found beyond the resources of the average amateur. Very often an old wheel and crank shaft or a wheel which will run on a stud pin can be picked up at a scrap-iron dealer's. An old sewing-machine treadle might be pressed into service, the wheel being weighted up with lead pipe. The writer has seen a very respectable treadle made up out of layers of $\frac{3}{4}$-in. floorboards, laid cross grain, with a centre bearing made by driving in a piece of iron gas barrel and nutting the same at each side. Two diameters are required for this lathe, the smaller one being not more than 10 in. diameter, while the larger should be about 2 ft. diameter.

The next operation will be to bore the back poppet for its centre. For accuracy nothing is better than the conical centre, and if the Morse taper (1 in 20) is adopted a standard chuck may be fitted in either the mandrel or the back poppet. A master chuck, consisting of a piece of brass or iron, may be drilled and tapped to suit the lathe mandrel nose, and in this a $\frac{3}{8}$-in. drill may be fixed, and the poppet drilled up for a distance of at least $\frac{1}{2}$ in. A coned " D " bit or a Morse taper reamer may be used to finish the hole. This bit should then be reversed and used in the mandrel hole to ensure their being of exactly the same taper.

Tee-Rest for Hand Turning.—The tee-rest for hand turning is shown in Fig. 64. This may be used in conjunction with the boring table, or by arranging two slabs of iron as shown at A. With a square-necked $\frac{3}{8}$-in. steel coach bolt and fly nut a good fixing may be obtained without damaging the surfaces of the bed-bars. The square neck of the bolt should be $\frac{3}{8}$ in. deep. This neck will then prevent the bolt from falling through the hole in the top slab of iron, and yet allow the bolt to draw down on the tee-rest fork. Further, by inclining the fork of the foot of the tee-rest, the latter should readily slide under the head of the bolt. The square neck also holds the bolt while the fly nut (or wing nut) is being tightened up. The tee-rest may be swivelled in any desired position and the height adjusted to requirements. The tee-rest itself is best cast in malleable iron, but it may, of course, be built up of rectangular iron bar and a piece of $\frac{5}{8}$-in. round steel rod.

Boring Table.—As an improvement on the two flat bars, a boring table is illustrated in Figs. 56 and 65. This is a step in the direction of finally making the tool a screw-cutting lathe. The same system of adjusting the bearing on the bed-bars as used in the headstock mandrel bearings is employed. The casting is sawn after boring and after the $\frac{1}{4}$-in. holes for the adjusting screws have been drilled and tapped. The latter holes, it will be noticed, are drilled and tapped right through to the upper surface. This may as well be done at the outset, as the holes may subsequently be found of service in bolting work down to the boring table. The boring table will require to be planed, filed, or turned up quite true with the surface of the bed-bars. The table will just swing in the lathe itself, but unless the iron is very soft it would hardly do to attempt it. However, when a slide-rest is made, the latter may be rigged up on a temporary boring table and a cut then taken over its surface. For this work the table should be bolted to the faceplate, a casting for which can be obtained from any tool dealer. The faceplate casting should be drilled and tapped $\frac{3}{4}$-in. Whitworth, run on the nose, the boss faced at the back, and the plate then reversed. The front of the faceplate may then be faced.

The boring table has two lugs on the front for the bolt holding the slide-rest. These holes are used only when large diameter work, such as boiler shell tube, is in the lathe being skimmed up or trued at the ends. A stiffer support for the slide-rest can be obtained by bolting into either one of the two holes provided in the boring table between the bed-bars.

Slide-Rest.—With regard to further developments, the slide-rest that may be at some time fitted may be of the usual type with "vee" slides, or, if desired, the scheme adopted for making the bed of the lathe may be used, namely, two bars. These should be at least $\frac{5}{8}$ in. diameter and about 6 in. long, so that a traverse of $3\frac{1}{2}$ in. could be obtained. Fig. 58 is a sketch of the idea. For screw cutting, a bearing should be provided for the outer extension of the leading screw, this also forming a bearing for the "eye" of the quadrant, on which the change wheels are arranged.

CHAPTER III

NOTES ON LATHE WORK

Holding Work in the Lathe.—For woodwork the simplest form of chuck is a small faceplate with a taper wood screen in the centre, as shown in Fig. 66. On this chuck "headstock work," such as turning rings, bases, and other short but large-diameter cylindrical work, is easily

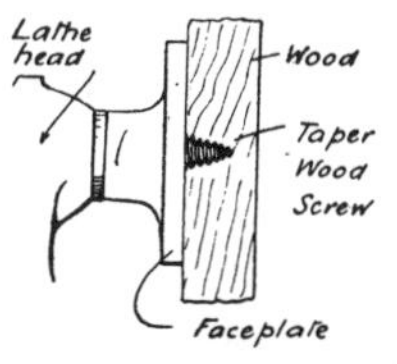

Fig. 66. — Taper screw chuck for wood

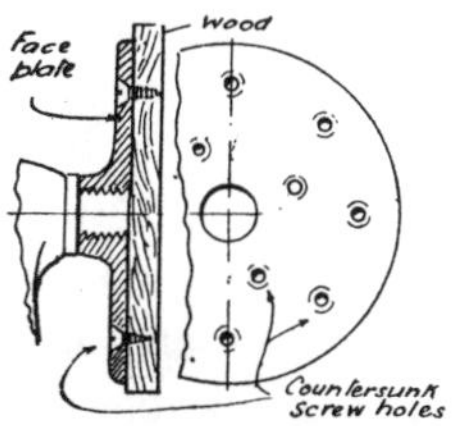

Fig. 67.—Wood work screwed on faceplate

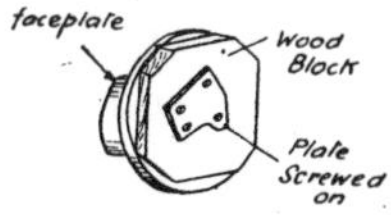

Fig. 68. — Metal work fixed to wood on face-plate

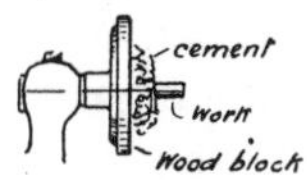

Fig. 69.—Metal work cemented to wooden face-plate

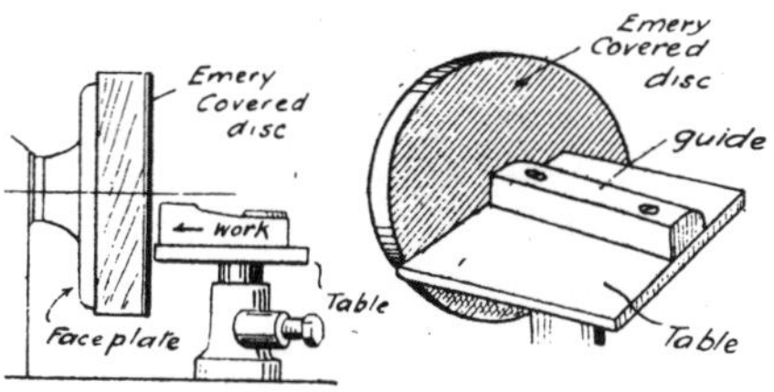

Figs. 70 and 71.—Grinding-disc

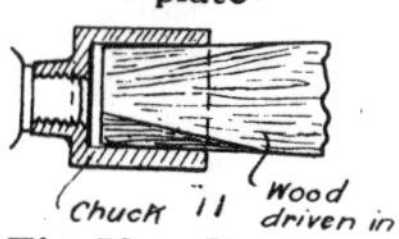

Fig. 72.—Cup chuck for wood

accomplished. An expedient often resorted to in a small job is to cut the head off an ordinary wood screw (a steel screw for woodwork) and to grip it, with the point of the screw outwards, in a self-centring or master chuck. A variant of the screw chuck is shown in Fig. 67. Here the wood is screwed on from the back, this being better suited to heavier and larger work, where a secure fixing is required.

The ordinary faceplate usually supplied with the lathe could, of course, be adapted to the same purpose, a few special screw holes being drilled in it if necessary. A piece of hard wood attached on the faceplate in this manner will be found useful for mounting, by nailing or screwing, awkward castings or parts, or machining over the whole surface a thin plate which may have holes drilled in it but cannot be attached by dogs or clips (see Fig. 68). Another use of the wooden faceplate is for cementing on small castings which cannot conveniently be clipped or screwed on (see Fig. 69). The cement used is any of the shellac cements which melt like sealing-wax with the application of heat. Such an expedient is, of course, only applicable to small castings. Abrasive material, emery powder on a glued surface, or emery cloth, may be fixed to such a piece of wood, and the disc used as a grinding and polishing machine, a suitable table being fixed up near to it, as indicated in Figs. 70 and 71.

For turning short lengths of wood a cup chuck (Fig. 72) is often employed. The other end of the work may or may not be supported by the back centre. Another chuck for "between centre work" is the prong chuck (Fig. 73). This chuck has a projecting centre and two chisel-shaped prongs which drive the work.

For metal work the ordinary faceplate (Fig. 74) is one of the most useful adjuncts of the lathe, and, if possible, should be obtained in two sizes. The work is attached as shown in Fig. 74, the clips A and B being two forms. Larger castings and parts of odd shapes which require machining over the entire surface may be held with screw dogs (Fig. 75) fitted on the faceplate. These dogs have set-screws to engage the edges of the work, and are secured to the faceplate by nutted tails which project through the slots of the faceplate, as shown. In some cases it will be found convenient to clip the casting on to the faceplate while it is being set in position by the aid of a scribing block. The clip may then be removed for machining the surface. A four-jaw chuck (Fig. 76) is a useful but expensive accessory to a lathe, and may be employed instead of separate dogs on the faceplate. The jaws are operated by a key and are quite independent of

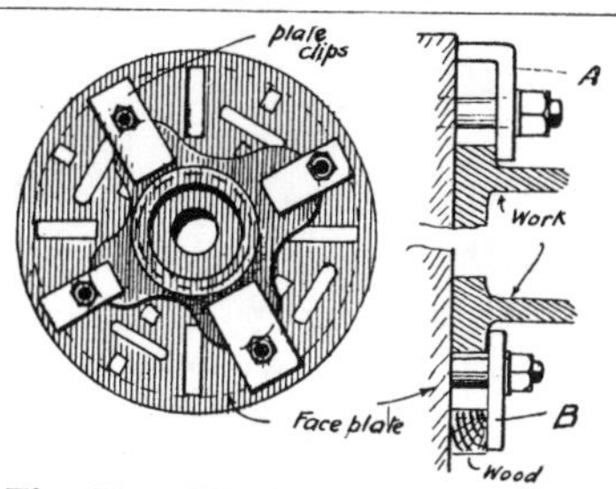

Fig. 74.—Clipping metal work to faceplate

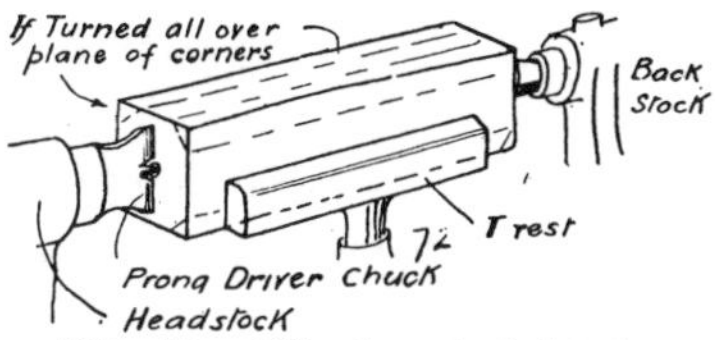

Fig. 73.—Woodwork held by prong chuck

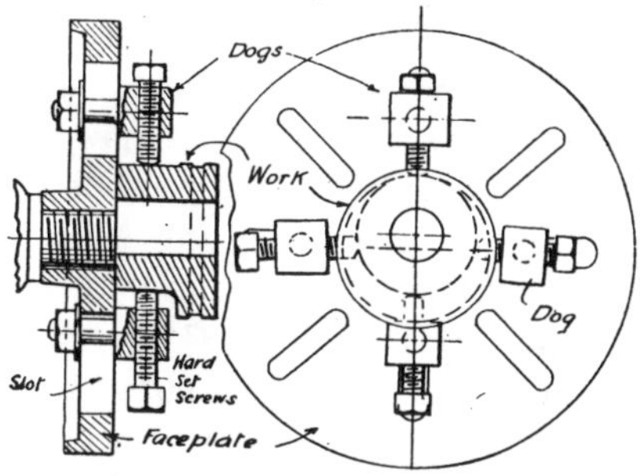

Fig. 75.—Screw-dogs holding work on lathe faceplate

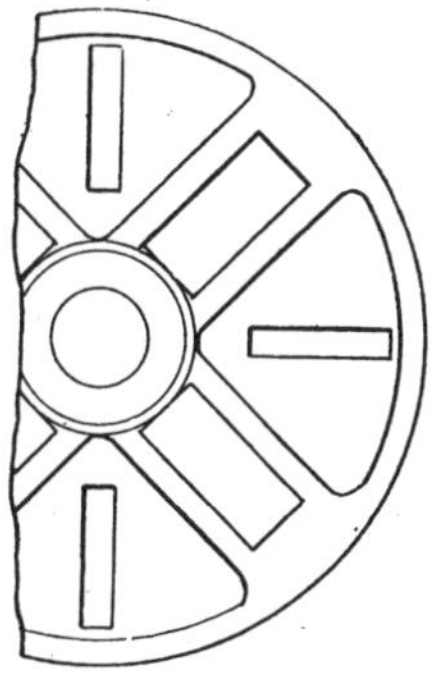

Fig. 77

Fig. 76.—Half-plan of four-jaw chuck, with one jaw removed

Fig. 77.—Part back view of body of chuck

Figs. 78 and 79.—Details of one jaw

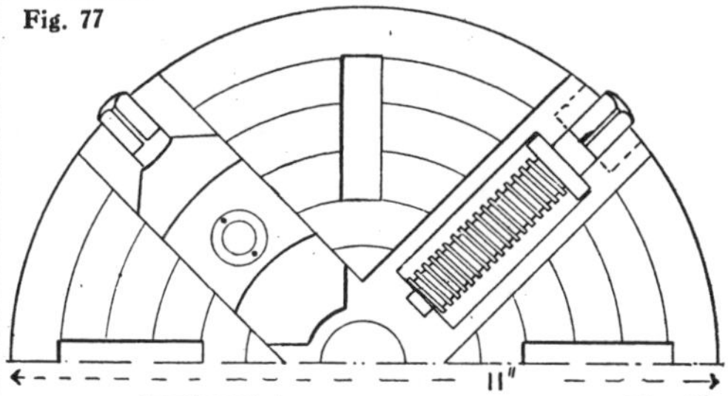

Fig. 76

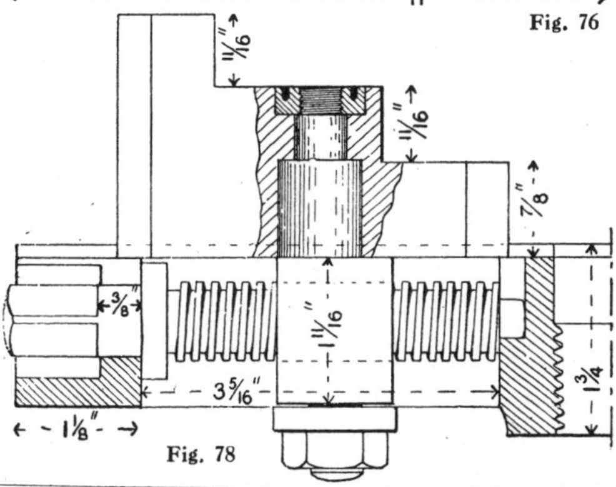

Fig. 78

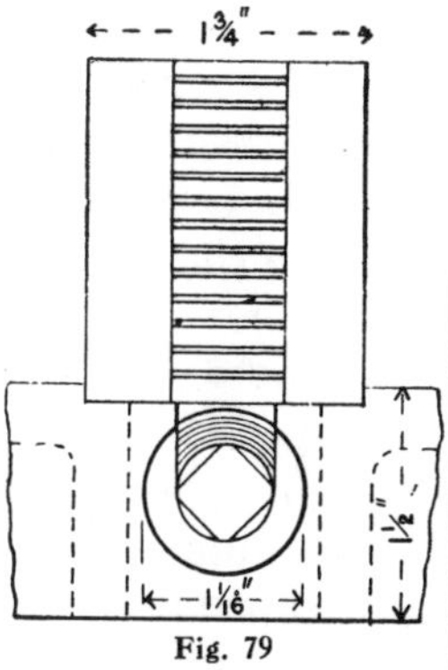

Fig. 79

each other. Irregular objects are therefore quite easily held. In chucking very rough round bars (such as cast gun-metal bars and bushes) there is always a danger of straining a self-centring chuck, and therefore the work should be turned, if only in the rough, in a chuck which will accommodate itself to irregular surfaces.

A simple bell chuck is shown in Fig. 80. It is like an ordinary cup chuck, but has set-screws fitted in its periphery as shown. The ordinary bell chuck is, however, " murderous " in appearance, and to protect the fingers from damage, the writer can recommend the design for an eight-screw chuck shown in Fig. 81, in which the screws are more or less encased. The screws should be made of tool steel, and have square heads made to fit the same key as is used in the self-centring (that is, where a geared chuck operated by a key is employed). The casting should be of iron for lathes over 2½-in. centres, and the only machining required is the facing, boring and tapping for the nose of the lathe, the boring and tapping of the holes for the set-screws, and the turning of the flanges for the protective casing. This protective casing may be of tinplate, with the joint lapped in a trailing direction, so that it does not catch when the lathe is running in the proper direction. A piece of thin brass tube would make a better covering, the flanges being turned to fit the inside of the tube, and the latter spun over at the edges to retain it in place without any further fixing, otherwise it may be secured by countersunk screws as indicated.

Another time-honoured chuck is the master chuck (see Fig. 50, page 31), but this *must* be truly bored and faced while on the lathe for which it is intended. It should be fitted with a hardened set-screw. It may be duplicated—say, in 1-in. and ½-in. internal diameters for a 3½-in. lathe—but, if not, special bushes may be made and fitted to it, with plain or tapped holes to suit the requirements of the moment. For example, a casting as A (Fig. 82) may have to be bored and tapped and faced accurately with the screw-threaded bore. One end of each pair of opposite arms may be drilled and tapped, then this tapped portion may be screwed on to the stud in the parallel bush fitted to the standard master chuck.

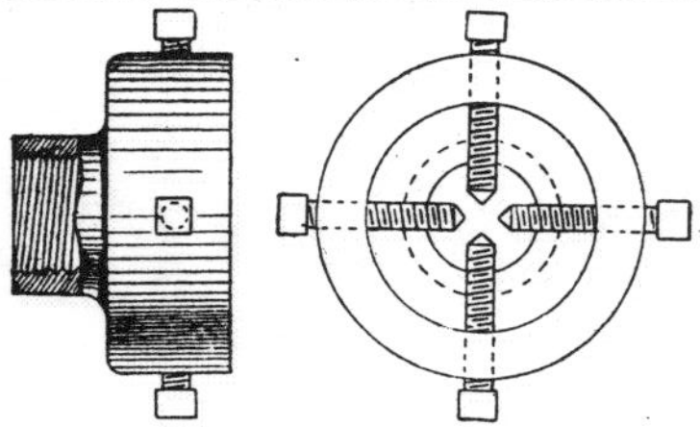

Fig. 80.—Ordinary four-screw bell chuck

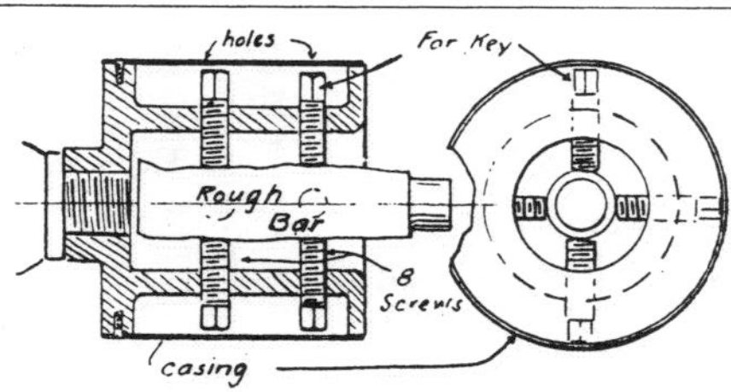

Fig. 81.—Protected eight-screw bell chuck

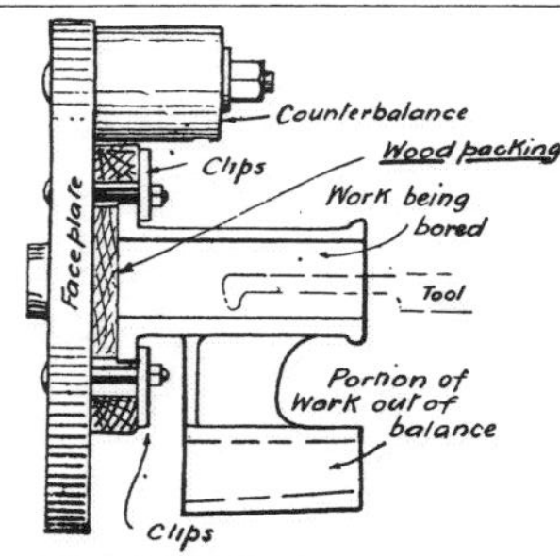

Fig. 84.—Boring work on the faceplate

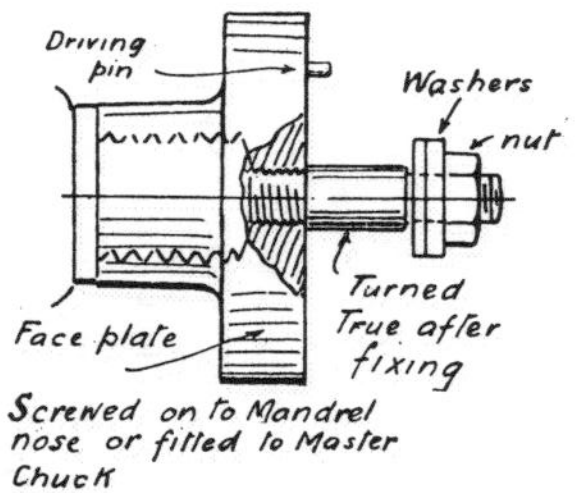

Fig. 85A.—Combined mandrel and faceplate for holding small wheel, etc., for boring and turning

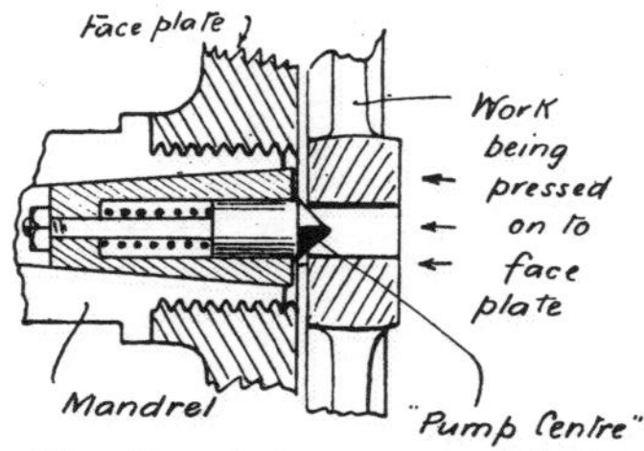

Fig. 85.—"Pump centre" for faceplate work

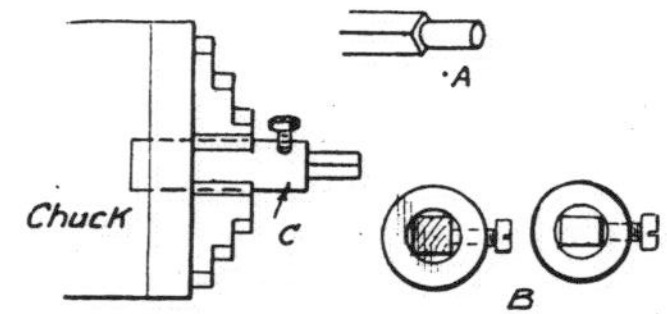

Fig. 83.—Method of holding square rods

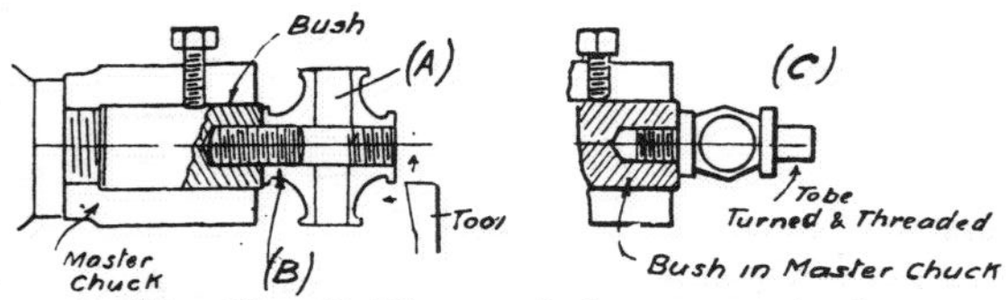

Fig. 82.—Holding work in master chuck

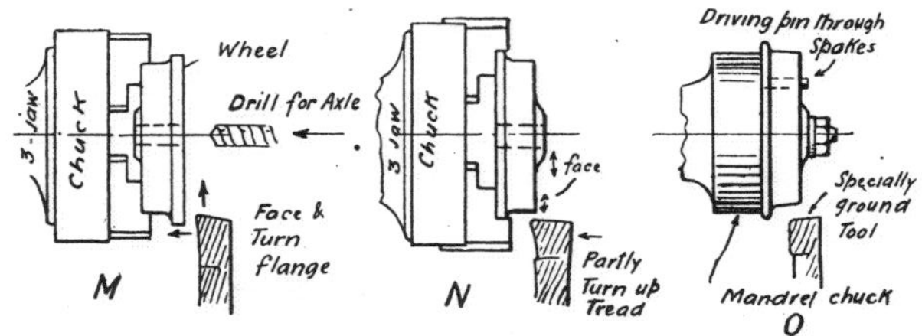

Fig. 86.—Turning and boring model flanged wheel

The opposite end may then be drilled and threaded, and faced. Reversing the work, the end drilled and tapped at first may be faced as at B. By making internal threads in a bush held in a master chuck, spigot ends may be turned up and faced truly (see C, Fig. 82). Indeed, the work, with reasonable care, is bound to be accurate, and while it may take a little longer, better results can be obtained by using such specially-made chucks than by doing the whole of it (where such can be held) in the self-centring chuck.

A master chuck is not required to hold small bushes. A piece of brass or steel rod may be held in the self-centring chuck and the particular internal or external thread cut on it. Of course, it must not be moved from the main chuck as a self-centring chuck cannot always be relied on for absolute accuracy. With a master chuck and well fitting bushes, the degree of accuracy easily obtainable will allow of the removal from the lathe. Permanent chucking pieces—that is, jigs and chucks which may be required later—are best made to fit one of the master chucks.

It is often necessary to turn down the end of a square or other rectangular rod, as shown at A (Fig. 83). The possession of an independent jaw chuck is a rare thing in a model-maker's workshop, and as it is impossible to hold square stuff in an ordinary three-jaw self-centring chuck, it is necessary to make a simple holder by drilling up a piece of round or hexagonal rod with a hole exactly the same size as the measurement of the square stuff over the corners. Where several short pieces are being dealt with, a blind hole may be drilled, this assisting in making every piece alike. A set-screw B is employed to secure the work while it is being turned. This method was adopted in turning up the ends of the slide bars for the model locomotive fully illustrated in Chapter XVI. The holder C should be gripped as near to the self-centring chuck as the set-screw will allow. The holder can, of course, be fitted as a standard bush to one of the master chucks in place of being gripped in a three-jaw chuck as shown.

Where a hole has to be bored clean through a casting attached to the faceplate, a flat and parallel piece of hard wood should be placed between the casting and the faceplate so that the tool may clear the inner edge of the casting. There is no need previously to bore the wooden packing. Unbalanced work should be balanced by a counterweight, bolted on to the faceplate as indicated. In setting up work on the faceplate—say, a model-engine flywheel which has been bored—a useful appliance is a spring or "pump" centre (Fig. 85). It is applicable to any lathe with a hollow or "drilled-down" mandrel. The centre has a spring plunger which normally projects beyond the surface of the faceplate. As the wheel to be turned and faced is pressed up to the faceplate in the process of clipping it on, it is retained in a concentric position, and will not require further centring. A development of the idea for small model railway wheels is shown in Fig. 85A. This special appliance is really a small faceplate with a truly turned face and a projecting mandrel, fitted with a nut and washer. The wheel is first held in the self-centring chuck with the outside jaws M (Fig. 86), and the back is faced, the flange turned down nearly to size, and the axle hole bored. The wheel may then be reversed and the face turned up as shown at N. While in this position any abnormal eccentricity or roughness may be removed from the tread of the wheel. The rest of the work is then done with the wheel on the mandrel chuck as shown at O (Fig. 86). In every case the faceplate portion of the chuck should be large enough to engage the tyre of the wheel so that the mandrel is not subjected to any bending strain.

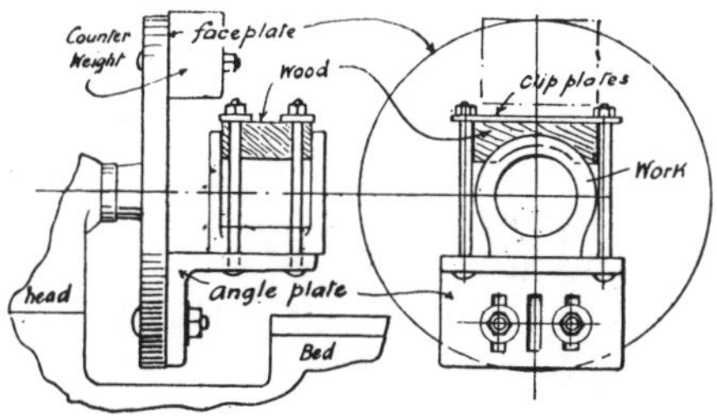

Fig. 87.—Boring work held on angle-plate

A method of fixing a steam-engine cylinder or similar object which has a flat surface parallel to the bore is by bolting the work on to an angle-plate, as shown in Fig. 87. The flat surface may be first planed or filed to the correct distance from the bore and bolted face down on the angle-plate. To prevent distortion of the casting, wooden blocks, roughly shaped to the contour of the outside of the cylinder, may be employed in the place of only the iron clip-plates. The unbalanced weight of the angle-plate will require a counter-balance on the faceplate as illustrated.

Where it is necessary or advantageous to bore a part out with the work stationary, it may be bolted to the slide rest or saddle of the lathe, the cutting tool being fixed in a mandrel revolving between the centres of the lathe. The arrangement is shown, with a connecting-rod end being bored out, in Fig. 88. A carrier is attached to the mandrel, and is driven by the driver chuck screwed over the live centre, as illustrated.

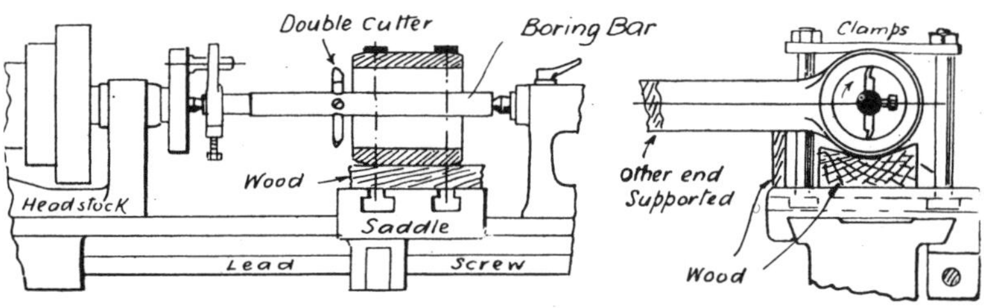

Fig. 88.—Boring cylinder on the saddle

Should the connecting rod or other piece of work required to be bored be very long, the overhanging portion can protrude over the back of the lathe and be supported on a temporary surface, so that it can slide along with the saddle.

The mandrel cutter revolves in the usual direction, and the work is traversed by means of the slide-rest. If the lathe is of the screw-cutting type, the change wheels may be set up to give a fine pitch, say 120 to the inch. To vary the depth of the cut, the cutter, if a single-edged one, may be made to project further from the mandrel. With a double-edged cutter (as more clearly shown in the detail diagram to the right of Fig. 88), various sizes must be used, although two will generally suffice, one for roughing and the other for the finishing cut. The hole to be bored must be cored out nearly to size, or be rough-drilled at the outset. The work must be accurately set up, and packed up with hard wood, care being taken to hold the work so that the hole is not distorted. The holding-down bolts may be slackened slightly for the last cut, as otherwise there may be a certain amount of distortion.

Without a slide rest there are greater difficulties. However, a cylinder or other small object which is not too unbalanced in general form may be supported on the cutter mandrel itself. The mandrel must be true, and preferably fitted with a double cutter. The cylinder to be bored should

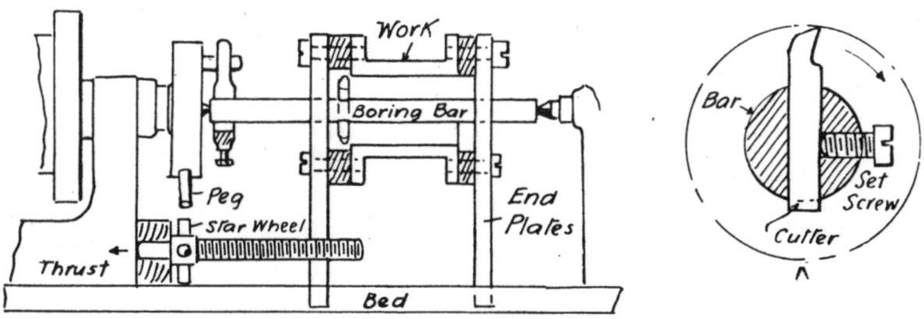

Fig. 89.—Boring cylinder without using a slide-rest ; A, detail of cutter

be provided with two end-plates, packed out with wood or metal distance-pieces, so that the cutter can emerge from the cylinder at each end. If the lathe has a bed with a central slot the plates may protrude into this slot, to prevent the work revolving. The boring-bar can then be placed in the cylinder and the plates screwed up with the cutter outside the right-hand end. A very good self-acting feed can be arranged by the star-wheel method, a stud with a gas thread being screwed into the left-hand end-plate, as shown in Fig. 89. The carrier engages the pegs or star wheel at every revolution, this having the effect of advancing the work a quarter of a turn of the threaded stud.

Centring Lathe Work.—In modern lathes the Morse taper centres are usually employed, and for driving work between centres, instead of the old-fashioned driver chuck shown in Fig. 49 (page 31) a catch-plate is used. The driving pin is often fitted in a slot in place of one of several holes at different radii from the centre, so that it can be adjusted to different sizes of carriers (*see* Fig 49).

The proper centring of the work preparatory to placing

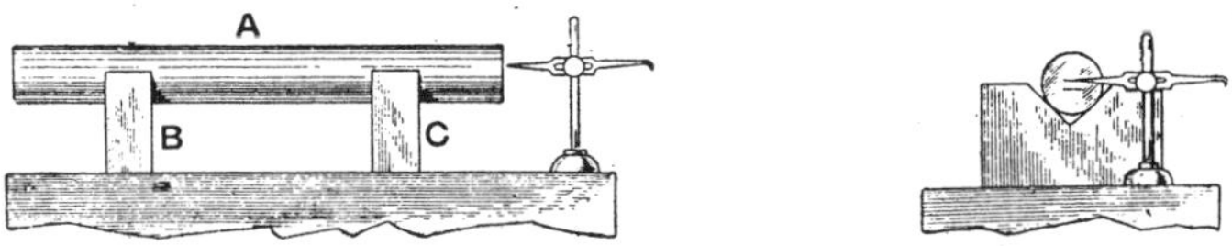

Figs. 90 and 91.—Marking centre with scribing-block

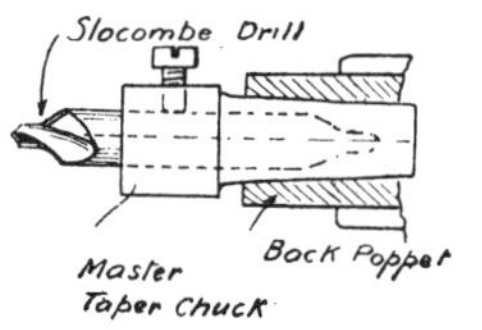

Fig. 93.—Centring work with Slocombe drill

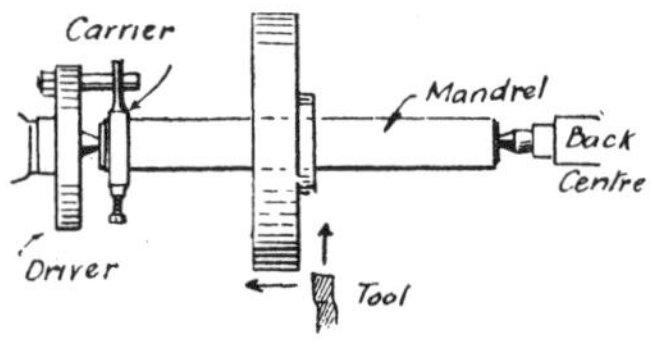

Fig. 94.—Wheel mounted on mandrel for turning

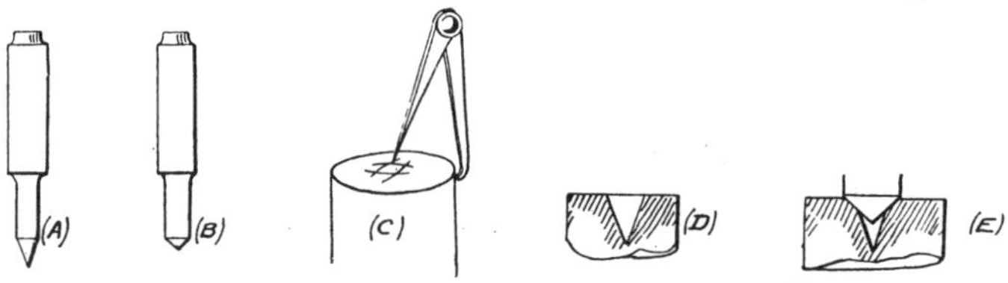

Fig. 92.—Centring a bar with "moph" callipers

it in the lathe is very important, tending to produce more accurate results with the least trouble. A bar which is reasonably true at the outset—for example, drawn bright steel rod—may be first marked out on V blocks with a scribing-block, as shown in Figs. 90 and 91. The V blocks B C are placed on a true surface (a proper surface plate or a piece of plate glass), and, with the scriber just above the actual centre, four lines are drawn on the end, the hole then being centre-punched in and afterwards drilled to form the perfect centre shown at A Fig. 95, the lathe centre being hardened. The series illustrations (Figs. 96 to 100) show specimens of centring to be avoided.

A rapid method of centring a bar of metal for turning is first to file the end of the bar clean and square, and then with the "moph" (hermaphrodite) callipers scribing the four lines (*see* C, Fig. 92). With a centre-punch, A, ground to a fine point, holding the bar in the vice, strike a centre-pop as nearly in the centre of the square as possible. If the punch is ground up by hand give it a turn or a part of a turn between each blow to prevent the hole taking up the imperfections of the punch. When satisfied with the depth of the

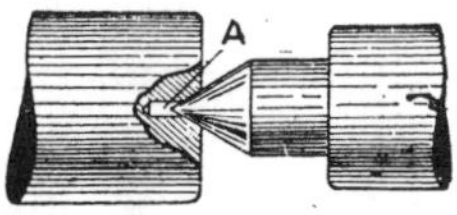

Fig. 95.—Correctly made centre

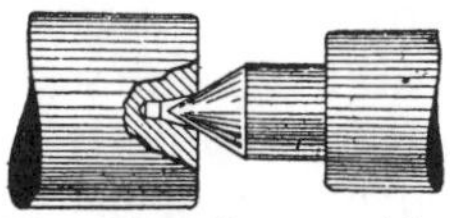

Fig. 96.—Centre with angle too acute

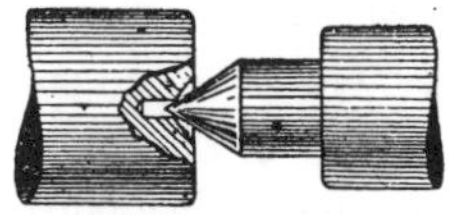

Fig. 97.—Centre with angle too obtuse

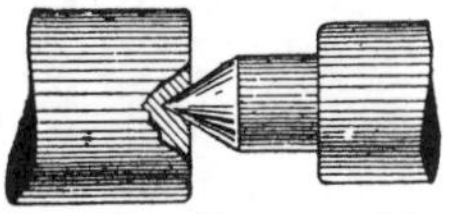

Fig. 98.—Centre with no point clearance

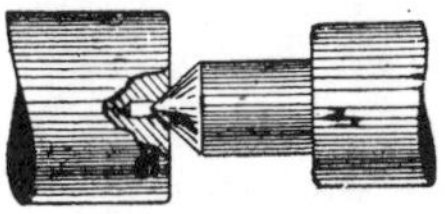

Fig. 99.—Centre-point too blunt

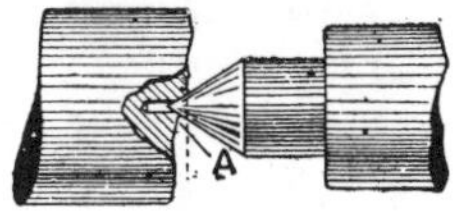

Fig. 100.—End of bar unfaced

hole D, a second punch with a blunter angle, B, may be used as at E. This requires a slighter blow—just enough to give a proper bearing of the *same* inclination as the lathe centres. Of course, a hole may be drilled up after the first centre is made, but the above method is quicker and will produce the same result—that is, it will prevent the lathe centre from bearing on the bottom of the hole.

For centring small bright bars, the best method, especially if a hollow mandrel is available, is to hold the stuff in a self-centring chuck and to start the centre with a pointed hand tool, taking care to remove the pip which tends to form in the centre of the recess. A drill and afterwards a countersink may then be employed properly to form the centre. A square back centre (Fig. 51D, page 31) or, better still, a fluted centre (Fig. 52B, page 3) may be employed. The well-known "Slocombe" combined centring and countersinking drill (Fig. 93) held in a chuck in the back centre gives a perfect result, but it must not be used roughly, and when steel or iron is being operated on it should be freely oiled. Fig. 93 shows such a drill fitted in a master chuck.

Large wheels and discs of metal that are bored for an axle should be turned on a mandrel when the hole is large enough to admit a stiff mandrel. The wheel is driven on tight, to ensure which the mandrel should be quite smooth, truly circular, and slightly tapering. In driving mandrels (these must be properly centred and turned upon these centres, *see* Fig. 94) care must be taken not to damage the ends and centres, a piece of hard wood or soft metal being interposed between the mandrel and the hammer. All facing and turning should be accomplished while the work is on the mandrel to ensure not only truth but perfect balance. The mandrel can be reversed for facing the opposite sides of the wheel.

Lathe Tools.—A set of lathe tools—about 12 to 15 in number—gives a model-maker a good start. It should include at least those shown from A to M (Fig. 101). The first two are roughing-out tools—front tools for wrought iron or steel and brass work respectively—they have a plain diamond point (viewed in plan), and in the case of the steel working tool a top and side rake is provided. For cast iron, a tool the same shape as for brass and gunmetal, B, may be used. As a general rule, the top surface of brass and cast iron working tools coincides with the horizontal surface of the work, although a little top and side rake may be provided for cast iron, and the clearance angle reduced so as to strengthen the cutting edge. When turning copper a top rake is advisable, the angles being much the same as for soft mild steel. Several of the diagrams herewith, being plan views only, do not show the proper cutting angles for the materials to be worked. As a guide to the turner, reference should therefore be made to the table on page 56. All tools should be designed with a view to their being reground several times, and care should be taken to see that the cutting edge is not formed too high above the body of the tool;

otherwise the spring of the tool may cause it to dig into the work. This precaution must be observed also in shaper and planer tools, otherwise uneven surfaces will be produced. The tools C and D are right and left-handed " side " or " hook " tools, while those shown in plan at E and F are used for the same purpose (that is, side cutting), and are sometimes called knife tools. Parting tools for iron and brass respectively are shown at G and H, the plan of the tool being the same in each case.

For boring work with the slide-rest, the tool J is suitable for smaller holes; for large holes, this tool may be fitted in

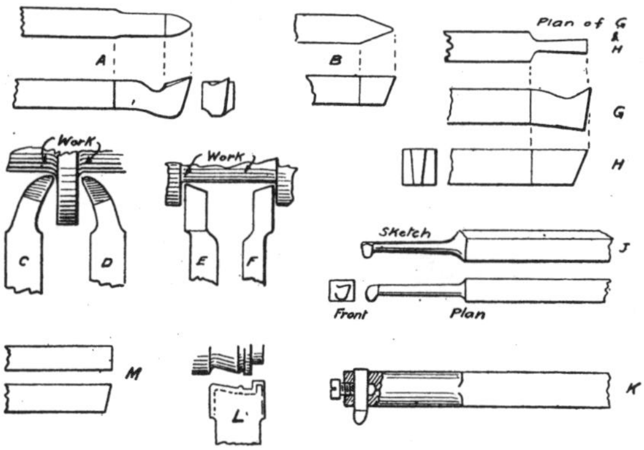

Fig. 101.—Slide-rest tools, etc.

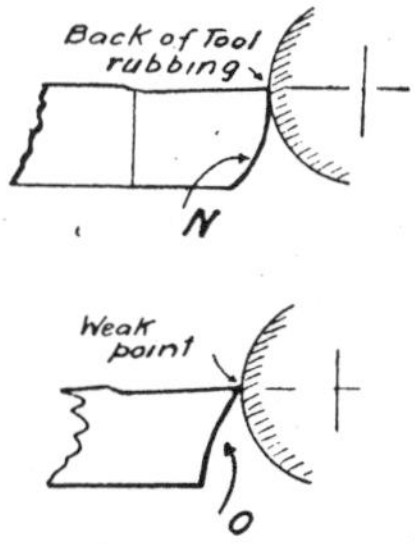

Fig. 102.—Badly ground tools

a holder or bar as at K. A special tool, called a former tool (see L), is shaped to the profile of the finished work and must of course be backed off on all sides. The square-ended tool M is useful for finishing iron and steel work, while the right- or left-handed hook or bent-nose tool, as C D, may have a pronounced " hook " to enable some special difficulty to be more easily overcome. The backing-off surface of a slide-rest tool should be quite straight; therefore the shapes shown at N and O (Fig. 102) should be avoided.

Setting Height of Tool.—Some skill and judgment are required to place a lathe tool correctly in the slide-rest. The material, the diameter of the work, and the depth of the cut compared with the strength of the lathe all have their influence. Nominally, the tool should point to the centre of the work. If it is too high a true cutting edge is not presented to the work and the point will be ground off. The noise made when a tool is set too high is a warning that the position needs modifying. In large diameters the height of the tool is not so important, as may be judged from the diagrams A and B (Fig. 103). In A, with small diameter work, the angle of the cutting edge to the horizontal is much greater than in B, although the height of the tool above the centres is the same in both cases. The same difference will be observed if the tool is below the centre line. There is greater danger, as shown in diagram C, of the work springing over the top of the tool when it is small in diameter, this being often noticed when using the parting-tool, and therefore the final cuts of the latter in parting off a fairly large bar should be lighter than at the outset, when the tool is operating on the largest diameter. The spring of the lathe work and tool is therefore a factor in the height of the tool. Careful and regular feeding up of the tool is a point to be watched, and the difference between an amateur's

TABLE OF TOOL ANGLES AND CUTTING SPEEDS

For meanings of terms *see* Fig. 104, page 57

Material and turning speeds in inches per minute	*Angles of*		
	Clearance	*Top rake*	*Side rake*
Wrought iron (300) Soft steel (250)	1 in 9	1 in 2	1 in 3
Tool and other hard steels (200 to 250)	1 in 10	1 in 2½	1 in 4
Cast iron (200) Hard gunmetal (250)	1 in 9	1 in 15	1 in 20
Brass (800) Soft gunmetal (600)	1 in 7	level	level

NOTE.—Unless the tool cuts at the side as well as at the front, as in the straight tool A, Fig. 101, then side rake is not required. In the knife tool (E and F) the angles of side and top rake are virtually transposed. The hook tool requires top rake only. In a parting tool the clearance angle is given to the three vertical sides of the tool. In planer and shaper tools the cutting edge should be lower than the top surface of the tool—that is, behind the latter. For very heavy cuts the clearance angle must be reduced to strengthen the tool point.

hand feeding of the slide-rest tool and the perfectly regular cut resulting from the use of the change wheels, is easily demonstrated on any screw-cutting lathe. Where the change wheels ordinarily supplied with the lathe are not adapted to provide a cut finer than 100 to the inch it is well to obtain an extra wheel to give the finest possible cut. The limits of the size of this wheel are determined by the position of the studs on the change-wheel quadrant.

Hand Metal-turning. — The amateur model-maker, unless he is an expert or professional hand turner, will find that the slide-rest generally gives the better results, for

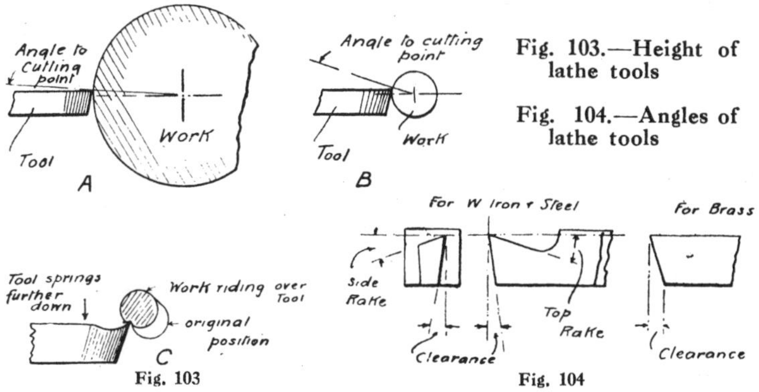

Fig. 103.—Height of lathe tools

Fig. 104.—Angles of lathe tools

Fig. 103

Fig. 104

which reason hand work is usually confined to those who have no slide-rest, or for preparatory work or finishing off some job which is otherwise turned out by slide-rest tools. A full set of hand tools is always useful, but the graver, parting, pointed, and flat tools, and a hook tool for iron and steel, and a tool shaped as shown in Fig. 110, include all the necessary types required by the model-maker. Heavy hand turning, such as is described in some instruction books, is not necessary in average model-making, and requires years of training to produce satisfactory results. To provide the maximum power the tools and handles should be long. The rest should be close to the work, the exact position depending on the size of the job, as will be seen from

Figs. 107 and 109. Work of medium diameter is quite easy, especially in brass. Shouldering-down a small steel spindle is, however, more difficult, as the tendency is for the tool to get under the work. No lubricant is required for turning brass, cast iron or gunmetal. Wrought iron and steel require either oil or turpentine. In parting off work by hand a steady hold is required, the tool being "rocked" into the work, but never allowed to go so far that the point is under the centre, otherwise the work will ride up over the point and

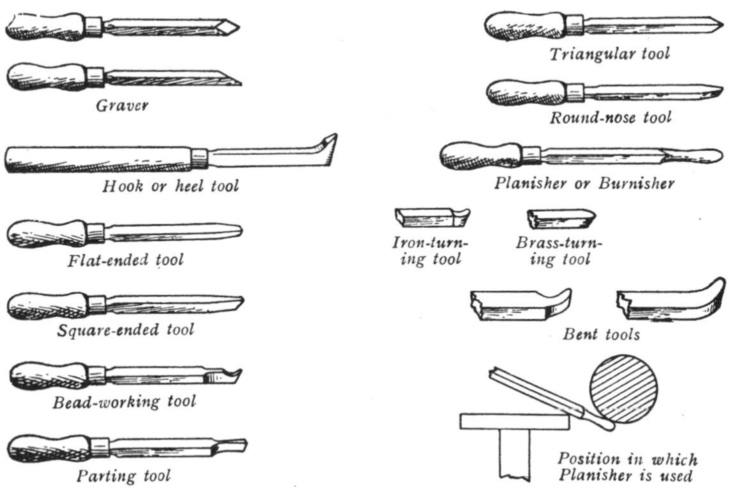

Fig. 105.—Hand turning tools

disaster to tool or work will follow. During the operation the parting tool should be given a slight lateral movement so that it cuts a groove a little wider than itself. The "arm-rest" (Fig. 111) is a useful accessory for internal work, and is employed as indicated in the sketch Fig. 112. The tool shown by Fig. 110 is handy for centring and facing brass work and for removing raw edges and arrises.

Drilling in the Lathe.—The model-maker uses his lathe extensively for drilling, and in the writer's experience the results obtained are superior to those accomplished on a hand drilling machine, which, without a self-feeding attachment, is difficult to manage, and has less range than a lathe.

There are several types of drills that may be employed in the lathe; indeed, any kind may be used if suitable fixings are provided. For larger holes the old diamond-pointed drill (*see* Fig. 113) fitted into a three-jaw or master chuck (or to a standard bush in the lathe) will be found satisfactory, and where an odd job has to be done will save the expense of a special twist or fluted drill. Diamond-pointed drills may

Fig. 106.—Method of holding hand turning tool

be made by the amateur, and their efficiency depends on whether they are finished with each facet true to the other in all cutting angles.

Twist and fluted drills are, however, mostly used, and in the lathe may be held either in a chuck (or expanding bush) in the mandrel or against or in a chuck in the back poppet. In the latter case the work revolves but the drill does not.

With a rotating drill several fitments are required. The first is a suitable self-centring chuck. The ordinary three-jaw chuck already referred to is usually employed, but it may be supplemented by a smaller drill chuck with Morse taper shank, so that it may be inserted in either the mandrel or in the back poppet as shown in Fig. 114. Where the lathe is not provided with taper centres, a straight shank drill chuck may be used and arranged to fit in a master chuck. The tailstock should be provided with drilling pads as at A B (Fig. 115), the first being used for large flat work and the V-notched pad, B, for drilling shafts and other round work. In drilling the bars and plates and other work which may be held in the hand, the work is often placed against a piece of wood backed up by the sliding poppet as indicated in Fig. 113. It is advisable to hold such work against a tee-rest or the bed of the lathe, otherwise

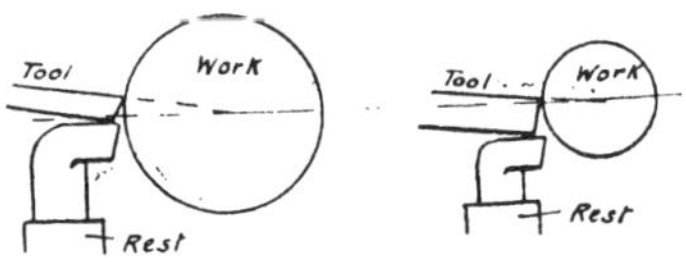

Fig. 109.—Height of hand-rest

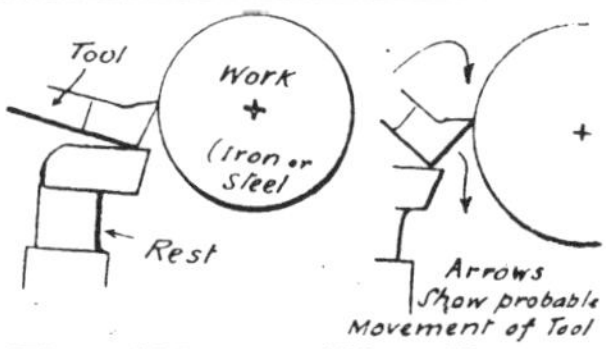

Figs. 107 and 108.—Correct and incorrect positions of hand turning tool

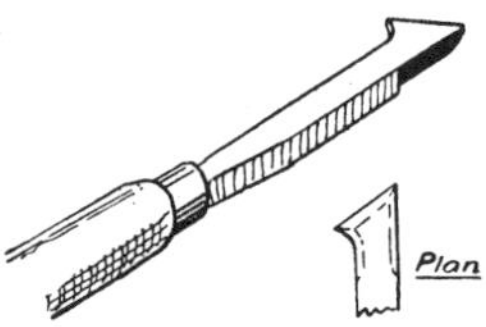

Fig. 110.—Useful tool for brass work

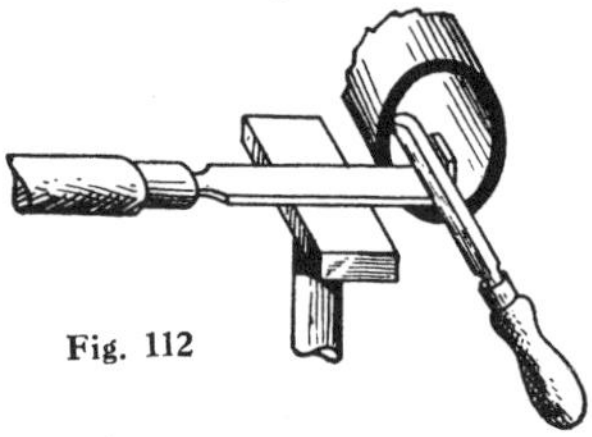

Fig. 112

Fig. 111

Figs. 111 and 112.—Arm-rest, and how to use it

should the drill " grab " the work it may be forced out of the hand, the operator possibly receiving personal injury. Where the work is revolving, the drill may be held in a drill chuck or master chuck attached to the back poppet. Large drills are centred at the back and may be held against the back centre as shown at C, Fig. 115. A lathe carrier is secured to the drill as illustrated, and to prevent accidents the drill should be firmly held up to the centre, both in driving it into the work and withdrawing it, and the resistance of the drill should be taken up by the carrier sliding on the top of the tee-rest. Small drills may be held up against a female centre as at D, Fig. 115.

A flat drill, held in the slide-rest as in Fig. 116, gives a good result if accurately centred both vertically and horizontally; but such a drill does not, as a rule, produce a hole of sufficient truth and finish for, say, a steam engine cylinder

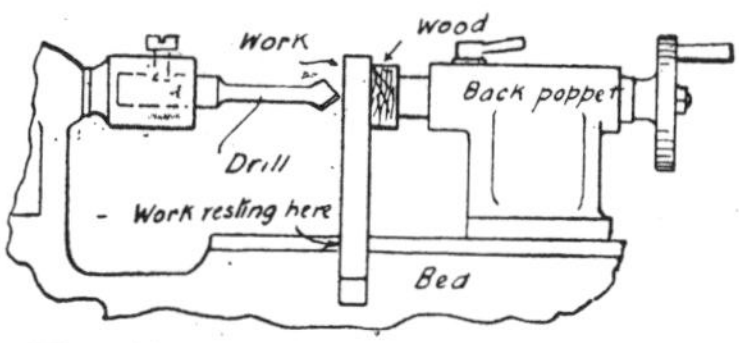

Fig. 113.—Drilling with revolving drill against back centre

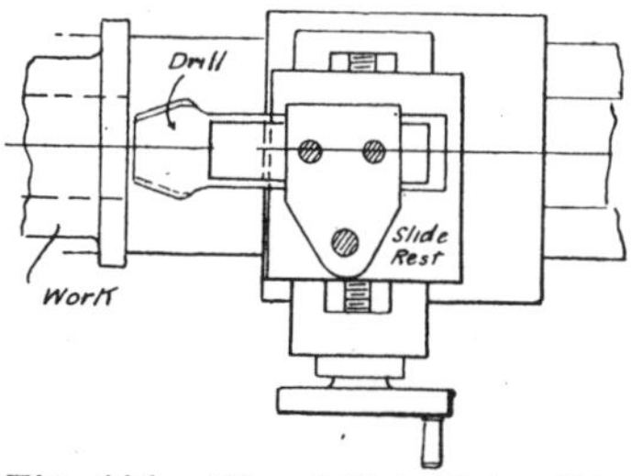

Fig. 116.—Flat drill held in slide-rest

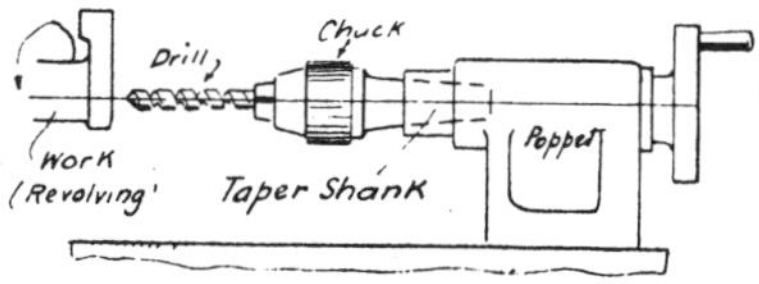

Fig. 114.—Drill held in chuck in poppet

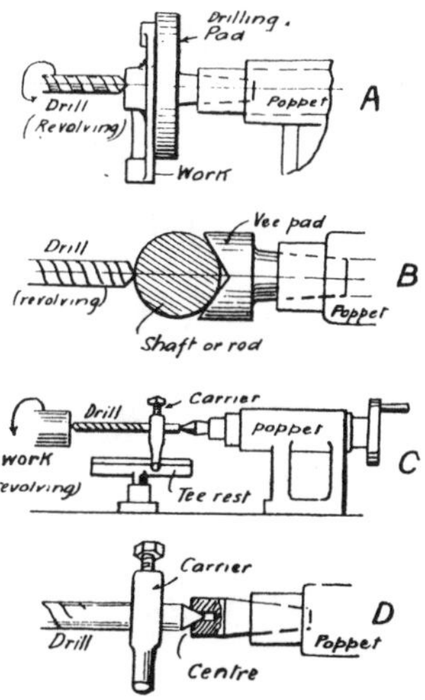

Fig. 115.—Four methods of drilling in the lathe

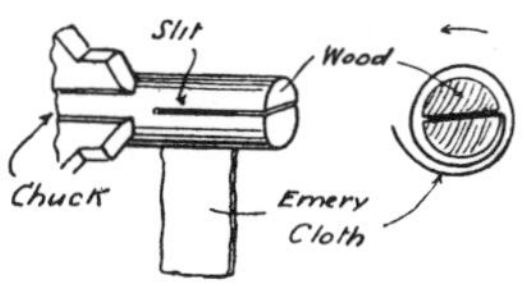

Fig. 117.—Lap for finishing bored hole

unless the work is subjected to further operations, such as reamering with a standard reamer, or lapping by mounting a piece of wood or lead, to fit the bore of the cylinder, on a mandrel and charging it with emery powder and oil. This lap is revolved and the cylinder is run up and down it—the whole length at each stroke—until a smooth surface is obtained. For a small cylinder, a lap is made by sawing down a round piece of wood with a longitudinal slot and inserting a strip of fine emery cloth as shown in Fig. 117, the cloth being rolled round as indicated.

A form of drill or boring tool that can be used where a greater degree of accuracy is required in the parallelism of a large hole is shown in Fig. 118. This " packed bit " cuts at the sides and front and is applicable to large holes that have been previously roughly drilled or bored out to a slightly smaller size ; it gives a very good finish. For smaller but true and deep holes a D bit (Fig. 119) is excellent.

A drill must not be unduly forced, and, with either the work or the drill revolving, the centres should be properly

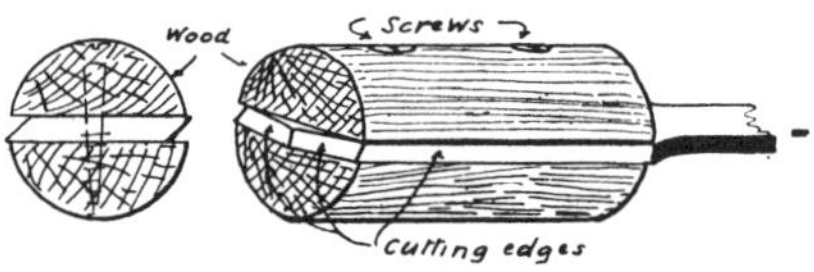

Fig. 118.—Packed bit

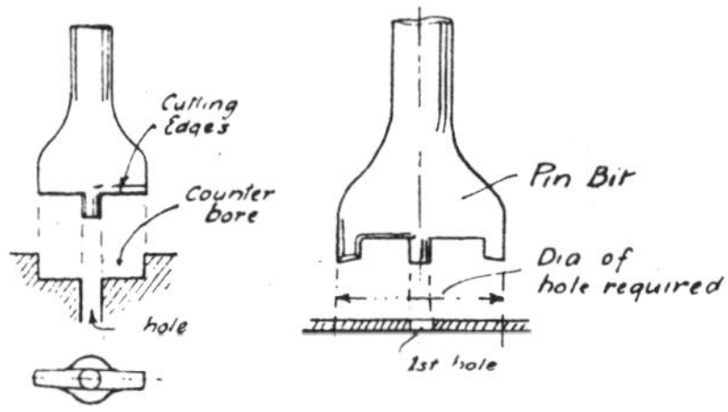

Figs. 120 and 121.—Two pin bits

Fig. 119.—D bit

formed in the work before drilling. In boring long holes the drill should be frequently removed to clear away the chips. In drilling steel or iron, the drill point should be lubricated. For brass and similar metals, the drill may be wetted to prevent seizing. The speed of small diameter drills should be high and the pressure light.

The pin drill is useful for counter-boring holes and also for making large diameter holes in sheet metal. The shape of the bit for the first-named purpose is shown in Fig. 120, the cutting edges being either at 90° to the centre line of the hole, as indicated, or made to suit the profile of the counter-bore required. Fig. 121 shows a bit used for large holes in metal that is too thick to be punched but cannot be drilled in the ordinary way. The prongs are provided with cutting edges on all four sides.

Metal Spinning in the Lathe.—There are many parts of a model for which the maker may desire to employ what are technically termed "spinnings." Spinning consists in moulding or pressing sheet metal into various shapes without resorting to cutting, piercing or fitting. Iron sheet $\frac{1}{32}$ in. diameter is spun at 600 revolutions per minute, while with thicker material the speed should be 400 revolutions. Zinc spins best at 1,200 revolutions, and copper, brass and aluminium at 800 to 1,000 revolutions. The tee-rest has closely spaced holes about $\frac{5}{16}$ in. diameter to receive steel pegs. The tools are long, both in the steel portion and the handle, so as to obtain leverage. Revolving back centres are more or less essential, and special centres and chucks are required to enable "formers" (pieces of wood or metal corresponding in shape to that of the work) to be employed. Hard and polished tools are used. A group of useful tools is shown in Fig. 122, and among these A is an auxiliary rest used in conjunction with the tee-rest, and in which the spinning tool is supported while doing some awkward internal operation; B and C are roller beading tools; D is a flaring tool, and is useful for smoothing over an already roughed-down job; E and F are tools for breaking down curves or flanges; G is a flat planisher or smoother; H is a cutting tool called a skimmer; I, J and K are mostly used for internal spinning. The tools the amateur would require for his initial experiments are D, E, F, G and K, together with an ordinary hand turning tool for skimming up. Copper of No. 18 S.W.G. lends itself best to the amateur's first efforts.

Before starting work the disc is lubricated with soft soap or vaseline, and everything being in order and the lathe running, grasp, say, a ball tool under the armpit with the steel end between the pins of the tee-rest. Set the nose of the tool a little below the centre, and, at a point towards the worker, apply the pressure and start to bring the tool outwards

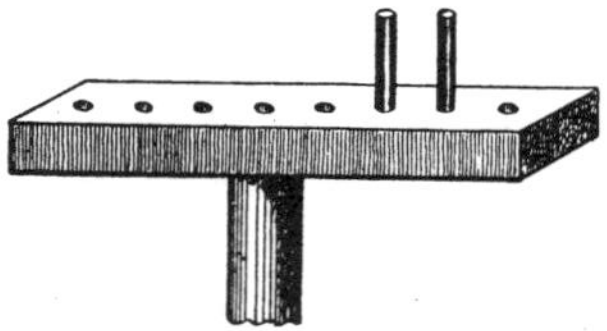

Fig. 123.—Tee-rest with fulcrum pegs

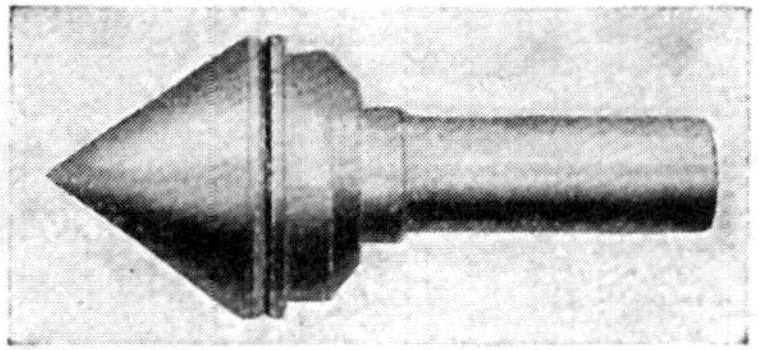

Fig. 124.—Ball-bearing revolving back-centre

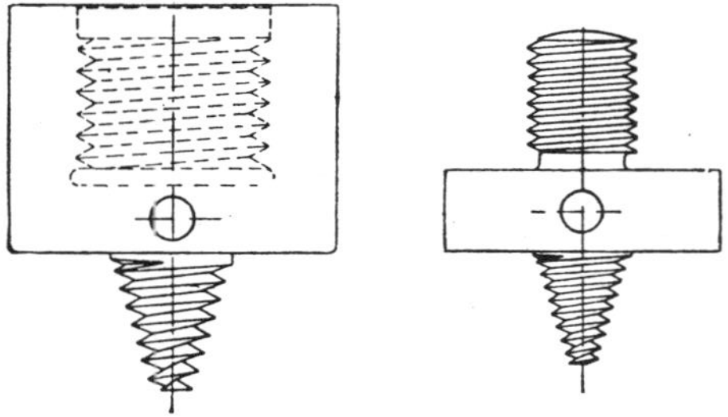

Figs. 125 and 126.—Internal and external threaded centres

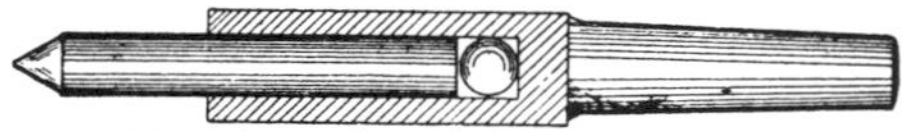

Fig. 127.—Revolving back-centre

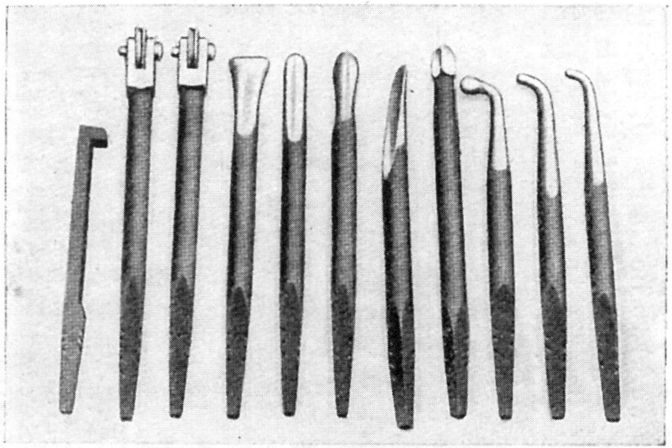

Fig. 122—Group of metal-spinner's tools

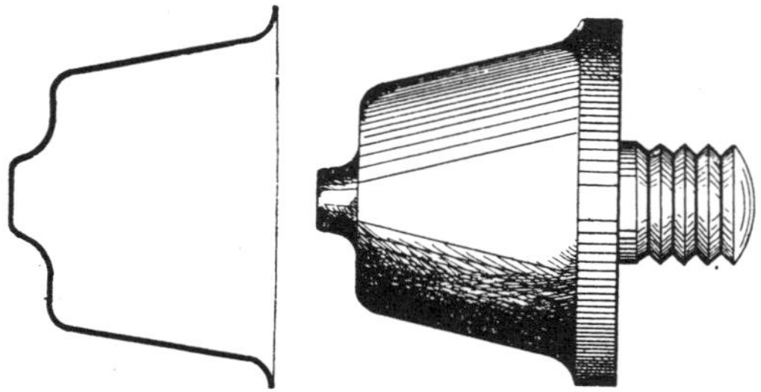

Fig. 128.—Spun metal object and its former

towards the periphery of the disc with a sweeping movement, constantly repeating the stroke, but applying some little pressure on the return movement. Do not allow the tool to rest in one position with the pressure applied, otherwise the metal will unduly stretch at this point.

A " back stick "—a short piece of round hardwood like an ordinary ebony desk ruler—is used in the left hand and is held fairly hard against the disc on the opposite side to that upon which the spinning tool is operating. This re-

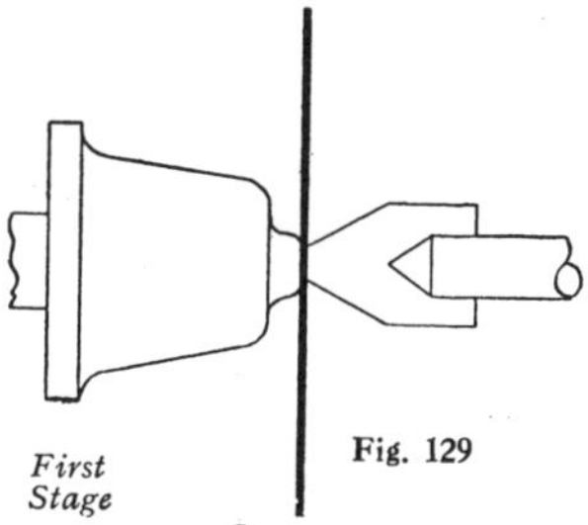

First Stage

Fig. 129

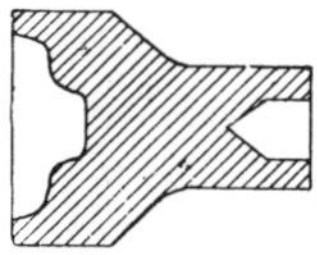

Fig. 132.—Follower for supporting partly-spun disc

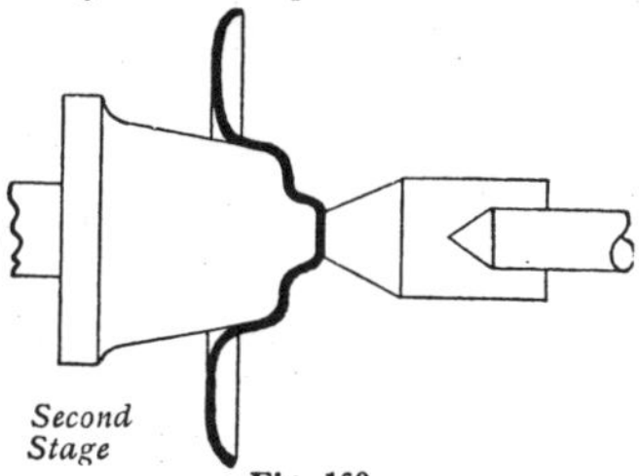

Second Stage

Fig. 130

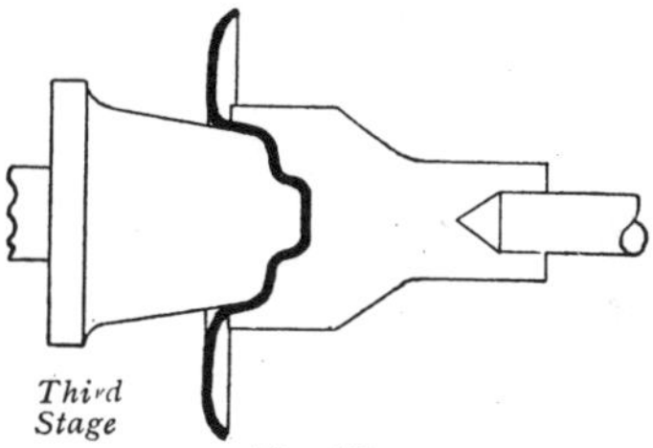

Third Stage

Fig. 131

Figs. 129 to 131.—Three stages of spinning

duces the liability of the metal to buckle. The illustrations show some of the chucks employed and also a disc being spun in its several stages. Where the work becomes too hard during any one of the stages, it should be removed and annealed. Hollow articles with a greater diameter in the centre are accomplished on sectional chucks ; but this is more or less beyond the scope of the requirements of a model-maker.

Running-down Cutters.—Where round rods or similar work have to be shouldered down, the running-down cutter, held in the poppet of the tailstock, is a most useful tool.

A master chuck may be made to hold them, the attachment of the chuck being arranged to suit the particular form of tailstock. Several standard sizes from $\frac{3}{32}$ in. upwards are procurable, the design being as shown in Fig. 134, but home-made cutters are usually made as shown in Fig. 135. The number of cutting edges should be at least four, and should be equally pitched, otherwise the work will not be true. The end of the rod to be worked on should also be trued up with a hand tool and edge chamfered off as at A (Fig. 133) before the cutter is brought up to it. This is very necessary where the reduction in diameter is considerable. The maximum reduction desirable in this process is about 30 to 50 per cent., i.e., say, from $\frac{1}{4}$ in. to $\frac{1}{8}$ in., or $\frac{1}{4}$ in. to $\frac{3}{16}$ in.

Wood Turning.—In model pattern making, wood turning is an operation frequently necessary. As a rule, the amateur will find that soft woods require sharper tools, higher speed, and more skilful handling than hard, close-grained woods. Beech, box and mahogany are useful woods to the beginner, box wood, especially, working more nearly like soft metal. Round work being turned out of square stuff should be roughly shaped with a hand chisel or spokeshave before mounting it in the lathe. The speed, compared with metal work, should be high.

The gouge and the chisel used by the wood turner are long, and have long handles so as to give greater power in using, and the cutting edges are as shown in Figs. 136 and 137. The tool is held more or less on the top of the work, and the hands give it a sweeping movement in parallel turning, with a rolling motion in cutting beads, etc. The chisel, as indicated, is bevelled on both sides so that it may be reversed. The edges of the tools must be very keen, as in the case of carpenter's tools. In sweeping along a piece of parallel work, the cutting must be done with the chisel between the portions A and B (Fig. 139); on no account should the point of the chisel, P, be allowed to touch the work; if it should it will very likely dig in and force the work out of the lathe or break the point of the tool. Beads and curved work are executed by slightly rolling the tool while moving it along, first to the left and then, with the tool reversed, to the right. For the hardest woods and ivory, tools much in the same position and shape as metal-working tools (as on brass) are employed.

Turning to Template.—In turning special shapes, such as a model locomotive chimney, where accuracy of outline

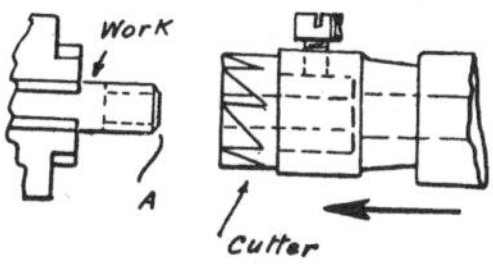

Fig. 133.—"Running-down" rods in the lathe

Fig. 135.—Home-made "running-down" cutter

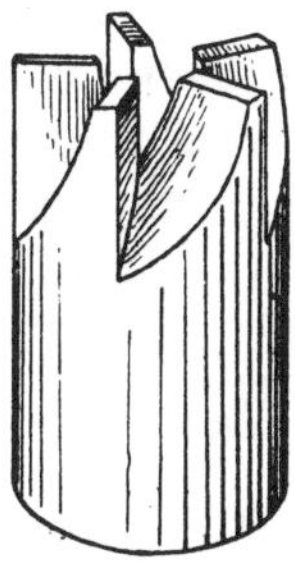

Fig. 134.—"Running-down" cutter.

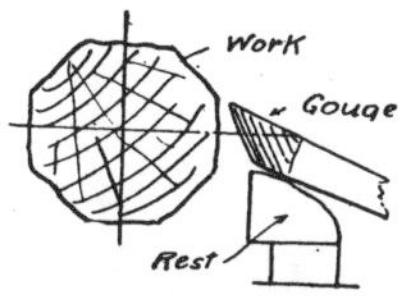

Fig. 138.—Position of wood-turning gouge

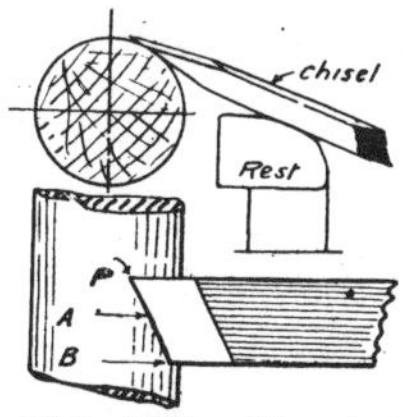

Fig. 139.—Turning soft wood

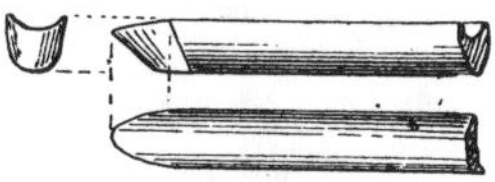

Fig. 136.—Wood-turning gouge

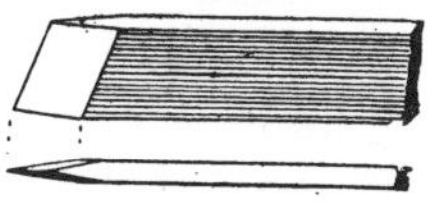

Fig. 137.—Wood-turning chisel

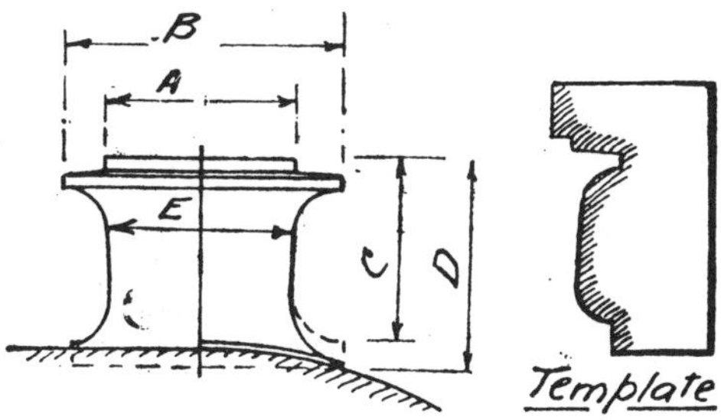

Fig. 140.—Turning work to template

is essential, a template should be cut out in thin tin plate from the full size working drawing. In a locomotive chimney the base fits on a round barrel, and therefore the bottom radius must be filed up by hand, the turned portion C (Fig. 140) being shaped on the lathe to the dotted line, the total length of the metal equalling dimension D. The important diameters are A B and E, which must be carefully callipered.

CHAPTER IV

The Various Processes Employed

Patterns and Pattern-making.—In model engineering as practised by the amateur, patterns should be reduced to the minimum, the work being built up out of raw material as much as possible. This method often saves both time and money, and, in addition, gives a much cleaner result. However, castings are in many cases essential, especially

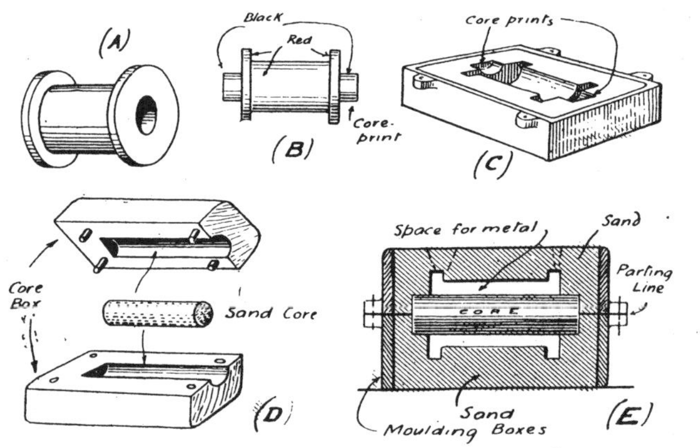

Fig. 141.—Processes of moulding and coring

in larger models and small-power engines. For cast-iron cylinders, patterns will require to be made in quite a professional style with core prints and core boxes. Proper patterns will also be necessary if the model-maker desires to market the castings, and in such cases wooden patterns would be made for all larger work, and metal patterns, often in duplicate, for the small parts. A composite pattern may also be used for several small parts, the castings being connected by sprays which are cut before machining (*see* Fig. 552, p. 261). This tends to prevent the loss of small patterns.

A core is necessary for making hollow castings, and to produce a core a core box or mould must be made at the same time as the pattern. To illustrate the principle of coring, A to E (Fig. 141) show a pattern and casting for a plain flanged hollow cylinder in the various processes. A shows the cored casting; B is the pattern, which has two projecting plugs equal in diameter to the cored box of the

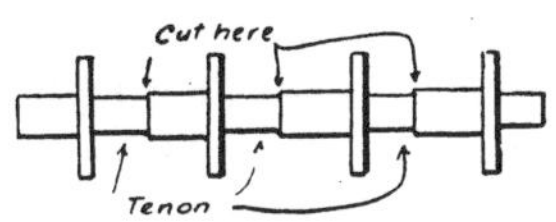

Fig. 145.—Multiple pattern

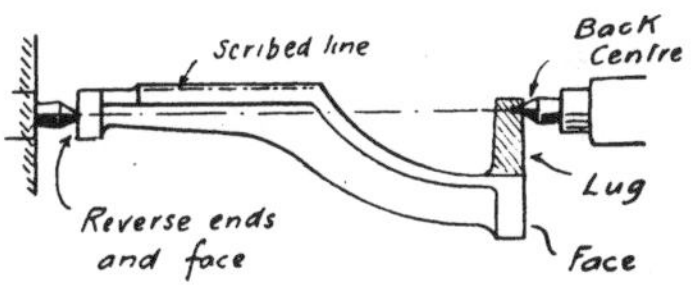

Fig. 143.—Chucking pieces

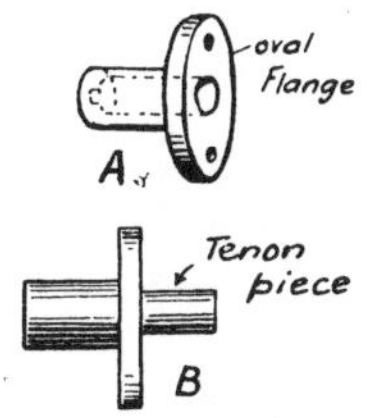

Fig. 144.—Tenons or spigots for chucking

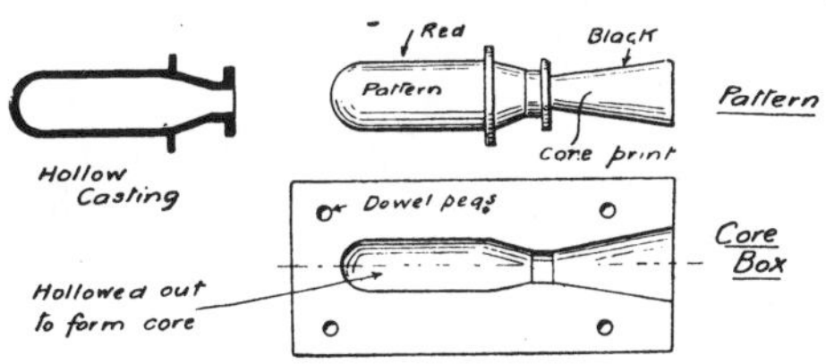

Fig. 142.—Pattern and core box for hollow casting

cylinder castings. These are called the "core prints," and serve to make two indentations in the sand; see the half of the mould after the pattern has been moulded. The core is made of sand in a box as shown at D, the core being baked dry after moulding. The core is then placed in the prints made in the mould by the core prints on the pattern, and the top half of the moulding box is put in place as shown at E. This gives a hollow casting, the core, of course, filling up the spaces made by the core prints. Such plain cylindrical cores can always be left to the founder, no core box being provided, an indication, by a special instruction or simply colouring the pattern as at B, being given to him that a cored casting is required. Of course, the pattern must have prints and the core required should be of a normal regular size.

In the above case the core is supported both ends, but in many instances there is only one opening to the inside of the hollow casting, as shown in Fig. 142. Here an overhanging core is required, and the print must therefore be longer to support it. Fig. 142 shows also the pattern and half of a suitable core-box.

The addition of spigots, tenon, and chucking pieces is always to be recommended in model work to facilitate holding the work during machining. Some of these additions will enable work to be done in the lathe. As an example, the cast standard of the vertical engine which forms the subject matter of another chapter may be taken. This standard is so supplied that filing is the only method of finishing it. By casting a lug on the foot (*see* Fig. 143) it could be placed between the lathe centres and the top and bottom faces could then be easily faced up truly parallel with each other. The lug could then be cut off, and failing the use of a shaping machine the crosshead slides could be filed up. While in the lathe a horizontal line could also be scribed on it to assist the fitter in filing the slide surface.

Small gland castings (Fig. 144A) are difficult to hold in the lathe unless a spigot is cast on them, as at B. Indeed, as there are generally several glands in one engine, a multiple pattern may be prepared as shown in Fig. 145, each casting being sawn off before machining. The casting is held in the chuck by the tenon piece cast on the front, and the gland turned, bored and faced. It may then be reversed in the chuck, the spigot cut off, and the front faced to finished dimensions. In making patterns for locomotive driving wheels it is the usual practice to make a master pattern in wood with a double shrinkage and ample machining allowances. Two or three brass castings are then obtained, and balance weights, which in locomotive work vary in position and magnitude, may be added to each of the two or three machined and finished brass patterns. From these patterns soft iron castings are obtained.

In all patterns ample "draw" must be allowed, and a certain knowledge of the foundryman's art is required to design patterns which will cast in a sound manner with the least possible trouble. In model patterns loose pieces (necessary for under-cut work) should be avoided. Plain, straightforward moulding is to be recommended. Small, flat, metal patterns should be bored with a $\frac{1}{16}$-in. or $\frac{3}{32}$-in. hole somewhere near their centre of gravity to enable the moulder the more readily to lift them out of the sand. The contraction of castings must be allowed for in all patterns, and a patternmaker's rule can be purchased with the neces-

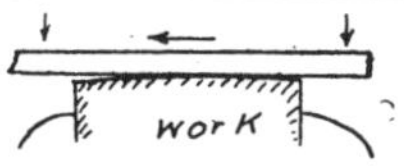

Fig. 146.—Improper movement of hand file

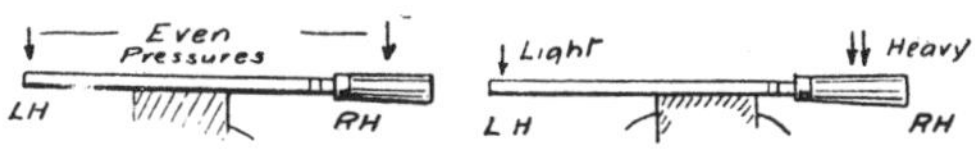

Figs. 149 and 150.—Pressures at middle and near end of stroke

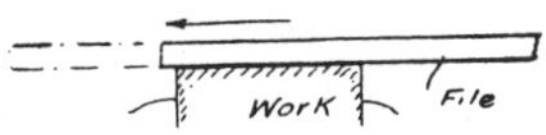

Fig. 147.—Proper movement of hand file

Fig. 148.—Pressure when beginning stroke

sary allowances for all materials. The contraction is roughly: Cast iron $\frac{1}{8}$ in., brass, steel and malleable iron $\frac{3}{16}$ in., and aluminium $\frac{1}{4}$ in. in the foot. Patterns should be made with well-rounded fillets, and wood patterns should be painted and finished with a hard shellac spirit-varnish. Large patterns are often made in two halves, the parts dividing at the parting line of the mould.

Filing.—Although all hand processes cannot very well be learnt from books, there are a few hints which may reduce the time it takes to learn to file a true surface. True filing requires considerable skill, the tendency being to produce a rounded surface, as Fig. 146. The back stroke needs no pressure, as the teeth do not cut; and the forward strokes should be made deliberately and with all the desirable pressure, the file being kept perfectly horizontal. It is obvious that to accomplish this the excess of pressure of the left hand at the beginning of the stroke must be transferred (automatically and without mental effort) to the right hand at the completion of the stroke, as illustrated in the diagrams

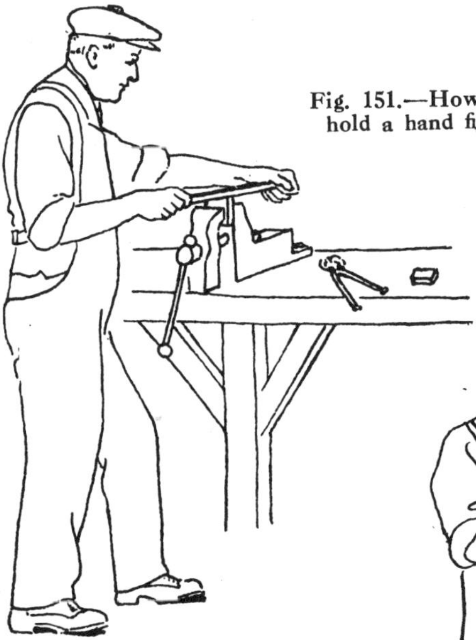

Fig. 151.—How to hold a hand file

Fig. 152.—Method of draw filing

Figs. 148 to 150. This is where skill is necessary, and such skill is only obtained by long practice.

As wrought iron and steel give a better grip on the file than do cast iron and brass, older files should be used on the former and newer ones on brass and cast iron. With regard to working cast iron, the outer skin should be first removed with an old, rough file or chipped off. Pickling cast iron in diluted sulphuric or hydrochloric acid assists in removing the hard skin. Chilled surfaces, however, must be ground off, as no file or machine tool will touch them.

Large flat surfaces should be checked for accuracy on a surface plate smeared with red lead or ochre and oil. To prevent the files "pinning"—that is, becoming clogged and scratching the work—the teeth may be filled with chalk. The

Fig. 153.—Triangular scraper

Fig. 157.—Section through half-round scraper

Fig. 154.—Another triangular scraper

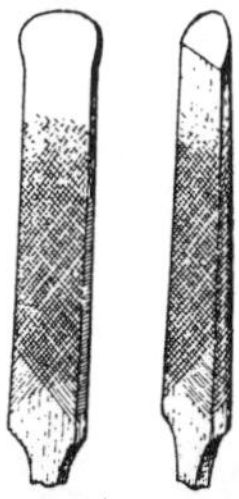

Fig. 158.—Two shapes of rounded-nose scrapers

Fig. 155.—Flat scraper

Fig. 156.—Half-round scraper

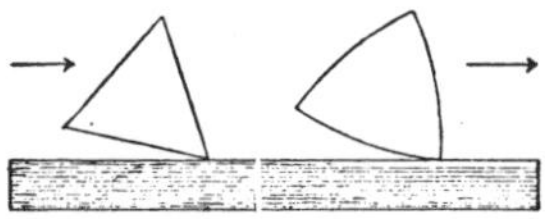

Figs. 159 and 160.—Triangular scraper, correctly and incorrectly ground

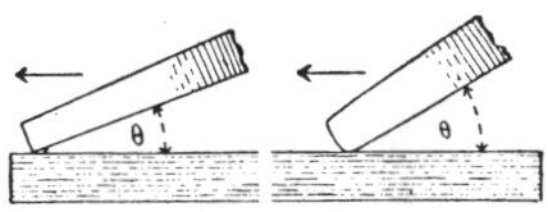

Figs. 161 and 162.—Flat scraper, correctly and incorrectly ground

illustrations show how to hold a file; draw filing (Fig. 152) is employed to smooth long, narrow surfaces, the file being rubbed on a piece of chalk to avoid scratching the work.

Scraping and Grinding.—Where a true surface has to be obtained, grinding or scraping must be resorted to. Scraping is adopted for larger iron surfaces, bearing brasses, etc. In 1840 Sir J. Whitworth demonstrated the superiority of scraping over all other hand processes for producing surfaces of a high degree of accuracy. Scraping is done by hand tools such as are illustrated in Figs. 153 to 166. These can be ground up on a grindstone (wet) from

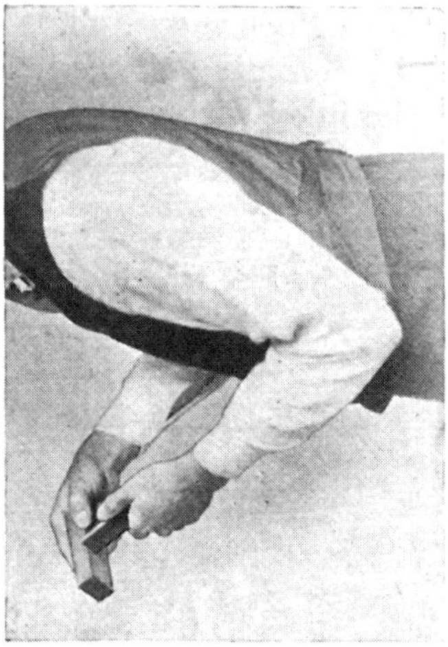

Fig. 164.—Rubbing square edge of scraper

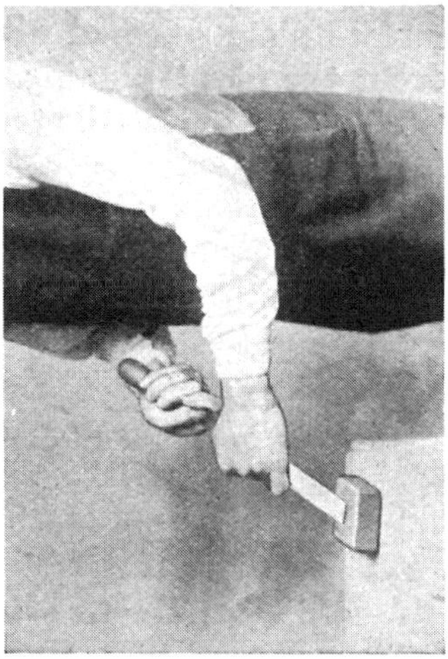

Fig. 166.—Holding flat scraper

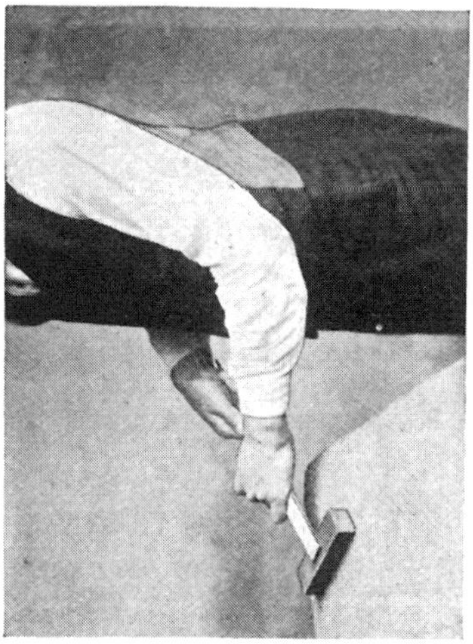

Fig. 163.—Rubbing flat face of scraper

Fig. 165.—Easing hole with scraper

old files and must be finished with a keen edge, such as produced on an oilstone. Scrapers should be dead hard, no tempering being required; in hardening, however, the temperature should not exceed a bright red. Scrapers must be used in conjunction with a true surface, a piece of plate glass sufficing for model work, and comparisons are made by thinly smearing the surface plate with red lead or ochre and oil, and applying the work; the high places will then

Fig. 170.—Using long-handled scraper

Fig. 167.—Edge of flat scraper

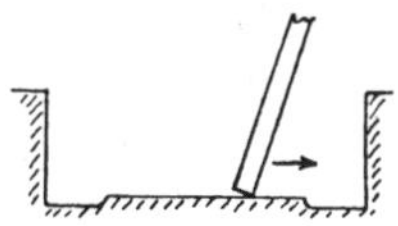

Fig. 168.—Use of draw scraper in recess

Fig. 169.—Long-handled draw scraper

Fig. 172.—Case-hardening small part

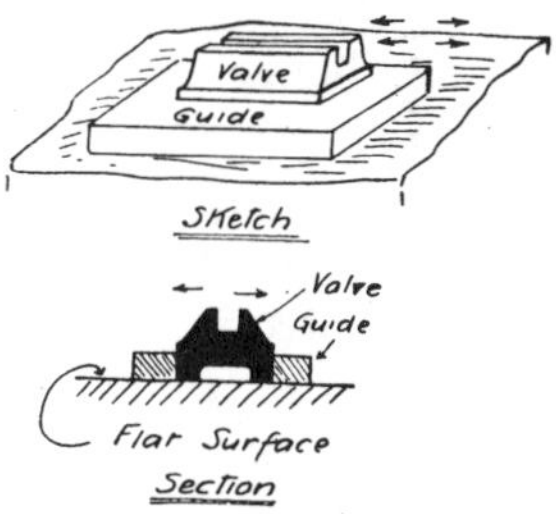

Fig. 171.—Grinding up small slide valve

be observed by the red contacts. In the case of a bearing brass, the oil is smeared on the journal of the shaft or crank pin. In oilstoning a scraper, rounded surfaces should be avoided. Figs. 159 to 162 show the angle at which scrapers should be used, and also why badly ground scrapers will not cut. The edge of a flat scraper should be slightly curved, as shown in Fig. 167, and should be used with a push stroke, but to get at a slide-valve port face in a recess a long-handled flat scraper (Fig. 169) should be used with a draw stroke, as illustrated in Figs. 168 and 170. A small surface plate will also be required. The strokes, in all cases, whether draw or push, should be short, never exceeding ½ in. For facing up very small valves and surfaces, such as are common in model work, grinding is frequently resorted to. Sometimes the grinding surface is formed on a disc revolving in the lathe, and the work is held on a table up to the disc. This method is quite all right for ordinary jobs, but where accuracy and steam tightness are required a good method is to face a valve finally with flour emery, or, better still, fine pumice powder and oil on a piece of plate glass (not the piece or the side of the piece used as a surface plate for measuring). To prevent rocking a small object and the production of a rounded surface, a guide plate may be made.

A slide valve for a model steam engine is shown being surfaced in such a guide in Fig. 171. In grinding in petrol and gas-engines valves, a rotary motion is given to the valve with a screwdriver held in a slot in the top of the valve. The valve should be lifted periodically to prevent grooves being cut by any large particle of emery in the seating or valve. Brass valves should be ground in with pumice powder or other mild abrasive material with water, not with oil and emery.

Case-hardening.—This is a process of giving a coating of hard steel to soft mild steel or wrought iron, which substances do not harden simply by quenching owing to the deficiency in carbon. After machining and polishing, objects made in these materials may be made to absorb carbon by being placed in an air-tight box or case and heated to redness while in contact with some substance rich in carbon. Only the outer skin is converted into high-carbon steel, and this is hardened on quenching. In large work animal charcoal—that is, bones, leather, and hoof scraps—are used; in small work, yellow prussiate of potash is used, and the work is often done by heating in a tin lid full of powdered prussiate in the open forge (*see* Fig. 172), the operation taking only a few minutes. To create a thick skin of steel the work must be boxed (to prevent scaling), and a regular heat continued for about twelve to fifteen hours. While red hot, the work is quenched, and if any warping is apparent the piece must be straightened and reground to shape. Pins and long objects should be plunged endways to prevent warping as much as possible.

Hardening and Tempering Tools.—Tools are made of varieties of steel (high-carbon) which will harden on being heated to redness and quenched. Tool or cast steel is the commercial name for the ordinary kind, while for small cutters a fine crucible cast steel, called silver steel, is much used by model-makers. Tool steel should not be heated above a bright red, as otherwise the strength of the metal is liable to become impaired.

As a rule, tools are forged and roughly ground or filed to the shape desired. The tool must then be hardened by heating to redness and quenching in water. In this state the steel is very hard, but so brittle that it would not stand the strain of turning or cutting metal, and it therefore requires tempering or "letting down." This is done by heating it and observing the different colours which the heated tool assumes, which colours extend from a very pale straw colour, through dark straw to brown-yellow, yellow-purple, purple, dark purple, dark blue to blue. Steels vary a little, but the colour observation is sufficiently correct for ordinary purposes. The tool should be heated away from the cutting edge, which is usually the less massive end, so that the back (the non-cutting portion) is softer and therefore tougher, the colour changing by virtue of the heat conducted from the back to the front of the tool. When the working point reaches the desired stage in the letting down, the tool should be quenched. To judge the colour easier, the tool should be brightened with emery cloth at the working point. Some tools—for instance, a cold chisel for metal—may be hardened and tempered at one heat, only the working point being immersed in the quenching water. The point is then quickly brightened, and the remaining heat in the stock of the tool will travel up to the point through all the colour changes until it reaches the dark purple when it should be dropped into the water. In all cases of quenching the tool should be moved about in the quenching water. Some steels harden best in a strong solution of common salt ; others in a stream of running water.

Tools may be hardened in oil, but only one degree of hardness, equal to that of steel tempered down to a dark straw, is obtainable ; although the nature of the oil will make some difference.

TABLE OF COLOURS IN TEMPERING TOOL STEEL

Dark Blue .	Springs, screwdrivers, wood chisels.
Dark Purple .	Chipping chisels.
Purple-brown .	Brass turning tools, drills, centre punches, lathe centres.
Brown-yellow .	Reamers, turning tools, punches, and dies, drills.
Dark straw .	Chasers, taps, and screw dies, drills, turning tools.
Medium straw .	Shaper and planer tools, milling cutters.
Light straw .	Scrapers for brass only (iron scrapers are not tempered down).

Special tool steels, known as self- or air-hardening steels, do not require any tempering or hardening ; after being heated to a high degree these steels cool in air at such a rate that leaves them hard enough and sufficiently strong for all machine-tool purposes. There are various brands of these " high-speed " steels, and each should be treated as instructed by the makers. As a rule, great care must be taken not to overheat them in the preliminary forging to shape.

Drilling Metal Work.—The notes in the last chapter on the subject of drilling may be supplemented by some hints on hand drilling. The flat drill already referred to and illustrated by Fig. 173 should be ground up with exactly equal length of cutting edges, the 30° angles A and B (Fig. 173) also being exactly alike. The sides of the drill may be scraping sides (that is, they have cutting edges as shown at C), but while this drill is much used it is liable to produce taper holes. The sides of the drill should ordinarily be quite parallel as at P, so that when reground the size of the hole formed by the drill will not be altered, as would be

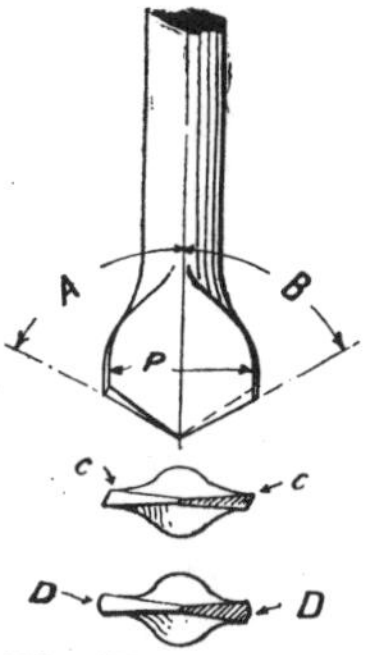

Fig. 173.—Flat or diamond-pointed drill

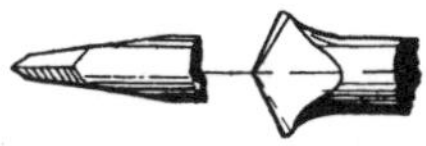

Fig. 174.—Drill with two cutting directions

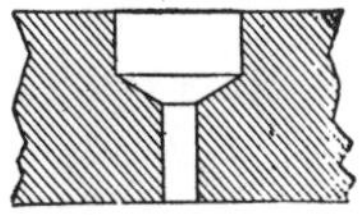

Fig. 179.—Small leading-in hole

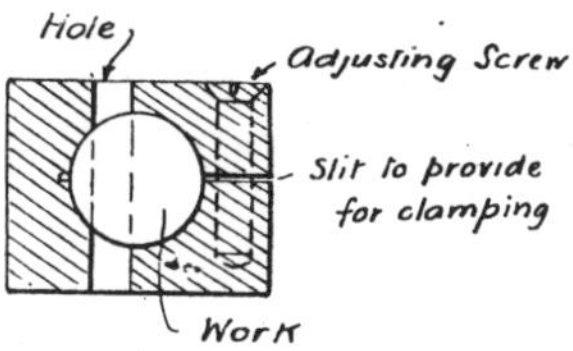

Fig. 182.—Drilling jig (*see* Fig. 180)

Fig 180

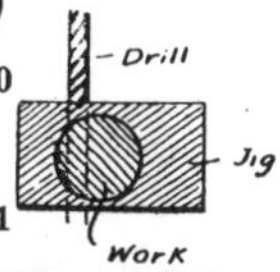

Fig. 181

Figs. 180 and 181.—Hole in side of round rod and method of drilling it

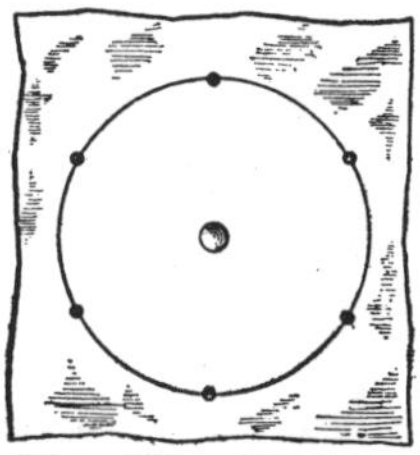

Fig. 175.—Marking out centre for drilling

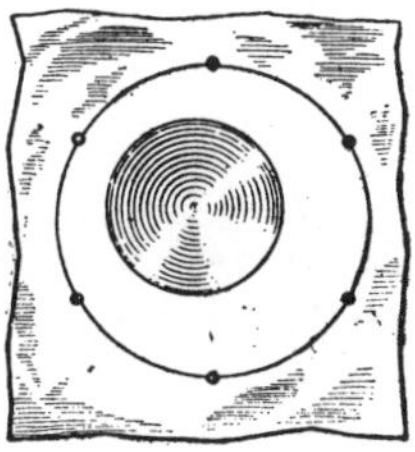

Fig. 176.—Eccentricity of drill recess

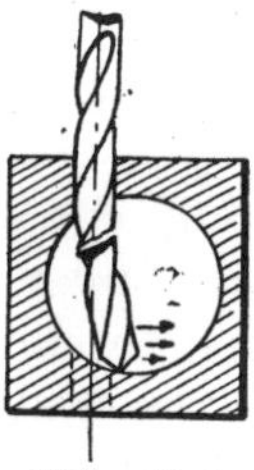

Fig. 183.—Bad result of drilling into cavity

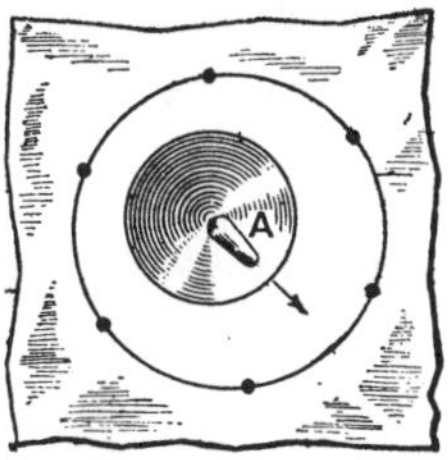

Fig. 177.—Method of drawing centre

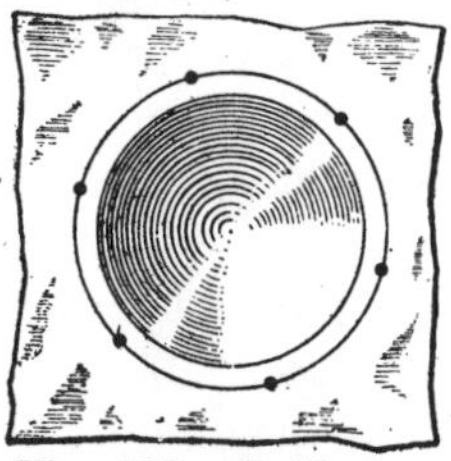

Fig. 178.—Drill correctly placed in marked-out circle

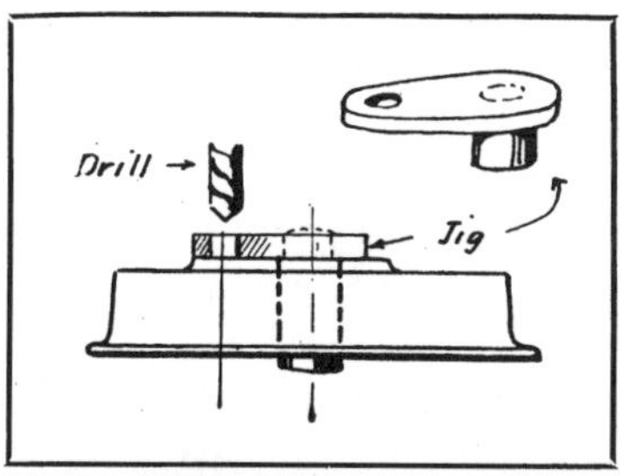

Fig. 184.—Drilling jig for crank-pin holes of locomotive wheels

the case with a drill shaped as Fig. 174. The sides should also be rounded (*see* D, Fig. 173) to the same (or less) radius as that of the hole to be drilled. No cutting or scraping can then take place. Where the fiddle-string hand drill is used, or the Archimedean or any similar drilling appliance in which the direction of the drill is reversed, the drill may be ground as in Fig. 174. Naturally, such a drill is slower in action, and does not really cut, but scrapes the metal away. In using the geared hand drill, a short drill should be used if the work will allow. This applies to the twist and fluted drill as well as the diamond-pointed kind just referred to. Steadiness in holding the hand drill is another point to observe, and while the speed should be high enough, rushing the drill through is likely to cause disaster by the unsteady hold on the drilling appliance produced. In drilling thin stuff the speed should not be too slow, but the pressure light, especially at the period in the operation when the point of the drill is breaking through. If the drill "grabs" at this moment, then by holding the main gear wheel of the hand drill in all the fingers and with a repeated forward and reverse movement, feeling for any dangerous resistance and immediately stopping the motion should it be felt, a clean hole (and an undamaged drill) will result. Straight-fluted drills are recommended for plate work and in brass and soft gunmetal. The twist drill acts, in such work, like a screwed bolt in a nut, and seizes the job to the detriment of both drill and work. Before operating on a large hole, the diameter should be marked out as shown in Fig. 175, and a centre popped as nearly as possible in the middle of the ring. If the application of the drill shows that the centre is out of truth, then by making a groove with a fine chisel as at A (Fig. 177) the drill will be drawn into the correct position. A leading-in hole of small diameter is often made to guide the large drill and to relieve its point of any strain (Fig. 179).

Drilling through Jigs.—Where a hole has to be drilled in a round rod or from a slanting surface in such a position (Fig. 180) that the drill tends to run off, then the only safe method is to make a temporary drilling jig, or to drill it while it is inside a piece of rectangular metal as shown in Fig. 181, the position and direction of the hole being carefully marked out and provided for. A permanent drilling jig is recommended, irrespective of the position of the hole, where several pieces have to be drilled. This jig (*see* Fig. 182) may be made in tool steel, so that it may be hardened and tempered, the small hole being drilled first and the larger hole drilled or bored afterwards. Where the two

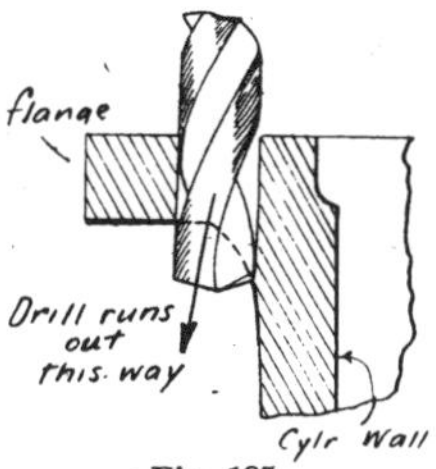

Fig. 185

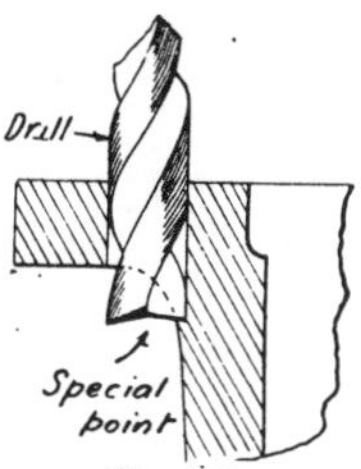

Fig. 186

Figs. 185 and 186.—Drilling cylinder flange

Fig. 187.—Broach or taper reamer

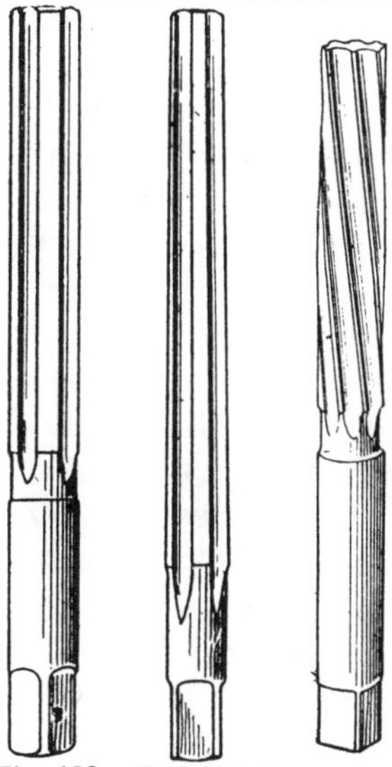

Fig. 188.—Parallel, taper, and parallel-twist fluted reamers

holes are nearly the same size and the smaller one is to the one side, then a plug should be placed in the hole. This is a precaution which should be taken in drilling any single piece of hollow stuff where the drill emerges and re-enters a hole with the surfaces not at right angles to the drill. Otherwise, the drill may be broken, as shown in Fig. 183.

In drilling model locomotive wheels for coupling rod crank pins a high degree of accuracy is desirable to prevent the coupling rods binding on passing the horizontal dead centres. To ensure the correct throw, a drilling jig should be made from a piece of steel rod turned to fit the axle hole, this rod having a steel plate riveted to it as shown. This plate is accurately marked, drilled the required size, hardened or case-hardened, and then used to guide the drill as shown in Fig. 184.

Where a flange must be drilled and the hole is likely to emerge near to the wall of the pipe, cylinder or chamber there is danger of the drill running out, as shown in Fig. 185. This may be prevented by grinding up a twist drill with a point of reverse angle, as shown in Fig. 186.

Reaming Holes.—Where a hole is drilled too small, a broach or reamer or " rimer " may be used to open it out. The name " broach " is given to the smaller five-sided reamers as illustrated by Fig. 187. These tools are rather long, and have a slight taper, and are sold on cards in sets of six. The tangs are square and may be fitted into handles. Fluted reamers (Fig. 188) are made in the parallel and taper forms, the latter being usually employed for opening out holes of $\frac{1}{4}$ in. diameter and above. The parallel reamers have either straight or spiral flutes, and are used for finishing holes dead to size. In model work their chief use is for truing cylinder and pump plunger bores, and for bearings and bearing bushes. The spirally fluted reamers are most likely to give, in an amateur's hands, a clean surface to a bored hole. Fluted reamers, however, are expensive tools, and great care should be taken in storing them to prevent damage to their cutting edges.

Bottoming Holes.—Where it is necessary to square the bottom of a hole as left by the drill from the shape A (Fig. 189) to shape B, a special drill may be made as shown in Fig. 190. The flat part of the drill need not be too thin and should be parallel with rounded edges. The two cutting edges are divided by a slot, cut at an angle as indicated; the cutting edges therefore overlap each other and give a smooth hole without leaving a central pip.

Cutting Large Holes and Discs.—For large holes in plate stuff and also for making discs of metal, a cutter bar as shown in Fig. 191 may be used. The pin A works in a small hole drilled in the plate, and the bar B may be extended

Fig. 189.—Hole before and after bottoming

Fig. 190.—Bottoming drill

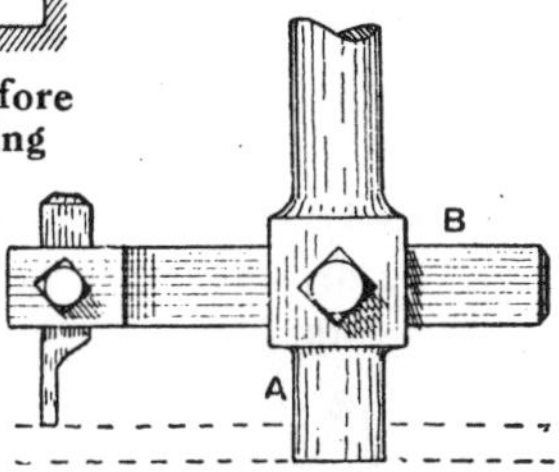

Fig. 191.—Cutter bar for large holes

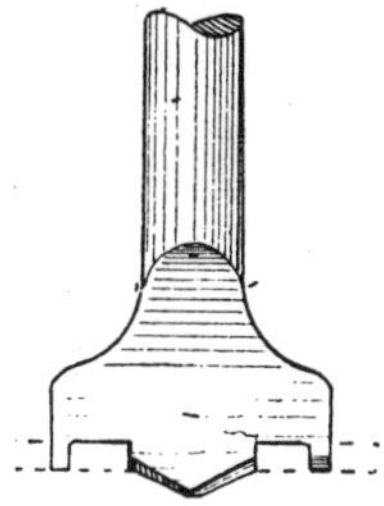

Fig. 193.—Drill for cutting large holes

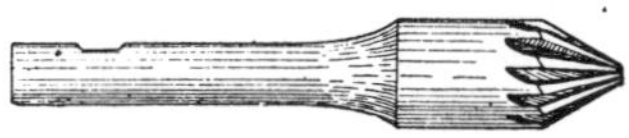

Fig. 194.—Rose-bit countersink

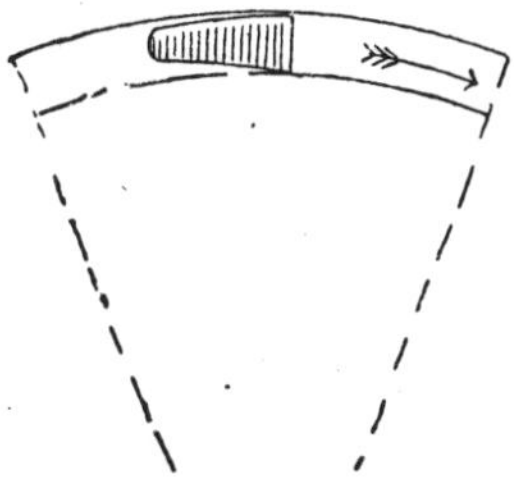

Fig. 192.—Diagram showing angle of cutter

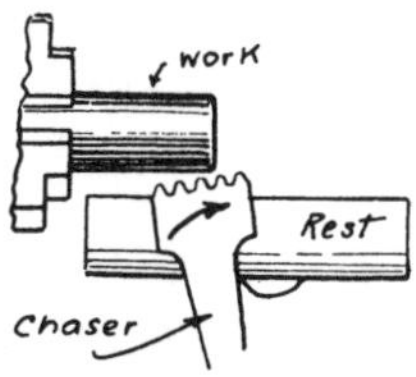

Fig. 196.—Using screw chaser in lathe

Fig. 195.—Arboring tool

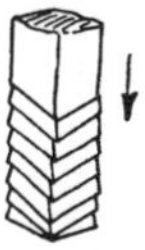

Fig. 198.—Large drift

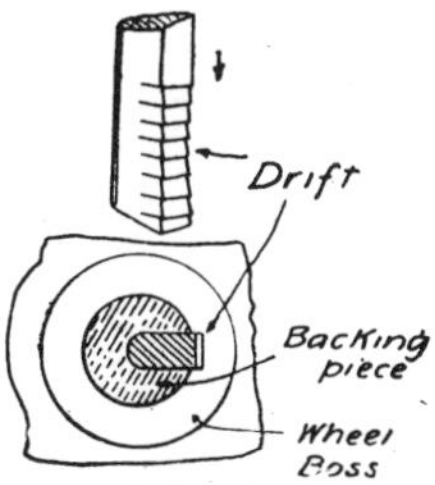

Fig. 199.—Drifting a key-way

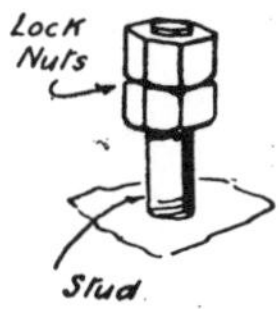

Fig. 200.—Driving a stud with lock nuts

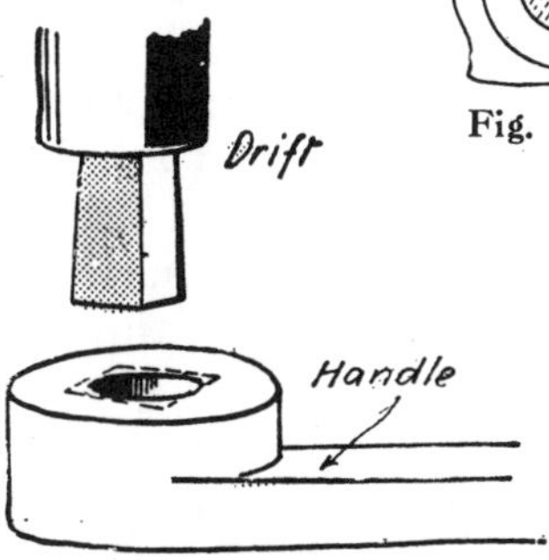

Fig. 197.—Drifting square hole

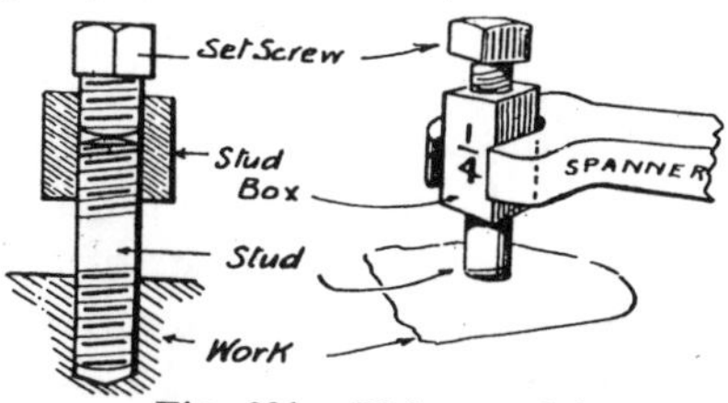

Fig. 201.—Using stud box

to cut any size hole required. In plan the working edge of the cutter must be shaped like a parting tool with clearance on both sides as well as on the bottom edge (*see* Fig. 192). Fig. 193 shows a type of drill that cuts the smaller and larger diameters at the one operation. It is a useful appliance for making washers from thick plate.

Countersinking and Counter-boring.—For countersinking a hole for a screw or bolt with a flush head it is better to use a rose cutter (Fig. 194) than an ordinary drill of larger size, a more regular hole being produced, especially in brass, copper, and soft steel. If a drill must be used, choose a twist or straight-fluted drill in preference to a diamond-pointed one. For counter-boring large work a milling cutter on an arbor, as shown in Fig. 195, should be used. The ordinary pin drill, however, is usually found to be quite satisfactory in ordinary model work (*see* Fig. 120, page 62).

Chasing Screw Threads.—In model engineering, ability to use a screw chaser is an immense advantage. The chaser is made in two forms—for external and internal threads; and may be considered as a part of a screw-thread die on the end of a handled tool. The difficulty to overcome is "striking" the thread. The tool should be brought up to the work slightly on the slant, as if the operator were using a flat-ended turning tool to chamfer off the edge of the work. It should also be given a swing, the magnitude and rate of travel being such as suits the pitch of the thread being cut (*see* Fig. 196). If the start of the thread is struck properly no difficulty will be encountered in finishing it, as the chaser automatically travels as it cuts, and it should be allowed to travel without resistance. Internal threads are a little more difficult. The advantage of the chaser is that a large or any odd diameter may be given to the threaded portion. Finer threads than Whitworth can therefore be used on a given diameter of work. A chaser is also largely employed to finish a thread which has been roughly screw-cut on the lathe with the change-wheel gear. Indeed, if a screw-cutting lathe is available, this is the best method of cutting the thread, and, if desired, following the single pointed tool, the chaser may be mounted in the slide rest. If the thread is a short one it can, however, be easily finished off by hand.

Taper threads, so useful for boiler tubes and fittings, may also be produced with the chaser. A range of inside and outside chasers, including 40, 32, and 26 threads per inch, is the most useful to the model maker.

Drifting Square Holes.—It is often necessary in model work to cut a square hole in a hand lever or similar part, or to cut a keyway in the bored box of a small pulley wheel. This may be accomplished by means of a drift. A round hole, equal to the diameter of the desired square hole measured over the corners, is drilled in the part being operated on, and then a square punch (with serrated sides in larger examples) is driven into the hole as shown in Fig. 197. This punch removes the metal at the corners. The drift may be made to cut the finished size of hole, so that no further cutting and filing is required. In the case of larger work two drifts —one first-cut and one finishing size—are employed. To make a key-way, a narrow drift with teeth only on one side may be used. To save damage to the hole a backing piece (Fig. 199), made by slitting a piece of steel, the same material as the shaft, is placed in the hole as shown. Only one drift is required; the work may be done in two cuts by using different backing pieces.

Screwing and Unscrewing Studs.—To screw in a stud without damage, some method of locking a nut on the uppermost threads must be adopted. The ordinary double lock nuts (Fig. 200) will usually suffice, the two nuts being locked together as firmly as possible with two spanners. A better appliance, which can be easily made, is what is termed a stud box (Fig. 201). A piece of hexagonal or square stuff is drilled and tapped to suit the particular standard thread of the stud. A set-screw is fitted in the top, and to use the appliance it is screwed on to the stud until it touches the half driven-in set-screw. The latter is then tightly locked down on to the stud, as shown, and then the stud box may be turned with a spanner until the stud is screwed in sufficiently far. A release of the set-screw will enable the stud box to be removed. The stud box may be marked with its size of stud, as shown in the sketch.

Silver Soldering and Brazing.—In model work, as in the jeweller's and silversmith's art, the use of a high-melting point solder, such as that known as silver solder, is in many cases a necessity. Soft or pewter solders are useless if a strong joint is desired, and positively dangerous if employed as the *sole* means of uniting the parts of a model boiler working at anything over, say, 10 lb. to 20 lb. per square inch. It must be remembered that the water and steam in the boiler increase in temperature with the pressure, and their temperature at 60 lb. to 80 lb. per square inch will be approaching the melting point of ordinary tinman's solder.

Silver solder is termed a hard solder, and is a material used in the same way as "spelter" is used by cycle makers in brazing up the steel frames. Silver solder, however, melts at a lower temperature (according to its exact composition), and can, therefore, be employed to unite brass, copper, and silver objects. An old shop method of making silver solder is to melt up old silver (using current silver coinage is an expensive method of obtaining the silver, and is said to be illegal) with some *brass* pins, not the iron ones so common now. Two formulæ are given below which will be found to give good results for copper and brass respectively. The "finer" solder is the one that melts at the higher temperature. The other is more suited to brass, which is easier to fuse than copper. (1) 2 parts silver to 1 part brazing spelter; (2) 7 parts silver to 2 part brazing spelter. (No. 2 is whiter than No. 1.)

The methods of silver soldering vary with the size of the work. The ordinary jeweller holds the work in the hand, on the end of a piece of binding wire or on a square of charcoal, and applies the heat by a mouth blow-lamp from a horizontal gas-jet, as already described. Larger work demands a flame of greater intensity, and sufficient air can only be supplied by a foot-blower or some similar device, or, as an alternative, from the flame of a suitable petrol or paraffin blow-lamp. Silver solder can be purchased at from 2s. 6d. to 3s. 6d. per ounce in sheet form, about $\frac{1}{32}$ in. thick. Where the solder is melted down by the amateur, a good way to obtain the sheet form is to turn the globule of molten metal on to the bench and to place a flat-iron on it. Of course, the result will not be equal to a rolled ingot.

For the lighter variety of work the special tools (*see* Fig. 202) and materials required are as follows: Suitable

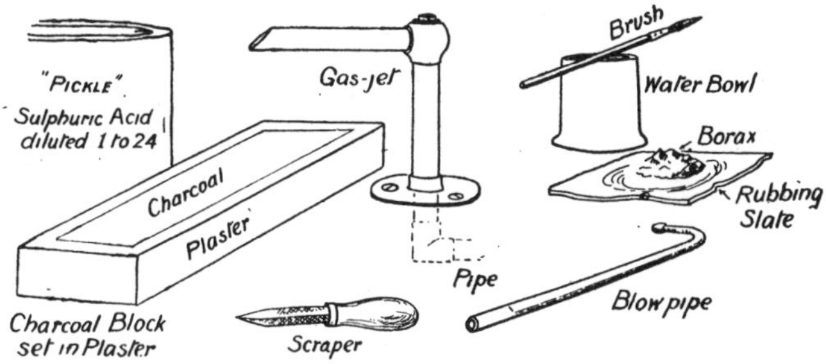

Fig. 202.—Requisites for silver soldering

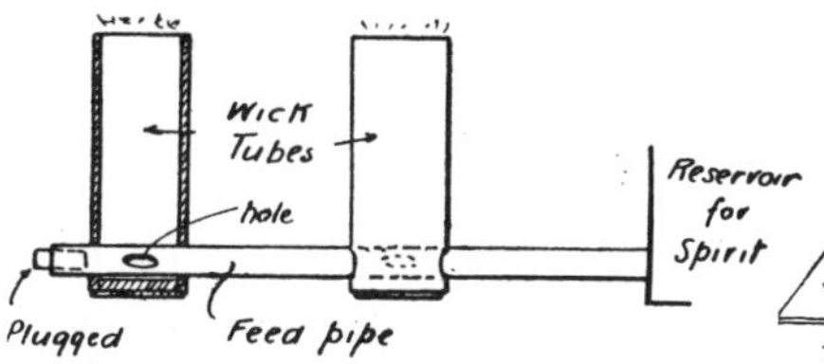

Fig. 203.—Spirit lamp

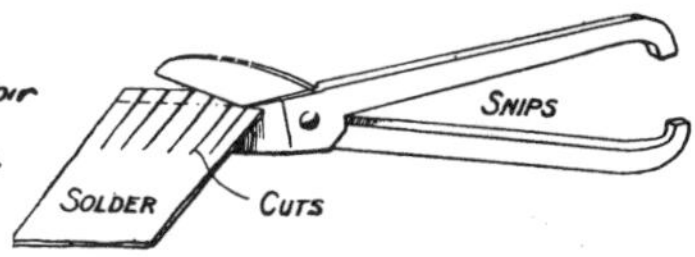

Fig. 204.—Cutting up solder into paillons

gas-jet or other flame; mouth blow-pipe; scraper; jar containing a sulphuric acid "pickle"; piece of slate; camel-hair brush; pieces of lump borax; two grades of silver solder; charcoal block; iron binding wire.

The pickle should be made by pouring 1 part of common sulphuric acid into 20 parts of water, and its function is to remove all dirt and borax from the metal being operated. Silver soldered articles should not be thrown into the pickle until they are nearly cold, as otherwise the joints may crack, but in the preparatory annealing (that is, softening) of plain metal, wire, rod or tubing, the article may be put into the pickle when hot—but take care of the splashes! Plunging hot copper or brass into cold water does not have the effect of hardening it. Always remove an iron binding wire before placing a job in the pickle.

In many cases it is advisable to heat the work and put it "through the pickle" before working on it, especially in the case of tubing that has been lying by for some time and has become dirty. As an example of the process of silver soldering, take the making of a methylated spirit lamp (Fig. 203). The wick tubes, of $\frac{3}{8}$-in. or $\frac{1}{2}$-in. light copper piping, may be cut off to the required length and drilled for the $\frac{3}{16}$ in. diameter horizontal feed pipe. The ends may be small discs of copper or brass, either purchased stamped out to size or turned off a bar; in the latter case they may have a slight flange. The tubing may be cleaned in the manner already mentioned, and the tube should, in addition, be scraped inside and on the edge so that the solder will run properly. This scraping is only required to the extent of soldering the joint. The most suitable scraper is made by grinding down a piece of an old three-cornered file and putting it into a handle.

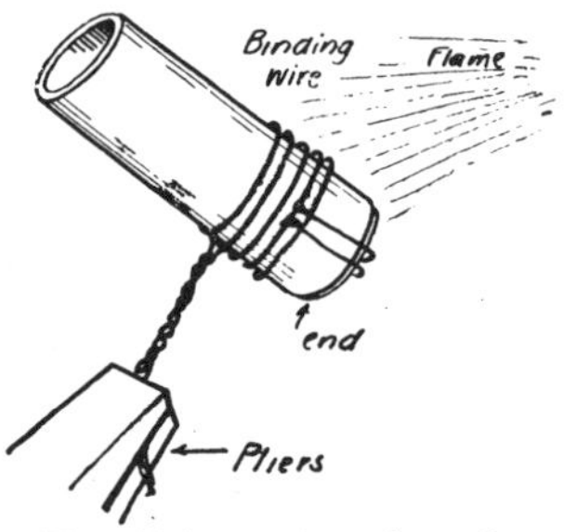

Fig. 205.—Tube wired for silver soldering

Before putting the disc in place make up the flux on the slate by rubbing on it a piece of lump borax moistened with water. This paste may be applied to the parts where they are proposed to be jointed with the camel-hair brush. The parts are then fitted together. As a precautionary measure it is a good plan to now fill the brush up again with the paste, and run it round inside the tube to make quite sure of there being enough. The flux prevents the oxidisation of the surfaces, which would resist the amalgamation of the metals and solder. The work is now ready for the silver solder. This may be cut up into $\frac{1}{8}$-in. squares or paillons (see Fig. 204), and well covered with the borax paste. It may be applied with the tip of the brush, the knack of easily placing in position coming after a little practice.

The solder should be clean (if not, clean by passing it through the fire and pickling), and four or five pieces may be put in equal distances outside on the disc, and over the place where the solder is intended to run into. The solder may be placed inside the tube, and, if so, a few strands of the binding wire should be put round the centre of the tube and carried over the end to prevent the same falling off. A few strands should also be placed round the centre and twisted up to form a handle (Fig. 205), this being held in the pliers. If the solder is put on the outside, then the tube may be wired on to the charcoal block with the end

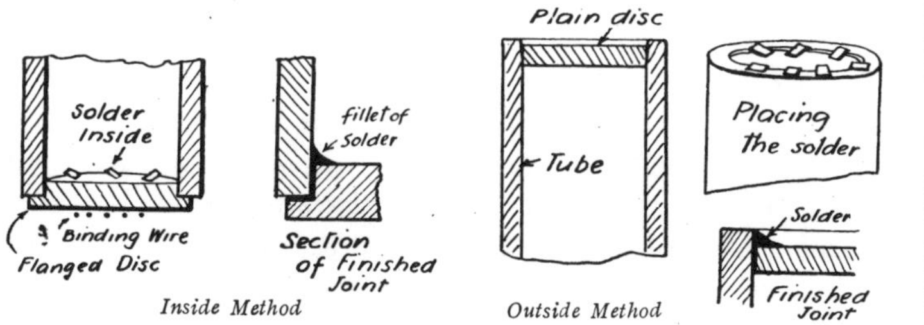

Fig. 206.—Silver soldering ends into tubes

to be soldered upwards. The charcoal block returns the heat of the flame to the work, and speeds up the work.

Now *slowly heat the work* by blowing the gas jet on a part of the tube farthest away from the solder; the borax will dry, and should the solder have moved, return it with a suitable tool or the point of the wet camel-hair brush. The heat must not be applied too suddenly at first, otherwise the borax will boil up and push off the pieces of solder. The heat may be increased when the bubbling has ceased.

Do not hold the work too far away, or it will get dirty in the smoke of the flame, or yet too near, else the gas will not be used to advantage. As the tube begins to get hot, slowly work the flame to the end of tube until the solder melts and runs into the joint. Give it now a little extra heat to thoroughly get the solder down into the crevices of the joint, and then let the work cool down. When nearly cold twist off the iron wire and put the job into the pickle. Leave the work in the pickle about ten minutes, when all the borax will be dissolved. After removing from the pickle, rinsing, and drying, the soldered joint should show a whitish line outside the tube, and if sufficient solder has been used, the inside should finish with a good fillet of solder, making the joint really the strongest portion of the work. A disc with a flanged end is to be preferred where the joint is made with the solder inside. If a plain disc is used it may be pressed into the tube a little lower than the edge and the solder applied to the outside as in Fig. 206.

The following notes on the composition of silver solders are due to W. H. Jubb : (1) 12 parts standard silver and 1 part brass ; (2) 6 parts standard silver and 1 part brass. These two solders are compulsory for silver articles that have to be sent to assay for hall-marking. No. 1 has a very low melting point, and is termed " quick," and No. 2, which requires a higher temperature, is called " stark " (in some parts of the country, " fine "). No. 2 should be used at the first heating and No. 1 at the second. These should make ideal solders for amateur use, as the chances of burning the work, even thin brass, are almost nil. (3) 2 part brass, 1 part standard silver ; (4) 5 part brass, 2 parts standard silver. Whereas Nos. 1 and 2 are silver solders, Nos. 3 and 4 are termed " German silver solders," as they are not so white and are used on German silver. Both Nos. 3 and 4 are good, have a comparatively low melting point, are much less expensive than Nos. 1 and 2, and, if plenty of wet borax is used, will " strike up " well. No. 3 is recommended. (" Standard silver " is about 95 per cent. pure silver. Old " sterling silver " is 92·5 per cent. pure silver. German silver is an alloy of copper and nickel.)

In making any of the above solders the brass and silver should be melted together, and care should be taken to see that the metal is clean before melting down. Where large quantities of solder are made the metals are scoured with emery cloth before they are put into the crucible.

While the foregoing methods are for quite small jobs, say for $\frac{1}{4}$-in. or $\frac{5}{16}$-in. copper pipe and fittings attached thereto, heavier articles require entirely different arrangements. A foot-bellows and gas blow-pipe, or else a paraffin or petrol (benzoline) blow-lamp is essential. An "Aetna" paraffin blow-lamp with horizontal burner, of one pint capacity, is of

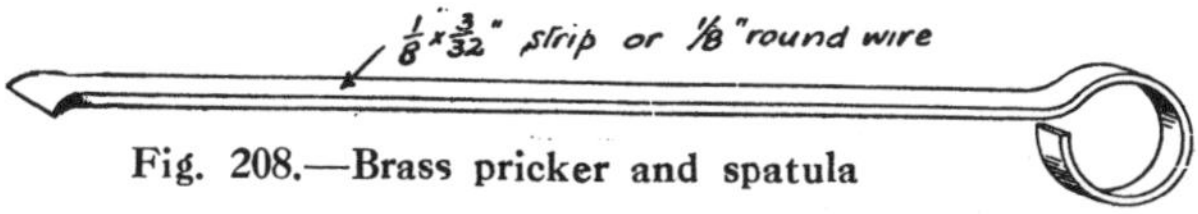

Fig. 208.—Brass pricker and spatula

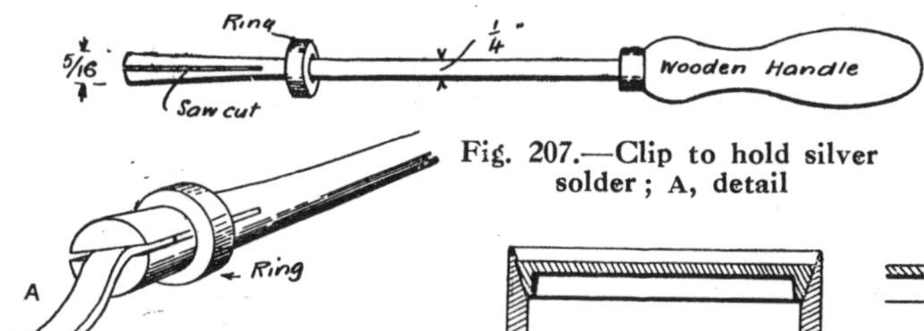

Fig. 207.—Clip to hold silver solder; A, detail

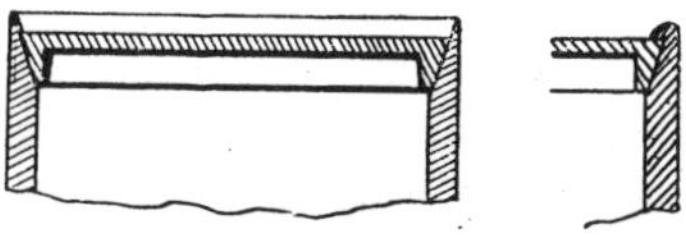

Fig. 211.—Boiler end silver soldered in place

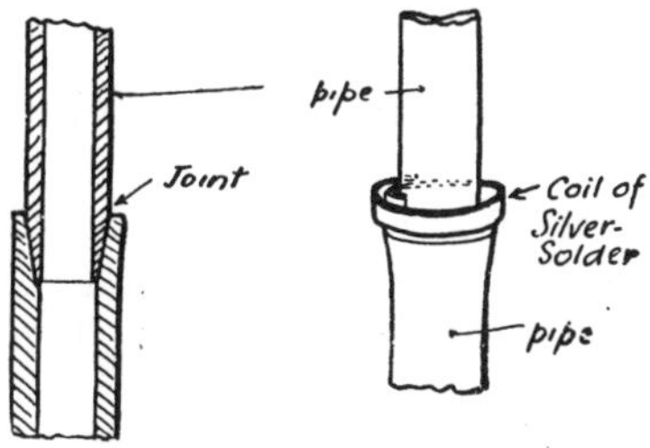

Fig. 209.—Silver soldering two pipes together

Fig. 210.—Boiler buried in coke

ample power for average model work. These lamps are made by the "Primus" firm, and are quite satisfactory, although, of course, if a gas supply is available in the workshop the user will find that a foot bellows and blow-pipe is a much more convenient arrangement. A blow-lamp or blow-pipe requires a suitable tray or "forge" of sheet-iron in which coke and odd pieces of brick or tile may be laid and used to pack round the object whilst the flame is being played on the part to be soldered. Among the smaller additional tools that will be required will be one or two pots (tooth paste pots) to hold powdered borax and also for brass spelter, where the brazing of iron or steel is contemplated, a clip to hold the solder and a brass pricker, both of which are made as shown in Figs. 207 and 208. These tools will be referred to in describing various operations requiring the same.

To take a few examples of silver soldering larger work : say it is necessary to silver solder two pipes together, one smaller than the other, and one or both are *in situ*. The best course to adopt is to file or scrape the end of the smaller and the inside of the larger (reaming and filing them if necessary) until a good-fitting joint is obtained as sketched in Fig. 209. A strip of solder is then cut off, and after the joint is well coated with borax paste (from the rubbing slate) this solder may be wound round the smaller pipe. If possible, the joint should be soldered in a vertical position, the larger pipe being the lower one. The heat should be conserved by laying the work in the coke and building the same round, or, if the work is too large or the joint in an awkward part of the pipe, a shield of tin or iron should be placed behind the joint so that the flame is thrown back on to the work. Should the pipe be attached in close proximity to the joint to a heavy piece of metal, then warm this metal up first, otherwise all the heat will travel to this part, and the work will take much longer to get to the proper temperature. In all cases where one part of the joint is of heavier substance than the other that part should receive the greater amount of attention from the flame of the lamp. In fitting-in and soldering a boiler end the whole of the boiler except that being operated on should be buried in the coke. A section of the method of building up the coke is shown in Fig. 210. The joint should be fitted with the inside of the tube slightly tapered at the end, and the end casting similarly tapered and driven in until the edge projects slightly. This forms a ridge to work the solder against and ensures a better joint. Of course, it is not always permissible. Where exigencies of design stipulate that the face of the end must be projected beyond the barrel, while a less satisfactory arrangement from the point of view of silver soldering, it is better than a flush joint. However, if a flush joint is essential, the scraper should, when the end is fitted in, be used to cut a V-shaped groove all round the joint, reliance being placed on the solder filling up this groove again and providing the required flush end face.

But to return to the ordinary case. The end is fitted with the edge of the tube projecting. This may be slightly knocked over the end casting all round. The joint must then be coated with borax paste and the boiler placed in the coke in the forge, as already described. The heat is then applied, and with the pricker more borax is put on to the joint to take the place of any that becomes burnt. The solder is cut into long strips $\frac{1}{8}$ in. wide and 4 in. or 5 in. long, and held in the clip tool shown in Fig. 207. When the work is up to heat (cherry red), the solder may be applied, the end being dipped into the borax as occasion requires. Most of the 5-in. length of solder will have disappeared if the end is $1\frac{1}{2}$ in. diameter or over, and if it has not run into the joint increase the heat and assist the solder to flow with more borax at the end of the pricker.

With regard to cooling, many users of silver solder object to the cooling of the work by plunging into water or pickle whilst it is hot. No damage or cracking of the joint occurs, the writer thinks, if the work is not plunged when it is red hot or anywhere near red hot. Plunging into a pickle certainly cracks the burnt-in borax, which can be readily removed and the joint examined to better advantage. Many a silver soldered joint has been passed as quite sound when it has only been the borax that has been stopping the interstices, and only after it has been placed under service for some time does the faulty joint make itself apparent. It is important to note that silver soldering can only be done on work that has not been previously soft soldered. If it has, then the offending part must be cut away. Soft soldering can be readily accomplished after silver soldering or brazing so long as the work is clean and all burnt borax is removed.

Soft Solders.—Soft or pewter solders vary in fusibility according to their composition, and the alloy required will depend on the metal or alloy to be united. For model work a good or " fine " solder is recommended, the composition of 1 part lead and 2 parts pure tin being about the right thing. The bit must be maintained with the point properly coated with solder. This is done by heating the bit to a dull red, just above a full black heat, and then filing up the point and dipping the bit for an instant into a pot of killed spirits, the usual flux for model work, and then rubbing on a clean piece of tinplate, solder being applied at the same moment. A sharp pop, without a lot of smoke or spluttering, as the " iron " is dipped in the spirits denotes the right temperature. If the bit is damp and still unclean the temperature is insufficient. The soldering bit must not be overheated in subsequent use, otherwise its point will be burnt and require re-tinning. A lump of sal ammoniac is used by some workers and touched with the point of the bit to make the solder run well, but a clean pot of killed spirits (*see* page 17 for method of making this flux) is good enough for all purposes.

Typical Soft Soldering Jobs.—Figs. 212 to 216 show the best methods of holding bit and work for the various seams of a light, cylindrical object. The solder in such work is drawn along the seam by the heated bit. If it refuses to be drawn, then the bit is not hot enough or the joint is unclean. Some amateurs overheat the bit, but this results in discoloured work and spoilt solder, the latter assuming a sandy appearance. Others try to solder up hill. The work should be held so that the solder is running down hill, so that the molten solder collects round the point of the bit and travels with it. This, besides facilitating the work, makes a strong, clean-looking joint.

When the surface of an iron object is rusty and dirty, a liberal application of raw spirits (hydrochloric acid) may be applied, and after being washed off the working surface may be tinned. That any work should be scrupulously clean is essential to the success of the operation. Zinc and galvanised objects require diluted raw (not killed) spirits as flux.

Where a heavy copper sheet, or any other piece of work of such a large mass that it readily absorbs and dissipates all the heat of even a large copper bit, is being dealt with,

Figs. 212 and 213.—Incorrect and correct methods of gripping soldering-bit

Fig. 214.—Soldering an internal grooved seam

Fig. 215.—Soldering on can bottom internally

it may require to be heated with a blow-lamp or over a gas ring, the solder being led along the joint with the heated bit in the ordinary way. Small jobs may be united under the flame of a mouth blow-pipe, the solder being applied as in silver soldering—i.e. in small pieces laid on, or by applying a stick to the already heated joint. The joints in all cases should be scraped clean, be made free from grease or oxide, and coated with flux. Sweating two parts together is a common operation; the end of a pipe and a socket or other fitting may be sweated together. To accomplish this, after cleaning and fitting the parts, they are separately tinned by fluxing, heating, and applying a thin coat of solder. To obtain the thin coat necessary to get the parts to fit together all superfluous solder should be removed, while it is molten, with a damp rag. The parts are then assembled, and with a preparatory coating of flux heated up. When the two parts "sweat" together, solder is applied until it is observed that a sufficient quantity has run into the joint, and a good strong fillet forms outside. Care should be taken, in sweating pipes and fittings together, to fit the parts well. If the joint is badly made, from a mechanical point of view, then the applied solder may disappear inside the pipes and fittings, and block up the passages.

SOFT SOLDERS FOR MODEL WORK

Material to be jointed	*Flux*	*Composition of Solders*
Brass, copper, and gunmetal; Tinplate	Chloride of zinc,* resin, or "Fluxite" paste	2 parts tin and 1 part lead, or 2 parts tin and 1½ parts lead.
Iron and steel	Chloride of ammonia	1 part tin and 1 part lead.
Lead	Tallow or resin	1 part tin and 2 parts lead.
Galvanised iron and zinc	Hydrochloric acid	2½ parts tin and 2 parts lead.
Pewter	Gallipoli oil	1 part tin, 1 part lead and 2 parts bismuth.

* Chloride of zinc is "killed spirits."

Painting Models.—One of the most difficult processes in finishing a model is painting and enamelling, and because of the skill and care required not one amateur-made model in fifty is really well finished in this respect, the appearance of many otherwise excellent examples of work being ruined. The very best paints and enamels should be used in all cases. Wooden models must not be painted with common oil paints such as are supplied by the local chandler. Finely-ground paints are required, and flat tints ground in turps will be found to give good results, only sufficient oil to bind the pigments without producing a gloss being used. Some of the flat enamel paints, like flat "Velure," "Paripan," etc., although comparatively expensive, are the cheapest in the end. Especially in the case of model buildings, glossy paints entirely spoil the effect of the model, and flatted surfaces are recommended. A good model may take a month or more to paint. Work which has any inequalities of surface should be first filled with patent fillers used by coach painters, and rubbed down with fine or worn glasspaper. Very small models may be painted with artists' oil colours. For demonstration models which do not require to be finished in natural tints, french grey or lead colours are the most effective, and come out best in photographs. Enamelled models with glossy surfaces are the worst from the photographer's point of view.

Fig. 216.—Soldering a seam externally

Model locomotives are usually painted in the colours of the original, and require to be carefully lined out and lettered. Where the engines are subjected to heat, then stove enamels or japans must be employed, and the construction of the model should be such as will allow it to be taken to pieces as much as possible for the purposes of painting, and to stand the heat 100° to 150° F. of the stove. The first two coats of enamel should be allowed to dry thoroughly, say for a week or more, and each should then be rubbed down with pumice powder with felt rubbers. The work should have been previously rendered entirely free of all grease, oxide, or corrosion, the oil and grease being best removed with paraffin first, and then petrol or benzoline. The latter should, of course, be used in the open air and away from any naked light.

All painting work, tools, and colours should be kept

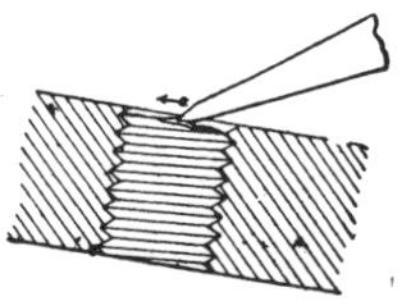

Fig. 217.—Turning out broken screw with blunt chisel

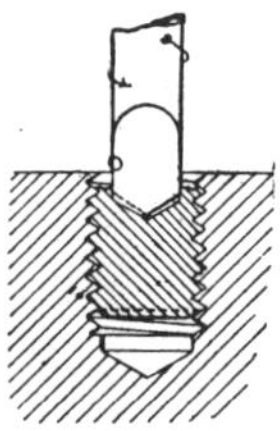

Fig. 218.—Drilling screw with left-handed drill

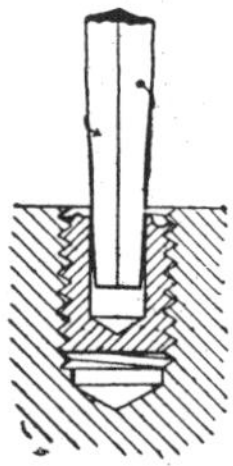

Fig. 219.—Turning out stump with squared drift

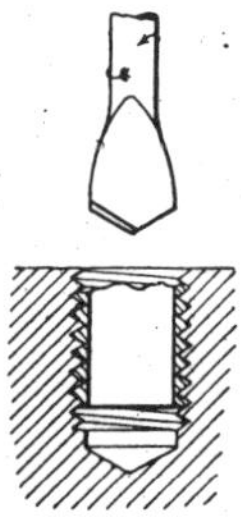

Fig. 220.—Stump drilled out to leave thin shell

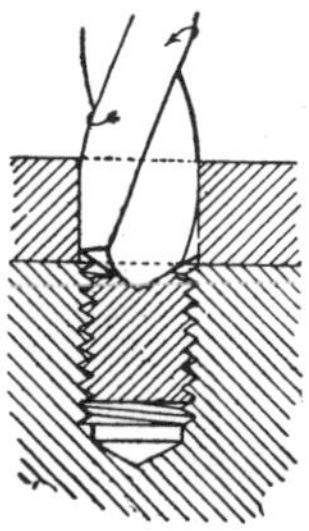

Fig. 221.—Method oi starting hole concentrically

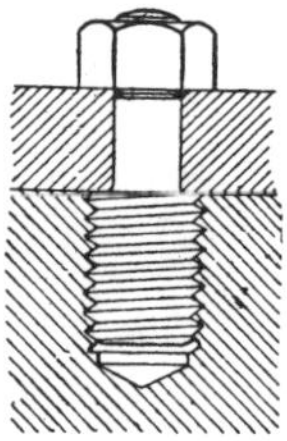

Fig. 222.—Special stud to fit re-tapped hole

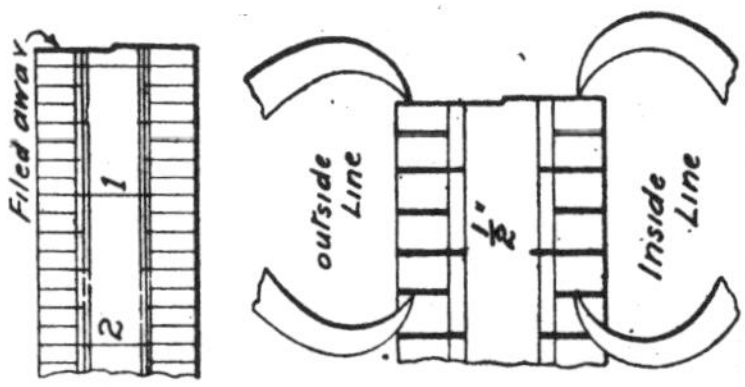

Figs. 223 and 224.—Making fine calliper measurements by means of a filed rule

free from dust and from particles of the skin which forms on opened tins of paint. Good brushes should also be obtained, and in laying on enamel just enough colour that will flow freely from the brush should be used. If the enamel is brushed out bare it will not flow together with an even surface, and will show brush marks. Too much colour will cause tear drops and will tail down in ridges. If brushed too much the enamel will gather in lumps. The essentials in skilful painting are cleanliness, quickness, and a steady, confident handling of the tools and colour.

Lining is an art difficult to acquire, and amateurs will find the draughtsman's ink-ruling pen a convenient tool to ensure even and straight lines. Plain artists' colours (not enamel) may be used for all thin lines and letters, and the consistency of the paint must be found by experiment, and be such as will cause the colour to run out of the pen without forming blobs of colour just as the pen touches the job. For "iron work" on model wagons and other rolling stock, "egg-shell black" gives an excellent finish, and several good brands can be obtained in small tins.

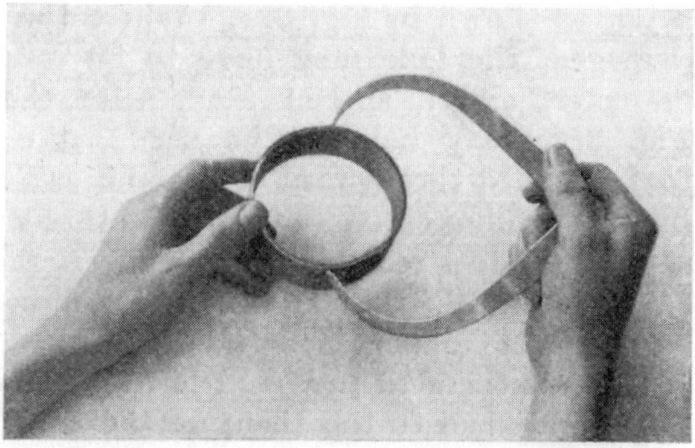

Fig. 225.—Using outside callipers

Fig. 226.—Using inside callipers

Removing Damaged or Rusted Screws and Drills.—In repair work, removing a rusted screw is an operation which is often necessary. If the job can be made hot the expansion will sometimes loosen it, while a liberal application of oil—preferably paraffin—will also assist. A broken screw of large diameter may sometimes be turned out with a blunt chisel. Drilling is, however, necessary with stubborn examples, a left-hand drill often moving the screw before it has penetrated very far. The shell of a drilled-out screw may sometimes be removed with a square taper drift, as shown in Fig. 219. Where the work is of brass and the screw steel, care must be taken to start the drill accurately, otherwise it will prefer to work on the softer brass. A straight flute or twist drill may therefore be used through a jig, as shown in Fig. 221. Where the internal thread is damaged, the hole may have to be re-tapped to a larger diameter, and a special stud, after the style shown in Fig. 222, may have to be used. A drill, if the hole is to be drilled through, may in some cases be knocked out by first drilling carefully from the other side and then using a piece of steel rod as a punch.

Using Callipers.—To take off a dimension from a rule by means of callipers is not an easy task. The usual method is to open them to just a little over the size required (say ½ in.) and then to tap them on the bench until they come as nearly as can be observed to the ½-in. mark on the rule; but greater accuracy is obtained by the following method. Procure a finely divided steel rule with the same divisions on each edge, and file away one half of the zero end as shown in Fig. 223, the amount being such as the callipers, on being placed as shown in Fig. 224 with the leg on the uncut end, show that the measuring point is on the inside edge of the mark, while from the filed-away end the point shows it to be on the inside of the line. To obtain an exact measurement the callipers can be set to any dimension, and when the measuring point shows it to come on the inside and outside of the mark when taken from each edge of the rule, the exact measurement is within the limits of the thickness of the line, and work which the callipers will just not pass is too large, while if it passes without resistance it will be within the limits of the thickness of the line.

Callipers should be held lightly and so that the heat of the hand and the pressure of the fingers do not alter the dimension. External callipers should fall over the work with the weight of their points. The points of "inside" callipers should be narrow and curved on the measuring surfaces,

CHAPTER V

Model Steam-Engine Cylinders

Oscillating Cylinders.—The cylinder and piston—a mechanical contrivance on which so much of the present civilisation depends—was invented by a French scientist, Denis Papin, in 1695, and it is strange that he intended to operate it as an explosive engine, employing gunpowder instead of the charge of compressed petrol and air used in the modern internal combustion engine.

In model-engine making, the cylinder and piston is perhaps the most important detail. The single-acting oscillating cylinder is the simplest form, as no extraneous mechanism is required to distribute the steam to the piston. The single-acting cylinder does not require any packed glands; but in a cylinder over $\frac{5}{16}$-in. bore the front end of the piston rod should be supported by an end cover in preference to obtaining the necessary support by a long piston. The two systems are shown in Figs. 227 and 228. The steam distribution in an ordinary model oscillating cylinder is also peculiar, in that it does not admit of advance in the timing of the various functions of admission and exhaust; therefore lap, lead, expansion, and variable cut-offs are more or less impossible.

Comparing the cycle of operations of a slide-valve cylinder and an oscillating one—both single-acting, by the way—it will be seen that the admission period is just as long as the exhaust, and that the slight amount of lap necessary to prevent a leakage from the steam to the exhaust sides makes both the point of steam admission and the exhaust late. With a slide-valve cylinder, in which the valve is operated by an eccentric, the valve may have a large amount of lap, and the eccentric may be advanced beyond the 90° point to suit, and to obtain the functions known as compression, lead, expansion, and early release, all of which tend to greater economy of steam. The two diagrams (Figs. 229 and 230) show the comparative cycles ; A represents the steam admission, X the valve closed, expansion period, E the valve open to exhaust, and C valve closed to exhaust, compression period.

The reason the advantages of the slide-valve cylinder cannot be obtained with the ordinary oscillating cylinder is due to the fact that the steam distribution and the valve mechanism is operated by the oscillation of the cylinder, and this movement is exactly at right angles to the thrust of the piston. Advance in the timing of the movements is impossible.

The usual method of arranging the steam distribution is by ports at the end of the cylinder. A single port is drilled into the cylinder, and the outer face slides over two other port holes formed in a steam block, which is a fixed portion, and usually forms the pivot bearing for the cylinder. One of the ports in the steam block is connected to the boiler, and the other is the exhaust. The setting out of the ports depends firstly on the size, and secondly on the extent of the oscillation. The amplitude of the oscillation is, in turn, dependent on the length of the stroke and piston rod. Figs. 231 and 232 show how to set out the ports, the size of the latter being not less than one-sixth of the bore of the cylinder ; therefore for a $\frac{3}{4}$-in. bore cylinder $\frac{1}{8}$-in. ports would be used. Where the cylinder and piston rod are long, it will be seen by this diagram that the distance from the centre of the ports must be increased in proportion. The ports in the steam block must be sufficiently wide apart to allow the port in the cylinder to clear both of them when in mid position. This is necessary to prevent leakage from the steam to the exhaust ports, as already mentioned. The exact width of this port bar will vary very slightly in the various sizes of engines. Just the same amount of lap will be necessary in a $\frac{1}{4}$-in. bore cylinder as in one 2-in. bore. Therefore in a small engine the travel of the ports will have to be greater in proportion to make up for this defect.

Another important point about oscillating cylinders is the method of pivoting and preserving the contact between

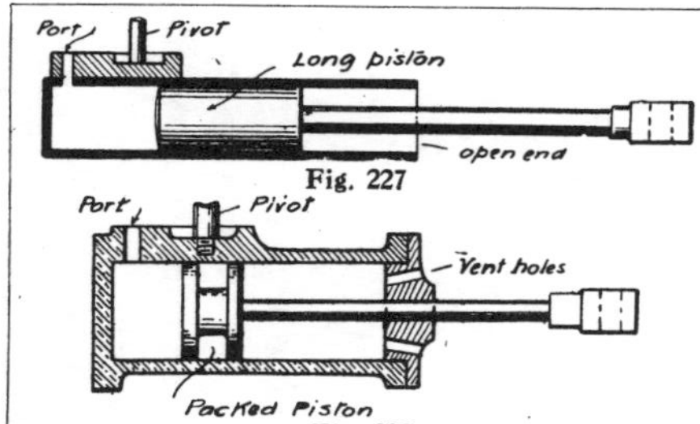

Fig. 227

Fig. 228

Figs. 227 and 228.—Cylinders with long piston and open end and with packed piston and guide respectively

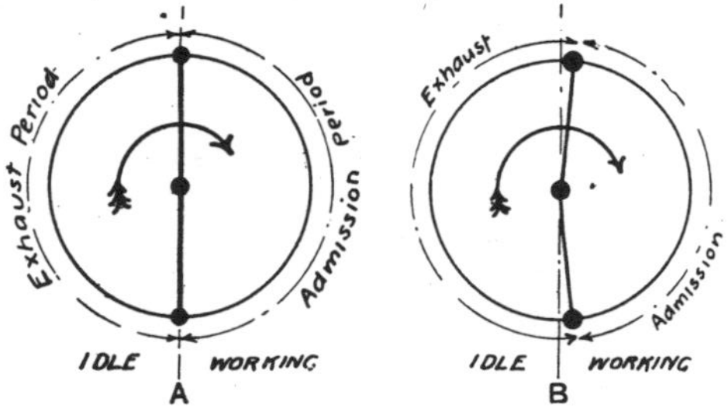

Fig. 229.—Cycle of operations of oscillating cylinder; (A) Theoretically perfect cylinder, and (B) as in practice with slight lap of ports

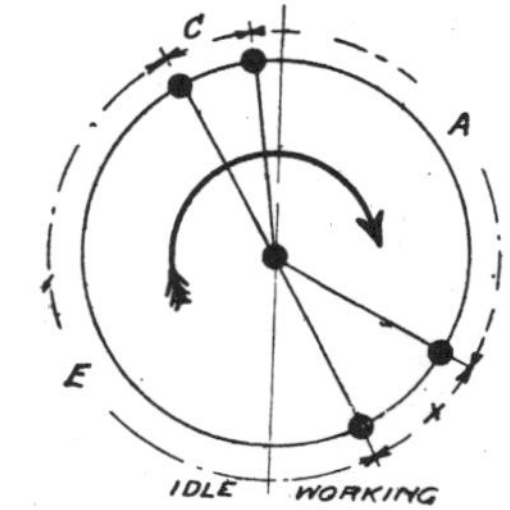

Fig. 230.—Typical cycle of slide-valve cylinder with lap and lead

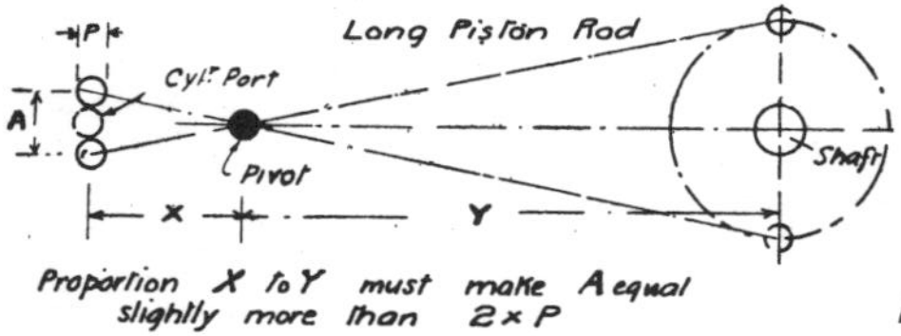

Fig- 231

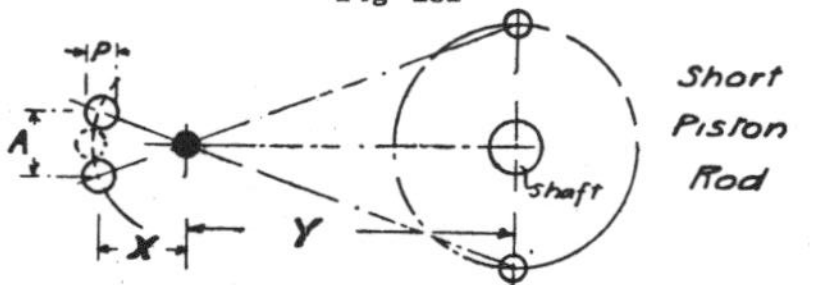

Fig. 232

Figs. 231 and 232.—Setting out ports of oscillating engine with long and short piston rods

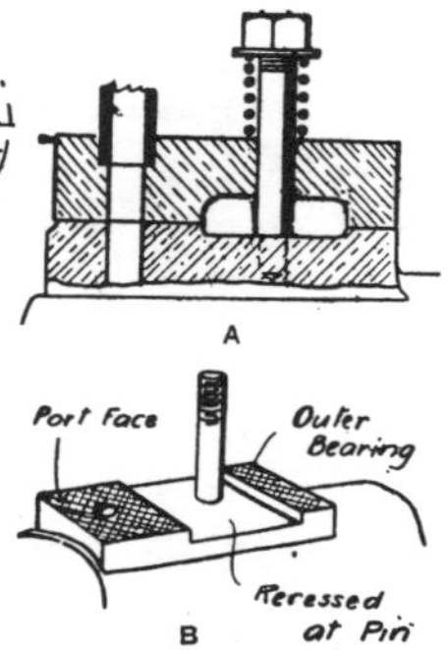

Fig. 233.—Bearing faces of oscillating engine

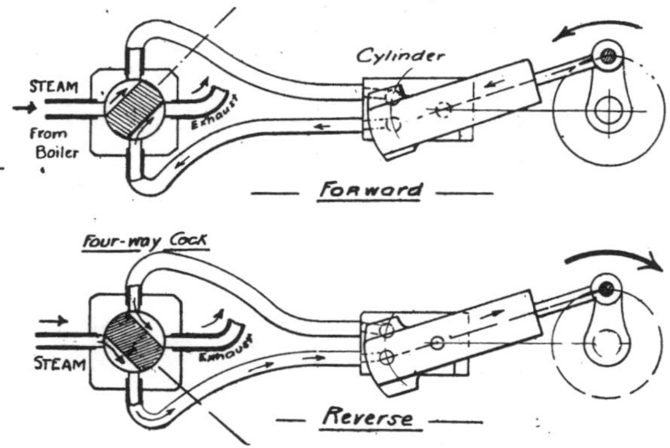

Fig. 234.—Reversing oscillating cylinder with four-way cock

the port faces. Spring contacts are the only satisfactory devices. The old-fashioned method, where the cylinder is pressed up against the steam block by a pointed set-screw, is to be avoided at any cost. In fitting the steam block, the whole of the centre portion immediately round the pivot spindle must be removed (*see* A and B, Fig. 233). The outer bearing faces should be small.

The pressure of the spring must be sufficient to overcome the opposing pressure of the steam, which at all times is tending to force the port faces apart. This force is in amount equal to the pressure of the steam per square inch multiplied by the area of the steam port, which if $\frac{1}{8}$ in. in diameter has an area of ·0122 sq. in. At 20-lb. steam pressure the forces tending to separate the port faces will thus equal about $\frac{1}{4}$ lb. The steam pressure in a model oscillating engine is therefore limited. The spring tension must not be too great, as the resultant friction will seriously reduce the efficiency of the engine, and in practice model oscillating cylinders are not usually worked at over 25-lb. or 30-lb. steam pressure.

Reversing arrangements for oscillating cylinders are extremely simple. It is for this reason that in model work oscillating cylinders are sometimes preferred. Reversing may be accomplished in two ways: (1) by changing over the ports in the steam-distributing block from steam to exhaust, and vice versa, by a four-way cock or similar device placed anywhere between the boiler and the engine; or (2) by providing a separate arrangement (in the form of a false port face between the cylinder and the steam block), in which the ports and passages are so arranged that the movement of this reversing plate at once changes over the direction of the steam.

Fig. 234 is a diagram showing a suitable four-way cock, which, of course, must have a large plug to enable the passages to be formed in it, and at the same time to provide enough lap to prevent cross leakage of steam.

In Fig. 235 all the working faces are shown shaded, and these must be ground in and be quite steam-tight. The port holes in the steam block, it will be noticed, are placed one beside the other on the centre line of the engine, not above and below this centre line on the arc of movement. The reversing plate may be of brass, and should be at least $\frac{1}{8}$ in. thick, and in addition to the pivot hole has three steam ports, at the same radius from the centre as the steam port in the cylinder. The grooves shown must then be cut, and should in depth be half the thickness of the reversing plate. These grooves must be chipped out with a fine chisel.

The only engines used in real practice that have valves or ports operated by the oscillation of the cylinder are hydraulic engines. These do not require the functions of expansion and compression, for the simple reason that water is practically incompressible.

Slide-Valve Cylinders.—The type of cylinder most used by model makers is the slide-valve cylinder, sometimes referred to as a " fixed " cylinder. The latter title is, however, not quite a correct one, as it is possible to fit a slide valve to an oscillating engine. Indeed, none of the devices just described are employed in real oscillating steam engines. As already shown, when the steam distribution is dependent on the oscillation, it cannot be arranged in such a way as to obtain the greatest economy of steam. Therefore, in all large oscillating steam engines, the ordinary slide valve operated by eccentrics is employed.

Fig. 236 shows the arrangement used in marine practice. Engines of 1,100 h.p. to this design were built as late as 1883 for H.M.S. *Sphinx* by the famous firm of John Penn and Sons. The trunnion on which the cylinders oscillate is used to conduct the steam to the valve chest, and the valve is actuated by Stephenson's link motion, the link of which is connected to a die block fitted to a large curved slide (shown shaded), which moves between two of the fixed columns of the engine. The fact that the cylinder oscillates does not matter, as the radius of the slot in this curved slide is struck from the centre of the trunnion. Therefore, in effect, the arrangement is the same as in a fixed engine, where the link motion is connected directly to the slide-valve spindle.

The slide valve was first employed in Watt's improved beam engines, and is sometimes called the "D" valve, owing to its shape being like the letter D (*see* Fig. 237). In an ordinary double-acting engine three ports are arranged in the cylinder, the centre one leading to the atmosphere and termed the exhaust port, and the two outer ones communicating with the respective ends of the cylinder. The exhaust port is generally twice the width of the steam ports, and is entirely covered by the slide valve. This slide valve is situated in a closed chamber called a "steam chest" or "valve chest," which is connected to the boiler by suitable pipes and a stop valve. The valve is of such a length that when placed in the centre of its travel it also covers both steam ports; but on being moved one way or the other opens one of the steam ports to the steam in the valve chest, never under any circumstances opening both steam ports at the same moment. The steam passing through the open port to the cylinder will press on the piston and drive it forward, and the piston being connected to the driving shaft by a piston-rod, connecting-rod, and crank, will cause the shaft to rotate.

When the one steam port is admitting live steam from the valve chest, the other port is in communication with the large central exhaust port, and the piston, during the time the used-up steam is passing away to the atmosphere, will recede. The proper movement of the slide valve is effected by an eccentric fitted to the crank shaft, and therefore the functions of the slide valve may be made to synchronise with the motion of the piston in any pre-determined manner.

The simplest form of slide valve is the one without "lap" or "advance." This type gives the same steam distribution as a model oscillating engine, because, having no lap, the eccentric is placed at exactly 90° to the crank. It is therefore "timed" in the same way as an oscillating cylinder, and reversing can be accomplished by similar methods.

The series of diagrams in Fig. 238 shows the "phases" of the valve and piston in a single cycle of operations. The valve is a simple one without "lap" or "lead." At A it is shown covering both ports. The piston is at the end of the

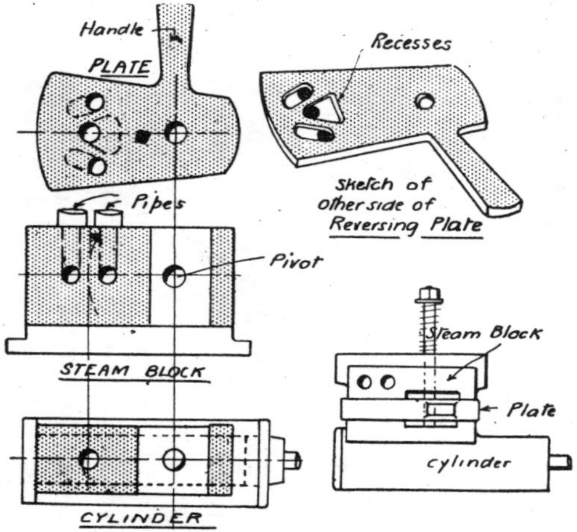

Fig. 235.—Reversing with moving port face (reversing plate)

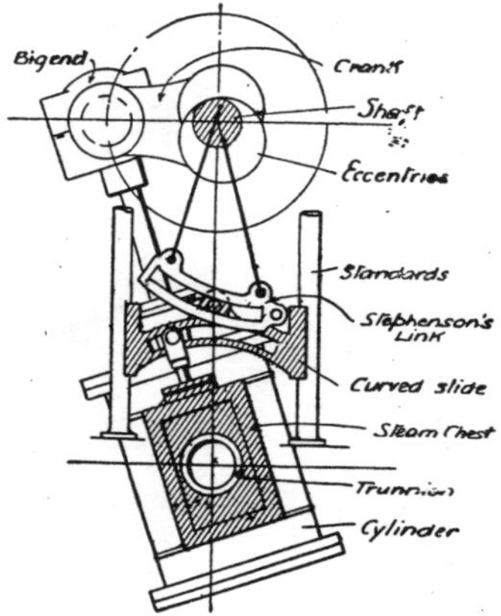

Fig. 236.—Slide-valve oscillating engine with Stephenson's link motion reversing gear

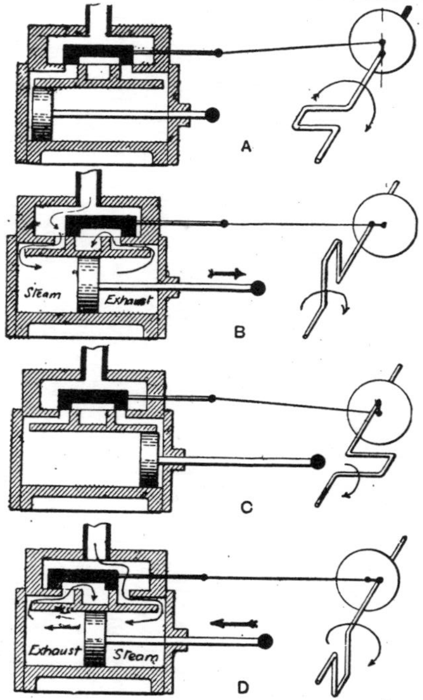

Fig. 238.—Diagrams showing the various phases of simple valve and piston

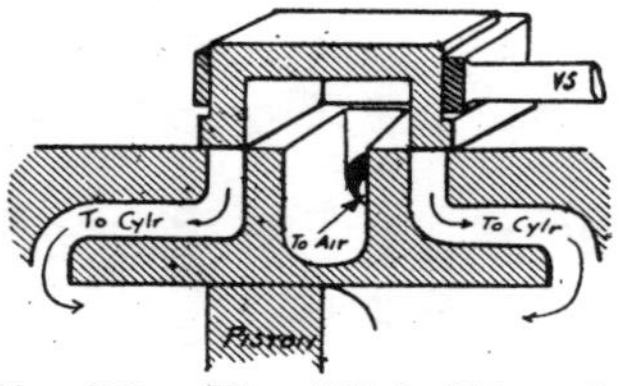

Fig. 237.—The "D" slide valve and steam ports

Fig. 239.—Lap added to normal slide

stroke; the crank on the dead centre, and not able to exert any turning movement in the axle. The steam cannot enter the cylinder, and any remaining from a previous stroke cannot get out. In the next diagram (B) the valve has moved from left to right, and during the time which would elapse in its changing from position A to position B it has been admitting steam from the boiler to the left-hand side of the piston, forcing it to the right, and moving the crank shaft in a clockwise direction. The crank is then in its most favourable position, and the valve is open to its maximum. The other end of the cylinder, it will be noticed, is exhausting the steam from the previous stroke.

Diagram C is the counterpart of diagram A, and that at D shows the movements directly opposite to that depicted in diagram B. The piston in D is moving from right to left, and is exerting its full force in turning the crank shaft.

Except in the smallest sizes, and where reversing is desired by some such simple device as a four-way cock, the simple or normal valve (a valve without lap) is to be avoided. Not only can greater economy be obtained by a better timing in the cycle of operations, such as shown in Fig. 230 (page 103), but a sweeter-running engine will also result.

To obtain this, "lap" should be added to the "D" valve (Fig. 237). This increase in the length is shown by the black portion in the sectional view of a slide valve shown in Fig. 239. If a paper model of the valve and ports is made, it will be seen that this addition necessitates an increased travel of the valve to fully open the port. The total travel, instead of being as in the normal valve equal to the port width $\times$ 2, must be, travel = (lap + port width) $\times$ 2. The reason why the sum of the lap and port width is multiplied by two is that the valve moves equally to each side of its central position.

The next point to consider is the position of the eccentric on the crank shaft when the crank is on the dead centre and the piston about to commence a new stroke. The valve should, with the piston in this position, either be on the point of opening the port to live steam, or the admission of the steam should have already commenced. The writer has already shown that with a normal valve the eccentric is 90° in advance of the crank, and to obtain the correct position of the valve (just about to open) when lap is added, the eccentric must be still further advanced. It is this extra amount that is termed by engineers " the angle of advance." The 90° is not considered, but only that in excess of the right angle.

If the valve is actually admitting steam when the crank is at dead centre, this amount of the opening is called the " lead " (pronounced " leed "). This function is necessary in fast-running engines to give the steam time to pass down the ports to get to its work before the piston starts on its new stroke. " Lead " is, however, only of use in engines with cylinders over $1\frac{1}{2}$ in. in diameter. The linear advance

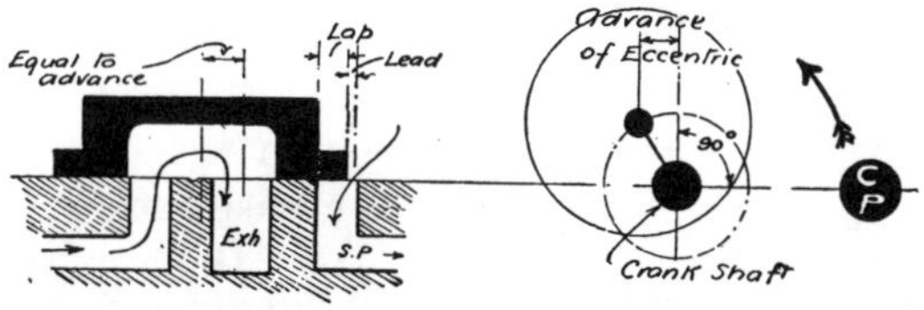

Fig. 240.—Diagrams showing angle of advance necessary with addition of lap to valve

of the eccentric where the valve has both lap and lead must be equal to " lap + lead."

The addition of lap to the valve gives it several new functions, all of which are shown in the cycle diagram (Fig. 230), and which may be enumerated as follows : (1) Earlier admission of live steam ; (2) full admission occurs earlier in stroke ; (3) earlier cut-off of live steam, this economising the consumption of steam ; (4) a period in which the steam is imprisoned in the cylinder, and during which the steam can do useful work by expanding ; (5) earlier exhaust, giving the steam more time to get out and reducing back pressure ; (6) a period of compression, in which the steam is compressed by the piston at the end of the exhaust stroke. This is called the cushioning effect, and is good thermally as well as mechanically.

All these effects are shown in the series of diagrams

(Fig. 241). At E the valve is shown open to lead, the crank being on the dead centre. At F the valve is fully open, although the piston has only just started on its stroke. Between G and H is the expansion period. The release of the steam occurs at H and continues to K, when the exhaust side of the valve closes and imprisons any remaining steam. This arrests the movement of the piston, and gets it ready for the next stroke; at the same time the compression of the steam increases the temperature of the cylinder walls, and reduces the inevitable losses by condensation.

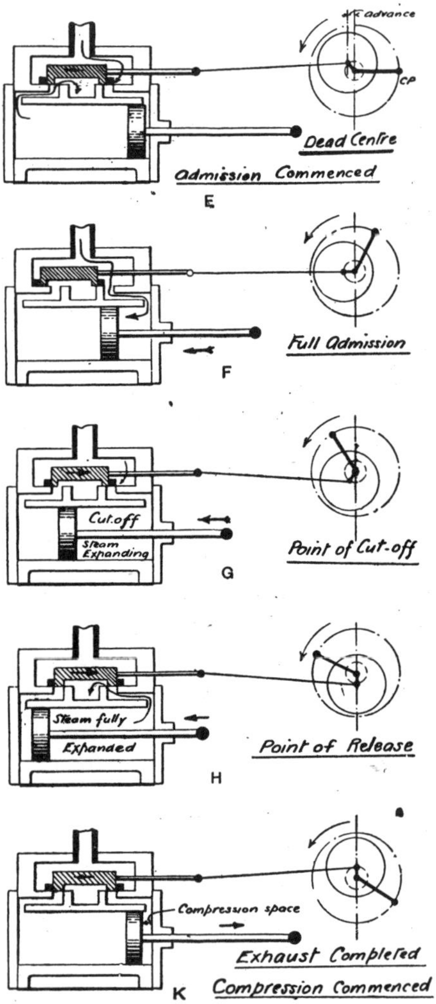

Fig. 241.—Diagrams showing various phases of valve with "lap" and "lead"

Fig. 242 shows the component parts of a double-acting slide-valve steam cylinder, and gives their more usual names.

Proportions of Steam Ports.—For high-speed model steam engines up to 2-in. bore it will be found that the best proportion for steam ports (*see* Fig. 243) is half the bore in length (L), and one-sixteenth the stroke of the cylinder in width (WS). For example, in a $1\frac{1}{4}$-in. by $1\frac{1}{4}$-in. engine the steam ports should be $\frac{5}{8}$ in. by $\frac{5}{64}$ in., although $\frac{5}{8}$ in. by $\frac{3}{32}$ in. would no doubt be used so as to eliminate "sixty-fourths." The port bars B_1 and B_2 should never be less in width than the steam ports; usually, where the ports are cast in, the writer makes the port bars one and a quarter times the width of the steam ports. The width of the exhaust ports (WE) should be twice that of the steam ports. Therefore, WE = one-eighth the stroke of the cylinder. The cavity C in a normal valve must be exactly $B_1 + WE + B_2$. The

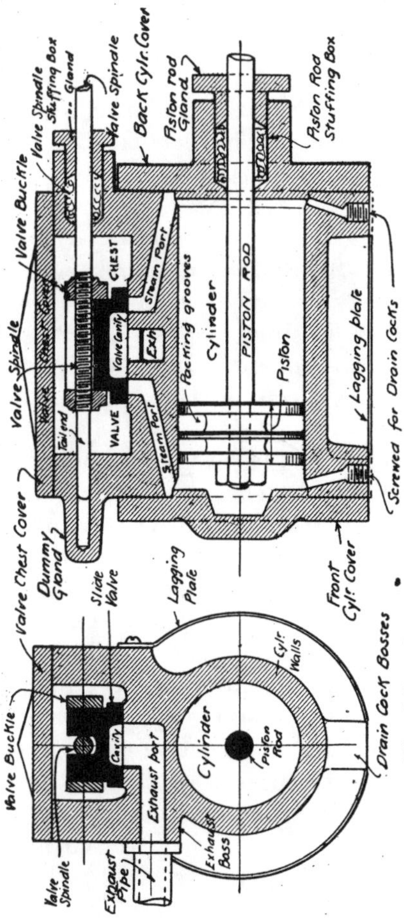

Fig. 242.—Component parts of model steam-engine cylinder

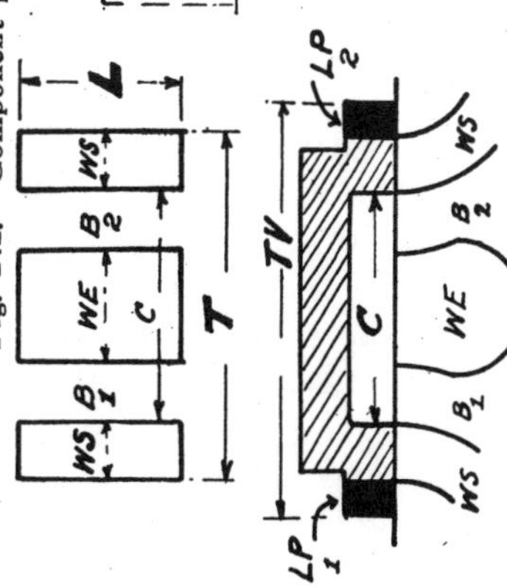

Fig. 243.—Proportions of steam ports

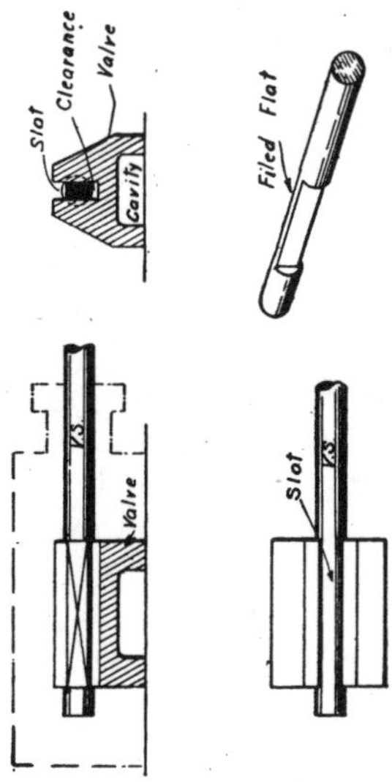

Fig. 244.—Simple method of fitting a slide valve to the spindle

total length of the valve (TV) depends on the lap adopted. The lap in a small-power engine should never exceed half the width of the steam port. TV therefore = T + LP_1 + LP_2. In small and slow-speed model engines and locomotives the length of the ports (L) may be reduced to $\frac{3}{8}$ or $\frac{1}{4}$ of cylinder bore.

Slide Valves and Attachments.—The simplest form of slide valve and spindle is shown in Fig. 244. Here the valve may be cast in brass or gunmetal from a pattern in wood, in which the cavity is formed. The cavity, in the casting, will of course be somewhat rough, and will require cleaning. After the face of the valve has been filed smooth and flat, and the rest of the valve reduced to nearly the finished size, it should be held in the vice and the limits of the cavity scribed on the face. The length of the cavity must be in a normal valve the same as the distance between the inside edge of the steam ports, and the width exactly the same as that of the steam ports. When marked out a small ($\frac{1}{8}$-in.) sharp cold chisel should be employed to cut down the edges of the cavity quite sharply, and as nearly square with the surface as possible (Fig. 245). After this the working face must be finished off. In model work this may be most readily done by grinding the valve on a piece of plate glass (*see* Fig. 171, Chap. IV.).

The fixing of the valve is shown in Fig. 244. The spindle should be of fair size. A good rule for the size of the valve spindle for model work is :—VS = one-eighth of the cylinder bore + $\frac{1}{32}$ in. So for a $\frac{1}{2}$-in. bore cylinder the size would be $\frac{3}{32}$ in. The valve is slotted at the back, and the spindle is filed with two parallel flats on it (the length of these flats being the same as the valve), so that the spindle will easily fit the slot in the valve. The latter should be deep enough to allow the valve to lift a little should any condensed water want to get out of the cylinder, the steam-tightness of the valve depending on the steam in the steam chest pressing the valve down on the port faces of the cylinder.

The adjustment of the relationship between valve and eccentric with this slotted valve fixing can be arranged by screwing on the forked joint to the eccentric rod (*see* Fig. 246).

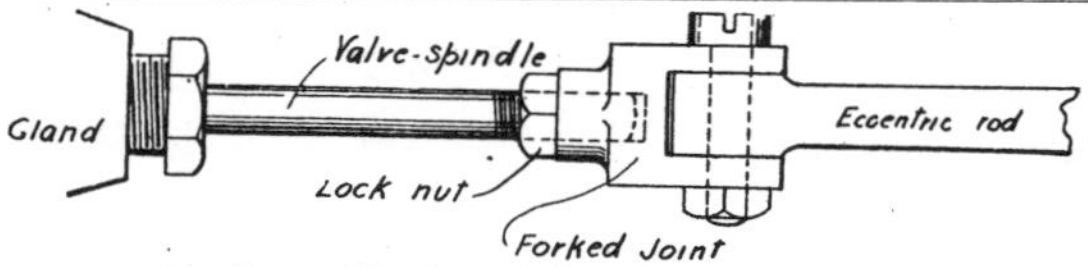

Fig. 246.—Forked joint for eccentric rod

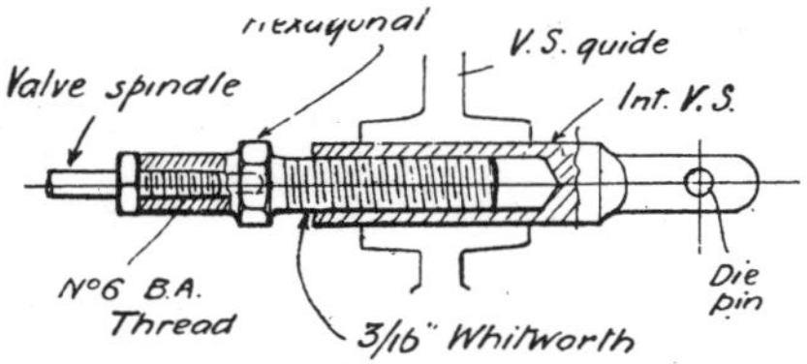

Fig. 247.—Adjustment for valve spindle

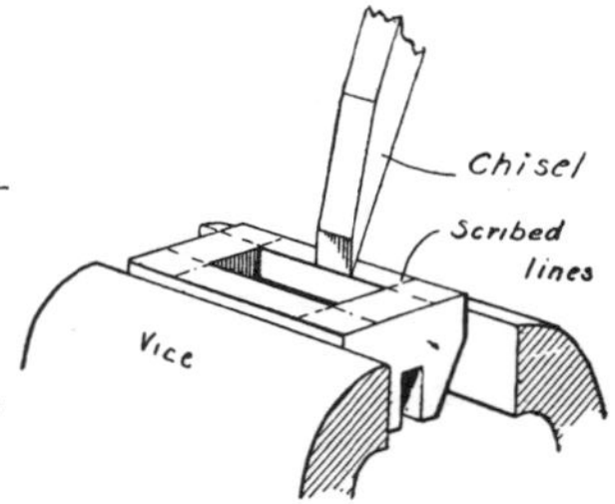

Fig. 245.—Cutting cavity with chisel

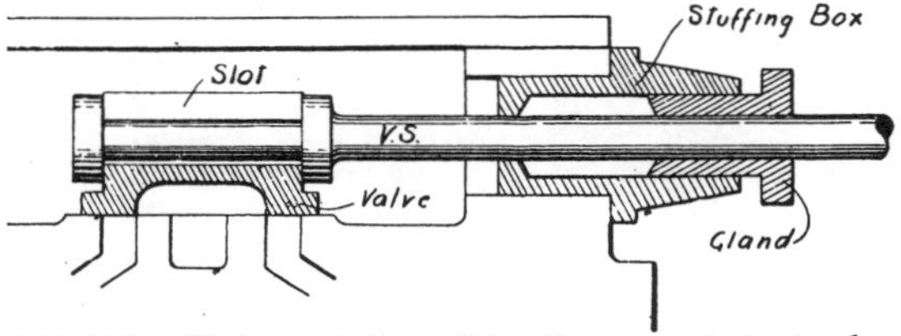

Fig. 249.—Valve spindle, solid collars and slotted valve

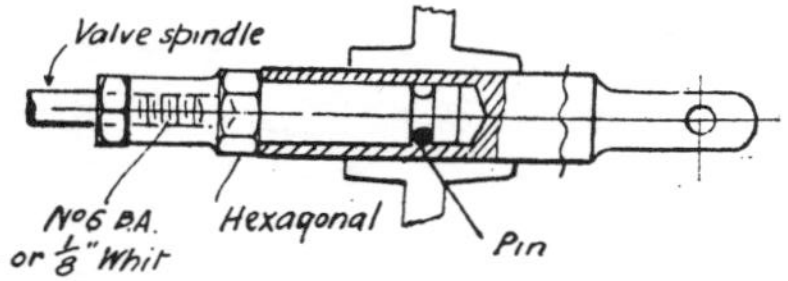

Fig. 248.—Another type of adjustable valve spindle

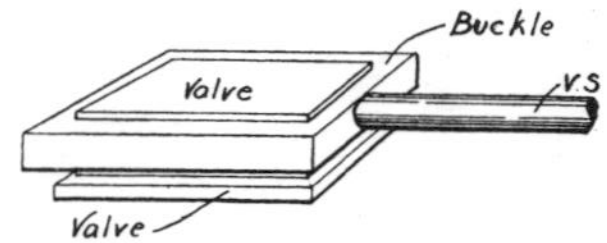

Fig. 252.—Valve spindle complete with solid buckle

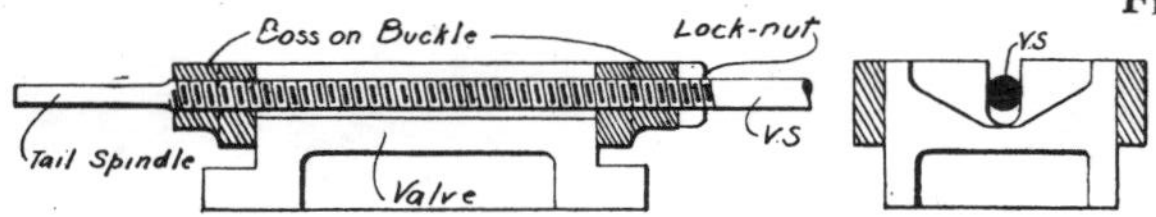

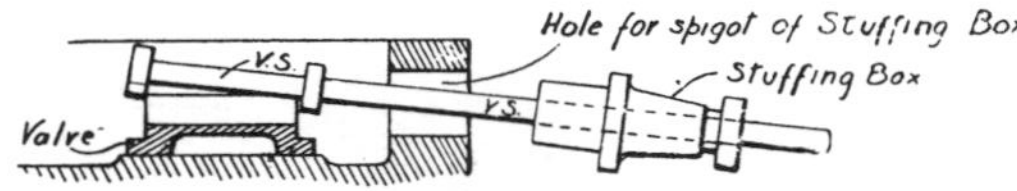

Fig. 250.—Fitting valve spindle

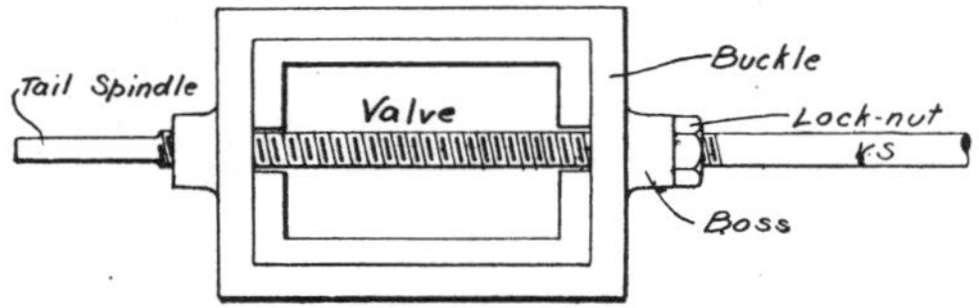

Fig. 253.—Buckle with screwed-in valve spindle

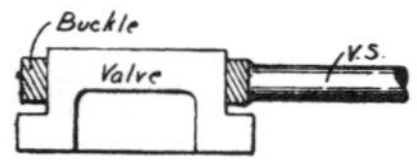

Fig. 252a.— Section through solid buckle (Fig. 252)

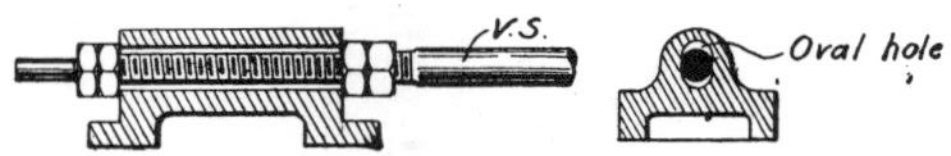

Fig. 251.—Valve spindle screwed and fitted with double nuts

To vary the position of the valve, the pin or screw through the joint must be withdrawn, and the eccentric rod dropped out of the fork. The fork can then be screwed up or unscrewed, according to whether it is required to lengthen or shorten the valve spindle. The thread on the spindle should be as fine as possible (B.A. preferable), and a lock-nut is an advantage, especially if the thread is at all an easy fit.

Where the valve spindle cannot turn round and an intermediate guide is employed, a very good idea is shown in Fig. 247. In this device the nipple has a fine thread inside and a coarser thread outside. Screwing or unscrewing the nipple gives a fine adjustment in length, due to the difference in the pitch of the two threads. A lock-nut on the spindle secures the nipple.

Another arrangement in which a revolving nipple, held in place by a pin, is employed is illustrated in Fig. 248.

A development of the same idea of attaching the valve spindle is shown in Fig. 249. In this arrangement, which, by the way, is suited only to larger models, the valve spindle is not filed flat, but is turned down to fit into the slot in the back of the valve. The collars which drive the valve being solid with the valve spindle, it is necessary to make the stuffing box removable, so that a hole may be obtained in the wall of the steam chest sufficiently large to enable the valve spindle to be tilted and placed in the slot in the back of the valve. This method of attaching the spindle to the valve is more clearly shown in Fig. 250.

Of course, the collars could be separate, and in large models (i.e. "small-power" engines) this is often done. The collars are fixed by set-screws or, preferably, small pins, which pass right through the collars and the spindle.

An arrangement giving greater strength and having the same effect is shown by Fig. 251. Here the spindle is threaded, and double nuts (nuts which are locked against each other) are fitted on each side of the slide valve. The slide valve may be slotted as shown in the previous diagrams; but the more usual device is to bore the valve with a slotted hole, the width of which is equal to the diameter of the valve spindle. The hole is bored this diameter first, and filed out top and bottom with a rat-tail file. In the case of very small valves, a larger round hole would have to be adopted in place of an oval one.

In real practice the most common method of attaching the valve to the spindle is by a buckle, which is forged solid with or welded on to the spindle (*see* Fig. 252). This construction entails a large door at one end of the valve chest, to enable both valve and buckle to be inserted together. The arrangement is something like the separate gland shown in Fig. 248, except that the door must be square. In some cases the door is on the opposite wall of the valve chest to the stuffing box. To get over the complication of steam-chest joints necessitated by a forged buckle, the writer uses the fixing shown in Fig. 253 in engines with cylinders up to 4-in. bore. Here the buckle is cast in gunmetal or brass, and is threaded for the spindle. It is better to make the spindle continuous, that is, solid with the tail spindle, and to do this the valve must be slotted at the back as shown. In all cases where there is no other guiding device or support for the valve spindle except the valve-spindle gland, a tail spindle is desirable; and, as a rule, this must be smaller in diameter than the other end of the spindle.

Another device which is much used by model-makers for attaching slide valves to their spindles is shown in Fig. 254. Here again the spindle is screwed and the adjustment of the valve is effected by turning the spindle. Only one nut is employed, and this is placed in a large slot in the back of the valve. Where the valve has no other guiding device, it is better to lengthen the nut as much as possible, and also to extend it at the sides, so that a lip or flange may be arranged in the nut to hold the valve square with the ports, as shown in Fig. 255.

Materials for Valves.—With regard to the materials which may be used for valves and valve spindles—with brass or gunmetal cylinders, valves of the same material are often used. Where the steam is superheated this should be avoided at any cost. A brass valve on a brass port-face rapidly wears, and very often in grooves, causing leakage of steam. Bronze, steel, or cast-iron valves will work much more satisfactorily. The drawback to an iron valve is that it may rust during the periods the engine is not in use. A thorough oiling directly the engine is stopped will, however, get over this trouble.

For cast-iron cylinders the valves may be of cast-iron (a softer grade of material preferably), bronze, or gunmetal. Where the steam is highly superheated, cast-iron should certainly be employed. Of course, steel or cast malleable iron might be tried, and there is no reason why either of these materials should not work very well. Brass, however, is out of the question with high-temperature steam.

Valve spindles under ordinary conditions are made of steel. Such spindles are, however, subject to corrosion; in smaller models more particularly. Therefore in any small-power engine which is only used intermittently, bronze or german silver (nickel bronze) valve spindles are to be recommended. German silver has the advantage, for scale model work, of looking like steel. Where a steel spindle is used in a model, much trouble is often experienced on running an engine for the first time after a lengthy period of disuse. The spindle rusts, and the oxide grips the valve, so that the valve is held off the port face, and the steam "blows through" to the exhaust without doing any work in the cylinder. The remedy is a liberal charge of paraffin until the rust is dissolved and the valve freed from the spindle.

In real practice, the pressure of the steam on the surface of the valve is considerable; so much so, that various devices are employed to relieve the valve of this weight. In model work the pressure on the valve is not so important from the point of view of the friction and the wear and tear it involves. It is often not sufficient to overcome the friction of the valve-spindle attachments, and therefore the engine sometimes has difficulty in starting. The grease and dirt accumulating on the spindle prevent the valve sitting down on the port face, and the steam blows past the valve to the atmosphere. Owing to this tendency, model slide valves are often provided with springs to keep them up to the valve faces whether steam is on or not. Figs. 256 to 258 show various methods of arranging the springs.

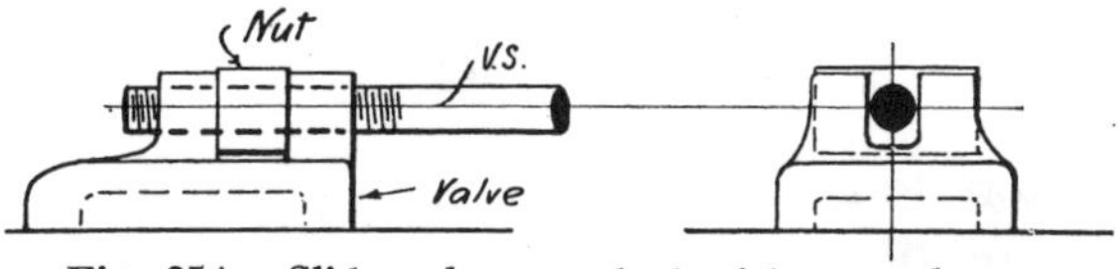

Fig. 254.—Slide valve attached with central nut

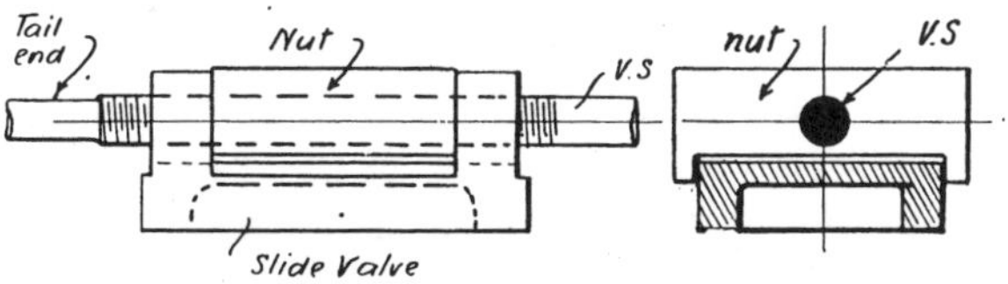

Fig. 255.—Slide valve with long flanged nut

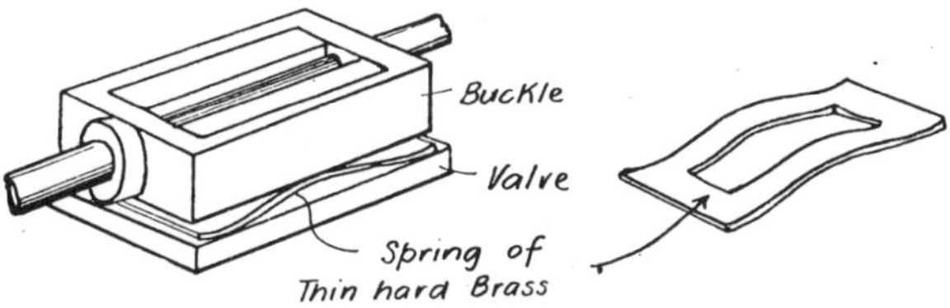

Fig. 256

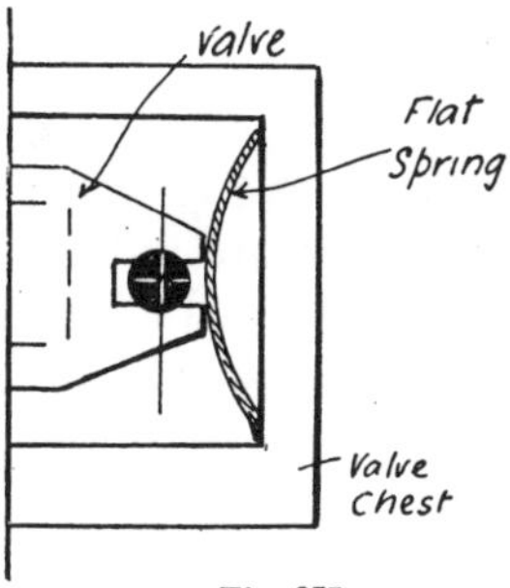

Fig. 257

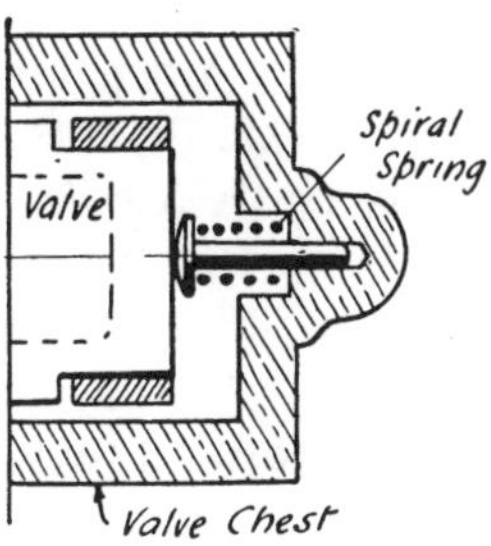

Fig. 258

Figs. 256 to 258.—Methods of fitting springs to back of valve

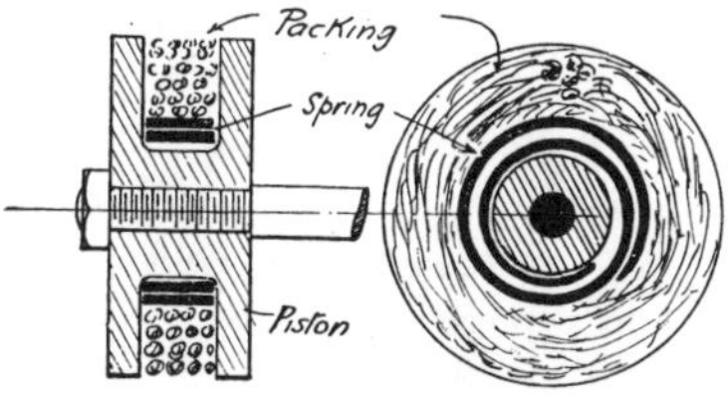

Fig. 262.—Woven packing assisted by spring ring

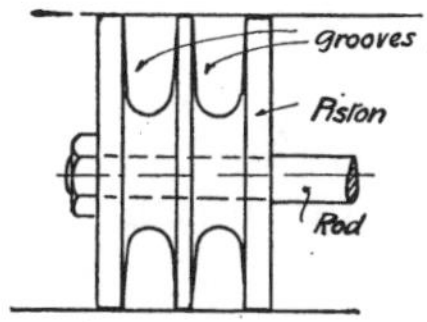

Fig. 260.—Double-grooved piston

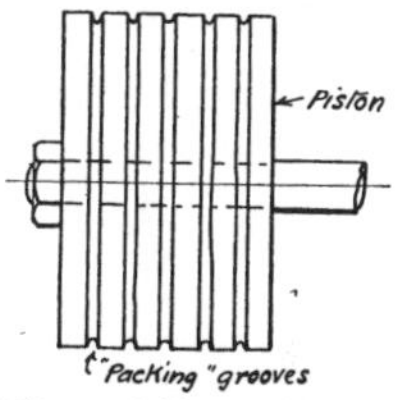

Fig. 261. — Piston with "labyrinth" grooves

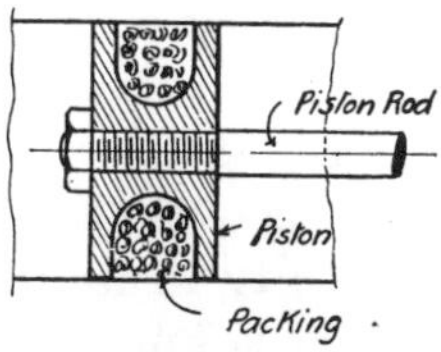

Fig. 259.—Grooved piston with woven packing

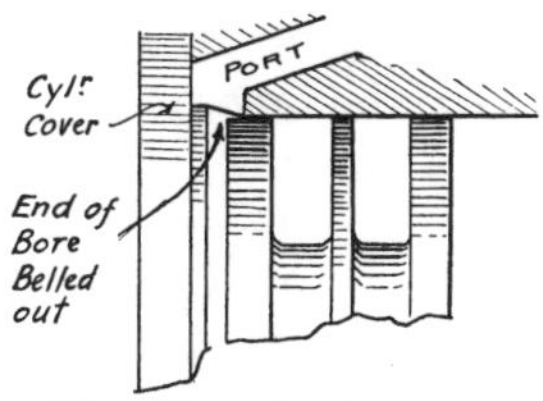

Fig. 263.—Setting out piston grooves

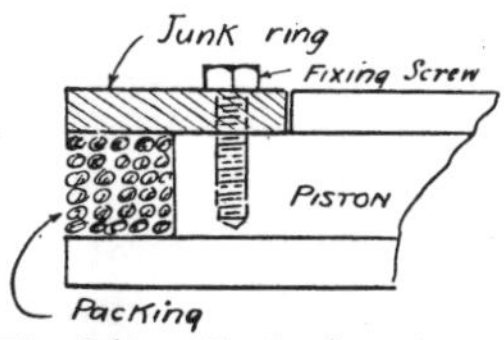

Fig. 264.—Junk-ring piston with woven packing

Pistons and Piston Packing.—The piston is one of the more important features of model steam-engine construction. Its proportions and details vary considerably from those adopted in real practice. In a large engine a piston 3 in. thick is ample for an 18-in. bore locomotive cylinder; this is a proportion of 1 to 6. In model work a $\frac{1}{4}$-in. piston would be used in a $\frac{1}{2}$-in. bore cylinder, the thickness and bore being in a proportion of 1 to 2.

The smallest models, especially those with brass cylinders, also widely differ from large modern confrères in the method by which the pistons are made steam-tight. One of the simplest devices is that most commonly used in small model pistons, namely, a deep groove filled with cotton or asbestos yarn packing, as shown in Fig. 259. Where the piston is large enough, say $\frac{5}{8}$ in. or $\frac{3}{4}$ in. in diameter and $\frac{3}{8}$ in. or $\frac{7}{16}$ in. thick, two grooves may be turned in it, the idea being to assist the steam-tightness by subdividing the packing (*see* Fig. 260).

It is well known that the presence of grooves alone is, especially in fluid engines, a sufficiently good packing. This system is known as "labyrinth packing." Therefore, where the maker is perfectly sure that the two metals which he employs will work together satisfactorily, a very fair degree of tightness can be obtained by cutting a number of small parallel grooves in the piston, as shown in Fig. 261. The explanation of the action of these grooves in preventing fluid under pressure passing through is simple. Any fluid or gas which tends to get from one side of the piston to the other must pass these grooves. For instance, a particle of steam under the full pressure passes along to the first groove between the small space which must be provided between the piston and cylinder. Directly it gets into this groove the volume of the space is increased. Now, an increase in volume means a corresponding decrease in pressure, and therefore the steam has lost much of its force. However, it may have enough pressure left to squeeze its way to the next groove. Here it encounters a further increase in volume, and the pressure falls again. It will, therefore, be seen that the larger the number of grooves employed the better. Of course, the device also depends on a good fit between the piston and cylinder, and this is why care has to be taken to use materials which will suit each other and wear for a considerable time. Cast iron on steel, iron on brass, or cast iron on cast iron works quite satisfactorily. With brass cylinders, pistons of the same material are likely to wear out very quickly, and where iron cannot be paired with the brass, it is better to use a hard phosphor or other bronze.

Small toy-engine pistons are for the most part made without any packing whatever. A sufficient degree of steam tightness is obtained by the use of a comparatively long piston and perfect mechanical fits. Everything works well while the engine is new and where saturated steam is employed. Considerable trouble was experienced when some of the German makers tried to use superheated steam. This was, however, mitigated by more efficient lubrication and by the use of different metals for cylinder and piston, namely, brass and phosphor bronze respectively.

One of the difficulties with yarn pistons is the necessity for the frequent renewal of the packing, and where superheated steam is employed cotton packings rapidly char and therefore asbestos is used. Another difficulty is that the packing, on becoming wet, swells, and excessive friction results. An arrangement which may be used to take up the wear of the packing and to give it more elasticity is shown in Fig. 262. The groove in the piston is turned very deeply, and a coiled spring, made of thin hard brass strip, is formed in the bottom of the groove, and the packing wound over it.

There is one additional point which should be observed in making small pistons, those of the packed variety more especially, and that is the position of the packing groove. The groove or grooves should not extend too near to the face of the piston, otherwise there is a danger, especially where the end clearances are small, of the packing getting entangled in the steam ports. Fig. 263 shows a suitable setting out.

In the old days hempen packing was, of course, the rule, and the steam-tightness of the piston was arranged much in the same way as shown in Fig. 264, with a removable junk ring covering in the packing groove. This idea is sometimes adopted in model work; but on larger model pistons model-makers now use piston rings.

Model flash boilers also demand engines with cast-iron cylinders and pistons, and either steel or cast-iron piston rings. Brass cannot be employed in any working part of the cylinder owing to the great heat of the steam supplied by a model flash boiler.

The simplest form of piston fitted with Ramsbottom rings is shown in Fig. 265. Here the piston is solid, and the rings are sprung over the piston. The objection to this arrangement in a small engine (say under 1½-in. bore) is that there is great risk of distorting or breaking the rings in fitting on or removing them, therefore the writer always recommends either of the forms of piston shown in Figs. 266 and 268. The body of the piston is in two parts; in the case of Fig. 267 one part being virtually the junk-ring idea, with metal rings instead of hempen packing. The piston rings are made with their inner and outer diameters eccentric, this form of ring being found to exert a more even pressure on the walls of the cylinder. Any number of rings may be used, the loose carriers (that is, the solid rings) being increased in number to suit. Two rings should be the minimum. The advantage of the arrangement is that rings may be placed in position without risk of breaking or distortion. The rings are, of course, split at the thinnest part, and should be turned a little larger than the bore of the cylinder, the excess being about 1 or 1¼ per cent. of the diameter of the piston. The rings may be cut on the slant with a small knife-edged file from the inside.

Model cylinders, except perhaps in the smallest sizes, should always bore with the ends tapered out to a larger diameter, as shown in Fig. 263. This facilitates the putting in of the piston, especially where piston rings are employed.

A simple method of making a trunk piston, suited say to a model hot-air engine or toy engine, is shown in Fig. 269. The materials and apparatus required will be some scrap hard type-metal or zinc; the cylinder, the bore of which is assumed to be polished and true; a piece of hard wood; and a ladle for melting and pouring the metal.

Cut the piece of wood to the shape shown in section at A in the accompanying illustration, so that it tapers towards the top. If rings are available, they should be sprung in so that they remain in position as at B. Next fit the cylinder with the rings as shown on the piece

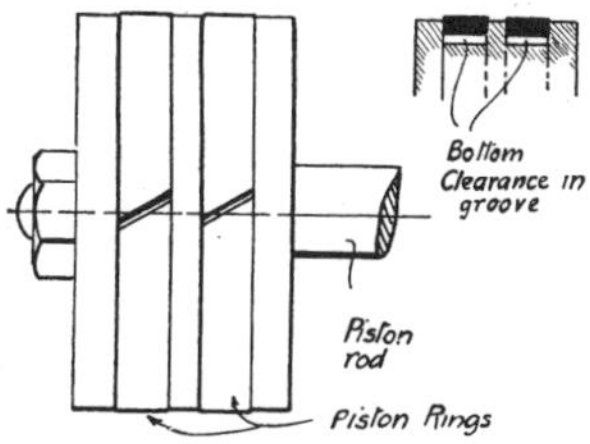

Fig. 265.—Solid piston with "Ramsbottom" spring rings

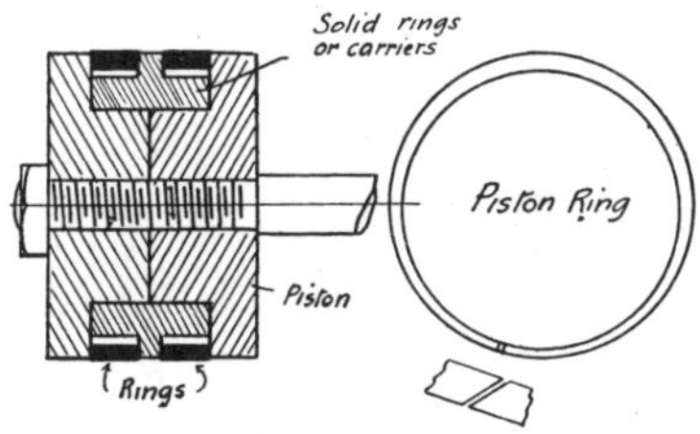

Fig. 266 and 267.—Built-up two-ring piston

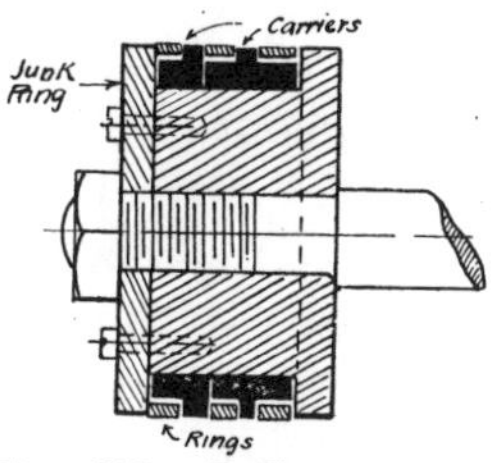

Fig. 268.—Built-up three-ring piston

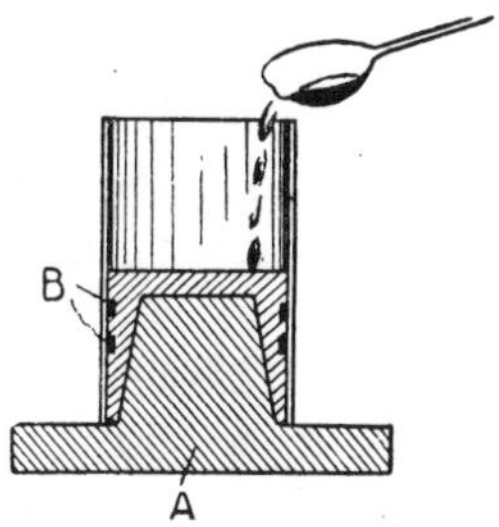

Fig. 269.—Casting piston in type-metal or zinc

of wood, and adjust it until the top of the taper appears quite centrally in the cylinder. Melt the metal and warm the cylinder thoroughly over a flame. Now fix it as quickly as possible in its proper position over the piece of wood (which, of course, should be placed on a horizontal surface), and pour gently the molten zinc into the cylinder as shown.

If the piston is to be packed a coil of strip tin may be used as a core for the grooves, and may be removed from the casting when cold. Such pistons wear very well where the heat is not excessive.

CHAPTER VI

Types of Model Steam-Engine Cylinders

General Design.—Although the design of the steam chest of a model steam cylinder largely depends on the particular type of engine adopted, and the general disposition of the parts, there are three distinct methods of construction which may be employed.

In small models, especially those of the commercial-made kind, the steam chest is a hollow box cast in one piece with a stuffing box and cover, attached to the cylinder, the joint being on the same plane as the port face (*see* Fig. **270**). While this type is very simple and necessitates only one steam joint, it does not make it possible to set the valve by sight without special jigs or other appliances. Furthermore, the valve cannot be examined without detaching the valve spindle from the link motion or from the eccentric rod, as the case may be. To set the valve by observation, the best thing to do, especially if several models with the same size of cylinder are likely to be required, is to make a dummy steam chest with no cover, which may be fitted to the cylinder in the same way as the final steam chest. When all the valve gear is erected, the movements of the valve may be observed, and the latter set correctly. The dummy steam chest can then be removed, and care must be exercised in taking down the valve motion to see that no alteration is made in any previous adjustment of parts, otherwise the proper timing of the valve will be upset.

One of the best methods of making model-engine steam chests is shown in Fig. **271**, and this arrangement will be found quite satisfactory in engines developing up to $\frac{1}{2}$ h.p. The only drawback to the design is that there are two joints instead of one; however, pattern-making is much simplified. One point worthy of special attention in all larger model cylinders is the recessing of the port face. Usually it is impossible to cast this recess in without resorting to complicated methods of pattern-making. Therefore, the face may be recessed by chiselling it away as indicated in Fig. 272 for a depth of, say, $\frac{1}{16}$ in. or $\frac{3}{32}$ in., according to the size of the cylinder.

The working face should be as wide as the valve, and

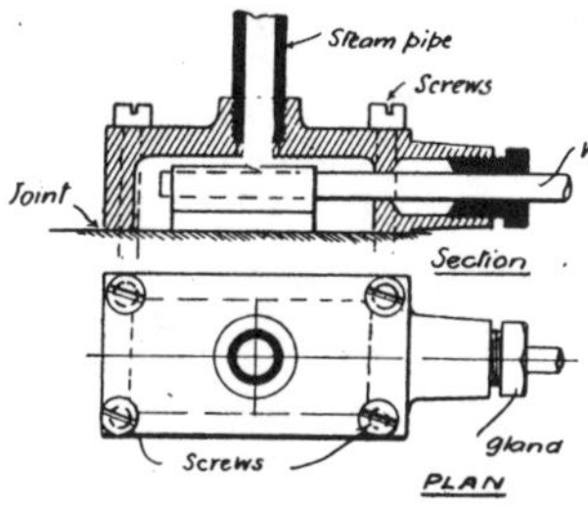

Fig. 270.—Ordinary model steam or valve chest

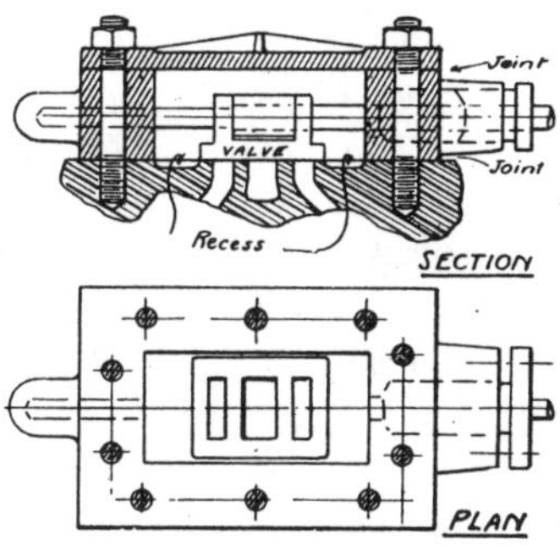

Fig. 271.—Valve chest for small-power engine

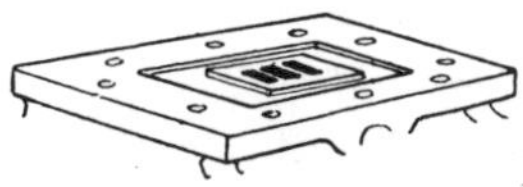

Fig. 272.—Recessed port face

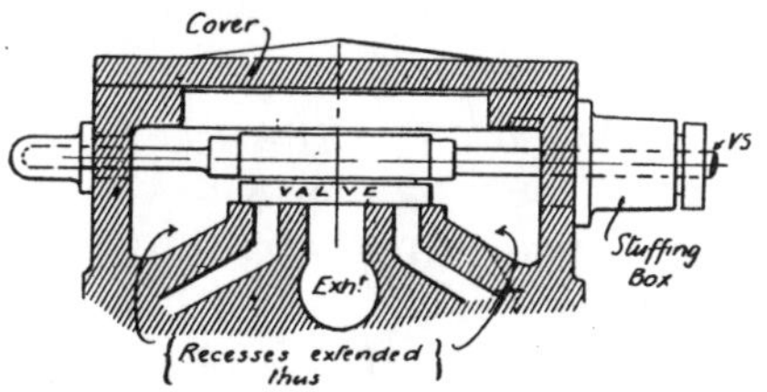

Fig. 273.—Valve chest (cored in casting) for large model or small-power engine

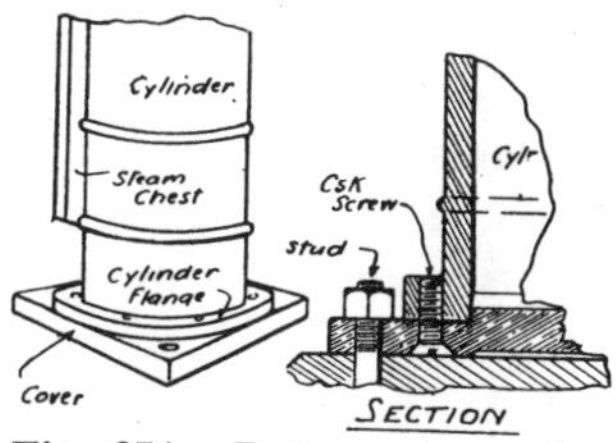

Fig. 274.—Bottom cover for fixing cylinder of model beam or vertical engine

sufficiently long to provide for the full travel of the valve without any possibility of the exhaust cavity being opened to the live steam.

Where the steam chest is cast solid with the cylinder, as shown in Fig. 273, a core box is necessary for the inside of the steam chest, and the port face over which the valve works can be easily recessed in the casting. Indeed, such recessing is necessary in any cylinder over, say, 2-in. bore, to lighten the casting at this point. To obtain a perfectly sound cylinder free from blowholes, it is essential that the metal be evenly distributed over the whole casting. Another point is the setting out of the studs. These must be arranged to miss glands, and possibly the exhaust-port opening or flange studs. So much for steam-chest details. The next thing for consideration is the variations in design that the special uses of the engine involve.

Types of Engines.—Stationary engines may be of several types: vertical, inverted vertical, horizontal, and those built on the boiler which supplies the steam, as in the case of portable and semi-portable engines. Marine engines are generally of the inverted vertical or diagonal types, vertical and horizontal engines having long gone out of fashion, although possibly some may still remain. Locomotive cylinders are almost always horizontal, or nearly so, and are special only in the methods by which they are fixed either inside or outside the frames, and in the arrangement of the steam and exhaust pipes. All of the above-mentioned kinds of cylinders may be simple or compounded, and in the case of marine engines arranged for three or four stages of expansion; that is, triple- or quadruple-expansion engines.

Beam Engine Cylinders.—The oldest type of vertical engine is the beam engine. Here the bottom cylinder cover may be quite square, and the projecting angles may be bolted down to the bedplate (*see* Fig. 274). The steam chest may be quite independent of any fixings to the base; and as beam engines have generally a very long stroke (often three times the bore), the slide valves may be divided, Watt's drop valves or Murdock's long "D" valve being hardly applicable to an ordinary working model. The live steam, of course, is in direct communication with both valves; but the exhaust steam must be connected by an outside flanged pipe connection, a fitting which will really enhance the appearance of the model. Fig. 275 shows a design typical of this. The steam chests are of the pattern shown in Fig. 271, and are coupled by an oval or square connection, which may be cast with the steam chest, or may be a piece

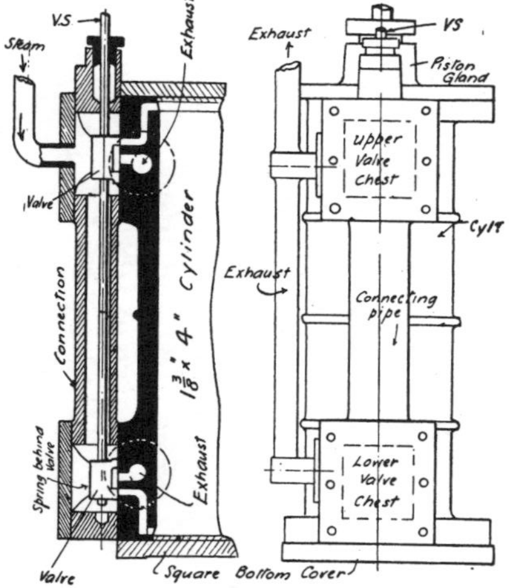

Fig. 275.—Valve chests for model beam engine

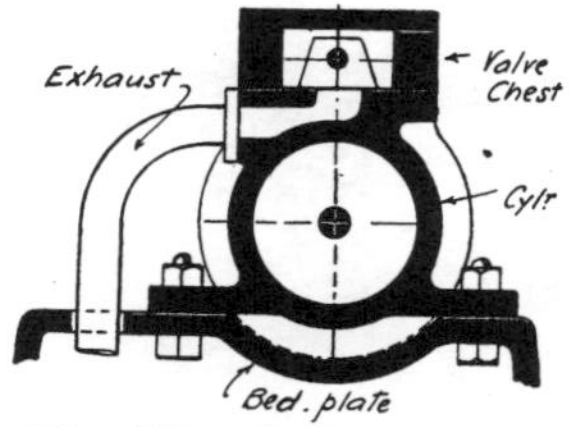

Fig. 277.—Cylinder fixing for model mill engine

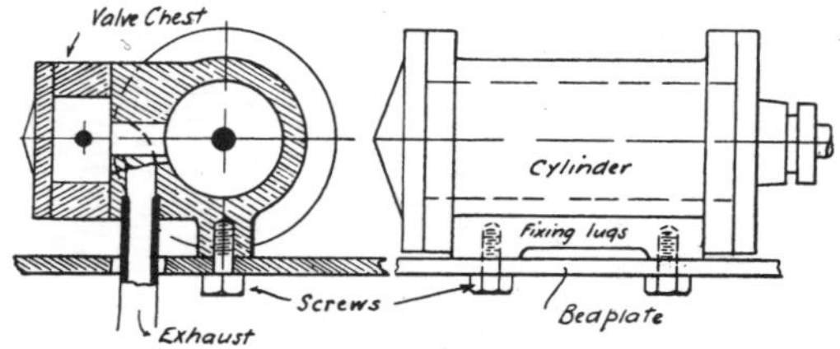

Fig. 276.—Cylinder fixing for small model horizontal engine

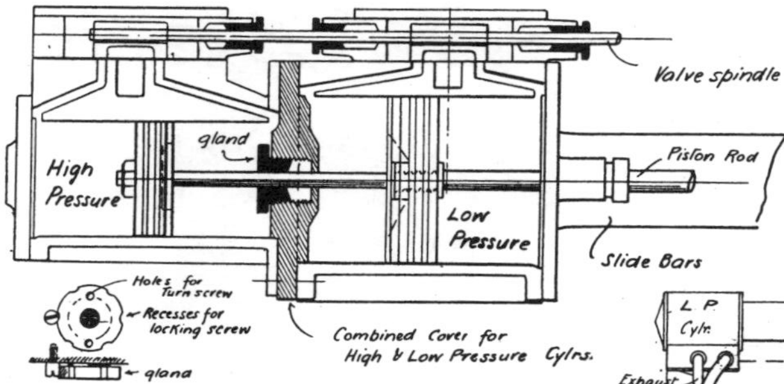

Fig. 280.—Section through cylinders of model tandem compound engine

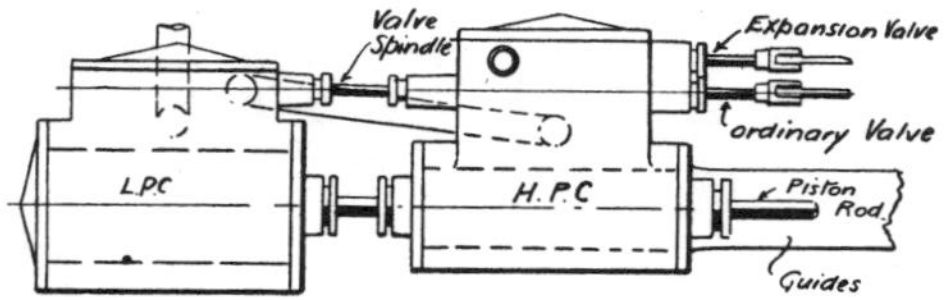

Fig. 279.—Plan of tandem compound engine

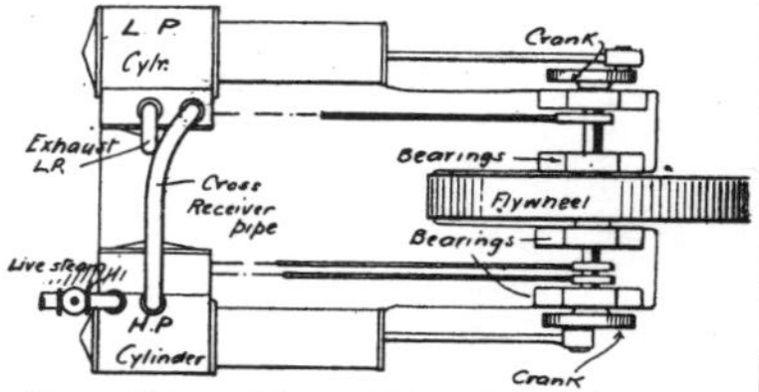

Fig. 278.—Plan of horizontal cross compound engine

of thick tube, or brass rod previously bored, silver-soldered in between two ordinary steam-chest castings. The exhaust may be led upwards or downwards, as occasion requires.

Where the cylinder is of normal dimensions, the valve chest will be of the ordinary type; the only difference in the design of the cylinder from one used in a horizontal engine will be the absence of any lugs on the side of the cylinder, and the use of the square-bottom cylinder cover already mentioned.

Horizontal Engine Cylinders.—Horizontal engines take many forms. The steam chest may be placed on the side or on the top of the cylinder, and in each case need not take any part in the holding down of the cylinder to the bedplate, and the exhaust being conducted downwards. Fig. 276 shows a typical device for fixing model cylinders up to, say, 1-in. bore. Fig. 277 shows a method of fixing the cylinder with side lugs, and Fig. 281 the attachment of a cylinder of a high-speed short-stroke engine, known as overhung type. The use of this fixing is exemplified in the design for the "Stuart" horizontal engine illustrated by the photograph, Fig. 282. Here the bedplate is extended vertically in circular form to embrace the back cylinder cover and gland, and special arrangements have to be made, in smaller engines more particularly, to obtain a proper steam-tight cover joint, and at the same time a satisfactory fixing to the bedplate. In Fig. 281 the cover is fitted to the soleplate with one countersunk screw first, and then the cylinder is put into place and secured with five or seven studs, according to the dimensions of the cylinder and the pressure at which it works.

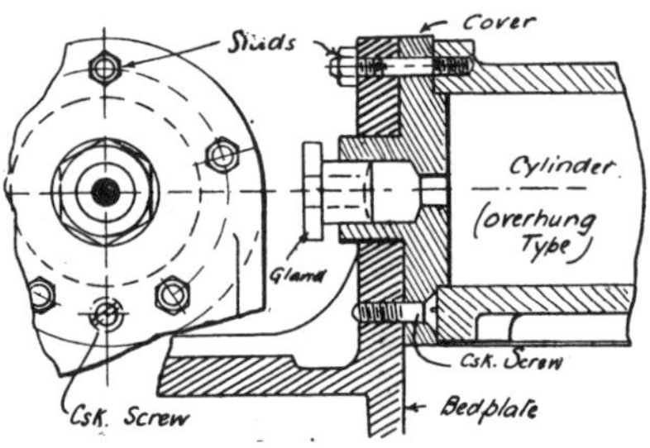

Fig. 281.—Cylinder fixing for high-speed overhung engine

The compounding of horizontal engines is very interesting, and enhances the value of the model from all points of view. The high- and low-pressure cylinders may be placed either side by side, as shown in Fig. 278, or in tandem one behind the other, as in Fig. 279. When placed laterally, the flywheel is generally between the two cranks, which are of the single-web or overhung type, and the engine is known as a cross compound, Fig. 278 showing the general disposition of the cylinders and pipe connections. Model tandem compound cylinders may be made with the high-pressure cylinder next to the crank and the cylinders entirely separated. The advantage of this arrangement is only marked when the

Fig. 282.—" Stuart " model high-speed horizontal engine

high-pressure cylinder is fitted with expansion valve gear, as shown in Fig. 279.

To save space longitudinally, and also to reduce the number of glands, a design such as that shown in Fig. 280 may be adopted. Here the low-pressure cylinder is placed next the crank, and the " front " cover forms the back cover of the high-pressure cylinder.

A gland is, of course, necessary ; but this can be arranged from the high-pressure cylinder side ; and if the stuffing box is sufficiently capacious, no trouble in the working of the engine will ensue. The steam chests must be separate, and, to provide enough room between them for a pair of glands and stuffing boxes, the chests may have to be placed at the opposite extremities of the cylinders, as shown. Both the

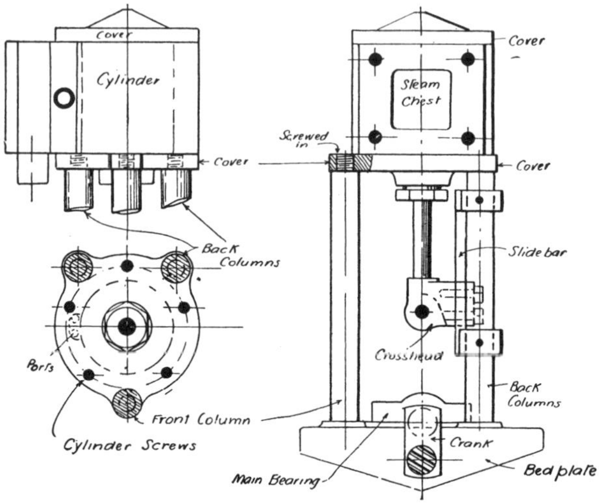

Fig. 283.—Cylinders and supporting columns for model launch-type vertical engine

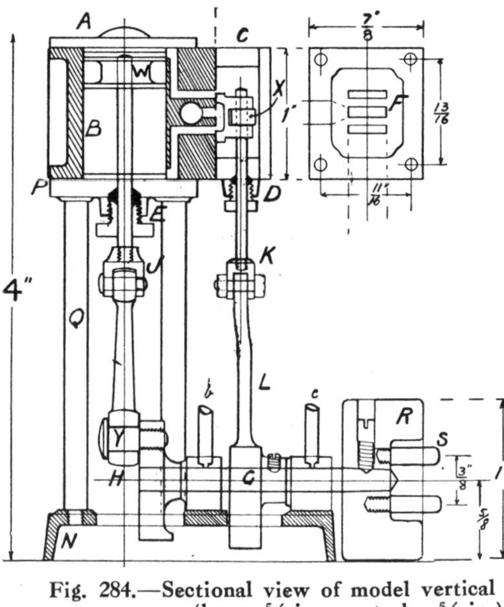
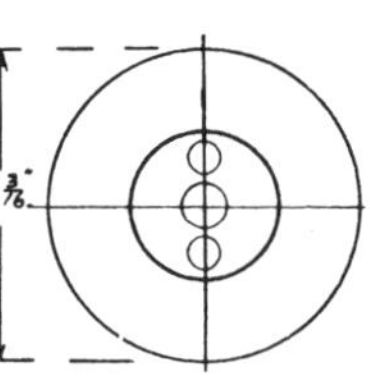

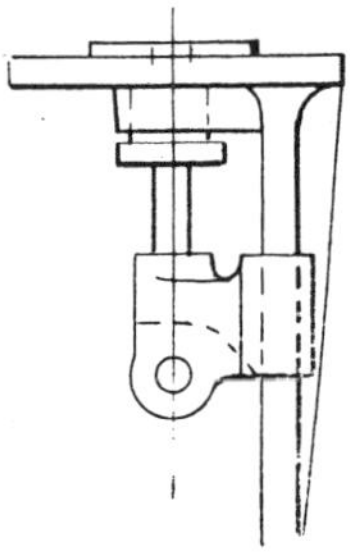

Fig. 284a.—Cast slide-bar for engine (Figs. 284 and 285)

Fig. 284.—Sectional view of model vertical launch engine (bore, 5/8 in. × stroke 5/8 in.)

high- and low-pressure valves work from the one eccentric, therefore the steam chests are best placed in line with each other. The internal gland will require a locking arrangement, a suggestion for which is shown by the small detail sketch in Fig. 280. A screw with a good long head is tapped into the combination cover, and engages recesses in the flange of the gland. The gland should have tommy holes driven in the face, to allow it to be tightened or unscrewed by a special turnscrew with two projecting pins.

Fig. 285.—Photograph of model vertical launch engine

Vertical Marine-type Engines.—The general arrangement of cylinder and steam chest may, in an inverted vertical engine, be very much varied, and cylinder fixings also often present some difficulty in design.

The simplest of all inverted vertical engines for amateur building is the launch type, in which the bottom cylinder cover is extended to take three or four columns of bright steel rod. Fig. 283 shows this method of construction, and it is adopted in real practice in all comparatively small engines where lightness and accessibility of parts are essential features. The slide bars involve a little more work than in cast column engines, as, unless the device illustrated in Figs. 284 and 285, in which the slide bar is cast on the cylinder cover as shown, is adopted, they have to be built out from the round columns on suitable brackets, as indicated in Fig. 283. The slides are usually of the single-bar type; but, especially in the case of reversing engines, which have also four column slide bars, they are often arranged on both sides of the crosshead. Great care must be taken in building up engines with round columns to tap the holes for the columns truly square with the cover, otherwise the alignment of the cylinder and motion will suffer. The engine will fail to run smoothly, and also rapidly wear out in subsequent service.

The design (Fig. 283) shows a small engine with three columns and a single slide bar. The columns are made of bright mild-steel rod shouldered down at each end, and screwed for the cover and for the nuts below the bedplate casting. The cylinder-cover studs are arranged to miss the columns, and as far as possible the steam ports. The latter is an important point, and the position of steam ports and drain cocks for the most part settles the position of the cylinder studs or screws. Figs. 284 and 285 are the commercial outcome of this main idea, and machined sets of castings can be obtained for this engine.

In larger engines the columns are turned all over, and where the brackets holding the slide bars have solid eyes bored for columns, the diameter of the columns at the places where the brackets are fixed must be equal in diameter to at least one of the flanges, as shown in Fig. 286. Otherwise the brackets must be split or fixed in some other manner to the columns.

In many cases, if not all, the maker of a model marine engine finds that the available height is extremely limited. To obtain a reasonable stroke, a lower centre of gravity, and an efficient piston gland, the piston is often coned as shown in Fig. 287. In this way the gland does not project so far below the cylinder cover, as a large proportion of the stuffing box is contained within the correspondingly coned portion of the bottom cover.

Figs. 288 and 289 are under-side plan and elevation of the

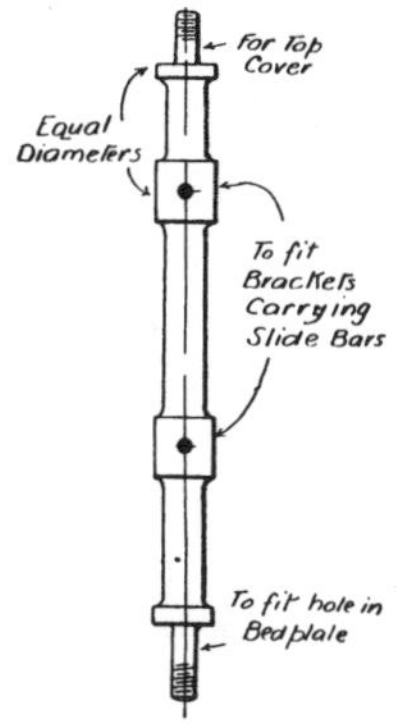

Fig. 286.—Turned column for launch engine

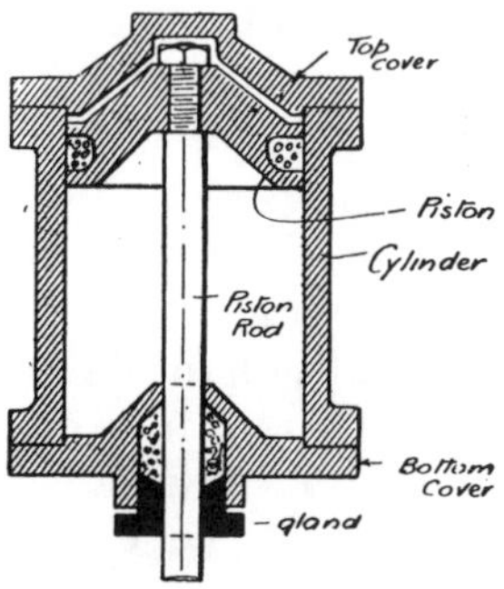

Fig. 287.—Coned piston of vertical engine

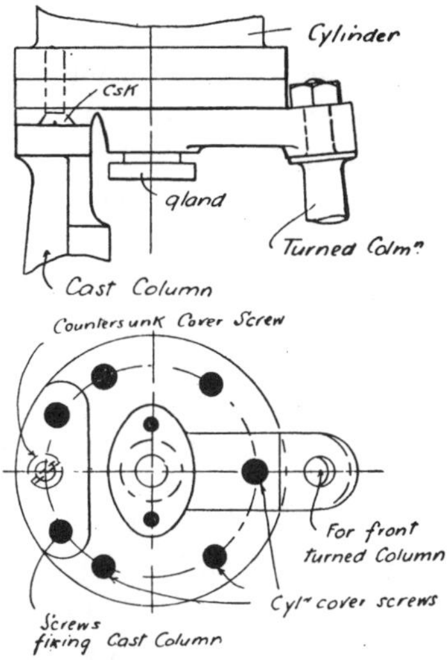

Figs. 288 and 289.—Cylinder fixing of cast-standard engine

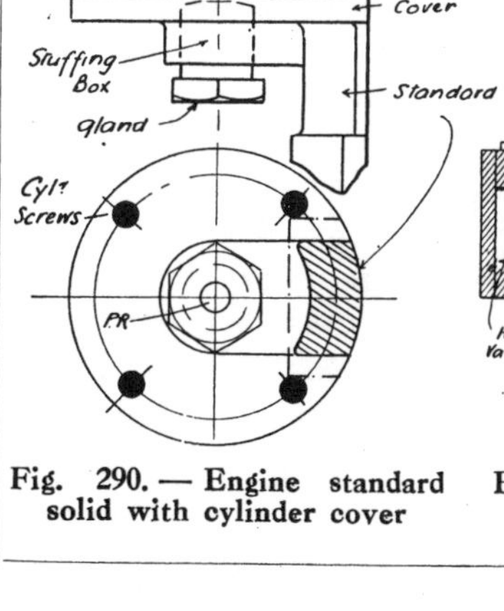

Fig. 290. — Engine standard solid with cylinder cover

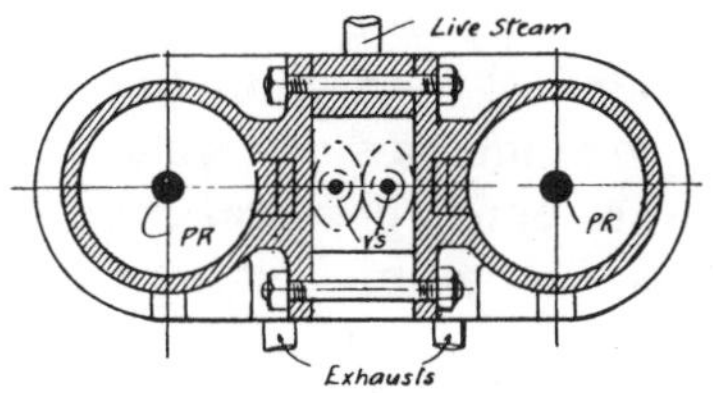

Fig. 291. — Section through twin-cylinder engine with central valve chests

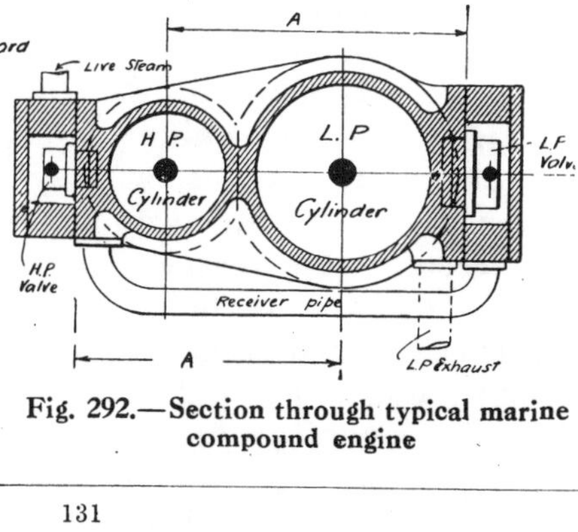

Fig. 292.—Section through typical marine compound engine

lower fixings of a cylinder of an engine which has one cast and one turned column. The cast standard is screwed (studded) on to the bottom cover on a facing strip provided in the casting, and the turned column in front fits a similarly formed lug. To securely fix the cylinder to the cover, six studs or screws may be necessary, and in such a case one of these may be a counterscrew fitted underneath the centre of the standard. This construction is suitable for engines with cylinders from 1-in. to 2-in. bore. Smaller models may have the standard and the bottom cover cast in one piece. This method is shown in Fig. 290, and it will be noted that only about four screws can be used to fix the cover to the cylinder. A front turned column can also be used and arranged as shown in Figs. 283 and 288. This construction covers most ordinary designs, and may be extended to twin- or triple-cylindered engines as required.

The next point is the arrangement of the steam chests in model marine type with multiple cylinders. The old-fashioned " twin launch engine " generally had its cylinders arranged as shown in Fig. 291. This is quite good from a constructional point of view, but the old difficulties of valve setting still exist; indeed, they are increased in a model vertical marine-type engine. It would be a rather troublesome matter to take down each cylinder in turn to set the valves by sight, and unless other methods equally troublesome and complicated are adopted, this must be done. The better plan is to place the valves outside the cylinders, casting the latter in one piece, as shown in Fig. 292. This figure shows the cylinders of a two-cylinder compound in sectional plan; but, of course, it is just as easy to arrange the valves and valve chest in the same way in a non-compound twin engine. The eccentric sheaves need not be split, as is necessary in the case of Fig. 291, more particularly where a solid forged crankshaft is used also. The sheaves may be of the ordinary pattern, and fit on to the ends of the shaft. In Fig. 292 the valve spindle of the high-pressure cylinder is closer to the centre of the cylinder than on the low-pressure side. The exact distance must be settled by the room on the crankshaft. For link motion the high-pressure valve chest may have to be extended to provide space for the two eccentrics, main bearing, and crank web.

Another point to remember in designing an engine for home manufacture is with reference to the boring of the cylinders. Unless the lathe has a boring table, the cylinders must be mounted on the faceplate, and dimension A marks the limits of the lathe. In almost any engine larger than a model, a gap-bed lathe will be necessary for this part of the work.

Fig. 292 also shows the pipe connections. The communication pipe between the high-pressure exhaust and low-pressure steam chest should be of ample size, so that it can act as a receiver. This is especially important in the case of a compound engine which has the cranks at right angles; and it may be found necessary to core the L.P. steam chest out to give a little more capacity than that shown in Fig. 292. In all two-cylinder compound models of small-power steam engines which do not require to be self-starting (as, for instance, an electric lighting engine), it will be found much better to more nearly balance the reciprocating parts by placing the cranks at 180° instead of in the usual angle of 90°, adopted in most marine engines.

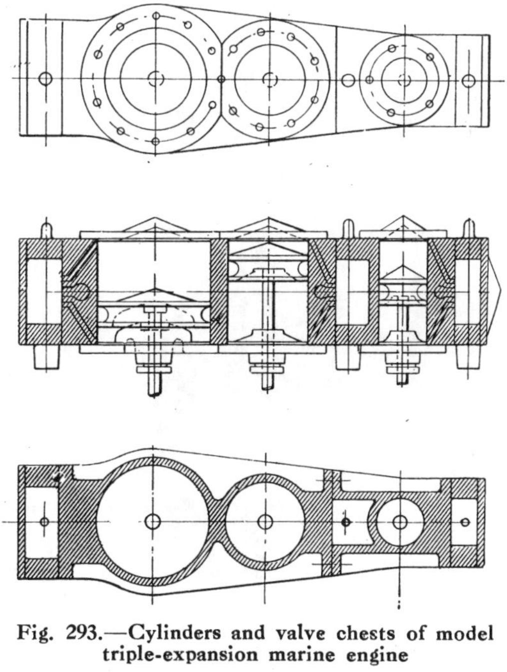

Fig. 293.—Cylinders and valve chests of model triple-expansion marine engine

In setting out a twin or compound engine with the valve

chests outside the cylinder, it may be necessary, to save longitudinal space and to lighten the whole engine, to place the cylinders as close as possible together, the cylinder covers being planed off on their adjacent edges, as indicated by the dotted lines in Fig. 292. The ports of the high- and low-pressure cylinders should be of the same width, but in length they will bear a direct proportion to the diameters of the respective cylinders.

Fig. 294.—Model twin-cylinder non-compound launch engine

Of course, one or more of the steam chests may be placed at right angles to the longitudinal centre line of the engine. This is sometimes adopted in the case of three-cylindered engines for the middle cylinder, simply to provide ready access to the valve and port face. Of course, it means that a radial valve motion or a rocking shaft must be employed for this cylinder.

Fig. 293 shows the arrangement of cylinder sometimes adopted in model triple-expansion engines. One valve chest of the intermediate cylinder is between two cylinders, the two others being outside. Fig. 294 illustrates a "Stuart" model twin-cylinder non-compound launch engine; while Fig. 295 shows a large model two-cylinder compound marine engine with reversing gear, complete with oil and drain pipes and link reversing gear. Both of them have outside valve chests. Fig. 296 shows a model triple-expansion engine with cylinders arranged as in Fig. 293, made by Mr. T. H. Cadwell, of Camborne.

Fig. 295.—Model twin-cylinder compound marine engine with reversing gear

Locomotive Cylinders (Inside Type).—Where locomotive cylinders are placed inside the frames, the question of the arrangement of the various steam passages is an important one. In the cylinders illustrated in Figs. 297 and 298 the writer got over all the difficulties which exist where it is attempted to place two separate cylinders within the narrow limits of width between model locomotive frames.

Fig. 296.—Model triple-expansion engine

The cylinders are cast in one piece, and in large sizes the steam ports may be cored out. The valve chest (or steam chest) is placed on top, with the slide valves s v directly over their respective cylinders. The exhaust passage E P is best drilled out of the solid; it must therefore have an opening in the side, which has to be plugged. This plug should be screwed for a fine thread, and should be driven home tightly, the threaded portion being slightly tapered. The exhaust is then conducted to the outer air by means of a pipe E X, which passes through the steam chest, the lower end being prevented from steam leakage by being screwed with a fine tapered thread, and the upper portion where it passes through the steam-chest cover S C being packed by a stuffing box and gland E G. The valve chest V C is shown its minimum width. Where the main frames at the top (where the smoke-box joins) will allow, it may be made wider and longer steam ports obtained.

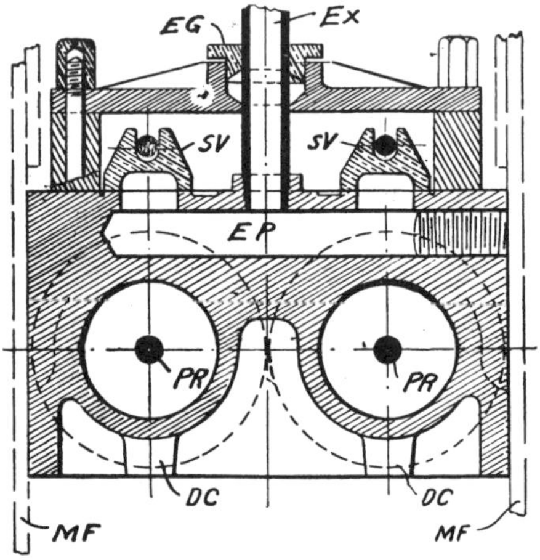

Fig. 297.—Cross section through locomotive "inside" cylinders

In the cylinders shown herewith, the tail of the valve spindle is supported by a dummy gland D G. The piston P may, where it is 1 in. in diameter or over, be packed by a pair of piston rings. Otherwise it must be turned with a deep groove for hempen or asbestos packing.

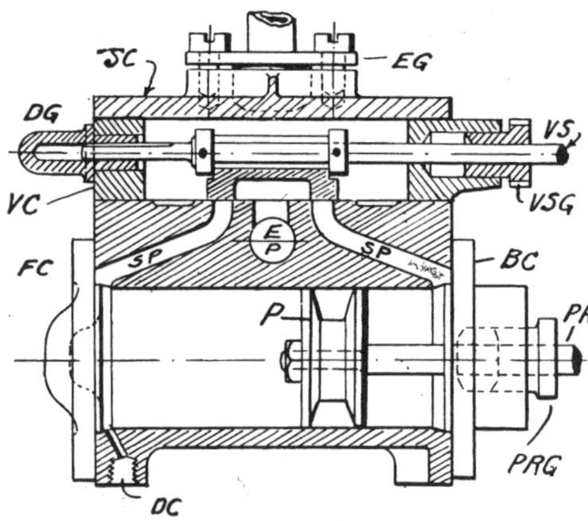

Fig. 298.—Longitudinal section through locomotive "inside" cylinders

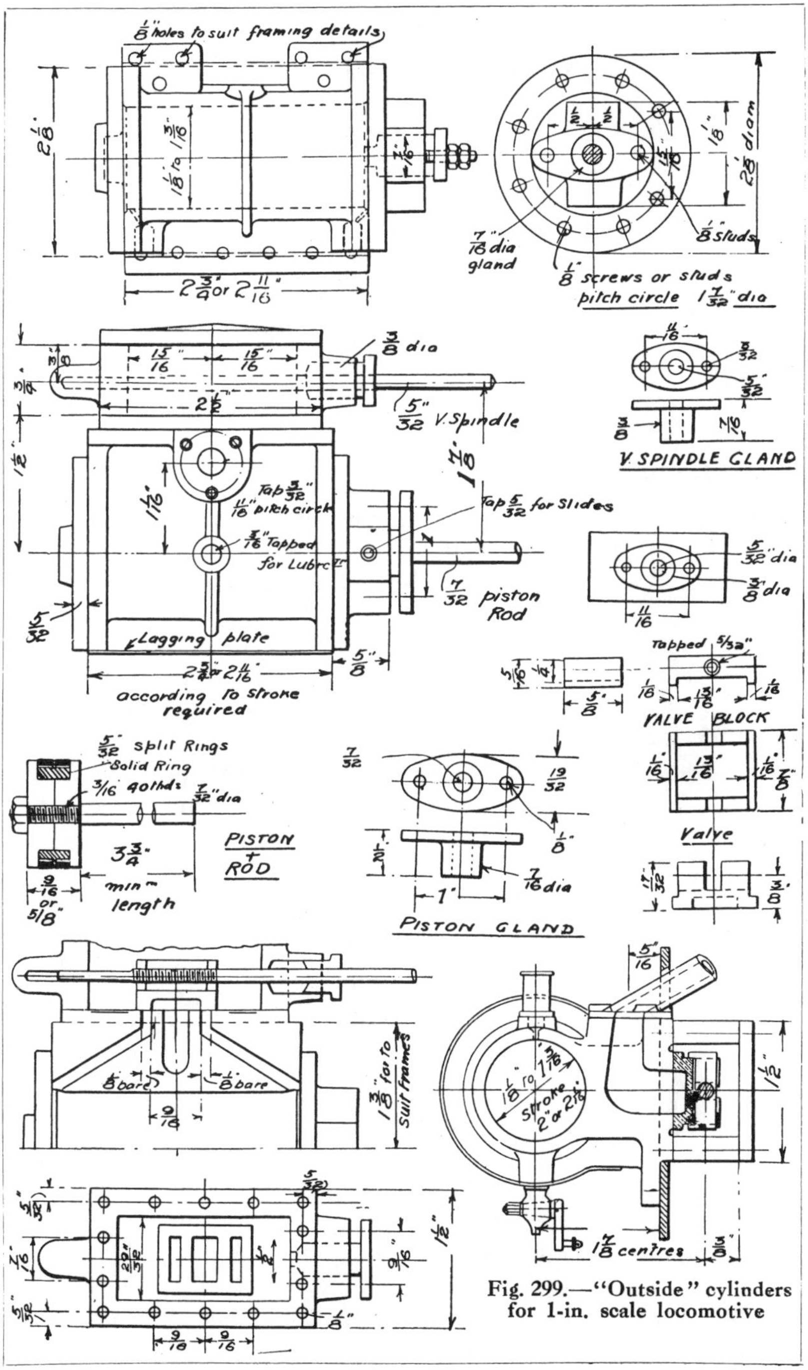

Fig. 299.—"Outside" cylinders for 1-in. scale locomotive

The following is a list of the letter references not already mentioned: P R the piston rod, P R G the piston-rod gland, D C the drain cocks, F C the front cover, B C the back cover, V S the valve spindle, V S G the valve-spindle gland, S P the steam pipe, and M F the main frames. In smaller engines the lower portion of the flange holding the cylinders to the main frames may be dispensed with. The cross section at this point is then as shown in the chapter describing the ½-in. scale M.R. single locomotive.

Fig. 300.—Locomotive frames with "outside" cylinders attached

Locomotive Cylinders (Outside Type).—Fig. 299 gives working drawings for cylinders which may be considered as a standard for models of most English-type locomotives having cylinders outside the frames.

As in the case of inside cylinders, the difficulty is the arrangement of the exhaust piping. This is got over by cutting away the flange of the cylinder at the top, and fitting on the exhaust pipe with a flange. The two exhausts must be joined in the centre of the engine to form a blast pipe, concentric with the chimney. In large models this blast pipe is cast complete with the exhaust flanges; but in models of 1-in. scale and under it may be made up from copper or brass tubing, silver-soldered. The cylinder body should, in a cylinder of the dimensions given, be cast in soft iron, the exhaust port being cored out. The steam ports may be drilled in the solid casting, the face of the ports being chipped out square, or milled out.

The steam-chest casting is separate, the stuffing-box and dummy glands cast on, and a separate cover. Unless a hole is cut in the main frames to clear the valve-spindle stuffing-box, the cylinder must be finally erected in the frames. The valve may be of hard gunmetal or with a highly superheated steam cast-iron is to be preferred.

The cylinder requires lagging. This is best done with sheet brass if painted, otherwise blue-surface Russian iron may be used. No fixing is required for the lagging; it

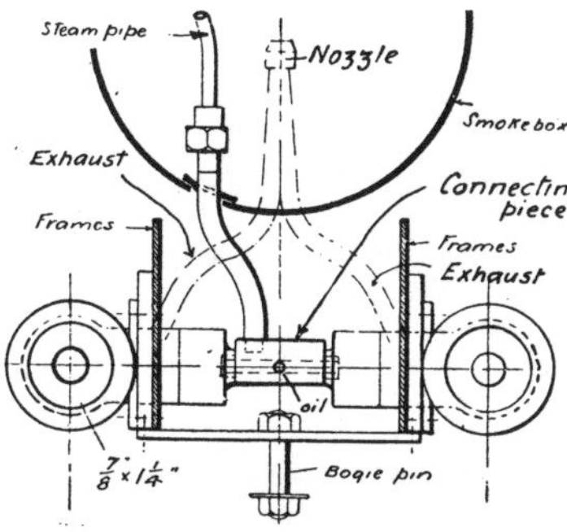

Fig. 301

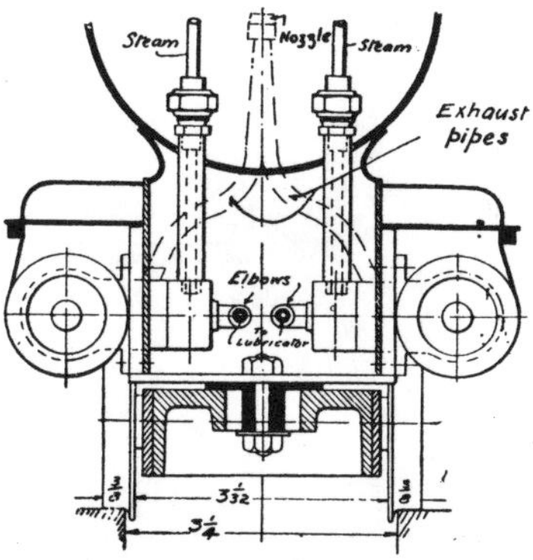

Fig. 302

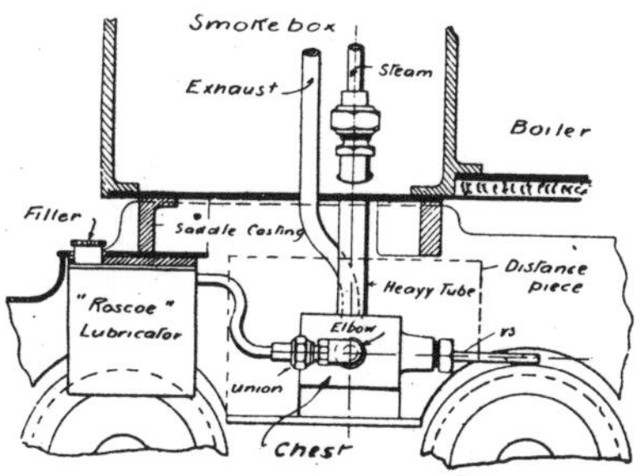

Fig. 303

Figs. 301 to 303.—Fixing and connecting up "outside" cylinders for $\frac{1}{2}$-in. and $\frac{3}{4}$-in. scale model locomotives

should be rolled round a suitable rod, and sprung into place, the cylinder covers holding it longitudinally.

The illustrations indicate how the cylinder drain-cocks may be operated from the driver's cab. A rod is fitted across the engine, about the centre line of the cylinders, and each end of this rod has a crank attached to it. The crank pins on these cranks engage in the flat rod which connects the "fore" and "aft" drain-cocks on each cylinder.

The steam pipe is screwed into the upper wall of the

steam chest. It should be made of stout tube, and have a back nut on to the face of the steam chest. The unions

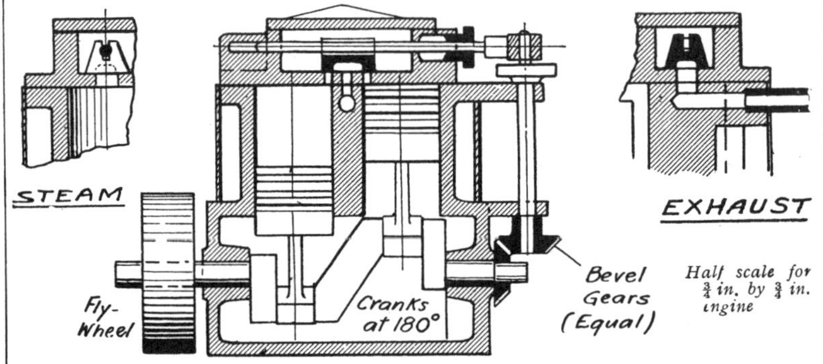

Fig. 304.—Twin-cylinder single-acting high-speed engine

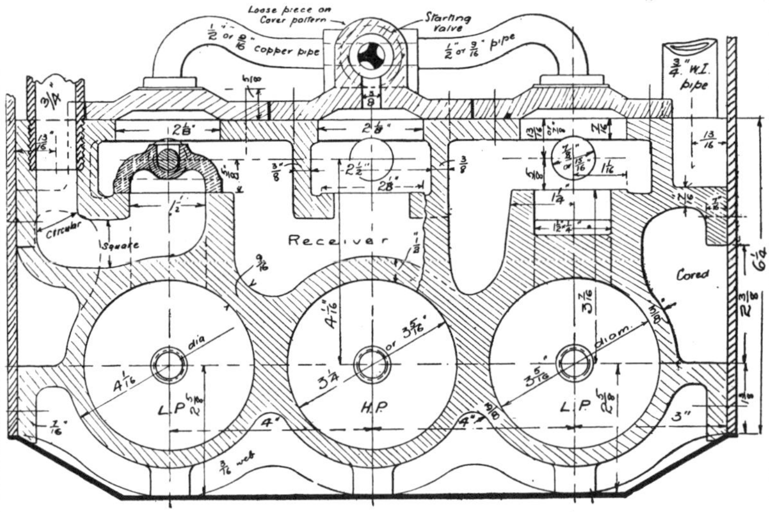

Fig. 305.—Smith's three-cylinder compound system

with the steam pipe or superheater should be well inside the smoke box, so that they can be got at through the open smoke-box door. For a $\frac{3}{4}$-in. scale model the cylinders may be $\frac{7}{8}$-in. bore by $1\frac{9}{16}$-in. stroke; for $1\frac{1}{2}$-in. scale $1\frac{3}{4}$-in. bore by $3\frac{1}{8}$-in. stroke. The other parts may be in proportion to the 1-in. scale cylinder illustrated in Fig. 299. The photograph (Fig. 300) shows the frames of N.E.R. Atlantic locomotive with a pair of the cylinders already fixed.

For smaller model locomotive, gunmetal cylinders of the same general character are obtainable. There are two methods of connecting these cylinders to the boiler: either as shown in Fig. 301 with a screwed connecting nipple, into which the steam pipe is silver soldered, or, preferably, as in Figs. 302 and 303, by separate vertical pipes with unions in the top. In the latter two pipes lead from the steam joint on the boiler to the respective unions.

Single-acting Engines.—The single-acting "Westinghouse" type of engine, introduced by the writer into model work some time ago, has proved successful for model racing boats and also as a high-speed stationary engine. Fig. 304 shows that the exhaust is drilled down into the metal between the two cylinders, and is led out at the side of the cylinder casting. The steam ports are drilled and slotted directly into the cylinder, and the slide-valve can be worked by a cam, an eccentric, or from a geared vertical lay-shaft, the top of which has a disc crank and a slotted connection to the valve spindle.

Three-cylinder Compound System.—A method (known as Smith's system) of arranging compound cylinders which is a very good one where there is frequent starting and stopping, is shown in Fig. 305. The cylinders may be all the same size, and the two L. P. cylinders should have cranks placed at 90° to each other, the central H. P. cylinder crank being between the other two. The engine may be started as an ordinary two-cylinder simple engine by turning live steam into the L. P. steam chests. This steam can be regulated at will, so that the engine may be worked as a simple, semi, or full compound engine. In a model reversing engine the high-pressure cylinder being in equilibrium when starting as a simple engine, slip eccentric gear is all that is necessary for the centre cylinder. In a locomotive the cylinders may be arranged with the high pressure (inside the frames) driving on to one axle and the low pressure (outside) driving on to wheels on a trailing axle. This is termed "dividing the drive."

CHAPTER VII

Engine Cranks, Connecting Rods, Bearings and Eccentrics

Cranks and Crank Shafts.—Steam engine connecting rod, crank, and crosshead depend largely on one another in the details of design. For instance, with a double-webbed crank, the "big end" of a connecting rod must be made in two halves to get it into place. It is only when a crank is of the overhung pattern that a solid big end can be employed, and even then split bearings are generally adopted in real practice to allow of an adjustment for wear.

Figs. 306 to 308 show the three patterns of cranks usually employed. The overhung type is made in two shapes, the disc pattern (Fig. 306) being least difficult for the amateur model-maker to make. Failing a casting to make this crank, a disc of metal—punched-out discs can be purchased in brass or steel, or a piece may be sawn off a bar of brass or steel—is chucked in the lathe, faced for the back, and drilled to suit the shaft.

In small engines the shaft may be screwed as shown at B (Fig. 309), and in larger engines (say 1½-in. bore and upwards) the shaft should be simply shouldered down and driven tightly into the crank disc, the latter being secured by a round key-pin, driven into a hole drilled half in the shaft and half in the crank. This method is shown in Fig. 310. The pin may be a screw-pin or quite plain; but in cases where a screw-pin is fitted, care must be exercised in tapping the hole. Forcing the tap—which should be a plug tap—may result in its breaking. When the disc crank is fitted to the shaft, the latter may be gripped in the chuck, and the front of the crank finally faced up and turned true on the edge. The throw of the crank pin may be scribed on the face at the first chucking, and, holding the disc down

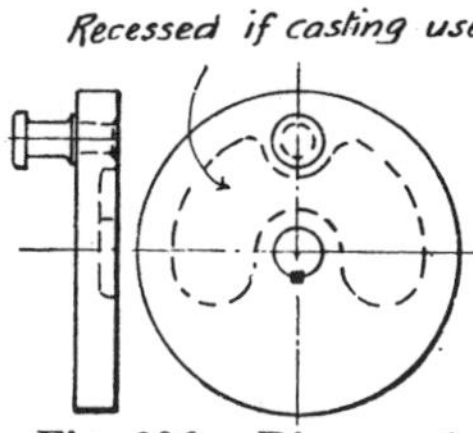

Fig. 306.—Disc crank

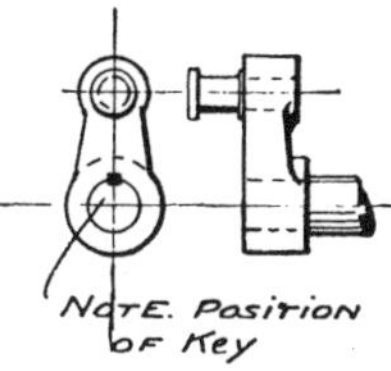

Fig. 307.—Overhung crank

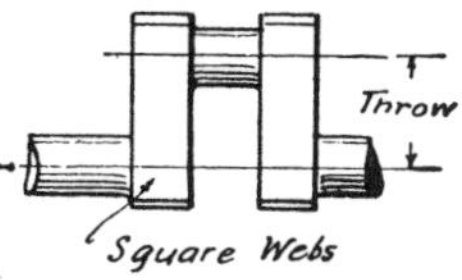

Fig. 308. — Double-webbed crank

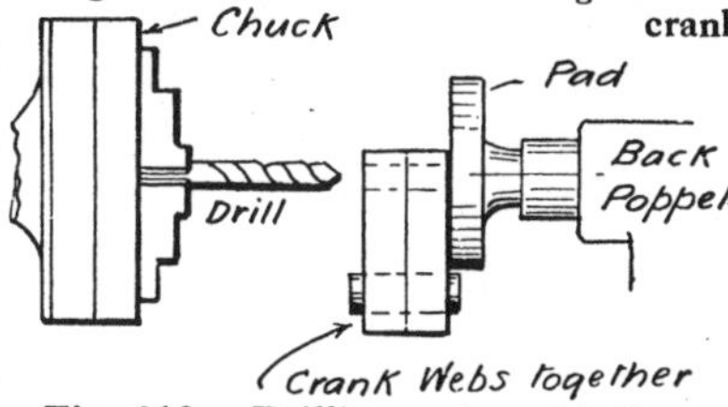

Fig. 312.—Drilling webs of built-up crank shaft

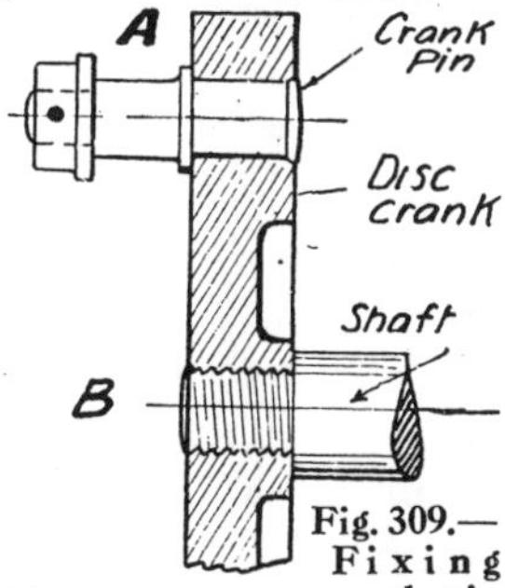

Fig. 309.—Fixing crank pin and shaft to crank disc

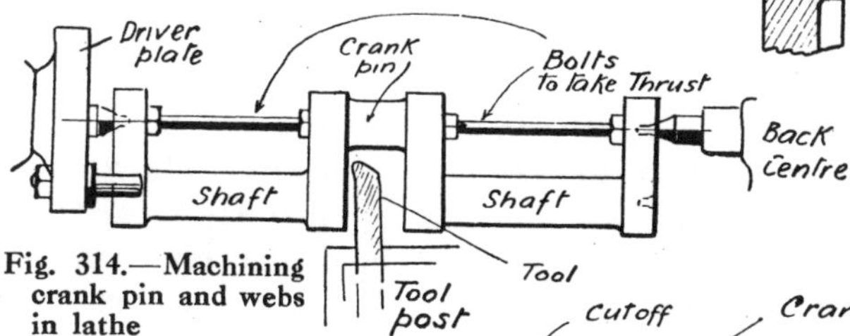

Fig. 314.—Machining crank pin and webs in lathe

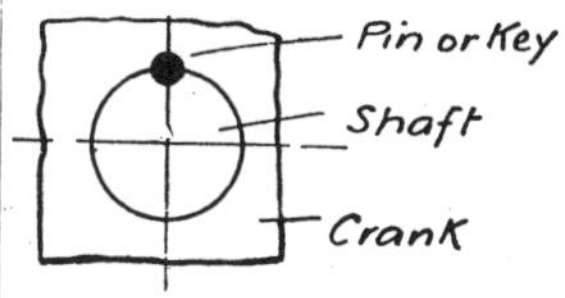

Fig. 310.—Shaft keyed to crank

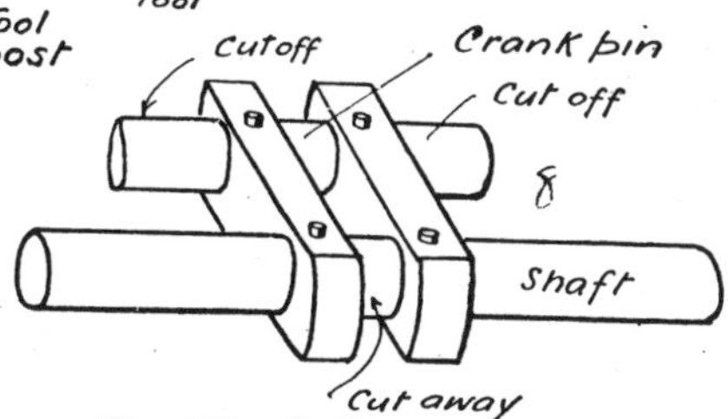

Fig. 313.—Built-up crank shaft

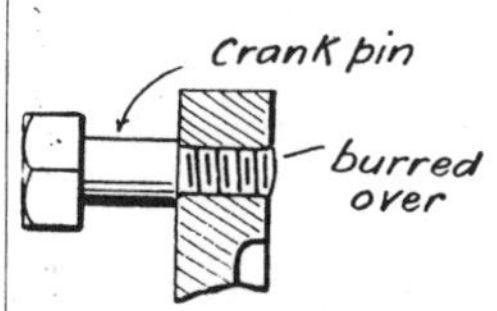

Fig. 311. — Crank pin for small engine

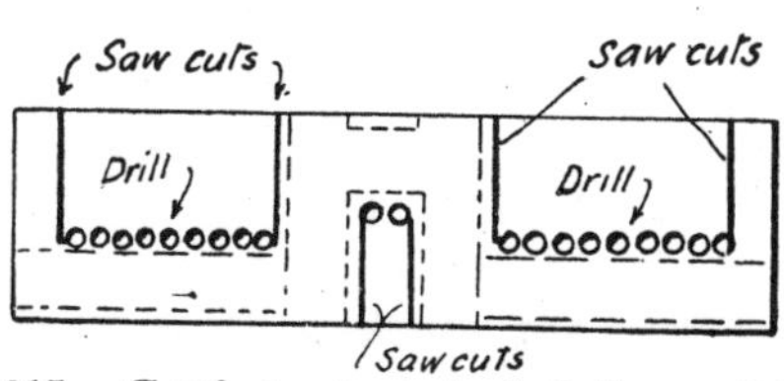

Fig. 315.—Cutting out crank shaft from solid slab

on the bed of the drilling machine or on the drilling pad, the hole for the crank pin may be drilled.

In small models a shouldered screw (Fig. 311) is used for the crank pin; but in larger engines the crank pin is best forced in and riveted over at the back as shown at A (Fig. 309). A key is unnecessary.

The type of crank shown by Fig. 307 may, as regards its fixing, be dealt with in a similar way, the crank itself being cast either in gunmetal or malleable iron. It is not so suitable for casting in iron as the disc type of crank. The key, where used, should also be placed in the position shown.

The web crank (Fig. 308) can be made up in different ways. The simplest and most suitable method for a small model—where a slide-rest lathe is not available—is to build it up from bright steel rod. Flat steel bar is obtained for the webs, and round stuff for the pins and shaft. At the outset enough material is cut off for the webs, and they are drilled at one end dead size for the shaft. They are placed together, and a piece of rod is pushed through to "jig" the holes, and the second set is drilled together (*see* Fig. 312) at the correct throw. Drill a small hole one-quarter the size of the final diameter first. This will guide the larger drill. The webs are then threaded on the rod as shown in Fig. 313, and soldered or brazed. Before doing the latter the webs may be pinned with small pins as shown. This is especially necessary in the case of a large engine. To finish, remove the piece of the shaft between the webs, and trim the crank-shaft up clean with the file.

Sometimes model-engine cranks are cast in malleable iron or steel alloy. Where this is done it is as well to cast on the throw plates at the ends, so that the crank can be turned without making special fittings. Where the crank is forged, special end throws must be made to turn the pins, as indicated, and if necessary the crank must be supported longitudinally to resist the thrust of the lathe centres.

Fig. 314 shows a crank between the centres of the lathe during the operation of turning the crank pin and facing the inside of the webs. This illustration shows the temporary thrust bolts already mentioned. To make these, cut off pieces of steel rod, which will just go between the webs and the throw plates. Screw both ends, and fit nuts. By screwing these nuts *off* the rod a pressure will be exerted on the throw plates and webs, which will take up that of the lathe centres and prevent the crank shaft being forced out of truth. In the photograph (Fig. 316) the three-throw crank for the model triple expansion engine (Fig. 296) is shown between the lathe centres. Two lathe carriers were used as throw plates.

For a single-web crank a slab of rectangular section mild steel should be marked out, and the superfluous metal removed by drilling, sawing, and chipping as shown in

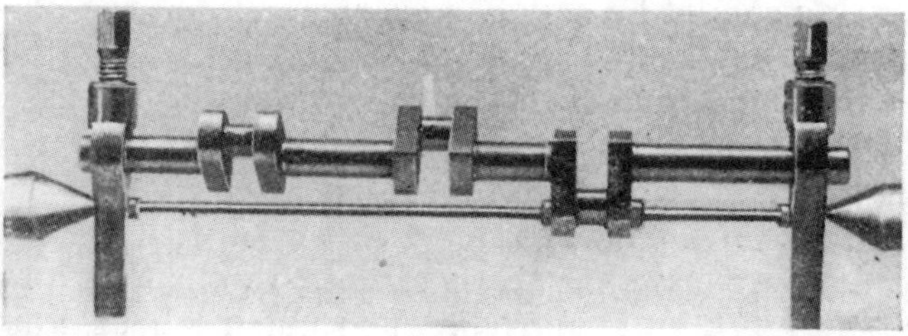

Fig. 316.—Three-throw crank shaft between lathe centres

Fig. 315, the throws at the ends being left in the solid metal, and removed when the crank pin is turned and the webs are faced up.

This method cannot be adopted with double-throw cranks, as three centres in each end are required. The crank shaft is first roughed out of the slab with the saw, and then the centre portion between the webs is heated and the shaft twisted until the webs stand at 90° to each other as in Fig. 317. Fig. 318 shows a cast double-throw crank with end plates cast on.

Connecting Rods and Crossheads.—For models of mill and winding engines with the overhung crank (Figs. 306 and 307), the big-end bush need not be split if the crank pin screws into the crank disc, or if it has an outer removable collar, as described.

Fig. 319 shows a connecting rod of " three times stroke " proportions, made out of flat mild steel bar. The rod portion is turned circular between centres, and a solid brass bush is used for the big end. This big-end bush is turned with a rectangular face to imitate square brasses, and it is driven in and riveted over. The cotter is a dummy, a round pin being driven through the big end and the visible ends filed flat. The little end has a plain eye, which need not be bushed unless the pin is over, say, $\frac{1}{4}$ in. in diameter. This part, however, may vary according to the arrangement of slide bars adopted. As it is, it suits the four slide-bar system (*see* Fig. 320).

The gudgeon pin (little-end pin) should not be less in diameter than the piston rod, and if possible the width of the bearing should be equal to or greater than the diameter of the pin. Such rules are more important in larger models ; but at the same time even the tiniest working model engine should be made with some eye to obtaining proportionate details in all working parts.

The forked slide bar, as sometimes used with the circular, single, and two-slide bar arrangements, means that a forging or casting must be employed. Too much labour would be involved in carving it out of the solid. Very good mild steel alloy and malleable castings can be procured, the only trouble being that several will require to be ordered, and castings cannot be put through under two or three weeks. Fig. 321 shows an adjustable form of little end, which may be used in larger models or small-power engines. Fig. 322 shows the single-bar crosshead. In actual fact, no slide bar is used, as the crosshead slide bears either on the bedplate in a horizontal or diagonal engine, or on the back column or standard in a vertical engine. It is not entirely suitable for reversing engines, as the slide strips are only retaining strips, and should not be subjected to the maximum thrusts of the connecting rod. The crosshead in this case is forged solid with the piston rod. A forked end attached to a two-bar crosshead is shown in Fig. 323. Here the slides of the crosshead are separate, and may be of brass or cast-iron working on steel bars. The crosshead should be fashioned

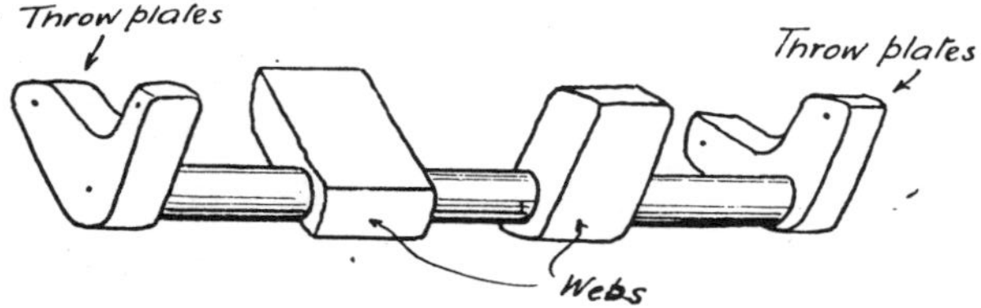

Fig. 318.—Double-throw crank casting

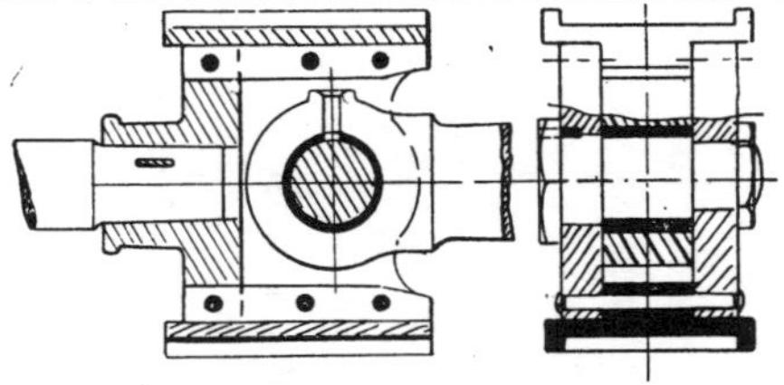
Fig. 324.—Two-bar crosshead (eyed-end) with separate slide

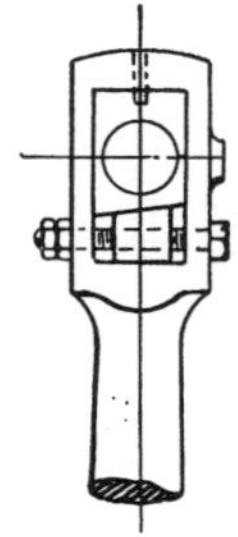
Fig. 321.—Eye-ended little end with adjustable brasses

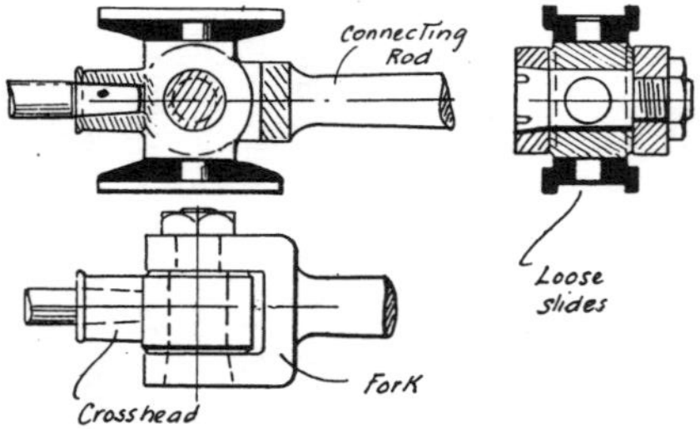

Fig. 323.—Two-bar crosshead (forked end) with separate slide

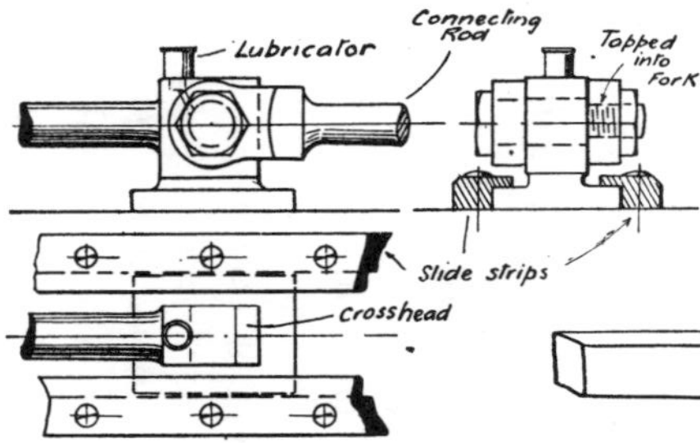

Fig. 322.—Single-bar crosshead and forked little end

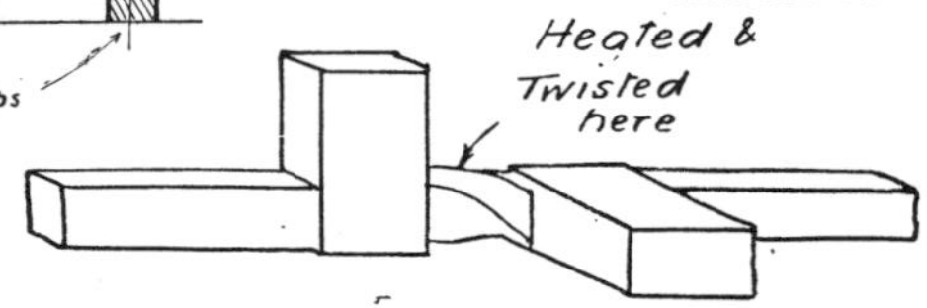

Fig. 317.—Double-throw crank shaft made from steel slab

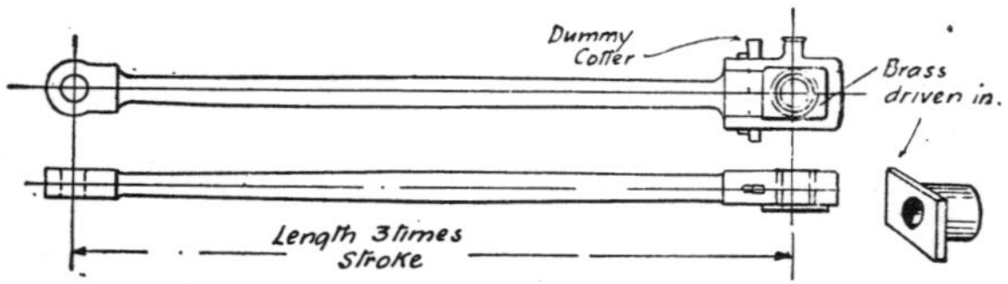

Fig. 319.—Connecting rod for model mill engine

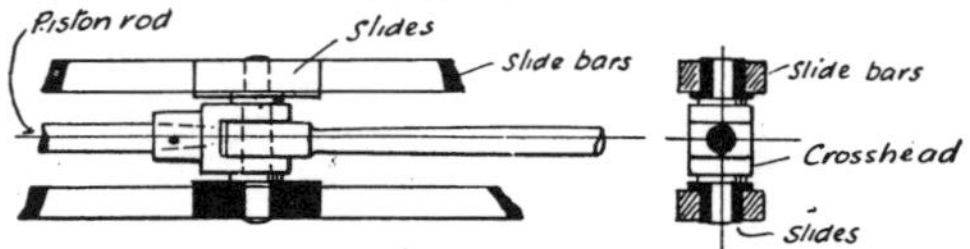

Fig. 320.—Four-slide bar crosshead for horizontal mill engine

out of the steel bar. The gudgeon pin is tapped into one fork, and lock-nutted outside.

A two-bar crosshead, with an eyed little end, is shown in Fig. 324. The slides are separate, and are riveted on to the forked crosshead. The advantage of this system of making is that the internal faces of the crosshead may be filed out. Otherwise milling gear will be required as well as a cored casting. The little end is bushed with a brass bush of drawn tube.

The split box end is a useful design for any overhung crank pin. The forging (that is, the steel part of the rod) is cut out to a box shape, and the bearing brasses are arranged so that there is ample play longitudinally to allow the brasses to slip over the collar on the crank pin, when they are being removed or inserted. To secure them, the outer brass has a lip or flange at the back to clip round the big-end forging, while the inner brass is secured laterally by a cotter. Fig. 325 shows the construction, the particular example being the big end used for a rather large (15-in. gauge) model locomotive designed by the writer, and of which eight engines have been built.

For small engines—locomotive models with inside cylinders in particular—a very good form of modified strap end is shown by Fig. 326, the rod, little end and big end, being cast in gunmetal in one piece. The casting as received from the foundry is shown at A (Fig. 327). The projecting big-end strap is then cut off and squared up with the file to fit over the big end as at B. Then the two parts are soldered together, and drilled and tapped for the big-end screw. The connecting rod is then hammered to stiffen and straighten it, and then bored for the big-end bearing as at C. To finish the end it is placed on a mandrel (*see* D) held in the chuck, and faced with the ring round the journal bearing hole left projecting beyond the main portion of the big end. The big end is reversed to face the other side.

The marine type big end is one of the simplest types for model work. In its most primitive and smallest form (*see* Fig. 328) the rod is cast solid with the end in brass or gunmetal. The cap of the big end is sawn off, soft-soldered on

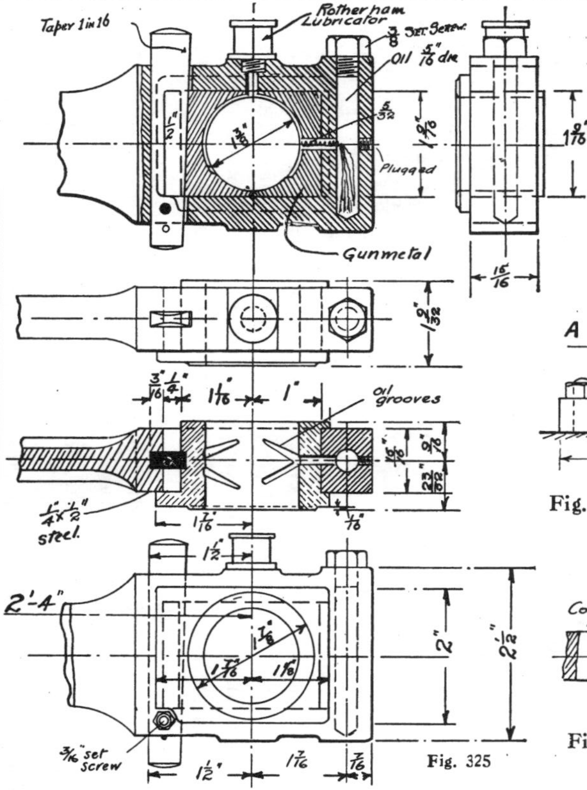

Fig. 325

Fig. 325. — Box big end with adjustable brasses

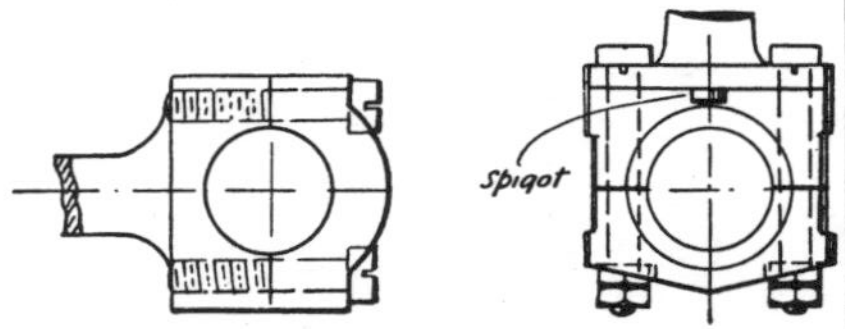

Figs. 328 and 329.—Big ends for model marine and larger engines respectively

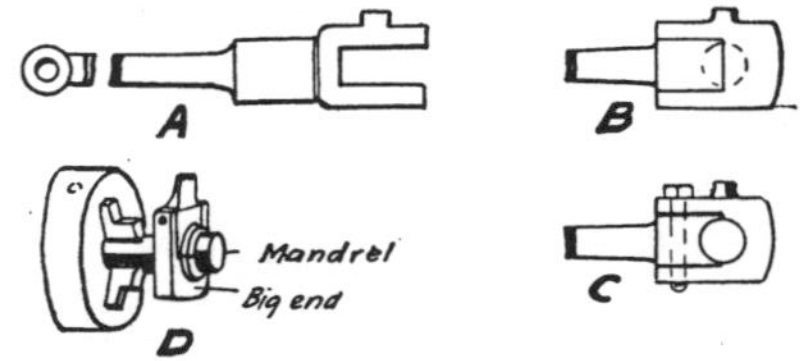

Fig. 327.—Making model strap big end

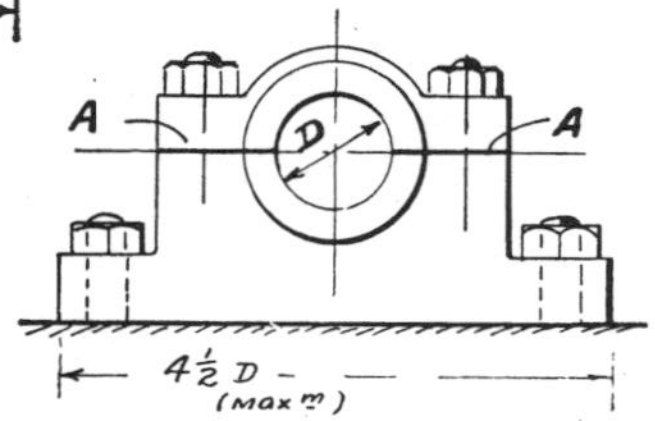

Fig. 331.—Pedestal bearing or plummer block

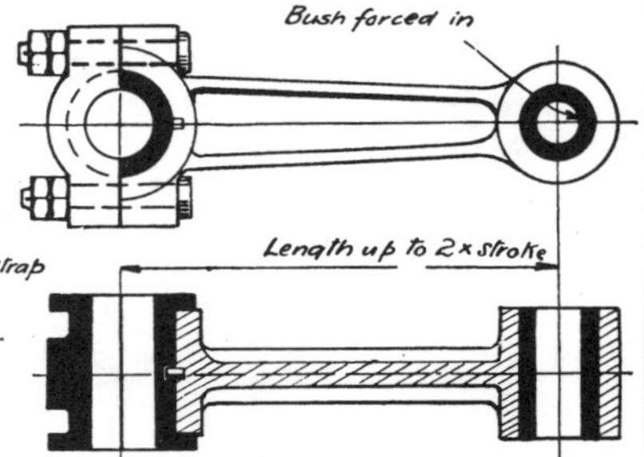

Fig. 330.—Connecting rod for model gas-engine, etc.

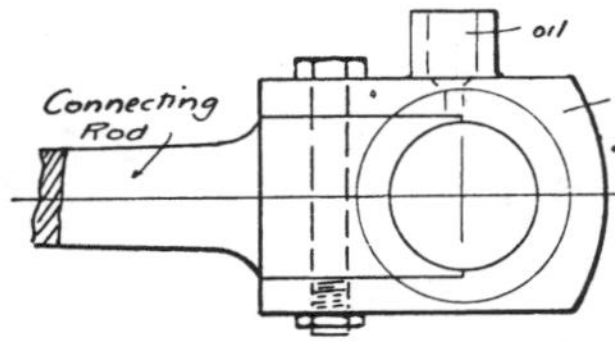

Fig. 326.—Strap big end for small model

again, and the fixing bolts fitted. The end is bored and faced as in the example last described. While this is quite a good method for small engines, the details of the design must be amplified for larger models. The rod should be of steel (forged or cast), with the two big-end bearings of gunmetal as shown in Fig. 329. The rod should have a "tee" end, and this "tee" may be faced between the centres of the lathe, a small spigot being formed to engage a hole in the back bearing brass. The bolts should fit perfectly in the holes in the bearings and the connecting rod, as they take other stresses besides those of the pull and push of the piston.

A type of rod with bushed ends, which is used for model gas and high-speed steam engines, is shown by Fig. 330. These connecting rods are cast in steel alloy, and the bushes are of gunmetal, the little-end bush being solid and forced in. The big-end bush must be prevented from turning round, and for this purpose a pin or key should be fitted in the top brass. Where the pressure is mostly on the top brass, that is, in small petrol and single-acting steam engines, only the top half need be separately bushed. The cap may be cast in the gunmetal.

In designing model and small-power connecting rods, the maker should be careful to consider the work transmitted through the big-end bearing. With high pressures and high speeds the bearings should be large, not in diameter only, as the mere increase in the diameter of the pin does not mean that a longer life will be given to the bearing. It must not be forgotten that the peripheral speed increases with an enlargement of the crank-pin diameter. The maximum length must be provided, as the wearing qualities will increase in almost direct proportion to the *added length* of the bearing.

Main Bearings and Axle-boxes.—For small models in which the crank shaft is so arranged that the bearings can be slipped on from the end, plain non-adjustable bearings are sufficient; these in a stationary or marine engine may be shaped out of the solid material to much the same external form as larger "plummer blocks," except that they are not split. Two forms are shown by Figs. 331 and 332, the latter being a simple plummer block, while the former has dummy studs to represent those used for holding down the cap. In both cases the blocks may be faced in the lathe—on a mandrel—in the manner already shown in Fig. 327.

Fig. 331 shows a split brass (*see* joint lines at A), which is made in the same way, except that the cap is first faced and soldered on, drilled, bolted up, and then bored and finished, the soldered joint then being unsweated and cleaned off. The dimension D is the diameter of the journal, and in any bearing, more particularly for high-speed shafts, the length of the bearing should be not less than one and a quarter times the diameter. Other proportions, such as total overall length, should not be greater than marked, smaller proportions being possible with the increase of size. The proportions are, however, dependent on the room the bolts take up, as, naturally in the tinier engines, screws are relatively more clumsy.

What may be termed "small-power" engines of, say, $\frac{1}{2}$ h.p. and upwards, require more elaborate bearings, and to reduce the cost of metal and to facilitate renewals, the brasses are made separately from the pedestal block. The body is cast in iron, with a square or polygonal recess to take a brass. The top brasses are cylindrical, and the cap is of cast-iron or mild steel. Figs. 333 to 335 show the general arrangement and proportions of a main bearing for an engine with a shaft $1\frac{1}{8}$ in. in diameter, the length of the bearing being not less than $1\frac{1}{2}$ in. The cap bolts may be either studs as shown at Z, or bolts with a round head and a pin as at X, or with a square head as at Y. The oil-box may be formed in the cap as at O, or a standard "Rotherham" cycle lubricator, with a spring lid, as at R (Fig. 335), may be screwed into the cap. These lubricators are nicely made, and improve the appearance of the model. Various sizes are readily obtainable.

In small and model explosion engines where the horizontal thrust of the connecting rod is considerable, and to a large extent in one direction only, the bearings are split at an angle. In most instances the bearings are cast solid with the frame or bedplate, and so arranged that the thrust of the piston is taken by metal in compression, as is shown by Fig. 336. Cast-iron is about seven times as strong in compression as it is in tension. The bearing brasses in this design (Fig. 336) are cylindrical, and the bottom one is restrained from turning in the cast-iron base by a small pin P as shown, or otherwise by a key or lug fitted in any convenient manner. The use of a small pin enables the maker to finish the bearings entirely in the lathe. The pin should be of brass, if the bearing is so small that it must project right through the bottom brass and is likely to rub on the journal of the crank shaft.

In many modern steam engines the adjustment for horizontal wear and tear of bearing brasses is provided for by splitting the brasses into three or four parts, and fitting screw wedges underneath or at the sides of the brasses as shown, in much the same way as in connecting-rod big ends (*see* Fig. 337). Messrs. Marshall, Sons and Co., Limited, in their 8-h.p. compound undertype engines, fit brasses which are split vertically in the manner shown in Fig. 338. This system to some extent corrects vertical as well as horizontal alignment.

For high-speed shafts, such as dynamo spindles, very long bearings are employed, and lubrication is effected by a loose ring of larger diameter than the shaft. The ring (*see* Fig. 339) hangs on the shaft and revolves with it, picking up oil from a well or " oil bath " formed in the bearing block below the shaft. To prevent oil running along the shaft and flying off, knife-edged collars K are arranged on the shaft at each end of the bearing. Such bearings are often in real practice made of cast-iron with " brasses " of white metal. This alloy is run in the cast-iron bearing block and cap, both of which have recesses so shaped to prevent the " brass " revolving. The metal is then bored out to size.

The collars K are encased by recesses formed in the bearing block, and the oil, flying off by centrifugal force, is returned to the oil well by suitable passages drilled in the

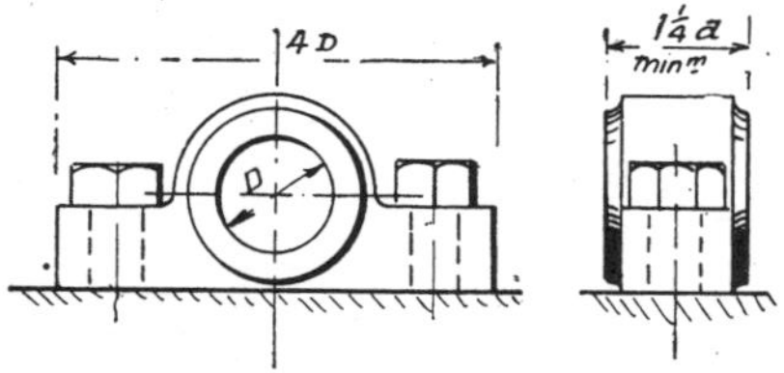

Fig. 332.—Simple pedestal bearing or plummer block

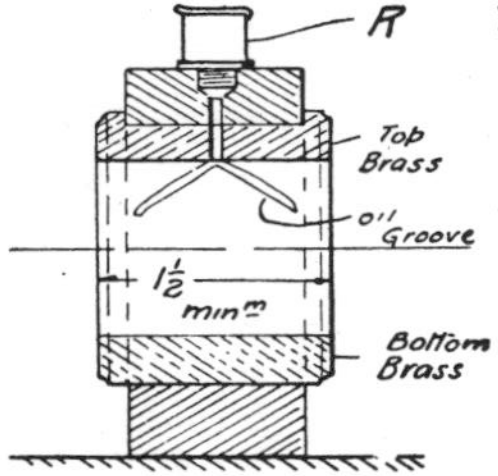

Fig. 335

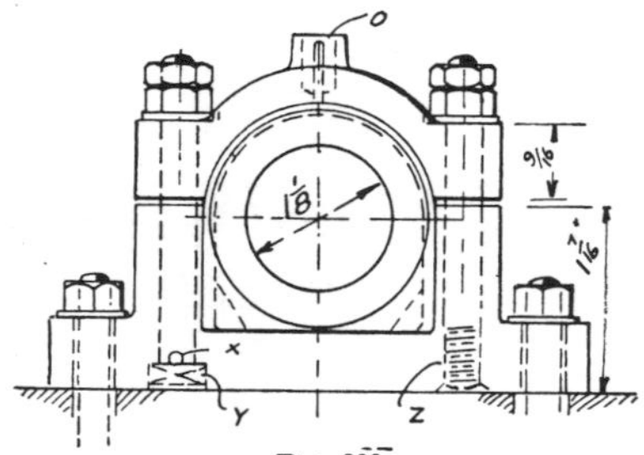

Fig. 333

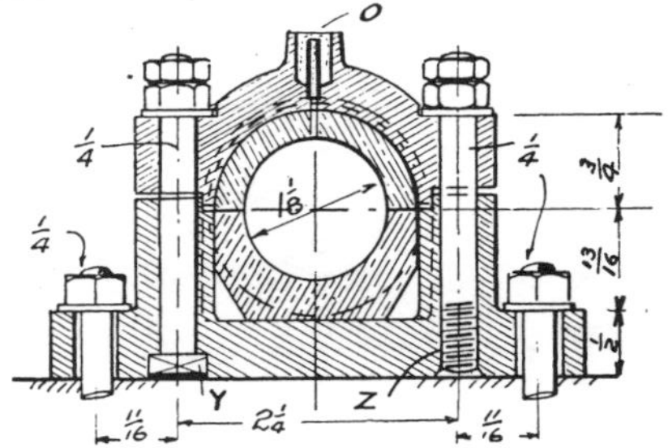

Fig. 334

Figs. 333 to 335.—Elevation and two sections of plummer block with separate brasses

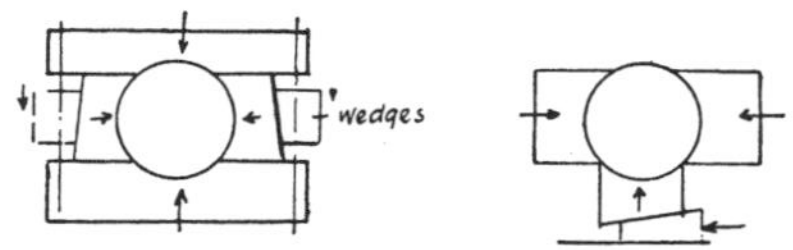

Fig. 337.—Bearing brasses adjustable by wedges

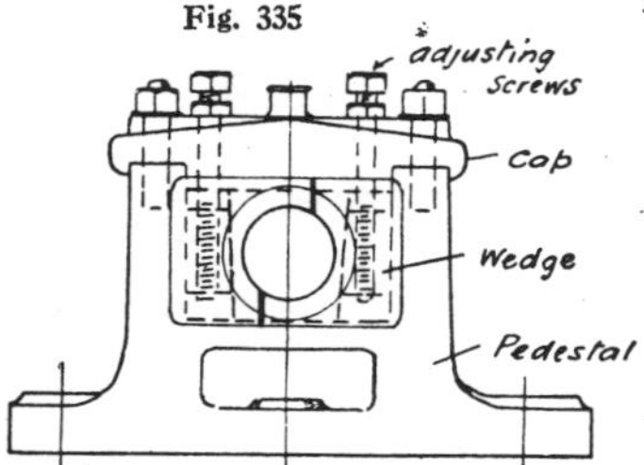

Fig. 338.—Model of Marshall's bearing

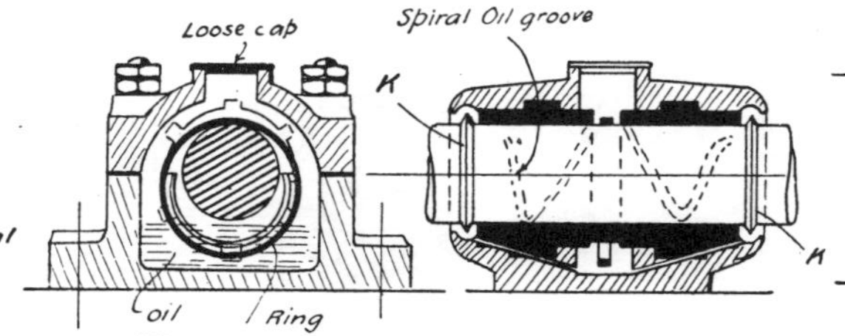

Fig. 339.—High-speed oil-ring bearing

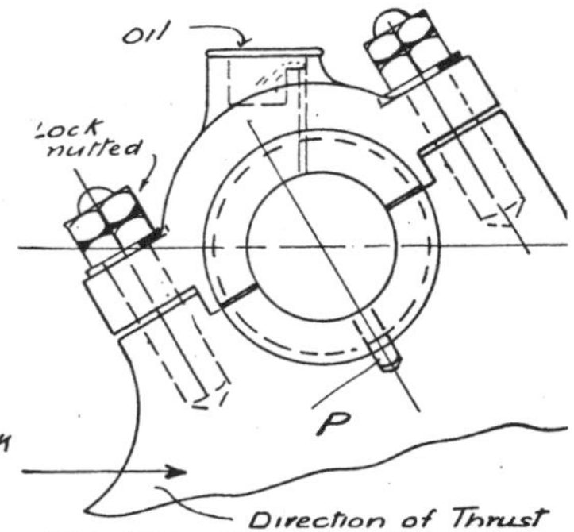

Fig. 336.—Main bearing with brasses split diagonally

casting. Such bearings will run for indefinite periods without attention. Oil grooves are chipped in the white metal, and these are generally of spiral form, so that the oil is automatically led along the bearing.

Locomotive shaft bearings or "axle-boxes" are quite different from stationary and marine-engine bearings. The

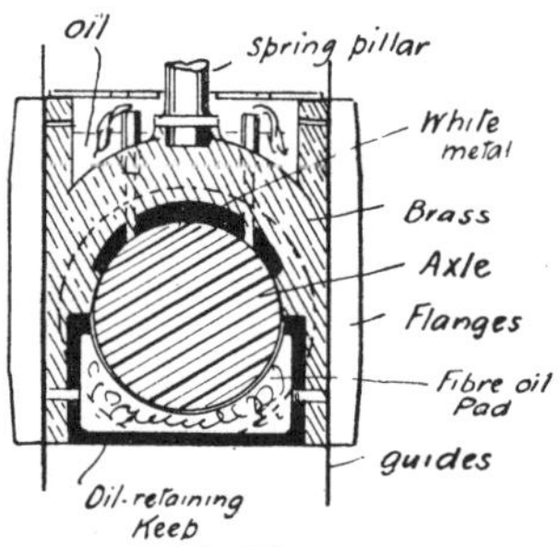

Fig. 340

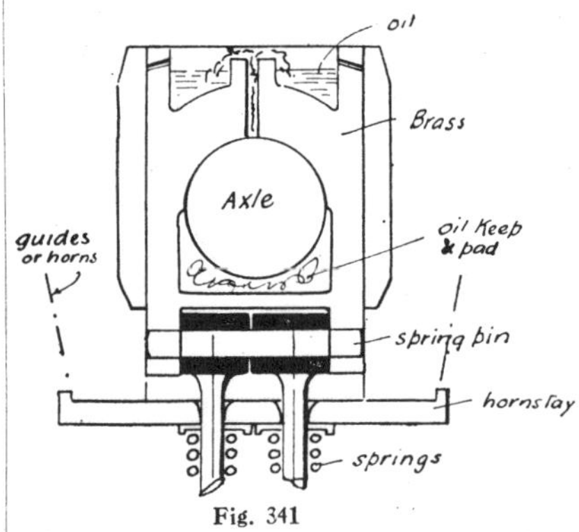

Fig. 341

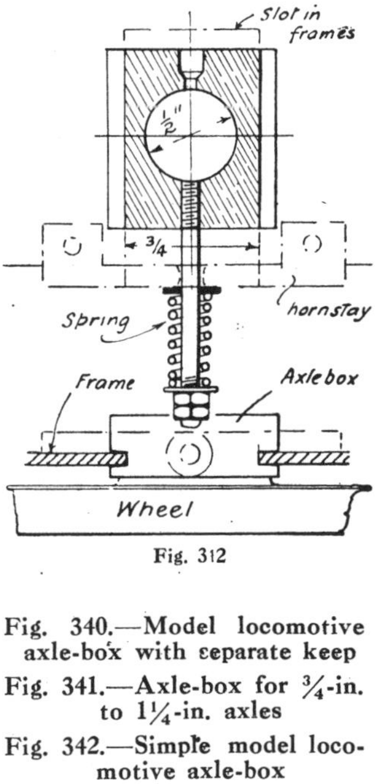

Fig. 312

Fig. 340.—Model locomotive axle-box with separate keep

Fig. 341.—Axle-box for $\frac{3}{4}$-in. to $1\frac{1}{4}$-in. axles

Fig. 342.—Simple model locomotive axle-box

pressure is upwards, and for this reason only the top half, or rather top third, of the bearing is in contact with the axle journal. In real practice the bearings are always white-metalled. Fig. **340** shows a typical bearing in which the springs are fitted overhead. The under-side of the bearing is encased by a "keep," to keep out dust and to retain the oil, a pad being placed in this keep to maintain the lubrication of the journal, even if the top oil-box is empty.

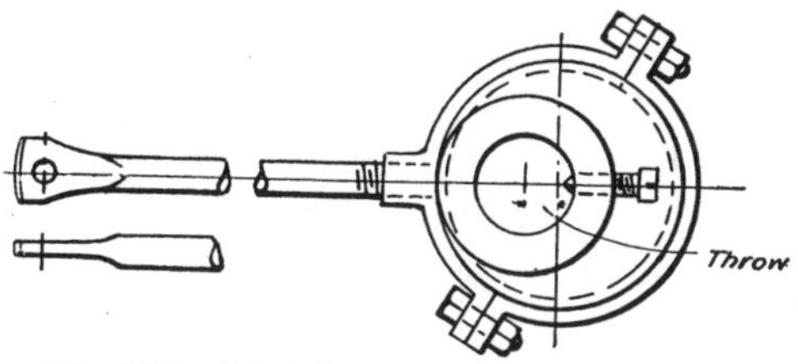

Fig. 343.—Model eccentric rod and strap

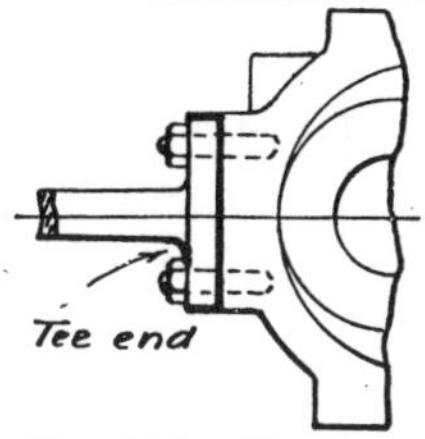

Fig. 345.—T-ended eccentric rod

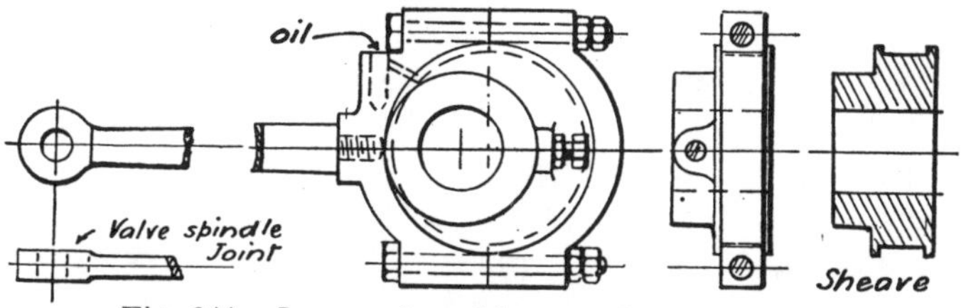

Fig. 344.—Improved model eccentric rod and strap

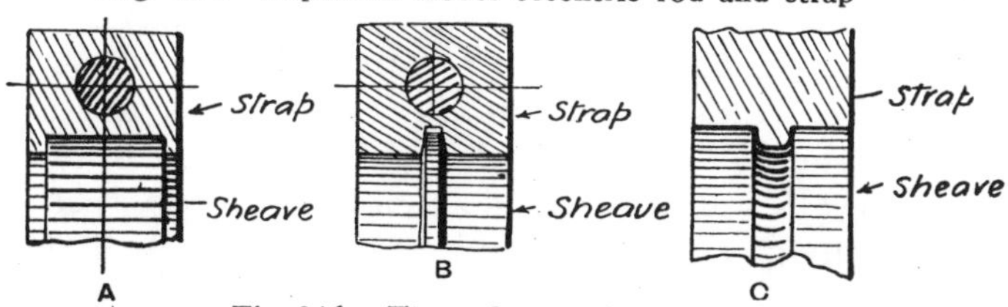

Fig. 346.—Three forms of sheave

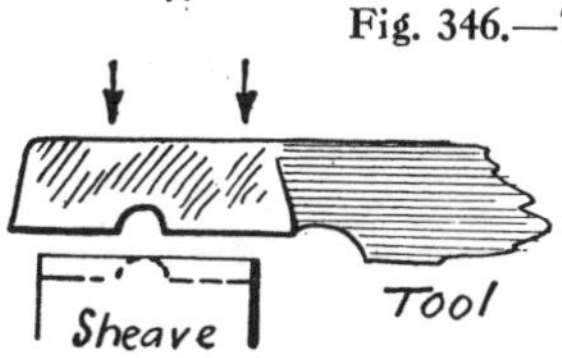

Fig. 347.—Forming tool for sheave C (Fig. 346)

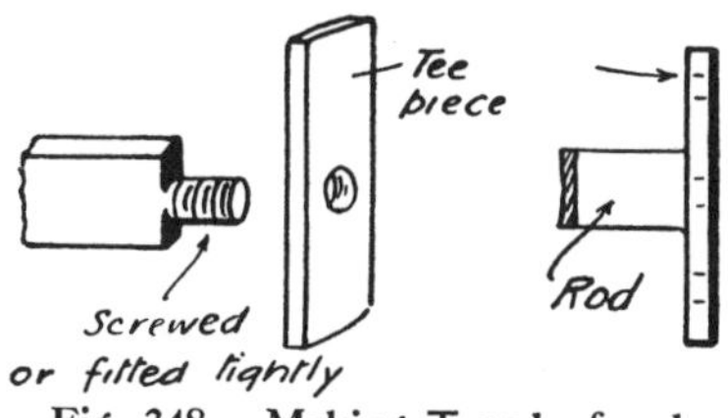

Fig. 348.—Making T-end of rod

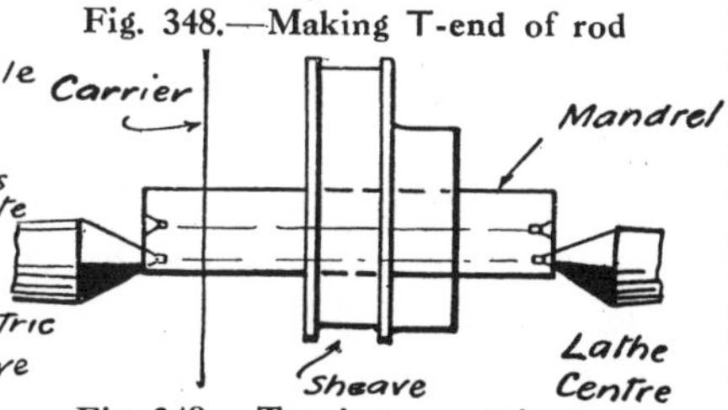

Fig. 349.—Turning eccentric sheave on mandrel

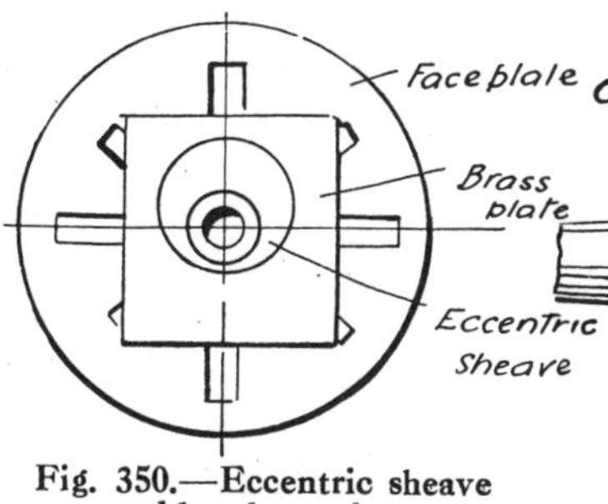

Fig. 350.—Eccentric sheave soldered on plate

Only very large models, such as the writer has designed for 12-in. and 15-in. gauge garden railways, would have such elaborate axle-boxes. A modification is shown in Fig. 341. Here the keep is cast in one with the axle-box, and once it is on the axle it cannot be removed, unless the wheels are taken off. This is not, however, a serious drawback in a model. Fig. 341 shows the axle-box arranged for underhung springs. In all cases the axle-box must be free to move up and down in the frames or frame guides.

Fig. 342 shows a simple axle-box such as would be used on models under $3\frac{1}{2}$-in. gauge. The axle-box is a block of brass drilled for the axle and grooved at the side to fit in the slot in the main frames. The hornstays allow the wheels and boxes to be taken out of the frames, and take the pressure of the spiral bearing spring.

Eccentric Sheaves and Straps. — The ordinary form of model eccentric sheave and strap seen in the shops is based on the design adopted by steam engineers a hundred years ago. They are usually made of brass throughout, and as will be seen by Fig. 343, there is very little metal in the lugs to allow for subsequently taking up wear. The use of brass for both the strap and the sheave is also to be condemned. A much better design of strap is illustrated by Fig. 344. Here the lugs are long and the centre of the bolt lies nearer to the sheave. The sheave may be made of mild steel or cast-iron. The rod is of flat steel, not simply a piece of round wire with the end flattened out and drilled, and in smaller models is screwed and soldered into the strap. The latter is also provided with a lubricating hole, the exact position of which depends on whether the engine is horizontal, vertical, or inclined.

For larger models, the eccentric rod should be forged with a tee end and secured by two studs and nuts as shown in Fig. 345. The sheave is sometimes turned with a central rib as shown at A, and sometimes as at B in Fig. 346. This rib retains the eccentric laterally, and while the proportions shown at A are more usually adopted in real practice, the periphery of the larger diameter taking the load, in model work it will be found easier to shape the eccentric and strap to the profile shown at B. In this form the rib does nothing but keep the strap in place laterally, the actual work of driving is accomplished by the faces on either side of the rib. The method shown at C (Fig. 346) is similar to B, but the eccentric sheave is incised instead of the eccentric strap. This will be found to simplify the machining of the sheave, as one cut can be taken straight across it, and then the groove may be incised with another tool of suitable shape. The internal diameter of the strap may be turned with what is called a "former tool," the broad face of the tool being grooved in the centre to the extent of the rib to be formed in the strap (*see* Fig. 347). The straps should be

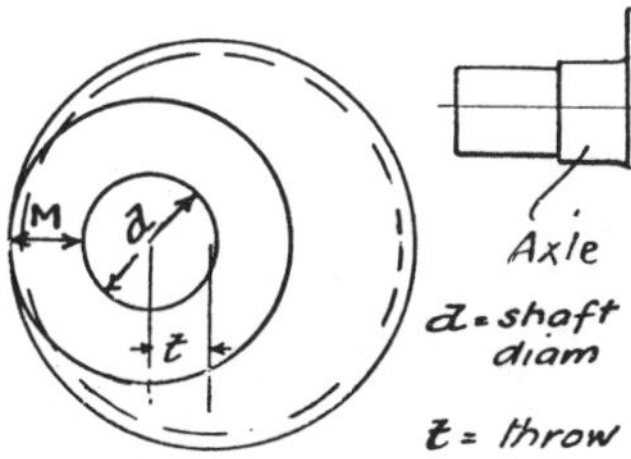

Fig. 351.—Setting out eccentric sheave

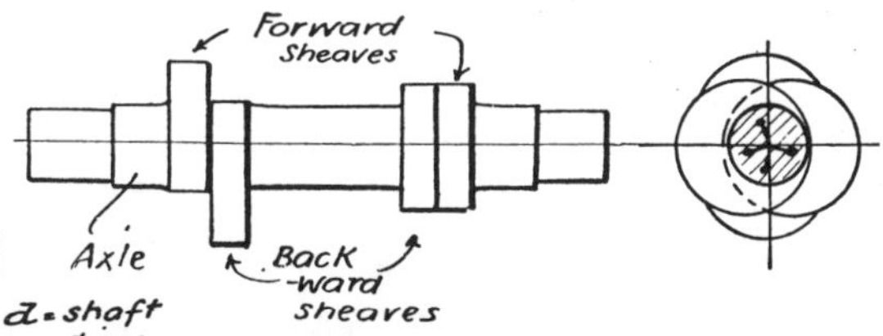

Fig. 352.—Elevation and cross section of axle with four eccentrics turned from solid

faced, soldered together, drilled, and bolted up. The soldered joint may then be broken and the two halves bolted up again for machining. Before breaking the soldered joints, the edges of the strap which cannot be filed up except when the bolts are removed should be cleaned up to the required shape and dimensions. The straps are best faced up at the sides by clipping them with their own bolts on a mandrel held in the lathe chuck, as already suggested for dealing with the big end of connecting rods.

To eliminate the forging necessary in making a tee-ended eccentric rod, the rod may be built up out of bright strip steel. This steel should be as thick as the required width of the boss at the valve spindle end and as wide as the depth at the tee end. The rod is then filed down to the working drawing, and the end shouldered and screwed to enter a hole drilled in the short piece of the same steel cut off to form the T-piece (*see* Fig. 348). The parts are then soldered or brazed together, and finished off in accordance to the required outline.

In setting out the sheave, the diameter of the shaft and the required eccentricity of the sheave must be known. The diameter of the sheave can then be determined, sufficient

Fig. 353.—Solid-turned four-eccentric axle mounted with wheels

metal (at least half that of the shaft diameter where a cast-iron sheave is used) being left at M (Fig. 351). If a projecting boss is used then the diameter of the boss is settled by the amount of metal at M, the periphery of the boss coinciding with that of the sheave. Where the sheave is made of steel or wrought iron, the metal at M may be somewhat reduced; but enough must be left to provide a boss with sufficient metal in its walls to allow of the usual set-screw, key or other fastening. Sometimes a lug is cast on the boss of the sheave to provide for the set-screw as shown in Fig. 344.

Eccentric sheaves may be machined in numerous ways. The casting or blank may be bored first and then have the sides faced and boss turned with the sheave driven on a mandrel. This mandrel (Fig. 349) may then be carefully re-centred with sheave centres and the periphery of the sheave turned up between the lathe centres. This, however, can only be done where the eccentric centres fall well within the diameter of the shaft. If they do not, then throw-plates, as required for turning crank shafts, may be used. Another method is to first turn the main diameter of the sheave and face the plain side truly square with the periphery of the sheave. The sheave may then be soft-soldered on a plate of brass (*see* Fig. 350), set and clipped in the required " out-of-centre " position on the faceplate of the lathe, and faced and bored. Large eccentrics can be, of course, bored while gripped in dogs on the faceplate or in an independent four-jaw chuck. Yet another method applicable in small work would be to hold the sheave in an ordinary three-jaw chuck, one of the jaws being put in the wrong scroll, the finer adjustments being made by packing. A further method is shown in Fig. 75, Chap. III.

Model locomotive reversing motions in which eccentrics are used often call for special treatment. For outside cylinder engines fitted with Stephenson's curved link motion, it is the writer's invariable practice to turn the sheaves on the axle or shaft out of the solid (*see* Fig. 352). This allows much smaller diameter sheaves to be used, this, in turn, allowing a longer firebox to be used. In any case, it reduces to a minimum the trouble in setting sheaves. Furthermore, the axle acts as a mandrel. If the labour of turning four sheaves and axle out of a solid bar big enough to contain them all is deemed too great, then rough sheaves may be brazed in position on a shaft, the whole finished in the lathe in the same way as if it were a solid forging. A photograph of a finished axle mounted on the wheels is shown in Fig. 353.

CHAPTER VIII

Steam-Engine Valve and Reversing Gears

The functions of the steam-engine slide valve are, as already explained, numerous. Obviously, quite small differences in size, timing, and arrangement will make or mar the efficiency of the engine. Reversing motions further complicate the issues. The diagrams included in Chapter V. clearly show the action of the slide valve and the effects of addition of lap and lead. In many of the simpler reversing gears applied to models lap and lead cannot be obtained; the steam distribution is of the simplest character, as in the normal valve shown by Figs. 237 and 238, and the same as that of the ordinary model oscillating cylinder (*see* Fig. 229). In actual practice such gears are used in steam winches and steam steering gear aboard ship, where economy of steam is sacrificed to extreme simplicity and reliability under the roughest service conditions. In a steam steering engine, piston valves are used because when, to effect the reversal of the engine, the live steam is transferred to the exhaust port and the exhaust steam to what were the steam ports, a piston valve will not lift off its seat.

Reversing Cylinders.—The cheap German-made model steam engines frequently have this type of reversing gear, Figs. 354 to 359 showing the usual arrangement, which has been modified in the illustrations to make their functions more apparent. The valve is a piston valve, ground in, the cylinder being built up out of tube and rod stuff, all passages being drilled holes. The wide central groove in the valve is the exhaust port and engages special exhaust ports. The outer grooves connect the steam passages with the outer set of ports. The cylinders have, as a rule, hollow valves. The internal passage is necessary to connect the left-hand ports with the steam passage B at the right-hand end of the cylinder. The exhaust cavity connects the port

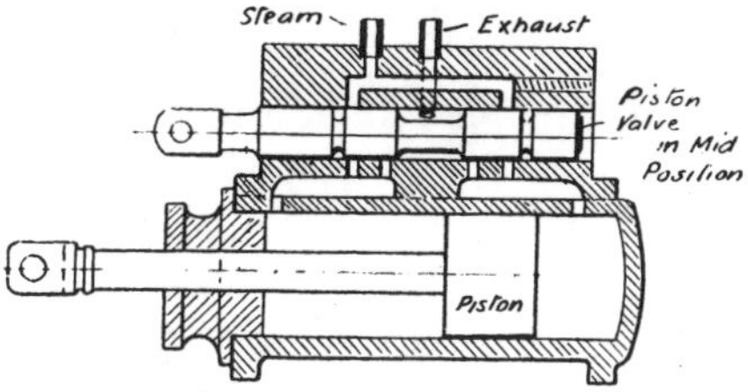

Fig. 354.—Piston-valve model engine cylinder

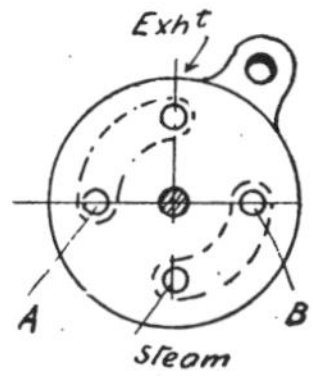

Fig. 356.—Plan of steam-reversing plate

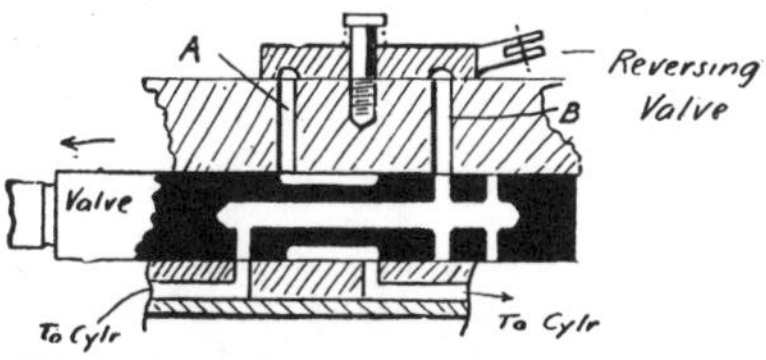

Fig. 355.—Diagram showing section of steam-reversing plate

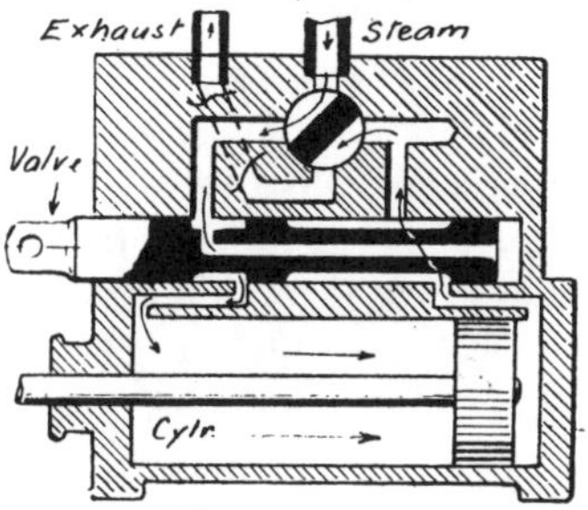

Fig. 357.—Piston-valve reversing cylinder: forward stroke

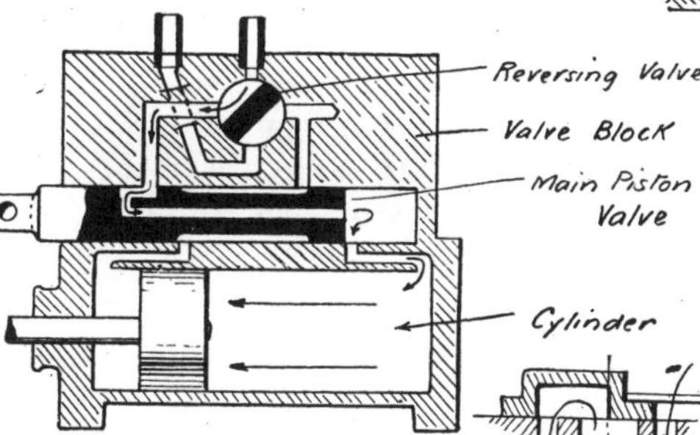

Fig. 359.—Piston-valve reversing cylinder: backward stroke

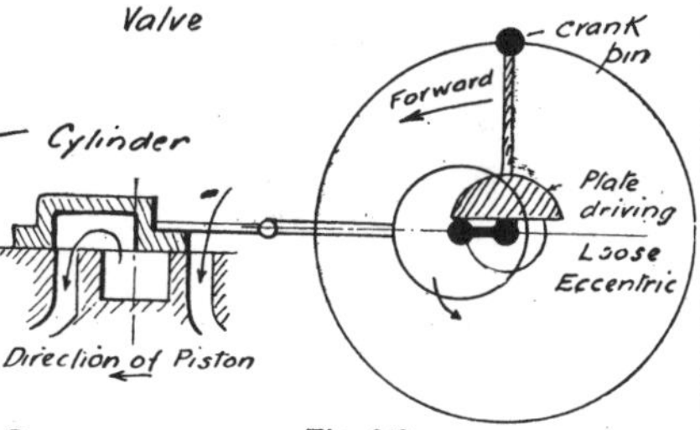

Fig. 360

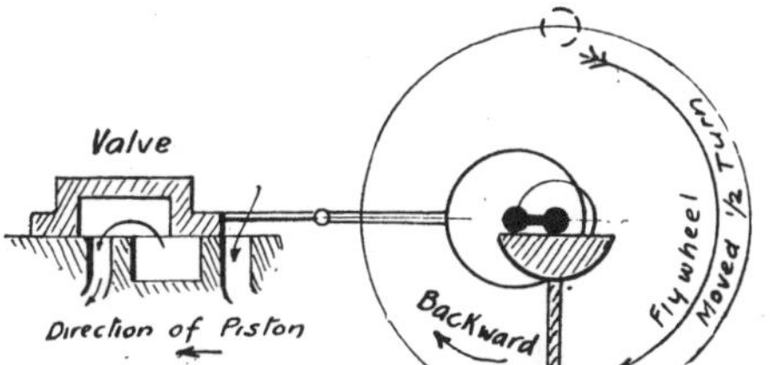

Fig. 361

Figs. 360 and 361.—Diagrams showing principle of loose eccentric reversing valve gear

Fig 358. — Steam passage with four-way valve in reverse

alternately with the passage A (Figs. 355 and 356). The reversing valve is a partially rotating circular plate with two grooves on its working face. The plate can be moved by the lug through an angle of 90°, and the exhaust and steam ports may then be connected to A or B at the will of the operator. In Fig. 356, A connects with the exhaust, and B with the live-steam port. The passages are all drilled in the steam block, and the entrances of the drill are in some cases plugged up. To explain the reversal of the steam distribution, diagrammatical views in which a 4-way cock is shown instead of the reversing plate are given by Figs. 357 to 359. These show the cylinder in forward and reverse gears. The eccentric is fixed on the shaft, and is placed at 90° to the crank. The valves and pistons of these model engines are beautifully fitted (ground in), and no packing whatever is used in piston, piston rods, and valves. The pistons and valves should be made of a grade of brass different from the steam block and cylinder. Needless to say, the steam should not be supplied at too high a temperature. The cylinders require a lubricator (using a thick oil) on the steam pipe. Any grit or insufficient lubrication causes these cylinders to seize.

"Slip" or Loose Eccentric Reversing Gear.—The simplest form of reversing gear applicable to small *slide-valve* engines is the slip or loose eccentric gear, and in this the expansive force of steam can in a measure be utilised. The writer has used this with success on launch engines up to 2 h.p. The only drawback of the gear is that reversing can only be accomplished when the engine is stationary. To start the engine in the reverse direction, the flywheel is given half a turn in the required direction. In a small steam launch or canoe this operation is easily done. The engine will continue to run or will restart in the direction it is initially made to run. This is clearly demonstrated in the diagrams (Figs. 360 and 361). The crank is shown with a driving plate attached, and engaging an eccentric in the two positions. The valve remains where it is until it is driven in the proper direction by the driving plate.

So much for general description; in small model engines

the method generally adopted is to file off half the boss of the eccentric sheave and to drive the eccentric by a pin fitted in the crank shaft, as shown in Fig. 362. The

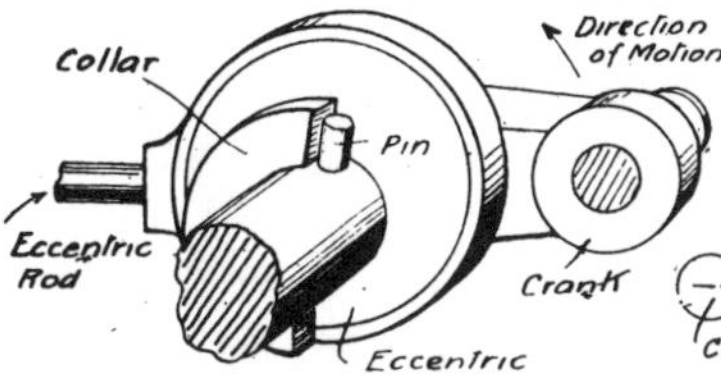

Fig. 362.—Pin in crank shaft for driving eccentric

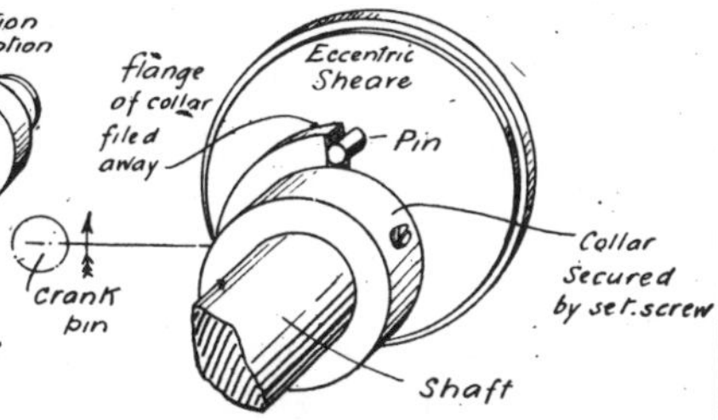

Fig. 363.—Stop-collar method of driving eccentric

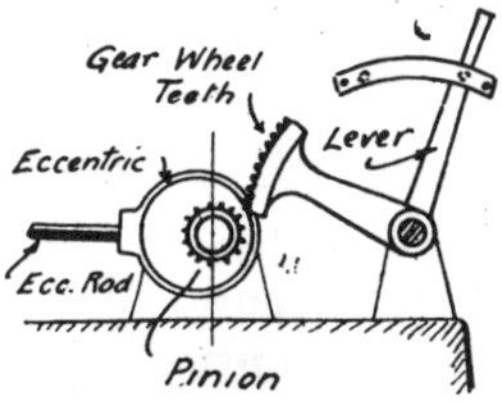

Fig. 366.—Reversing slip eccentrics

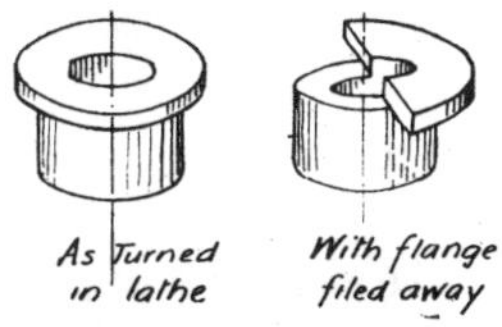

Fig. 364.—Making stop collar

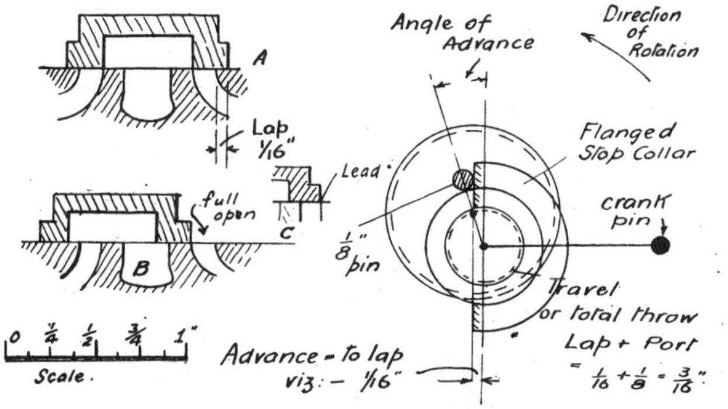

Fig. 365.—Setting out slip reversing gear

objections to this method are several. It is difficult to drill the shaft and to fit the pin with accuracy, and no adjustment is possible except by filing the pin or taking off he eccentric and filing off or adding to the halved boss.

The writer therefore always recommends the device illustrated in Fig. 363. The pin is fitted in the sheave and is driven by a halved "stop collar" which is set-screwed on to the crank shaft or axle. This collar is first turned up with a complete flange, the latter being filed off afterwards. The amount of metal left depends on the size of the pin and the lap of the valve desired.

As explained by the diagrams in Chapter V., in the normal or primitive valve (i.e. the valve with no lap or lead) the eccentric must be 90° *in advance* of the crank pin. The valve with lap must be advanced the amount of the lap more than 90°. In the setting out of the slip eccentric gear the lap of the valve may be provided for by the position and diameter of the pin in the eccentric sheave and the cutting away of the flange of the stop collar.

Fig. 365 shows a setting out that may be adopted for a valve with $\frac{1}{8}$-in. steam ports and $\frac{1}{16}$-in. lap. It will be found on making a drawing double or treble the full size of the actual model engine, that the pin in the eccentric if of $\frac{1}{8}$ in. diameter, will require to be placed $\frac{3}{8}$ in. from the shaft centre to provide the $\frac{1}{16}$ in. advance, the flange being cut away to a line $\frac{1}{16}$ in. in advance of the vertical centre line. If the pin is placed in the major axis of the sheave the collar will stand exactly vertical with the crank in a truly horizontal position. However, except that the pin should be $\frac{3}{8}$ in. from the shaft centre, its position relative to the eccentricity of the sheave is not an important matter. The flanged stop collar can be easily moved round on the shaft, and if the forward gear needs a little more advance than the backward gear it can be easily provided by adjusting the position of the stop collar. To set the valves the first thing to do is to get the slide valve to open each port to an equal amount; this may be done quite independently of the position of the crank, and is usually effected by screwing up or unscrewing the valve spindle. The valve gear may then be timed. Fix the crank pin on the exact dead centre, either with the piston right in or right out. The *movement* of the *eccentric* from forward to back gear should place the valve in exactly the same position on the port face.

Adjust the stop collar on the shaft until this happens, and then fix it with the set screw.

While in ordinary circumstances a slip eccentric engine must be first started in the required direction, it is possible to fit a lever to reverse the position of the eccentrics. This lever should have a part of a toothed wheel fixed to it, and this will engage in a pinion fixed to the eccentric sheave. The number of teeth should not be more than sufficient to move the eccentric through the required partial rotation, and may be arranged as shown in Fig. 366. The device should be used only when the engine is stopped, and it is more particularly applicable and desirable in small model locomotives with outside cylinders.

Link Motions.—It is obvious from the foregoing and from the notes in Chapters V. and VII. that if two eccentrics, one set in the correct position for the forward rotation of the engine and the other with the correct advance for the backward movement, could be used and the valve actuated by either one or the other, a reversal would be effected. This was done in early locomotive engines, the ends of the eccentric rods having hooks to alternately engage the valve spindle in forward and reverse gears. As in the loose eccentric gear, a variable port opening was, of course, not obtainable, and until the introduction of Stephenson's link motion (*see* Fig. 367), in which the fore and back gear rods were connected by a slotted link, satisfactory results were not possible. The Stephenson gear provides for a variable cut off as well as reversing, and is still largely used. With the form of link illustrated in the diagrams (Figs. 367 and 368), in which the eccentric rods are attached directly above and below the slot, the link must be considered as a lever reducing the valve travel. Therefore, for a required valve travel, a larger eccentric must be employed. The length between the centres and the available movement of the die (allowing a good clearance top and bottom) are the dimensions necessary to proportion the eccentric throw to the valve travel. To put the problem into a formula—

$$\frac{P \times V}{Q} = E$$

where P and Q are as indicated in Fig. 368, V the valve travel, and E the eccentric travel. To take a practical example, the link is $2\frac{3}{4}$ in. long between centres as shown

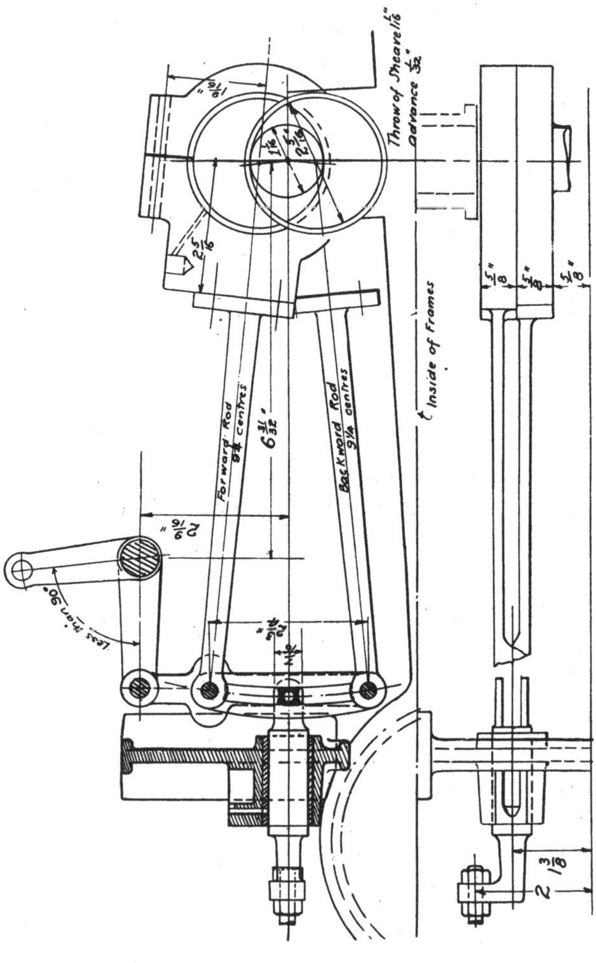

Fig. 367.—Link motion as applied to locomotive

in Fig. 367, and the total vertical movement of the die is $1\frac{1}{2}$ in.; then $2\frac{3}{4} \div 1\frac{1}{2}$ multiplied by the valve travel (say $\frac{1}{2}$ in. in this case) will give—

$$\frac{2\frac{3}{4} \times \frac{1}{2}}{1\frac{1}{2}} = \frac{11 \times 2 \times 1}{4 \times 3 \times 2} = \frac{11}{12} \text{ in. (say } \tfrac{7}{8} \text{ in.) eccentric travel.}$$

In very small engines the eccentric should have more, rather than less, throw. In small engines the eccentric should not be advanced so as to provide "lead." There are other functions too complicated to be dealt with here, which give all the lead required. The advance is increased by short eccentric rods. In $\frac{3}{4}$-in. and $\frac{1}{2}$-in. scale engines

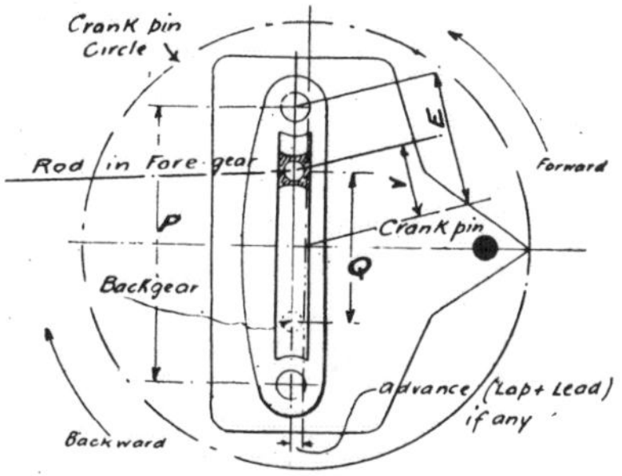

Fig. 370.—Setting-out for valve-gear model

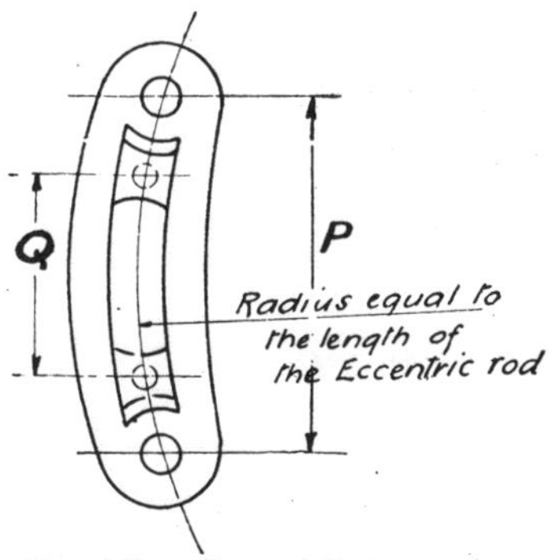

Fig. 368.—Curved link as used in locomotives

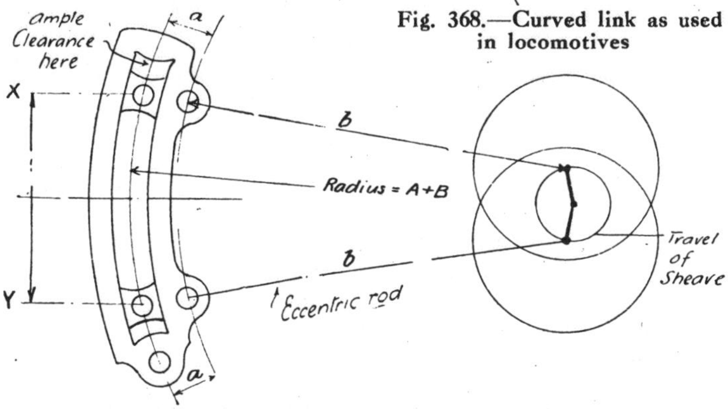

Fig. 369.—Curved link as used on steam launches

the writer always designs the eccentrics with a 90° advance only.

A model which the writer has designed for studying the effect of the reversal and expansion functions of link motion is illustrated in Fig. 371. The link without curvature is drawn on a piece of paper or card attached to a revolving piece of board, a very long connecting rod to the valve being used. The position of the die in the slot link coincides in full fore and back gear with the centres of the respective eccentrics. The model also automatically gives the excess of throw of the eccentric required for the type of link illustrated in Figs. 367 and 368. The diagram (Fig. 370) shows the setting out for this model, and in the case of a small engine the model may be made three or four times full size. The reference letters are made to agree with those in the formula above.

In launch engines and other models, and small-power steam engines which must have short eccentric rods, the type of curved link shown in Fig. 369 is often adopted.

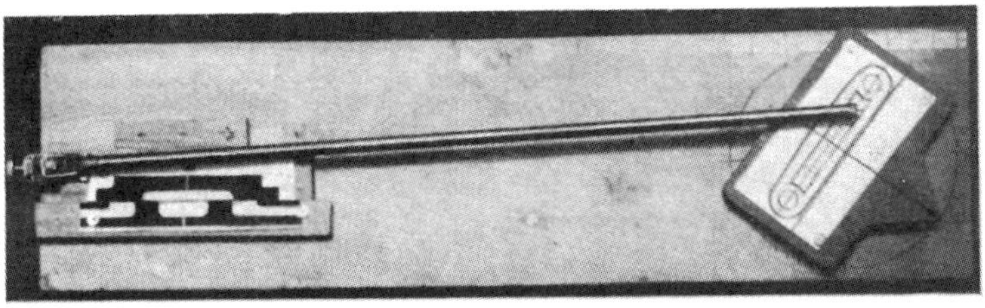

Fig. 371.—Photograph of experimental valve-setting model

With this arrangement the eccentric rod end comes right opposite the die in the link, and eccentrics may therefore be designed with the same throw as the travel of the valve, as in a directly connected non-reversing or slip-eccentric gear. The type of link is not altogether a good one in small engines, and ample allowance must be made for the excessive slip of the die block, which takes place at each end of the slot.

A simple form of reversing valve motion which needs only one eccentric is shown in Fig. 372. This gear has a slotted link which is pivoted to any portion of the main frame of the engine, the link being given a vibrating motion by an eccentric fixed at 90° in advance of the main crank pin. Being pivoted in the centre, the link is like an even-armed lever, and the die, which is connected to the valve spindle by a suitable radius rod, can be moved so that it is either opposite the end of the eccentric rod or at the other extremity of the link; in the central or "mid-gear" position no motion is given to the valve. When the die is at the top of the link, the direction of the motion provided by the eccentric is simply reversed, and the valve movement being reversed, the engine will travel in the opposite direction. No lap or lead can be given to the valve; any advance of the eccentric over the normal **90°** would be turned into so much "lag" in the backward

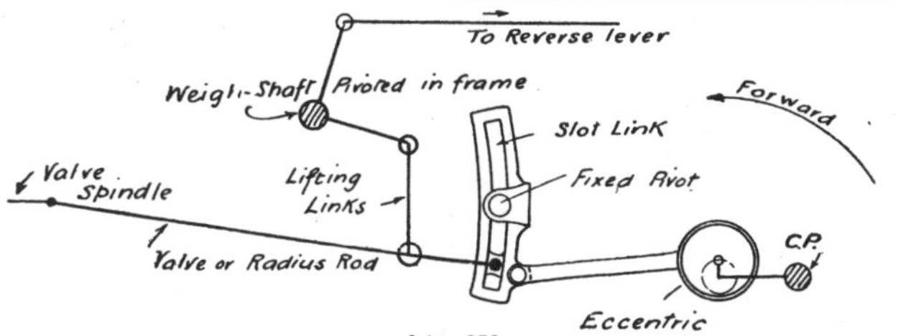

Fig 372

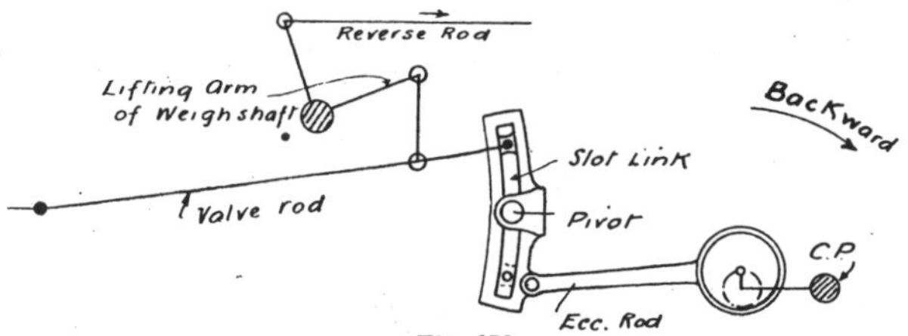

Fig. 373

Figs. 372 and 373.—Single eccentric link reversing gear, forward and backward positions respectively

gear. This reversing gear is therefore only suitable to small models in which the economy of expansion need not be considered. The gear is a part of the well-known Walschaert's reversing motion used in real practice. By fixing the eccentric in the opposite position (**90°** behind the crank pin C P), the position of the die in Fig. **373** will give the engine a forward movement, and that shown in Fig. **372** will be the back gear position.

Radial Valve Gears.—This term is given to valve gears which work wholly or partly from the vertical and horizontal motions of the crank, connecting rod, or crosshead. Hackworth's valve gear is the father of all these motions, a boom in which occurred in steam engineering circles in the 'eighties and 'nineties of the nineteenth century. Hackworth's gear (Fig. 374) can be worked from a point in the connecting rod or from a small crank or eccentric, which exactly coincides with, or is exactly opposite, the main crank pin. In

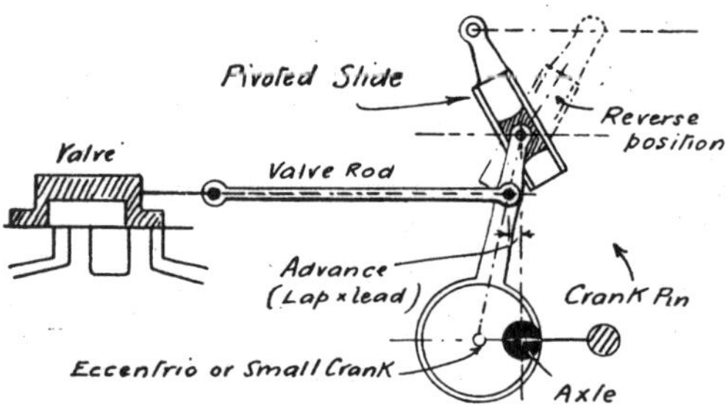

Fig. 374.— Diagram showing principle of Hackworth's radial valve gear

Fig. 374

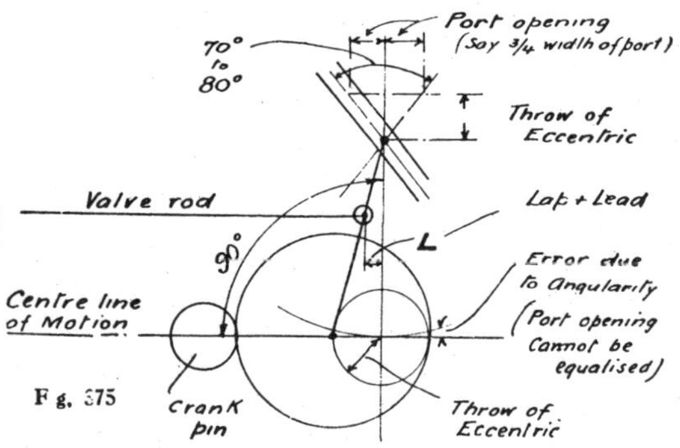

Fig. 375. — Diagram showing setting out of Hackworth's radial valve gear

Fig. 375

practice, the small crank or eccentric is usually necessary, as the valve spindle centre cannot be placed high enough above the piston rod centre to prevent serious errors in the port openings due to the angularity of the various links and rods, as shown in Fig. 375. The reversing is effected by a slide and slide block, the slide being pivoted in the centre and the reversing lever causing it to be inclined one way or the other at the engineman's will. Lap and lead can be provided for by utilising the horizontal movement of the vibrating rod, the valve rod being pivoted at the required distance below the die block to provide the proper amount of advance. With inside admission piston valves the crank pin would be in the position shown in Fig. 375.

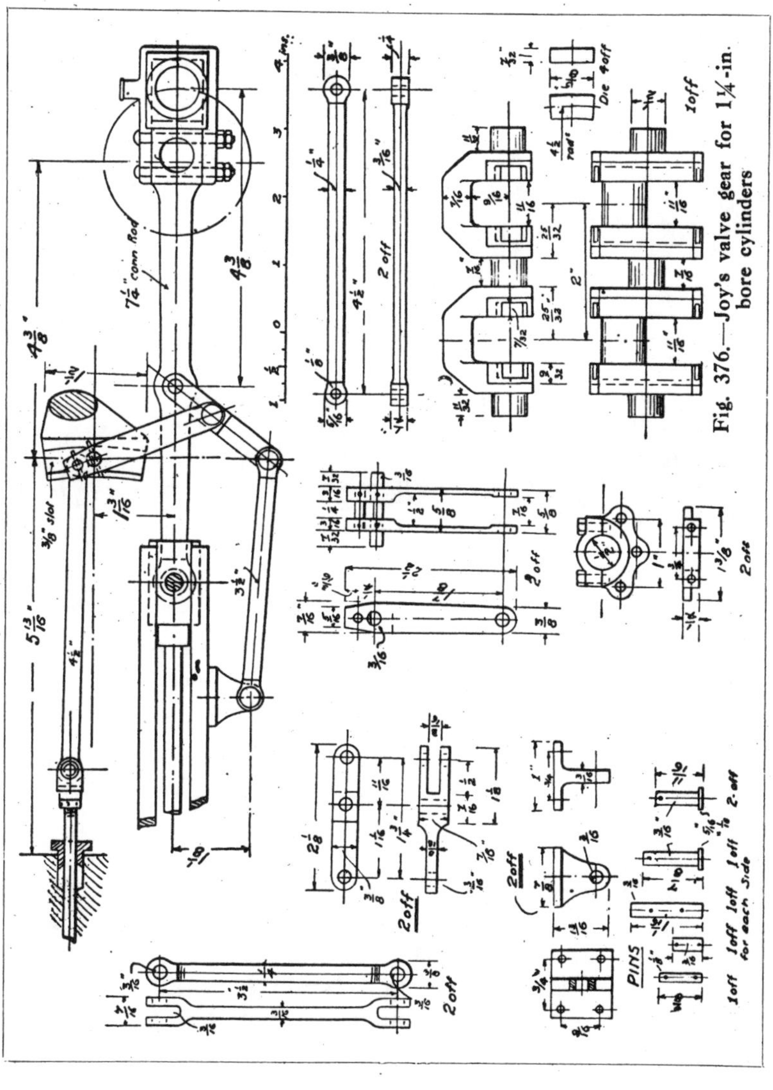

Fig. 376.—Joy's valve gear for 1¼-in. bore cylinders

Joy's valve gear, illustrated in Fig. 376 in a size suitable for an inch-scale model locomotive, or any engine with a cylinder about $1\frac{1}{4}$-in. bore by $2\frac{1}{8}$-in. or 2-in. stroke, is the best known and most used modern development of Hackworth's invention. To correct the inaccuracies of the link transmitting the motion to the die in the guide shaft, and to give an equal port opening, a system of correcting links is applied as shown. This gear also provides for the lap and lead of the valves.

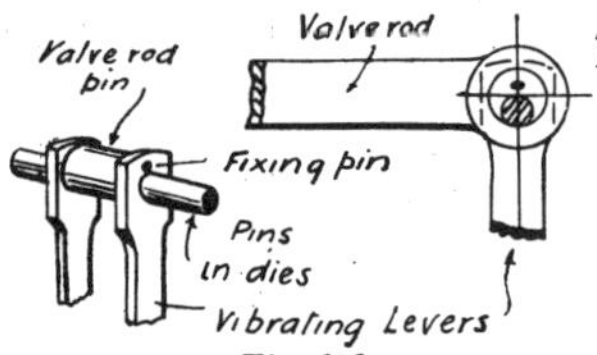

Fig. 378

Fig. 378.—Detail of eccentric "lap and lead" pin in Greenly's corrected valve gear

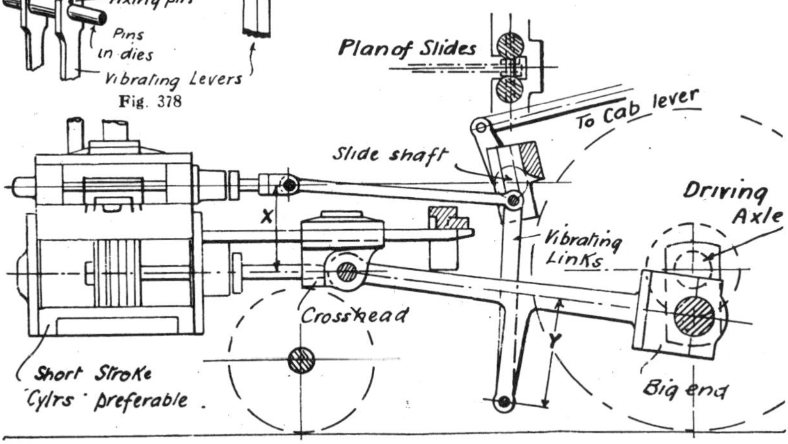

Fig. 377.—Simplified Joy's valve gear adapted to model locomotive

In small models these may be eliminated as well as the lap and lead portion, as illustrated in Fig. 378, and to reduce the angularity of the vibrating link, it is lengthened and attached to a lug dropped from the connecting rod. The slides may be straight and formed by first drilling holes in the slide shaft. The cylinders should have a short stroke if possible, and the bar between the steam ports should be as thick as possible. With $\frac{1}{16}$th ports, $\frac{1}{8}$-in. port bars and a $\frac{3}{32}$-in. exhaust port are suitable dimensions. Distances X and Y should be as much as possible, so that the longest vibrating link the engine will allow can be provided. To set the motion the crank should be placed on dead centres, and by bending the connecting rod the die should then be made to coincide exactly with the pivot of the slide shaft so that a movement of the reversing lever transmits no motion to the valve spindle. The valve should be adjusted so that it is exactly central and covering the ports. Fig. 379 shows the writer's later valve gear. In this motion a correcting gear is added which enables the designer to obtain a more compact gear in a vertical direction, and a perfectly equal port opening. The lap and lead functions may be added in larger engines as in Figs. 376 and 378. In Fig. 378 the lap is comparatively small, and the two adjacent pins used in the full Joy's gear are not possible. The movement is therefore provided by an eccentric pin fixed to the vibrating levers, the small diameter working in the dies and the end of the valve rod engaging the large diameter, as indicated in the detail (Fig. 378). The advantage in model work of the writer's gear over Joy's is that very large diameter working pins may be fitted.

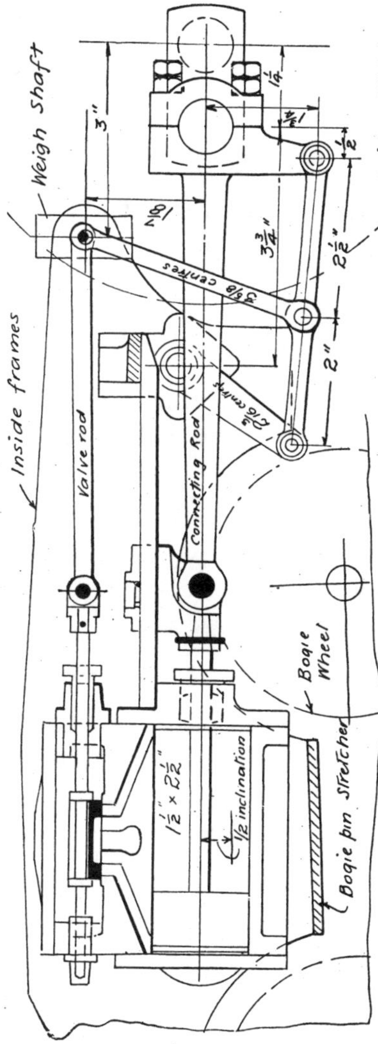

Fig. 379.—Greenly's corrected valve gear

CHAPTER IX

Model Boiler Design and Construction

Evaporative Power.—The following practical data as to the design and evaporative power of model and small-power boilers will be found useful to those who require to know what size of boiler a given engine requires, or what power may be expected from a given boiler under certain conditions.

The boiler is the source of the power; the engine is only the medium for converting the latent power in the steam into useful work. The power of a boiler may be made to vary by altering the rate at which the fuel is burnt, or the nature of the fuel. The design may make a large difference in evaporative power, and, further, causing the flame to impinge on the heating surfaces at a great speed will often increase the steam production.

TABLE I

Proportionate Evaporative Power of Full-size Steam Boilers

(*Terms reduced to model sizes*)

Type of boiler	*Heating surface*	*Grate area*	*Evaporation*
	sq. in.	*sq. in.*	
Externally fired ..	56	4	1 cub. in. per minute
Flash*	46	2⅔	,, ,, ,,
Cornish	50	2	,, ,, ,,
Lancashire	45	1¾	,, ,, ,,
Water tube (stationary)	64	1⅝	,, ,, ,,
Marine (Scotch) ..	48	1½	,, ,, ,,
Locomotive	32	½	,, ,, ,,

* This flash boiler was of about 3 to 4 h.p.

In the accompanying tables, which relate to larger generators, the rate of evaporation has been reduced to terms that can be used by the model engineer.

From the table on p. 174 it will be seen that, independent of the relative efficiencies of the boilers in the matter of coal consumption, the externally fired boiler is the least satisfactory type, and the locomotive boiler (not when used as a stationary boiler, but as actually fitted to the locomotive and under running conditions) gives out the most power for its size. The locomotive boiler is worked under a more intense draught than any other type of generator. Marine boilers are also largely fitted with forced draught, and in comparing with a locomotive boiler the advantage in grate area (*see* Table I.) should be noted. The water evaporated in pounds per hour per pound of coal consumed varies with the draught, but the following is useful.

TABLE II

EVAPORATIVE POWER OF FULL-SIZE BOILERS PER POUND OF COAL USED

Externally fired	=	4 to 6 lb.	water per hour.
Flash, coal-fired	=	5½ ,,	,, ,,
Cornish and Lancashire	=	8½ ,,	,, ,,
Stationary water tube	=	13 ,,	,, ,,
Marine	=	10 ,,	,, ,,
Locomotive	=	10 ,,	,, ,,

Here, again, the proportion is more or less preserved. In model work, however, other conditions have to be considered. The fuel is not always coal; methylated spirit, paraffin, and petrol are also used. Among the coal-fired boilers, however, the writer's experiments have shown that 1 cub. in. of water per minute can be turned into steam with a heating surface and grate area as in Table III., page 176.

In Table III the model locomotive boiler has, like the real one, a comparatively small grate area, and makes up for it by the stronger draught which is induced by the exhaust steam from the engine cylinders issuing up the chimney. This method of creating a draught is often essential in a model, as the length of the chimney (never less than 15 ft.) which must be employed to obtain any kind of a draught naturally is generally impossible. This is one of the difficulties in making small coal-fired steam launches of two- or three-passenger capacity. The exhaust steam must be employed for making a draught in the boiler, and therefore the advantage of condensing and compounding cannot be obtained. The same applies, more or less, to the smaller model stationary steam plants.

The ordinary "pot" boiler, that is, the horizontal cylindrical externally fired kind, used for the smallest toy models, does not, under the best conditions, evaporate more than $\frac{5}{16}$ to $\frac{3}{8}$ of a cubic inch of water per minute in the medium size (about 8 in. long by $2\frac{1}{4}$ in. in diameter). The effective heating surface may be reckoned at 20 sq. in. and its efficiency 1 cub. in. of water per 60 sq. in. of heating surface, compared with Table III., is due to the fact that a large amount of fuel is employed, and that the whole of the under surface of the boiler is directly subjected to the action of the flame. The fire may be methylated spirit or gas, and although with such fuel it is difficult to think of the furnace area as grate area, the latter is almost equal to the heating surface. At a rough estimate, the space occupied by the lamps or burners must not be less than half the heating surface.

When water tubes as shown in Fig. 381 are used, the efficiency rises enormously. This is due to better circulation provided by the tubes. The particular and enforced

TABLE III

	Heating surface	*Grate area*
	sq. in.	*sq. in.*
MODEL VERTICAL BOILER—		
Natural draught	100	10
Induced draught	70	6
MODEL LOCOMOTIVE BOILER—		
Induced draught	45	$1\frac{3}{4}$

direction of the convection currents (the movements of water up and down and to and from the heated under-surface, as indicated by arrows in Figs. 380 and 381, are called convection currents) ensures the greatest efficiency in the transmission of the heat from the flame to the water. In such a boiler as shown by Fig. 381 it is therefore easy with spirits or gas, or a wickless paraffin stove, to obtain 1 cub. in. of water from 70 sq. in. to 100 sq. in. of heating surface with a furnace area of 16 sq. in. to 20 sq. in.

In a small model steam locomotive with an enclosed fire—a model Great Central Railway engine was the actual example—tests have shown an evaporation of 1 cub. in. of water per minute per 97 sq. in. of heating surface. In this surface two-thirds of the whole of the inner barrel was

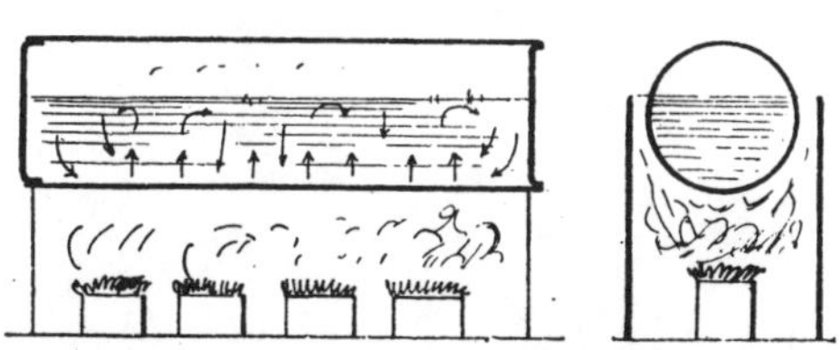

Fig. 380.—Model "outside fired" pot boiler

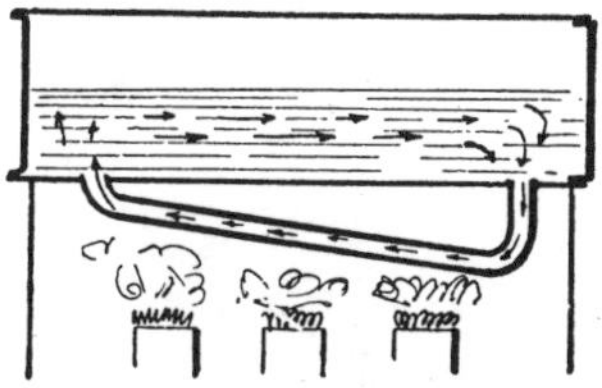

Fig. 381.—Model water-tube boiler

taken as being exposed to flames or heated gases, and was reckoned as heating surface. The furnace area would be about 15 sq. in. to 20 sq. in., or, proportionally, nearly twice the amount of the highest grate area in Table III.

Where oil fuel, paraffin, or petrol, in a blow-lamp is employed, the evaporation may easily rise to a value of 1 cub. in. for every 30 sq. in. of heating surface. This is entirely due to the flame being forced at a great rate on to the heating surfaces of the boiler. Of course, grate area or furnace area is of no use for comparisons in this case.

In flash boilers weight must be considered. Instead of having a heated body of water to steady the evaporation, heated copper or steel tube is utilised. The weight of a flash boiler may be as much as 1 lb. for every 15 sq. in. of heating surface. In model boat work this proportion of weight cannot be obtained, and therefore intense heat must be relied on, this resulting in erratic evaporation, the high superheat doing the engine little good.

One important experiment to be remembered in connection with the design of water-tube boilers is that made by Mr. Yarrow in an experimental model in 1896. He found that on heating a water tube at A (Fig. 382c), the circulation began in an upward direction in this tube; but

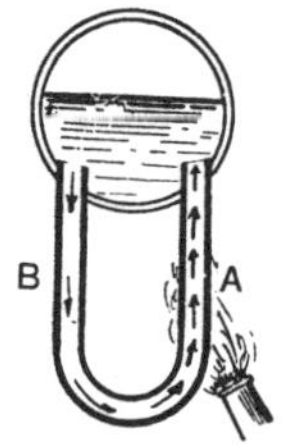

Fig. 382 C

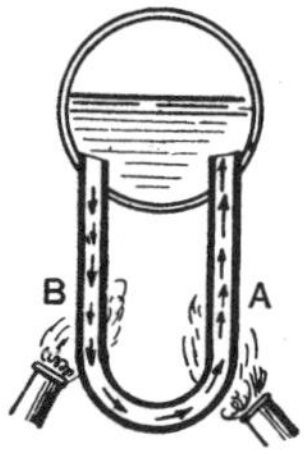

Fig. 382 D

Fig. 382.—Diagrams illustrating Mr. Yarrow's experiments with water-tube boilers

Fig. 383.—Model boiler, engine and dynamo

on heating the down-coming tube B (Fig. 382D) as well, the circulation was not altered, but was much increased in the original direction.

Types of Stationary Boilers.—In addition to the externally-fired boilers shown in Figs. 380 and 381, there are several types in which the fire and the hot products of combustion are wholly or partly surrounded by water. The simplest form is shown in Fig. 383. This tubular boiler may be made up of solid drawn copper tube 5 in. diameter for the shell and $\frac{7}{16}$ in. or $\frac{1}{2}$ in. diameter for flues, the ends being gunmetal castings. The lower casting (furnace crown) is shaped so that the mud deposited from the water will fall into the annular space provided. The tubes are screwed in at one end and expanded in at the other in the manner already described. This boiler is suitable for firing with a methylated spirit lamp, "Primus" oil burner, or gas

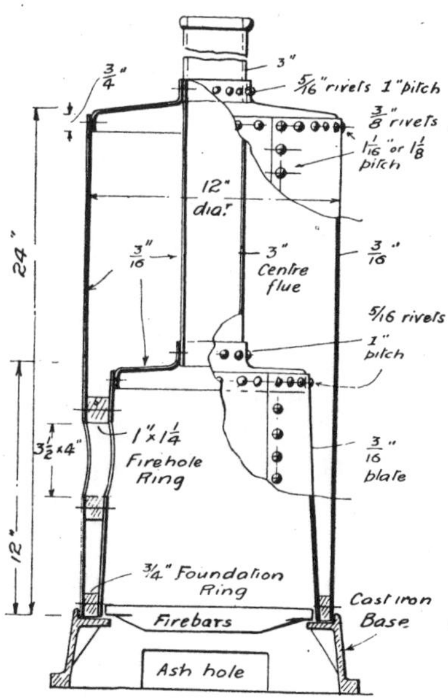

Fig. 384.—Vertical centre-flue boiler for solid fuel

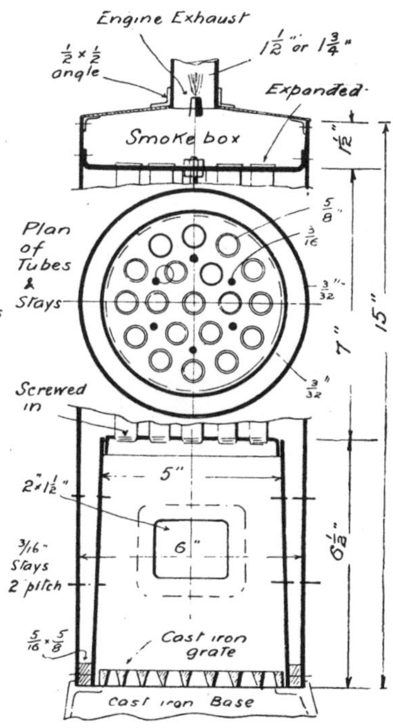

Fig. 385.—Vertical fire-tube boiler for solid fuel

ring. Spirit will, however, be found a very expensive fuel, and should be adopted only where either one of the two others are not available. The boiler is suitable for a 1-in. by 2-in. steam engine. Where solid fuel is employed, a vertical boiler should have a water-surrounded furnace.

Figs. 384 and 385 show two types of boilers, the vertical centre flue boiler and the multitubular type. The former, because of its relatively small heating surface, must for a given power be of larger dimensions. This means an increase in the cost of materials, but to some extent this is balanced by the simplicity of its construction. A centre-flue boiler is very useful in larger sizes (above 12 in. diameter) where it is required to reduce the attention it is necessary to bestow in working the boiler to the minimum. A natural draught as would be provided by a chimney 10 ft. to 15 ft. long, leading out to the open air, is to be preferred to a draught induced by the exhaust steam from the engine. While it would be necessary to instal a 12-in. by 24-in. centre-flue boiler to drive a 1½-in. by 1½-in. high-speed engine at full power, the same effect could be obtained with a multi-tubular boiler, made of copper instead of steel, 6 in. diameter by 15 in. high. Copper tube and castings for the ends might be employed, and with solid drawn tube $\frac{3}{32}$ in. thick (5 in. and 6 in. diameter respectively), a much higher working pressure, say 80 lb. or 90 lb. per square inch could be used. The ends should be ⅛ in. If the boiler is built up out of plate the longitudinal seams should be double riveted, in which case with $\frac{3}{32}$-in. material 65 lb. pressure would be within safe limits. If made of steel plate ⅛ in. in thickness should be used. The tubes should be 19 in number and ⅝ in. outside diameter. If $\frac{3}{32}$-in. tube is employed the inside firebox will require staying with $\frac{3}{16}$-in. screwed stays. This boiler could be worked with a short chimney, the exhaust from the engine being used to induce a draught. Of course, the boiler, by reason of its smaller firegrate and water capacity, would require constant attention; but as a model this would be reckoned as an advantage, and as part of the amusement obtained in working the plant. The centre-flue type of boiler may therefore be considered more of a small-power boiler than a model, and could not be so easily made by the amateur mechanic.

Developments of the simple boilers shown in the first two figures are illustrated in Figs. 386 to 388. The first of these is a gas- or spirit-fired boiler suited to a 1-in. by 2-in. horizontal engine or its equivalent. The barrel is made of 3½ in. diameter with cast gunmetal ends, riveted and silver-soldered in. The water tubes, made out of pieces of $\frac{7}{16}$-in. and $\frac{5}{16}$-in. copper tube, are silver-soldered together and into the boiler barrel. The casing is made of sheet iron lined with asbestos millboard. Where the engine is of suitable construction a superheater coil of good length (say 5 ft. to 7 ft. of tube) may be fitted as shown. If the engine has brass cylinders a shorter superheater is desirable. For larger engines a boiler using "Field" water tubes (Fig. 387) will be found very efficient, and at the same time easy to build. The construction is more in the nature of mechanical engineering than plate construction. The barrel, for a 2-in. by 2-in. single cylinder engine, should be about 7 in. diameter by 18 in. long, and if a coal or coke fire is employed steel can be employed throughout, except perhaps for the circulating pipes inside the "Field" tubes, which may be of brass. The water tubes (about 46 in number) should be of heavy-gauge solid-drawn tube $\frac{3}{4}$ in. outside diameter. The mild-steel shell should have

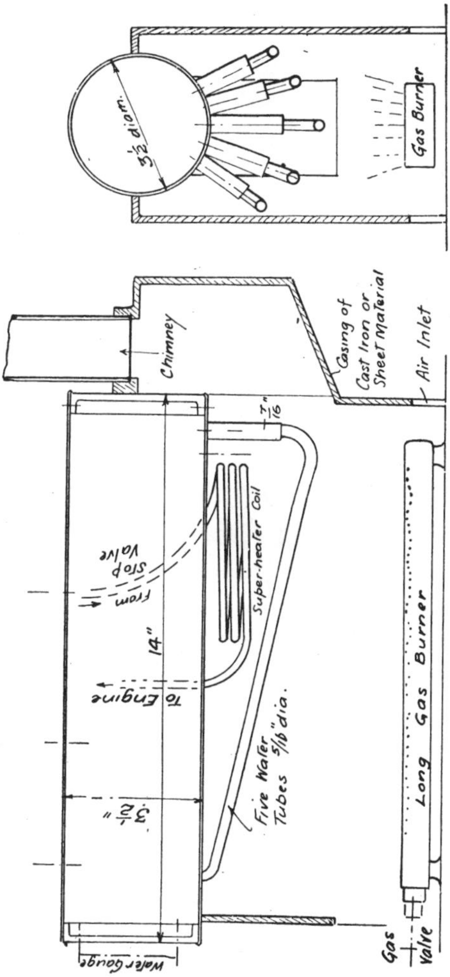

Fig. 386.—Model gas-fired water-tube boiler

a double-riveted longitudinal seam and be of at least $\frac{1}{8}$-in. stuff, to make up for the metal removed by the tubes. The seam should be outside the casing. The more nearly vertical water tubes should have central tubes $\frac{7}{16}$ in. diameter, while the almost horizontal one, on top, may have simply a strip of metal (a diaphragm) dividing the streams of water (convection currents) in the water tubes. The tubes should be in staggered rows as shown, and be screwed into the

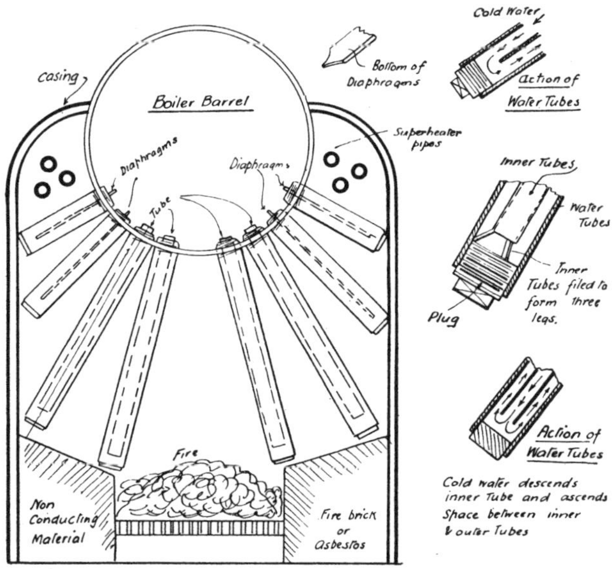

Fig. 387.—"Field"-tube horizontal water-tube boiler

shell with fine tapered threads (26 to the inch). They may with advantage be back-nutted inside. The inner tubes will require to be supported in a concentric position in the water tubes, and the sketches show how this can be done. The boiler is shown arranged for solid fuel, but a slightly smaller boiler, say 6 in. by 15 in. with $\frac{5}{8}$-in. tubes, would work quite well with a battery of Primus or other vaporising oil burners, and such a boiler could be made of copper throughout. Below, say, 4 in. or 5 in. there is no advantage in this type of boiler over that illustrated in Fig. 386. Its chief feature is that it can be built up without recourse to heavy boiler-making tools.

A type of boiler which also embodies an entirely mechanical construction is shown in Fig. 388, and this eliminates the silver-soldering or brazing process. The holes in the large steam drum are set out in zigzag formation, and are clearing holes. The water tubes are screwed into the mud drum with taper threads before they are bent up. The tube of which the mud drum is made should be at least $\frac{3}{32}$ in. or $\frac{1}{8}$ in. thick. For caulking the screw joints red lead or soft solder may be employed. The boiler must be fired with solid fuel coal or charcoal (the latter is the cleaner for small boilers), and the grate bars are built up out of strip iron or steel in a frame resting on the water tubes. The casing is made of sheet iron lined with asbestos millboard riveted on.

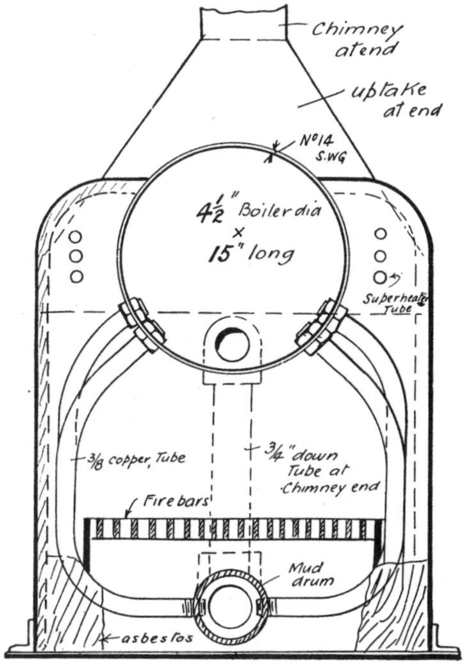

Fig. 388.—Horizontal water-tube boiler

In all vertical boilers where a smokebox is used a steam superheater coil should be fitted. Small steam engines suffer very much from cylinder condensation, and even if the engine is unsuitable for a high degree of superheat, the steam may be dried as much as possible. As in the ordinary way a centre flue boiler has no smokebox, a chamber can be made in sheet iron at the base of the chimney, as shown in Fig. 389, to take a coil of steam pipe.

Horizontal stationary boilers of the fire-tube type are

not, on the whole, very successful in model practice, and therefore nothing very great must be expected of model Cornish- and Lancashire-type generators. A suggestion for utilising a plain horizontal boiler to the best advantage is illustrated in Fig. 391. The boiler is in a lined sheet-iron casing or brick setting, and the lower portion is fitted with return tubes, a superheater coil being fitted in the combustion chamber at the back. The smokebox on the front end should have a door to allow the tubes to be cleaned out.

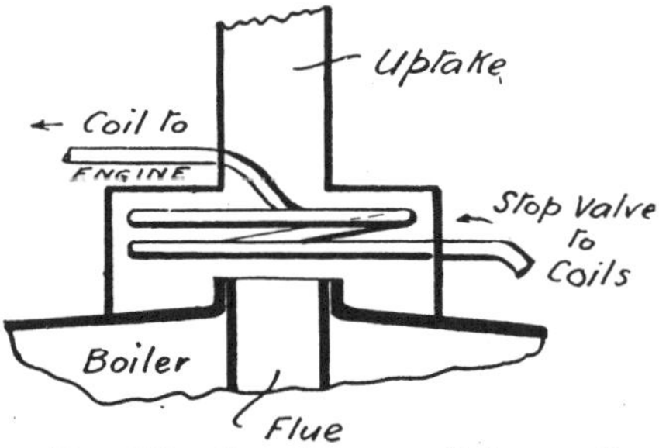

Fig. 389.—Superheater coil for small vertical boiler

Locomotive Type Boilers.—The locomotive-type tubular boiler is

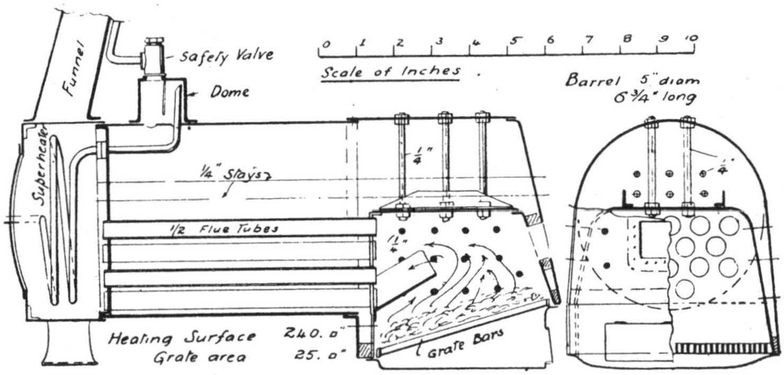

Fig. 390.—Locomotive-type boiler for model launch

expensive to make, and therefore should be adopted only in special circumstances. It is applicable to model undertype engines, and in some cases to model steam launches. In the earlier fast torpedo-boats the locomotive boiler was successfully employed. A solid-fuel boiler of this type can be recommended for reliability, coupled with a moderate power. The proportions of a suitable locomotive boiler for an open steam launch of, say, 30 lb. displacement are given in Fig. 390. To reduce the weight, castings should not be employed, but all the plates should be flanged up in sheet copper. With a little longer barrel and perhaps a deeper firebox the design would also do very well for a model undertype engine, but in this case castings could be used, as in the model express locomotive described in another chapter. For marine use the firebox must be shallow, to keep the centre of gravity of the boiler as low as possible in the boat. The grate is inclined and a plate is fitted as a " brick arch " under the tubes. This will prevent the piling up of the

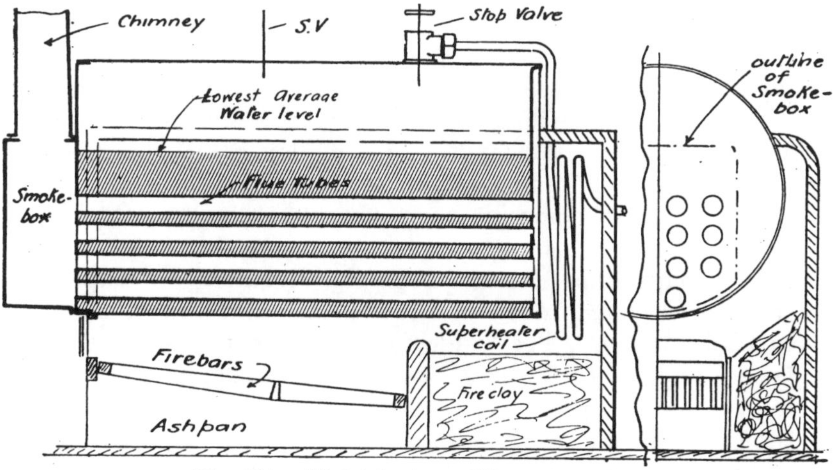

Fig. 391.—Model horizontal fire-tube boiler

fuel against the tubes and ensure an equal draught through each tube.

Model Marine Boilers.—The use of the marine boiler is limited by the necessity of a low centre of gravity and of light weight, and by the firing difficulties. A model launch of ample beam will work quite well with an almost rectangular boiler fired with charcoal. Such a boiler as this must be well stayed and worked at a moderate pressure, not exceeding, say, 30 lb. per square inch.

Fig. 392 shows a typical example, suitable for a boat of $5\frac{1}{2}$-in. or 6-in. beam. The plate is relatively thin (No. 18 S.W.G.), and the ends are best made of *light* gunmetal castings with the flanges cast on. Four water tubes may be inserted by nipples and double nuts to save any silver-soldering, as shown in the detailed sketches (Fig. 393, A and B, on page 187). The back portion of the furnace must be screened off so that the air drawn in by the exhaust must pass *through* the fire from the ashpit. The boiler should work a $\frac{3}{4}$-in. by $\frac{3}{4}$-in. engine with ease at a pressure of 20 lb. to 25 lb. per square inch. A superheater may be placed in the smokebox, and if the engine is fitted with an iron cylinder, as much tube as can be got into the smokebox may be employed. The boiler has a large grate area and small heating surface, therefore the smokebox temperature will be high, and a superheater can be used to advantage. All the joints (tube and riveted) may be caulked with soft solder. With the ends placed with the flanges as shown, screws will have to be employed on end instead of rivets.

The single-flue marine boiler (Fig. 394), really a Cornish-type land boiler, is popular for boats, and is usually fired with a blowlamp. The average size has a $3\frac{1}{2}$-in. diameter shell, 9 in. long, made of the lightest solid-drawn copper tube obtainable. The inside furnace is crossed with water-tubes, and is $1\frac{5}{8}$ in. or $1\frac{3}{4}$ in. diameter. This leaves the upper half of the boiler for water and steam. The water-tubes ($\frac{5}{16}$ in. diameter) *must be silver-soldered* in place, and the furnace similarly secured to the ends. The ends may be cut out of copper plate a little thicker than the shell, and be driven into the shell and silver-soldered. As the boiler is not riveted in any way, the silver-soldering must be carefully done so as to save every ounce of weight. This boiler will supply a $\frac{3}{4}$-in. by $\frac{3}{4}$-in. double-acting cylinder or its equivalent.

Where the boiler must be larger, then trouble will be experienced with the furnace. Unless unduly thick, the furnace tube will have a tendency to collapse at the higher pressures of steam usually employed. The limit of the furnace tube diameter would appear to be about $1\frac{3}{4}$ in. or 2 in. Therefore for bigger boilers than that shown in Fig. 394 the furnace may be duplicated, as in a Lancashire boiler, and a duplex blowlamp employed. An oval

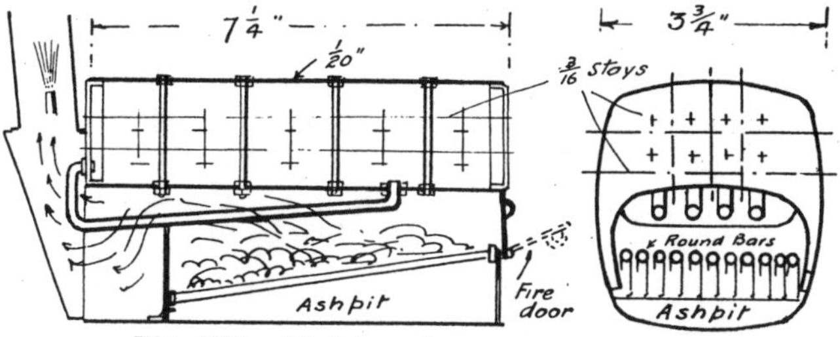

Fig. 392.—Model marine water-tube boiler

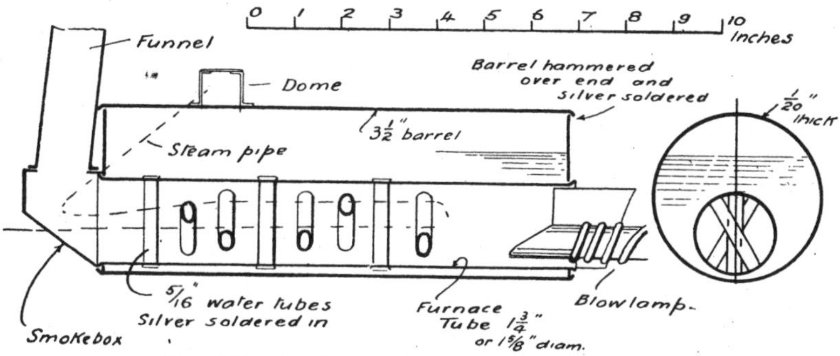

Fig. 394.—Small model single-flue marine boiler

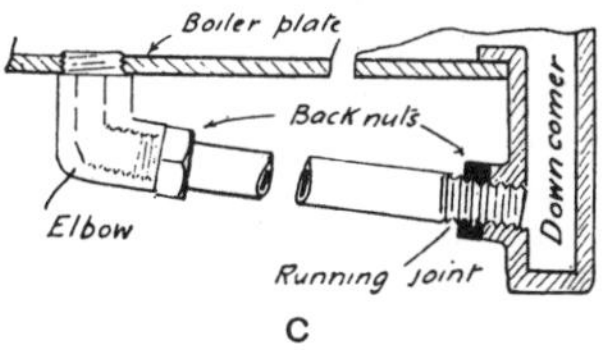

C

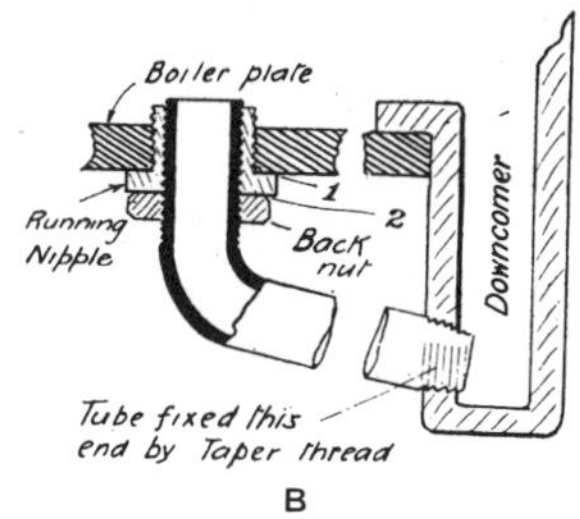

B

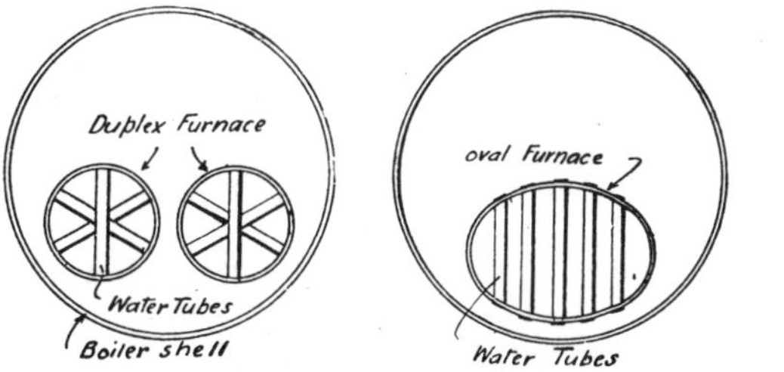

Fig. 395.—Furnace tubes for large model horizontal boilers

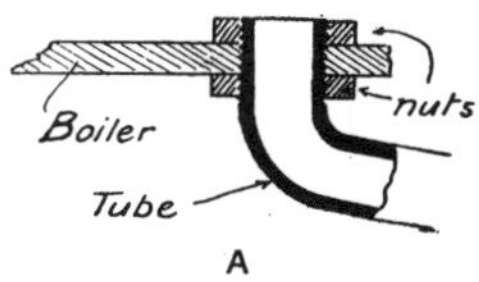

A

Fig. 393—(A, B and C).—Methods of fixing model water tubes

section may, however, be adopted, and the tubes arranged in a vertical direction only, to stay the flatter sides and prevent their collapsing. The radius of the smaller ends of the oval should not be more than ¾ in., and for this boiler a duplex lamp with the burners close together may be employed, or a single burner with a flame tube pinched into an oval shape at the outer end.

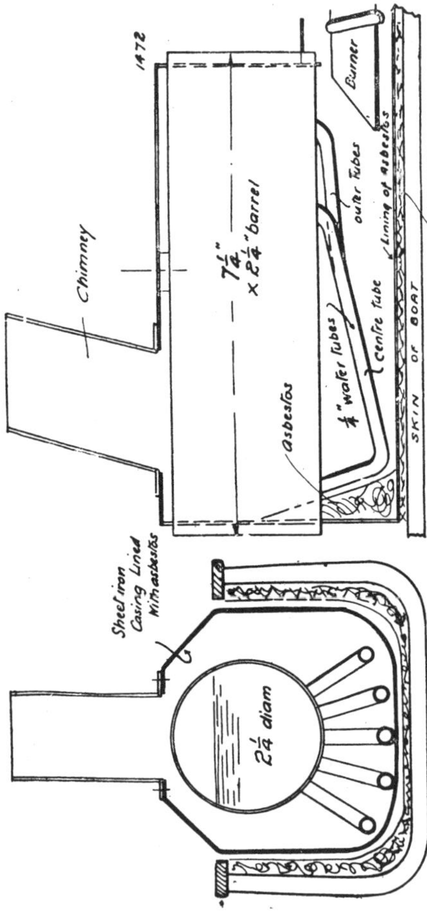

Fig. 396.—Position of marine boiler influenced by use of blowlamp

Small model steamers are often driven by boilers of the water-tube pattern as shown in Fig. 386 for land work. The difficulty with spirit firing is head room, and, therefore, while the boiler is comparatively light, it may have to be placed so high as to make a small boat, or one of narrow beam, quite unstable. By using a petrol blowlamp, as shown in Fig. 396, the boiler can be placed much lower down in the boat.

Fig. 397 is a photograph of a model Cornish-type marine boiler having a central flue fitted with cross water-tubes. It is fired with a petrol blowlamp.

Strength of Model Boilers.—As in the case of details of working model engine construction, the steam pressures cannot be reduced to scale. It is common practice to run a model at 50 lb. to 70 lb. pressure, the steam supplied in the prototype being only a few pounds per square inch higher. A comparatively high pressure is advised in a model for two reasons. In the first place, steam at a low pressure requires a larger surface to rise from than at a high pressure, and this is why boilers often fail to steam satisfactorily when fitted to engines with big cylinders. Large cylinders tend to lower the pressure rapidly, and

Fig. 397.—Model of Cornish-type marine boiler

owing to the small surface from which steam can rise in a model boiler the reduction in pressure leads to a violent ebullition, and causes what is known as "priming."

Steam at low pressure has a correspondingly low temperature, and as in a model cylinder condensation is a factor to be reckoned with it should be mitigated by the use of as high a temperature steam as can be conveniently handled. The drying of the steam in heated coils, if not actually superheating it, is therefore to be recommended in addition to the use of a fairly high pressure of steam in the boiler. One method of preventing priming is to reduce the orifice of the supply pipe—at the boiler end, so that the steam is kept back in the boiler. This arrangement partially superheats the steam, or at any rate ensures its dryness.

The materials for boiler making are copper, brass, in tube, rod and sheet form, gun metal castings,and mild steel plate. . Tin plate and sheet iron are also used for casings and for lagging boilers, both of these materials not being

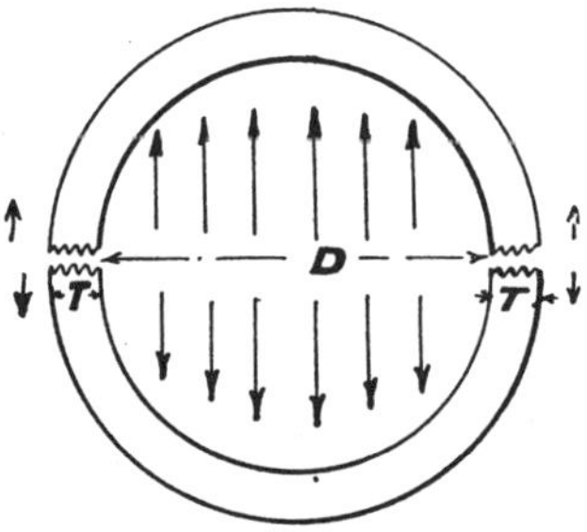

Fig. 398.—Failure of cylindrical boiler

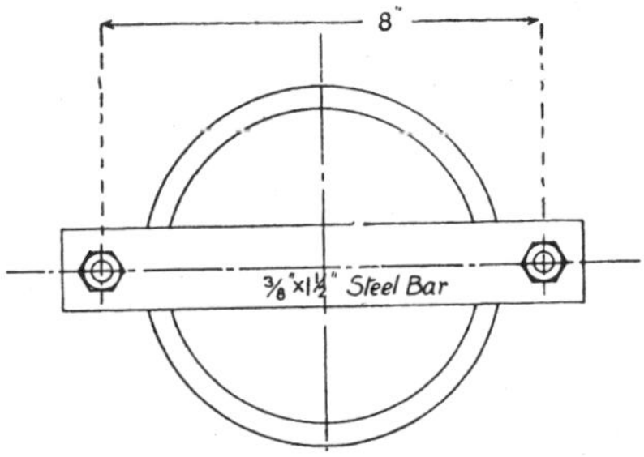

Fig. 401

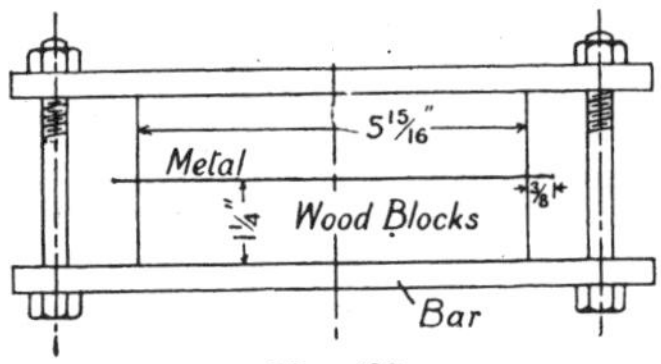

Fig. 402

Figs. 401 and 402.—Blocks and clamps for flanging boiler end

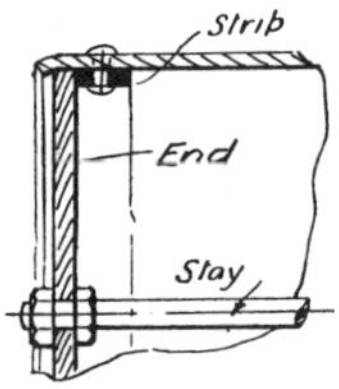

Fig. 400.—Substitute for flanged joint

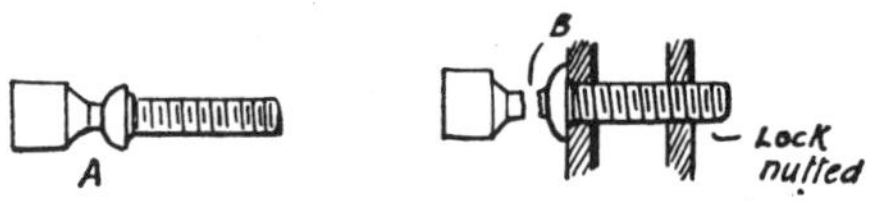

Fig. 399.—Method of turning and fitting stay

recommended, under any circumstances, for any parts subjected to steam pressure. Copper and brass are much used because they do not rust or corrode, and are easy to work and solder.

The strength of a boiler is an important consideration. For cylindrical portions solid-drawn tube will make the strongest job. Where a shell is rolled up out of sheet and the joint riveted up, the strength depends on the kind of joint employed. A single-riveted lapped joint has only 55 per cent. of the strength of the original plate. Where the joint is double-riveted the strength rises to 75 per cent. Another point to remember is that copper and brass are reduced in strength at high temperatures, and while copper may be said to have a tensile strength of 29,000 lb. (13 tons) per square inch under ordinary conditions, at 350° F. (the temperature of steam at 100 lb. pressure) the tensile strength may be taken as only about 25,000 lb. For brass not more than 18,000 lb. to 20,000 lb. should be allowed, while for steel 40,000 lb. per square inch is a fair figure to work on. In all small steel boilers the effect of corrosion must not be forgotten, therefore as a new boiler one made of steel may seem to be absurdly strong. In no case is steel of anything less than $\frac{1}{8}$ in. thickness recommended.

In calculating the working strength of a cylindrical boiler a certain factor of safety is allowed. The usual factor is 8, which means that the working pressure is only one-eighth of the pressure which the boiler would stand before it actually failed. The diameter of the boiler and the plate thickness are the important factors, together with the allowance for the reduction in strength due to riveting and for safety. As shown by Fig. 398, it is assumed that the boiler will fail in both walls, and the pressure is exerted across the whole diameter in the direction of the arrows; in calculating the diameter and twice the plate thickness must be stated. The formula works out as follows, for a 4-in. copper boiler made with $\frac{1}{16}$-in. thick plate—

$$\text{Working pressure per square inch} = \frac{\text{SM} \times \text{PT} \times 2}{\text{DIA} \times \text{FS}} \times \text{RA}$$

where SM is Strength of material
PT = Plate thickness
DIA = Diameter
FS = Factor of safety (say 8)
RA = Riveting allowance.

$$= \frac{20{,}000 \times \frac{1}{16} \times 2}{4 \times 8} = \frac{20{,}000}{256} = 80 \text{ lb.}$$

If the barrel is single-lap riveted, then the working pressure is 55 per cent. of this, viz. about 44 lb.; with double riveting it would be 75 per cent. (i.e. $\frac{3}{4}$) = 60 lb. per square inch. For solid drawn tube the riveting allowance may be disregarded. Sometimes it is desired to know the plate thickness required; the formula is then—

$$\text{PT} = \frac{\text{DIA} \times \text{working pressure} \times \text{FS}}{\text{SM} \times 2}$$

Double the result if a single-lap joint is intended, and add 50 per cent. if the joint is to be double riveted.

The ends of boilers should, as a rule, be thicker than the barrel, but here some judgment is required. The size and shape must be taken into account as well as the plate thickness.

Stays for Model Boilers.—Usually all flat ends over 4 sq. in. area are stayed unless the ends are very thick; for instance, gunmetal castings. Even then a stay relieves the rivets or brazed joint of some of the strain. Small boilers are usually stronger in this respect than large ones. However, a good rule is to put an $\frac{1}{8}$ in. diameter stay in for every 1 sq. in. unsupported flat surface in smaller models, and a $\frac{3}{16}$-in. stay per inch in larger ones. If bigger stays are employed, then the supported area may be increased in proportion to the area of the stay, taken at the bottom of the screwed thread.

It is important that stays should be supported in both plates. A plain bolt is insufficient. In the firebox stays of a locomotive boiler both plates are drilled and tapped in each operation. As a small head on the outside is desirable in such models, because of the limits of overall width, a very good way of making such stays is to turn them up out of larger rod than the nominal diameter (say $\frac{3}{16}$-in. rod for $\frac{5}{32}$-in. stays), and to form the head as shown in Fig. 399. When driven right home the superfluous portion will break off, and then the ragged edge may be filed off. Stays should be soldered up in small boilers; in larger ones they may be smeared with red-lead and oil before being driven home. In either case an inside lock-nut may be fitted wherever possible; this, however, is only important where red-lead is employed to caulk the joint. A piece of cotton should be dipped in red-lead and wound round under the nut before it is tightened up.

To save threading lengthy stays or stay tubes all the way along, the running nipple idea B (Fig. 393) may be adopted.

Fig. 403.—Inside and outside fireboxes of model locomotive during construction

Riveted Joints.—The rules of riveting commonly adopted in real practice may be slightly modified in model practice. The diameter of the rivets should be *at least* $1\frac{1}{2}$ times the plate thickness; for $\frac{1}{16}$-in. plate $\frac{3}{32}$in. or $\frac{7}{64}$ in. diameter should be used. The pitch (distance apart, centre to centre) should not be more than four times the diameter of the rivet; that is, $\frac{3}{8}$-in. pitch for $\frac{3}{32}$-in. rivets; three times the diameter is a safe rule where no strength is obtained from soldering. Silver-soldered plate joints need only be riveted sufficiently to hold the work together during the soldering, as the solder takes the strain.

Flanged Joints.—To save flanging plates, an operation requiring some skill, cast boiler ends with flanges cast on are sometimes employed. For simple boilers which have to stand only a moderate pressure and where solid drawn boiler tube is employed, a piece of strip metal may be riveted inside the tube and the end may be a brass or copper disc turned to a driving fit. When in place the copper boiler tube may be hammered over the end as shown in Fig. 400. Where the end is flat and is over 2 in. diameter and comparatively thin, a central stay should be used.

Flanging Plates.—The flanging on locomotive boilers, if made in the orthodox manner, is comparatively heavy and requires great care. The best results can be obtained only by the previous preparation of flanging blocks, made in hard wood or iron. The blocks should be accurately made from the drawings, all plate thicknesses being allowed for. The plates (copper for models) should be screwed or bolted on to the block, the holes chosen for the screw being holes which will subsequently remain. Where a hole is not desirable the plate to be flanged may be clamped between two blocks, the sketches (Figs. 401 and 402) showing the blocks and clamp used for flanging the circular end of a 6-in. copper boiler. Once or twice during the operation the plates should be annealed by heating to dull redness and plunging in cold water. Fig. 403 shows the inside and outside fireboxes of a 1-in. scale (5-in. barrel) model locomotive boiler during construction. The thickening up of the tube plate where the tubes screw in is accomplished by riveting on and silver-soldering another piece of plate. The firehole joint is flanged out. This job can be done with washers and plates in a heavy vice, the process being analogous to plate flanged by hydraulic press in real practice.

Fixing Boiler Tubes.—Fixing model boiler tubes is another point that demands attention. Especially where the firebox is small and it is impossible to get at the ends of the tubes to use a drift or expander, it is a good practice to screw the tubes with a fine taper thread of say 40 to the inch (*see* Fig. 404). A special tap must be made, but this will always come in useful for other similar purposes. The tube plate into which the tubes are screwed should be thicker than the rest of the boiler, and this is one of the advantages of using cast tube plates, as they can easily be thickened at the portion into which the tubes are screwed. The thread on the tubes should be chased, the end being worked upon running *on* the back lathe centre. The other ends of the tubes should have a slot cut in them with a hack-saw to facilitate screwing home. The threads may be red-leaded or soldered. If the latter, they should be tinned before driving home and the firebox made hot during the process. The plain ends may be expanded in, a smooth taper drift being employed for this purpose. Where the tube plates are large—as, for instance, in the 6-in. boiler (Fig. 384)—the tubes may be arranged to act as stays. After driving them home the plain ends may be expanded in with an ordinary conical drift; and with the special expanding tool, made of tool-steel hardened and tempered spring hard, shown in Fig. 405, the tubes

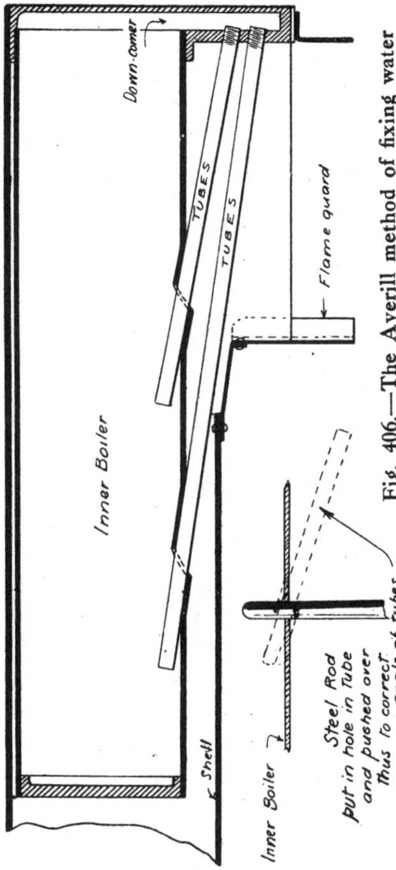

Fig. 406.—The Averill method of fixing water tubes

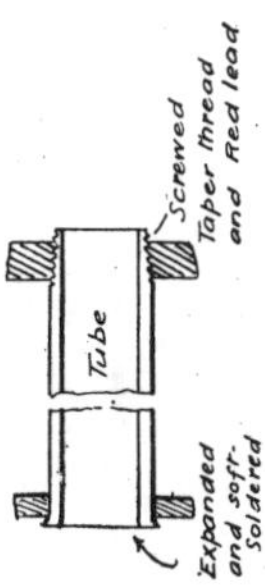

Fig. 404.—Method of fixing boiler tubes

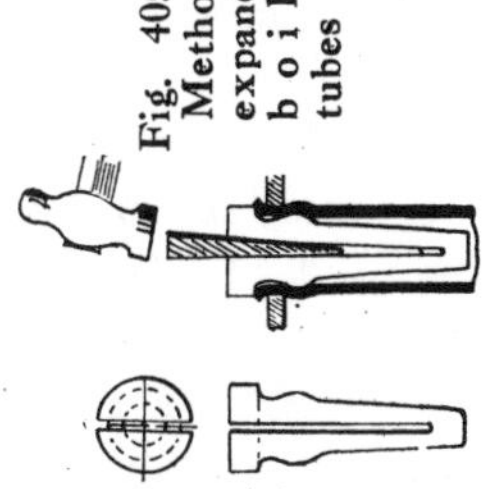

Fig. 405.—Method of expanding boiler tubes

may be expanded behind the tube plate. The expander is turned up to the shape shown, the bulged portion just fitting inside the tube. When operated on in one direction, the wedge should be pulled out and the expander turned round a quarter of a turn. The tubes, treated in this manner, will be found to support the tube plate as well as if they were double nutted. The ends of the copper tubes should, of course, be previously softened.

An ingenious method (due to T. W. Averill) of fixing tubes to model locomotive water-tube boilers is shown in Fig. 406. The holes are drilled in the bottom of the boiler barrel and the plates bent to shape by a steel rod. The tubes can then be screwed into the down-comer and soft-soldered into the barrel. Of course, if soft soldered—an expedient which should only be resorted to if no brazing apparatus is available—the water in the boiler must be kept well above the level of the tubes.

Water tubes in small copper boilers are generally secured by the safe and convenient method of silver-soldering them in. Indeed, the whole of the joints are silver-soldered, including the bushings for the boiler fittings. A silver-soldered boiler is immune from any danger arising from shortness of water, and it is not unusual, in the case of small locomotives with water-tube boilers, fired by methylated spirit, to work the boiler until it is quite dry. Amateurs will, however, find that large boilers are difficult to silver-solder, and where extreme lightness is required, as in small boat boilers, the thinness of the plates which it is desirable to employ increases the danger of burning the plates during the process of soldering.

In these circumstances other methods of construction (riveting, screwing, etc.) are resorted to. Water tubes may be secured by double nuts, as at A (Fig. 393), and if the threads are fine and the joints screwed up tightly, a little soft solder will caulk the tubes so that they will not leak, even if the boiler is run dry and the solder melted. When fitting up the tubes the nuts should be screwed up while the solder is in a melted state, so that no crevices presenting any appreciable area for the steam to press against are present. The diagram B shows a method of fitting a tube where the other end is fixed. The nipple is screwed with the same pitch of thread as on the tube. It runs off the tube into the boiler, and the flange forms the jointing surface (No. 1). To provide a further flat joint, which can be grummeted with red-lead or soft solder, a back nut is employed, forming joint No. 2. Elbows and back nuts may be used where the tube is screwed into a down-comer casting, as shown at C. The tube is screwed into the down-comer twice as far as it need be for ordinary purposes. The elbow at the higher end is then fixed to the boiler. The tube is screwed back again into this, and the back nuts run up to form the joint.

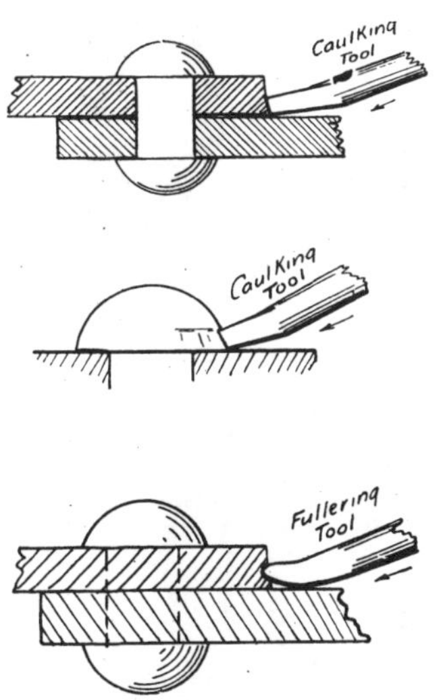

Fig. 407.—Caulking riveted joints

General Notes on Boiler Construction.—In attaching fittings or any other fixture into copper boilers, brass screws should be used. If steel or iron screws are employed, a fault which even professional model-makers have committed in building expensive working models, electrolytic action soon destroys them and may possibly cause a troublesome leakage.

Copper boilers, especially large ones, which are too big to have the joints caulked with solder, often develop small leaks, due to internal strains opening the joints. In the case of steel boilers the corrosion of the metal causes the joints "to take up"; this corrosion is not present in copper boilers, and the only thing that prevents leakage is the dirt forced into the seam. Where minute leaks occur, to increase the volume of this "dirt," the finest oatmeal, mixed into a thin paste, may be introduced into the boiler,

This remedy must not be over-done, however; a tea-spoonful is enough in a small boiler to half a cupful in a very large one. In building riveted copper boilers which cannot be soldered up, the rivets should be comparatively large and at all events closely spaced.

Fig. 408.—A flash-boiler power plant for model steamer

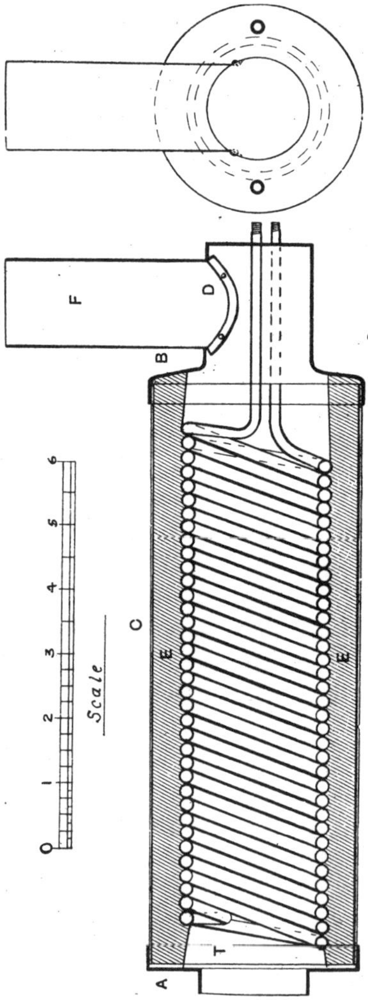

Fig. 408A.—Sectional view of marine flash-boiler

Fig. 407 shows how the plates and rivets are caulked with a caulking tool. On the water test all leaky places should be marked and caulked as shown. This tool and

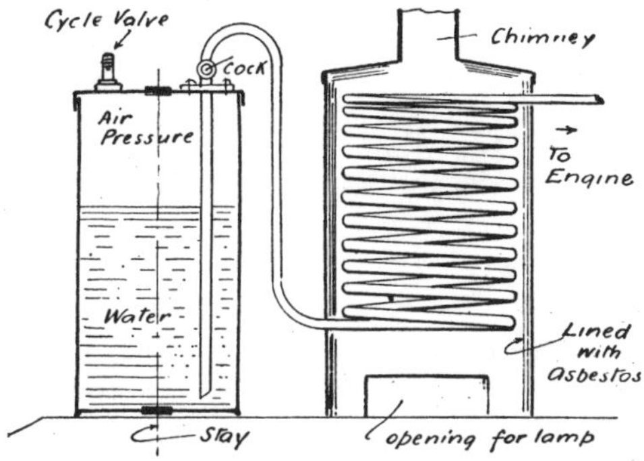

Fig. 409.—Simple flash-boiler with air-pressure feed

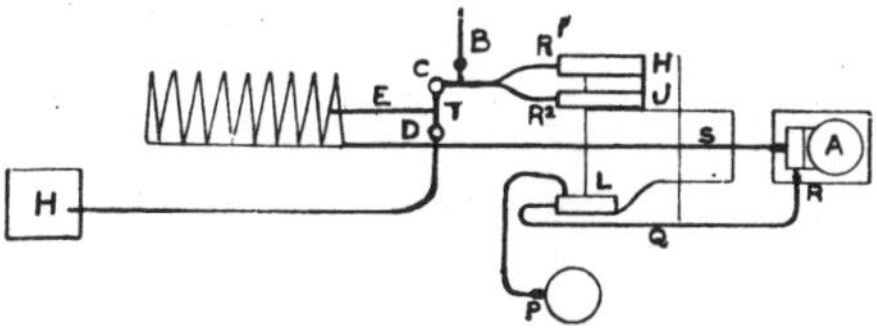

Fig. 410.—Diagram of pump system

Fig 411.—Photograph of pumps, etc., for model racing steamer

the fullering tool burr the plates and rivets, so closing the leaking crevices. In the case of steel boilers the joints may be sponged with a solution of sal-ammoniac to make them take up more rapidly.

Flash Boilers.—As already mentioned, flash boilers are dependent on a weight of heated metal. In model boats weight is a disadvantage, and therefore the reduction in metal is made up by the intensity of the flame. A highly superheated steam is the result, and only specially-built engines with iron or steel cylinders, pistons and valves will stand the heat. The degree of reliability is not great; a few hundred yards run, and then an accident to boiler, engine, or petrol lamp, and a complete conflagration is not uncommon.

There are two systems: the balance tank system and the pump system. Theoretically, the latter is the better, and a typical plant is illustrated in Fig. 408, the boiler being arranged as in Fig. 408A. In small sizes, however, the friction of all the pumps, etc., absorbs most of the power, and lightweight craft are best fed by the air pressure system of boiler feed, which is explained by Fig. 409. The pump system (Fig. 410) includes a lubricating pump, the geared water pump being duplicated to equalise the intermittent and heavy load on the engine. This is a drawback in a marine engine. In the pipe diagram (Fig. 410) the pump takes oil from tank P, and delivers it through pipe Q and check valve R to the engine A. The water from the two pumps H and J is delivered through the fork pipe R_1 and R_2, passing the by-pass or release automatic or safety valve B to the check valve C, the starting being accomplished by pumping water by the hand pump from the tank at H to the other check valve D, which is connected with the T-piece T to the pipe E leading to the boiler. From here the steam pipe S leads directly to the valve chest on the engine. A balance tank or air vessel may also be required between the boiler and check valves C D. Fig. 411 is a photograph of the pumps and oil tank as tried on a model racing steamer, and shows how complicated the pump system may be.

Steel tubing is used for model marine flash boilers, and the joints are screwed, socketed, and brazed. A coil or coils of about 30 ft. of $\frac{3}{16}$-in. or $\frac{1}{4}$-in. pipe is usual in a model steamer boiler. Copper may be used for a stationary boiler, as Fig. 409, which is fired by a spirit lamp or gas flame.

CHAPTER X

Model Boiler and Engine Valves and Fittings

In the fittings described in this chapter some of the designs are, of course, only applicable to models. Others are suitable for small-power engines.

Safety Valves.—The safety valve is a controlled valve fitted to a boiler, that will relieve the pressure which may accumulate therein over and above a certain predetermined amount. To be efficient, the safety valve should not blow off, weep, or leak until that pressure has been attained. It should then lift and release the steam, and not allow any appreciably higher pressure to be maintained. If by any cause—the shutting off of the fire or the supply of the steam to the engine—the pressure should fall below the set figure, then the valve should close promptly and effectually. In large plants the ordinary valve does not attain perfection in all these points, and in model work many types do so in none.

The cheapest valves are those fitted to toy boilers, as shown in Fig. 412. Very often to preserve tightness below the working or lifting pressure, the valve is fitted with a rubber washer, such as is shown in Fig. 413. So far as it goes this is all right, but unless every time the engine is used the valve is removed and tried by hand, there is a danger of the washer vulcanising up and preventing the valve from obeying the pressure. Such valves should therefore be eyed with suspicion, and if possible a metallic valve and seating should be used in preference.

The action of the valve shown in Fig. 412 is simple. The spring may be adjusted to any degree of compression, and the blowing-off pressure depends on the area of the valve orifice and the strength of the spring. The two forces just balance each other when the pressure in the boiler reaches the maximum working (or blowing-off) pressure.

The moment the pressure exceeds this amount the valve lifts, and allows the surplus steam to escape. Any tendency for the parts to jamb or stick, of course, will cause an increase in the pressure contained in the boiler before the steam is released.

A valve of too small an area will also allow the pressure to accumulate, even if the valve has lifted and is blowing off. The correct area in smaller models is perhaps difficult to settle by formula; in large models and small-power plants, using coal or other solid fuels, the Board of Trade rule for actual boilers may be employed. The rule is $A=\frac{37{\cdot}5 \times G}{P+15}$, where A = area of valve in square inches, G = area of grate in square feet, and P = gauge pressure to blow off at. Taking, say, a 12-in. by 24-in. vertical boiler, which would have a grate 10 in. in diameter ($\frac{1}{2}$-sq. ft. area), the size of the valve according to the above rule would be as follows for, say, a working pressure of 60 lb. per square inch:

$$A=\frac{37{\cdot}5 \times \frac{1}{2}}{60+15}=\frac{37{\cdot}5}{75 \times 2}. \quad A=\tfrac{1}{4} \text{ sq. in. area.}$$

Referring to a table book of areas, it will be found that the valve should be $\frac{9}{16}$ in. in diameter to give this area. This size is, in the writer's experience, a reasonable one. It is on the safe side as regards size, as very probably a valve $\frac{1}{2}$ in. in diameter would suffice under ordinary conditions of working.

One fault of the cheap valve, as usually supplied, is in the seating of the valve. As a rule this provides a comparatively large area of contact, as shown exaggerated in Fig. 414. With such a seating the presence of a speck of dirt or deposit from the water will cause the valve to refuse to shut down tight after it has relieved the boiler of the accumulated pressure. This leads to waste of steam, which commodity cannot be spared in a model engine. Better results are obtained by making the seating as shown in Fig. 415. This form of seating is known by model-makers as the knife-edge seating. The edge, however, is not quite sharp, but is chamfered off to engage the 45° angle of the valve. The area of this chamfer (the contact with the valve)

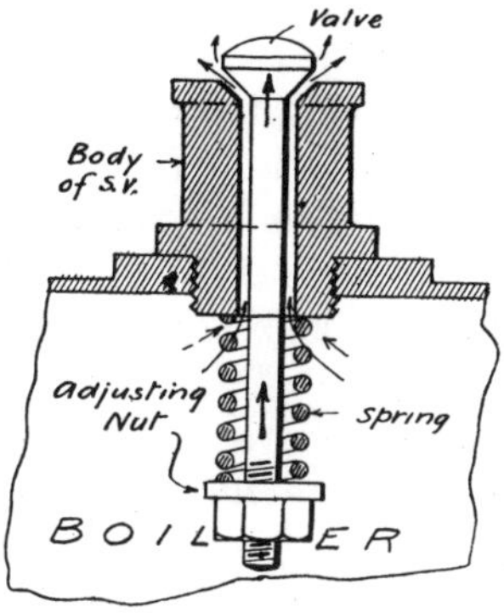

Fig. 412.—Simple model safety valve

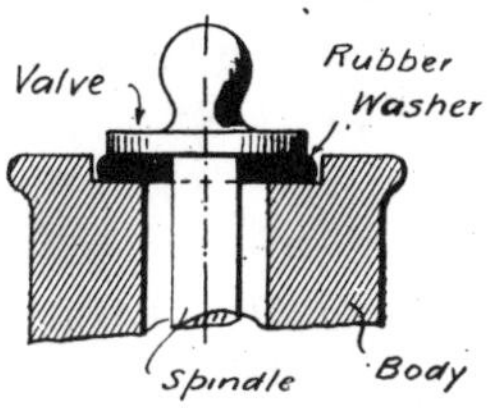

Fig. 413.—Safety valve with rubber seating

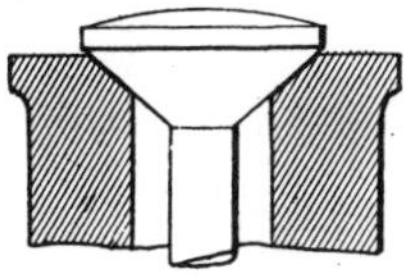
Fig. 414.—45°-angle valve and seating

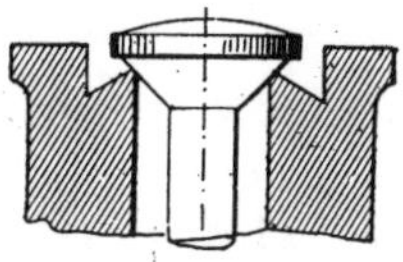
Fig. 415.—Valve with knife-edge seating

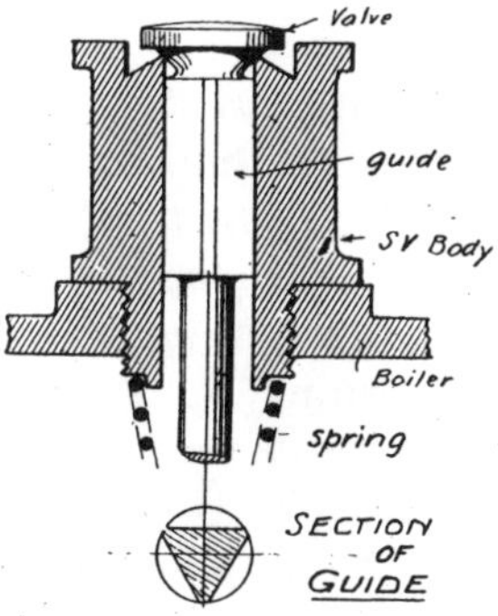

Fig. 416.—Valve with three-cornered guide spindle

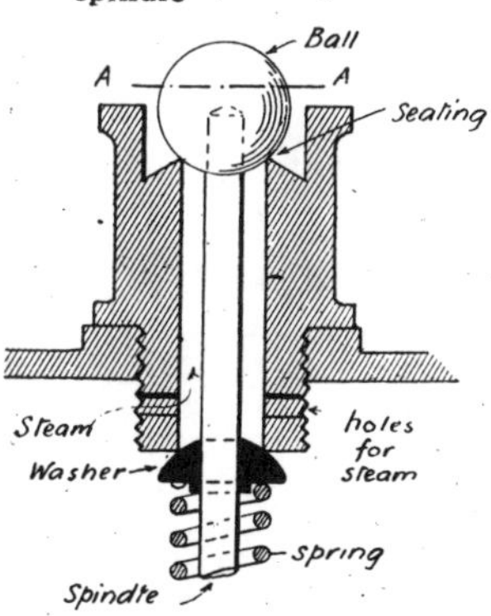

Fig. 417.—Safety valve of ball type

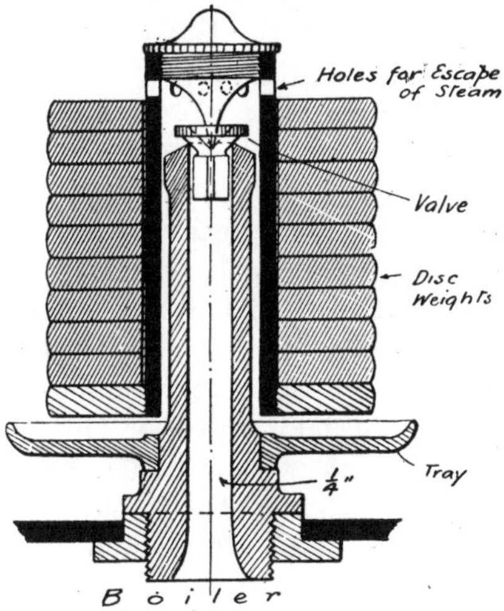

Fig. 418.—Model dead-weight safety valve

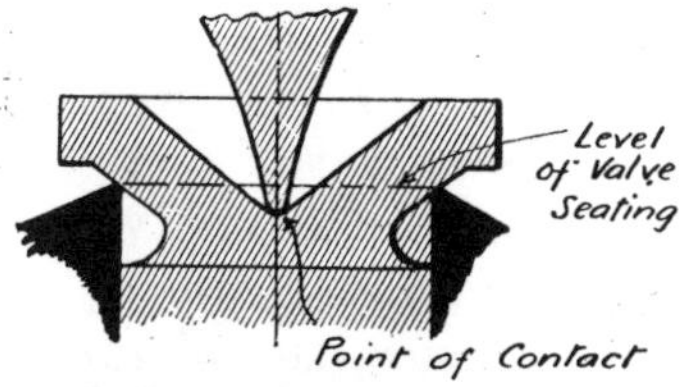

Fig. 419.—Contact of safety valve and load spindle

is relatively small, and the power of the spring is more likely to squeeze out any dirt or deposit quite clear of the surfaces touching each other, and to provide the necessary perfect metallic contact between valve and seating than with the valve shown in Fig. 414. A suitable cutter for making the seating is shown in Fig. 420.

Another fault of the model safety valve in which the valve and the spring spindle is made in one piece, is that unless the spindle is truly in line with the centre of the valve and square with the seating, the valve will not sit properly and will leak at all pressures from zero. Fig. 416 shows a valve which has a triangular guide, this shape providing a passage for the steam to escape when the valve lifts. Except for the friction the guide must create, a fair degree of tightness can be assured by this method.

A better idea is embodied in Fig. 417. Here the valve is a bronze ball, which is a commercial article. It has screwed into it a spindle of the requisite size. The seating is of the knife-edge variety, and after turning up as truly as possible, a steel cycle ball of the same size as the bronze ball is placed in the seating and given a smart tap. This will form a true seating, and at the same time render it unnecessary to grind in the valve and thereby spoil the truly spherical shape of the bronze ball. The valve being a sphere, it will always take up its proper seating, even if the spindle is slightly out of alignment. The only drawback to a ball valve which is fixed so that it practically has only one position on the seating, is that after a time a ridge is formed in it and its character (a perfect sphere) is spoiled. A bronze-ball valve should therefore never be ground in. The seating may be ground in by another ball, if thought desirable. This ball may be of steel or bronze, and be soldered on a rod of metal. The arrangement of the steam passages in the safety valve (Fig. 417) may be noted. If the washer at the top of the spring is of spherical form, this will ensure the alignment of the spindle. The top of the ball may be filed off to line A A if desired.

All the above valves are such that have the springs inside the boiler. This is not very objectionable in small models ; but in larger plants it is desirable that the spring should be outside, and also that the blowing-off pressure may be adjusted to the correct working pressure while the boiler is in steam. The objections to the internal spring safety valve are obvious. The spring cannot be of steel or other corrosive material, and even the hardest brass or bronze spring wire is not so elastic as one made of steel.

Of course, there is another method of loading a safety valve. For stationary engines a weight is quite satisfactory, and a design for a " dead-weight " valve is shown in Fig. 418.

This valve is suitable for, say, a large model or small-power stationary boiler of the vertical or horizontal type. In this valve the weight of the valve and its load in pounds should exactly equal the working pressure in pounds per square inch, multiplied by the area of the valve orifice in square inches. The valve is designed for a $\frac{1}{4}$-in. orifice and at 50 lb. ; this requires a weight of about $2\frac{1}{2}$ lb. This the discs shown allow for ; but any lower pressure can be accommodated by removing one or more of the discs. Each one removed would represent a drop in the blowing-off pressure of about 4 lb. per square inch. The valve pillar may be screwed into a pad piece in the boiler, and be provided with a drip tray as shown. The latter is used in large dead-weight valves. The valve fits in a knife-edge seating, and the weights are supported on a piece of $\frac{3}{4}$-in. tube having the bottom disc screwed and soldered or brazed on the bottom. This disc forms a shelf for the remaining discs. The top of the tube has holes drilled in the side for the escape of steam, and a centre pivot cap screwed and soldered to it.

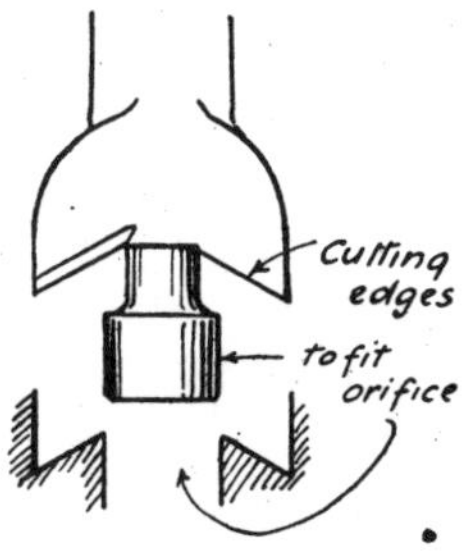

Fig. 420.—Cutter for making valve seating

When a safety valve is fitted with a valve of the wing type and loaded from above, care should be exercised in arranging the point of contact below the level of the seating. Fig. 419 indicates, to enlarged scale, how this may be done.

The valve is accurately countersunk as much as the metal will allow, and at a flatter angle than the centre pivot. When made like this the wings need not be so tightly fitted into the valve orifice. The valve will then be found to remain steam-tight, and at the same time work well and not stick.

Owing to the fact that the steam pressures are not usually reduced in proportion to the scale of the model, a weighted valve is usually fitted with a lever. The lever valve enables the model maker to provide an easy adjustment in the working pressure. With regard to the latter point, it goes without saying that no safety valve should be made in such a way that the user of the boiler can screw or weight it down so that the pressure at which it will blow off is above the safe limit for the particular boiler.

The lever valve is peculiarly susceptible to being tampered with. It is an easy matter to hang a weight on the lever. In the early days of steam engines, the overloading of safety valves by attendants and drivers caused many a disaster. For this reason "lock-up" valves are required by the legislature and insurance companies. In model work, of course, such restrictions are not met with; but all the same it is as well to fit valves which are pre-eminently safe.

The pressure at which a lever valve works is dependent on the distance of the weight from the fulcrum or joint of the lever. The enhanced value of the weight over a dead-weight valve is in direct proportion to the length between the weight and the joint and the centre point of the valve and the aforesaid joint.

If, as in diagram Fig. 421, the distances are 6 in. and $1\frac{1}{2}$ in. respectively, the weight is of $6 \div 1\frac{1}{2} = 4$ times its nominal value as a load on the valve. Of course, the weight and length of the lever add to the load on the valve, but this factor may in models be neglected. Fig. 422 shows the construction of a weighted lever valve. Even in this type it will be noted that it is important to apply the load in the centre of the valve and below the level of its seating, and, further, the lever should not be rigidly fixed to the valve. A pin, as shown, or a pivot pinned to the lever so that it can rock, should be used. The fulcrum pin should also be nicely fitted, and to protect this from damage the lever should work in a fork on the opposite side of the valve as shown in Fig. 422. Sometimes this is looped over the top of the lever, so that the lever can only lift a limited amount. The lever may be easily graduated with the pressures. The best way is to work out the gradations by arithmetic, and then to check such gradations with a pressure gauge—that is, if the latter is a reliable one.

The use of a ball in connection with a lever valve will involve some device which will allow the lever to roll over the ball. One idea is shown by Fig. 423. A flat-bottomed recess is made in the lever, and a cup-shaped pad loosely fitted into it. This will allow the ball and pad to take up a proper position without any tendency to shift the ball off its seating.

Another type of lever valve is the spring-loaded variety, often called Salter's spring-balance type (Fig. 424). It was largely used on the Great Western Railway and Midland Railway locomotives. On the former the spring was inside the driver's cab, and its casing had a scale which showed the pressure to which it was screwed down. In all such valves the screw threads should be so arranged that it is impossible to screw down the milled nut beyond a certain point. This will prevent anyone turning the nut so far that the spring is squeezed up into a solid mass and the valve rendered inoperative.

Among direct-loaded spring valves, the type shown by Fig. 425 is the most used. It is very suitable for stationary boilers, as it may be cased with a piece of tube, and the escaping steam conducted to the outside of the building as shown at A. The spring pillar is quite separate, and the cross-bar is tightened down with nuts. This compresses the spring, and transmits the load to the valve. As already mentioned, the point of contact between the spring pillar and the valve should be below the level of the seating of the latter.

An enclosed type of valve for model marine boilers is shown in Fig. 426. The cap or casing has a facing at the side, to which a flanged or screwed-in pipe is connected. This pipe leads up alongside of the funnel of the boat. To adjust the pressure, a screwed nipple with hexagonal head is fitted to the top of the casing. In both types of valves (Figs. 425 and 426) the spring pin may be made either by turning it out of the solid bar or by fitting on a collar to a piece of steel or bronze rod. The collar should be both screwed and soldered. In place of the exit for the steam at the side, the top of the casing may be pierced with several small holes after the fashion of a pepper box. These holes tend to muffle the noise of the exhaust. Such pepper-box valves are used on London and South Western Railway and North British Railway locomotives. The springs, however, are of a peculiar shape, ending in a pivot point both at the top and the bottom. No spring pin is therefore necessary.

The "Pop" Safety Valve.—A valve invented by the writer, and which gives a quite successful "pop" action without adding in any way to the mechanism of the valve, is shown by Fig. 427. The casing and spring arrangements may be of any convenient form, preferably the type with a direct-acting spring and a pepper-box muffle casing. A "pop" valve is one which lifts rapidly and to a considerable extent, and when the steam has been released, shuts just as rapidly at a pressure a few pounds below that at which it blew off. In the writer's valve this action is obtained by making the valve with a piston head loosely fitting a cylinder formed in the upper part of the seating. When the valve starts to blow off, the steam thereby encounters a larger area, and the load being the same, the pressure, of course, easily lifts the valve until the piston head clears the top of the cylinder as shown in the detail. A large amount of steam is released, and as the pressure rapidly falls the valve soon sits down again. The extent of the loss of pressure is regulated by the fit of the piston head in its cylinder, and the amount it has to lift to clear the top edge. The writer has made these valves down to $\frac{1}{4}$ in. diameter of orifice.

Model Blow-off and Try Cocks.—Model steam cocks are of innumerable types and shapes, and are used for the

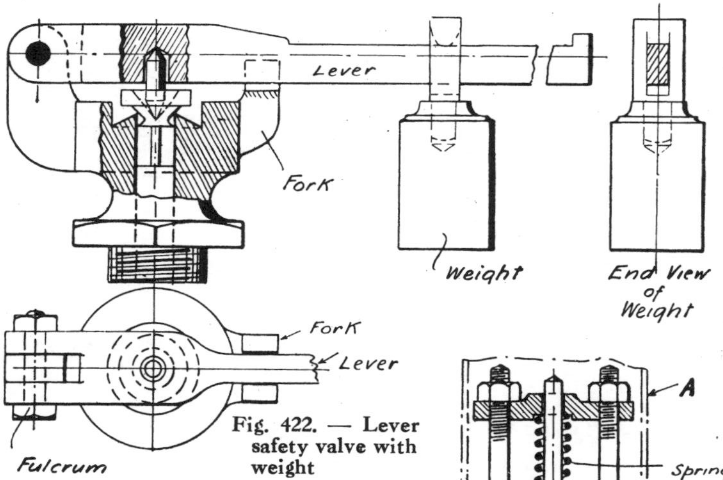

Fig. 422. — Lever safety valve with weight

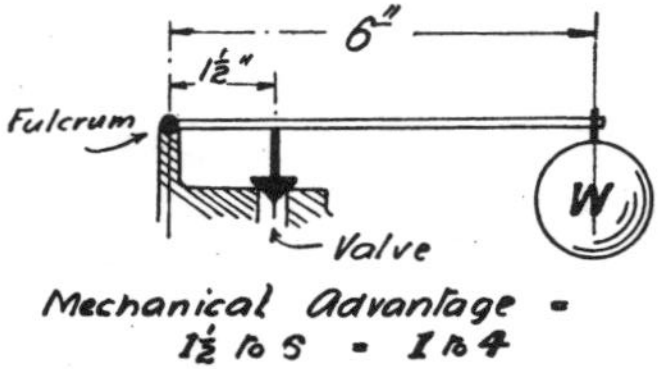

Fig. 421.—Calculating mechanical advantage of lever valve

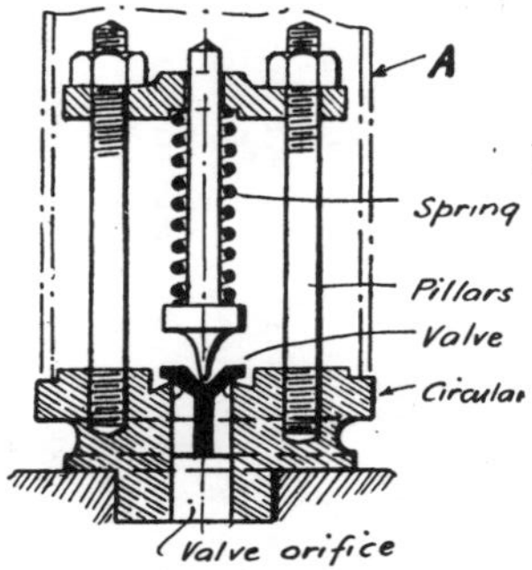

Fig. 425.—Direct spring-loaded safety valve

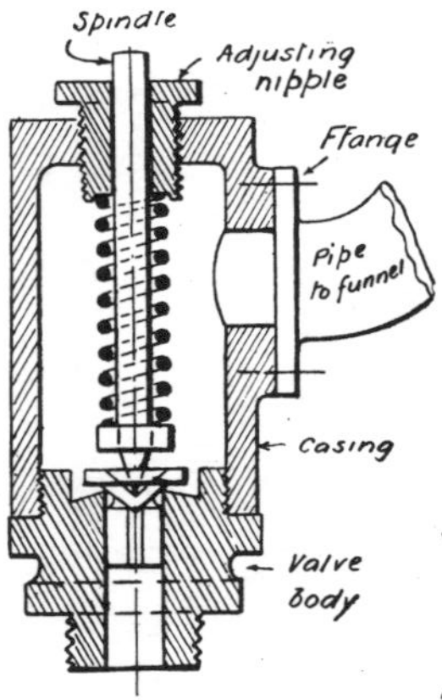

Fig. 426. — Marine - type safety valve

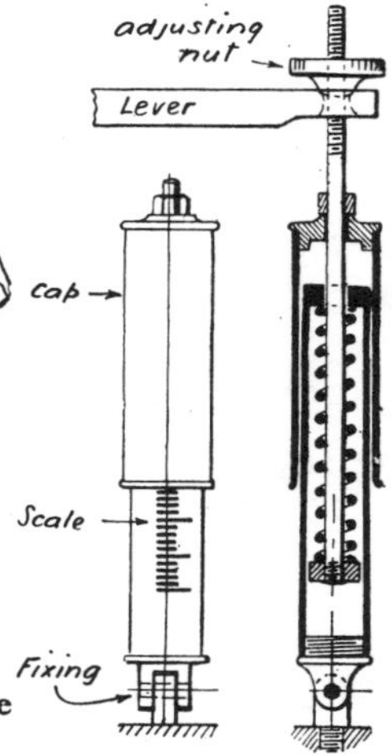

Fig. 424.—Spring balance for lever safety valve

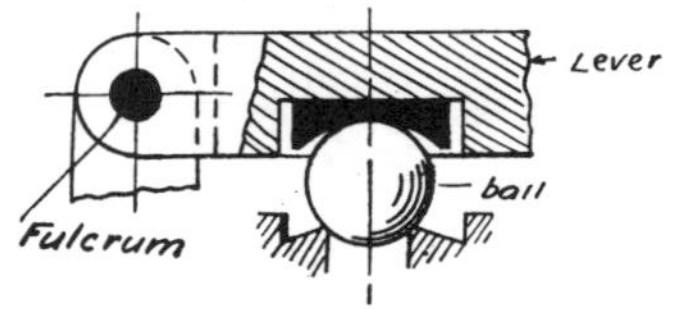

Fig. 423.—Lever safety valve with ball

following purposes: (1) Cylinder and steam-chest drains, (2) taps for tanks and other reservoirs, (3) blow-off and try cocks for boilers.

The most common pattern is the straight-nose cock shown by Fig. 428. In making plug cocks it is essential that the metals used for the body and plug should be of different kinds or qualities. If cast gunmetal is procured for the body of the cock, then drawn rod brass or bronze may be used for the plug. Bronze and best brass rod also work well together, these materials enabling the maker to employ them in the very convenient commercial "drawn" form, and to avoid the difficulties of chucking rough castings. Another point in which care must be exercised is that the diameter of the plug should be such that it will provide sufficient lap to ensure a complete stoppage of the gas or fluid when the plug is placed in the "shut-off" position. Fig. 429 shows an imperfectly proportioned plug, and Fig. 430 indicates about the correct diameter of plug for the given size of waterway.

The special tools for making are not numerous or difficult to make. Where the plugs are made from rod material on a hollow spindle lathe, then the headstock should be set over (this can be arranged in the 3½-in. Drummond lathe); or the compound slide-rest set to the required taper shown in Fig. 431. This position should be marked for further reference when making reamers for the plug holes. These reamers should be turned up out of silver steel rod, half of the section filed away as shown in Fig. 432, and then hardened. This form of reamer will be found to give a smooth hole, and if used by hand will be less likely to chatter and make an irregular hole than a 4- or 5-corner rimer.

To bend the handles of plugs, a socket to hold in the vice should be made as shown in Fig. 433, and the plugs bent with a wooden hammer, or with wood intervening between hammer and work, after turning the plug in the straight.

It is also essential that a square-hole washer should be used between the body of the cock and the nut, and a square neck should be formed on the plug just above the part tapped for the nut. The nut should be deep, so that there

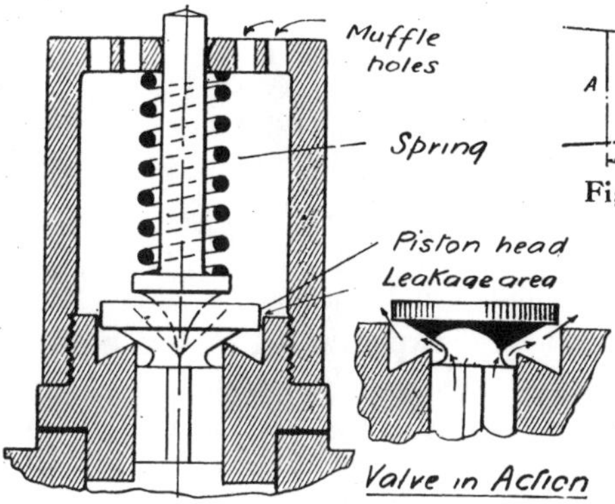

Fig. 427.—Greenly's "Pop" safety valve

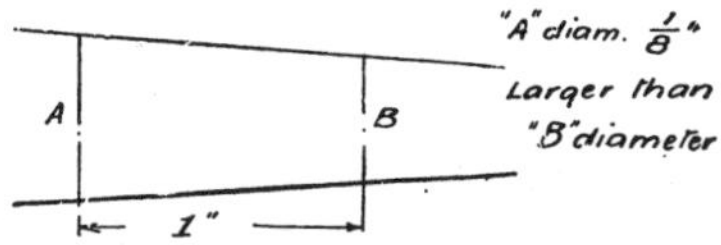

Fig. 431.—Taper for plug cocks

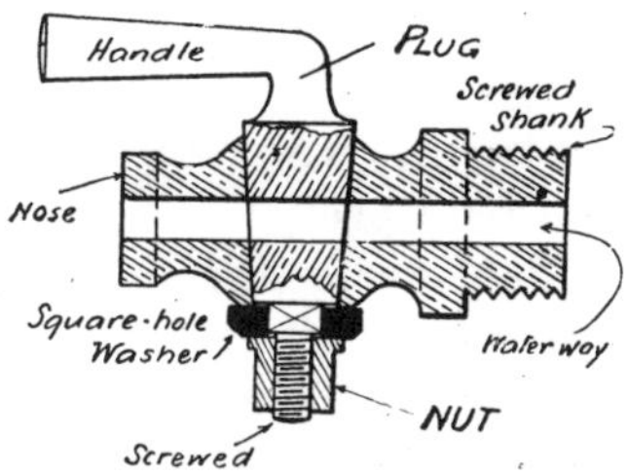

Fig. 428.—Straight-nose plug cock

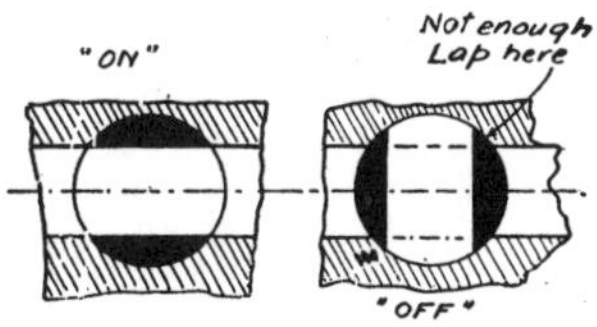

Fig. 429.—Plug too small for hole.

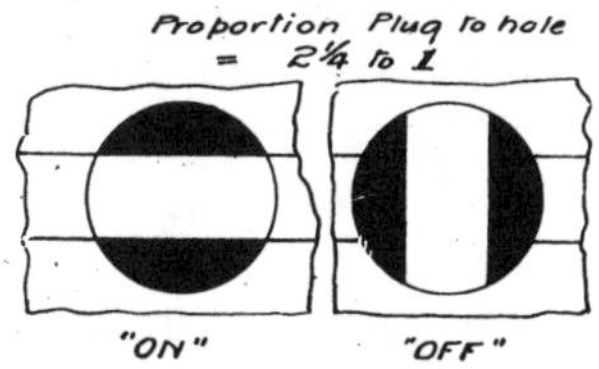

Fig. 430.—Plug correctly proportioned to hole

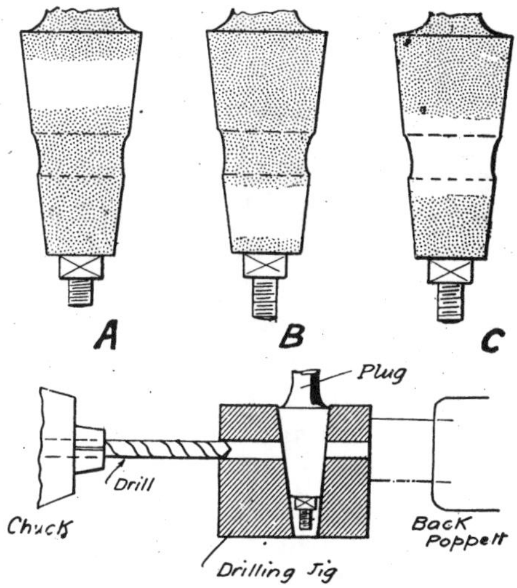

Fig. 434.—Drilling and grinding-in plugs

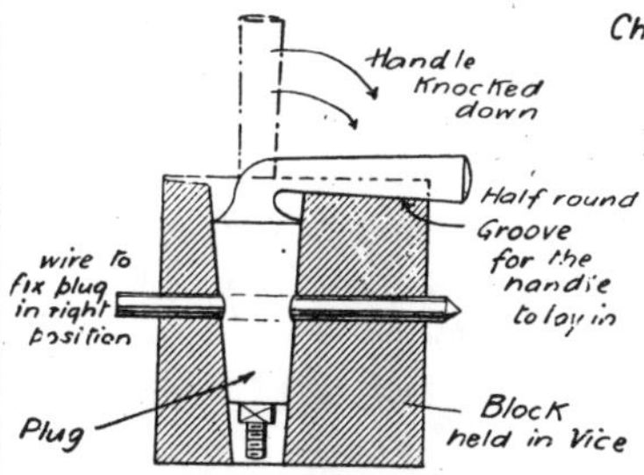

Fig. 433.—Jig for bending plug handle

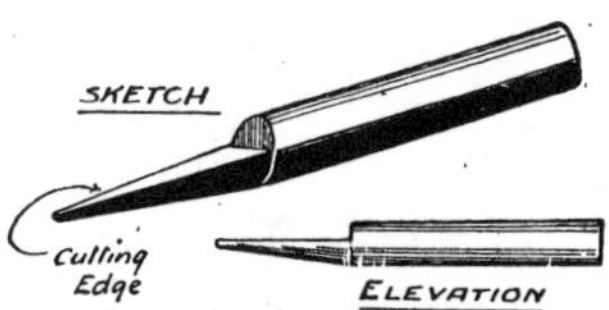

Fig. 432.—Reamer for conical hole in cock

is less risk of stripping the threads. The use of the square hole washer is to prevent the nut being screwed up or loosened when the plug is rotated one way or the other.

Where more than one cock is required, as it will be found difficult to turn up several plugs exactly the same dimensions in all respects, gauges with holes reamered out to exactly the same diameter and taper as the cock bodies may be prepared to test and mark out the position of the square neck, otherwise it may be found impossible to tighten up the plug. This gauge, which may be of steel, may also form the drilling jig for making the hole in the plug in the correct position. It is shown in use in Fig. 434. In bending the handle of the plug a similar cross drilling of the jig may be resorted to, so as to enable the handle to be bent exactly in line with the hole in the plug, a piece of wire being pushed into this hole during the operation of bending the handle (*see* Fig. 433).

Small bent-nose or "bib" cocks are made in the same way as straight-nose cocks, and after turning and drilling the nose is bent down in a jig. Larger cocks are cast with a bent nose, the hole being cored out in the casting. Sometimes cocks are made with loose handles; but for these and other external variations of the ordinary blow-off plug cock, readers can consult any model-makers' catalogue.

From time to time the plugs of cocks require re-grinding. The cock should be unscrewed from the boiler or tank. This should be done cautiously, grasping the cock with a pair of pliers with a piece of thick rag or paper between the jaws of the tool and the fitting, if necessary tapping the top of the plug with a piece of wood to loosen it.

Remove the nut and washer from the plug, and examine how the latter is taking its bearing in the conical hole in the body of the cock, giving it a few twists to make the bearing surfaces more distinct. At A (Fig. 434) the plug is bearing too hard at the top, and at the bottom in diagram B; in C it is bearing too much at the centre. The ideal state is when the cock bears equally hard at the top and the bottom and lightly over the hole.

When the cock has been much used, a ridge is sometimes

formed at the bottom of the hole (Fig. 435), thus spoiling the fit. The ridge may be removed by the rimer before referred to, or by an ordinary broach. Where the plug is found to be worn as shown in Fig. 436, a new one should be fitted, the hole being rimered out before the same is fitted, and a special drilling jig prepared. Of course, in such a case it may be found quicker to make a new cock entirely.

Any fine silicious substance may be used for grinding in the plugs after machining, and for re-grinding after service. It should be well washed and sifted. Brass-finishers employ a species of loamy clay. This is an ideal material for brass and other copper alloys. A piece about the size of a shilling is crushed to a powder and stirred in water, and the heavier particles allowed to settle. The rest is poured off, and the excess water in the remainder allowed to evaporate until a thick paste is formed.

The plug after being turned (and before the drilling) should be finished off carefully while in the lathe with a superfine file. When ready to be ground in, it should be tried in the hole and twisted round to show how it is bearing. Put a small quantity of the grinding substance on the bright portion (that is, where it is bearing hard), and grind with rapid half turns of the wrist, using water to keep the grinding material wet. If the shoulder at the bottom of the hole is formed as in Fig. 435, remove this as already described. Wipe the plug and the body clean, and then try for the bearing mark. If not perfect continue as before. Before screwing the plug up finally lubricate it with a mixture of tallow and very fine graphite. A "B B" black-lead pencil may be rubbed over the plug, and then coated with tallow. There is no need to screw up the plug too tight, as it will become tighter as it gets hot. The use of graphite will do much to prevent the "scoring" or "cutting" of the wearing surfaces, which in model fittings made of brass or similar alloys is always the trouble.

Plug cocks are often made with three or four ways. Fig. 438 shows various methods of arranging the passages in the plug to connect different pipe lines. In designing a three-way or four-way cock, care must be exercised to see that there is sufficient lap. It is also obvious that the plug must be much larger in proportion to the diameter of the passages than in the case of an ordinary two-way valve as illustrated in Fig. 430.

A type of "blow-off" or "try" cock which does not suffer from the defects of the plug cock is shown by Fig. 437. This the writer has for many years recommended for use on high-pressure model boilers. It is easily cleaned, and never leaks. Furthermore, such cocks are very easily made by the amateur, and can be provided with comparatively large passages.

Screw-down Stop Valves.—For many purposes plug cocks are quite unsuitable, more especially for petrol or paraffin and high-pressure and temperature steam, therefore model-makers must use some form of screw-down valve. The ordinary "needle" valve is made in two forms, and each is useful where the amount of fluid to be transmitted is not large or is impelled by a higher pressure than actually required. The ordinary straight-way valve—termed in many model catalogues a "globe" valve because of its globular body—is, of course, not a straight-way valve in the proper sense of the word. The passages are comparatively small, and have to be made during the machining operations, as they are too small to core out. Fig. 439 shows the necessity of this. The valve stem in the smallest valves is a plain conical-ended "needle." In the larger models (upwards of those for a $\frac{1}{4}$-in. pipe) they may have a valve shaped as shown at A. To preserve the packing from a continuous contact with the higher-pressure fluid or steam, the supply side is generally arranged to be that connected to the under-side of the valve, as indicated in the illustration. In fitting up model "globe" valves the fitting should therefore be carefully examined before connecting it to the pipes to see that this is so.

A form of angle valve is shown in Fig. 440. This is a very convenient fitting to attach to the side or the top of a tank, and although it would appear to offer a greater resistance to the flow of a fluid than the fitting shown in

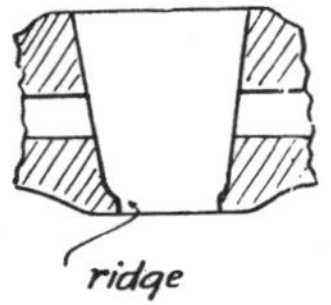

Fig. 435. — Imperfect hole in cock

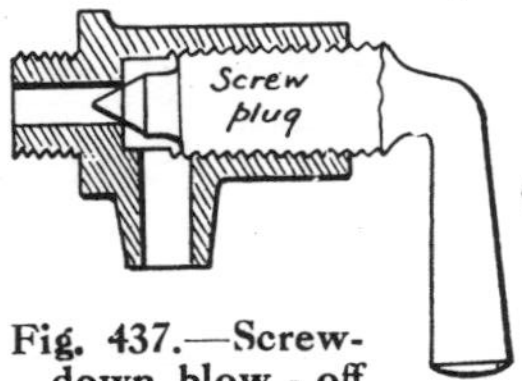

Fig. 437.—Screw-down blow - off cock

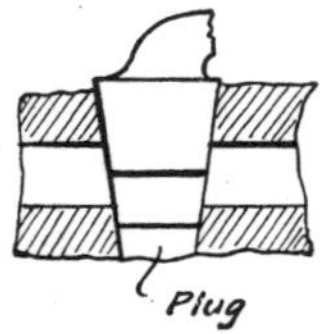

Fig. 436.—Badly-worn plug and hole

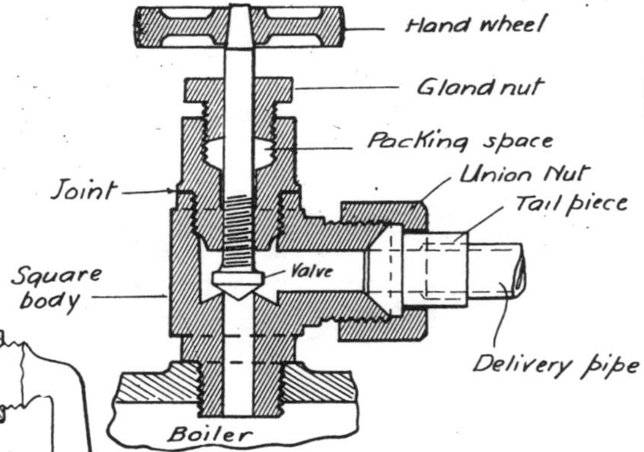

Fig. 440.—Angle screw-down stop valve

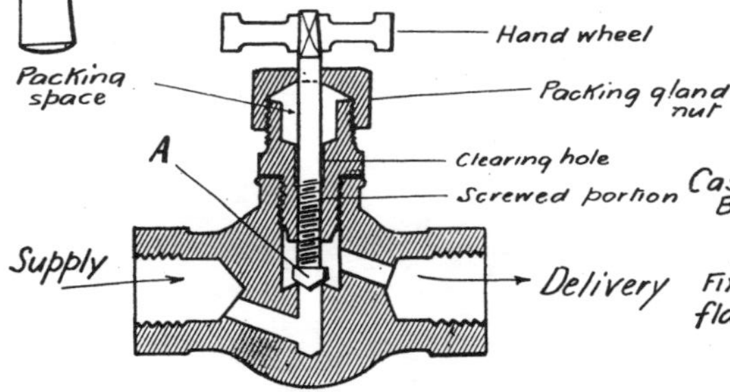

Fig. 439.—Screw-down "straight-way" or globe valve

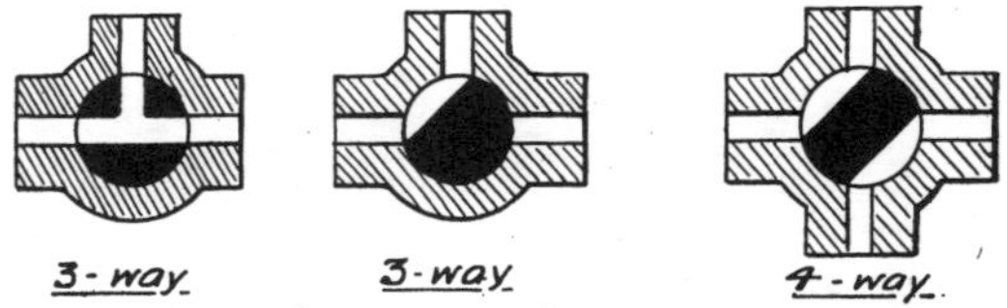

Fig. 438. — Diagrams of three multiple-way plug cocks

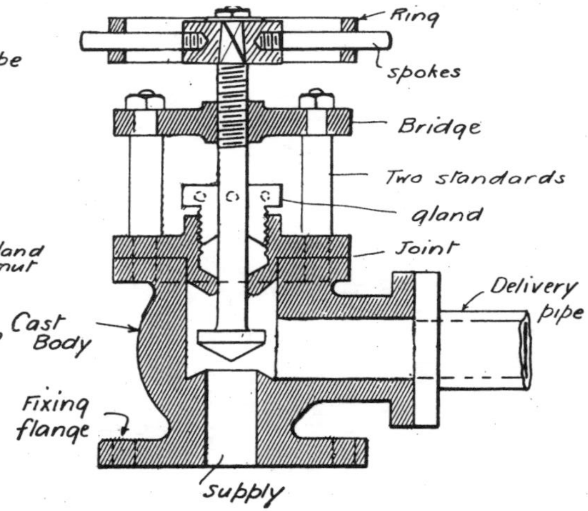

Fig. 441.—Flanged angle stop valve with bridge

Fig. 439, its passages are less tortuous. Furthermore, they are much easier to drill out. The supply side need not be fitted with a union, as the valve can be screwed directly into the tank or boiler as shown. The valve body may be made from a casting, and to facilitate the machining it should be provided with a tenon or spigot piece as shown in Fig. 442, so that the union connection branch may be turned up and threaded. This tenon may be afterwards removed, the fitting being reversed and placed in a screw chuck to cut and clean off this face.

Another point to notice in the design of the valve is that the lift need not exceed one-quarter of the diameter of the orifice of the valve. When this elevation of the plunger is obtained, the valve is fully open. Therefore, with an eye to this fact, the screwed portion should be so set out that it does not work up into the packing space. A further item to be noted is that on the accuracy of the machining the tightness of the valve will depend, the actual valve being solid with the stem, and not loose as in full-size work.

For larger marine and stationary models, the outside screw may be adopted. This arrangement of stop valve is shown in Fig. 441. As will be seen, it is more ornate, and therefore suitable to a fine-scale model. Flange connections are used. For working models these are only recommended for pipes, etc., over $\frac{5}{16}$ in. in diameter. In smaller sizes they are apt to be both weak and clumsy in appearance. For marine work the valve is sometimes inverted, and the spindle extended down to what would be the starting platform of the engine. In that case the bridge which engages the screwed part of the spindle may be placed down near to the handle, bracketed from any convenient part of the framing of the engine (*see* Fig. 443).

In the valve (Fig. 439) the gland nut is outside; but in the example (Fig. 440) it fits inside the stuffing box. The advantage of the former is that some head room can be saved, otherwise the writer prefers the inside gland. Hand wheels are best fitted on squared stems. The latter may be slightly taper, and the wheel secured by being fitted tightly and driven on. Otherwise a nut may be used

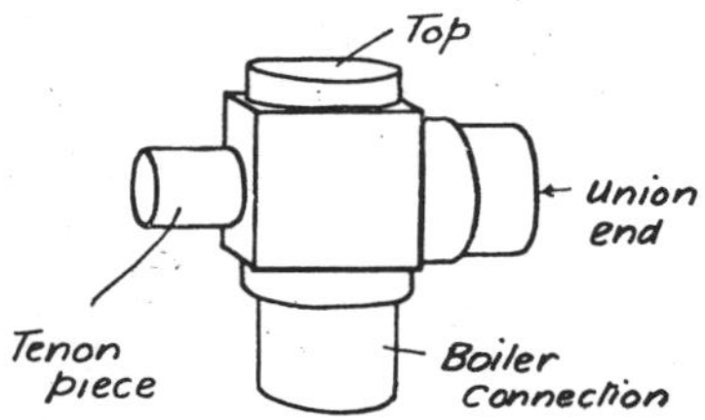

Fig. 442.—Pattern for body of angle valve

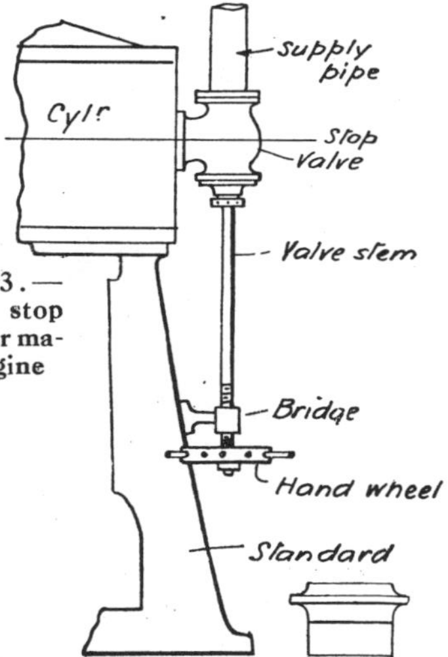

Fig 443

Fig. 443.—Flange stop valve for marine engine

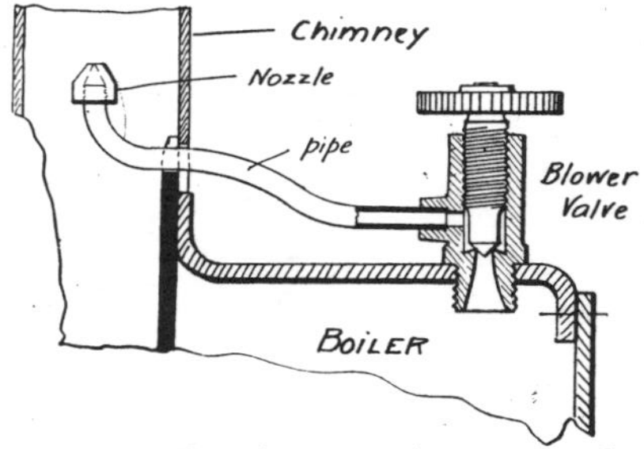

Fig. 445.—Simple screw-down valve for blower of vertical boiler

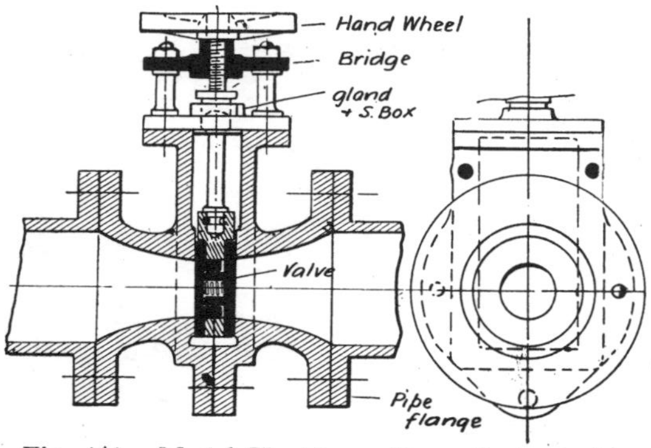

Fig. 444.—Model Hopkinson-Ferranti stop valve

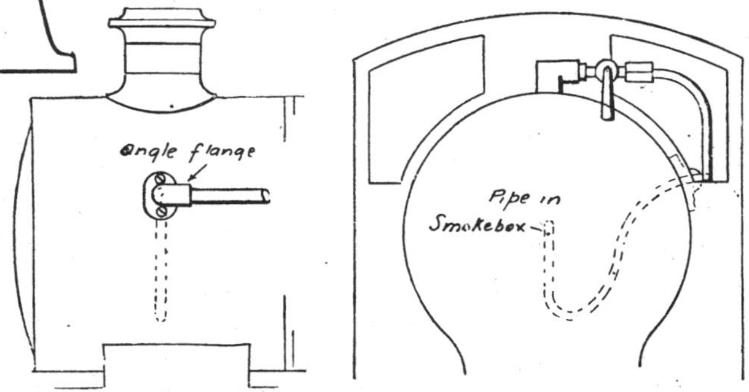

Fig. 445A.—Steam blower pipe in locomotive smokebox

to fasten it in place. To make the square hole in the wheel, first bore a suitable round hole, and with a serrated square drift, or series of drifts, the hole may be cut to fit the square stem. The combined cap and stuffing box in the valve (Fig. 441) is fitted with four or more screws.

The sluice or gate type of valve suitable to modelling is the "Hopkinson-Ferranti" valve (Fig. 444). Compared with the size of the pipe, a small valve only is required, the converging nozzles preventing to a large degree any waste of energy in the throttling of the steam through so comparatively small an orifice. The body of the valve must be made in two halves to enable the seatings of the valve to be faced. The valves have telescopic spigots, and are pressed against the faces by a strong spiral spring. The two valves are carried in a cradle to which is attached the spindle by a swivelling joint. The hand wheel may, if desired, form the nut, in which case the spindle may be solid with the valve cradle. This type of stop valve should, of course, be either fully opened or closed.

Threads for Model Fittings.—In making all brass engine and boiler fittings it is best to adopt a fairly fine series of threads. Coarse threads mean coarse, clumsy, and large fittings for the size of the passages in them. The writer recommends the following standards: $\frac{1}{4}$-in. diameter and below, 40 threads per inch; above $\frac{1}{4}$-in. to and including $\frac{5}{16}$-in. diameter, 32 threads per inch; above $\frac{5}{16}$-in. diameter, 26 threads per inch.

Steam Blowers.—Simple stop valves are sometimes required for blowers of model steam engines. For this purpose the work that a gland and stuffing box entail may be saved by adopting the simple form of screw-down valve shown by Fig. 445. The body of the valve is practically the same as that of the blow-off valve shown in Fig. 437, except that the screwed portion of the valve stem should be made a little longer to prevent leakage. A wheel with a knurled edge may be used in place of the plain handle as shown.

A common fault in making a steam blower is, it may be here mentioned, that too large a nozzle is employed. This leads to waste of steam. Another fault is that it is often not placed low enough in the smokebox or chimney, and owing to the jet not filling the chimney, the efficiency of the blower is lessened. A jet only $\frac{1}{32}$ in. in diameter will in a funnel of $\frac{7}{8}$-in. inside diameter produce quite a good draught. The pipe leading to the blower

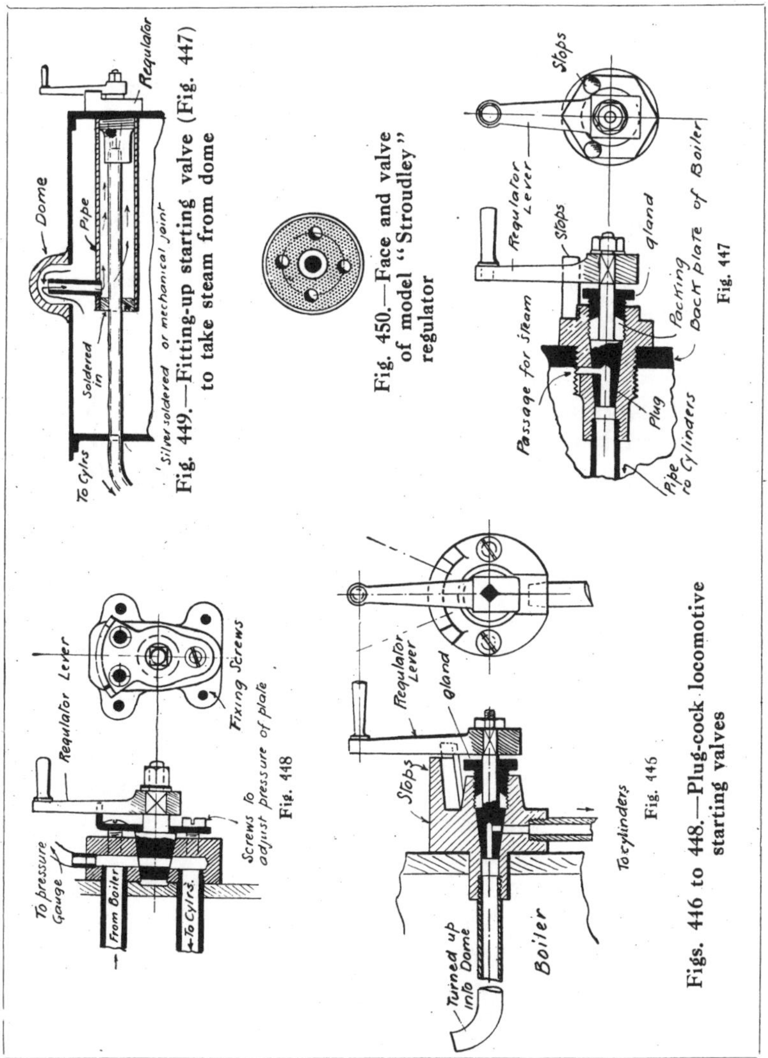

Fig. 449.—Fitting-up starting valve (Fig. 447) to take steam from dome

Fig. 450.—Face and valve of model "Stroudley" regulator

Figs. 446 to 448.—Plug-cock locomotive starting valves

should, however, be of ample dimensions, otherwise it is always likely to become blocked up. The nozzle may be screwed on to the end of the pipe, and then if the fine hole in it becomes choked by a particle of foreign matter it can be readily removed.

In a locomotive the blower is placed in the smokebox, and as chimneys are now short the jet should be placed sufficiently low down. The valve or cock is arranged in the driver's cab, the pipe being carried forward to the smokebox either inside or outside the boiler. Fig. 445A shows the latter method.

Steam Regulation in Engines.—The regulation of the steam supply in model locomotives and other steam engines may be of three kinds: (1) Plug-cock type; (2) slide-valve type; (3) rotating-valve type. Piston valves and poppet valves have been tried, but the first named are difficult to make steam tight, and the poppet valve has to rely on the tightness of the packing of the spindle.

The plug cock is by far the most used for small locomotives and engines, and may be of various designs, according to the requirements. In the model G.C.R. locomotive shown on pp. 398 to 400, the regulator may take the form of a simple angle cock screwed into the back plate of the boiler, with an internal pipe leading to the top of the middle part of the boiler barrel.

Fig. 446 shows an improvement of this idea, and provides a lever working in the orthodox way. The plug cock has also a packing gland which will prevent any leakage to the outer air. The body of the regulator may be screwed into the boiler, or it may be secured with two brass screws as shown. The handle should be made of German silver. This looks more like steel than brass, and has the advantage that it will not rust.

Regulators of this kind are sometimes made with an outlet extra pipe to serve a blower. A hole is made in the plug to communicate with this pipe so that there are three positions of the handle: (1) Central or shut-off position; (2) to the right, the steam being turned full on to the cylinders; (3) to the left, which allows boiler steam to flow to the blower. The steam pipe in the fitting (Fig. 446) is arranged to pass through the back plate of the firebox, as in the G.C.R. " Sir Sam Fay " model, through the fire to the cylinders. It is therefore only suited to outside-fired engines, and to those fitted with the water-tube boiler.

The kind of regulator cock usually fitted to small model locomotives having the locomotive-type boiler is shown by Fig. 447. The disadvantage it has is that the steam is

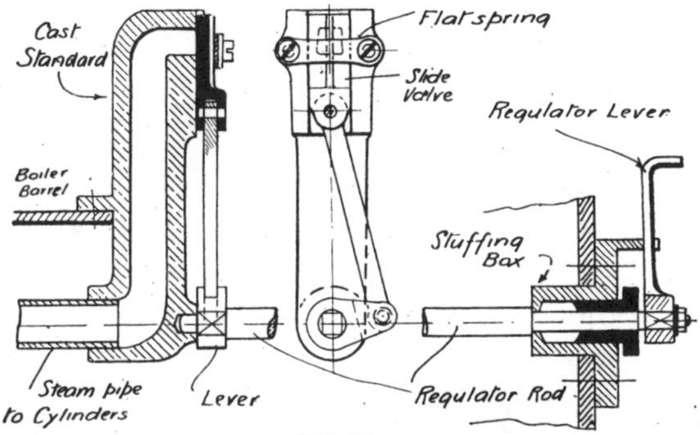

Fig. 452

Fig. 452. — Model slide-valve locomotive regulator

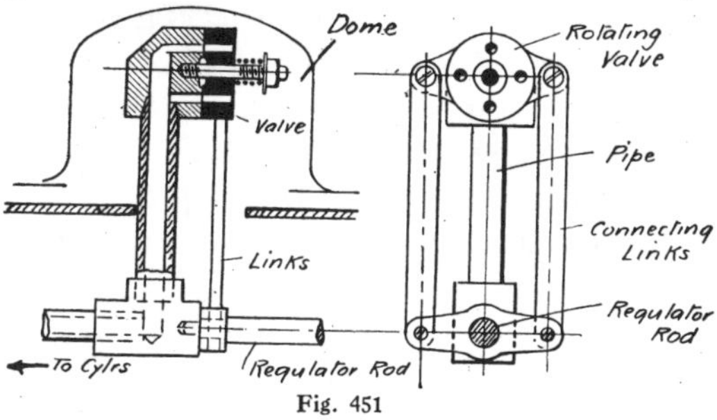

Fig. 451

Fig. 451. — Model " Stroudley " locomotive regulator

taken from the back end of the boiler, and when the locomotive starts in a forward direction, the water surges up against the inlet holes and causes priming. This regulator is the commercially made modification of that illustrated in Fig. 448. In the latter the steam may be taken from the dome. The plug is kept tight by a plate screwed to the body of the regulator with three screws. This plate also forms the stops for the handle.

Where it is deemed essential that the steam shall be taken

from the dome, or, at least, from the centre of the boiler barrel, the regulator illustrated in Fig. 447 may be fitted up as shown in Fig. 449. The encasing pipe conducts the steam from the upright pipe in the dome to the small hole in the top of the regulator.

The slide-valve regulator is shown by Fig. 452. This may be made with a cast and cored standard, or built up as shown in Fig. 451. The slide valve should be retained in its position by a flat spring in small engines, all parts, including this spring and the screws, being made of brass or gunmetal or other non-corrosive material.

The rotating type of starting valve—known as the "Stroudley" regulator—is good for models. Care must, however, be exercised to see that the centre of the valve is recessed so that it does not bear on the seating in the centre. It is better to recess both the valve and the seating. Four holes may be drilled for the ports, sufficient lap being provided in both valve and seating when the valve is shut off. The valve should be ground in, and if possible the valve should be of a different alloy to the seating, the valve being the softer of the two. This will lessen cutting up of the ground surfaces when the engine is in service.

The portion of the face and the valve which should bear is shown shaded in Fig. 450. As shown in Fig. 451, this regulator may be easily built up out of tube and raw material. The regulator rod should be squared into the handle and the lever at each end respectively, and, further, the rod should be stout enough not to twist when the valves offer any resistance to turning due to the pressure of steam on it. A short spiral spring should be used to keep the valve to its face when there is little or no steam in the boiler.

CHAPTER XI

Force Pumps, Injectors, and Gauges

Check Valves.—The ordinary model check valve used on pump feed pipes and injector deliveries (**Fig. 453**) has a square or hexagonal body, and screws into the boiler by a right-angle connection. The valve is usually a ball, and the valve chamber is bored out, the casting for the valve being quite solid before it is machined. The top is capped by a screw plug, which enables the ball to be changed and the seating cleaned when there is no steam in the boiler. A tenon piece (**Fig. 454**) should be cast on to the valve body to enable the screwed spigot which enters the boiler to be turned, bored, and threaded. It may then be reversed and inserted in a screw chuck, and the tenon piece cut off.

The best possible seating for a check valve is shown at **Fig. 455**. This allows any sediment to fall off the seat, whereas in the ordinary valve (**Fig. 456**) the seating is liable to become coated, and the valve will not remain tight. A tool for cutting the seating is shown on p. **205**.

To enable the check valve to be examined while there is steam in the boiler, a cock is often placed behind the valve as shown in **Fig. 457**. The hole in the plug of the cock is arranged so that when the handle is straight down as illustrated, the passage is open to the boiler. This is perhaps the most convenient method, but there are obvious drawbacks. To make a neat fitting, the hole in the cock is necessarily small, even if the usual proportions of hole to plug are exceeded, as they may be in the case of a check valve where the cock is only required occasionally. Moreover, it is not always advisable to have a cock in a delivery pipe which is fed from a pump which is geared from the engine crankshaft. If the engine should be moved while the cock is shut, there is danger of the pump bursting the feed pipe. On the other hand, should the check valve be fitted to an injector feed, then a further means of cutting off the latter from the boiler will be found very advantageous.

Check valves often leak, and the small injector especially is peculiarly liable to temporary failure if it gets hot. A screw-down valve, independent of the check valve itself, is therefore advisable. The design (Fig. 458) is the best the writer has tried in small sizes, and provides, in addition

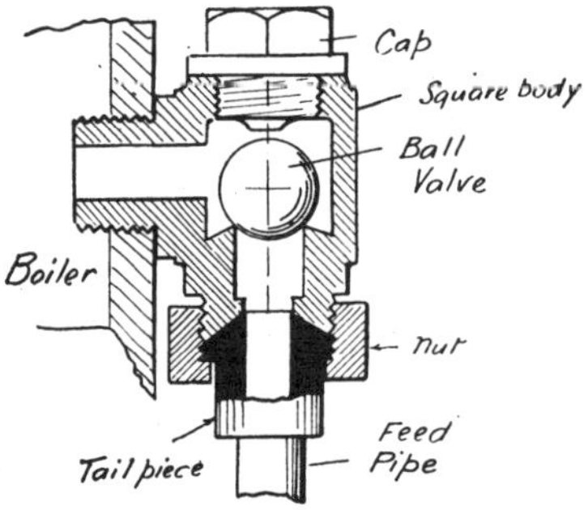

Fig. 453.—Simple ball check valve

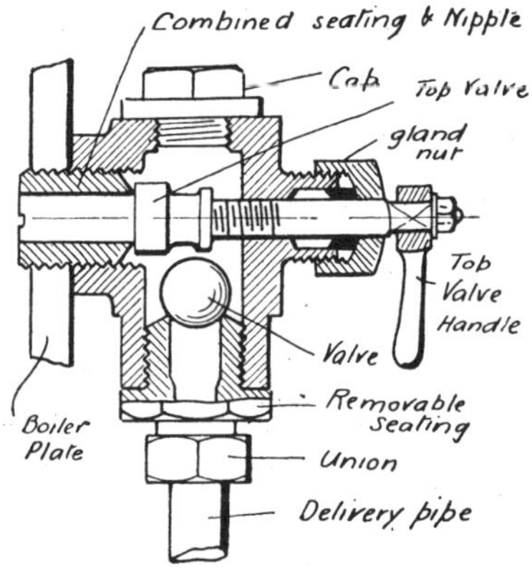

Fig. 458.—Check valve with screw-down shut-off cock

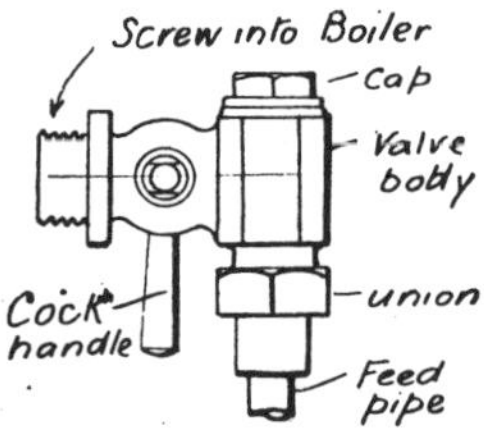

Fig. 457.—Check valve with cock

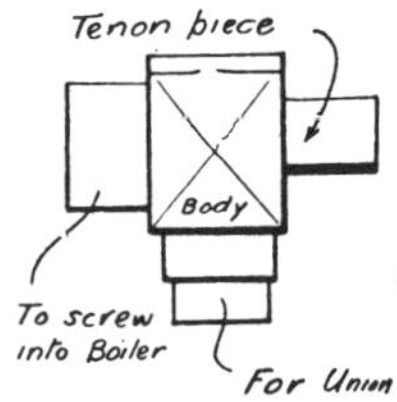

Fig. 454.—Pattern for check valve

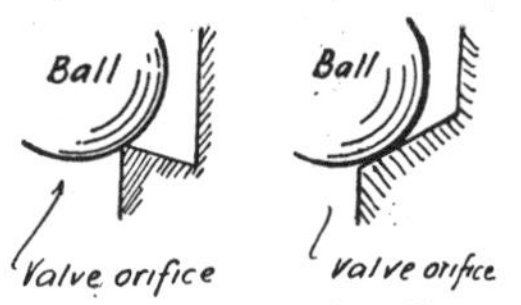

Figs. 455 and 456.—Check valve seatings

to the shutting off of the valve from the boiler above the check valve, for the removal of the valve seating while the boiler is under steam. The fitting is, of course, large; but on a *working* model appearances must be sacrificed to reliability in action. A wing valve may be used where the orifice is over $\frac{3}{8}$ in. in diameter. Otherwise a bronze ball, which is a commercial article, is more satisfactory, as it is less liable to stick.

Water Gauges.—Water gauges are very popular model fittings, and also in small sizes cause much disappointment. Where the glass measures less than $\frac{3}{16}$ in. outside diameter, capillary action often resists the force of gravity and prevents a correct reading of the water level in the boiler. As most readers are aware, the functions of the water gauge depend on gravity or on the fact "that water will always find its own level." The pressure of steam does not enter into the calculations at all, as will be seen by Fig. 459. The pressures on the top and bottom of the column of water in the gauge glass are equal, and therefore, as in the boiler, only gravity has to be considered. The level of the water in the glass, except for the phenomenon of capillary action in very small tubes, and in the boiler will be the same.

Figs. 460 and 461 show two common forms of model water gauges fitted to cheap German-made model steam engines. The first is very simple; but the glass is very liable to be broken, both in use and in fitting it to the boiler. It also projects considerably, and if the new glass is not exactly in line with the nipples in the boiler, then it may break in getting it in place. The other kind (Fig. 461) must have a special recess in the boiler back to receive it. In both cases rubber is used to make a steam-tight joint.

A model water gauge of more characteristic design is shown in Fig. 462. It can be made on an amateur's lathe out of hexagonal brass rod, the nipples into the boiler being silver-soldered on to the hexagon rod. The chief care of the maker of the gauge should be to get these square, and the portion which bears up against the boiler both exactly the same distance, in the top and bottom fittings, from the centre line of the glass; otherwise there will be difficulty when it comes to fit the glass. The top fitting is open, and has a cap, and the glass can be inserted through this orifice.

In the other type (Fig. 463) three cocks are fitted. Those behind the fittings, next the boiler, are used to shut the gauge should a glass break. The bottom tap is employed to clear the glass of mud or other obstructions. Steam travelling faster than water at the same pressure, the glass is cleared from the top, and when the cock is shut again the water should rise to the proper level. This to some extent tests the accuracy of the reading of the water level. Clearing plugs are sometimes fitted. These are useful additions, and the screwed holes in which they fit may be employed during the machining of the castings for purposes of chucking. The writer has also used them to attach a sheet-metal guard of the form shown by Fig. 464. A small glass can do almost as much personal damage as a large one should it burst, and therefore a guard is always to be recommended. The glands are of the outside type, and the glass is inserted from the top. The best packing for a water gauge is a small ring made by cutting slices off the end of a suitable piece of thick rubber tube.

Pumps.—One of the simplest forms of hand-force pump for boiler feeding is shown in Fig. 465. As the direct pressure of the hand is limited the area of the plunger cannot be large. At 60 lb. steam pressure without reckoning frictional resistances, the knob will require over 7 lb. to move it. One feature of the design is the means provided for preventing the plunger, which is packed by a gland, from being accidentally withdrawn. The plunger is flanged at the bottom, and this restricts the upward stroke. The knob is screwed on after the plunger is in place. The screw S is a stop for the suction valve, and it will be noticed that the valves are of large diameter and have a small lift. This is an important point in all small pump work, and its non-observance explains the reason why so many model pumps fail. The delivery valve has a $\frac{1}{16}$-in. raised rib across the top to prevent its blocking up the passage to the union when it rises.

The pump is intended to screw down in a tank or in a locomotive tender. As it is what is called a "drowned" pump, a slot must be filed or milled along the bottom of the body to allow the water to pass to the suction valve. With regard to the stroke of the plunger, the maximum movement at A should be less than distance A A. The gland nut should be threaded only so far as to allow of this being

Fig. 459.—Action of water gauge

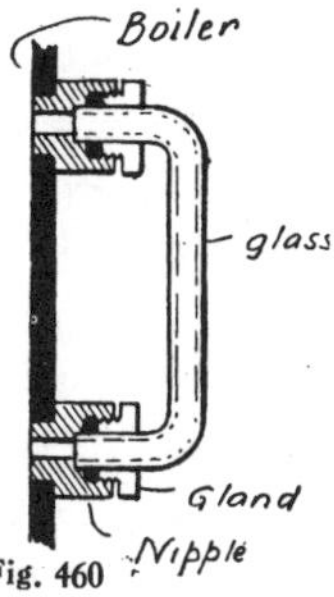

Fig. 460.—Bent-glass water gauge

Fig. 460

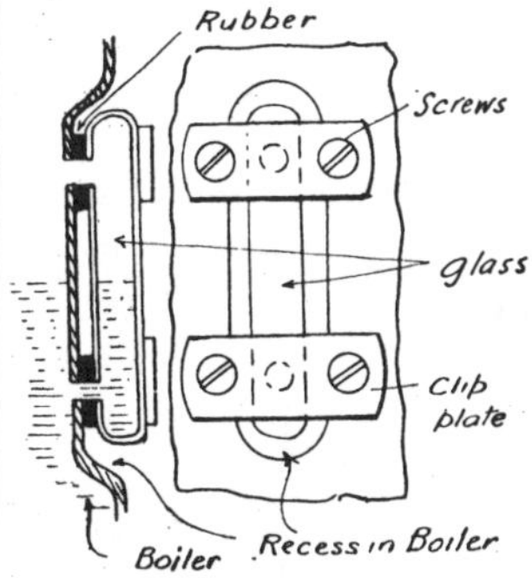

Fig. 461.—Clip-on water gauge

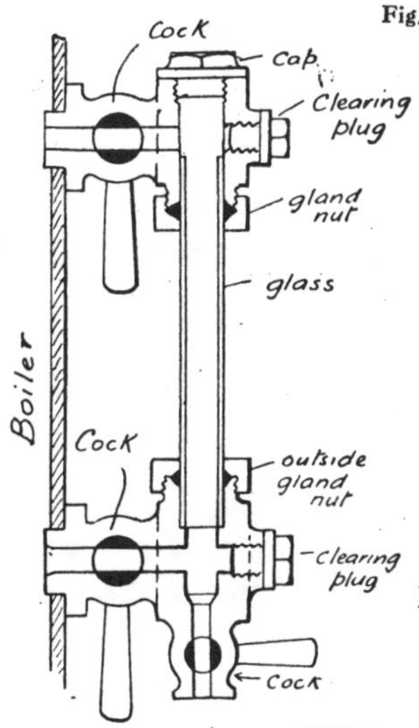

Fig. 463.—Three-cock water gauge

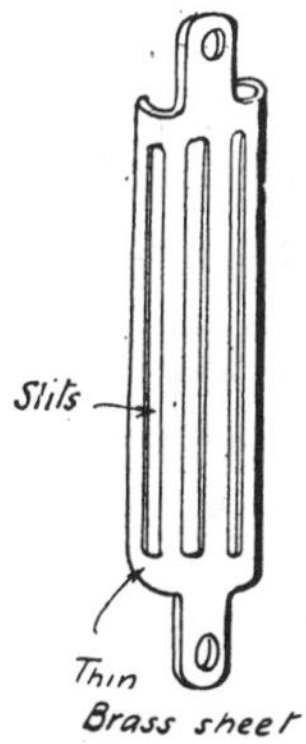

Fig. 464.—Sheet-metal guard for water gauge

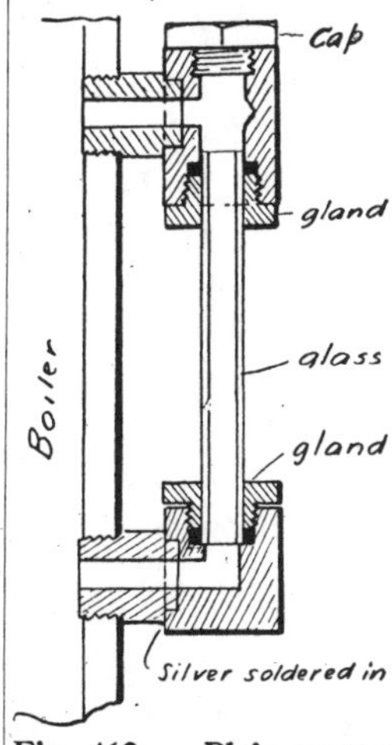

Fig. 462. — Plain water gauge without cocks

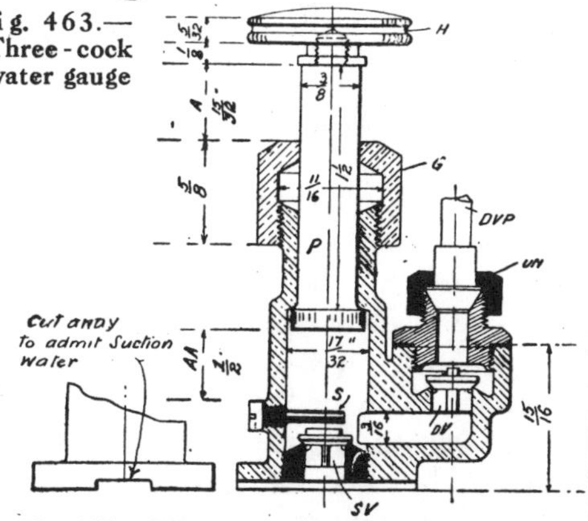

Fig. 465.—Hand force pump for boiler feeding

the case when it is screwed right down. In calculating the displacement of the pump, the enlarged diameter of the flanged end must not be considered; the actual capacity of the pump is measured by taking the area of the $\frac{3}{8}$-in. portion of plunger by the stroke. With thirty strokes per minute the capacity of the pump (allowing for a certain amount of inefficiency) is about $1\frac{1}{4}$ cub. in. per minute, that is, enough for a boiler with 100 sq. in. of heating surface.

With small steam engines it is often required to drive the pump from the engine shaft. This can be done where the speeds are less than, say, 350 revolutions per minute. In any pump which is to be run at speeds approaching the above figure the valves should be almost as large in diameter as the plunger, and where the above speed is exceeded a geared pump (Fig. 468) will be found essential. A fairly heavy flywheel on the engine is then desirable to take up the load of the pump as it comes every two or three revolutions of the engine shaft. A simple shaft-driven pump, which can be made out of rod material with not more than two castings, is shown by Fig. 466. Simple patterns may be first made for the valve chamber and for the top cap. The pump barrel is of brass tube screwed with a fine thread into the boss on the valve chamber. The plunger is of the trunk type, and is made of a piece of thick tube, turned, if necessary, to slide inside the tube forming the pump barrel. This tube is plugged at the end with a forked piece of brass rod (*see* the details, Fig. 467), and packed with a cup leather. The cup leather is secured by a specially made shouldered brass screwed into the plug. The suction-pipe flange and valve seating is in one piece, and screws into the large vertical tapped hole in the valve chamber. The delivery-valve seating is, however, screwed in first and soldered. The delivery-chamber cap may be secured with four screws, and provides for fixing an air vessel, also built up from brass tube and rod. The air vessel steadies the flow of the delivery. With a plain eccentric driven pump it is also difficult to get sufficient travel for the plunger and ensure success; the valve lift must be restricted to about one-eighth of the diameter of the valve orifice. The system of gears is shown in Fig. 468.

For a larger model the detail of the pump may be

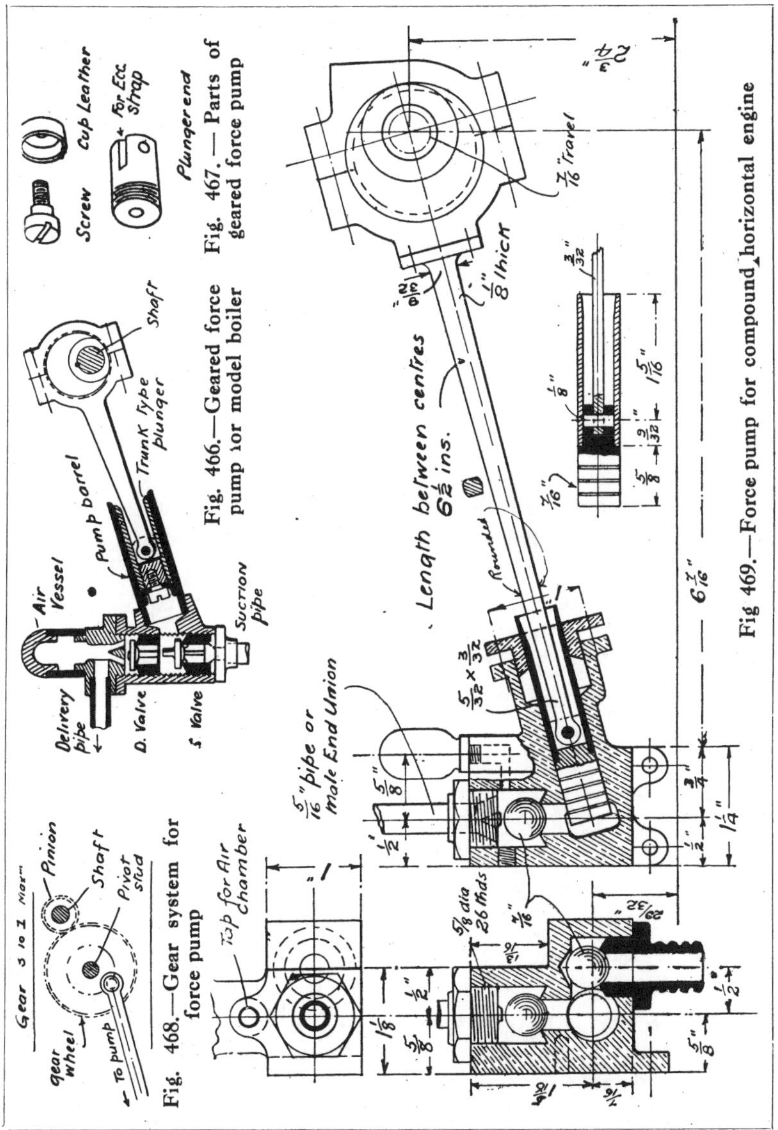

Fig. 466.—Geared force pump for model boiler

Fig. 467.—Parts of geared force pump

Fig. 468.—Gear system for force pump

Fig 469.—Force pump for compound horizontal engine

improved, Fig. 469 showing a pump used for a compound horizontal engine with a $1\frac{1}{4}$-in. by 2-in. H.P. cylinder. The trunk plunger can in this case be packed by the usual gland. The body of the pump is cast solid, and all the passages are drilled and pin-bitted in them. The cap of the delivery valve provides for inserting the ball valve, while the suction valve seat is removable and may be arranged for a rubber connection as shown, or for an ordinary metal pipe union. The air vessel is relatively small, and the plunger is arranged to displace as much of the space between the valves as is possible. The latter is an important feature, especially in a pump which has to lift as well as force. If the space between the valves and plunger is very large, then the pump will not start well, as a less perfect vacuum will be formed on the suction stroke. Ball valves are used in the pump, and comparatively little lift is given to them. The passages (three in number) in the delivery valve chamber cap are arranged so that the valve cannot close or restrict them.

Hand pumps intended to force larger volumes of water and higher pressures demand a lever action, and a home-made force pump embodying this arrangement is illustrated by Figs. 470 and 471. The valves are large and are superposed in a chamber turned out of brass rod. The plunger is long and has packing grooves and double cup leathers, and although the particular pump was arranged outside the supply tank, it had no lifting to perform, as it was placed below the level of the water. Used in this way or as a drowned pump, the design is an excellent one. The hand lever is detachable, and can be made any length according to the working pressure of the boiler to which the pump is attached.

Injectors.—Injectors are very convenient for feeding boilers where the feed water is clean and cold. They work by virtue of the fact that the speed of steam issuing from a hole at a given pressure is much higher than that of water at the same pressure, the ratio being as about 20 to 1. In an injector the feed water is made to meet a jet of steam, and the latter gives the feed water some of its high velocity, and forces it against water at same initial pressure. The steam condenses on meeting the feed water.

In an injector it is essential (1) that the areas of the various nozzles should be correctly proportioned, accord-

Figs. 470 and 471.—Home-made lever-action force pump

Fig. 470

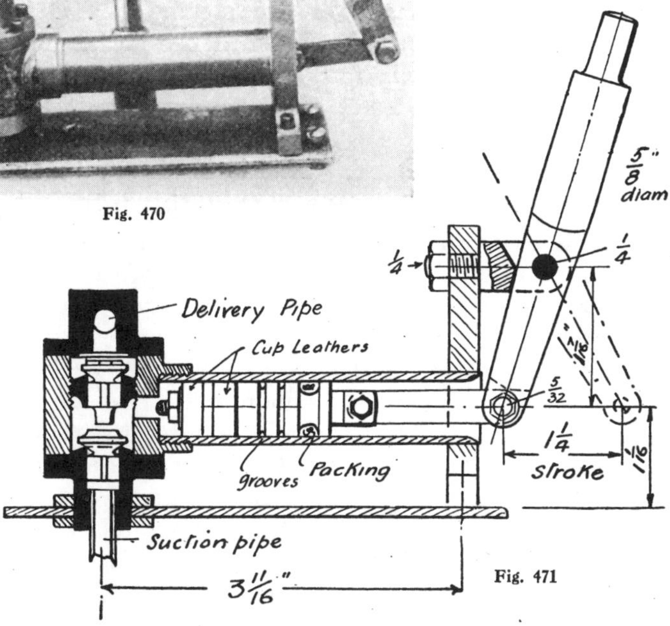

Fig. 471

ing to the boiler pressure; (2) that all pipes and passages should offer the least possible resistance to the flow of the steam and water; (3) that the feed water should be cold and condense the live steam; (4) that any pressure forming in the apparatus is immediately released by suitable overflow passages; (5) that the steam supply should be dry, and that the feed water should be delivered below water level. Sharp angle bends in the pipes are therefore to be avoided, and all pipes and passages in fittings should be large. There are one or two model injectors on the market, and full instructions as to fitting up are sent out with them. Care should be taken to fit all pipes quite soundly, especially with the suction pipe (from water tank), as the slightest air-leak will cause failure. Fig. 472 shows a model injector of the the automatic type (not requiring any adjustment in working except by curtailing or opening out the steam and water supply). This is the smallest one that can be recommended as satisfactory, and the workmanship must be perfect. The shape of the steam cone is important. It is important that it expands in the steam nozzle. The "combining" cone is fairly long and converges. This is because the steam takes time to condense and the final volume is smaller. In the combining tube an overflow passage must be formed. This is necessary to allow fluids (steam or water) to escape should there be any pressure in the mixing cone. When the injector is working properly there is a vacuum here, and the auto-valve which governs the first overflow is drawn down tightly on its seat. The auto-valve gives perfect starting and restarting should the injector "knock off." The second overflow consists of three holes drilled into the valve chamber. The steam nozzle is adjusted to the correct pressure by screwing in or out, a screwdriver slot being provided in it. The delivery cone may also require some adjustment and is similarly provided. It will be noted that the smaller diameter is slightly smaller than the end of the combining nozzle.

An injector with non-adjustable cones has a limited range of action, and to get the best results with a varying pressure more steam should be supplied as the pressure drops. The water may be partly cut off at the commencement. Fig. 473 shows the arrangement of the pipes. It is better to place a model injector below the feed tank level, as it can then be readily cooled by turning on the water before the steam.

Pressure Gauges.—Most model gauges which are obtainable down to $\frac{3}{4}$ in. diameter and at various pressures are made on the "Bourdon" bent oval tube principle, as shown in Fig. 474. The steam pressure inside the tube tends to straighten out the oval tube, and in this way pulls the

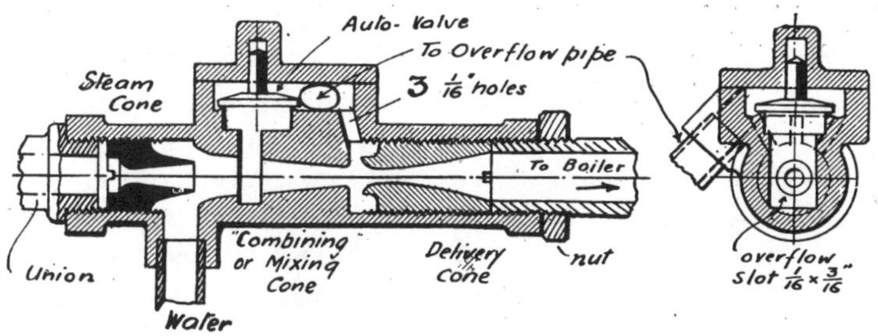

Fig. 472.—Section of steam blower for vertical boiler

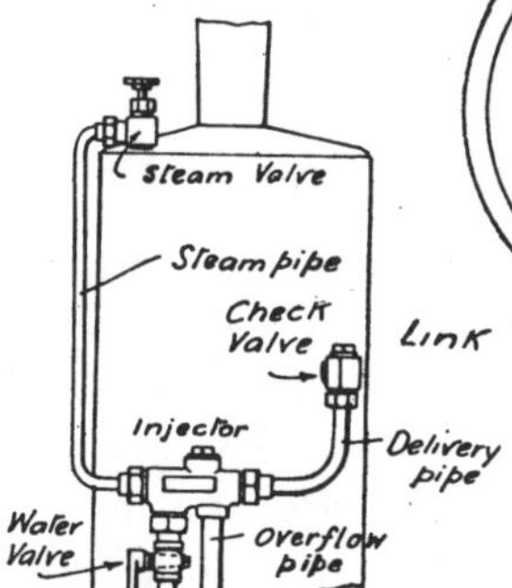

Fig. 473.—Arrangement of injector and pipes

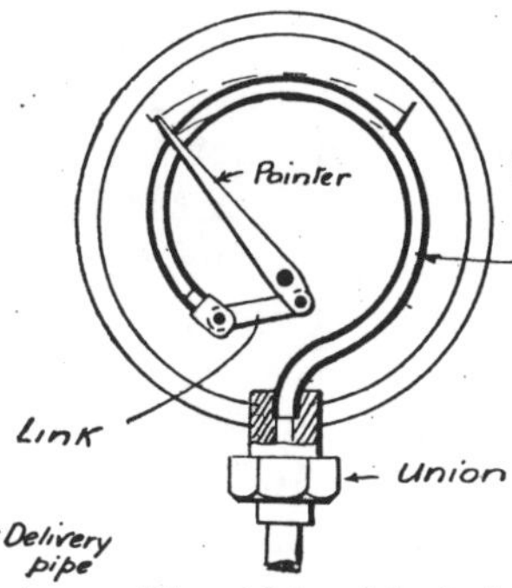

Fig. 474.—Model Bourdon pressure gauge

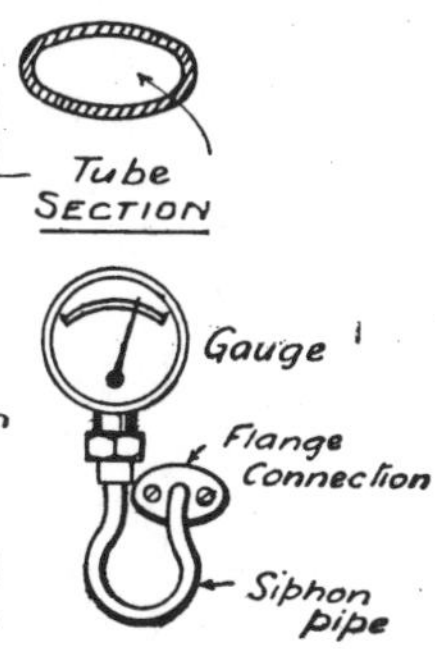

Fig. 475. — Gauge connection to model boiler

pointer over the scale on the dial. As heat seriously affects such gauges, they must be kept cool, and steam is prevented from entering the tube by connecting the gauge to the boiler by a siphon pipe (Fig. 475). This pipe then contains water (condensed steam), which screens the heat of the steam from the Bourdon tube.

CHAPTER XII

Firing Model Boilers

No subject in model steam engineering admits of so many varying ideas and conditions as the firing of model boilers. In real practice coal, coke, and oil are the more usual fuels, the solid fuels being generally burnt in water-surrounded furnaces, and oils being injected into furnaces by various kinds of spray burners. In model-work, coal and coke can be supplemented or substituted by charcoal or any other of the similar patent fuels, like the " Dalli," used in heating domestic irons and warming pans. Charcoal has the advantage of burning without smoke, and while the heat value per pound of fuel is much lower than that of coal, it more readily ignites and requires less draught. It is, however, satisfactory and economical only in fireboxes of 3 in. or 4 in. square, in which coal would not burn very well. Coal, if used in models, requires to be of the best " steam " quality, say, Welsh navigation coal. The house coal from Midland collieries is of no use, as it is very smoky and coats the firebox and tubes with a tarry deposit. Anthracite " peas " as used in slow combustion stoves is very good coal for the larger model boilers; the fire should, however, be started with a little ordinary coal, and a little of the latter afterwards mixed with the anthracite, this requiring a fierce draught and igniting slowly. The coal does not give out its heat for some time after it has been placed on the fire, a point to be observed and acted upon in firing a model locomotive.

Other fuels for models include methylated spirit (spirits of wine rendered unpleasant to the taste), refined paraffin oil as used for lighting, petrol, or benzoline, and coal gas. The use of acetylene has been suggested, but the results of any experiments with this fuel have not been recorded.

Methylated spirit is an expensive fuel, and therefore

used only for the smallest boilers. It is convenient and not dangerous unless spilt and ignited—that is, it does not give off at normal temperatures an explosive vapour. It requires a large amount of air completely to burn it, and when used in closed fireboxes it is generally found that half the spirit is vaporised and passed off unburnt through the flues. Methylated spirit can be burnt in an ordinary wick lamp, as shown in Fig. 476. In a model G.C.R. express locomotive two of the wick tubes are square and all have holes near the top. These holes allow the escape of vapour, which ignites and is ventilated by the fresh air passing up between the wick tubes. Wick tubes in a spirit lamp should be evenly spaced, so that the air is able to get at each wick. Where a forced or induced draught is employed, it should not be too fierce, as an excess of incoming cold air may retard the evaporation of the boiler. In a closed or internally fired boiler, such as on the G.C.R. model locomotive, the exhaust, which induces the draught, should not be nozzled down too much. Smaller models, however, are not likely to suffer in this respect as locomotives of $3\frac{1}{4}$ in. or $3\frac{1}{2}$ in. gauge with which it is attempted to haul a passenger. The difficulty of the spirit lamp is regulating the heat; with an ordinary wick lamp one cannot moderate or increase the volume of flame except by arranging the wick in sets and feeding them by separate pipes with cocks to cut out any one set of wick tubes. This is not a bad idea, as the wicks may be placed close enough to ignite one another; and charring of wicks, as the flame dies out when the supply of spirit is cut off, does not occur if wicks of asbestos yarn are employed.

Vaporising spirit burners (Fig. 477) are made for outside fired model locomotives, stationary and other boilers, in which a perforated tube is fed with spirit vapour by the conduction of heat from the burner tube to a wick tube. As methylated spirit vapour will *not keep ignited* when issuing from a plain jet unless it impinges on some red-hot surface, a pilot light is fitted to these vaporising burners. This pilot light also supplies the heat to start the burner. These burners are of doubtful value under an induced draught.

A regulating burner which combines the wick and vaporising principle is shown in Fig. 478, which gives an external and sectional view of two of several burners fitted on one supply pipe. The outer wick is the initial vaporiser and pilot light. The outer sleeve can be lifted and cuts down the volume of the outer pilot flame. This reduces the vaporising heat, and less gas issues from the holes in the central vapour tube. The latter is provided with a wick of asbestos yarn. Paraffin and petrol are usually employed in vaporising burners or blow-lamps. The respective advantages are (1) the comparative safety and cheapness of paraffin; (2) the cleanliness of petrol or its equivalent, benzoline. Paraffin is a good fuel, but, as the nipple of all blow-lamp burners is very small, if for any reason the fuel is not perfectly vaporised, particles of carbon will form in the nipple and block it up. This is an annoying trouble, especially in a boiler in which it is difficult to get at the burner in the firebox.

Paraffin burners are best purchased from a reliable maker. The "Primus" burners, which are the best known and most used, are in two patterns, the "silent" and ordinary; silent burners have a muffled flame, and for model locomotive purposes can be arranged as shown in Fig. 479.

For an ordinary vertical boiler the "Primus" stove can be used just as it is purchased, except perhaps that the kettle-supporting frame may have to be cut off. If the boiler is fitted up on a bench, a hole can be cut in the latter, and the burner of the stove passed through from underneath when it has been lighted. The oil tank being below the burner, no supply valve is required, the flame of burner being regulated by the air release valve and air pump. When the air is released the oil in the burner flows back into the tank, and a fruitful source of the "burner-blocking-up" trouble is eliminated. In lighting, the burner is heated by a methylated spirit flame, and the oil should not be allowed into the burner until it is thoroughly hot.

The model locomotive demands special arrangements; the oil tank must be specially made to suit the tender or bunker of the engine, and as a rule a separate cycle pump will have to be used to supply the air pressure. The standard

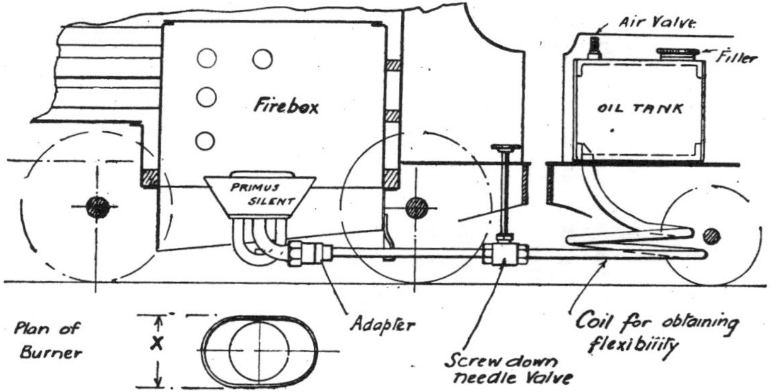

Fig. 479.—Primus burner arranged for model locomotive

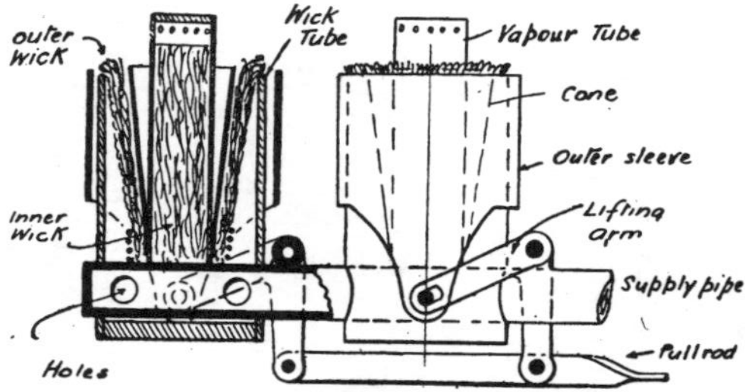

Fig. 478.—Variable-flame semi-vaporising wick spirit lamp

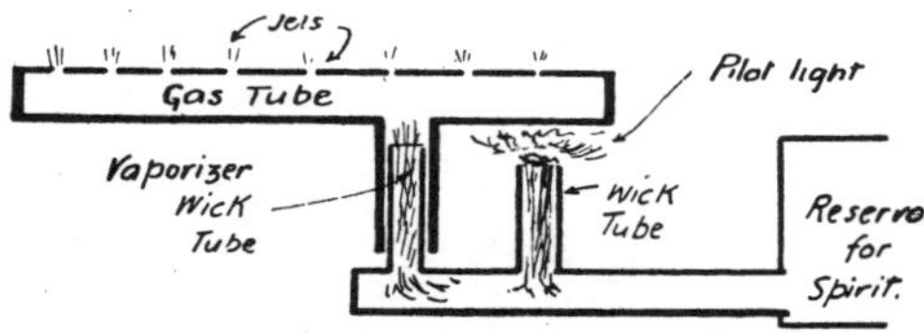

Fig. 477.—Vaporising spirit lamp

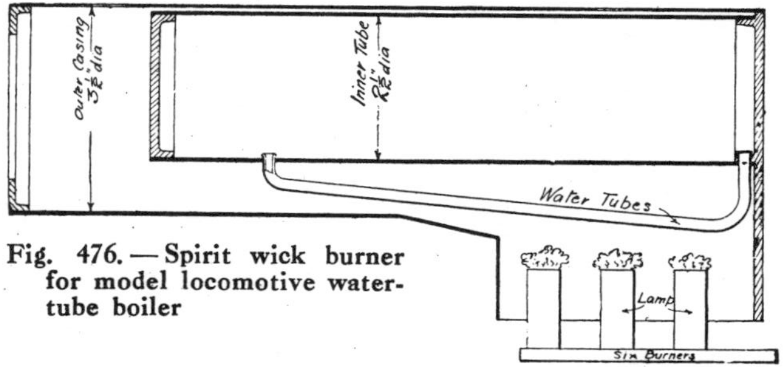

Fig. 476.—Spirit wick burner for model locomotive water-tube boiler

"Primus" air valve (all parts of tanks and burners are supplied separately) can be fitted into the top of the tank, and will require a screwed nipple suiting the ordinary cycle-pump connection. A combined oil filler and air-release valve is also obtainable. The burner itself will require modification in a small firebox. The top flame lip may require to be pinched in as shown at x (Fig. 479). The oil supply pipes underneath the burner must be bent (they are quite soft), so that an adapter may connect the burner to the horizontal $\frac{3}{16}$ in. or $\frac{5}{32}$ in. copper oil tube. An oil valve of the screw-down type (plug cocks are of no use with oil or petrol under pressure) should be placed as near to the burner as possible, so that the burner can be made hot before the oil is supplied to the burner. Where the oil reservoir is on a separate tender a flexible connection is desirable, but small flexible metallic tubing should be avoided for this purpose. It is better to use a coiled copper pipe as indicated. The "Primus" burner works well with a loco-type boiler having water tubes in the firebox, or with a standard water-tube loco boiler which has a double casing. The effect of blast pipe should not be so fierce as in a coal fired engine, and a blower as well as an auxiliary steam-raising blower is essential.

The "Primus" silent burners are made in two sizes, $2\frac{1}{2}$ in. and 3 in. diameter, the noisy type having a smaller diameter of flame ring. Prickers are supplied by the makers of the burners, also separate screw-in nipples.

Petrol Blow-lamps.—These are usually employed in model boats, as they are generally designed to give a powerful horizontal flame (as long as 9 in. or 10 in.). In marine boilers, which have to be light and small, this advantage makes success possible, but blow-lamps are not recommended for stationary boilers. The heat delivered is too local. A design for a model marine boiler petrol blow-lamp is given in Figs. 480 and 486. This lamp has a pressure gauge so that the air pressure, which may be as much as 25 lb. per square inch, may be made known to the operator. If a cycle valve is used, one of the Lucas type should be employed; and if this is not readily obtainable, the "Primus" air valve with a threaded nipple to suit cycle standards may be employed. The ordinary cycle valve with rubber sleeve cannot be used with oil or petrol. The other fittings and materials necessary are a screw-down supply valve, filling plug and release valve, pressure gauge, 3 ft. of $\frac{1}{4}$-in. diameter copper tube, one " Primus " nipple, and a flame tube $1\frac{1}{4}$ in. external diameter $4\frac{1}{2}$ in. long, five dozen copper rivets $\frac{1}{8}$-in. diameter by $\frac{1}{4}$ in. long, a piece of scrap brass about 3 in. by 2 in. by $\frac{1}{8}$ in. for supporting the flame tube. The pressure gauge should read up to 45 or 60 lb.

The vaporising coil of the burner ends in a brass block $\frac{3}{8}$ in. square, and drilled up through the centre as shown in Fig. 480. Into the side of the block, and opening into the hole, another hole is drilled and tapped to take the " Primus " nipple (*see* Fig. 480). This nipple fits into the hole in the block and protrudes through a flanged cap fitted over the back end of the flame tube. All these fittings, including the nipple (the most important part) should be purchased. The container is a piece of light brass tube $2\frac{1}{2}$ in. in diameter with flanged or spun ends (which should not be quite flat if very thin) driven into the ends of the tube, riveted, and soldered.

For bending the vaporising coil get a block of wood, and through the centre drill a hole which will be a nice tight fit for the flame tube (*see* Fig. 483). As close to this hole as possible drill a $\frac{1}{4}$-in. hole for the coil tube. The first bend can be made in the vice (after annealing the tube) round a piece of $\frac{3}{8}$-in. or $\frac{1}{2}$-in. round iron or steel. The centre of this bend should be about $3\frac{1}{2}$ in. from one end, and the bend should be at right angles. Now fix the fire-tube into the block, and put the short end through the $\frac{1}{4}$-in. hole alongside the fire-tube (*see* Fig. 483). The block should be held in the vice or bench, and then the three coils pulled round the tube, and half a coil, finishing up on the opposite side to which the bend was started. Now drill another $\frac{1}{4}$-in. hole exactly opposite to the first, and put a piece of $\frac{1}{4}$-in. iron about 4 in. long down into it. This iron should be bent on one end, and the bent portion inserted in one of the air holes, then tied to the flame tube, and the next bend in the pipe pulled round it as in Fig. 484. Now turn the coil the other way up on the block, still keeping it round the flame tube, and the last bend can be pulled up along the top of the coils (*see* Fig. 485). The remaining bends are easily made. Care should be taken that these other ends are taken round a good radius, so as not to crack the pipe.

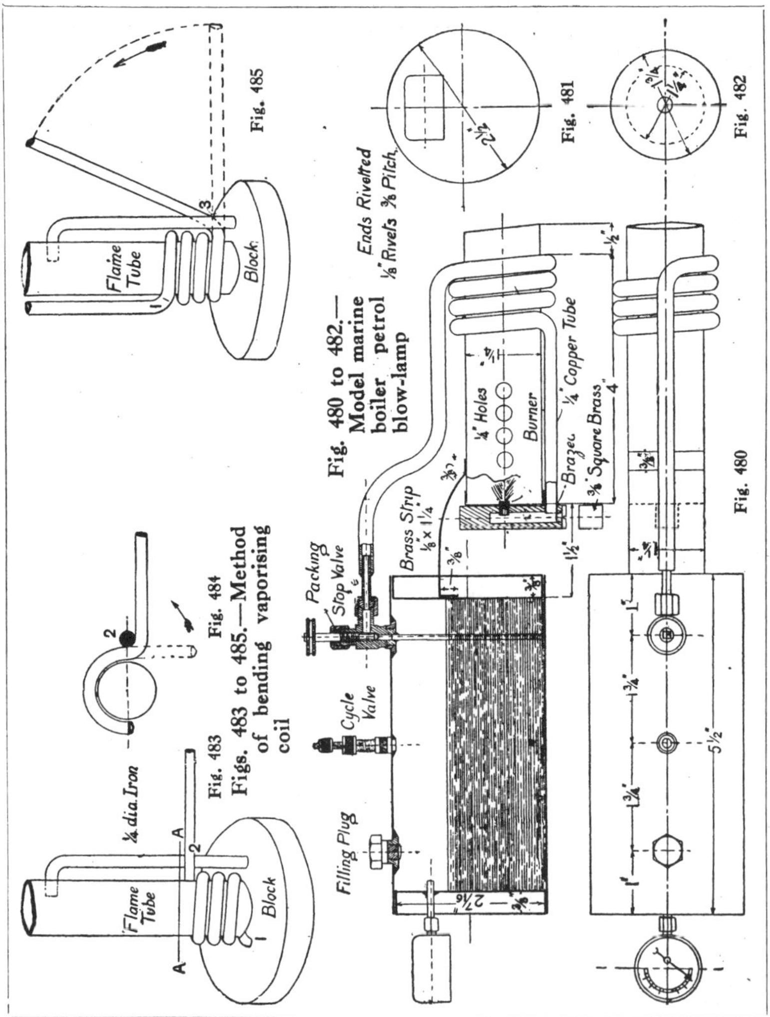

Fig. 480 to 482.—Model marine boiler petrol blow-lamp

Figs. 483 to 485.—Method of bending vaporising coil

One end of this coil goes to the stop valve as shown in Fig. 480. The short end is brazed into a piece of $\frac{3}{8}$-in. brass, which is drilled out $\frac{3}{16}$ in., and holds the "Primus" nipple. The brass has a screw cap on the bottom, which may be undone for cleaning purposes.

All the vaporising gear can now be assembled. All that is left to be done is the making and fitting of the flame-tube support. It is made from a piece of $\frac{1}{8}$-in. brass $1\frac{1}{4}$ in. wide, narrowed down to $\frac{5}{8}$ in. at the flame-tube end. The air holes in the flame tube may be put in practically anywhere near the back end of the burner tube. Put a few in first, say half a dozen $\frac{1}{4}$-in. holes. A trial will soon determine if more are wanted. It is also advised to have the flame

Fig. 486.—Photograph of petrol blow-lamp

tube about $1\frac{1}{2}$ in. longer than shown, and to cut a little off at a time until a good long flame is obtained. A lamp made to this design gave a flame of about 6 in.

Before putting any petrol into the container give it a water test by filling it quite full and heating it to make the water expand. If it is quite tight at 40 lb. it will do. Now drain all the water out of the vessel and fill up with petrol. Replace the plug again, and with a cycle pump put about 15 lb. pressure in the container, making sure beforehand that the valve is screwed down. Put a little cotton waste or rag in the lid of a cocoa tin, and soak the waste with petrol or methylated spirit. Take the lamp, lid, etc., out into the garden for preference, and set light to the cotton-wool. Put the lamp on the ground with the coils in the flame of the wool, making certain the coils get hot (they should get almost red hot); then ease the valve off its seat just a fraction. At once a long string of flame will shoot out of the tube in jerks. If the flame dies down, open the valve a little more; but as long as the flame stops do not touch the valve. Presently the flame will get shorter, and instead of burning yellow it will change to a blue flame, hardly visible in the daylight. At the same time the tube will get hot, and the lamp will make a buzzing noise. The flame can then be regulated by the valve; but do not touch the valve until the lamp is burning properly; that is, when the yellow flame has disappeared and its place is taken by the blue flame. Take care to maintain the stop valve tight by a little asbestos packing round the stem; also the joints where the valves screw into the shell.

The cap through which the nozzle protrudes on the back end of the flame tube is essential. It was found that when air is admitted at the back end of the flame tube and no cap fitted, it was difficult to keep the lamp alight. The air should be admitted at the side by means of the holes.

A short length of $\frac{1}{8}$-in. copper tube must be soldered to the main supply valve leading as nearly as possible to the bottom of the container.

Gas Firing.—Gas firing may take the place of spirit or oil nearly in all the smaller stationary boilers. It should be applied to boilers which have plenty of flue tube or water tube heating surface rather than to vertical centre flue and similar generators (*see* Chapter IX.), which are intended solely for solid firing. Oil fuel can also be used in boilers designed to suit solid fuel by spraying the oil with a steam jet in a suitable ejector. The ordinary fire grate is retained, and the oil spray is introduced just above the level of the incandescent coal or coke. The oil should not be allowed to impinge on the bare firebox plates. Either a bank of asbestos or fireclay should protect these plates. The system, however, offers little advantage over the simpler handled solid fuel. Steam must be raised in the ordinary way before the oil burner can be used.

Solid-fuel Fireboxes.—These should be as deep as possible, to admit a good layer of fuel, and as in the case of a locomotive firebox the grate may slope from the back plate to the tube plate to prevent the open ends of the tubes being blocked up by fuel. A thick steel plate to take the place of the brick arch used in real practice can then be placed over the fire to deflect the flames as indicated in Fig. 487, and more thoroughly consume all the smoke. With charcoal these last precautions are, however, quite unnecessary. Charcoal burns without smoke and with little ash, and the firebox can therefore be filled to the top independently of the position of the tubes. A deep firebox is, however, an advantage in any case, as it will hold more fuel.

Draught.—Natural draught for ventilating fires and furnaces is promoted entirely by the heated products of combustion rising in the chimney, and to get the best results the chimney should be long so that the weight of the column of hot air, etc., inside is much less than a similar capacity outside. Mere length, therefore, settles the intensity of the draught. Another point is that the chimney should not lose too much heat, and as a small tube has greater radiation surfaces in proportion to its internal capacity, very small boilers will not ordinarily work with natural draught. If the chimney or flue must be less than $1\frac{1}{4}$ in. in diameter, natural draught is not a very successful proposition. Natural draught may, however, be improved by casing the chimney if it is out of doors, and is also better if only part of the chimney—say the upper half—is in the open. The chimney may be warmed with a blow-lamp to assist in steam raising or a piece of oily waste may be burnt in the *smokebox* (if it can be opened) at the outset to start an up-draught.

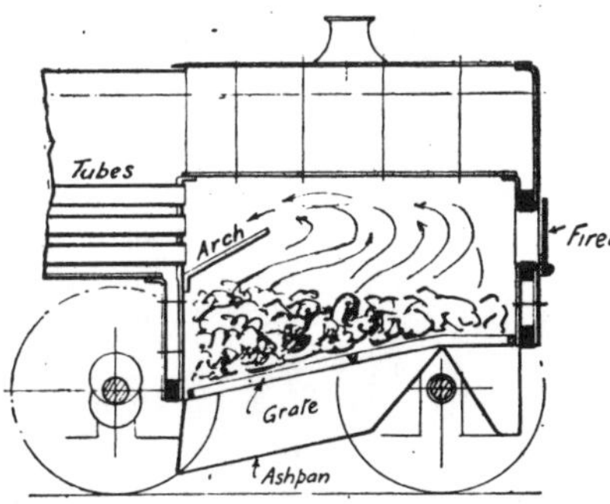

Fig. 487.—Solid-fuel firebox with arch to deflect flames

Locomotives, small stationary boilers, and *model* marine boilers having short chimneys require the power of the exhaust steam to induce a draught. To obtain the best effect the position of the blast pipe (the name given to the end of the exhaust pipe) should be sufficiently low so that the steam fills the chimney. It should not be nearer to the top of the chimney than shown in Fig. 488, the angle of the jet being about 1 in 12. The orifice should be nozzled down to an area $\frac{1}{20}$th (in large engines) to $\frac{1}{30}$th (in small engines) of that of the piston.

For example, the nozzle should be not more than $\frac{3}{32}$ in. diameter for a model locomotive with $\frac{5}{8}$-in. by 1-in. cylinders. Of course, nozzling down the exhaust takes power from the engine, as it causes some back pressure, but this is in

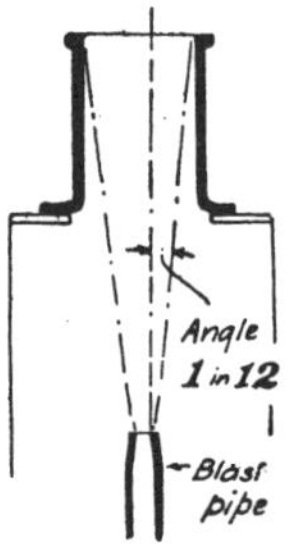

Fig. 488.—Artificial draught in locomotive chimney

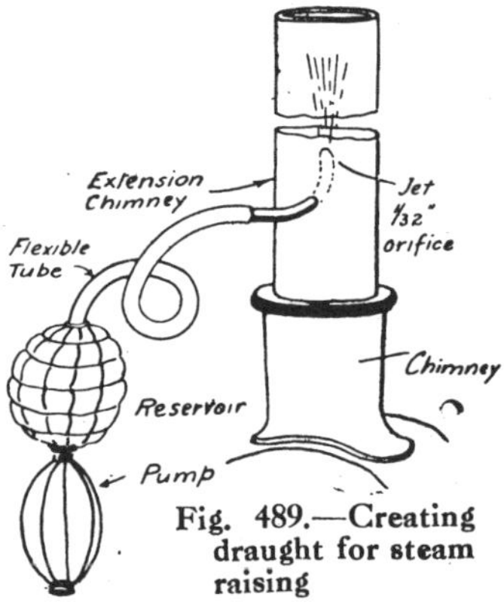

Fig. 489.—Creating draught for steam raising

some respects an advantage in a model. With an induced draught the needs of the engine are regulated by the exhaust; if the engine works hard the draught is made most intense, and the evaporation of the boiler is increased.

Steam Raising.—All internally-fired engines in which the exhaust is used to create the draught when working will require auxiliary means at the outset. Large boilers with funnels over $1\frac{1}{2}$ in. diameter can have the steam raised by natural draught, an extension chimney 10 ft. or 15 ft. long being placed temporarily over the ordinary one, and the joint made secure from air leakages. For small boilers a hand air-blower (scent-spray pump) may be employed as in Fig. 489, or a cycle pump may be connected to the boiler by a special union and the boiler pumped up with air, the steam blower being used to induce the draught. This is a very satisfactory method. An easier one is shown in the photograph (Fig. 490); a small spirit- or gas-fired boiler which will get up steam easily and quickly may feed the extension chimney with steam. This leaves the engine-driver free to tend the fire and other needs of the engine. For the ½-in. scale solid-fired M.R. single locomotive illustrated in another chapter, a Lyle's syrup tin, soldered up

Fig. 490.—Steam raising by means of auxiliary boiler

and placed over a gas-ring, served the purpose very well. No cock or other stop valve should be placed on the steam pipe; the pressure in the syrup tin cannot therefore rise to any dangerous degree. When steam in the main boiler reaches 10 lb. or 20 lb., the permanent steam blower (*see* Figs. 445 and 445A, p. 217) may be manipulated.

Large coal-fired model boilers may be started with wood. A gas jet or a spirit flame under a grate filled with charcoal suits many of the smaller generators.

CHAPTER XIII

Historical and Other Scale "Glass-case" Models

No treatise on model engineering would be complete without some reference to the methods employed in building "glass-case" models of the earlier types of engines. In making scale models the chief difficulty arises where it is

Fig. 491.—Model Maudslay table engine and boiler

attempted to make the model an accurate replica and at the same time a satisfactory working engine. This is especially the case where the boiler is made to the proper scale, comparatively to the engine. A case in point arose in connection with the fine model of the "table" engine shown in the photograph (Fig. 491). In the Maudslay engine (invented in 1807 by the famous Henry Maudslay) the cylinder is placed on a table above the crank shaft and two return connecting rods are employed, one on each side

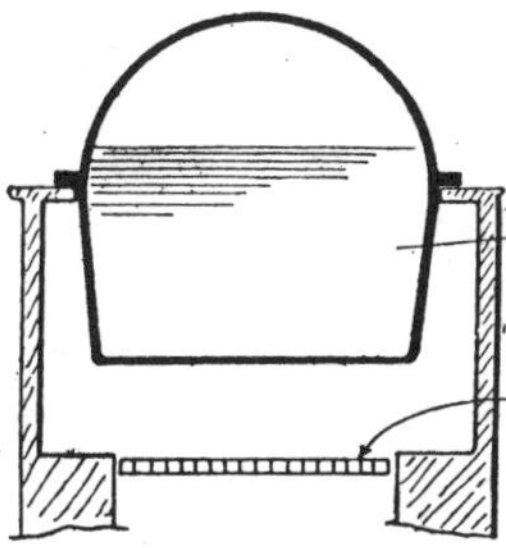

Fig. 492

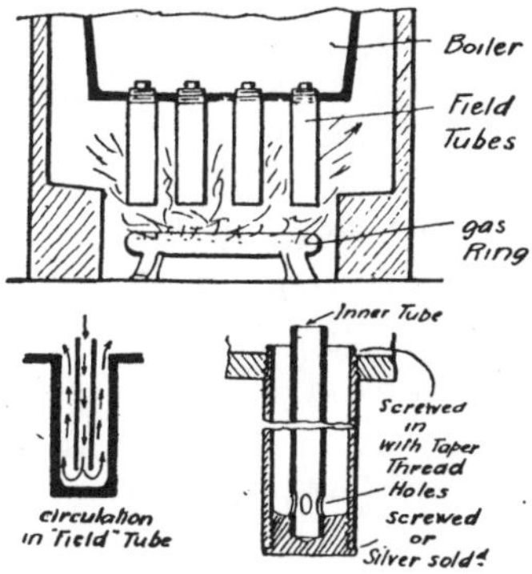

Fig. 493

Figs. 492 and 493.—Haystack-pattern boiler before and after adding Field tubes

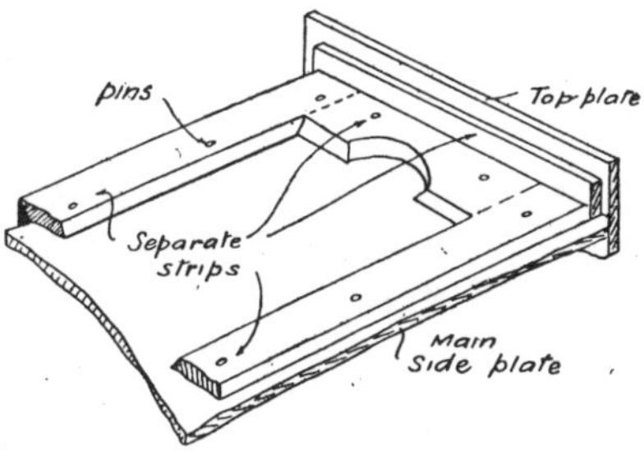

Fig. 495.—Building up model engines

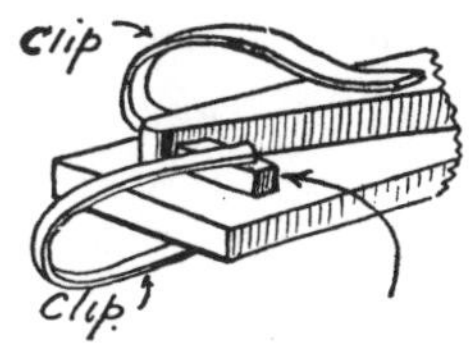

Fig. 496.—Work for soldering held down by clips

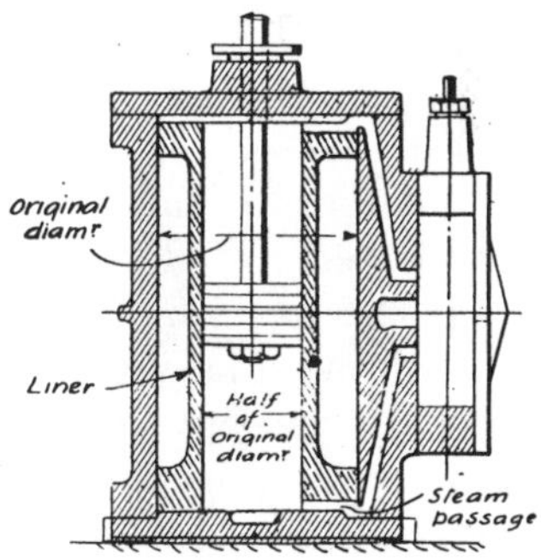

Fig. 494.—Lining-up a cylinder

of the cylinder. The model in question was fitted with a haystack-pattern boiler placed in a suitable setting with a grate underneath. The writer was called in to report why it could not be shown working continuously, and he proved that the failure was due entirely to insufficient heating surface compared with the size of the cylinder; but he was able to demonstrate it working without alteration by first raising a good pressure and then throttling the steam down so that the engine only used a part of the pressure. This in effect tended to dry or superheat the steam by supplying low-pressure steam at the increased temperature of the higher pressure steam in the boiler. While a charcoal fire with a sharp exhaust from the engine would have no doubt improved the working, an ordinary bunsen burner was desired to supply the heat for the model, which being well preserved was to be kept as clean as possible. The writer therefore recommended the addition of "Field" tubes (Fig. 493). These tubes enormously increased the heating surface and circulation without detracting from the historical value of the engine.

Where conditions are favourable, a very good method of ensuring success would be to reduce the bore of the cylinder or cylinders of a scale model by inserting a liner in the cylinder, as shown in Fig. 494. Such a liner might be soldered in, where the cylinder is of brass. With an iron cylinder, if the liner is a good driving fit, the rusting of the surfaces in contact will soon prevent any small leakage of steam from one end to the other.

In construction, to obtain the best effect without resorting to elaborate pattern making (patterns are to be avoided unless several models or similar pieces are required), building up the parts out of raw material is largely resorted to. For example, many of the earlier steam engines were decorated with classical ornaments, as will be observed in the bedplate or table of the engine illustrated in Fig. 491 and in the vertical engine Fig. 499. These features may be added with the least possible trouble by layering one part on to another, soldering them together, and priming parts where there is any danger of the heat applied in subsequent operations loosening them. In soldering such parts together the spring clips, as shown in Fig. 496, are very useful. By the built-up method the resulting work is much cleaner and sharper, and altogether more suited to exhibition and showcase models of engines of all kinds. One of the finest of these models is the sectional model of the "Rocket" at South Kensington, illustrated in Fig. 497.

Another engine, made in a different style, namely in brass and lacquered, is shown in the same museum, and is illustrated in Fig. 498. This is a fine model of the Norris

Fig. 497.—Sectional model of the "Rocket"

American engine as supplied from 1839 to 1841, for operating the Lickey incline (Midland Railway).

The locomotive is a very fascinating type of engine for modelling to scale, and the American engine, by virtue of its wealth of visible machinery, affords the model-maker the greatest possible scope for his ingenuity as a craftsman. Mr. René Bull, the well-known artist and war correspondent,

Fig. 498.—A fine model of the Norris American locomotive engine

has built several very fine model locomotive engines which exhibit the highest degree of skill and finish. The model Baltimore and Ohio Railroad articulated compound locomotive illustrated in Fig. 500 is his masterpiece, and it is made entirely on the built-up principle. In describing the making of this engine, Mr. René Bull said that if two or more pieces had to be made he constructed a jig, or if holes were required to be drilled to the same size and in the same relative position in two pieces of metal, then they were done through a jig. Similar appliances were made to cut off several pieces of metal to exactly the same length in a little circular saw fitted up in his lathe. The model is made to a scale of ½ in. to the foot, and measures 3 ft. 7 in. long. It is made principally of brass sheet and rod, the only castings being the wheels (soft iron), and for the steel parts of the original drawn german silver is employed. Although it is complete in all the external machinery, the model is driven electrically, the motor being concealed in the boiler. This motor has a 40-section ring armature, and can be reversed.

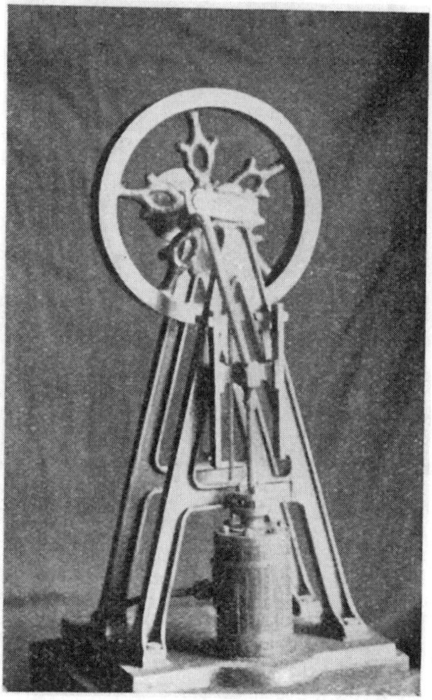

Fig. 499.—Model of an old type of vertical engine: cylinder, 1¼ in. × 3 in. Made by Mr. H. H. Ward

Making a Working Model Watt Beam Engine.—The beam engine of James Watt makes a most impressive working model, and while apparently complicated, the parts are numerous rather than difficult to construct. Where a working model is desired, the cylinder should be made of smaller bore than a mere scale reduction from the original would suggest. Otherwise, under even a moderate steam pressure, the work developed in the cylinder will be greater than is desirable, and a boiler entirely out of scale with the engine will be required. If the outer diameter of the cylinder must be preserved, for the sake of the external accuracy of the model, then the liner device illustrated in Fig. 494 may be adopted. In the design Fig. 501 a cylinder of small bore is employed, $\frac{5}{8}$ in. instead of $\frac{7}{8}$ in., the general construction of the cylinder being the same as illustrated in Figs. 274 and 275 in Chapter VI., two separate slide valves being used. The box bed may be built up out of sheet material, and also the entablature supporting the beam. This frame, which may also be constructed out of raw material, plate and strip, is carried on eight turned columns of Doric or other classical design. The beam may also be built up; indeed, there is no need for any castings in the whole model excepting perhaps the cylinder and fly-wheel. The chief feature of Watt's double-acting beam engine is the connection of the piston rod with the beam. The piston

Fig. 500.—Model Baltimore and Ohio R.R. "Mallet" articulated compound locomotive. Made by Mr. René Bull

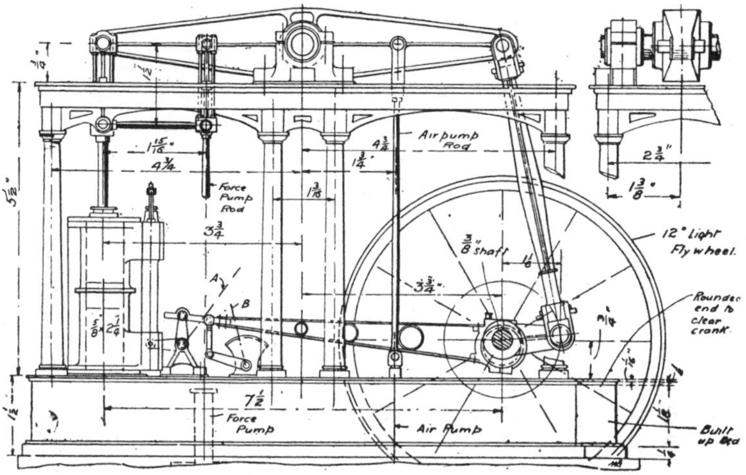

Fig. 501.—Model Watt beam engine of rotating type

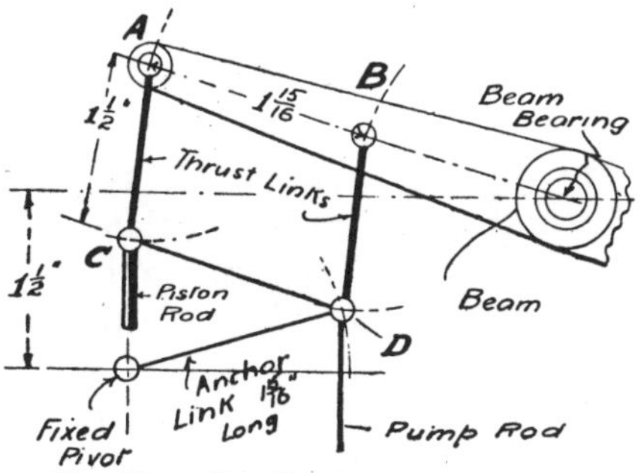

Fig. 503.—Parallel motion for beam engine

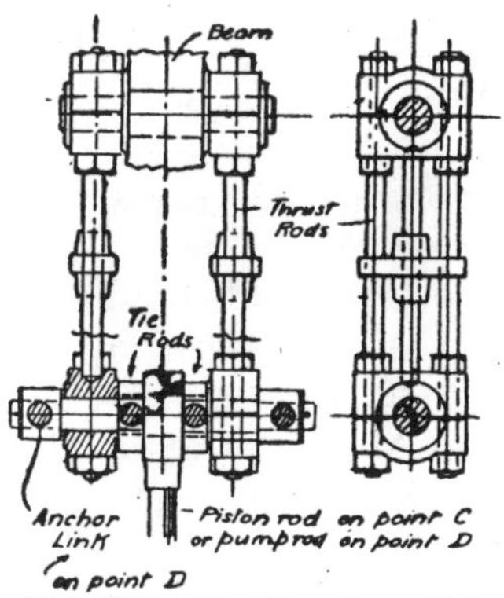

Fig. 504.—Details of parallel motion for beam engine

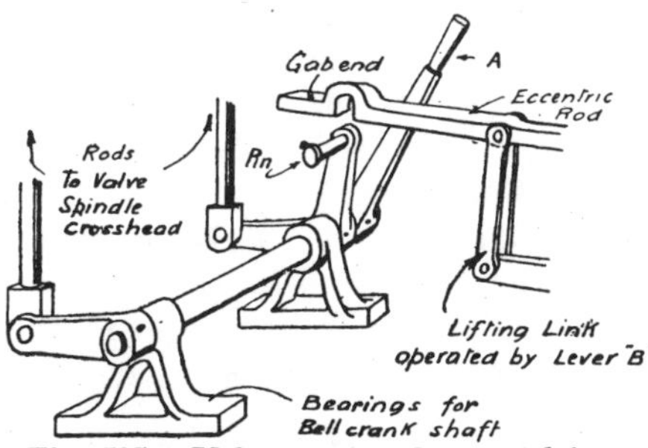

Fig. 505.—Valve motion for model beam engine

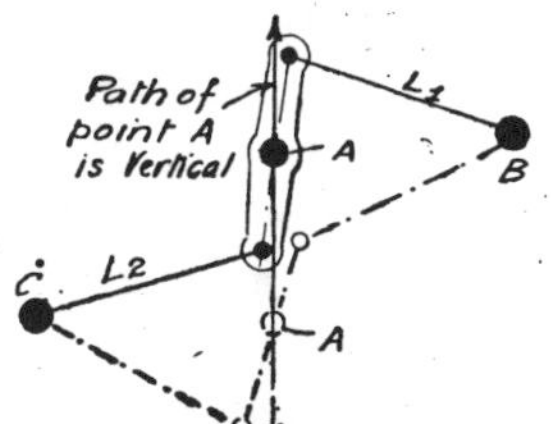

Fig. 502.—Diagram showing principle of Watt's parallel motion

rod has no sliding crosshead, and its alignment is preserved by a beautiful piece of mechanism known as Watt's "Parallel Motion." The beam has attached to it a system of links which ensures the parallelism of the piston rod, as shown in Fig. 502. Within certain limits of movement the point A in the link gear shown will move in a straight line path, B and C being fixed points. In the motion fitted to the model under consideration the links are given a rectangular arrangement, as shown in Fig. 503, and also provide (at point D) for driving the force pump. The anchor link (replacing links L_1 and L_2 in Fig. 502) is in duplicate, and is attached to pins fixed in the sides of the frame. The links which take up the thrust of the piston and pump rods are built up out of rod material and have adjustable bearings, as shown in the details (Fig. 504), and the tie and anchor links are plain round rods with eyed ends. The details of connecting rods, cranks, bearings, and slide valves may be worked out according to the information given in the chapters dealing with these fittings, the parts being rather light. The eccentric rod is of typical construction, and may be built up out of bar stuff and slices off the ends of various pieces of brass tube. The engine may be made to reverse by a shifting eccentric (*see* Chapter VIII.). The end of the eccentric rod has a gab or notch, which engages a pin on the vertical levers of the bell crank actuating the valve spindle. The eccentric rod may be lifted off this pin by the lever B and the crank and link attached to it. This lever may be arranged to fit in a notch to retain it in this "out-of-gear" position. The valve may then be operated by a hand lever (A) on the bell crank shaft, and with this the engine can be started in the desired direction. As soon as half a turn of the crank is completed the lever B may be released, and the gab will engage the pin in the bell crank lever, and the eccentric, now in its new position, will continue to drive the valves.

Condensing may be adopted, and in this case an air pump must be fitted up in the box bed and operated by the rod shown in the general drawing. The boiler supplying steam to this model must be fitted with a force pump.

CHAPTER XIV

Making a Model 1-in. by 1-in. Vertical Steam Engine

The engine shown by Fig. 513, and described in this chapter, can easily be made by the metalworker who has the use of a 3-in. gap-bed lathe and a drilling machine. A shaping machine would also be useful; but failing this, the surface work can be otherwise accomplished.

This model is of simple design; and by adopting the "Stuart" set of castings it can be constructed without much trouble.

The elevations (Figs. 506 and 507) give dimensions for machining the bed, column, cylinder, and covers; Fig. 513 is a photograph of the complete engine; and all details are illustrated by Figs. 508 to 512 and 514 to 567. Figs. 506 and 507 are reproduced half full size.

Making the Model.—Starting with the cylinder (Fig. 508), the cored hole should first be bored. The casting (Fig. 534) should be held either in a chuck or on the faceplate. If the latter method is adopted, packing must be put under the casting in order to hold it clear of the faceplate, so that the boring tool can go right through. The holding-down clips should project over the flange about $\frac{1}{8}$ in., and the nuts should be screwed up with care, in order to prevent breakage of the casting. It will be an easy matter to set the cylinder true with the partly circular portion, which portion must not appear to wobble when revolving.

The method of boring out the cylinder while held on the faceplate is shown in Figs. 535 and 536, A being the faceplate, B the cylinder, C the clips, D the steel packing, and E the wood packing. Owing to its elasticity, hard wood is very suitable for packing up holding-down bolts. Before taking the finishing cut through the cylinder bore, the clamping nuts should be slightly loosened. It frequently happens,

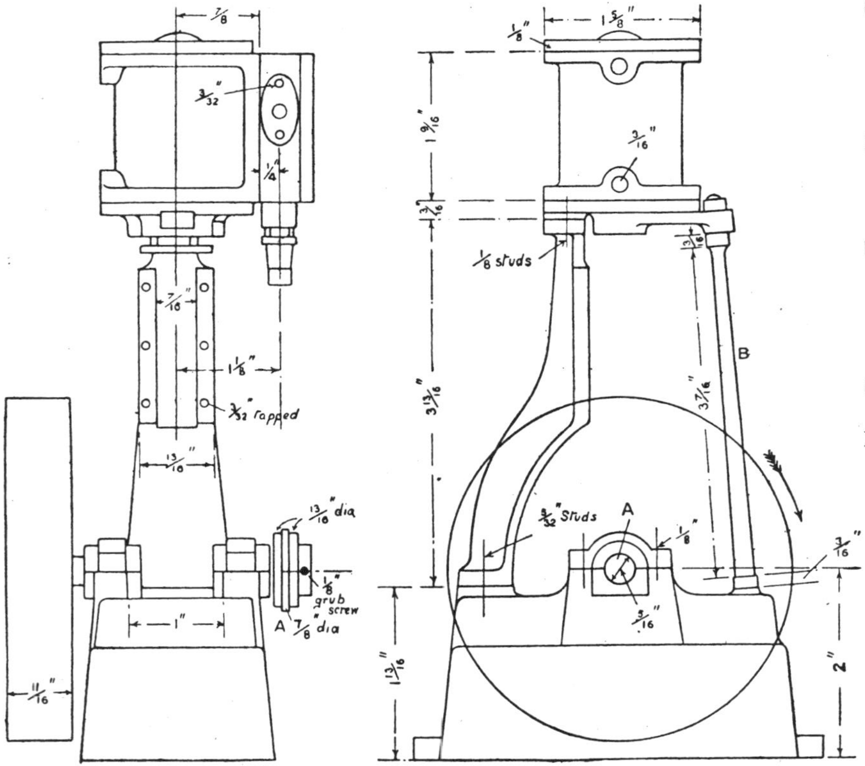

Figs. 506 and 507.—Elevations of partly-assembled vertical steam engine

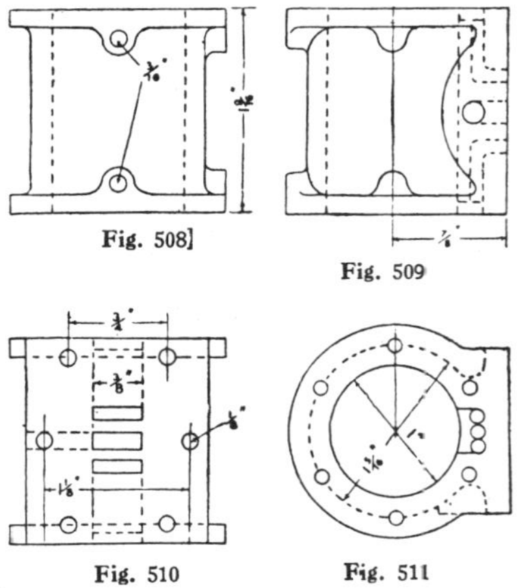

Figs. 508 to 511.—Details of cylinder

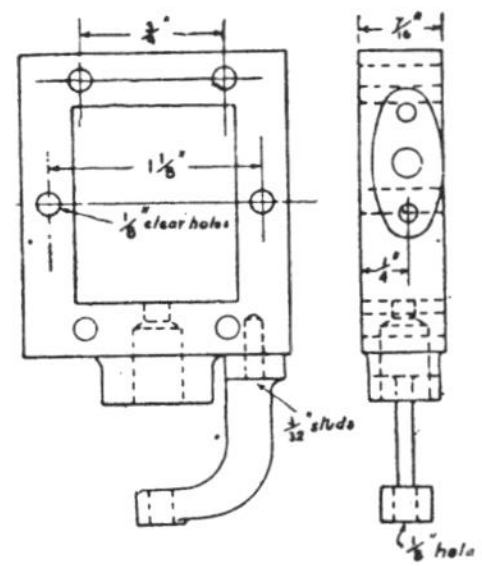

Fig. 512.—Details of steam chest

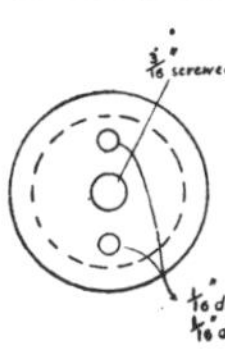

Fig. 514

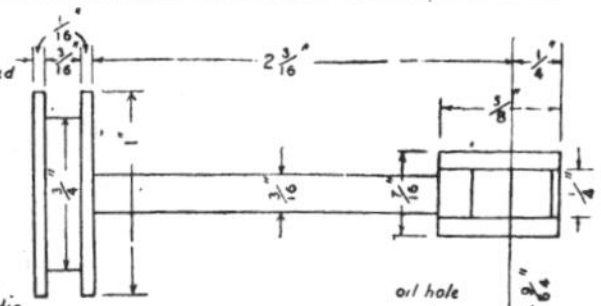

Fig. 515

Figs. 514 to 516. — Piston, piston rod and crosshead

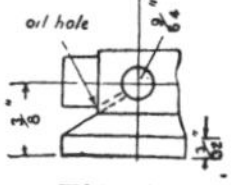

Fig. 516

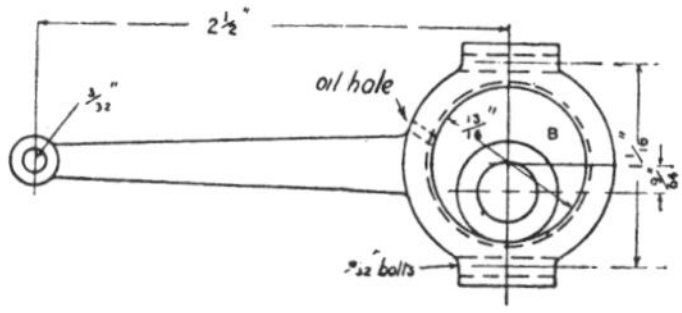

Fig. 518.—Eccentric rod

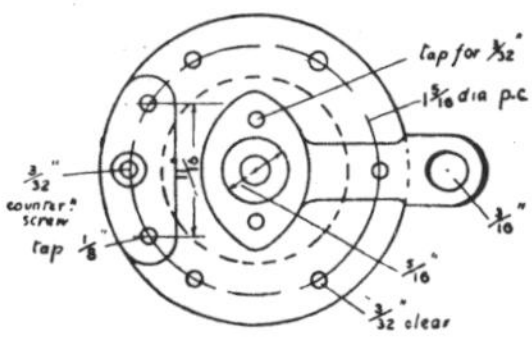

Fig. 517.—Plan of bottom cylinder cover

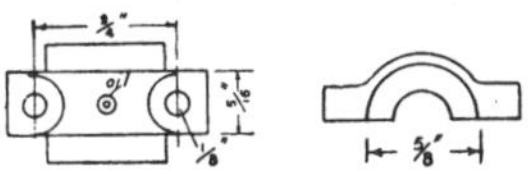

Figs. 519 and 520. — Top half of bearing brasses

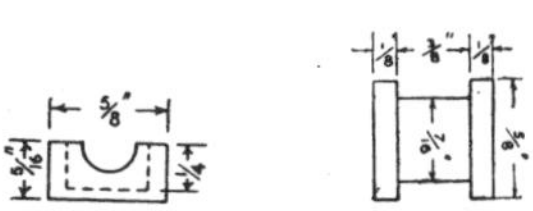

Figs. 521 and 522.—Bottom half of bearing brasses

Fig. 513.—Photograph of model vertical steam engine

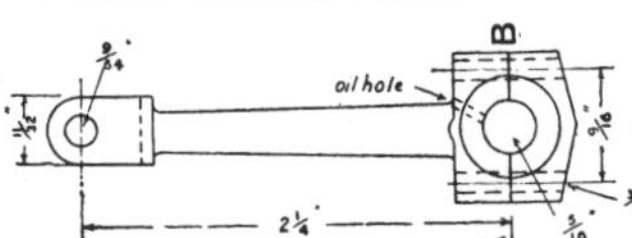

Fig. 523

Fig. 524

Figs. 523 and 524.—Connecting rod

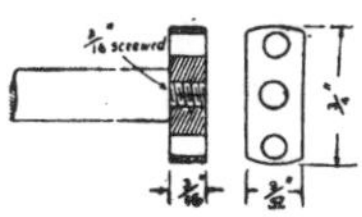

Figs. 526 and 527. —Column foot

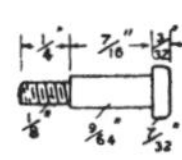

Fig. 525.— Crosshead pin

in work of this character, that the casting is slightly distorted during the clamping operation, with the result that the casting regains its original shape when the pressure of the clamps is taken off. The bore is then out of truth or twisted.

For facing the cylinder flanges in the lathe, a perfectly true and smooth mandrel is lightly driven into the bore. A smooth mandrel is essential, its surface affording a larger amount of grip. If a rough mandrel is used it will fit the bore in a few places only, and should the cylinder slip the roughness will be worn off, and it may then be necessary to make another mandrel. The operation of driving in the mandrel is shown in Fig. 537. Two square strips of steel, A and B, are placed in a convenient position, and the mandrel is pushed into the cylinder bore by hand, and afterwards struck gently on the end C by means of a lead hammer or a wood mallet. The ends of the mandrel should be shaped as shown at D, this preventing damage to the centre recess; if the ends are not recessed the mandrel will probably run out of truth after having been dropped on any hard surface.

The valve seating on the cylinder should be faced in the lathe in the manner indicated in Fig. 538. A small and accurate angle-plate A is fastened to the faceplate B, and on this is placed the cylinder C, which is securely held by means of the set screw or stud and clamp D. In order that the facing tool E can finish the face level, a small hole should be drilled in the centre of the valve face and where the exhaust port will ultimately be formed. However, in these castings the steam ports are generally cast in, so no drilling will be necessary. Care must be taken in setting up the cylinder on the angle-plate, and a piece of smooth, thin paper should be inserted between the faceplate and the angle-plate, and between the cylinder and other touching parts. The faceplate will require counterbalancing; a piece of heavy material such as lead should be fastened to the faceplate on the opposite side to the unbalanced work.

The casting having been marked out, and the facing finished to size, the metal should be carefully filed smooth, and afterwards scraped and fitted to the surface of a surface

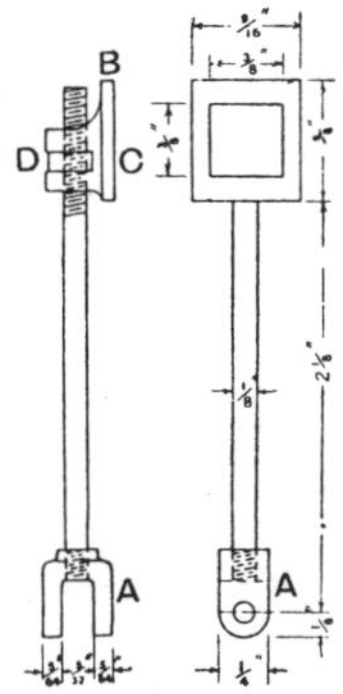

Figs. 528 and 529.—Slide valve and rod

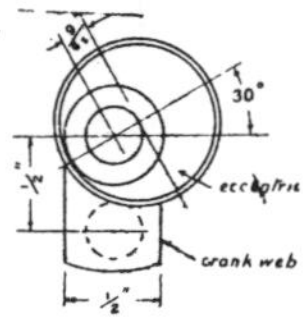

Fig. 531.—Eccentric fixed on crank

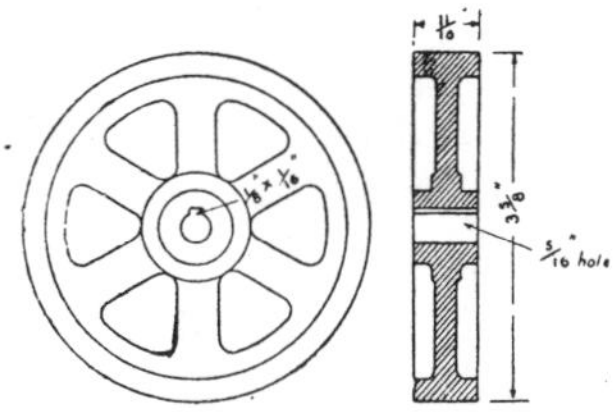

Figs. 532 and 533.—Flywheel

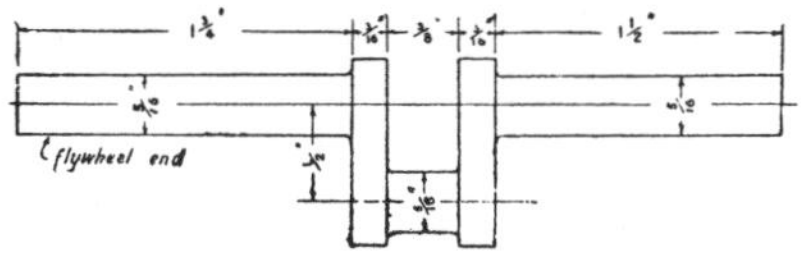

Fig. 530.—Crank

Fig. 534.—Photograph of cylinder casting

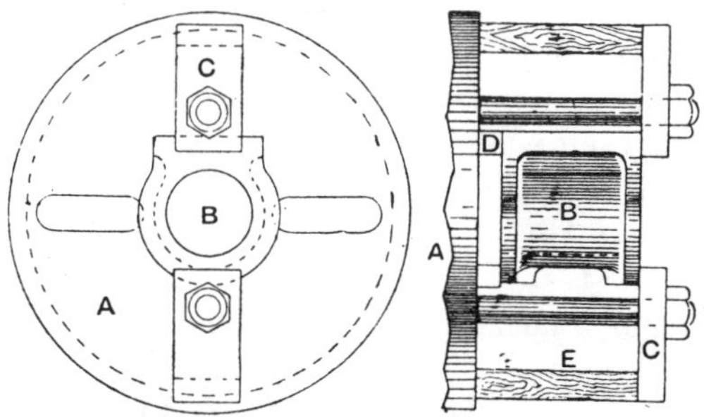

Figs. 535 and 536.—Boring the cylinder

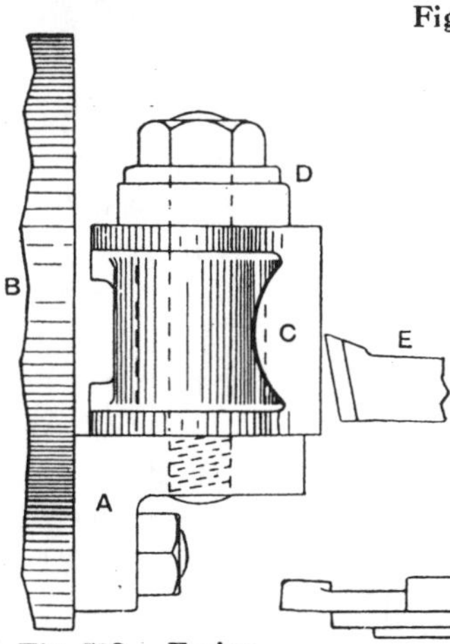

Fig. 538.—Facing valve seating in lathe

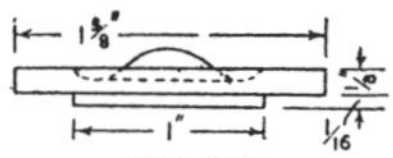

Fig. 539

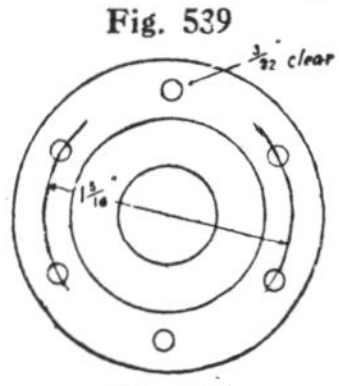

Fig. 540

Figs. 539 and 540.—Details of top cylinder cover

Fig. 541.—Callipering thickness of bottom cylinder cover

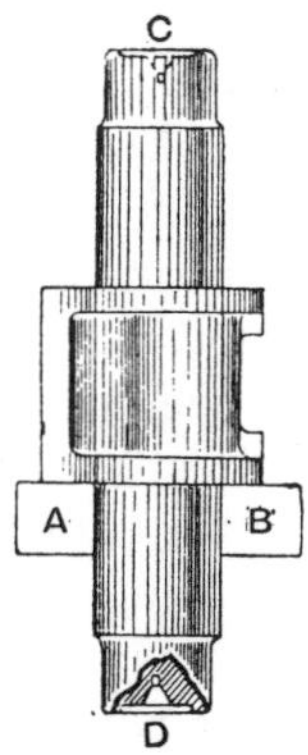

Fig. 537.—Fitting mandrel in cylinder

plate; failing which, however, the face can be finished with a smooth file only.

Regarding the drilling of the cylinder flanges and the holes for the steam-chest studs, this should be left until the covers are drilled. The holes can then be marked off, or even drilled through those already made, this method ensuring the fit of the parts over the studs.

The top cylinder cover should be held in a three- or four-jaw chuck as indicated in Fig. 542, A being the chuck, B, C, and D the jaws, and E the cylinder cover. After the top side has been finished, the cover can be taken out of the chuck, reversed, and the other side finished. The stud holes can then be marked out; the diameter of the pitch circle is $1\frac{5}{16}$ in., and the number of holes six. When the under side of the cover is being machined, a small centre should be made in order to facilitate working out the position of the stud holes. If it is decided to fit a lubricator on the top of the cylinder, a hole must be drilled and tapped through the cover to receive its stem.

To turn the bottom cover, hold it in the jaws of the chuck as shown in Fig. 543. First drill out the hole for the gland and the piston rod, and face the top of the gland seating. The cover can then be taken out of the chuck, mounted on a mandrel, turned over the top, and the spigot finished. An alternative method is to hold the cover in the chuck the reverse way to that indicated in Fig. 543, finish the spigot first, and then turn over and drill the gland and piston-rod hole (Fig. 544). After all the turning is completed, the stud holes can be drilled, Fig. 517 giving all the necessary dimensions. The hole for the front stay requires to be drilled at an angle, and one of the stud holes must be countersunk. The portion that rests on the column must be carefully filed flat, a pair of callipers being used for testing purposes as shown in Fig. 541. It is important that this face should be parallel with the other side of the cylinder cover, as otherwise the engine will not run smoothly.

Steam Chest.—The steam chest can be filed level on both sides, and tested in a similar manner for parallelism to that adopted for the bottom cylinder cover. If an accurate

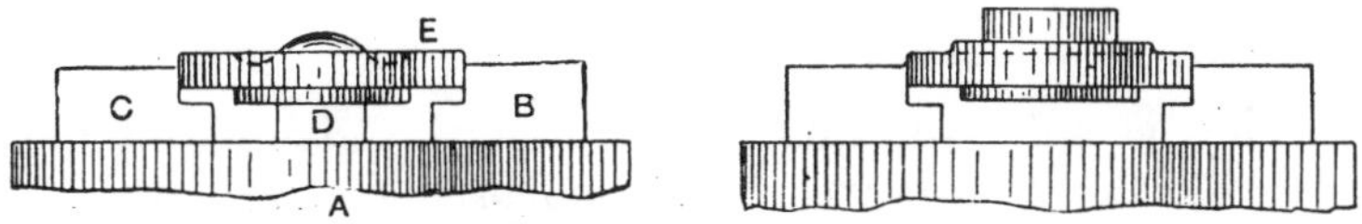

Figs. 542 and 543.—Machining top and bottom cylinder covers

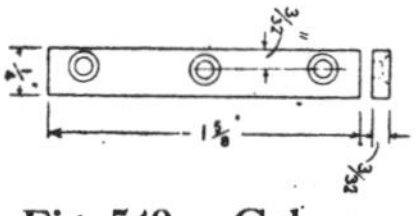

Fig. 549.—Column strips

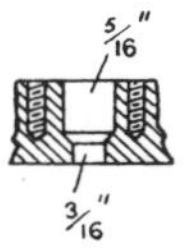

Fig. 544.—Section through gland

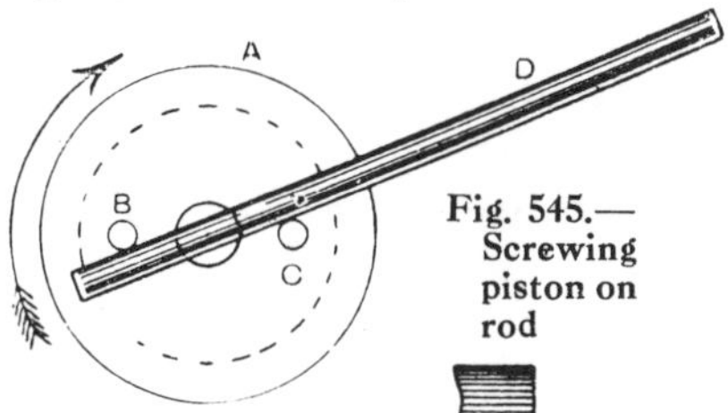

Fig. 545.—Screwing piston on rod

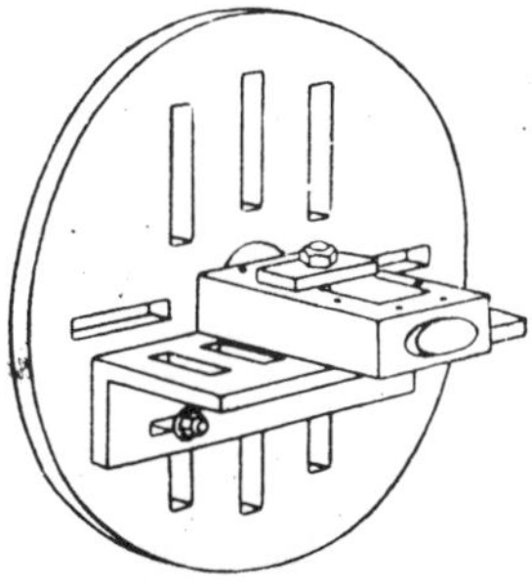

Fig. 546.—Boring gland hole in steam chest

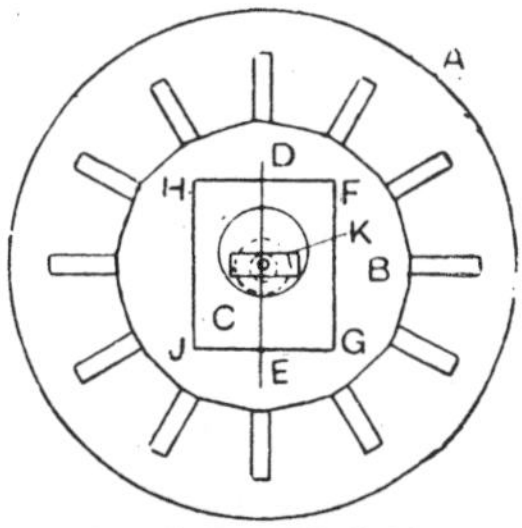

Fig. 547.—Finishing eccentric

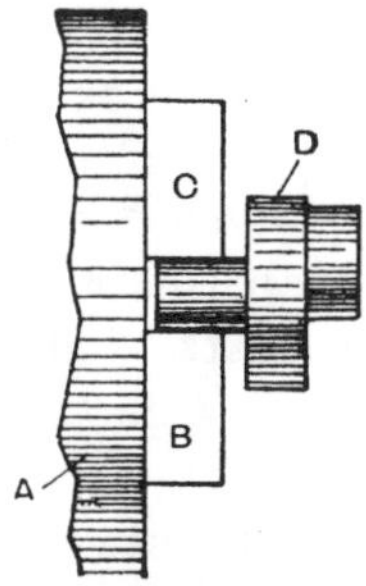

Fig. 548.—Machining eccentric

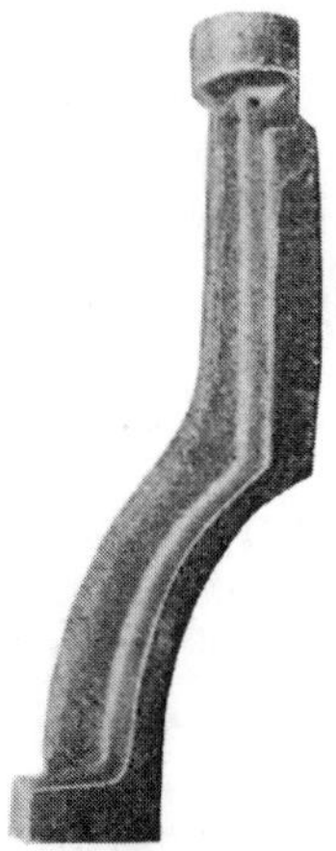

Fig. 550.—Column casting

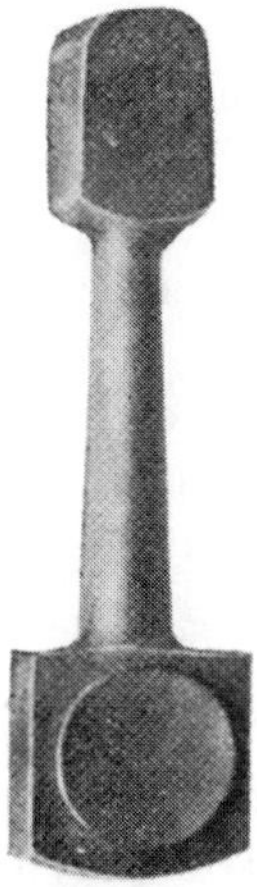

Fig. 551.—Connecting rod casting

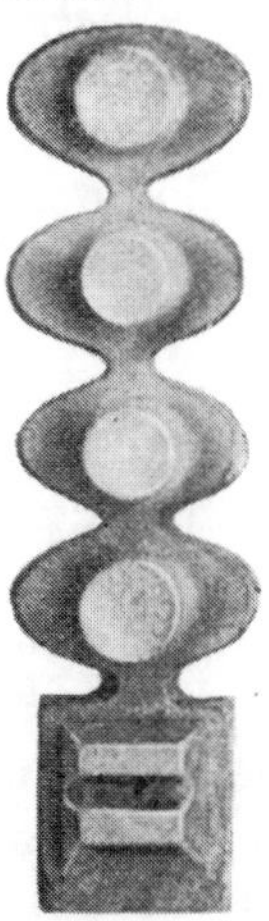

Fig. 552.—Slide valve and flange casting

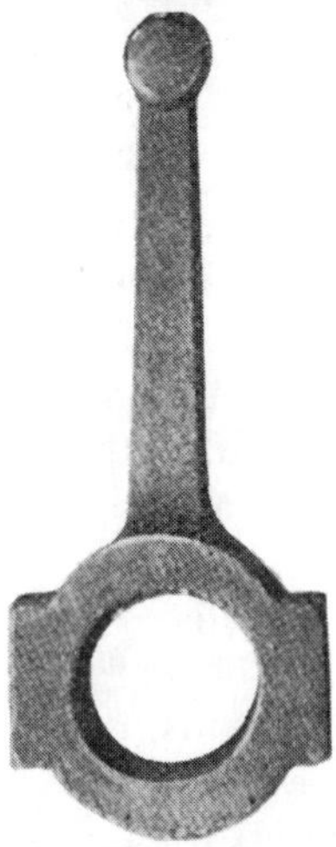

Fig. 553.—Eccentric sheave and rod casting

machine is not available for drilling the gland and valve-rod hole, this had better be drilled or bored out in a lathe, being securely fastened on an angle-plate during this operation, as shown in Fig. 546. The cover for the steam chest requires filing flat on both sides, and should be finished parallel; the parallelism is not of great importance in this case, but otherwise the nuts will not fit very well.

If the holes for the studs are now drilled in the cover, the steam chest can be drilled from it; or, if desired, the two could be clamped together and drilled at one setting. The *tapping* holes on the valve seating can next be drilled. At the same time as the stud holes are drilled in the bottom cylinder cover and the steam chest, the stud holes for the steam gland in the former, and for the exhaust flange in the latter, should be made. If the holes for the cylinder drain taps are now made, this practically completes the cylinder and its ports.

Piston.—The piston requires a $\frac{3}{16}$-in. Whitworth thread to be tapped through the centre. It should then be placed on a screwed mandrel and turned to the sizes given in Figs. 514 and 515. It is advisable to leave it a small amount over size, so that it can be finished after it is tightly screwed on the piston rod. For the purpose of screwing on the piston, two holes should be drilled in it as shown. Two pieces of iron or steel can be driven into these holes, and the piston screwed on as shown in Fig. 545, A being the piston, B and C the pins, and D a round bar. After the piston is screwed sufficiently far on the rod, the pins can be pulled right out by means of pliers. If the piston rod is held in a vice, care must be taken that it is not bent, scratched, or otherwise damaged. The crosshead is made of gunmetal, and necessitates accurate workmanship. A hole is tapped in the bars for the reception of the piston rod, and a hole carefully drilled at right angles for the fitting of the crosshead pin. The flat foot fits in between the column strips (Fig. 549), and requires careful filing up.

Standard.—The cast-iron standard (Fig. 550) must be carefully chipped and filed up. The top and bottom must be level and parallel, and the portion on which the crosshead slides must be made perfectly vertical, and at right angles to the top and bottom. Frequent use of the square will prevent any great error. After the filing is completed, the bolt holes in the top and base, and the screw holes in the column, can be made. The two steel strips (Fig. 549) for holding the crosshead require only filing and drilling. If the model-maker prefers, the strips can be made first and the holes marked on the column through those already made in the strips.

Connecting Rod.—The connecting rod (Figs. 523 and 524) should have the bolt holes drilled, and be then sawn in half across the line A B (Fig. 523). The bolts should now be fitted, and the crank-pin hole bored out in the lathe and one side of the brass faced. The rod is next turned end-for-end, and the hole for the crosshead pin drilled. Care must be taken that this hole is in line with the crank-pin hole; the same care should be applied to the finishing of the forked end.

Slide Valve.—The crosshead on the spindle A (Figs. 528 and 529) should be filed from an oblong piece of brass and tapped one end with a $\frac{3}{32}$-in. thread. The valve B must be slotted to receive the valve rod and nut D, and to be faced at C. The valve is cast in one piece with other parts (*see* Fig.552).

Eccentric.—The eccentric strap and rod (Figs. 518 and 553) should be treated in a similar manner to the large end of the connecting rod, that is, the bolts fitted, sawn in half along the centre line, bolted together, and then bored out while being held on the faceplate. The hole in Fig. 518 for the valve pin should be in line with the eccentric hole, and at the exact distance from the centre. The eccentric (Fig. 554) should first be turned on the large diameter, it being held between the jaws of a chuck by means of the tenon piece provided on the casting, as shown in Fig. 548, A being the chuck, B and C the chuck jaws, and D the eccentric. Care must be exercised when turning the eccentric in this manner, or the casting may be forced out of the chuck; one half of the eccentric strap may be used for testing the size.

A method of boring and turning the boss would be first

to hold the casting on a faceplate or in a chuck in such a manner that the small boss runs true. Then bore out the $\frac{5}{16}$-in. hole for the crank shaft, for which purpose the chucking pin on the casting should be sawn off. After removing the eccentric from the chuck or the faceplate, fit it on a mandrel and place this between the centres.

The sides of the eccentric and the outside of the boss can now be finished. The large diameter can now be machined while being held on a faceplate A (Fig. 547), with a flat piece of hard wood B on it, truly faced up. Procure also another piece C of hard wood $1\frac{1}{8}$ in. or so thick, and about 4 in. by 4 in., with the edges squared. Put two long screws through the corners, and screw it on the middle of the first piece, sinking the heads of the screws below the surface, so that the wood can be faced up. Now bore a hole $\frac{9}{16}$ in. in diameter in the centre of this piece, and into it press the boss of the eccentric. The line of the eccentric D E which joins its two centres must be placed parallel with two sides F G and H J of the squared-up piece. Now the two screws holding C to B may be taken out, and the piece C moved down $\frac{9}{64}$ in. along the lines F G and H J, and refixed. Thus the piece C acts like the slide of an eccentric chuck. In order to prevent the casting moving while it is being turned, an iron clamp K may be placed across the hole and secured with a screw passing through the wood. The half of the eccentric strap will, of course, be used to test the work, and the eccentric must be made to fit.

Crank Brasses.—The space for the reception of the bottom half of the crank brasses in bedplate (Fig. 555) should be filed out. Care must be taken that both spaces are in line; a narrow rule can be used for testing when a parallel strip is not available. When the bearing spaces have been finished the bottom half of the bearing (Fig. 561) can be filed up to fit. The bearing caps (also shown in Fig. 561) should then be filed up and machined as described in Chapter VII.

To bore out the holes in the crank brasses the bed may be held on an angle-plate, and the square recess in the bed for the reception of the brasses used for setting purposes.

Fig. 554.—Eccentric

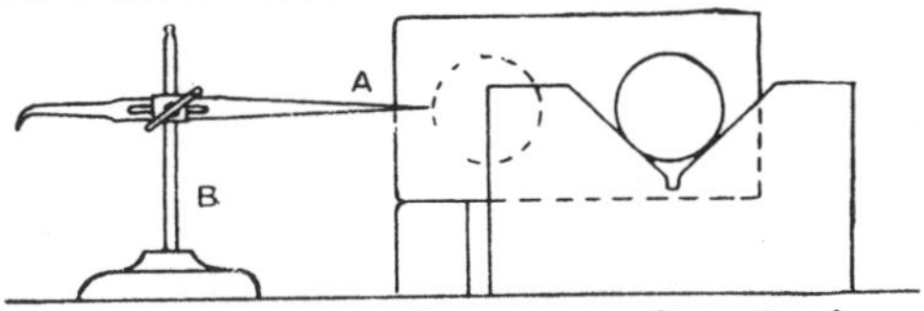

Fig. 563.—Testing for centre of crank pin: first stage

Fig. 555.—Engine bed

Fig. 556.—Piston casting

Fig. 557.—Crosshead casting

Fig. 558.—Crank casting

Fig. 559.—Flywheel casting

Fig. 561.—Top and bottom halves of bearing

Fig. 560.—Method of machining flywheel

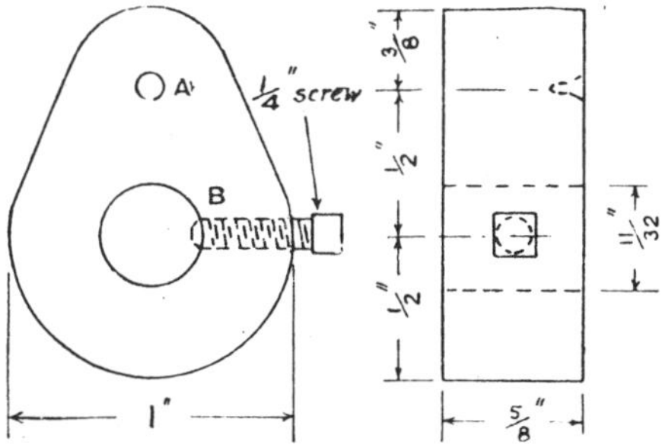

Fig. 562.—Throw plates for crank

After the holes are bored and finished, the portion to which the column and foot are bolted can also be finished. In order that this work may be done correctly, the bearings may be removed, a square parallel strip inserted, the bed placed on a surface plate or a marking out table, and the column facing tested from time to time by means of a scribing block in order to ascertain its relationship to the parallel strip. Unless the facing strip is perfectly horizontal, and in the correct position in relation to the centre of the crank shaft, the cylinder will be thrown out of line.

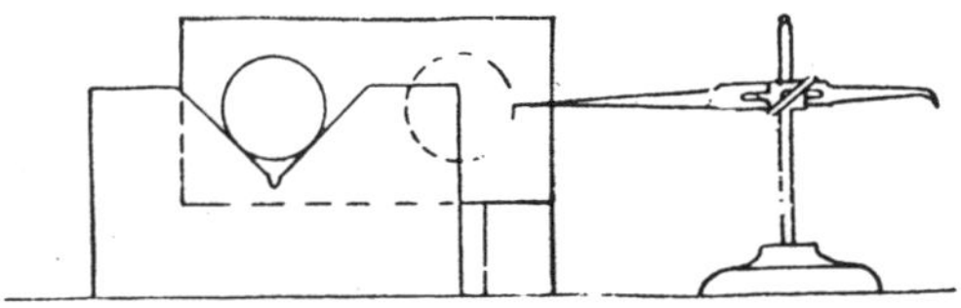

Fig. 564.—Testing for centre of crank pin: second stage

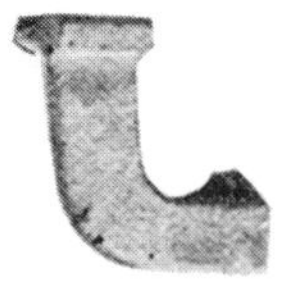

Fig. 566.—Bracket for slide-valve rod

Fig. 566A.—Piston ring

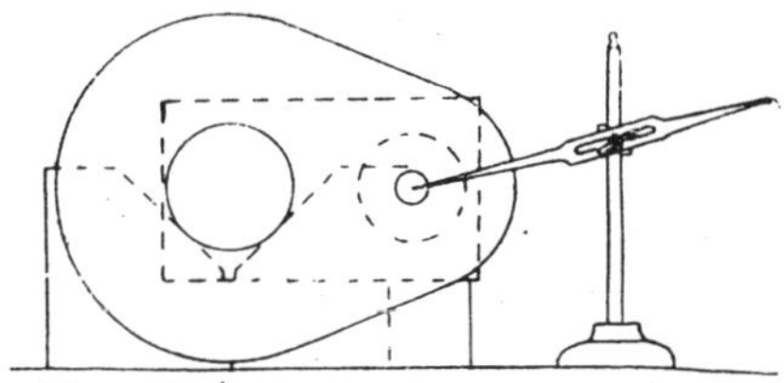

Fig. 565.—Testing for centre of crank pin: third stage

Flywheel.—To turn and bore the flywheel (**Fig. 559**), hold it on the faceplate by means of clips and screws in the manner shown by **Fig. 560.** If a small faceplate is used, or if the flywheel is packed clear of the face of a large faceplate, the casting can be finished completely while in this position. An alternative method is to hold the flywheel in a chuck, bore the hole, and then, after removing from the chuck, to turn the outside, the casting being fixed for this purpose on a mandrel held between the lathe centres.

Crank Pin.—Before turning the pin of the crank (Fig. 558) it is necessary to make two dogs, or throw plates, as already described in another chapter. With a centre recess at A (Fig. 562), at $\frac{1}{2}$-in. pitch, the casting is turned down to $\frac{11}{32}$ in. in diameter. The crank is then taken out, the carrier fixed on the other end, the crank replaced between the centres, and the process repeated. It is now necessary to mark out the centre of the crank pin, and for this operation the crank dogs are taken off and the crank removed from the lathe centres. The crank is then laid with the turned ends resting in V blocks as shown in Fig. 563. The crank pin is then packed up so that it is approximately on the same horizontal centre line as the shaft, as indicated at A. A scribing block B is then used to scratch a line on the crank pin. The crank is then turned half round, so bringing the crank pin into the position indicated in Fig. 564. Another line is made without changing the height of the scriber needle. Now the centre line of the crank pin is between the two scribed lines, and at an equal distance from each; but it might happen that only one scribed line is made, and if so this is the centre line.

Fig. 567.—Unassembled finished parts of model vertical steam engine

The dogs must now be not too tightly fixed on the turned-down ends, and the crank replaced in the V blocks; but this time with the blocks between the dogs and the crank webs. The scriber point must be set to the centre of the recess in the crank ends and the throw packed up, so that the centre line marked thereon coincides with the point of the scriber. Each dog must be then fixed so that the centre of the recess is exactly level with the point of the scriber, as shown diagrammatically in Fig. 565. The screws must next be tightened up, and the crank is now ready for placing between the lathe centres. Before this is done, however, it is advisable that the process of setting be again gone over, as the crank might be moved when the screws are tightened.

When the crank pin has been turned the crank must be taken out of the centres, the dogs removed, and the casting replaced in the lathe, with the centres in the recess on the ends of the crank and a thrust rod between the webs; the shaft can then be completely finished.

The bracket for the slide-valve rod (Figs. 566 and 512) can easily be machined either in a lathe or with a drilling machine. The same instruction applies also to the slide-valve gland, the piston-rod gland, and the steam and exhaust flanges. The size of the steam pipe is $\frac{3}{16}$ in., the exhaust pipe $\frac{1}{4}$ in., the valve travel is $\frac{9}{32}$ in., and the cut off $\frac{3}{4}$ in. of the stroke. The piston ring (Fig. 566A) is supplied already finished with the sets of castings referred to.

Having now completed the machine work for the whole of the parts (most of them are shown in Fig. 567), all that remains is the assembling, the grinding in of the slide valves, and the jointing with thin paper of all the cylinder and steam chest cover joints.

CHAPTER XV

A High-speed Compound Condensing Engine and Coil Boiler

The Engine.—As already mentioned, a condensing engine is from an efficiency point of view advantageous. Of course, the system would work with a single-cylinder non-compound engine; but the full value of the vacuum created by the ejector condenser would not be obtained. Furthermore, the average single-cylinder small-power engine is too much of a model to work for prolonged periods without showing signs of wear. For instance, a 1½-in. by 1½-in. vertical engine with a single cylinder (double-acting), such as are usually sold, may be made to give ½ h.p. with ease. But as a rule they are more or less models of large engines, and, the steam pressures and speed not being also to scale, the power developed with pressures of 50 lb. to 100 lb. per square inch is such that the bearings and other working parts will not withstand if the engine is put to continuous use.

By making a compound engine the work is split up between two cylinders. The amount of steam the engine can consume is halved, and, in addition, by using single-acting cylinders a much larger and heavier engine is obtained. Another point which is perhaps more important than all the above is that by employing two cylinders with cranks at 180° a more perfect balance is obtained. The reciprocating forces can be balanced by equal and opposite reciprocating forces. This follows proper engineering practice where high speeds are desired. The usual single-cylinder high-speed engine, as illustrated in Chapter XIV., hops all over the bench when one attempts to run it at speeds required by the average small-power dynamo.

The writer has designed specially the twin-cylinder single-acting compound engine in Fig. 568 as a part of a novel automatic condensing steam plant. The crank shaft is made up of a plain slab of metal $2\frac{1}{4}$ in. by $\frac{5}{8}$ in. (or $\frac{3}{4}$ in.) thick. No forging is required. Only one valve is used for the two cylinders. The exhaust from the high pressure is conducted through a cavity in the valve. The valve gear is extremely simple, and, furthermore, being provided with suitable castings with the cylinders bored, crank case and valve face machined, any amateur should be able to finish off the engine in quite a short time.

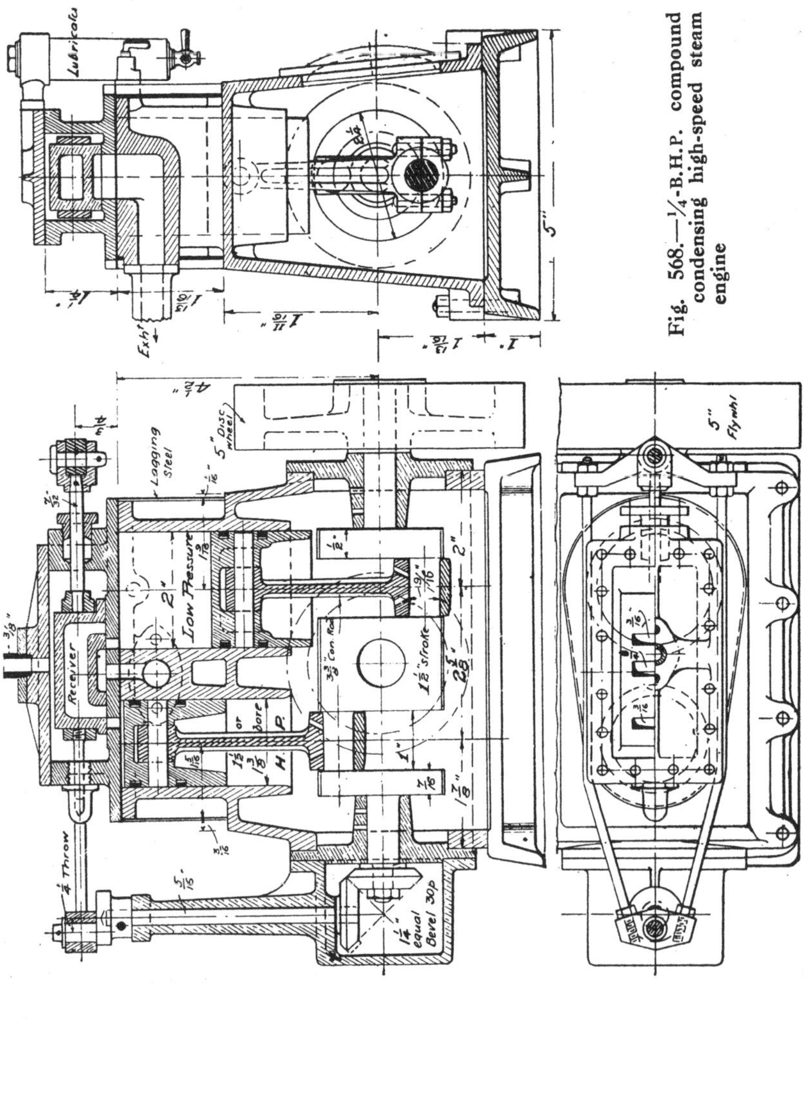

Fig. 568.—$\frac{1}{4}$-B.H.P. compound condensing high-speed steam engine

In the matter of castings, Mr. Furmston, engineer's pattern maker, of Letchworth, and Messrs. Baldwin and Wills, Hatfield Road, Watford, can supply either in the rough or machined for this engine.

The main body of the engine is a combined casting of the cylinders and crank case, and should be made of nice soft iron. This requires accurate machining, and for this

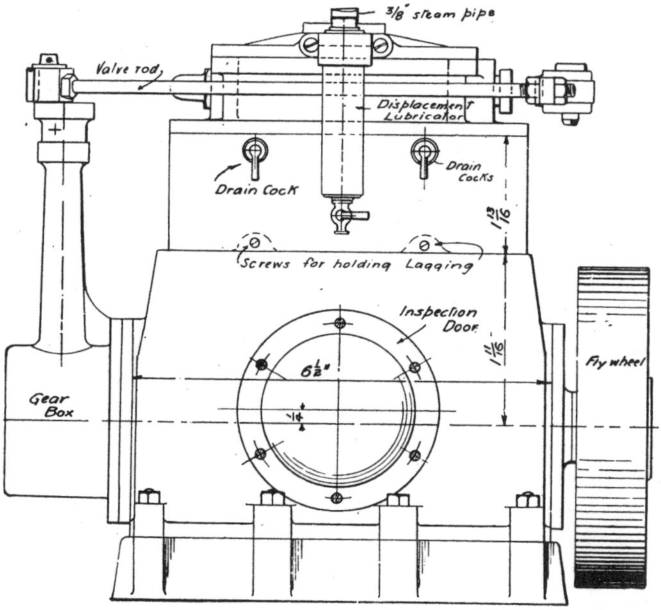

Fig. 569.—Elevation of ¼-B.H.P. compound condensing high-speed engine

a 5-in. gap lathe will be necessary, the casting being first filed or planed square and clean on the bottom, and then clipped on the faceplate. After the two boring operations the casting may be clipped on the boring table, and have the holes for the circular bearings bored out and faced at the one setting. The hole should be $2\frac{1}{4}$ in. in diameter, so that the crank shaft can be inserted from either end.

The illustrations are marked with alternative dimensions for the high-pressure cylinder bore. This is intended to allow for variations in the steam pressure. Where the pressure is low the larger size of high-pressure cylinder should be adopted. Where it is high, say over 50 lb., the bore of the high-pressure cylinder may be $1\frac{3}{8}$ in. Where it is very high, the low-pressure cylinder may be bored out as large as the castings will allow in addition. This adjustment of bores is necessary, as with low pressures the ratio of expansion must be lowered. For instance, the ratio of capacity of the $1\frac{3}{8}$-in. or 2-in. cylinder is as 1·48 is to 3·14. Therefore, with 50-lb. gauge pressure, which with the atmospheric pressure is 65 lb. absolute, the low-pressure cylinder pressure will be $65 \times 1{\cdot}48 \div 3{\cdot}14 = 30$ lb. approximately. With 30-lb. gauge pressure the absolute pressure would be 45 lb. and the low-pressure pressure 20 lb., whereas by making the high-pressure cylinder $1\frac{1}{2}$-in. bore, the ratio of expansion will be 1·76 to 3·14, and the low-pressure cylinder steam pressure maintained at about 30 lb. per square inch.

The bearings may be made of either cast iron or gun-metal; the latter is probably the best material, and represents only a plain turning and boring job to complete. They are very long, and no adjustment for wear is required. The lubrication is effected by sawing a couple of slots in the upper surface of the bearing as shown in Fig. 571.

Trunk pistons are used. The construction of these are the same as in petrol engines; but there is one variation—namely, to preserve the balance the high-pressure casting is proportionately much heavier. The idea is to equalise the weights of the low-pressure and high-pressure pistons in spite of their different diameters. The piston rings may be of cast-iron or steel, and should be of the eccentric form. Fig. 573 shows at A the high-pressure piston and connecting rod, and at B the low-pressure piston.

The valve may be a bronze or iron casting, and the receiver port should be cored as small as possible on the face, so that it can be accurately chipped to size. The exhaust port in the main cylinder body casting may be cored out; but the three ports in the valve chest should be drilled and filed out. The bevel gears should have an equal number of teeth in each wheel, and should be securely fixed to the respective shafts, the setting of the valve gear being accomplished by rotating the small disc crank on the top of the vertical countershaft. Until the final testing is accom-

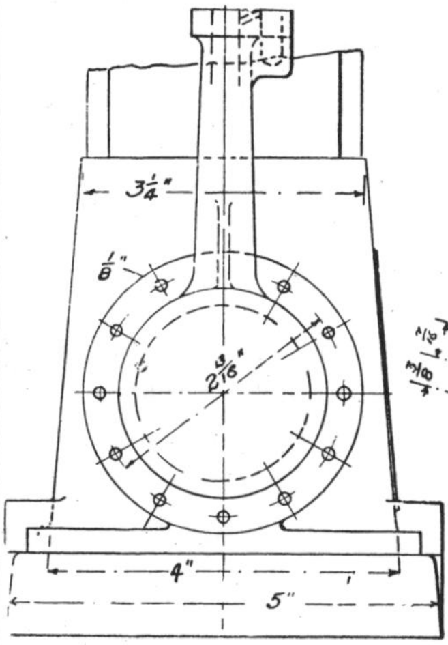

Fig. 570.—Part end elevation of compound engine, showing gear box

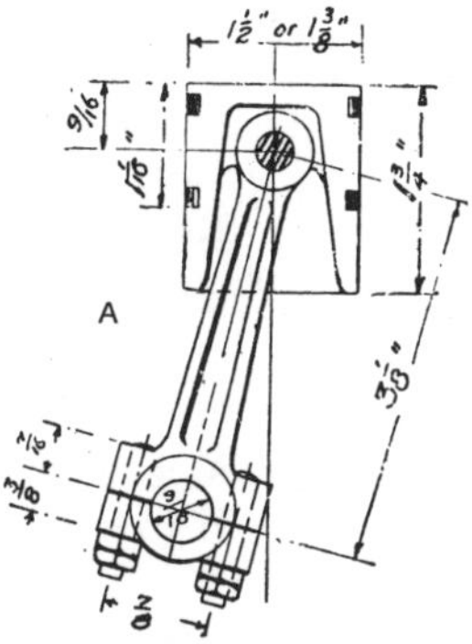

A

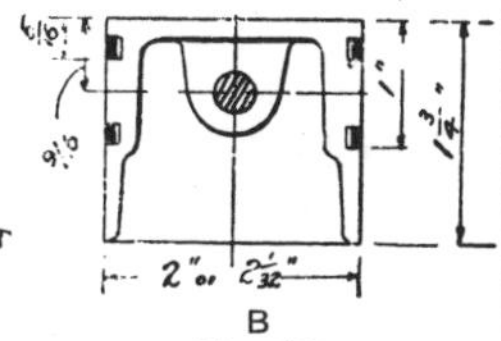

B

Fig. 573

Fig. 573.—High-pressure (A) and low-pressure (B) pistons, etc.

Fig. 571.—Lubricating-slots in main bearings of engine

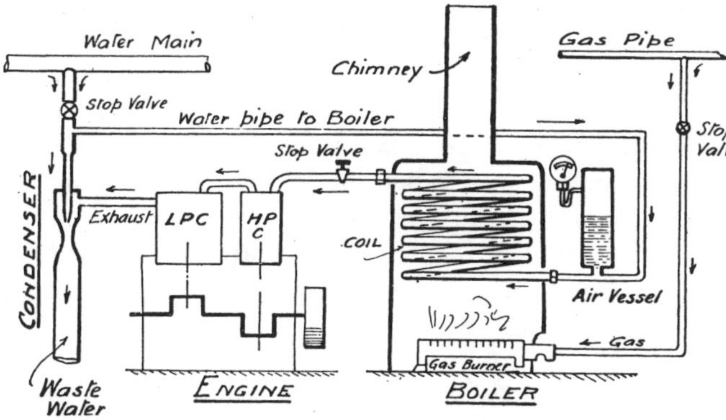

Fig. 572.—General arrangement of automatic steam plant, including compound engine

plished, this crank should be held by a small set-screw. Afterwards it may be fixed with a pin driven right through as indicated. The connecting rods should be bronze castings. The valve spindle is driven by a stirrup formed of two $\frac{3}{16}$-in. steel rods. This is made adjustable by the double nuts on the cross-bar which pivots in the valve spindle cross-head. Splash lubrication is provided for; but there is nothing against fitting forced lubrication to all bearings, the oil being introduced into the gear case at the end. It is estimated that speeds of 3,000 revolutions per minute are well within the capabilities of the engine, so that direct driving of either a small dynamo or a centrifugal pump will be quite possible without undue vibration or noise. The working parts are entirely enclosed, and the engine should therefore work without creating any mess.

The valve is held in a buckle, and the spindle is tailed through to the back end. In fitting the buckle to the valve spindle, the latter should be fixed in one piece; the tail end should be soldered in, and then the part in the centre, where the valve comes, should be filed or sawn away. The tail-end bearing is screwed into the steam-chest wall.

The lubricator is of the "Roscoe" displacement type. It is a cylindrical vessel made of brass tube, bolting on to the steam chest and having a draining cock at the bottom. The outlet is a small hole at the top, and the action is one of water displacing the oil. The water is introduced by steam entering the lubricator and becoming condensed.

In pursuance of an idea not only to cheapen the small-power steam plant, but to render its use more convenient and less messy, the writer has made some interesting experiments with a novel combination of boiler, engine, and condenser, which, even with the rough apparatus then available, proved quite a success. With the better engine just described there is no reason why a high degree of efficiency should not be obtained. Taking the ordinary $1\frac{1}{2}$ in. by $1\frac{1}{2}$ in. steam engine for example, to supply it with steam an outlay of £4 or £5 will be required for a copper or steel boiler, to say nothing of the cost of pumps, fittings, water gauges, etc. And when all is complete, it will be found that one has to stand by the engine practically all the while, either tending the fire, adjusting the draught by damper or blower, working or regulating the pump or injector. Then there is the difficulty of the exhaust steam. If it is used to induce a draught in the chimney as in a locomotive, a smaller and cheaper boiler may be used; but the attention required is increased. To simply lead it out into the atmosphere is a waste of heat energy, and in any case the steam should not be allowed to exhaust into a room where there are tools or other appliances which can rust.

The Automatic System.—With the system illustrated by Fig. 572 there is no mess, and no attention is required. No boiler fittings are required, except, perhaps, an emergency safety valve and a pressure gauge. With the first experimental plant neither pressure gauge nor safety valve was used, and the engine was started in a few minutes and then left to run all day. Not a vestige of steam was visible; the engine might have been revolving by a hidden electric motor or clockwork mechanism as far as the casual observer could tell.

The system the writer has invented combines in a single unit three separate component parts—the boiler, which is of the coil or semi-

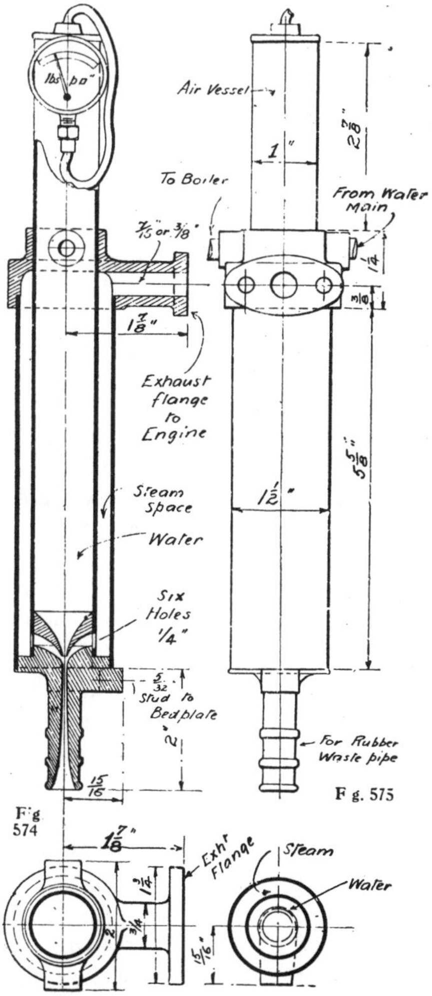

Fig 574

F g. 575

Fig. 576

Fig. 577

Fig. 574 to 577.—Arrangement and details of ejector condenser

flash type; an engine, preferably compound; and an ejector condenser, and necessitates the use of the house-water supply. Gas is the best and simplest fuel, and when properly installed it is possible to put one flexible pipe on the gas bracket and the other on the water tap, and after heating up the boiler coils, the water may be turned on and the engine immediately set going. The pressure in the water tap continuously supplies the boiler as it requires water. The pressure should be at least 30 lb. or 40 lb. per square inch, the higher the better. A compound engine is recommended for two reasons—(1) that it regulates the consumption or extraction of steam from the boiler, and (2) that it enables the expansive force of steam to be utilised and still further separates the condenser from the boiler.

The condenser is a simple piece of jet apparatus like an injector in which the force of the jet is utilised to extract the air and vapour and create a vacuum.

A general idea of the plant is obtainable from the diagram (Fig. 572). The water, it will be seen, is attached to the house service in any convenient manner. The writer, for his temporary experiments, converted an ordinary 4½d. anti-splash nozzle to take a flexible tube. The water from the house supply takes two courses, one to the ejector and the other to the boiler. The boiler is a coil or gridiron of tube; for small model plants copper tube can be used, and for larger installations steel tube is to be preferred. Before passing to the boiler coils the water passes an air vessel or balance chamber. This forms a flexible cushion between the water service and the boiler. From the engine the exhaust steam is conducted to the ejector condenser, and here it meets the other branch of the water supply. The force of the jet sucks out the steam from the low-pressure side of the engine and also condenses the steam, at the same time creating a vacuum.

Ejector Condenser.—The ejector condenser is a simple piece of jet apparatus made up of brass rod gunmetal castings tube as shown in Figs. 574 to 577. It acts as a surface condenser, jet condenser, air vessel, and to some extent also as a feed-water heater. The inner tube contains the cold water from the main. This enters at the flange casting near the top, and on the opposite side another pipe leads to the boiler. The steam is conducted outside the cold water containing tube. In the bottom of the latter the jet is fixed. The jet apparatus communicates with steam space by six holes drilled through at the bottom of the 1-in. tube. The orifice of the jet should not be more than $\frac{1}{16}$ in. at 60-lb. pressure, or $\frac{5}{64}$ in. at 30-lb. pressure, and both the jet and the mixing cone should be truly concentric. The main water pipe to the condenser should have a bore of at least $\frac{1}{4}$ in., otherwise there will be a pressure drop in the condenser, and the boiler will not get its proper share of the water.

The principal thing in making the ejector nozzles is to see that the parts are truly concentric, and also that the bores of the nozzle and combining cone are smooth. The tools required are simple, and may be made out of flat steel for the water nozzle. The steel is cut to the exact shape of the internal size of the nozzle and cutting edges formed on it, like those on an ordinary diamond-pointed drill. The work (or the drill) should be run at high speed. The mixing cone may be cut with two conical D bits, one for each end, made by turning up a piece of silver steel to the shape and filing half of it away. The diameter of the smallest part of the mixing cone should only be a shade above $\frac{1}{16}$ in. in diameter. There is no need for rivets or screws in the construction of the ejector condenser. Plain turned fits and soft solder are sufficient. The only exception to this is the fixing of the water pipes, which should be screwed on or secured by unions, and the water nozzle, which should be pinned in place as well as soldered.

Flash Boiler.—The boiler is not the least important part of the automatic plant. The type of boiler is the coil, or, as it is sometimes called, the " flash " boiler. As a light boiler means that there is little reserve of power, the coils easily becoming either cooled down and " flooded " with variations in load, the largest and heaviest possible generator (within reason) is recommended, and in place of a fierce fire, such as a blow-lamp, the mild heat of an ordinary gas burner or that of a slow-combustion coke or anthracite fire.

Flash or coil boilers are not any more economical of fuel than the best water-containing generators, but their quick steam-raising qualities, absolute safety and simplicity, and—a most important consideration—their ease of manufacture, give them many favourable points in the eyes of the amateur engineer.

Material is the next consideration. In the writer's experimental gas-fired boiler, copper was used. This material is quite satisfactory for toy steam plants fired by spirit or

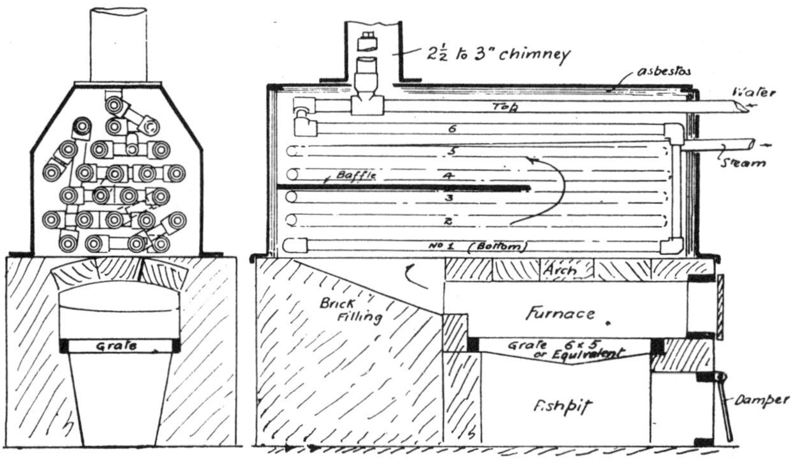

Fig. 578.—Stationary flash boiler for ⅛-B.H.P. compound engine

gas ; but the cost, and the fact that copper loses its strength to an alarming extent at high temperatures, make the use of iron or steel imperative in the present plant.

Fig. 578 shows a boiler made up of grids of steel or iron piping. As it is difficult to procure solid-drawn steel tubing of a heavy gauge (that is, with walls at least $\frac{1}{8}$ in. or $\frac{5}{32}$ in. thick), it is proposed to employ best-quality $\frac{1}{4}$-in. bore steam barrel and standard steam-quality elbows, tees, etc. Of course, it would be possible with a forge and suitable tools to bend up the grids without joints ; but as these may not be available, the writer is suggesting the built-up method. The tubes must be cut to varying lengths, and carefully screwed with the stocks and dies with a tapering

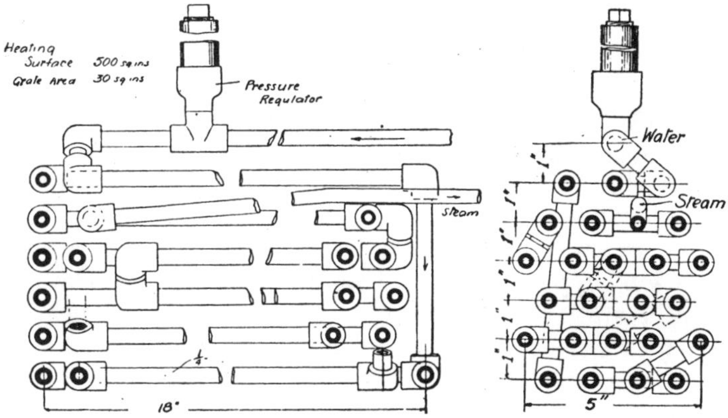

Figs. 579 and 580.—Grids or coils of flash boiler

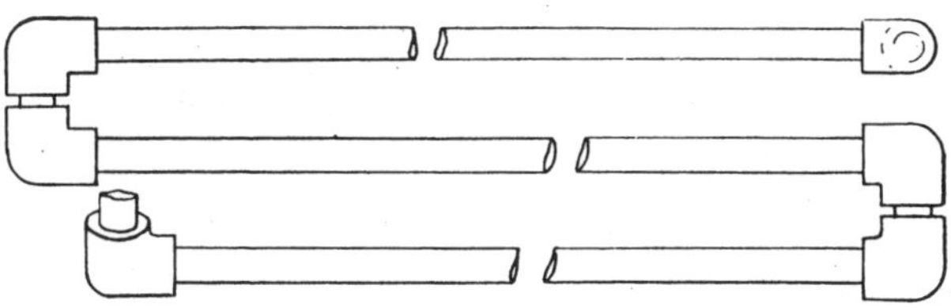

Fig. 581

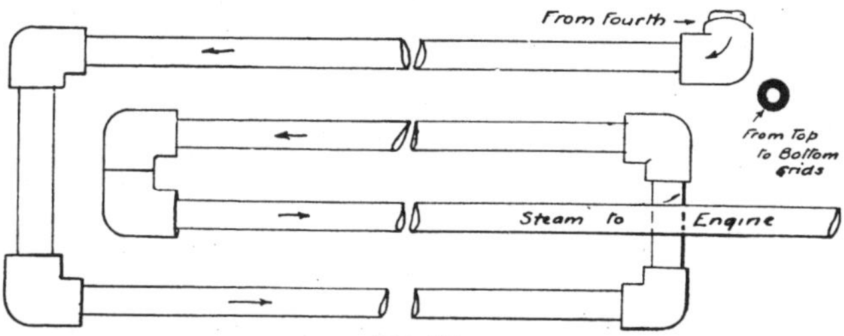

Fig. 582

Figs. 581 and 582.—Plans (enlarged) of boiler grids or coils, Nos. 6 (top) and 5

thread, so that they jam up quite tightly. To caulk them, red lead may be used, and, furthermore, the joints may be "rusted up" by passing some sal-ammoniac solution through the coils, leaving them for a few days for the chemical to take effect.

The design (Fig. 578) shows the boiler arranged in a combined sheet-iron and brickwork setting; and to protect the iron from the direct contact with the flame, the boiler is set in the flues, so to speak, and not directly over the fire. The water enters at the top, and in the top tube an air vessel or regulating chamber is arranged. This consists of a length, say 4 ft. or 5 ft., of ½-in. or ⅝-in. steam barrel, which is "teed" on to the top pipe. This forms a cushion between the water service and the boiler, and takes up any fluctuation of pressure. It has been found that the steam will not readily blow back into the water pipe. The water-delivery pipe is connected to (top) grid No. 6, and thence to No. 1, the bottom. The two top grids therefore act like feed-water heaters, and the early entry of the water to the bottom grid tends to prevent the burning of this set of tubes. The steam emerges at the fifth row from the bottom. A baffle plate of iron or asbestos sheet is arranged between tubes to distribute the heated gases throughout the whole of the tubes.

No fittings are really required on the boiler; but if desired, a safety valve or release valve set at double the usual working pressure may be fitted on the pipe which conducts the water to the coils. The draught should be natural, as obtained from a 10-ft. or 12-ft. chimney, as a mild heat is desired rather than a fierce quick-burning fire, which would cause the tubes to become red hot. The "flashing" of the water into steam is more effective if the tubes are only black hot. Water poured upon a red-hot surface takes a globular form surrounded by a film of steam, and therefore does not absorb the heat so readily.

The upper part of the generator casing is made of sheet-iron lined with asbestos card. This may be riveted on with copper rivets and washers.

There is no objection to increasing the weight of the boiler or the number of the grids; both of these modifications will tend to steady the steam supply and to reduce the required intensity of the fire.

CHAPTER XVI

A $\frac{1}{2}$-IN. SCALE MODEL MIDLAND RAILWAY EXPRESS LOCOMOTIVE

WHILE there are smaller types of locomotives to choose from, the design (Figs. 583 to 587) represents one of the simplest forms of express engine. The engine is short and will traverse curves of 6-ft. or 7-ft. radius. The external features resemble the older Midland Railway single locomotives brought up to date with a modern Belpaire fire-box. The cylinders are inside, and the boiler is a proper loco-type tubular boiler arranged for burning charcoal or other solid fuel.

Wheels and Frames.—The first consideration is the wheels and frames. All the castings are standard, and are readily obtainable from Messrs. Baldwin and Wills, 46 Hatfield Road, Watford, Herts, or A. W. Bond, 245 Euston Road, N.W. For the frames, $\frac{1}{16}$-in. thick hoop steel, which is made in 2-in. by $2\frac{1}{2}$-in. widths, is excellent material. The frames are what are known as double frames; but in the model the inside frames extend only so far as the valve motion requires them. They are secured to the outside frames, which run from end to end at the buffer planks, and by distance pieces (blocks of brass) placed just in front of the driving wheels. The arrangement of the frames is shown in Figs. 584 and 588. The buffer planks in the engine actually built are standard gunmetal castings, and have flanges cast on the top for fixing the footplating. Additional lugs or make-up pieces were therefore required to fix the outside frames. These lugs were made of blocks of brass soldered and riveted to the buffer planks. The centre-lines of motion and other centre-lines and holes should be marked on the frames at the outset, so that little or no drilling is required when the frames are erected. The most important of these is the cylinder centre-line. This is inclined, and at the centre of the cylinders measures $1\frac{15}{16}$ in. above rail level. All motion parts are square with this inclined centre-line and not with the level of the rails. Care must be more

Fig. 583.—Photograph of finished model M.R. express locomotive and tender

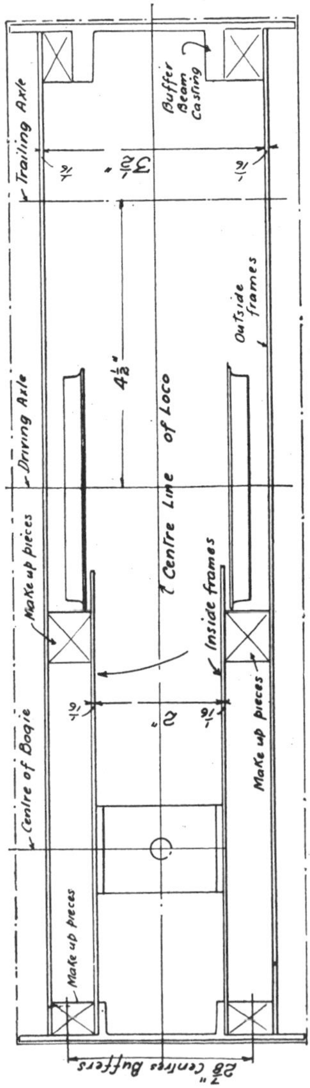

Fig. 584.—Plan of framing of M.R. engine

particularly exercised in correctly drilling the hole for the "slide" or "weigh" shaft of the valve motion, and also that of the correcting link, as on the accuracy of these much of the success of the engine depends. Another point is that the correcting links of the valve gear should be made at an early stage, so that they may be fitted on as the frames are being built up. At any rate, it is necessary to consider the fixing of the pivot pin owing to the proximity of the distance piece which attaches the inner and outside frames.

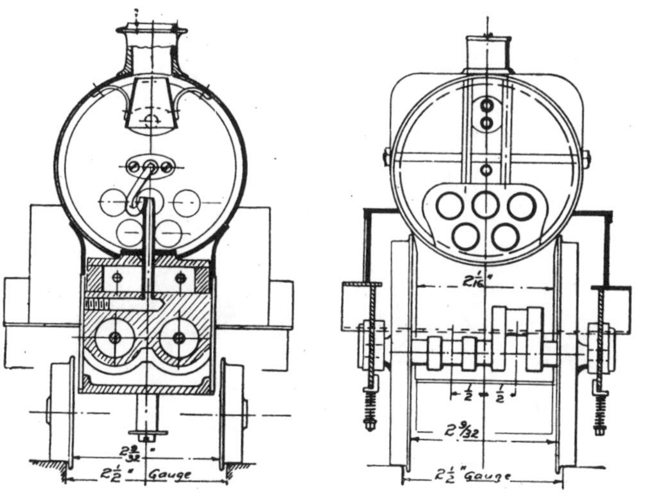

Fig. 585.—Cross sections of model M.R. engine

The bogie frames are of the same kind of steel as the main frames. These are cut out to shape and screwed with three $\frac{3}{32}$-in. countersunk screws to the central slotted casting. This casting has a lug on each side which overhangs the side frames and forms abutments for the spiral springs of the equaliser. The equalisers shown in perspective in Fig. 591 are castings with the centre part thickened up to take two spiral springs. The holes for these are blind holes drilled nearly to the bottom, if possible, a drill with a flat point being used to finish the holes. The holes in the equalisers are $\frac{9}{32}$ in. in diameter—to fit the axles easily—and when all the parts are finished, one bogie wheel only being fixed to each axle, the latter are threaded through the equalisers and the slotted holes in the frames and the other wheels finally driven on.

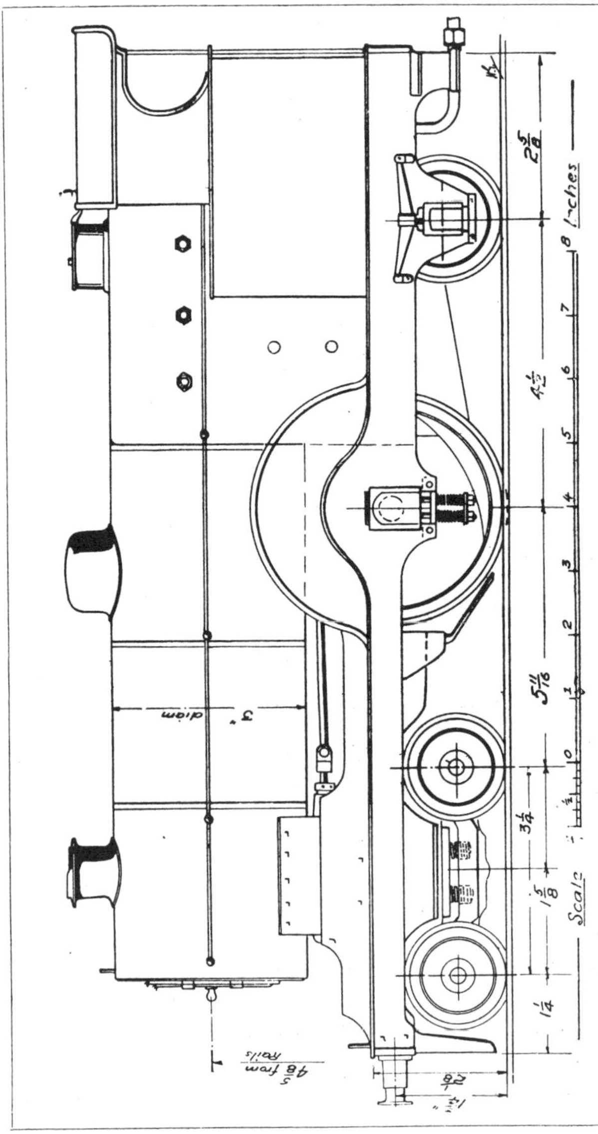

Fig. 586.—General arrangement of model M.R. express locomotive engine

Cylinders.—With larger bogie wheels, which are recommended where the curves to be traversed are not sharper than 7-ft. radius, the outline of frames in Fig. 588 may be

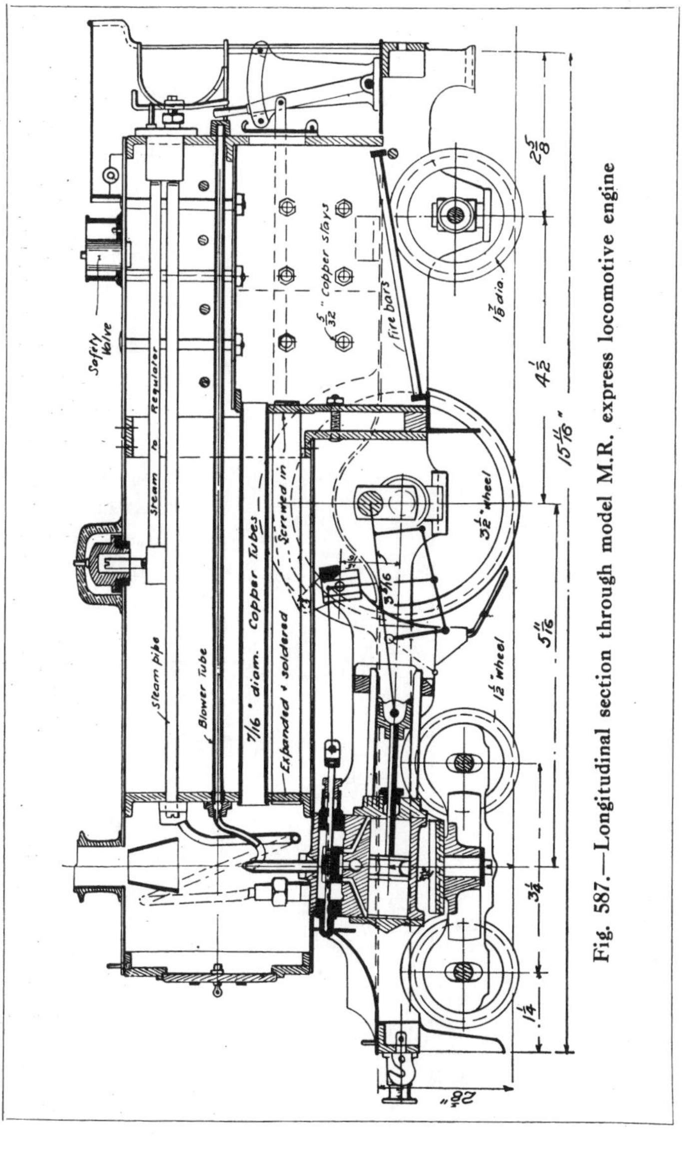

Fig. 587.—Longitudinal section through model M.R. express locomotive engine

adopted. The cylinders (Figs. 590 and 592) are of a well-known design, as described in Chapter VI., and where the home mechanic has no facilities for making them accurately, they can be purchased complete. The exhaust pipe is coned at the top to sharpen the puff. This is best done with a light hammer in a groove filed in the edge of any convenient iron block. The back end of the valve spindle has a guide. This is an important feature, and is to be recommcnded where any form of Joy's valve gear is employed.

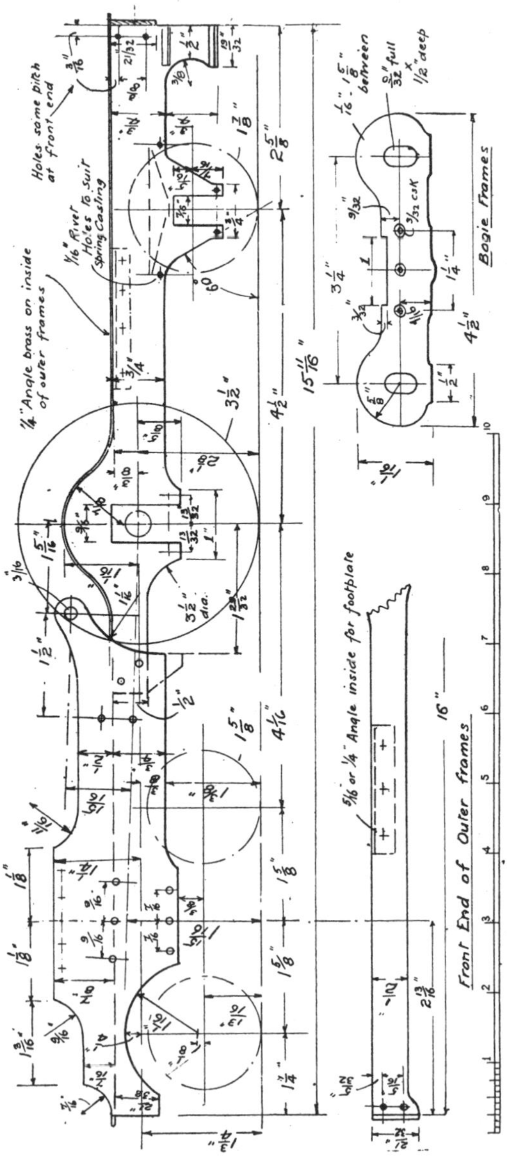

Fig. 588.—Arrangement of frames in model M.R. locomotive

The slide valve is adjustable, the spindle being screwed into a square nut fitted in a slot in the back of the nut. The valve spindle should be screwed with the finest thread available, so that an accu-

Fig. 589.—Photograph of locomotive parts and castings

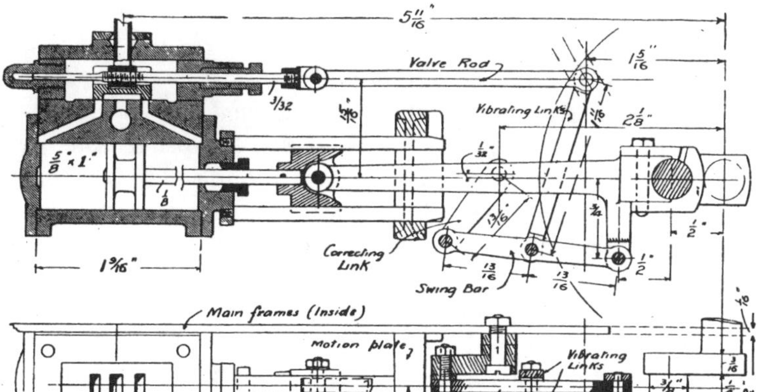

Fig. 590.—Diagrams of valve gear

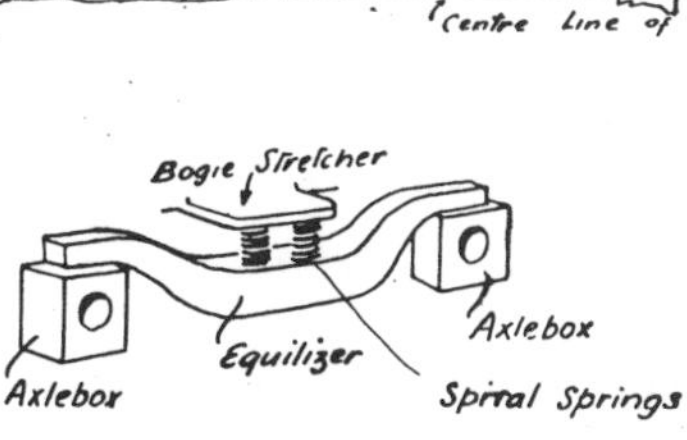

Fig. 591.—Bogie equalisers

rate adjustment of the valve may be obtained by undoing the valve rod from the forked crosshead, and turning it a half or complete turn one way or the other.

Crank Axle.—The crank axle may be forged or built up. The latter method was adopted in the engine illustrated. The shaft is of $\frac{3}{8}$-in. bright mild-steel rod, and the webs of $\frac{3}{16}$-in. by $\frac{1}{2}$-in. steel bar. The ends of the axle are turned down to $\frac{1}{4}$-in. diameter at the ends to fit in the brass bearings outside the wheels. This work and the shouldering down to $\frac{5}{16}$ in. for the wheels was done before the axle was cut away between the webs. The crank pins were not turned; but to give a good finish the tips of the crank webs may be cleaned off in the lathe.

Driving Wheels.—The driving wheels are turned up to the largest diameter the castings will allow (not exceeding $3\frac{1}{2}$ in. on the tread), the distance between the backs of the tyres when finished and fixed being $2\frac{9}{32}$ in. The flange should be a bare $\frac{1}{8}$ in. deep.

Slide Bars.—Two slide bars are of $\frac{1}{8}$-in. by $\frac{3}{16}$-in. mild steel turned down at the cylinder ends as described in Chapter III. (Fig. 83), and then screwed; $\frac{1}{8}$-in. holes are tapped in the cover to receive the bars, the other ends being supported by the motion plate illustrated in detail in Fig. 595.

Connecting Rods.—The connecting rods are cast in gunmetal, and have a species of "strap" big end. The lug for swinging bar of the valve motion is cast on to the stock end of the rod. This is forked, and a shouldered countersunk screw or a riveted pin secures the end of the swing bar. The anchor link, or correcting link, is slung from the frame, and has an overhung pivot pin. The swing link should be as thick as the connecting rod, so that, by relieving the sides of the vibrating links, the connecting rod will not touch these links. The vibrating links are in pairs, and at the top end embrace the valve rods. The distance between the side blocks should therefore equal the thickness of the three links.

Weigh Shaft.—The weigh shaft is a standard casting, and it should be first bored out with the four $\frac{1}{4}$-in. holes. The end pivots should then be marked out, centred and turned up, and when this is done the centre portion to clear the links may be filed out. Care must be exercised in holding the weigh shaft in the vice, so that the shaft is in no way

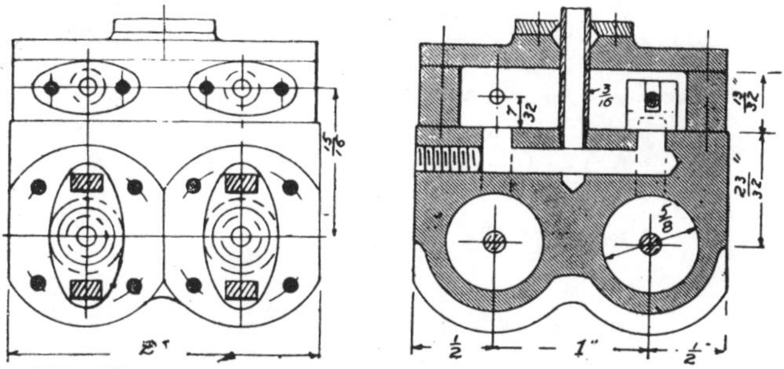

Fig. 592.—End view and cross section of M.R. locomotive cylinders

Fig. 593. — Trailing wheel, showing spiral spring in buckle of dummy spring

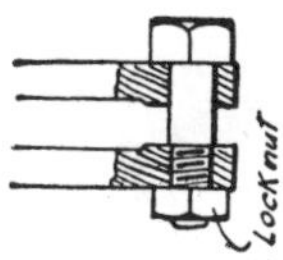

Fig. 594.—Typical pin joint for valve motion parts

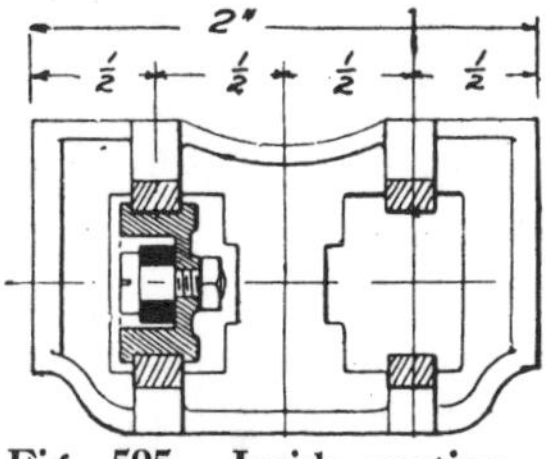

Fig. 595.—Inside motion-plate and crosshead

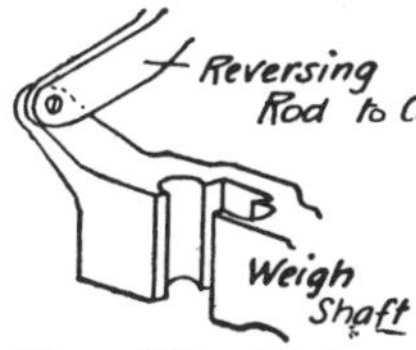

Fig. 596.—Fixing reversing rod to weigh shaft

bent or sprung out of alignment. Although a solid piece of metal at the outset, most of it is cut away at the centre-lines of the motion. In this particular model, owing to the

Fig. 597.—Photograph of front of chassis

Fig. 598.—View of valve gear

large size of the driving wheel it is not possible to carry the reversing rod outside or over the top of the wheel splasher. The reversing rod must therefore be fixed on the inside of the arm, as shown in Fig. 595, and the rod (made of $\frac{1}{16}$-in. by $\frac{1}{4}$-in. steel strip) must be bent outwards over the tread of the wheel tyre and then back close up against the fire-box. The splasher conceals the bends thus formed. The valve rods, swing bars, and vibrating links are best made out of strip steel, and the bolts should have a thread in one

Fig. 599.—Underside view of valve gear

Fig. 600.—Chassis finished and boiler in course of construction

of the three portions of the particular joint, lock-nuts being fitted on the outside. An enlarged section of a typical pin joint is shown by Fig. 594. One fork or link must therefore be tapped, while the other is drilled with a clearing hole. This is the only satisfactory method for pin joints in model work. Using an ordinary screw as a pin joint should be avoided.

Setting the Gear.—To set the gear the first consideration should be to get the link gear right. This is very simply done. The big end of the connecting rod is set on one of the dead centres. The slide block should then fall exactly in the centre of the slide or weigh shaft, so that when the latter is moved from backward to forward positions the valve spindle does not move. Adjustments are easily made by bending the swing bar either up or down in the centre. This, in effect, lengthens or shortens the vibrating links, and it is almost certain that, however careful the maker is in marking out the links and rods, some such adjustment will be necessary. When the link gear has been trued up, all that is required is to place the valve exactly in the centre of its travel when the big end is on dead centre. The valve should be *not more than* $\frac{1}{20}$ in. longer over all than the total over-all width (over the outer edges) of the steam ports. The cavity should also be shorter than correct for a normal valve. The setting of the valve in the centre of its travel is accomplished by taking the valve rod out of its forked crosshead and turning the spindle one way or the other.

Testing Chassis under Steam.—When the valve motion is fitted up and the pistons are packed, the chassis, having arrived at the state of completion shown by Fig. 600, may be tested under steam from a separate boiler. For this purpose the writer used a Lyle's syrup tin, soldered up and heated over a gas stove. Care is necessary in using such a boiler; but if only employed once or twice it is quite safe up to 15 lb. or 20 lb. pressure. Another and much safer temporary boiler is a coil of copper pipe heated over a gas ring, and fed with water either from the house water-main or from a tin tank in which an air pressure is maintained by means of a cycle pump.

Boiler.—The boiler is a coal-fired loco-type generator. It is, however, more simplified and has water spaces on three sides of the firebox only. The back plate is "dry," the comparatively large firehole occupying most of the lower portion of the plate. The barrel of the boiler is a piece of

3-in. solid-drawn copper tube with No. 18 gauge walls. The firebox is of the square-topped kind—known as the Belpaire firebox—and the outer shell is of No. 18 gauge copper fitted on to flanged gunmetal castings for the throat plate and back plate. The circular throat-plate flange is turned up

Fig. 601.—Parts of model M.R. locomotive boiler

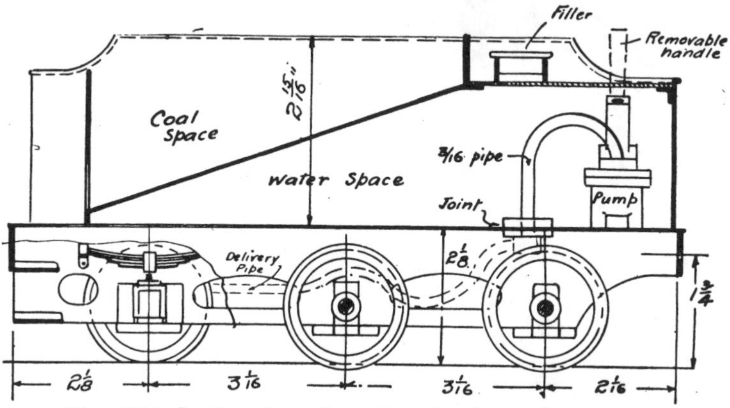

Fig. 602.—Section through tender, showing tank and pump

a driving fit for the barrel tube, and the latter riveted on with $\frac{3}{32}$-in. copper rivets, flush riveted on the outside. When riveted, the joint is caulked with soft solder. The firebox wrapper is formed up to shape on a block of wood of the exact section of the firebox, the copper being softened preparatory to shaping up. It is then riveted on to the throat plate. The inner firebox is built up on the back plate, a flange being cast on the inside of this plate. The firebox should be riveted and silver soldered. This is important, as it is the inner firebox that suffers should the boiler be allowed to become low in water. The tubes are screwed into the firebox tube plate in the manner already referred to. At the smokebox end the tubes are expanded in with a taper drift and then soft soldered.

Fig. 603.—Underside of finished M.R. locomotive; also showing firebars

The firebox having several flat sides, it will require staying. For this purpose direct stays are required of $\frac{5}{32}$ in. diameter, screwed 40 threads per inch (*see* Chapter IX). The four stays which cross the upper part of the firebox are of $\frac{5}{32}$-in. rod, threaded all the way along and lock-nutted with thin brass nuts on the outside.

The regulator is the writer's latest design, and is a standard fitting. It is a plug cock arranged with a hollow plug, fitting eccentrically in a circular body, after the pattern of the regulator illustrated in Fig. 447 (Chapter X.). It is also arranged to take steam from the dome. The dome is removable, and acts as a filler. The safety-valve is screwed into the firebox top and soldered. It has an oval ornamental casing which lifts off.

The smokebox is in one piece with the boiler barrel. The front is a flanged casting, and is turned to fit a disc forming the door. This disc is fitted with steel straps for hinges, which fit in eyes riveted on to the smokebox. The

Fig. 604.—Model M.R. locomotive boiler made and fitted

fastening is a latch operated by a knob on the outside. The fittings comprise a water gauge with not less than $\frac{3}{16}$-in. glass, pressure gauge $\frac{3}{4}$ in. in diameter and reading to 100 lb. per sq. in., and a check valve for $\frac{3}{16}$-in. pipe. The check valve is connected to a pipe which passes under the footplate and has a union at the end for attaching the pipe from the pump in the tender.

Tender.—The main frames of the tender are of steel

Fig. 605.—Model M.R. locomotive engine finished, with dome removed and smoke-box door open

$\frac{1}{16}$ in. thick, and are cut out as shown. They should be shaped up together, and when finished and parted, the horn plates, made of commercial $\frac{1}{4}$-in. by $\frac{1}{4}$-in. angle brass, should be riveted on. The laminated springs are dummy, as on the trailing end of the locomotive, and have small spiral springs, wound up out of pianoforte wire, concealed in the buckle. This is a very effective device, which reduces the amount of work considerably. It is not possible to make a plate spring to scale and at the same time to work with sufficient resiliency. The frames of the tender are fixed to angles on the end buffer planks, and light steel or brass angles are riveted to the top to form a fixing for the tank.

The tank is made of brass sheet; but, of course, where expense must be considered, stout tinned plate may be employed. One half of the tank has a sloping top, while the other is flat and removable (*see* Fig. 602). It allows the pump to be fixed into the tank and its valves to be attended to should anything go wrong. The delivery pipe ($\frac{3}{16}$-in. copper) is brought out of the bottom by a grummeted joint, the delivery pipe below the tank being entirely separate and having a double coil in it to give the necessary flexibility. This pipe fits that on the engine with a $\frac{3}{16}$-in. union.

The pump is a "drowned" pump, and, being immersed in the water, requires no suction pipe. It is operated by a lever which has a removable handle passing through a slot in the top of the tank. The only fittings of the tender are handrails, two spring buffers, and drawhooks. The tender is attached to the engine by the flap footplate, which is dropped over a stud on the tender. The edging of the tanks is of half-round $\frac{3}{32}$-in. brass wire.

In steam raising a good method is to use a Bunsen gas flame under the firebox, a draught being created by pumping air into the boiler with a cycle pump, through the feed pipe and check valve. The steam blower is turned on fully and the tender is separated from the engine, the cycle pump having a replica of the union on the end of a rubber flexible connection. When steam is nearly raised a few knobs of charcoal may be placed in the firebox. The gas will ignite this. The pressure arriving at 20 lb., the steam boiler can be turned on. The working pressure should not be less than 50 lb., and skill in stoking and feeding the boiler, which will soon be acquired, will enable the model-engine driver to maintain this pressure under all conditions of load.

CHAPTER XVII

A Working Model Metropolitan Railway Electric Locomotive

Electric locomotives are not so numerous in England as on the Continent and in America, but the engine illustrated in Fig. 606 is very representative of its order. The peculiar external design was first exemplified in the fine 95-ton machines made for the tunnel section of the Baltimore and Ohio line (U.S.A.) in 1895. Since then the use of the electric

Fig. 606.—Metropolitan Railway No. 1 class 50-ton 1,200 h.p. Westinghouse-type electric locomotive

locomotive has extended considerably, and externally similar engines have been built for the Central London, London Metropolitan, and the North Eastern Railways, to say nothing of the many other American electric lines, the Paris-Orleans and the Valtellina Railways.

The salient features of the Metropolitan Railway type of engine are the use of double bogies, which in the original have two motors on each, and a superstructure with a large central cab and two sloping ends encasing the controlling resistances and other operating gear. In the model to be

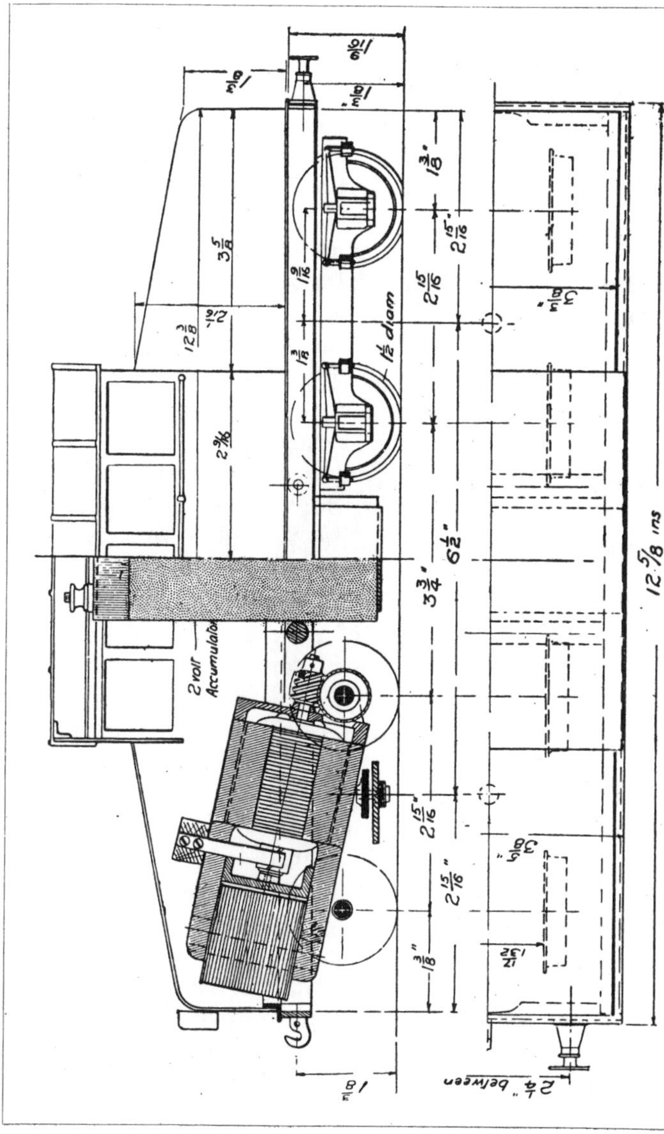

Fig. 607.—Part elevation, part vertical section and half plan of model electric locomotive

described, the external design can be as faithfully reproduced for a railway with a gauge of $1\frac{3}{4}$ in.—that is, the standard No. 1 gauge adopted by all model-makers. If the locomotive is intended to be only the beginning of a series of railway models, one of the smaller scales, such as that chosen, will be found much more satisfactory than a large one. In addition, the materials, castings, and tools required will not be so expensive.

It will be as well first to examine the various practical systems on which a model electric locomotive can be made to operate.

The current is collected from a fixed source by means of a central conductor rail and the running rails form the return circuit. This "third rail" system is in extensive use, but sometimes the return is made through a separate rail, the running rails not being sufficiently well bonded at the joints to provide for the return current. In a model there is no need for the extra return rail.

Reversing.—To provide for the reversing there are two or three well-known methods which may be adopted. The circuit through the rails may be provided with a starting and speed-controlling switch only, as in Fig. 610. This may be placed at any point on the supply wires between the battery and the rails; but, of course, will not enable the operator to reverse the engine from that point. It is a characteristic of the ordinary direct-current motor that a reversal of the direction of the current through the circuit will not reverse the direction of the rotation of the motor. This will be seen from Fig. 612. It is, of course, well known that a current in a coil of wire wound round a bar of iron causes that piece of iron to become a magnet, and also that the polarity of the ends of the bar for a given coil depends on the direction of the current impressed in the coil. The reversal of the current, therefore, reverses the polarity, and as the rotation of the electric motor is caused by the mutual attraction and repulsion of the poles of the field-magnet and armature, if the current through the coils on both the latter is changed over, no difference in this attraction and repulsion is effected. Only one portion of the motor-coil circuits requires to be changed to provide for a reversal in the direction of rotation.

This can be accomplished by the following methods: (1) The provision of a hand switch in the cab of the locomotive, which rearranges the current in the windings of the field-

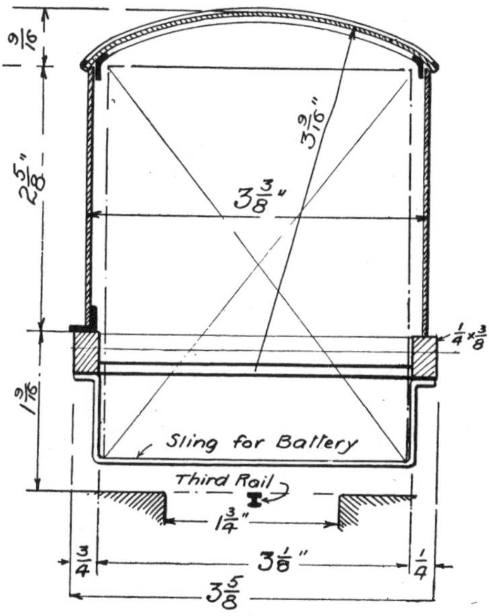

Fig. 608.—Cross section through electric locomotive (half-scale)

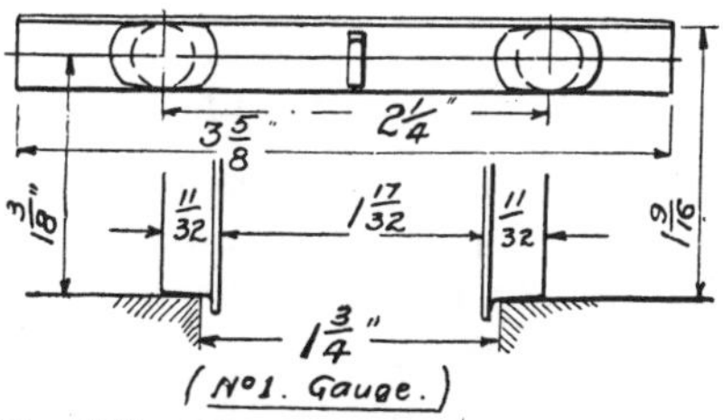

Fig. 609.—Diagram showing No. 1 gauge buffer and wheel dimensions

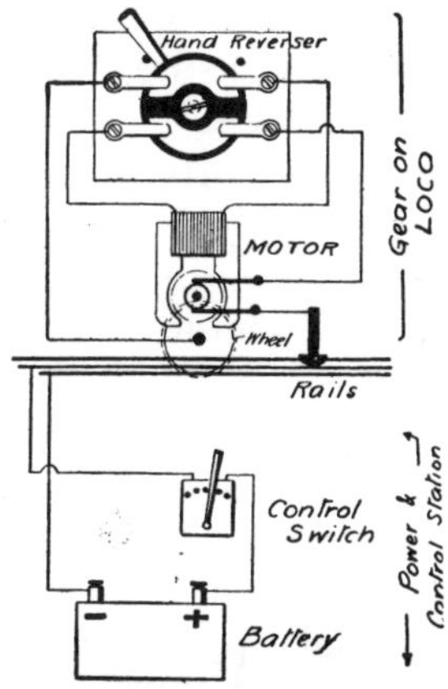

Fig. 610.—Series motor with hand reverser on locomotive and control on track

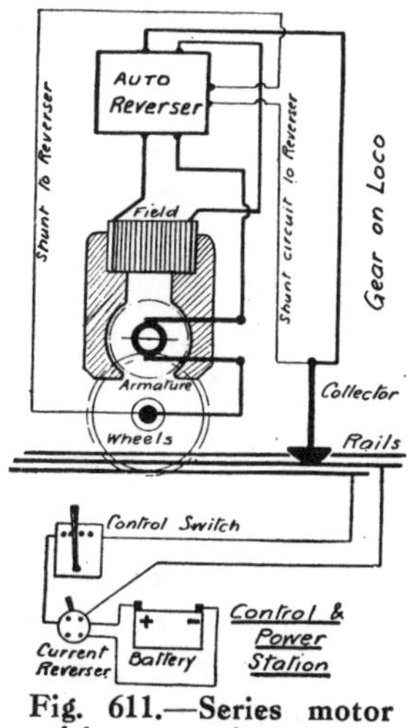

Fig. 611.—Series motor with automatic reverser

magnet and armature. This can only be effected by the operator going up to the locomotive. (2) The provision of an automatic polarised reversing switch which rearranges the current in the windings of the field-magnet and armature automatically, when the operator from any part of the line reverses the current in the conductor rails. (3) The use of a motor with permanent field-magnets. The field-magnets being of constant polarity and requiring no current and the armature fed from the line, the commutation (reversal) of the track current will reverse the locomotive. (4) The use of a motor which has its field-magnets supplied by a separate battery or accumulator (preferably the latter) on the locomotive and the armature from the rails. This is virtually the same as No. 3, except that a more powerful field is obtained by using a separately excited wound magnet.

Figs. 611 to 614 give the typical circuits involved in each arrangement of the motor.

In the model as described there are employed two traction-type motors, one on each bogie, with wound field-magnets, triple-thread worm gearing; a small accumulator in the central cab to excite the fields; underslung bogies with the pivot pins set back to give the greater amount of adhesive weight to the driving wheels; side spring-buffers; and a readily removable roof to the cab.

Polarised Auto-Reverser.—Among the several types of auto-reversers the pendulum type is shown in Fig. 615, and is eminently suited to the system in which there are two field coils, wound in opposite directions for running the motor forward and reverse respectively. In this system the connections are very simple. There is only one contact for the apparatus to make, and destructive sparking is practically eliminated. The motor should be of such a design as will allow a field-magnet with plenty of space for windings. This is necessary because double the usual amount of wire is necessary on the fields. The "Manchester" type would be very suitable, as the winding cores can be almost any length. The reverser consists of a circular permanent magnet made of square-section steel glass-hardened and then magnetised. In the gap between its poles swings a soft-iron pendulum

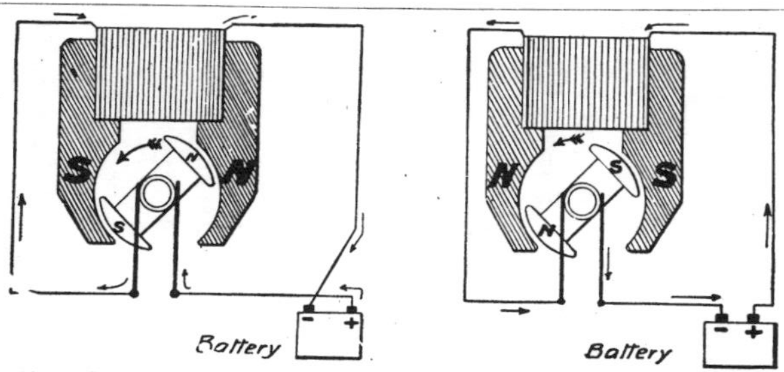

Fig. 612.—Two diagrams showing current reversal in ordinary-wound direct-current motor (the direction is not reversed)

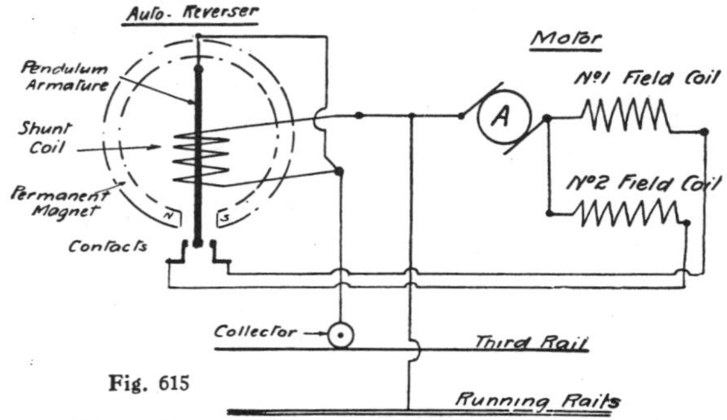

Fig. 615

Figs. 615 and 615a.—Auto-reverser for model electric locomotive

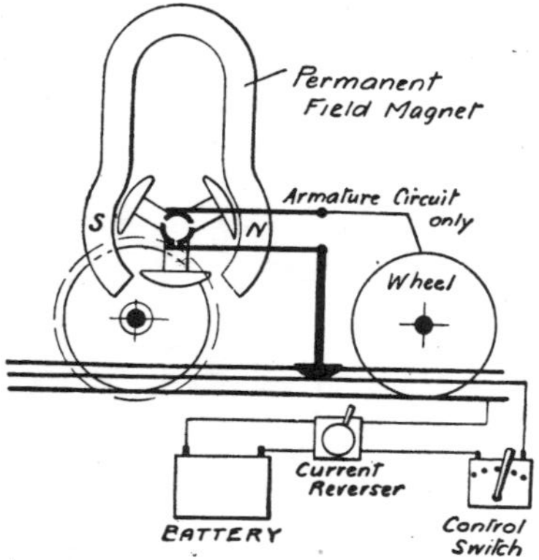

Fig. 613.—Permanent magnet motor system

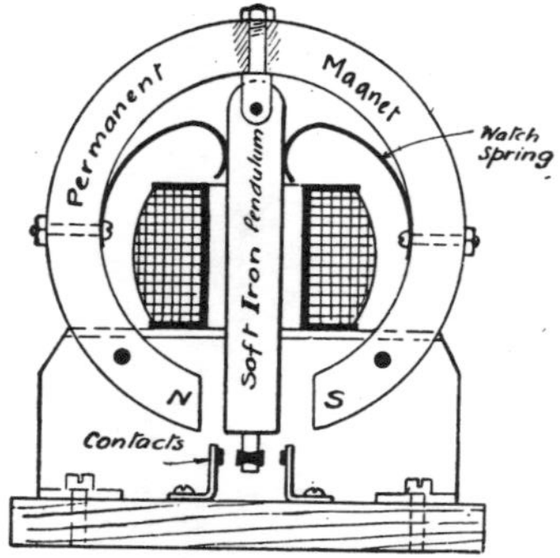

Fig. 615a

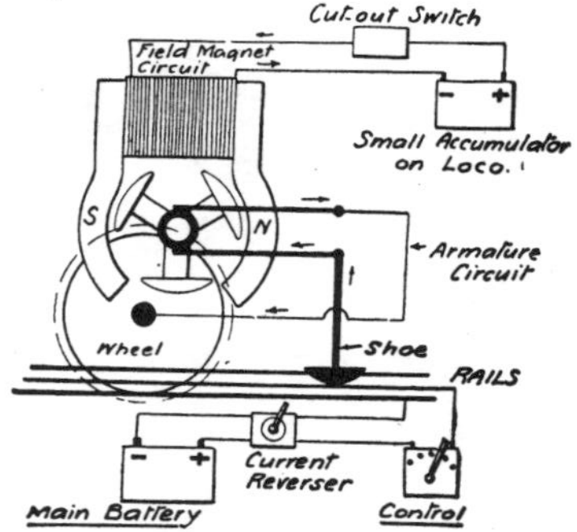

Fig. 614.—Separately excited motor system

armature. This armature is energised by a fixed coil having a core hole of sufficient diameter to clear the pendulum armature and to allow the latter to swing freely. The pendulum armature may be kept in its neutral position by gravity, but where the locomotive has to negotiate inclines it is better to control it by very light watch springs. The armature coil is a shunt circuit, and should be wound to take about $\frac{1}{8}$ ampere to $\frac{1}{16}$ ampere. The end of the armature carries the contacts, which should be of platinum. In action, either one coil of the field-magnet or the other is energised according to the direction of the current supplied to the rails. Although the direction of the current to the fields is changed on reversing the locomotive, the magnetism of the fields is constant in matter of polarity. The motor used with this reverser, except for the double field winding, has the same characteristics as an ordinary series motor, which form is of course the best for traction purposes.

Controlling Switch for Electric Railway. — With an electric locomotive fitted with permanent magnet or self-excited field, or with polarised relay switch, a reverser or commutating switch must be used in conjunction with the resistance switch on the side of the track. If it is arranged that the reversing and speed control may be operated by one handle, so much the better. The illustrations (Figs. 616 to 619) show how a combined reversing resistance switch may be made. This switch gives four speeds in both directions, and a stop position in the centre. Fig. 616 is the front elevation, and shows the stops and the curved commutating strips. The handle should be made of ebonite, vulcanite, or hard wood. The upper contactors A and B are plungers of $\frac{3}{16}$-in. brass rod with rounded ends pressed up to the strips with hard brass springs. The stud contactors are made by bending over two or more brass strips C, so that the ends of the metal engage the studs. The metal should not be wider than that of one stud plus one space. Stops S (Fig. 616) should be provided to limit the movement of the lever. The baseboard should be bushed with a brass bush (*see* Fig. 617), and should be fixed to a box containing the resistance wires (German silver or platinoid wire). The resistance wire should be hung on hooks (*see* Fig. 618). The two sets of studs 1 to 4 should be cross-connected, No. 1 to No. 1 and No. 4 to No. 4. The hooks x (Fig. 618) are not electrically

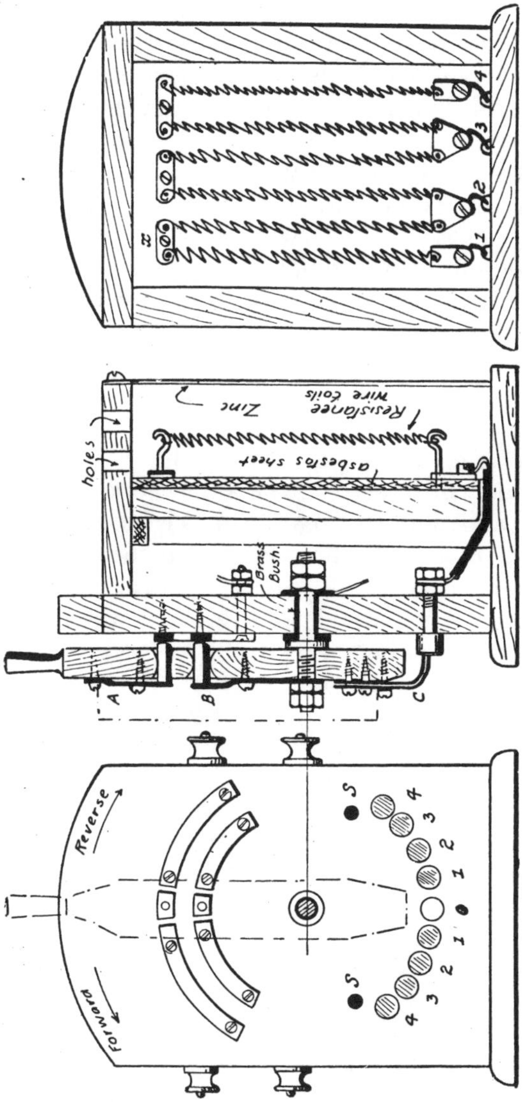

Fig. 616 Fig. 617 Fig. 618

Figs. 616 to 618.—Elevation, cross section and resistance frame of reversing and controlling switch for model electric railways

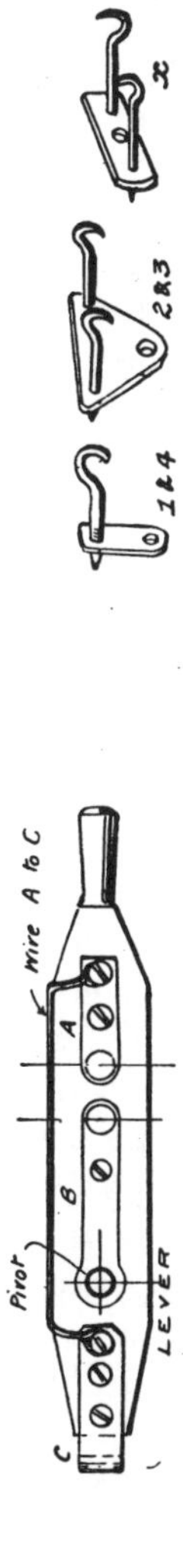

Fig. 619a.—Details of wire hooks

Fig. 619.—Details of handle

connected to any other part of the instrument, and are simply used to connect the tops of each pair of wires, and at the same time to keep the coils apart. The box enclosing the resistance frame may be lined with asbestos, a sheet of perforated zinc being fitted as the back cover. This, with holes at the top, will ventilate the resistance wires. Fig. 619 gives details of the handle and Fig. 619A of the hooks. The gauge of resistance wire will depend on the current to be passed.

The Motor.—The first consideration in the construction of the model will be the motor, and at the outset the standard arrangement illustrated in Fig. 620 will be dealt with. This motor may be made either of wrought-iron, with stampings for the armature, or of cast-iron for both fields and armature, the bearing brackets being castings, of course, in gunmetal. For electric motors of the traction type wrought-iron is very advantageous. The magnetic permeability of this metal is very superior to that of cast-iron, and therefore with a given expenditure of electric current the strength of the field-magnets is enormously increased. The same applies to the armature, and in addition this part can be made up of standard wrought-iron laminations built up on the armature spindle. Such an armature will stand a heavier current without heating up. The laminations prevent to a large extent the production of what are known as "eddy" currents, which represent so much wasted energy.

Of course, a casting for the field-magnets of the two motors can be obtained from the one pattern; but as this pattern involves a core-box for the tunnel, the amateur will find that it involves just as much labour to make the necessary pattern and clean up the castings as to saw the magnets out of raw material (as Fig. 621). The other alternative is to cast the limbs from one simple wooden pattern and to use a wrought-iron winding core.

The field-magnets may therefore be shaped out of $1\frac{1}{2}$-in. by $\frac{5}{8}$-in. good wrought-iron bar. If good, soft, and homogeneous stuff like Swedish iron is not readily obtainable, a very mild quality of steel may be employed. The bar should be cut into $3\frac{3}{8}$-in. lengths, and then marked out as shown in

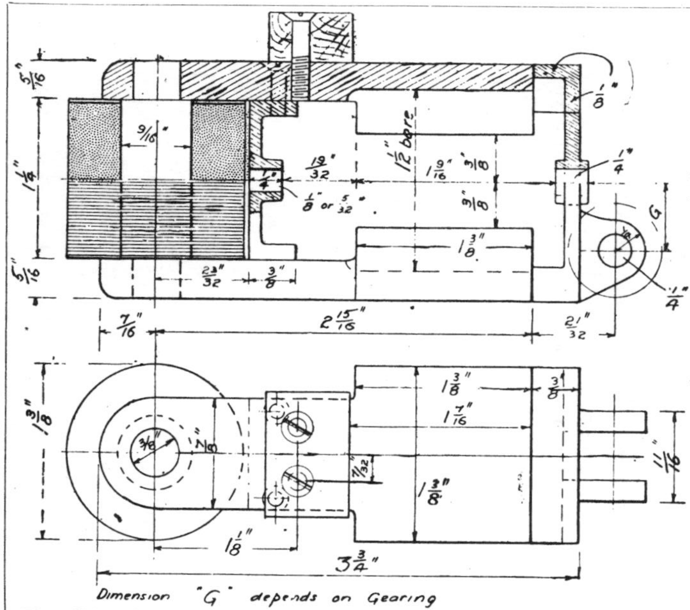

Fig. 620.—Standard type of motor for model electric locomotive

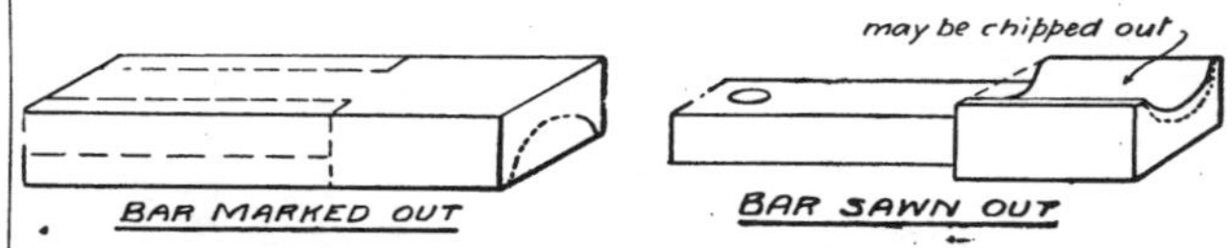

Fig. 621.—Sawing out field-magnet

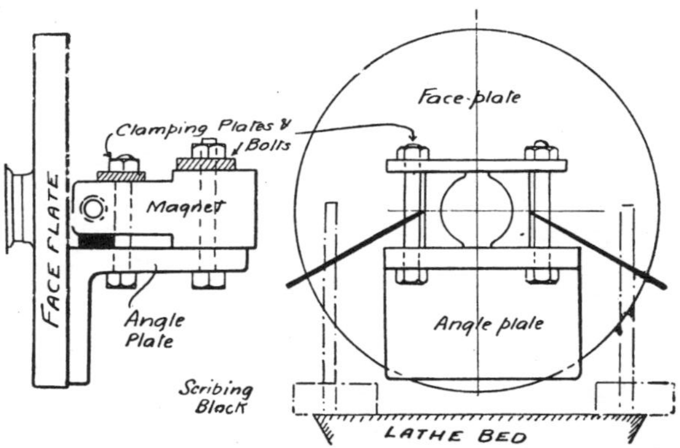

Fig. 622.—Field-magnet mounted in lathe for tunnel boring

Fig. 621. The limbs may then be sawn down to the reduced section, and to ensure accuracy the bars may be placed on the faceplate of the lathe after a small hole, say $\frac{1}{4}$ in. in diameter, for the winding core has been drilled. Then with the same setting the inside face may be machined true, and the winding core hole bored out to finished size. All the limbs (four for the two motors) are the same, and therefore the work can be very easily planned out.

The next operation would be to make the two winding cores out of Swedish iron bar to finish $\frac{9}{16}$ in. in diameter, shouldered down to $\frac{3}{8}$ in. in diameter at each end, as shown. The shouldered-down portions (or, at least, one) should be a driving fit on the magnet limbs. Before, however, this work is completed, to lighten the labour of boring out the tunnel the inside may be roughly chipped to the size marked out on the end. This work is optional, as the metal can all be removed in the lathe after the magnet is built up.

The method of setting it up on the lathe is shown in Fig. 622. The magnet limbs should be squared up if necessary, and bolted down on an angle plate, so that when the latter is level—that is, parallel with the bed—the centre-line of each pole-piece when tried with a scribing block is exactly the same height above the lathe bed. When this degree of accuracy is obtained, the bolts may be tightened up and the work proceeded with.

For wrought-iron or mild steel the tool should be as shown in Fig. 623, with plenty of clearance to prevent the back rubbing on the tunnel during the boring process.

The bearing-plates are cast in gunmetal, or fashioned out of sheet material, the necessary bearing bosses and lugs being soldered on. The back bearing-plate, the one nearest the field-magnet windings, is quite a simple plate with a fixing flange top and bottom and a central bearing boss. It fits in between the limbs of the magnet, and is secured by two $\frac{3}{32}$-in. countersunk screws at each end. This bearing-plate may, if so desired, be fitted before the tunnel is bored, as then it will be possible to drill it at the same setting, and ensure accuracy in the alignment of this bearing and the armature tunnel.

The outer bearing-plate provides a certain amount of clearance for the projection of the end windings of the armature, and limits the length of the latter. As will be seen from the main drawing (Fig. 607), there is none too much room for the motor, and these bearing-plates must not be too thick or clumsy. In addition to the above and the central boss, the outer plate also provides a transverse bearing for the shaft, this making it possible to obtain a direct connection between the bearing and the axle, and to ensure

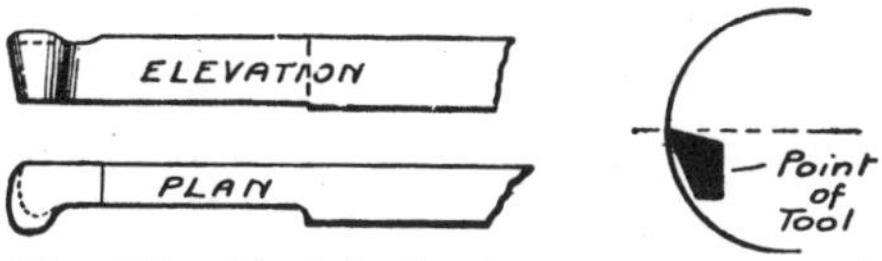

Fig. 623.—Tool for boring armature tunnel

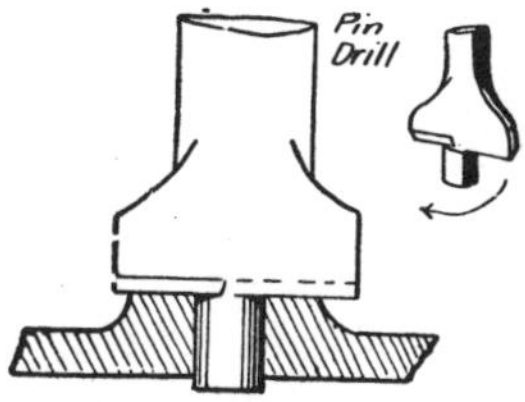

Fig. 625.—Facing bearing bosses with pin drill

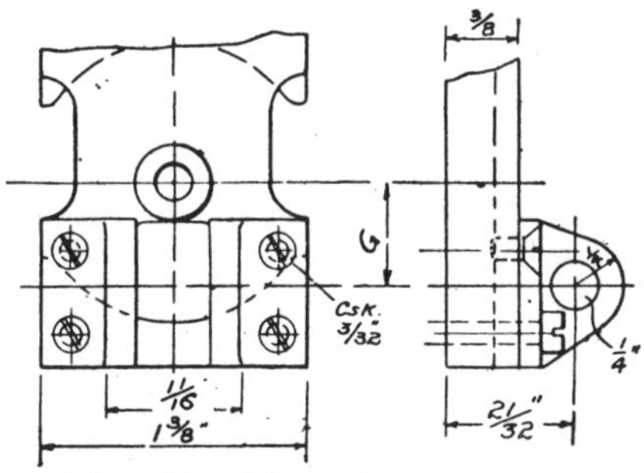

Fig. 624.—Alternative scheme for adjustable bearing lugs

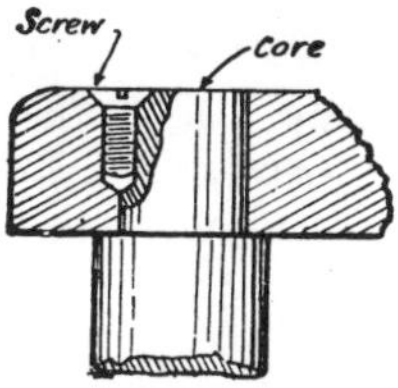

Fig. 626.—Limb screwed to core

an accuracy in the meshing of the gears almost impossible in the more usual arrangement.

The bearing-plate being faced up, either with a file or in the lathe (the latter is a somewhat tentative suggestion, as it will be found difficult to set up), it may be drilled for the armature shaft, and the bosses faced with a pin-drill (Fig. 625). Then it may be drilled for the four $\frac{3}{32}$-in. fixing screws driven in the corners of the pole-pieces. Following this come the transverse bearing holes in the lugs. This hole should be bored slightly under size, so that it may be rimered out to suit the gears. Admittedly this is one of the most difficult jobs in the whole mechanism of the locomotive, and one on which much of its success depends. Indeed, it is an open question whether it would not tend to a better result if these brackets are made loose, and in this way provide an adjustment of the depthing of the gears. A separate detail (Fig. 624) demonstrates this idea.

As the field-magnet coil in a built-up wrought-iron motor can be "former wound," only one end of the winding core should be fixed. This is the end which drives the more tightly into the bored hole. The other end should be a good fit, and the parts may be finally secured with a small steel screw as shown in Fig. 626.

This completes the carcass of the motor, the work of filing up the parts to the required dimensions being done in accordance with the drawings at the respective and proper stages in the construction. Where a one-piece casting is employed, the field core must be wound through the tunnel of the armature; this can be done between the lathe centres.

Armature.—Although the tripolar armature is, theoretically, not the most efficient, it has certain characteristics which often, in model electric traction work, make it the only one which can be employed without involving a high degree of skill. Without going into elaborate explanations, the inefficiency of the tripolar armature is due to the fact that the windings do not take up the best possible positions in the magnetic field. However, the tripolar armature is easy to wind, it is the simplest self-starting armature that can be used, and, furthermore, stampings or castings are, in certain regular sizes, obtainable from most electrical and model dealers.

In the motor under discussion either one of two kinds of tripolar armature may be used, the cast or laminated, the latter being the better. The cast armature is usually employed where the windings have to be flush with the ends, and also where cheapness in construction is an important consideration. Fig. 627 is a diagram showing the difference which may be made in the shape of cast and laminated armatures.

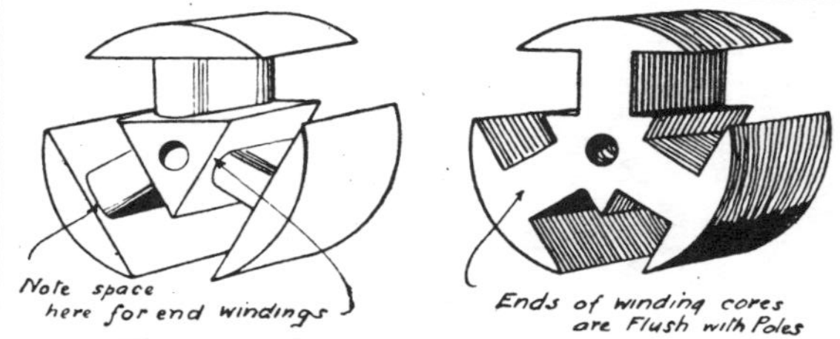

Fig. 627.—Cast and laminated armatures

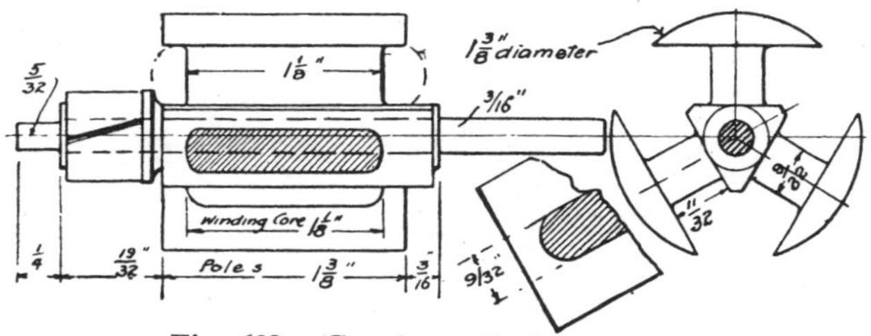

Fig. 628.—Cast-iron tripolar armature

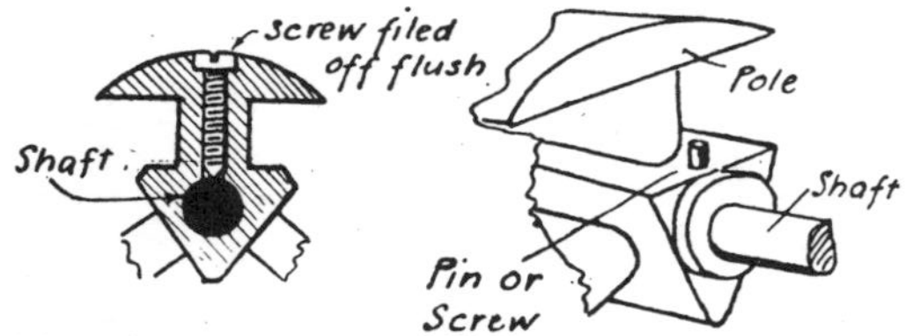

Figs. 629 and 630.—Fixing cast armature to shaft

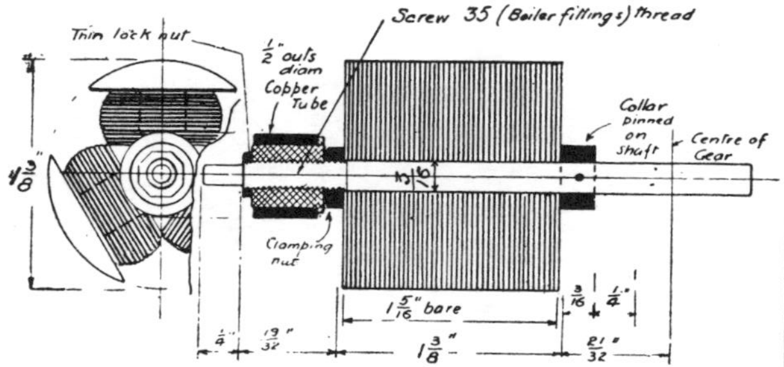

Fig. 631. — Laminated armature for model locomotive motors

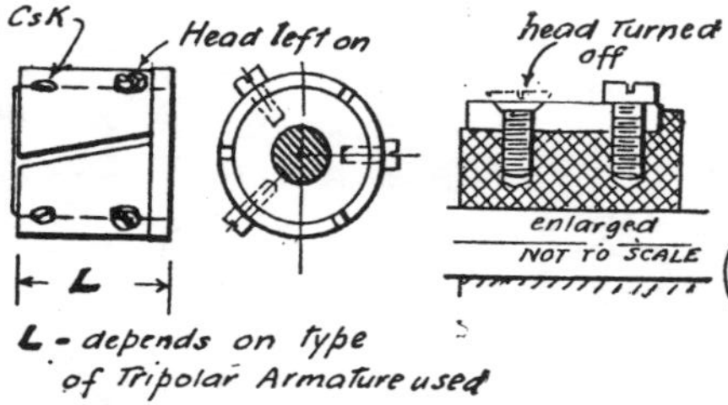

Fig. 632.—Making the commutator

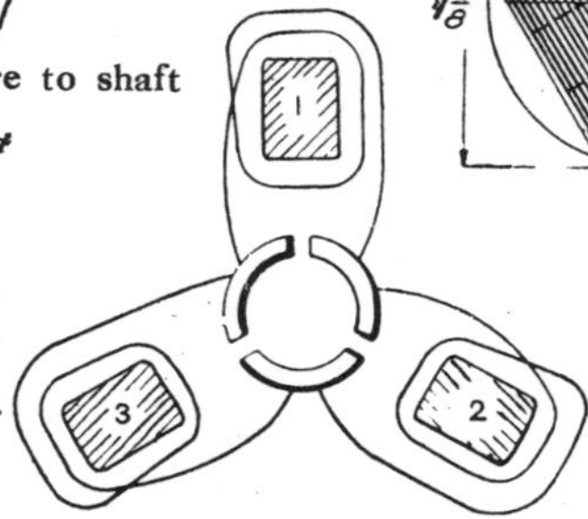

Fig. 633.—Armature winding diagram

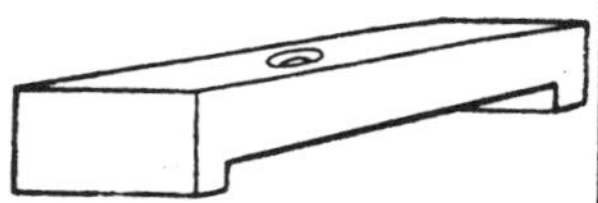
Fig. 634.—Insulating block for brushes

Fig. 628 shows a suitable cast-iron armature; but it will be noticed the necessary checking-in of the winding cores is very slight—only $\frac{1}{8}$ in. at each end—as the design of the motor provides for the extension of the windings. In addition, the armature may be fully $1\frac{3}{8}$ in. long at the poles. A solid cast-iron armature can be fixed to the shaft by being drilled a driving fit for the shaft; but if a further security is required, either a screw may be fitted in the centre of one of the poles as shown in Fig. 629, or as an alternative a pin or a set-screw may be driven into the projecting boss at the ends as shown in Fig. 630.

When fixed on the shaft and centred at one end, one end of the shaft may be held in a three-jaw chuck, and with the other one in the dead centre, light cuts may be taken over the pole-pieces, so as to reduce the armature to the required $1\frac{3}{8}$-in. diameter. Care must, however, have been taken to drill the shaft hole concentric with the other parts of the casting. Nothing gives so much dissatisfaction and trouble in subsequent working as a badly balanced armature. Therefore, care must be taken to see that a good balance is obtained both mechanically and electrically; and after the casting is examined for general truth and soundness and any excrescences removed from the surface of the poles with a suitable file, it may be held in the self-centring chuck for drilling. Before this latter operation is actually accomplished, any glaring inaccuracy can readily be observed and remedied by filing either one or the other of the poles.

A laminated armature requires different treatment. In this case the windings extend to the amount of their whole depth at each end. Therefore, the armature cannot in the present motor be longer than $1\frac{5}{16}$ in.; indeed, it had better be $1\frac{1}{4}$ in. long rather than exceed the first-mentioned dimension.

In a small armature the stampings are, if necessary, flattened and coated with a shellac varnish partially to insulate them from each other, and in this way resist the longitudinal flow of "eddy" currents. Then they are threaded on the armature shaft, which, as shown in Fig. 631, is of special design, with a collar at one end and a clamping nut at the other. The centre hole, which is usually provided in the stampings, should be a good fit on the shaft; and if it is not of the size chosen, the shaft will have to be turned down from a bar of sufficient diameter. If this has to be done, then the collar may be in the solid, and not a loose collar pinned on to a piece of commercial bright steel rod $\frac{3}{16}$ in. in diameter, such as is shown in Fig. 631.

When the armature stampings are in place and the clamping nut about to be tightened up, the stampings may be squared up and the nut screwed down. No further fixing should be required, and if the stampings are of good quality they should run reasonably true on the shaft, any slight burr in the periphery being easily removable with a smooth file. The winding core of the armature may then be cleaned up preparatory to the winding, any burrs or spikes which might pierce the insulation of the wires wound over them being carefully removed, and, as far as possible, the ends of the cores should be rounded off to prevent any similar electrical failure.

In Fig 620 the back (inside) bearing is dimensioned for either a $\frac{1}{8}$-in. or $\frac{5}{32}$-in. journal. The laminated armature, where a $\frac{3}{16}$-in. diameter shaft is employed, will necessitate the adoption of the smaller dimension.

The commutator may be built up in a variety of ways. The simplest method is to bore a piece of ebonite or vulcanite fibre for a driving fit on the shaft, or else to a tapping size to suit the thread cut on the shaft (*see* Fig. 631). This insulating bush is then turned with a slight flange at one end (to keep the metal surface from touching the armature), to suit a piece of thick brass or copper tube. This tube is then driven on, and six screws as shown in Fig. 632 driven into the insulation; but not, in any circumstances, into the hole for the shaft. The outer screws should be countersunk; but the inside ones may have projecting heads, and be afterwards used for attaching the windings to the commutator segments. The countersunk screws should not be fully countersunk into the metal tube. The tube may then be sawn into three equal segments, as indicated, preferably by an inclined cut. The metal should be just separated, and that is all. The commutator may then be put in its place with the three saw cuts opposite the respective poles.

With regard to the windings of the motor, the exact gauge of wire used for fields and armature respectively will depend on the electrical system adopted. For the moment, therefore, only a diagram (Fig. 633) showing the direction of the armature winding and commutator position is given. This method of winding is known as the closed-coil system, and is much to be preferred to the arrangement common to most toy motors, in which the starting ends of each coil are connected together, and the finishing ends to the nearest commutator segment. In the diagram the winding cores are shown in section and numbered 1, 2, and 3 respectively. As will be seen, the beginning and end wires of each adjacent coil are joined together and attached to a segment between the coils.

Brush Gear of Motor.—The brush gear for the traction motor under discussion is very simple. It consists of two spring brushes, clubbed at the ends which bear on the commutator, screwed to an insulating block of vulcanite fibre, ebonite, or hard wood (for preference, either of the first two materials), which in turn is fixed to the uppermost limb of the field-magnet, as already illustrated in the general arrangement drawings of the locomotive. In Fig. 620 this insulation is shown fixed to the field-magnet with two $\frac{1}{8}$-in. steel countersunk screws. However, if the block is made as shown in Fig. 634, with a lip or flange at each end to fit over the magnet limb M (Fig. 635), only one screw will be required. The brushes should be about $\frac{1}{32}$ in. thick and sheared out of hard springy brass sheet.

The blocks of metal K (Fig. 635) at the ends may be of brass or copper, and should be soldered on. When new they should be filed to a smaller radius than that of the surface of the commutator, so that the points bear on the commutator rather than the middle. This is important to the success of the motor, as unless the brush contact bridges the slots in certain positions of the armature it will not start readily.

There are two methods of fixing the brushes to the in-

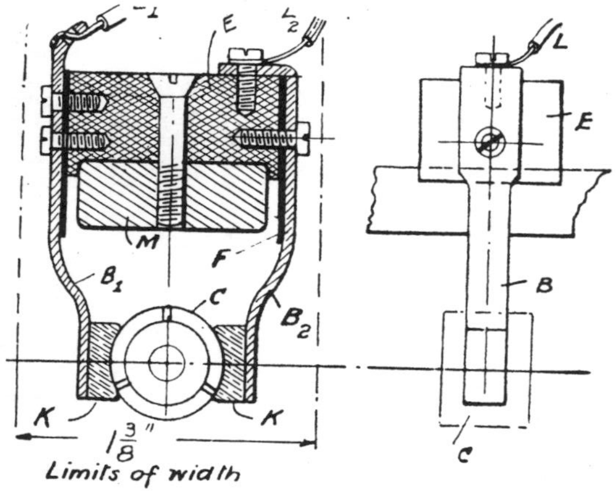

Fig. 635.—Brush gear complete (full size)

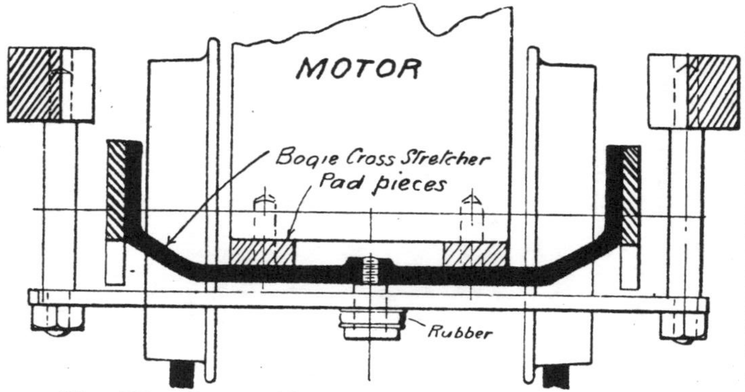

Fig. 637.—Cross section through bogie, showing fixing of motors (full size)

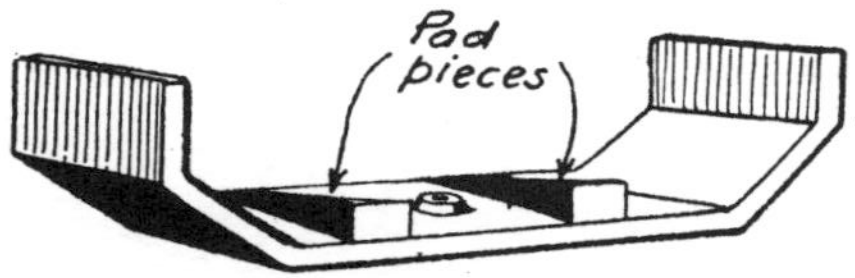

Fig. 638.—Bogie stretcher plate

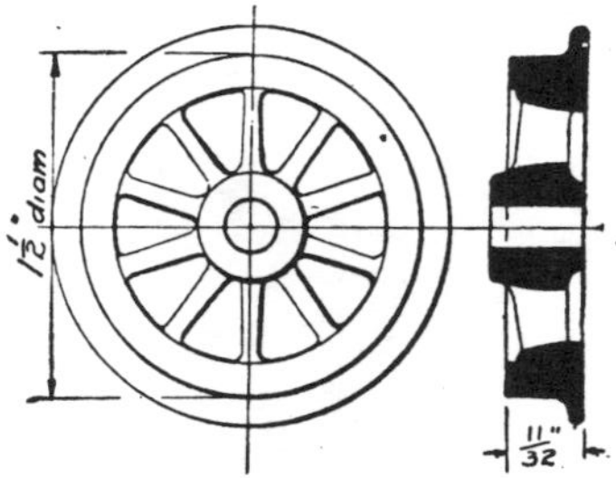

Fig. 639.—Wheel for electric locomotive

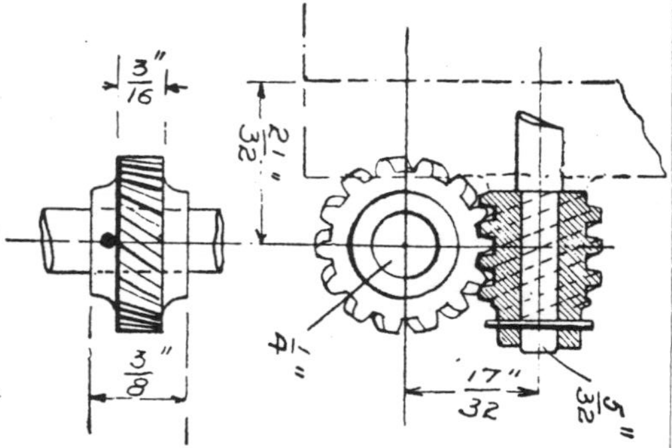

Fig. 636.—Worm gear (full size)

sulating block, shown respectively on the right-hand and left-hand sides of the full-size sketch (Fig. 635). The brush B_1 is shown fixed with two screws into the side of the insulating block, the connecting wire L_1 being threaded through a hole in the top of the brush and soldered. The right-hand brush B_2 is attached with a screw in the side and one in the top, the latter being used as a connection for the looped end of the lead L_2. The strip F is a piece of insulating material (thin sheet fibre), which is intended to prevent the brush touching the field-magnet, and causing a short circuit through the motor to the return (running) rails.

Windings.—For ordinary purposes and pressures of 4 volts to 6 volts, the field-magnets may be wound with No. 20 cotton-covered or No. 18 silk-covered wire, and the armature with either No. 22 cotton-covered or No. 20 silk-covered wire. These windings should be connected in series. For 8 volts to 10 volts the sizes given in the following table would apply:—

Series-wound motors fitted with hand or automatic reversing switch.

Armature, No. 24 cotton; fields, No. 22 cotton. Armature, No. 22 silk; fields, No. 21 silk.

Separately excited motors (fields, 2 volts; armature, 6 volts to 8 volts). Field-magnet, No. 24 cotton or No. 22 silk covered. Armature, No. 24 cotton or No. 22 silk covered. (Fields, 4 volts; armature, 12 volts to 16 volts.) Field-magnet, No. 26 cotton or No. 24 silk covered. Armature, No. 26 cotton or No. 24 silk covered.

Gearing.—The gearing chosen for the motor now being described is the well-known worm gearing. This gearing is perhaps the most simple arrangement that can be devised where a speed reduction of over 6 to 1 is necessary. A pair of wheels only is required, one termed the worm, which is the " driver," and the worm wheel, which is the " driven " wheel of the gear. Worm gear has only two disadvantages for such purposes. In the first place, it is, in ratios of greater disparity than about 1 to 5, an irreversible system of gearing. By this is meant that the worm will only drive the worm wheel. The reverse is impossible; the worm wheel cannot be made to drive the worm. The other drawback of worm gearing is that the friction absorbed by a badly made or badly matched pair of wheels is, comparatively speaking, excessive. In addition, the design of efficient worm gearing is considered among engineers as a difficult and complicated subject.

The speed ratio of the simplest form of worm gear is easily calculated. Where the worm is a single-threaded one, the speed ratio depends on the number of teeth in the worm wheel. If there are 20, then the ratio of the gear is as 1 is to 20. But worm wheels may be cut with two or more threads, when the ratio, instead of being with a 20-toothed wheel 1 to 20, would be as 2 is to 20 or 1 to 10 in the case of a double-threaded worm, and as 3 to 20 or 1 to $6\frac{2}{3}$ in the case of a triple-threaded worm.

For model-work a coarse-toothed worm wheel is best; Fig. 636 shows to full size a double-threaded worm working in a wheel having 14 teeth. The outside diameter of the worm is a trifle less than $\frac{1}{2}$ in., or to be exact $\frac{17}{32}$ in. The pitch of the thread is 4 to the inch.

There are two methods of cutting the worm wheel. One is to cut the wheel with a wheel cutter directly across the circumference at an angle, which angle must be measured from the worm. The other is the hobbed system. Here a facsimile of the worm is reproduced in steel, and cutting edges are formed on it, so that it is to all intents the same as a tap. This " hob " is revolved in the lathe, and a disc of metal, which is free to rotate on its axis, is brought near to it until the worm wheel is fully formed. For model-work it is a question whether the scientifically less accurate method first described is not the best, especially if the worm and worm wheel are of hard material and quite smooth.

The motor is intended to be fixed to the cross stretcher of the bogie. This stretcher may be of rolled brass sheet $\frac{1}{16}$ in. thick, bent to the shape shown in Figs. 637 and 638, and attached to the side frames of the bogie. The motor being at an angle, pad-pieces filed to the correct angle must be soldered on to the upper surface of the stretcher, and also a small centre boss for the screw which acts as the bogie pin.

The driving wheels of the locomotive are a standard size, and can be obtained in cast iron from most dealers. Gun-metal wheels are not used very much nowadays, as reliable, clean, soft castings in iron can be obtained; indeed, iron wheels are usually cleaner than those cast in brass or gun-metal. Owing to the gear ratio adopted, the wheels are slightly larger than the scale reproduction of the original locomotive. Fig. 639 is full size, and shows the proper shape of the flange and tread.

Frames.—The main frames of the locomotive are of very simple construction, and are made up of four strips of $\frac{1}{4}$-in. by $\frac{3}{8}$-in. rectangular section brass rod. Of course, iron could be used; but brass is not much more expensive, and is more readily soldered.

The side members are quite plain except for the projections which carry the supporting pillars of the bogie. These projections are formed by screwing and soldering on, on the inside, short strips of the same metal as the frames. When this is done, the frames can be drilled and tapped $\frac{1}{8}$-in. Whitworth for the pillars, the position of the latter being shown in the detail drawing of the main frames (Fig. 640). To stiffen the frames near the centre, two round stay rods are suggested. These may also be of brass, and alternative methods of jointing them are shown in Figs. 641 and 642. In the first, the $\frac{5}{16}$-in. rod is simply turned down at each end to $\frac{3}{16}$ in., the distance between the shoulders being the same as that between the frames, namely, $3\frac{1}{8}$ in. The holes in the side frames should be bored a good fit, and the joint secured by the rod being riveted over and soft soldered. The other method is obvious from the illustration; but although screws are used to brace the work together, the joint may be further secured by being soldered.

The buffer planks are rebated at each end so that the projecting ends are only $\frac{3}{32}$ in. thick. The centre portion is also cut away to clear the field-magnet windings of the motor. The clearance must be sufficient to provide for the swinging of the bogie when the locomotive is on a curve.

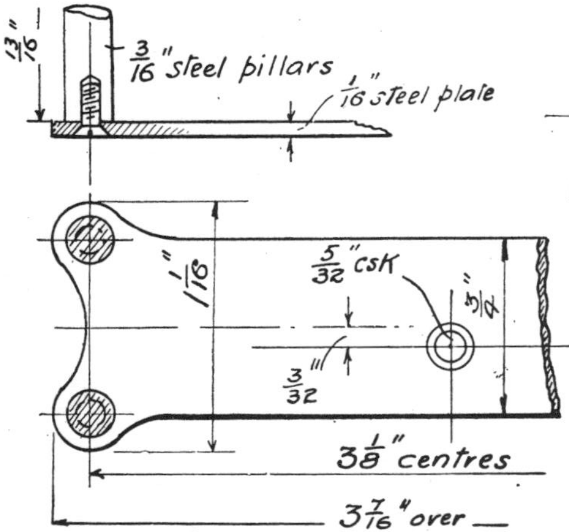

Fig. 643.—Bogie cross-plate and supporting pillars (full size)

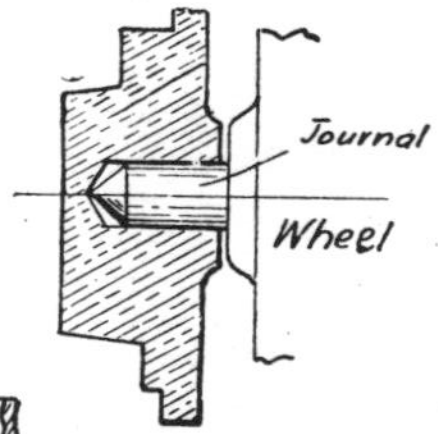

Fig. 645.—Section through axle journals and bearings

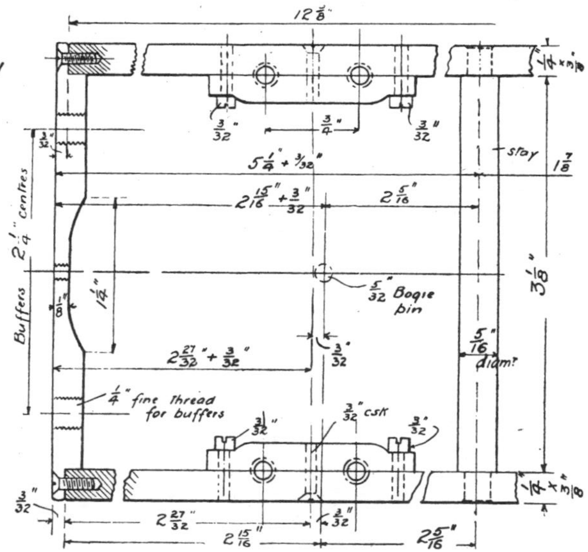

Fig. 640.—Details of main frames of electric locomotive

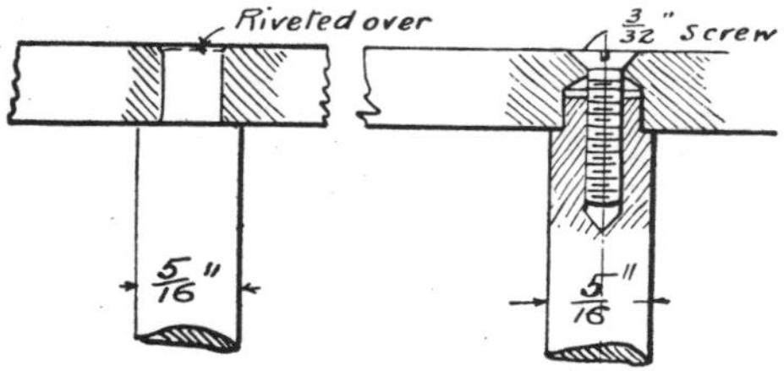

Figs. 641 and 642.—Cross-stay joints, riveted and screwed respectively

Fig. 644.—Bogie pin

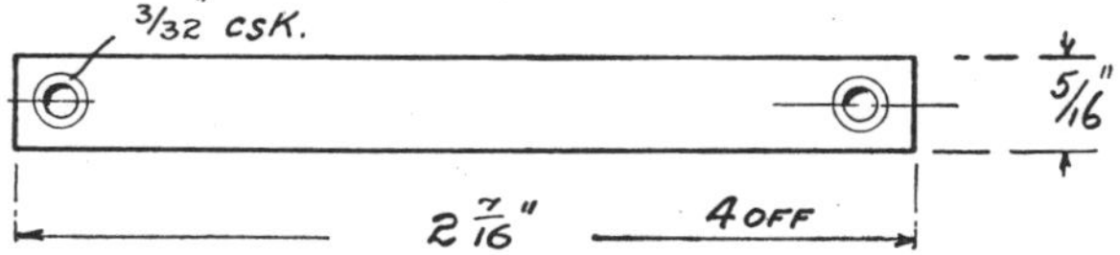

Fig. 646.—End plates of bogie frame

The bogie supporting pillars should be made of $\frac{5}{32}$ in. or $\frac{3}{16}$-in. steel rod, turned at each end to $\frac{1}{8}$ in., and screwed Whitworth thread. The distance between the shoulders should be $\frac{13}{16}$ in.; but where the centre conducting rail is raised above the level of the running rails, a better method of fixing the bogie cross-plate to these pillars is shown in Fig. 643. This increases the clearance by the depth of a $\frac{1}{8}$-in. Whitworth nut. The bogie cross-plate may be of $\frac{1}{16}$-in. steel plate. It will be clearly seen that the bogie pin is placed slightly to the rear of the centre of the bogie wheels.

On referring back to Fig. 637, it will also be noticed that a space is provided between the bogie cross-plate and the bogie stretcher. The idea of this is to provide for a certain amount of flexibility between the bogies and the superstructure of the locomotive. The bogie pin is, therefore, arranged with a rubber washer between the head and cross-plate, and if any tendency to instability or looseness is noticed in the finished engine, a similar (but larger) washer may be inserted between the bogie cross-plate and bogie stretcher. The hole in the former for the bogie pin should be countersunk both sides, and the tapped hole in the bogie stretcher should be such as to fit the bogie pin tightly. The head of the bogie pin must be very shallow—indeed, the lower rubber washer will have to be dispensed with if a raised third rail is employed—and to enable it to be easily driven home the design shown in Fig. 644, or even a countersunk screw, may be adopted.

Bogies.—For the side frames of the bogies, castings are required, and, failing their being obtained from a trade firm, the builder of the model must make a pattern. This pattern should be in metal to get the best results. A piece of $\frac{3}{32}$-in. brass plate should be cut to the shape shown in Fig. 645, an ample allowance being made for shrinkage and working up the final casting. On this plate the dummy springs, spring hangers, and axle-boxes must be soldered, the plate and attached parts being provided with " rake " or " draw " to ensure a clean casting. Clips should be employed to prevent parts which have been soldered from moving while adjacent parts are being operated on. Superfluous solder should be removed with a scraper. Inside the frame pattern two $\frac{1}{4}$-in. in diameter by $\frac{1}{16}$-in. bosses should be arranged, to provide a facing for the wheels and axle journals. In addition flanges for fixing the end stretcher plates should also be provided. These flanges are shown on the plan view of the bogie frames in Fig. 647. The end stretcher plates are shown in Fig. 646, and are fixed with one $\frac{3}{32}$-in. countersunk screw to each flange. The axles run in plain holes drilled from the inside of the bogie side frames, the axle-ends being pointed to lessen side thrust friction (see Fig. 645). The journals need not exceed $\frac{1}{8}$ in. in diameter.

Care should be taken in fitting up the side frames of the bogie, and in drilling the journal holes accurately. Otherwise the four wheels may not all touch the rails. The holes for the journals of the idle wheels may be larger than those of the drivers, to give a certain amount of vertical slackness to the wheels. This is more or less necessary where springs are not used, as it is impossible to obtain a perfectly level road even with the best permanent way.

Buffers.—Fig. 648 shows the standard type of buffer for No. 1 gauge vehicles. The socket is turned out of bar material, and the spigot threaded with a suitable fine thread, $\frac{1}{4}$-in. outside diameter, 40 threads.

The buffer head may also be turned out of bar material, steel or german silver being preferable to brass, as the heads should be left bright, and brass does not give the correct colour. Fig. 648 represents the circular type of buffer head; but as on the Metropolitan engine a form of oval head is employed, the writer provides an alternative design in Fig. 649. In this the stock and springing arrangement are identical; but as the buffer plank in the present model is only $\frac{3}{8}$ in. deep, the stock should be turned with its largest diameter $\frac{7}{16}$ in., as shown in the left-hand part of Fig. 649, and after fixing, the upper and lower portions of the flanges should be filed down flush with the plank. The head should be turned $\frac{1}{2}$ in. in diameter, and filed down to the shape shown in the right-hand view, all sharp square edges being eliminated during the filing process.

To retain the oval heads in the correct horizontal, the slots in the two screwheads of the plungers may be tied together as shown in Fig. 650.

Fig. 651 shows the drawhook to full size. In the present model exigencies of space prevent a more elaborate fixing into the plank. However, if the threaded portion fits tightly, and the hook is also sweated in with soft solder, the arrangement will be found quite satisfactory. The links should be bright and, with the hook, be made of any material which will represent steel. The central link should be shorter than the two others, and when hanging down the chain should not reach the level of the rails by at least $\frac{3}{16}$ in. This is more important where the "third" or conducting rail is raised above rail level, as should the coupling chain be too long and hang down, it may cause a short circuit through the frames of the locomotive to the return (running) rails.

Superstructures.—To make up the cab and end bonnets, reference must be made to the general arrangement drawing. The cab and bonnets may be built in one piece, if desired, in which case the plate forming the side of the cab (Fig. 652) must be extended a further $3\frac{5}{8}$ in. on each side. The most convenient arrangement, however, is to build the upper works in three pieces. The cab should be the full $3\frac{3}{8}$ in. in width, and the bonnets barely $3\frac{3}{8}$ in. (say $3\frac{5}{16}$ in.) wide, so as to obtain a definite shadow line at the joints between the parts. The superstructures are, as shown in the earlier drawings above mentioned, not fitted to the usual bedplate, but inside the bottom edge $\frac{1}{4}$-in. by $\frac{1}{4}$-in. angle-brass is soldered, the horizontal member of the angle projecting and forming the footplate line of the locomotive.

The windows are pierced as shown in Figs. 652 and 653. Except where the extra labour involved is not objected to, the openings are not edged with wire; but in the case of the door, a strip of half-round $\frac{1}{16}$-in. brass wire should be soldered on to represent the door frame. The panelling of the door may be shown by paint lines in the finishing processes. To fix the end plates of the cab to the sides, angle-brass riveted to the parts should be employed where required, and the joints afterwards well sweated with a soldering bit of ample size and used inside the joint. The roof should be made removable, so that the accumulator for working the fields may be readily removed. Retaining

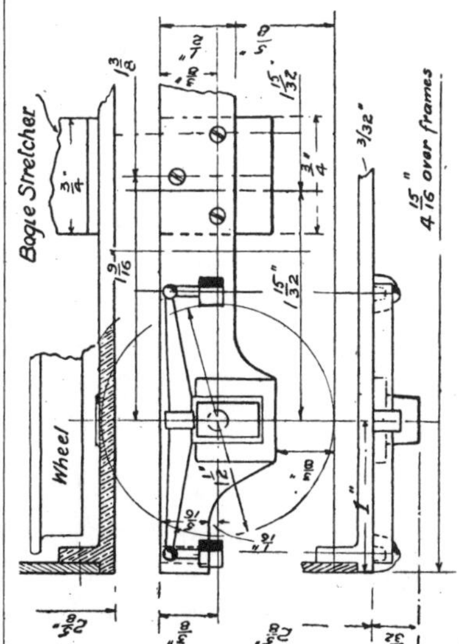

Fig. 647.—Details of cast bogie frames

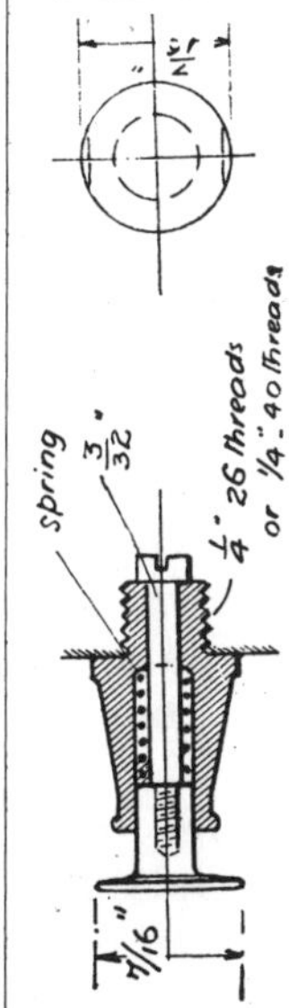

Fig. 648.—Standard round-headed spring buffer

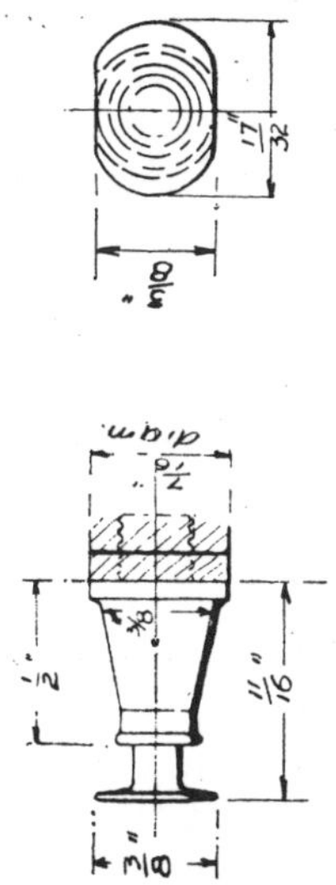

Fig. 649.—Oval-headed spring buffer

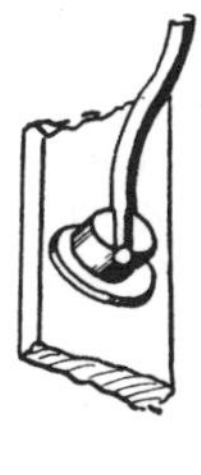

Fig. 650.—Method of retaining oval buffer in correct position

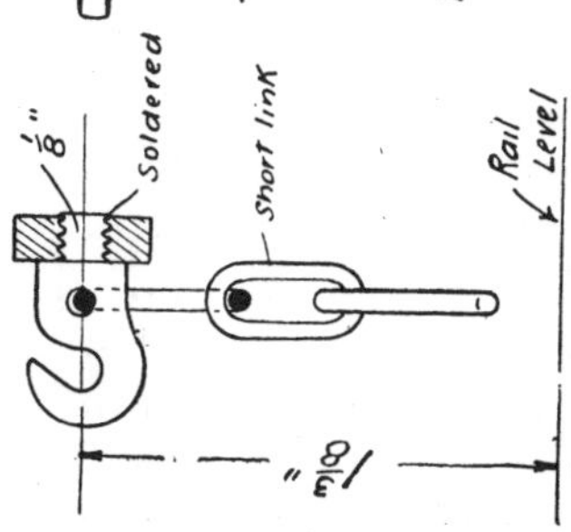

Fig. 651.—Drawhook and chain

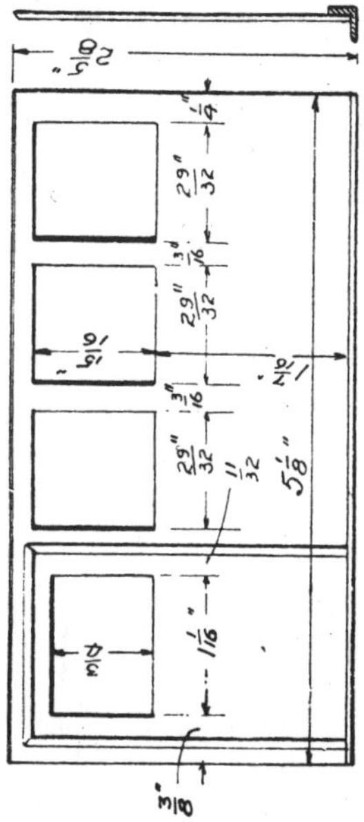

Fig. 652.—Cab side plates

angles should be riveted and soldered on inside as shown at A and B (Fig. 654). The side angles B should be well short of the end plates, and to keep the roof in place longitudinally the smaller pieces A may be fitted. The top of the roof should be edged and panelled as shown in the photographic illustration.

To fix the superstructures to the frames, pegs, dowels, or studs should be attached to the upper works, and fit into holes in the frames, the studs being long enough to allow of nuts being fitted underneath. Four studs should be sufficient for the cab, and the same for the bonnets, although the latter could be fixed with two studs fitting in holes in the buffer planks, and with one screw driven into a bracket fixed inside on the end plates of the cab.

The destination board may be screwed to the bonnets, and to enable the names of the stations to be altered as in the prototype, an arrangement to hold, say, about three or four cards is shown in detail in Fig. 656. The front is made of $\frac{1}{16}$-in. brass and pierced as shown, the top edge being rounded off. The back may be of thin brass or tinplate, in one piece with the bottom. The sides should not extend quite to the top to enable the cards to be more readily changed.

The superstructures may, of course, be made of tinplate. But some model-makers find this difficult material to work, and prefer brass. For this model No. 20 or No. 22 S.W.G. brass is quite thick enough. The handrail should be of steel or german silver wire, and the knobs may be of either material, the last-named being the easier to work. The knobs should be screwed or soldered into the side plate, care being taken to get the holes in perfect alignment. To drill the knobs for the handrail, use a jig consisting of two pieces of metal countersunk as shown in Fig. 657 and placed together over the knob, clamping it firmly. This jig has a guiding hole for the drill as shown.

Current Collectors.—The details of the collectors are shown in Fig. 658. This is perhaps the simplest form of collector, and it works quite well in practice.

In arranging current collectors for model railway vehicles, it must be remembered that to provide a continuity of supply

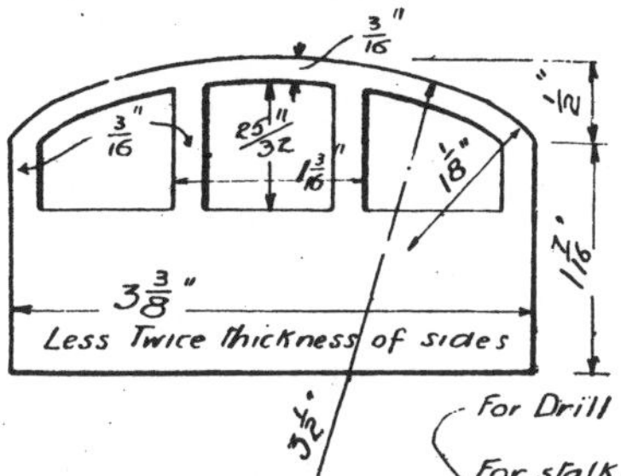

Fig. 653.—Cab end-plates

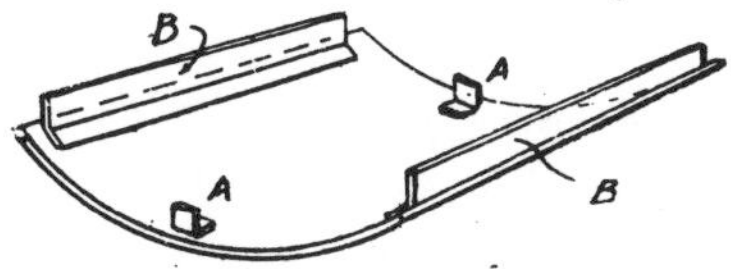

Fig. 654.—Underside of cab roof

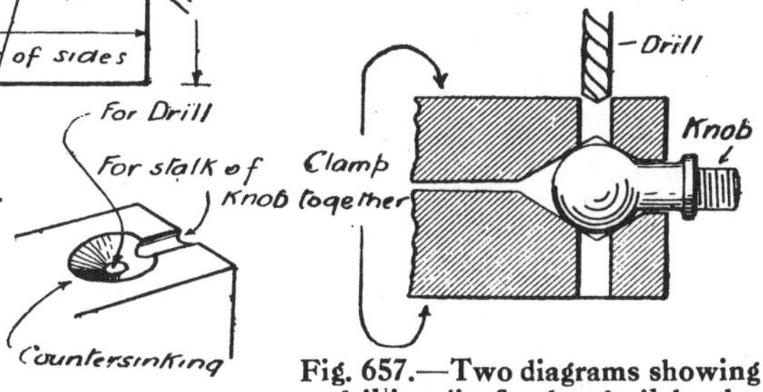

Fig. 657.—Two diagrams showing a drilling jig for handrail knobs

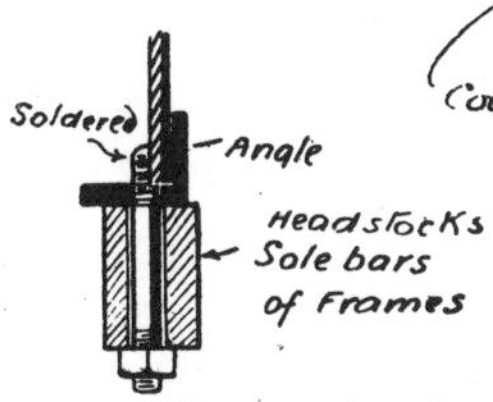

Fig. 655.—Fixing for cab and bonnets

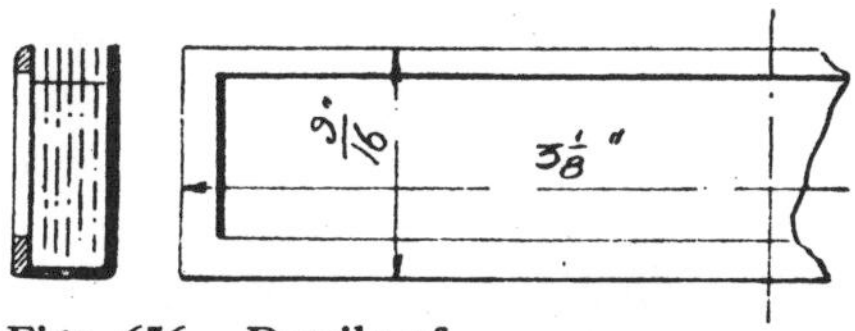

Figs. 656.—Details of destination board

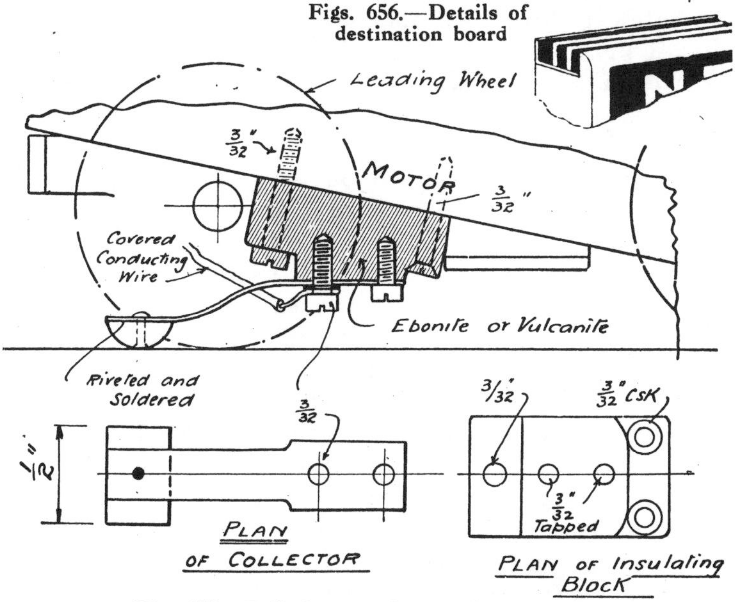

Fig. 658.—Full-size details of collecting shoe

to the motors when the engine or motor carriage is passing over points and crossings, two collectors are imperative. As will be seen by Figs. 659 and 660, at points and crossings the centre conducting rail must be broken, and to bridge this gap two collectors, which are cross connected, must be used. The distance between these collectors must also be greater than the longest gap in the " third " rail existing on the particular railway system installed. Another important point is that, where bogies are used, the collector should be placed on the bogie frames, so that the shoe may better follow the centre rail. If the collectors are placed on the main frame, the overhang of the latter on sharp curves may cause the collector shoe to leave the " third " rail and derail the locomotive, to say nothing of the resultant short circuiting and damage to the collector attachments.

Wherever possible, the writer always recommends his new " all level " system of arranging the centre conductor rails. This renders a raising of the third rail and careful vertical adjustment of the shoe quite unnecessary. The gaps at points and crossings may also be shorter than with the older arrangement, in which the third rail is raised $\frac{5}{32}$ in. or $\frac{3}{16}$ in. above the running rails, and the shoe must be adjusted so that it can on no account fall to the running-rail level and cause a short circuit. At all parts of the track where the centre rail crosses the running rails (as shown shaded in Figs. 659 and 660), the latter are cut on both sides of the crossing point, so that electrically it has no connection with the rest of the track. It is a " dead section," and, therefore, no short circuit can occur.

The collecting shoe is in the present model best attached directly to the motor. A block of insulating material is attached as shown with three screws to the lower limb of the field-magnets, and is tapped for two $\frac{3}{32}$-in. or $\frac{1}{8}$-in. screws. If a wooden block is employed, then wood screws may be used. To this block the collector—made of hard springy brass with a half-round shoe riveted on the end—is fixed with the two screws above mentioned. One of these screws should be provided with a washer, so that it may be used as a connection for the wire conducting the current to the motor. The ends of these wires should be connected together, so that it does not matter which shoe is collecting the current. The wires to and from the motor and the

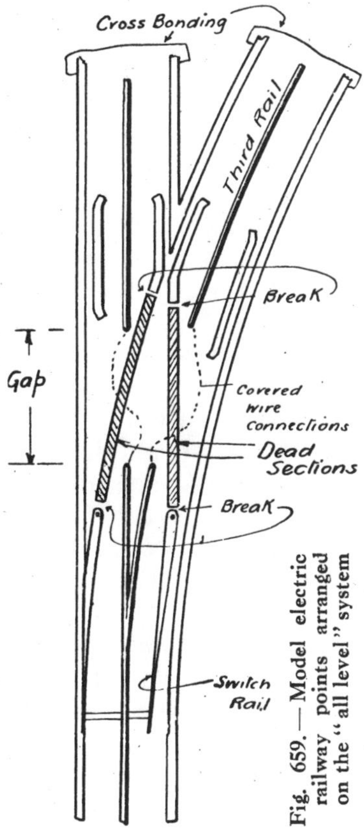

Fig. 659.—Model electric railway points arranged on the "all level" system

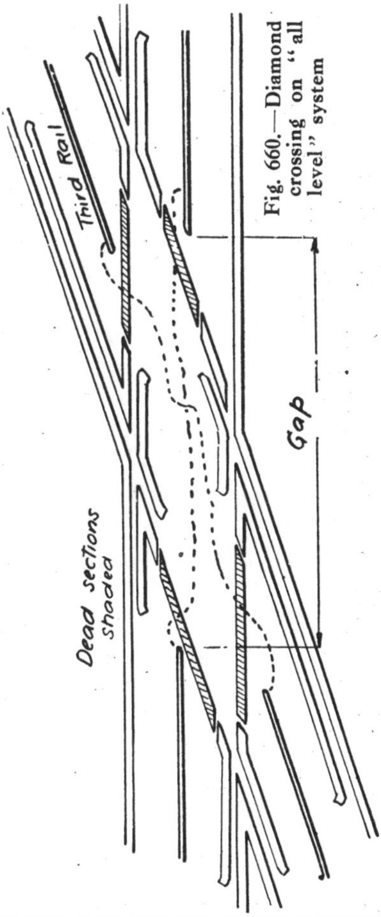

Fig. 660.—Diamond crossing on "all level" system

shoes are best covered with small-diameter rubber tube, to prevent any likelihood of an abrasion and a consequent short circuiting to the frames of the engine.

As the wheels and frames of the locomotive are in direct electrical connection with the running rails no live wire must touch the metal frames, except the one wire from the motor or switch on the locomotive. In the present engine the motor provides the best electrical connections to the wheels. However, a return wire may also be soldered to some part on the frames. As the current must pass through oil-laden bearings, which may offer a resistance, many builders of electric locomotives arrange a separate brush connection to one of the axles, as shown in Fig. 662.

Switches.—Presuming that wrought-iron field-magnets are employed, coupled with good workmanship in the mechanical parts of the motor and gearing, the minimum amount of exciting current will be required for the fields. An automatic cut-out may be arranged in the field circuit to cut in and out the accumulator, and should be energised by the armature current—that is, that from the rails. The coil of the cut-out should offer as little resistance as possible, and for this reason, and to keep the dimensions of the coil as small as possible, the windings may be duplicated or triplicated. The coil of the cut-out when energised by the flow of the current to the motor armature should attract a small iron armature with suitable contacts thereon, and in this way cause the field current to flow. When the rail current is shut off, the weight of this armature should allow it to fall away from the contact, and prevent the power of the accumulator being wasted.

A series-parallel switch worked by hand should be fitted in the cab to control the field-magnet circuit. By this means the field strength can be varied—roughly, in the proportion of two to one—and in this way the speed and hauling power of the engine can be altered to meet requirements. With the fields of the two motors in series, the engine will run at a higher speed, while in parallel a much higher tractive effort can be obtained.

To eliminate reversers and the exciting accumulator, a couple of permanent magnet motors (Fig. 664) could be used. Two of the small No. 0 ($1\frac{1}{4}$-in.) gauge motors are sufficient, the driving shafts being lengthened to suit the $1\frac{3}{4}$-in. gauge. The complete locomotive is shown in Fig. 665.

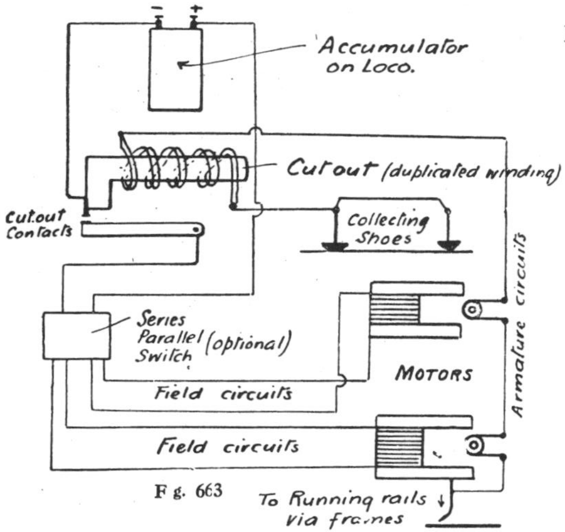

F g. 663

Fig. 663.—Diagram of connections for two motors on the separately excited system

Fig. 664.—Model locomotive motor with permanent magnet fields

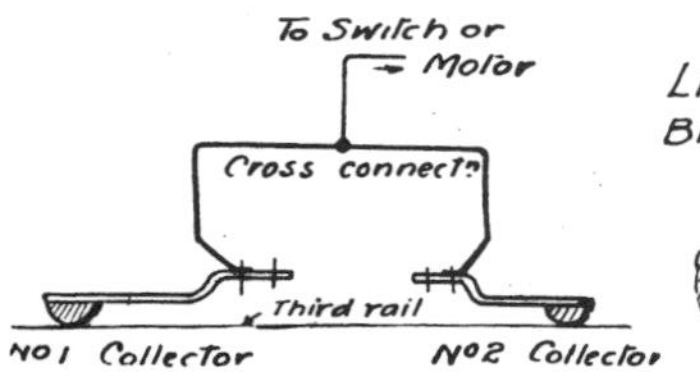

Fig. 661.—Diagram showing cross connection of the two collectors

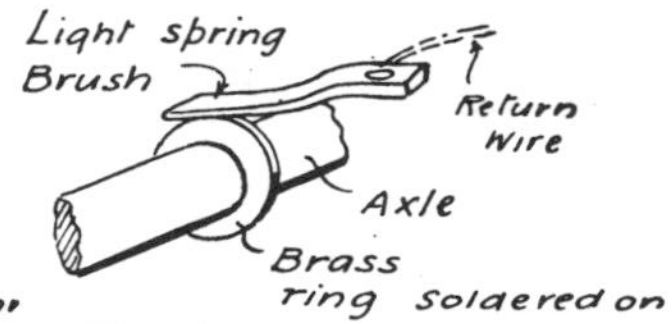

Fig. 662.—Return current brush

Fig. 665.—Model electric locomotive complete

CHAPTER XVIII

Internal Combustion Engines

The working model gas or petrol engine is a very popular form of prime mover among amateur engineers, and if carefully made provides the greatest power for the least expenditure and weight. The amateur should, however, avoid the sets of castings for model gas engines in which the function of the compression of the charge is absent. There is a class of engine being advertised in which the power obtainable is overstated, working on a very ineffective two-cycle principle.

These engines fire every stroke and have no compression stage and a very late firing point. In fact, they are merely flame engines, and at the most only toys. They are usually fitted with an automatic air valve, a gas valve and the exhaust being actuated from a gear-driven cam shaft, and are air-cooled.

The cycle of operations is as follows: At the commencement of the stroke the gas valve opens, and the suction of the piston takes in the gas, and also draws in a certain amount of air, this amount depending on the sensitiveness of the spring-loaded air valve. At about $\frac{3}{8}$-in. or $\frac{1}{4}$-in. stroke the piston uncovers a small port in the side of the cylinder. Outside of this port is burning a gas-jet, and a portion of the flame is sucked in, thus igniting the charge. As will readily be understood, with a permanent hole in the side of the cylinder, a mixture not compressed, and the late firing, no appreciable power is obtained, and such gas engines must not be expected to drive dynamos.

A word of warning may be added with regard to sets of parts for small engines using ordinary paraffin oil; readers must not think that they will be able to finish them satisfactorily without using a lathe. The cylinder may require lapping out, and it will be better if the piston is ordered to be a tight fit, or even supplied not turned at all, so that a perfect working fit, after lapping out the cylinder, may be ensured. A blank-ended ignition tube is preferable to the ordinary tube sent out with the sets of parts, which has to be plugged up or capped at the end. This may be made by boring up a piece of solid iron or mild steel bar and chasing the end screwed into the back of the cover of the vaporiser in an oil engine, or into the cylinder in a gas engine, with a fine tapering thread.

In starting an oil engine, see that the vaporiser, as well as the tube, is sufficiently hot, and, as a rule, an Ætna lamp with an inclined burner will be found best. As to governing the speed, even with a 2-in. bore engine, a governor is essential, and one of the most successful kinds for a small engine is that in which the exhaust is either held open or otherwise kept shut until the speed falls. In each case a new charge is prevented from entering the cylinder. Governing by altering the amount of oil supplied will be found difficult.

Where the castings have not actually been purchased, the writer would recommend a petrol engine in preference to a small oil engine, as the superior economy in fuel cost obtained with oil engines is not felt in below, say, 1 h.p. The vaporing and ignition lamp will be found to use as much oil as the engine; even more in some cases.

Two-cycle Engines.—The two-cycle system properly worked out is a very good one for stationary purposes, and may be used with gas or petrol, electrical ignition being recommended in both cases. Tube ignition is out of the question owing to the comparatively low compression obtained in the two-cycle engine (that is, one power stroke every revolution), there not being enough pressure to force the charge up the heated tube. The capacity of the crank chamber should be small, and to fill it up it is usual to have internal fly-wheels, or to make the crank large and of disc form for the same purpose. The crank chamber must be quite air-tight; a very long bearing or else a packing gland must be fitted. Only one valve, an automatic inlet, is used, the exhaust taking place through ports in the side of the cylinder. A characteristic of most two-cycle engines is that they run either way, according to the direction in which they are started. Figs. 666 to 668 show the main features of the cycle of operations. In the first sketch the piston is ascending and drawing into the crank chamber a new charge, the automatic non-return valve allowing the entry of the mixture. When the piston gets to the top, the sparking plug fires the charge and the piston descends, as in Fig. 667. During this, the working stroke, the piston also slightly compresses the crank chamber charge, and on arriving at the position shown in Fig. 668 the side ports open. The exhaust port, being larger, should open a little in advance of the

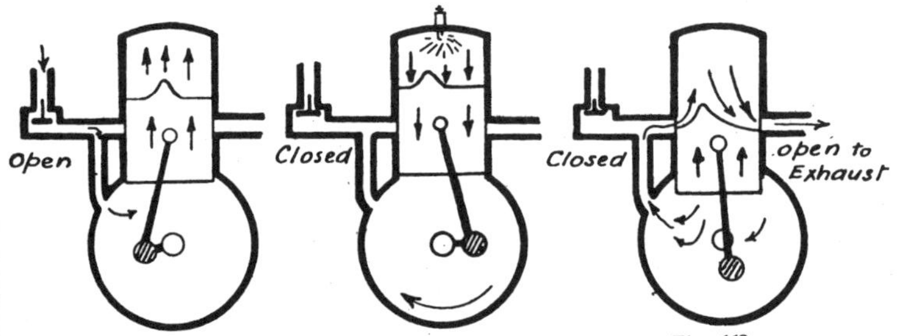

Fig. 666 Fig. 667 Fig. 668

Figs. 666 to 668.—Two-stroke cycle of internal combustion engine : compressing mixture and drawing new charge into crank chamber ; firing stroke and compressing crank-chamber charge ; and exhausting and new charge passing to cylinder

inlet. The horn or fin on the top of the piston divides the two currents, and the charge in the crank chamber being under some pressure, it rushes into the space above the piston. The piston rises and shuts off the side ports, the charge above the piston being compressed further, as indicated in the first diagram, Fig. 666. Probably Fig. 669 gives a better idea of the construction of this type of internal combustion engine. For stationary work over $\frac{1}{2}$ h.p., water-cooling is advisable, and sets of castings for engines from 2 in. by 2 in. upwards are obtainable.

Four-cycle Engines.—The Otto or four-cycle system has one working stroke every two revolutions, and the functions are more distinct and positive than in the two-cycle engine just described. The cycle of operations is shown in Fig. 670, this indicating the proper timing. In petrol engines the sparking point is commonly arranged so that it can be altered to give a variation in speeds. In very fast-running engines the ignition nominally takes place before the dead point is reached, but, of course, the engine should be started with the ignition well retarded, the spark afterwards being gradually advanced. In the Otto cycle the first revolution starts at A (Fig. 670) and the second at B. The movement of the valves is effected by cams designed

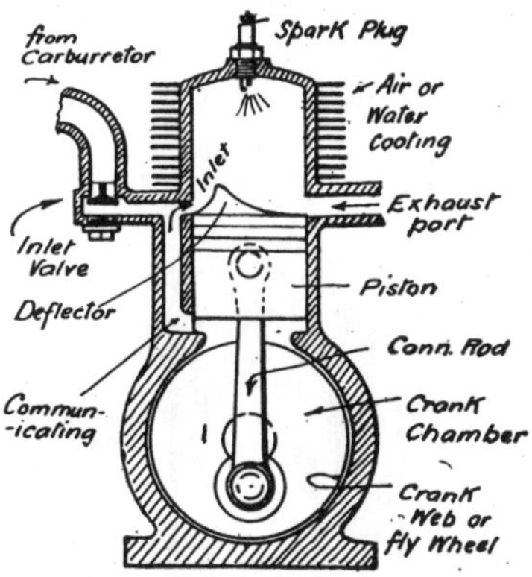

Fig. 669.—Section through two-stroke cycle engine

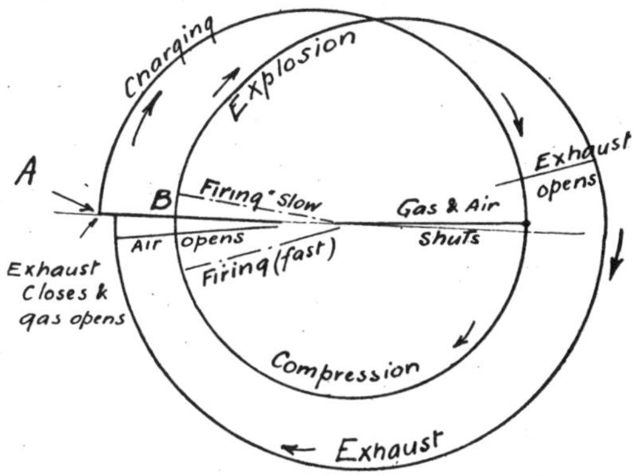

Fig. 670.—The Otto four-stroke cycle

to give a rapid opening and closing. Every stroke is distinct, and the compression stage—which occurs in the second one—compresses the charge to a much higher pressure than in a two-cycle engine, and in this way economises the fuel. There is also no mixing up of the charge and the exhaust, as must occur to some extent in the two-cycle engine.

Gas engines are usually of the horizontal type, while petrol motors are nearly always made with vertical cylinders. Small power and model gas engines may be made to work with petrol, but as a rule the extra power given by petrol is likely rapidly to wear the main and big-end bearings. A wick carburettor is the most suitable in such cases, as a weaker mixture can be more easily provided. A design for a wick carburettor is given in Fig. 671. Where a large engine is being fitted up for petrol, the level of the spirit in a wick carburettor can be maintained by placing it on a level with a larger supply tank, or by a float feed. The richness of the mixture can be regulated by the two air ports.

Vertical Gas Engines.—A design for a simple vertical gas engine is given in Fig. 673.

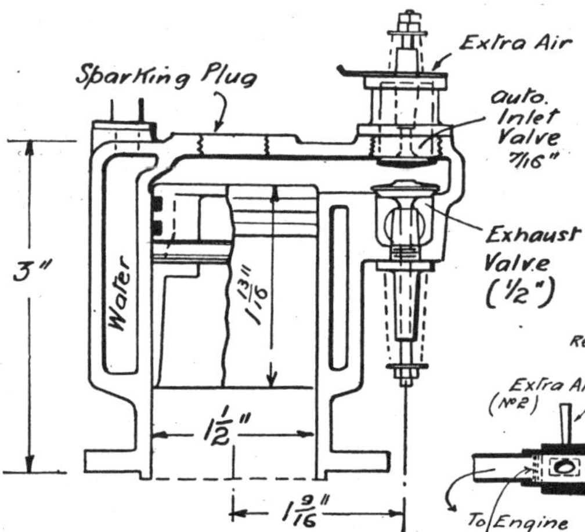

Fig. 672.—Cylinder for model petrol engine

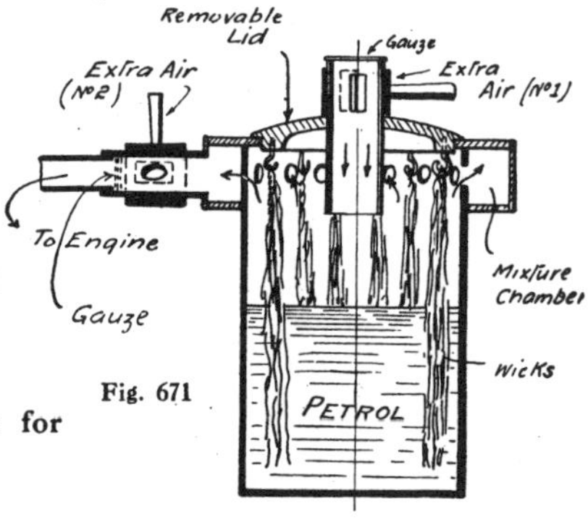

Fig. 671

Fig. 671.—Wick carburettor for model petrol engine

This engine could be made smaller, say with a $1\frac{3}{4}$-in. by 2-in. cylinder; but in that case petrol would be the better fuel, and under any circumstances with smaller dimensions electrical ignition would be advisable. Where an engine designed for gas is converted with a view of using petrol, the compression may be reduced by shortening the connecting rod or turning a slice off the back of the piston. This will lessen the increment of power of the engine due to the use of the more powerful fuel.

The engine shown in Fig. 673 has an overhung crank, the head of the crank pin actuating the two-to-one valve gear, which is arranged in the removable cover. The cylinder is water-cooled at the sides only, a water jacket of thin copper or brass tube being spun on to two flanges provided on the cylinder casting. The cylinder cover contains the two valves, the inlet being automatic and the exhaust operated by a rocker pivoted on a bracket cast on the cover. A tappet rod hardened at each end connects the rocker with the cam. The valves should be as large as the cylinder diameter will allow, and a clip should be provided on the inside of the cylinder to prevent the valves falling should the spindles break.

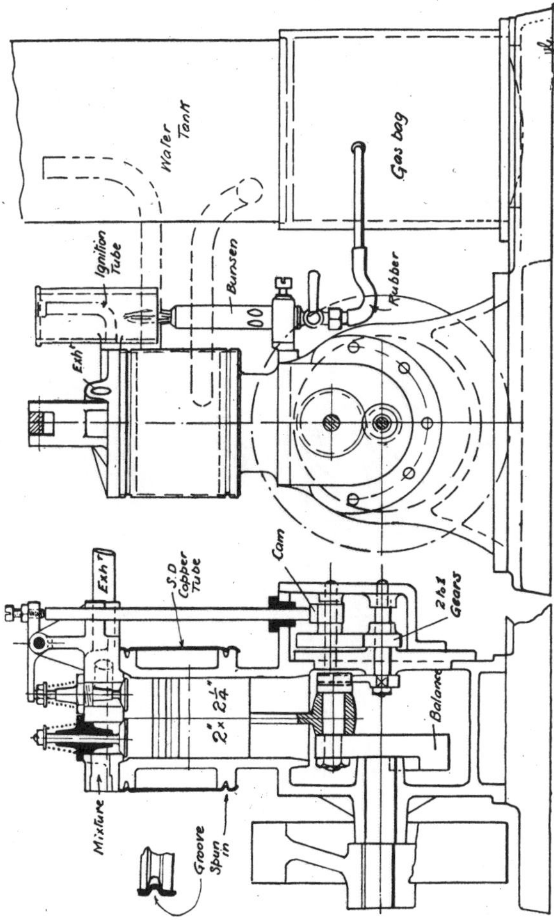

Fig. 673.—Small vertical gas engine

Tube ignition is provided for in the drawing, but, if possible, electrical ignition should be fitted. A cast-iron base with a cylindrical support for the water tank is indicated, this support having a rubber diaphragm in the bottom and acting as a gas-bag. Where tube ignition is used a gas-bag is essential, as it steadies the flow of gas to the bunsen burner. In small engines minute leakages through the valves and past the piston may prevent a high compression being obtained, and the charge may not be forced sufficiently far into the tube to ignite it. Electrical ignition is not dependent on the degree of compression, and therefore the latter may be lower, and the engine need not run at so high a speed.

Another arrangement of a water-cooled cylinder is shown in Fig. 672. Here the exhaust valve does not require a rocker, but is actuated directly by the cam tappet rod.

Making a Small Horizontal Gas Engine.—A neat and

Fig. 673A.—Photograph of ⅛-B.H.P. horizontal gas engine

simple design for ⅛-b.h.p. model gas engine is reproduced in Figs. 673A to 675. This engine may be made on the same lines up to 2-in. bore, and for the size illustrated "Stuart" castings are obtainable either in the rough or machined. On petrol the engine will give ¼ h.p. The crank is overhung, the crank shaft being supported in a long bearing cast in the bedplate. The water jacketing of the cylinder is accomplished in a very simple manner—the water-space is open at the bottom and is closed by bolting the body casting down to the sole plate. The horizontal valves are contained in a cover casting, which bolts on to the cylinder body casting. Tube or electrical ignition is arranged for; the latter, of course, is to be preferred.

Having obtained the machined castings and finished parts for this engine, the first operation should be to prepare the box bedplate casting and the frame or body casting, so that they may be bolted together—not perhaps finally,

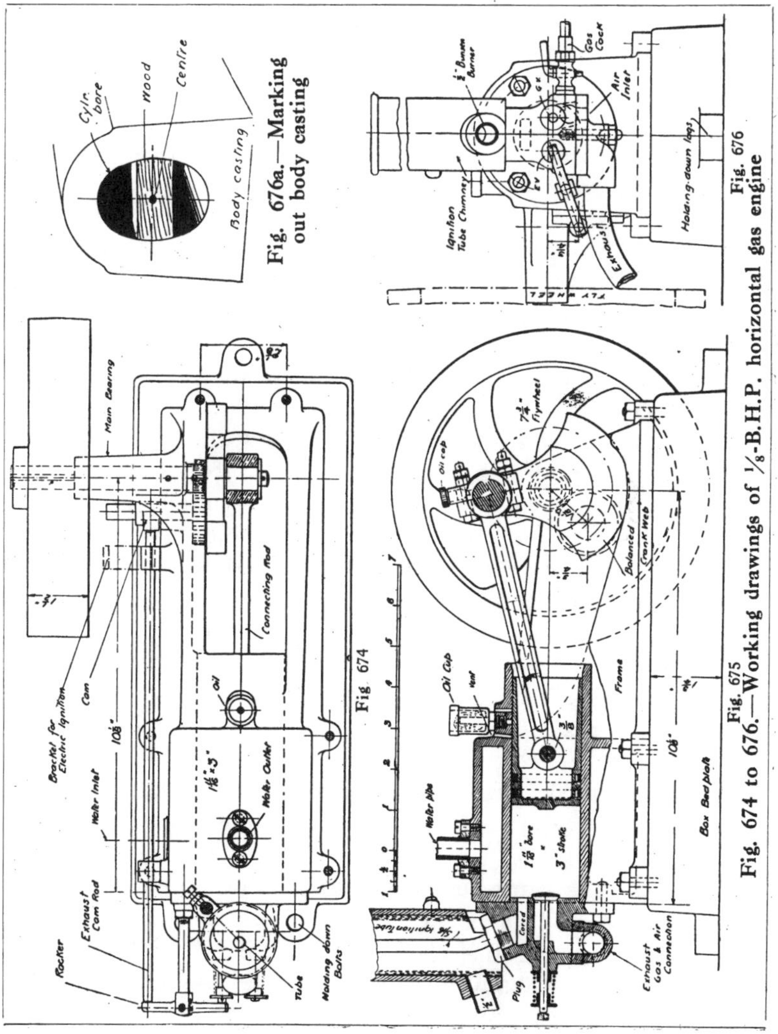

Fig. 676a.—Marking out body casting

Fig. 674

Fig. 675

Fig. 676

Fig. 674 to 676.—Working drawings of 1/8-B.H.P. horizontal gas engine but to enable the erection to be accomplished more conveniently.

The castings will be found sufficiently clean to require no planing where they join, and as the body casting is already machined in its main features—that is, cylinder bore, crank shaft, and two-to-one shaft bearings—it will therefore not require much in the way of " lining " or " marking out." If there are any excrescences on the casting these may be filed off.

The casting should then be rigged up on a flat, true surface, such as a piece of plate-glass if a surface plate is not available, and the parts which are required to be drilled, bored, etc., whitened with chalk. Before this is actually done, the outer or back end of the cylinder bore should be plugged with a piece of hard wood, as shown in Fig. 677. With the dividers the centre of the bore should be found and marked by a centre-pop. Both ends of the main bearing hole should be treated in the same way, and when done the casting may be arranged on the surface plate, and the bottom packed up with paper or tin, so that the centres of all three holes are quite parallel to the surface of the plate.

The scribing block used may be quite a simple contrivance. Failing a more orthodox appliance, all that is wanted is a block of brass or iron with one truly flat side. On this a pointer of strip steel is pivoted, as shown. This arm or pointer should work sufficiently stiff to enable it to resist the action of the scriber as it rubs a line on the metal. Figs. 677 to 679 show the scribing block in the three positions, and with the given position of the point of the scriber all three centre points should coincide with it. When the casting is in this proper position, then the builder can mark out any other level line either above or below the centre-line of the cylinder. The most important of these lines is the centre-line of the exhaust tappet rod, which is on the same level as that of the two-to-one shaft.

While the casting is set up, the centre-line of the water inlet on the tappet rod side of the engine may also be marked, and also the vertical and horizontal centre-lines of the cylinder bore on the back cover face. Wherever the casting will

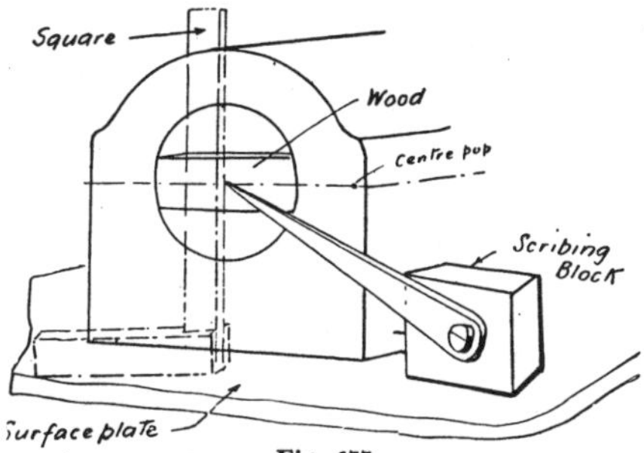

Fig. 677

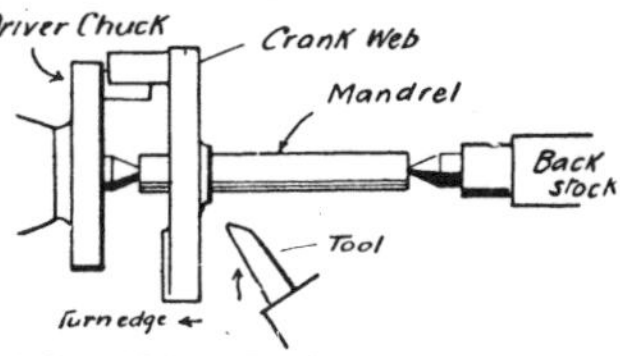

Fig. 686.—Facing crank web on mandrel

Figs. 677 to 679.—Scribing casting set up on level plate

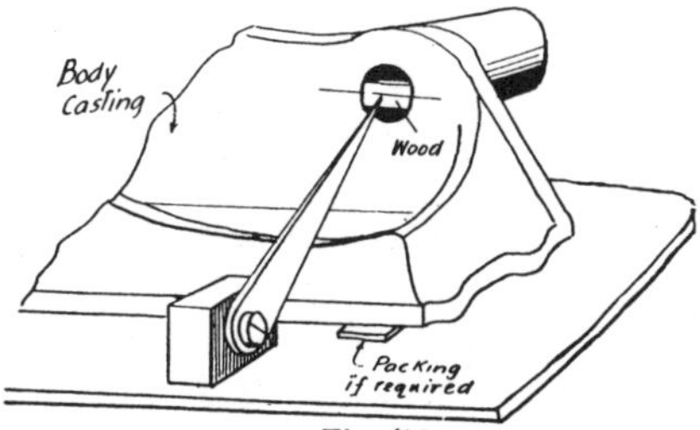

Fig. 678

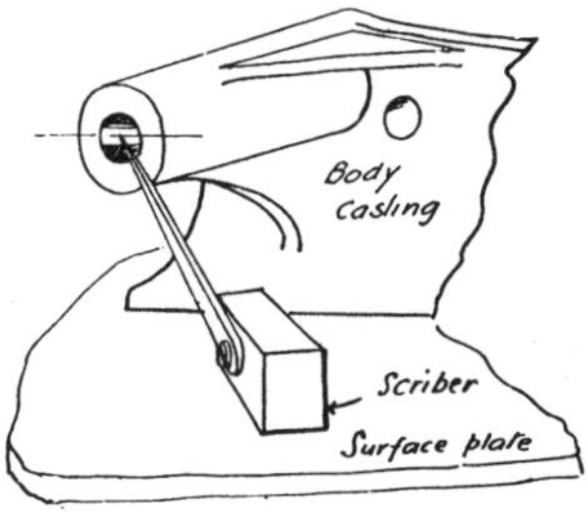

Fig. 679

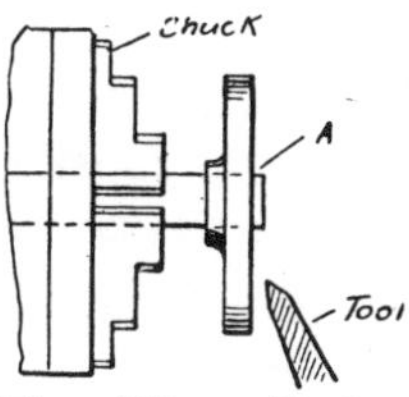

Fig. 680. — Facing water flanges

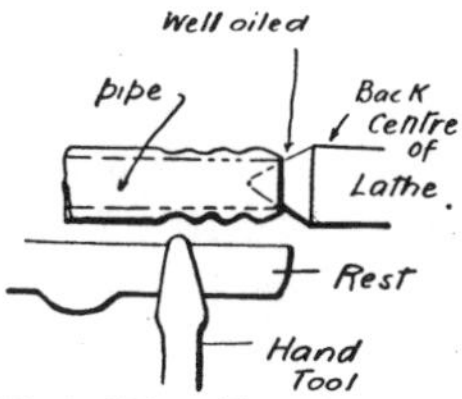

Fig. 681.—Turning end of pipe for rubber connection

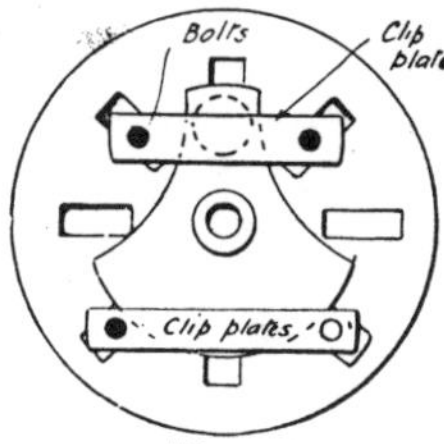

Fig. 685

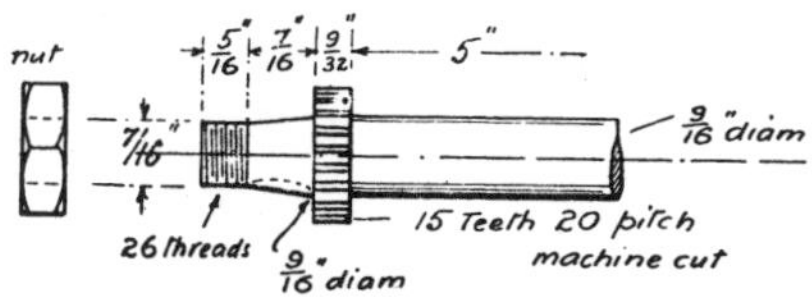

Fig. 682

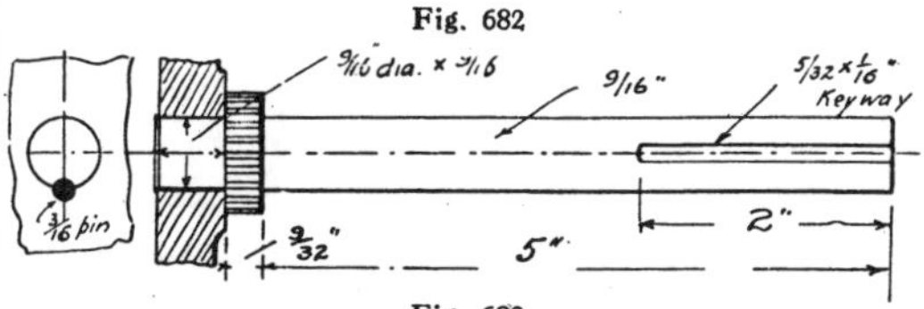

Fig. 683

Figs. 682 and 683.—Cone fitting and riveted fitting to crank web

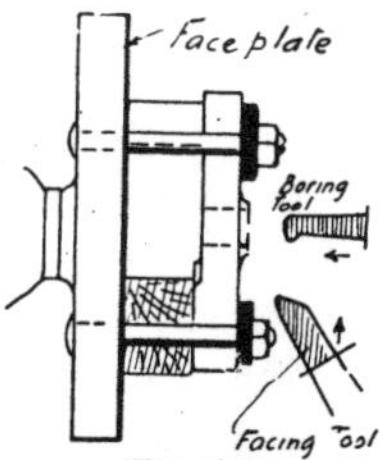

Fig. 684

Figs. 684 and 685. —Boring crank web

allow a square to be used to scribe vertical centre lines, these should be marked as indicated by the dotted lines in Fig. 677.

The body casting can then be lifted, and the important parts of the lines marked out on the chalked surface may be "centre-popped" at intervals along the lines with a fine centre punch, to prevent the obliteration of the marks. In the case of marks on the back end of the cylinder, only four are required, and these may be at the extreme edge of the casting. Their only use is in setting the cover on square when marking for the drilling of the stud holes.

The holes for the $\frac{3}{16}$-in. studs holding down the body casting to the bedplate may then be drilled $\frac{3}{16}$-in. clearing, and having filed the top surface of the box reasonably flat and clean, the three $\frac{3}{8}$-in. holes for the holding-down bolts, which, when the engine is completed, it will be necessary to fit. Six studs are used to join the body casting to the bedplate, four of which are at the cylinder end.

The joint between the casting and the box bed must be watertight, if the surfaces are not planed dead true, then a fairly thick piece of jointing material must be used, with the superfluous portions in the centre cut away.

The holes in the water flanges (Fig. 691) and in the jacket, which, as will be observed on receipt of the castings, are not cored, may next be drilled $\frac{3}{8}$ in. in diameter. After drilling the two water flanges to fit short lengths (say 4 in. to 6 in.) of $\frac{3}{8}$-in. copper or brass pipe as tightly as possible, and also with two $\frac{5}{32}$-in. clearing holes, as shown, they may be offered up to the cylinder or body casting, and the tapping holes on the facings marked out. Of course, before drilling or tapping these holes into the water jacket, the facings cast on the body should be filed up reasonably flat. To ensure accuracy in marking out the screw holes, and to take any shearing strain off them, the copper pipe may protrude through the face of the flange slightly, as shown at A (Fig. 680). The flanges may also be faced in the lathe as shown in Fig 680. The pipe should be soldered into the flange, and as it is intended to recommend a rubber connection with the water tank, the other end of the pipes may be skimmed up with a hand tool, as shown in Fig. 681.

The crank shaft may be fitted into the crank web in one of two methods shown in Figs. 682 and 683. In the first method the end is coned and threaded with a fine thread. A keyway is also cut with a chisel in the coned portion, a thin nut outside finally securing the whole of the parts. The second arrangement (Fig. 683) is simpler, and, if well

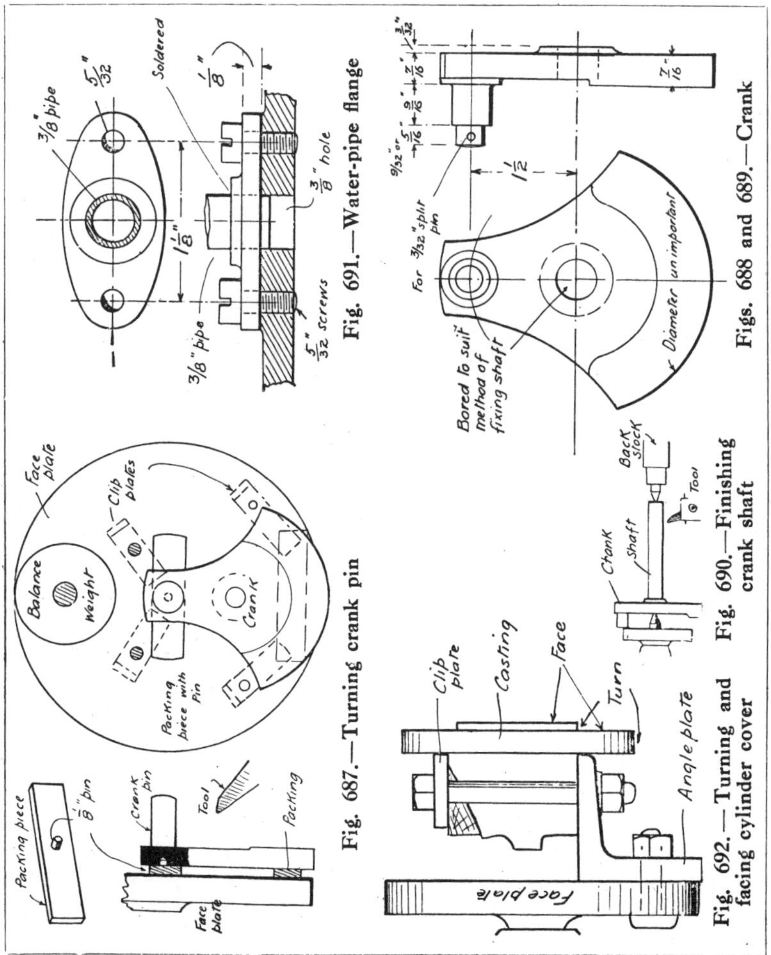

Figs. 688 and 689.—Crank

Fig. 690.—Finishing crank shaft

Fig. 691.—Water-pipe flange

Fig. 687.—Turning crank pin

Fig. 692.—Turning and facing cylinder cover

fitted, is quite as effective. The end is turned a driving fit into the crank, and is riveted over and secured by a $\frac{3}{16}$-in. parallel pin fitted so that it must be driven home with a hammer.

There are several different ways of tackling the work of finishing the crank. As will be noticed, the crank pin is cast solid with the web, and, before machining it, the casting should be examined to see if the pin is reasonably square with the web, as sometimes in the annealing process such mild-steel alloy castings warp. It may then be mounted on the faceplate, as shown in Figs. 684 and 685, and the boss turned and the $\frac{9}{16}$-in. hole bored for the shaft. The casting may then be placed on a mandrel and the back faced up (Fig. 686). The original position is then reversed, and with two pieces of parallel packing of equal thickness placed behind the casting, so that the boss is not touching, the casting will run quite true. It may be clipped on, and, when set, bolted up through the hole for the shaft. A pointer or scriber held in the slide-rest may be employed to check the distance between the shaft hole and the pin.

One of the pieces of parallel packing is fitted with a $\frac{1}{8}$-in. pin projecting, say, $\frac{1}{8}$ in. from the face. This packing is clipped on to the faceplate so that the pin runs quite true. The back face of the crank pin is then marked out, if this has not been done previously, and $1\frac{1}{2}$ in. from the centre of the $\frac{9}{16}$-in. shaft hole, and on the centre-line of the casting, a $\frac{1}{8}$-in. hole is drilled not more than $\frac{3}{16}$ in. deep, but at least $\frac{1}{8}$ in., to fit the pin on the packing piece. The job in this way sets itself correctly on the faceplate, and when the crank web is secured, the pin may be turned to the dimensions on the working drawings. The crank is shown in Figs. 687 to 689.

The crank shaft as supplied is roughly turned to size, and has solid with it the valve and timing-gear pinion, the teeth of which are machined with fifteen teeth of No. 20 diametral pitch (that is, to pitch of twenty teeth to a pitch diameter of 1 in.). The shaft is also already centred. The end which fits into the crank need, at the moment, only be turned up, unless the lathe will conveniently allow the shaft to be finally trued up with the job rigged up as shown in Fig. 690.

The cylinder cover is a rather complicated cored casting with a large projection for horizontal exhaust and inlet valves, and will be found rather difficult to hold by the periphery in an ordinary chuck. Therefore, where a suitable chuck or faceplate dogs are not available, the best method is to file the lower face of the valve box quite square and clear of all the fins left on the casting by the core prints.

The casting may then be clamped down on an angle-plate, as shown in Fig. 692, and the face which abuts the cylinder turned up, the spigot being fitted to the bore of the cylinder. The $\frac{1}{4}$-in. tapped hole for the exhaust flange may also be requisitioned to assist in holding the casting to the angle-plate. When this is done, the angle-plate and the casting may be shifted, and the exhaust and inlet valves bored out with a hook tool to $\frac{9}{16}$ in. diameter and $\frac{13}{16}$ in. centres. The two operations may be repeated in the case of the lower portions of the cored passages, the casting being placed face down on the angle-plate. As the hole for the valve spindles must be bored quite accurately with the valve orifice, a drilling jig should be made and inserted in the $\frac{9}{16}$-in. hole. This may be turned up out of a piece of $\frac{3}{4}$-in. iron or brass rod.

The holes for the cover bolts are $\frac{1}{4}$ in. in diameter clearing size, and are on a pitch circle of $2\frac{11}{16}$ in. diameter. They are approximately 120° apart; but as it is necessary on the left-hand side to clear the lug which holds the burner pillar, this hole may be placed slightly lower down on the pitch circle. The holes in the cylinder should be marked out from those already drilled in the cover.

The burner pillar is a piece of $\frac{5}{16}$-in. steel rod, and is fitted into a vertical hole drilled into the lug provided on the casting. To secure it, a $\frac{1}{8}$-in. or $\frac{5}{32}$-in. set-screw is fitted into the side of the lug.

The hole marked "Tap $\frac{1}{4}$ in. 26 threads or Whitworth" in Fig. 693 is a hole for the rocker fork or pillar. The finer thread is suggested as providing a stronger fixing. For tube ignition only, the top face of the valve box is drilled and tapped $\frac{5}{16}$ in. 26 per inch to receive the iron tube which is supplied. The tube is screwed in while it is straight, and is heated and bent to the vertical position after fixing. Some red lead and oil should be smeared on the thread before it is fixed.

The combined exhaust-pipe flange and inlet-valve cap (Fig. 694) requires facing to fit the valve box. When this is done it may be tapped for the exhaust pipe, and drilled $\frac{1}{4}$ in. and $\frac{5}{16}$ in. as marked. The $\frac{5}{16}$-in. hole is chamfered inside to fit a $\frac{7}{16}$-in. ball valve. A $\frac{1}{4}$-in. stud fitted between the exhaust and inlet passages in the valve box secures the flange in place, and to ensure a gas-tight joint a thin sheet of asbestos should be inserted between the flange and valve box.

The piston (Fig. 695) is of the usual trunk type, and the casting has a chucking piece cast on its outer end. To turn the piston it is therefore held in the lathe, as shown in Fig. 696, and while in this position it is finished a good fit for the cylinder bore, and the grooves turned for the rings, to the dimensions given. When the outside is finished, the casting may be reversed in the chuck, the tenon piece removed, and the mouth of the piston finished off. The little end pin is of $\frac{3}{8}$ in. diameter mild steel. The centre of the inside bosses should be carefully marked on the outside by the aid of a scribing block and V blocks, and centre-popped on both sides. The drill may then be held in the lathe chuck, and, holding the other side with the back centre in the centre-pop, the hole may be drilled in each side separately. If there is any doubt about getting the two holes truly in line, a slightly smaller drill may be used and the hole reamed out afterwards with a $\frac{3}{8}$-in. reamer. Extreme care must be exercised in finishing the piston casting, as it is necessarily light and fragile.

For the piston rings (Fig. 697) a casting large enough to make two rings and also leave a piece for spares is available. It should be chucked in the self-centring chuck, turned up to $1\frac{3}{4}$ in. bare outside diameter, and faced on the other side. The casting may then be loosened and packed out with a piece of plate about $\frac{1}{32}$ in. thick, this

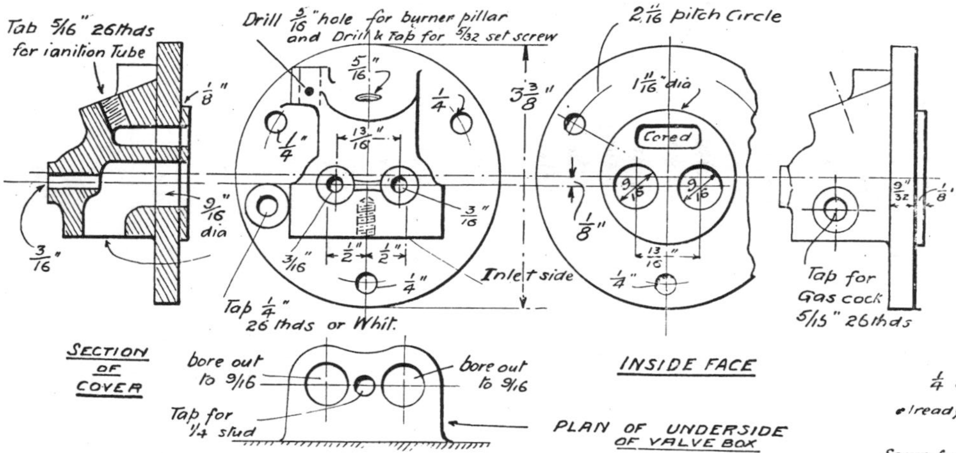

Fig. 693

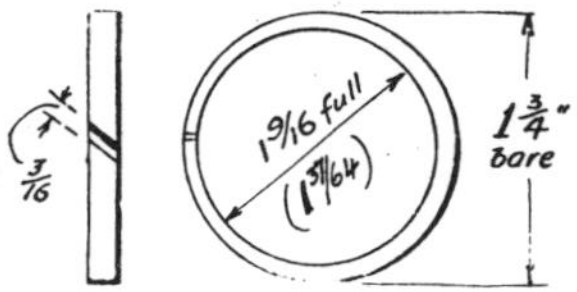

Fig. 697.—Piston ring

Fig. 693.—Details of back cylinder cover

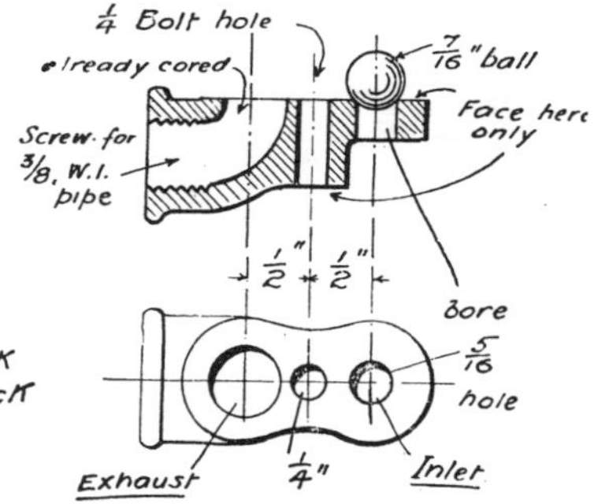

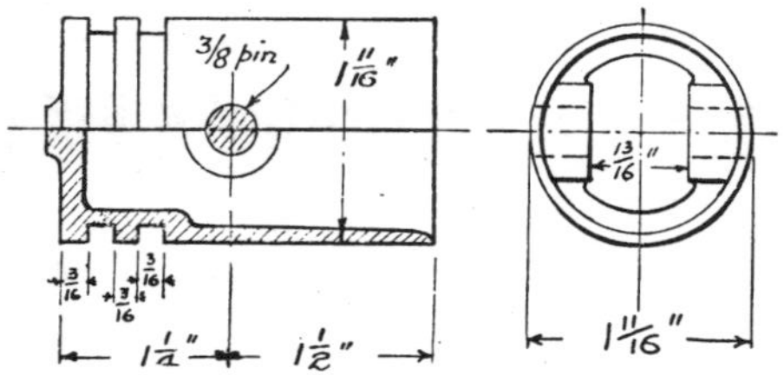

Fig. 695.—Details of piston

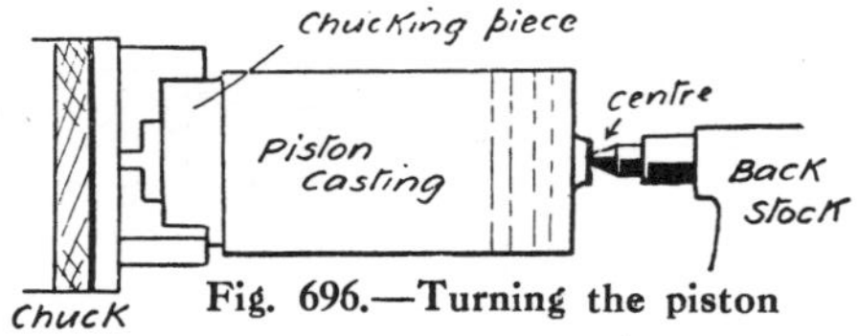

Fig. 696.—Turning the piston

Fig. 694.—Inlet cap and exhaust flange

causing the casting to run eccentrically. With a scriber held in the tool-rest, test the outer face to see that this runs quite true; correct, if necessary, by a slight knock with a piece of wood. The inside may be turned $1\frac{9}{16}$ in. in diameter full, and the rings parted off with a narrow tool to exactly $\frac{3}{16}$ in. wide. The length of the outside turned at the outset should be enough for all the rings—that is, the whole of the metal overhanging the jaws of the chuck should be machined on the outside at the first chucking. The rings are filed through at an angle at their thinnest part, the width of the slot being nearly $\frac{3}{16}$ in. The rings must be sprung over the piston, and being small, if they are warmed, the operation will not be so likely to end in the breakage of a ring as otherwise might be the case.

The valves are of mild steel, and are turned out of the solid bar. They are supplied roughed out, and should be centred at each end at the outset, held by a carrier, and the head then finished off as shown at A (Fig. 698). Instead of turning up the spindle with two diameters, the larger being next to the head and extending for $\frac{1}{2}$ in. or so (*see* Fig. 699), the $\frac{3}{16}$-in. portion of the spindle is arranged to grow into the head as shown in Fig. 700. This makes a stronger valve, and involves no extra work. The carrier is then placed at the other end of the spindle, and the $\frac{3}{16}$-in. diameter turned up to fit the holes in the back cover easily, but without any shake. The tool should be keen, and the height quite central.

Two valves which are alike in every particular are required, and, as shown in Figs. 699 and 700, the projection in the top of the head should be provided with a slot (a saw-cut) to engage a screw-driver during the operation of grinding in.

In grinding in valves, by the way, a continuous rotation of the valve and a continuous pressure is not the best method. Do not, therefore, just put one part in the lathe and hold the valve up against it. This may only form rings in the bearing portions of the valve and seating. The valve should be inserted as if it were being finally fixed, spring nuts and all being attached. The cylinder cover may then be held in

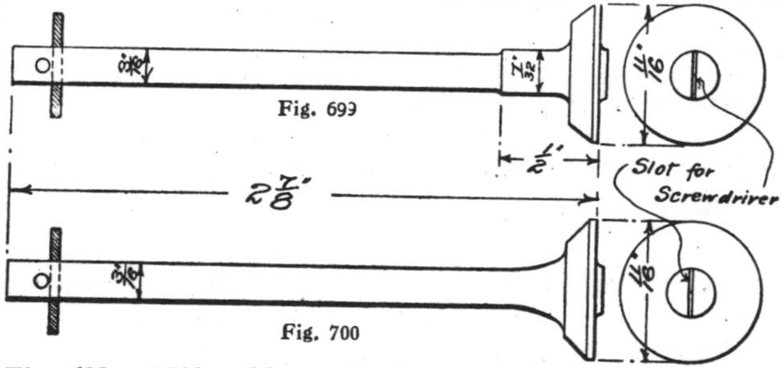

Figs. 699 and 700.—Alternative form of inlet and exhaust valves

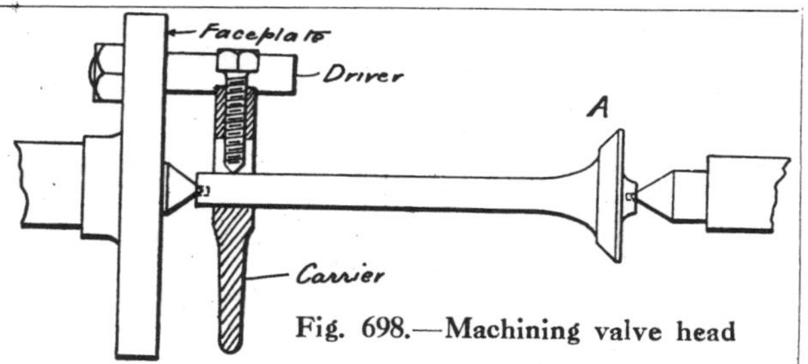

Fig. 698.—Machining valve head

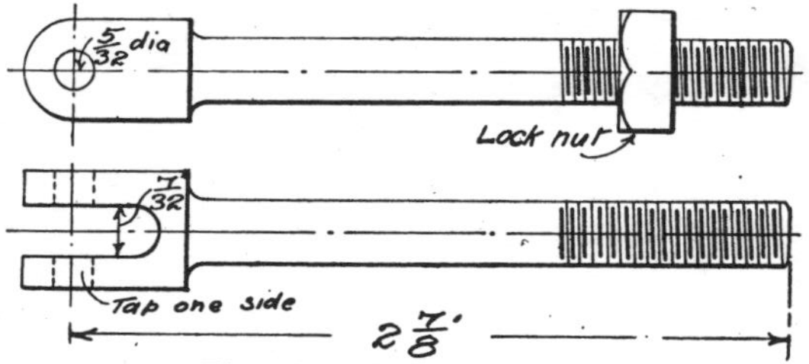

Fig. 704.—Rocker fork

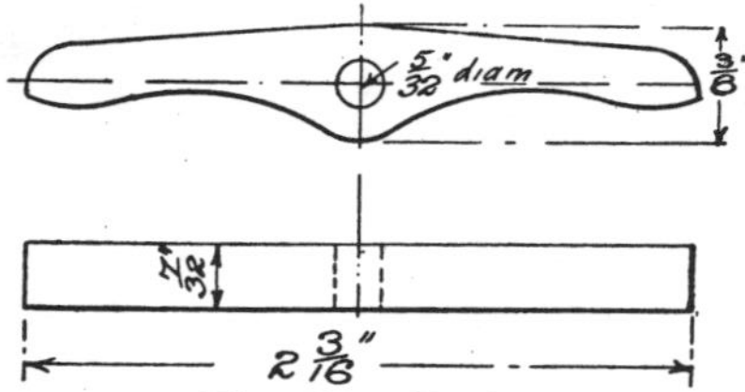

Fig. 703.—Rocker

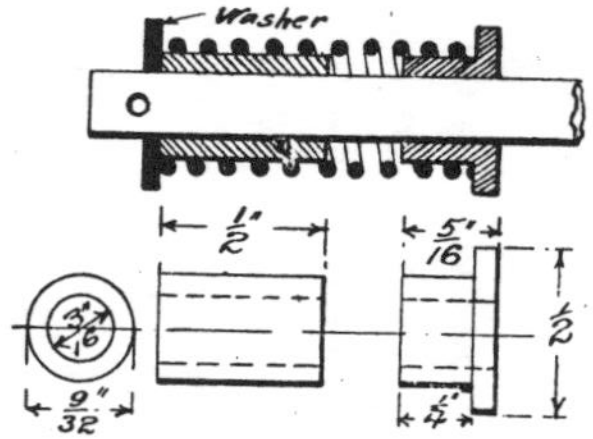

Fig. 701.—Inlet valve collars

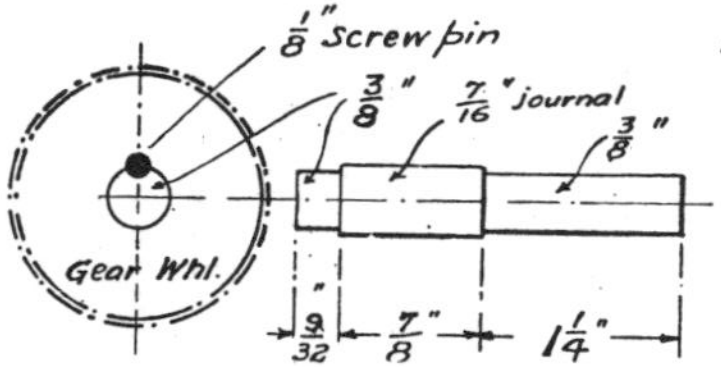

Fig. 705.—Cam shaft and gear wheel

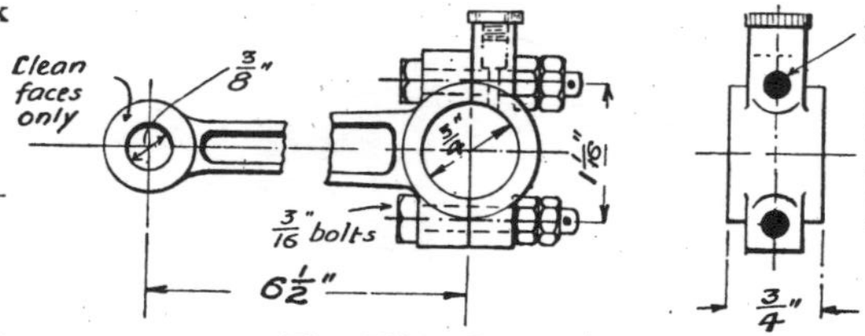

Fig. 706.—Connecting rod

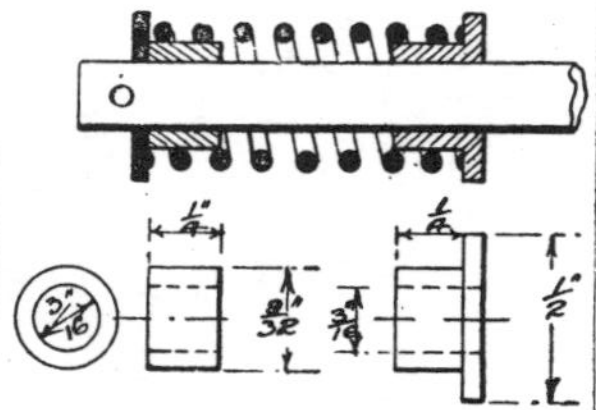

Fig. 702.—Exhaust valve collars

the vice, and fine emery powder and oil applied to the valve. The valve should be turned with a screw-driver or its equivalent, and the rotation reversed occasionally. Now and then the valve should be lifted off its seating and dropped in a new place if possible, so that the particles of abrasive material (emery) are shifted.

To complete the valve mechanism, brass spring collars should be fitted on the outer end of the spindles as shown in Figs. 701 and 702, and the rocker and rocker fork fashioned as shown by Figs. 703 and 704. The rocker, which is out of a piece of mild steel, may be case-hardened.

The end of the valve spindle and the end of the cam tappet rod may be treated in the same way.

The cam shaft is a short piece of rod which fits in the already bored hole in the body casting. This hole is drilled $\frac{7}{16}$ in., and the machined gear wheel $\frac{3}{8}$ in. In turning up the shaft to Fig. 705, an eye should be given to the fitting of the shaft in these holes more than to the dimensions on the illustrations. In the case of the gear wheel, the shaft must be a driving fit, as once it is fitted on it need not be removed, but may be secured by a $\frac{1}{8}$-in. screwed pin as shown. The $\frac{7}{16}$-in. diameter portion which forms the journal should be a good working fit. The bearing is a single one, and necessarily short. Therefore, accuracy in fitting must be aimed at. Although the projection of $1\frac{1}{4}$ in. beyond the journal is not required in a tube-ignition engine, the overplus need not be removed. The engine may subsequently be required to be fitted with electrical ignition, when this extra length of metal will be found useful for mounting the wipe contact.

The connecting rod (Fig. 706) is a mild-steel casting. The big end is bushed with a solid gunmetal bush; but to enable the rod to be assembled the end is arranged in two parts. The end of the rod and the cap should therefore be faced up, and by a suitable clamp or by holding the two parts together in a vice, a $\frac{3}{16}$-in. hole should be drilled through one of the lugs, and the bolt inserted. The other hole may then be drilled.

The boring out of the end of the rod to fit is a more difficult job, and the best method entirely depends on the

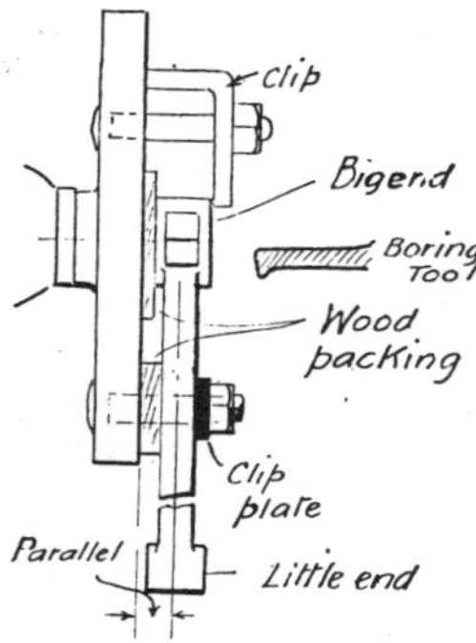

Fig. 707.—Method of boring connecting-rod end

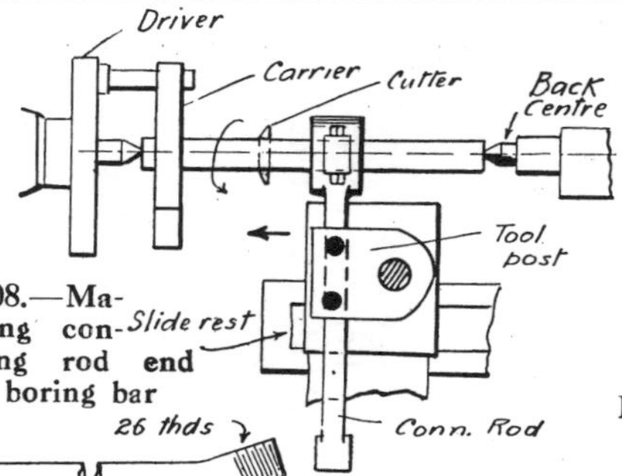

Fig. 708.—Machining connecting rod end with boring bar

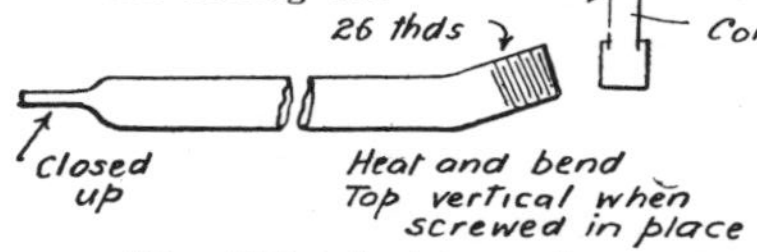

Fig. 716.—Ignition tube

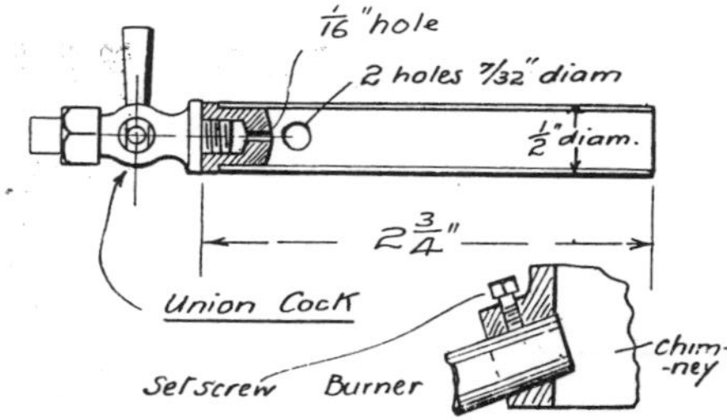

Fig. 715.—Burner tube

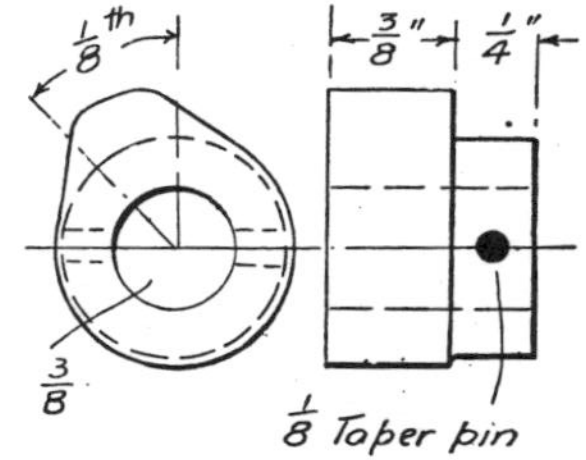

Fig. 712.—Exhaust cam

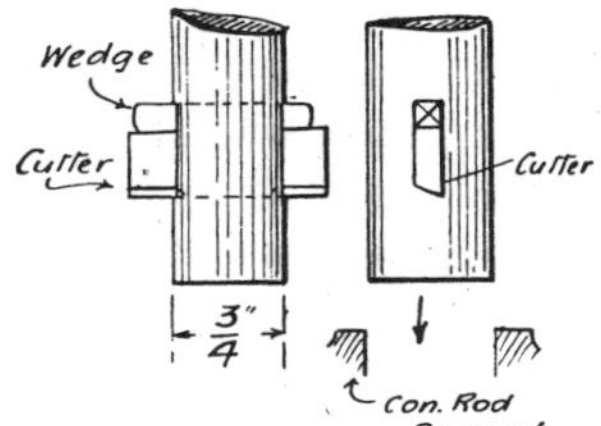

Fig. 710.—Cutter for facing hole in connecting rod

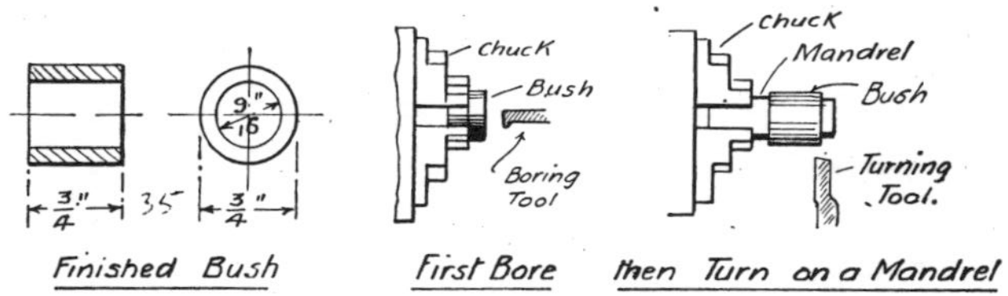

Fig. 711.—Gunmetal big-end bush

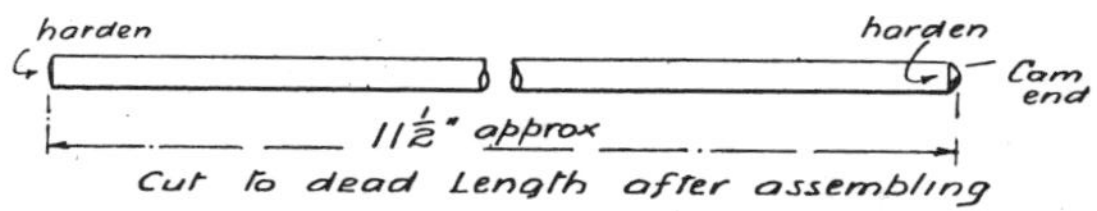

Fig. 713.—Tappet rod

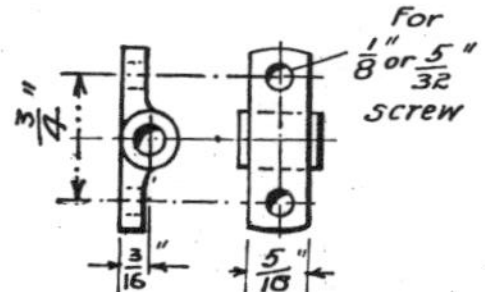

Fig. 714.—Tappet-rod guides

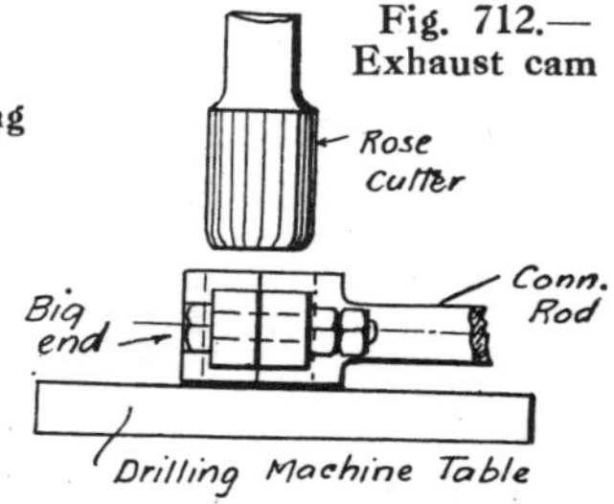

Fig. 709.—Boring connecting rod with rose cutter

available tools. Where the lathe will swing the rod, it would be an easy matter to mount it up on the faceplate, taking care that the centre-line of the rod is parallel to the plane of the faceplate, as shown in Fig. 707. Another way would be to hold it in the tool rest, and to use a boring bar running between the lathe centres (*see* Fig. 708). Except for the making of the tool in the first instance, a good way is to bore it out with a rose cutter as shown in Fig. 709, and then to face it with another cutter made as shown in Fig. 710. All these are useful accessories, and once made will be found to be of service in other jobs.

The gunmetal bush (Fig. 711) is turned a good working fit for the $\frac{9}{16}$-in. diameter crank pin, and a tight fit for the $\frac{3}{4}$-in. hole in the big-end casting, so that the bolts will have to be slackened to get it in. Should the grip of the cap be deemed insufficient, then a few strokes of the file on the joint face of the cap will provide the necessary hold on the bush.

The exhaust cam, as soon as the connecting rod is finished and fitted, can be made and secured to the cam shaft. It is made of mild steel, and may be "potash hardened" in the manner already described. Otherwise a piece of cast (tool) steel may be used, and after finishing, hardened a dark straw. The duration of the exhaust opening being for one stroke out of the four which completes the cycle of operations, and the cam shaft running half the speed of the main shaft, the rise of the cam only covers one-eighth of its circumference. This is shown in Fig. 712. The tappet rod (Fig. 713) is rounded at both ends, and, especially at the cam end, should be hardened. The approximate length of the rod is $11\frac{1}{2}$ in., as shown; but it should be filed to the dead length required after the engine is erected, and then have the ends hardened. The tappet rod is carried in gunmetal guides (Fig. 714), which are screwed to the side of the body casting.

The cam is secured to the shaft by a $\frac{1}{8}$-in. taper pin; it should, however, fit fairly tightly at the outset, so that it can be adjusted into position before drilling the hole in the shaft for the pin.

The bunsen-burner tube (Fig. 715) is of $\frac{1}{2}$-in. brass tube with two side holes $\frac{7}{32}$ in. in diameter and with the end plugged up with a nipple piece. This nipple is drilled $\frac{1}{4}$ in., a suitable thread for the gas cock. The ordinary size is $\frac{5}{16}$ in. in diameter, 26 threads. The ignition tube (Fig. 716) is screwed the same thread, and is bent to the required angle when fixed in place. The chimney is supported on a piece of $\frac{5}{16}$-in. rod. A hole is bored in the lug provided, and a small hole ($\frac{5}{32}$ in.) drilled and tapped in the side to receive a screw, which shall hold the chimney in any desired position on the rod. The chimney is also drilled $\frac{1}{2}$ in. at an angle to receive the bunsen-burner tube as shown in the general arrangement drawing. The burner is secured by a $\frac{1}{8}$-in. or $\frac{5}{32}$-in. screw. The chimney must be lined with a piece of asbestos card to conserve the heat of the flame. As most readers know, the tube type of ignition depends for its efficacy on the compression. If the piston or rings are faulty, the charge will not be squeezed sufficiently far into the tube to cause an explosion. This squeezing of the explosive mixture into the hot tube enables the firing point to be regulated within certain limits. The lower down the tube is heated, the earlier will the explosion occur.

Converting an Engine from Tube to Electrical Ignition.—The necessary extra fittings that are required to convert the gas engine just described, or any other engine, to electric ignition are not numerous, expensive, or difficult to make. The only trouble that may be experienced is in fitting the plug. Standard sparking plugs are screwed with a metric thread, the nearest English equivalent being $\frac{11}{16}$ in. diameter, $17\frac{1}{2}$ threads per inch. If not tapped by the makers, the fitting of the plug may mean the making or purchasing of a special tap or an adaptor to fit the plug, or sending the casting out to be tapped.

Not only does electrical ignition make a cleaner-running engine, but the power obtained is enhanced considerably. If the engine is coupled to a dynamo for accumulator charging, then the difficulty of providing the current for the coil is lessened, as two of the cells, if the voltage is not more than 4 volts, may be tapped to supply the trembler coil. Otherwise, a battery of three sack Leclanché cells (not an ordinary Leclanché) or a good 4½-volt ignition dry battery may be used.

The diagram of the connections (Fig. 717) shows the electrical apparatus required. A trembler coil is recommended, and a miniature coil measuring 3⅞ in. by 2⅛ in. by 1½ in., weighing 7¾ oz., and giving on 4 volts a spark ¼ in. long, can be obtained for 7s. 6d. to 10s. A full-size trembler coil costs about 10s. 6d. ; the switch will cost less than 3d. The positive wire and the earth wire may be short pieces of electric light wire No. 1/20 (cost about 1½d. a yard), or special L.T. ignition flexible at 3½d. a yard, and for the high tension the special heavily covered flexible used for H.T. ignition leads on motors at 1s. a yard.

Although four terminals may be thought necessary, two for the primary and two for the secondary, most ignition coils only have three terminals in all. The one marked P is the primary to which the positive wire from the battery or accumulator is attached. The high-tension wire terminal is marked S P (sparking plug). The terminal lettered M (mass or earth) serves as a return connection for both the high- and low-tension currents, and may be connected to any part of the engine frame, either under a holding-down bolt or under any other screw or nut in the metal part of the engine. Fig. 718 illustrates the fixing of the sparking plug, a copper asbestos washer being recommended to ensure a gas-tight joint. The engine attachments are shown in Figs. 717 to 721. The tappet-rod guide nearest to the crank shaft is arranged with a lug to carry a block of fibre. The screw holding the fibre block is well countersunk, so that the brass contact strip attached on the top cannot touch the screw and short-circuit the primary ignition current. One end of the block is tapped for a ⅛-in. pin, and the other for the screw of the contact blade. This blade (Fig. 720) is made of hard strip brass, so that it will have a certain amount of elasticity, and is slotted as shown. These slots allow for a certain amount of adjustment in the firing point.

The wipe contact is shown in Fig. 721. A piece of brass rod is bored to fit tightly the extended portion of the two-to-

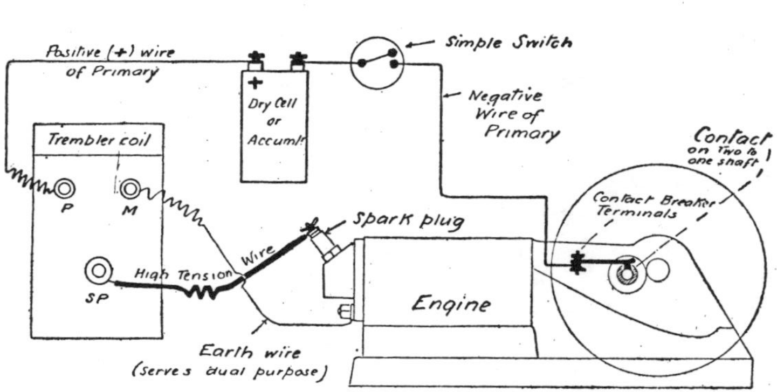

Fig. 717.—Diagram of connections and apparatus for electrical ignition

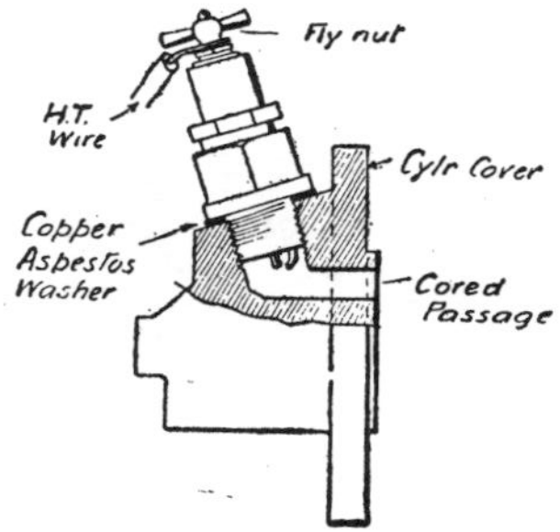

Fig. 718.—Fitting of sparking plug

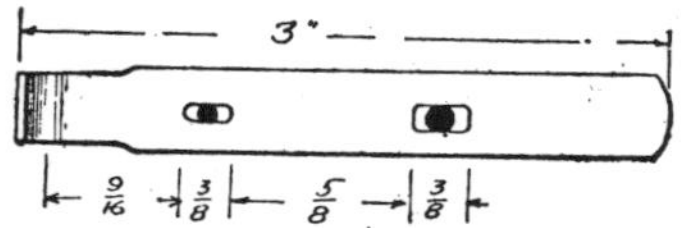

Fig. 720.—Contact blade

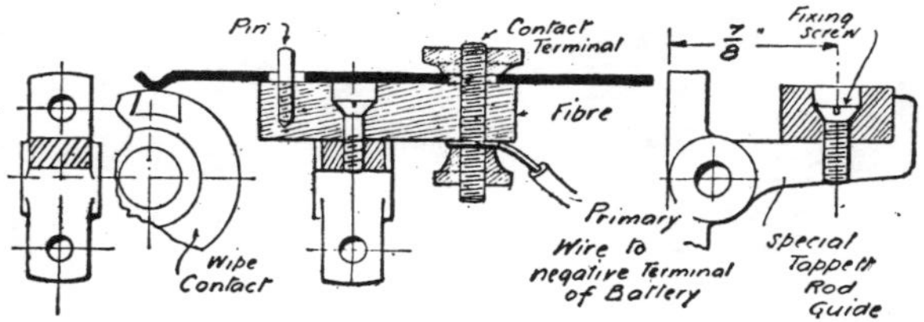

Fig. 719.—Tappet-rod guide, contacts and insulation

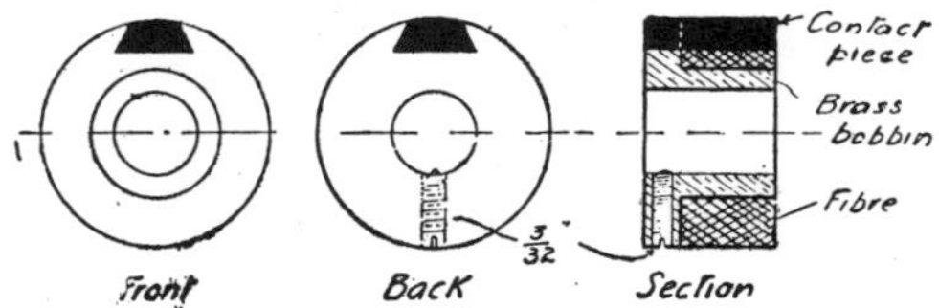

Fig. 721.—Wipe contact on two-to-one shaft

one shaft and tapped for a $\frac{3}{32}$-in. grub screw at one end. Using a piece of rod of the same size as the two-to-one shaft as a mandrel and the grub screw as a means of securing it, thc outside is turned down to fit a ring of fibre previously prepared. This ring is fitted on, and then a dovetailed slot is filed in the periphery to a depth of about half the thickness of the fibre ring, and a brass contact piece is carefully and tightly fitted into this slot. It may be secured by tacking at the back (that is, the all brass face) with soft

Fig. 722.—Parts of $1\frac{3}{16}$-in.-bore model petrol engine

solder. The whole contact may again be placed on the mandrel, and with a very sharp tool the whole of the outside may be skimmed up to run dead true.

While it is quite possible with electrical ignition to speed the engine up to a number of revolutions impossible with hot-tube ignition, it is not wise to do so; 500 to 600 revolutions per minute is the maximum satisfactory speed. To adjust the speed, slacken the top nut of the contact blade and move the blade forwards or backwards according to requirements. The switch may be placed on either the positive or negative wire of the primary circuit, according to which is the more convenient; and should there be any suspicion that the oil in the bearings is offering a resistance to the path of the low-tension current, then a collecting brush made of a piece of strip brass could be attached to the tappet-rod guide and arranged to wipe on the end of the two-to-one shaft.

Petrol Motors for Model Boats.—Small or "model" petrol engines are extremely popular for driving racing boats, but success can only be obtained with this form of engine by perfect workmanship in all the component parts. Where the cylinder is, say, $1\frac{3}{8}$-in. or $1\frac{3}{16}$-in. bore, as in the case of the engine illustrated by Figs. 722 and 723, the valves and piston must fit freely and without the slightest leakage. Otherwise the engine will not suck the charge or properly compress it. The engine shown was made by Mr. F. Westmoreland, of the Manchester Society of Model Engineers, for driving a "metre length" motor-boat. It is built on the general lines of that illustrated in Fig. 673, but instead of a tube being used for the water jacket, the latter is cast, and the working cylinder is a steel liner forced into the casting. Mr. Westmoreland has built one engine with a $1\frac{3}{8}$-in. by $1\frac{3}{8}$-in. cylinder weighing only 5 lb., and another $1\frac{3}{16}$ in. by $1\frac{3}{16}$ in. weighing less than $3\frac{1}{4}$ lb. They are water-cooled, have electrical ignition, and their speed is 4,000 revolutions per minute; they lie horizontally in the boats, and drive through bevel gearing.

Fig. 723. — $1\frac{3}{16}$-in.-bore model petrol engine, built by Mr. F. Westmoreland

CHAPTER XIX

Model Railway Engineering

The construction of model railways is a phase of miniature engineering to which many amateurs devote the whole of their spare time. It is undoubtedly a fascinating hobby, and embraces work of many kinds which it is impossible within these covers to describe in full. Further, it may occupy one's energies summer and winter, and both indoors and outdoors. Where an outdoor line is decided upon, the locomotives, carriages, wagons, signals, and other accessories may be built during the winter, and in the light evenings that follow the track may be laid and operated. An indoor railway may be constructed in an attic or other spare room, which also forms the workshop. Realistic effects can be obtained with an indoor line; due to the protection from the weather the scale and gauge of the line may be small, and the detail put into the permanent buildings and accessories of the line is only limited by the skill of the amateur. Railways of 1¼-in., 1¾-in., and 2-in. (Nos. 0, 1, and 2) gauges are usually laid indoors. The standard gauges, No. 3 (2½ in.), 3¼ in., 3½ in., 4¾ in., 7¼ in., and 9½ in., are usually employed out of doors.

Standard Scales and Gauges.—In railway vehicles certain standards of widths between rails and flanges are adopted, the rail gauge now universally employed for main lines in England being 4 ft. 8½ in. In models the desire to use even figures has resulted in the nearest regular dimension to the scale chosen. The smaller gauges are also numbered, and the scale is a metric one. The table reproduced on page 358 gives all the standard dimensions in each gauge, and includes the height and width between buffers and overall dimensions or "loading gauge" of the vehicles. (*See also* Fig. 724.)

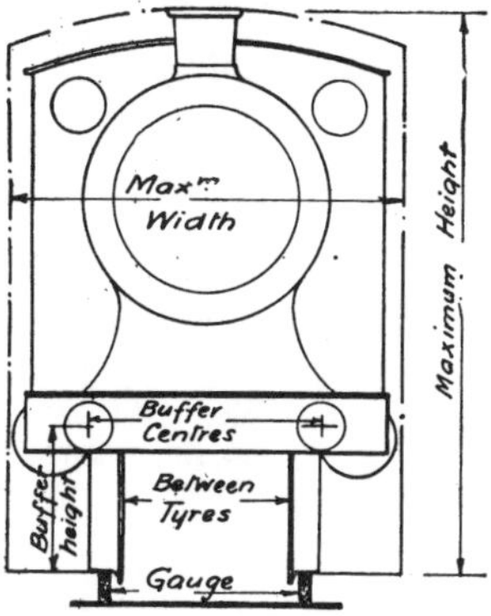

Fig. 724.—Diagram showing meaning of gauge terms

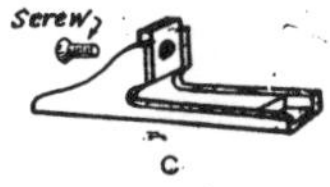

Fig. 728.—(A) Single chair; (B) double or check-rail chair; (C) slide chair

Fig. 726.—Joint of hollow tin-plate rail

Fig. 729.—Spring "fishplate" rail-jointing piece

Fig. 727.—"Rustless" solid steel rail

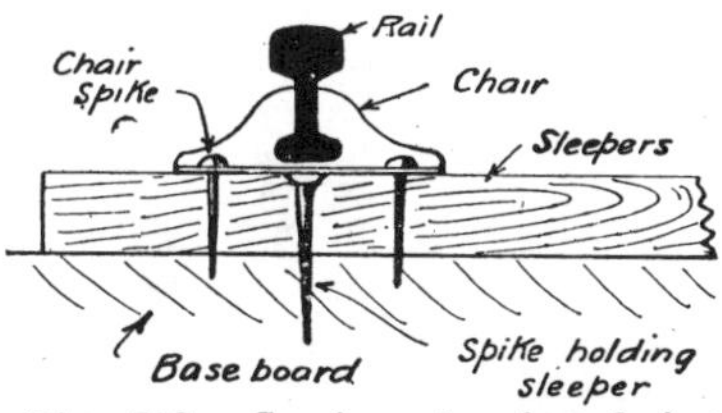

Fig. 730.—Section showing fitting of solid steel rail

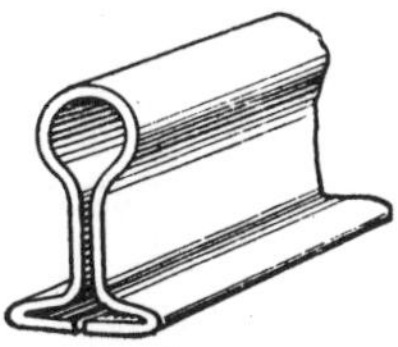
Fig. 725.—Hollow tin-plate rail

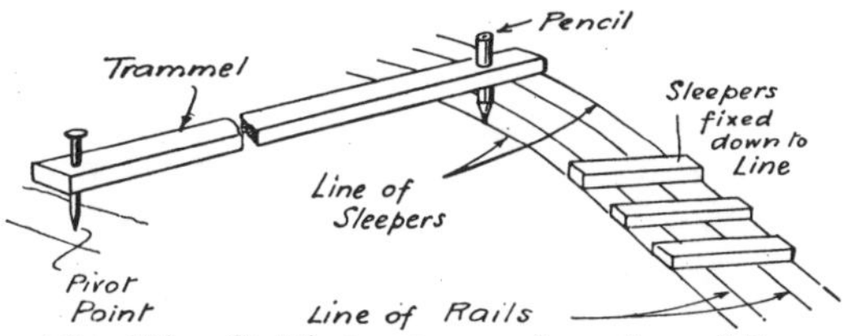

Fig. 731.—Striking out curved portion of line

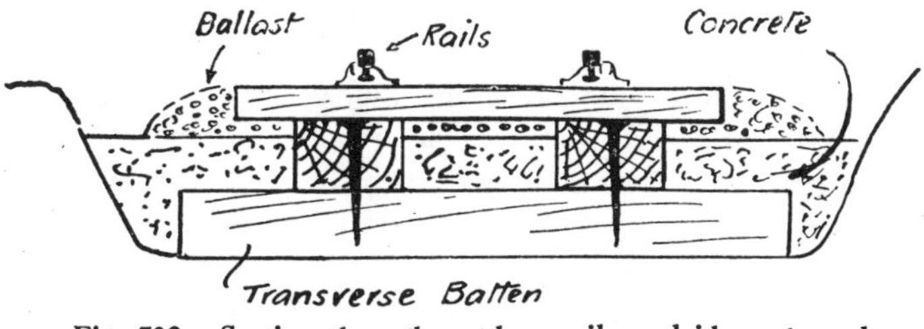

Fig. 732.—Section through outdoor railway laid on ground

TABLE OF MODEL RAILWAY AND LOCOMOTIVE STANDARD DIMENSIONS

Scale to the foot	*Rail gauge*	*Wheels*		*Buffers*		*Over-all dimensions*	
		Width between tyres	*Depth of flange*	*Height above rail*	*Width*	*Height above rail*	*Max. width*
No. 0 (7 mm.)	$1\frac{1}{4}$ in.	$1\frac{1}{16}$ in.	$\frac{3}{32}$ in. or $\frac{7}{64}$ in.	24 mm.	40 mm.	96 mm.	66 mm.
No. 1 (10 mm.)	$1\frac{3}{4}$ in.	$1\frac{17}{32}$ in.	$\frac{7}{64}$ in. or $\frac{1}{8}$ in.	35 mm.	57 mm.	135 mm.	95 mm.
No. 2 ($\frac{7}{16}$ in.)	2 in.	$1\frac{25}{32}$ in.	$\frac{1}{8}$ in.	$1\frac{1}{2}$ in.	$2\frac{1}{2}$ in.	$5\frac{13}{16}$ in.	$4\frac{3}{16}$ in.
No. 3 ($\frac{1}{2}$ in.)	$2\frac{1}{2}$ in.	$2\frac{9}{32}$ in.	$\frac{1}{8}$ in.	$1\frac{3}{4}$ in.	$2\frac{7}{8}$ in.	$6\frac{3}{4}$ in.	$4\frac{3}{4}$ in.
$\frac{11}{16}$ in.	$3\frac{1}{4}$ in.	$3\frac{1}{32}$ in.	$\frac{1}{8}$ in.	$2\frac{3}{8}$ in.	$3\frac{15}{16}$ in.	$9\frac{1}{4}$ in.	$6\frac{1}{2}$ in.
$\frac{3}{4}$ in.	$3\frac{1}{2}$ in.	$3\frac{9}{32}$ in.	$\frac{1}{8}$ in.	$2\frac{5}{8}$ in.	$4\frac{5}{16}$ in.	$10\frac{1}{8}$ in.	$7\frac{1}{8}$ in.
1 in.	$4\frac{3}{4}$ in.	$4\frac{1}{2}$ in.	$\frac{9}{64}$ in.	$3\frac{1}{2}$ in.	$5\frac{11}{16}$ in.	$13\frac{1}{2}$ in.	$9\frac{1}{2}$ in.
$1\frac{1}{2}$ in.	$7\frac{1}{4}$ in.	$6\frac{3}{4}$ in.	$\frac{5}{32}$ in.	$5\frac{1}{4}$ in.	$8\frac{5}{8}$ in.	$20\frac{1}{4}$ in.	$14\frac{1}{4}$ in.
2 in.	$9\frac{1}{2}$ in.	9 in.	$\frac{3}{16}$ in.	7 in.	$11\frac{1}{2}$ in.	26 in.	19 in.

Note.—In the gauges Nos. 0 and 1, the scales used are 7 mm. and 10 mm. to the foot. A wheel 6 ft. in the original would therefore be 7 × 6 = 42 mm. in No. 0 gauge, or 10 × 6 = 60 mm. in the No. 1 gauge.

Track and Track Materials.—Indoor tracks may consist of hollow tin rail. This in the past has been practically all of German manufacture. It is certainly a cheap track, and the rail is supplied loose with stamped chairs, which may be spiked down with gimp pins to the baseboard of the track, or to sleepers previously placed. This hollow rail is also made in rolled brass, but there is no advantage in this material for indoor work. The rail joints are maintained in alignment by a spike in one rail fitting into the hollow head of the other. Points and crossings may be made up of this material, but naturally the switch rails, when pointed at the ends, are not as strong as might be desired. A solid rail is therefore recommended, and the British-made "rustless" steel rail (Fig. 727), sold by model-dealers, makes a firm and excellent track of scale appearance. The rail is drawn mild steel, in 3-ft. lengths, specially treated with a non-corrosive surface. It is of the proper Bull-headed section, and can be supplied complete with three standard types of chairs, spring fish plates, spikes and sleepers. Parts all ready for laying points are also supplied. Where sleepers are not used, it is necessary to see that the wooden substructure is planed perfectly level. The line of the proposed track is then marked out on the baseboard by two lines representing the centres of the respective rails. These lines will be slightly wider apart than the exact gauge or distance between rails. The chairs are then threaded on the rails, the ordinary number per rail being 16 per rail-length, but, of course, more, say 20 or 22, will give a better appearance to the finished track. The chairs should be placed so that the overhang of the rail from the chairs at the end is half the usual space between the chairs. The rails are then fitted with chairs and one rail laid down first, the two ends being tacked down—not firmly—and then the centre directly over the scribed line. The rail should then be faired up by eye, the chairs between the ends being put in as this "fairing up" proceeds. A dead straight line can be obtained by punching the rail at or near the chairs one way or the other. The spikes are driven with a small hammer and finally with a hollow punch when the line is faired up. The opposite rail is laid with a gauge from the one already down. The gauge may be a piece of metal filed with two slots to fit the head of the rails when at the proper distance apart.

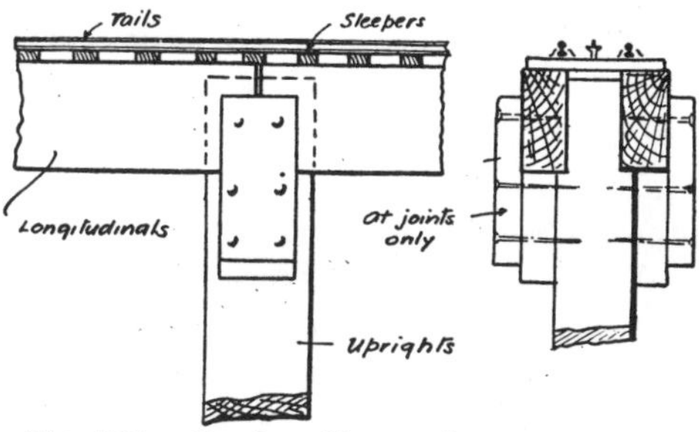

Fig. 733.—Outdoor line: rails supported on edge battens

For curves, a lath of suitable length should be made, according to the desired radius of curve, and a nail or screw fixed in one end as a centre point. In the other end may be drilled two holes to fit a pencil, the distance apart of the two holes being equal to the space between the centres of the rails. This lath, or "trammel," the idea of which is illustrated in Fig. 731, may be pivoted to some temporary support at the level of the rails, and with the pencil point on the mark representing the commencement of the curved lines may be scribed representing the centres of both rails. Care should be taken to see that the curve is truly tangential to the straight length of line from which it leads off.

The rails need not be bent, and they will take a better curve if sprung into place. The ends for a length of 1 in. or 2 in. may, however, require a little setting over, as the rail may not otherwise take the proper radius at the ends. A bad joint at the rail ends, especially on a curve, may cause frequent derailments. The writer usually adopts a 1½-in. scale rail for a 1-in. scale locomotive, and a 2-in. scale rail for a 1½-in. scale engine, and so forth.

The best possible construction for railways which are laid on the ground is shown in Fig. 732. Longitudinal frames are made up with suitable wood coated with a preservative. These frames are laid on the surface and concreted in to prevent weeds growing through the track. The sleepers are nailed to these battens, and the track ballasted up with spar or granite chips in the usual way, this ballast being, of course, only ornamental. Elevated tracks are usually built up on 2-in. by 1½-in. battens fixed, say, 1 in. to 2 in. apart on edge and bracketed from a fence or else supported on wooden posts, as shown in Fig. 733. The sleepers are then nailed to the battens. Of course, such railways are tracks only, and scenic effects are hardly possible, except perhaps in hilly sites, where the line is on posts at one point and below or on the level of the ground at another.

Fig. 734 shows a method of building a post-supported track, side walls being provided in case of a derailment. The superelevation on a curve is arranged as shown in Fig. 735, a tapering strip giving the required elevation of the outer rail. A method of building an outdoor tunnel with creosoted boards is shown in Fig. 736.

Points may be made on the steel rail almost entirely without solder, the only solder used on those shown in the photograph being at the rod connection to the point "blades" or "switch rails." The drawings for cross-over are applicable

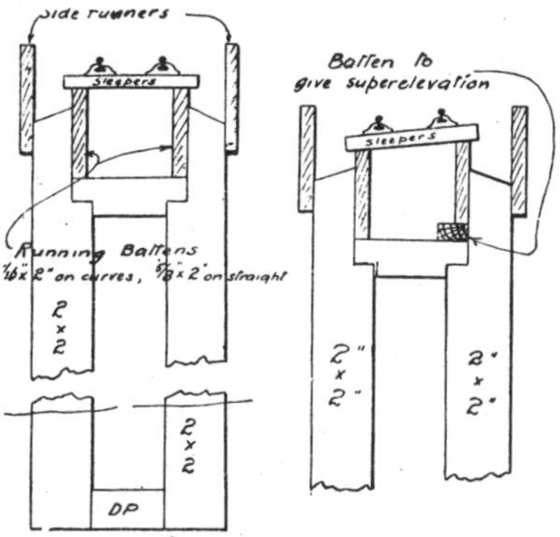

Figs. 734 and 735.—Post-supports for outdoor track

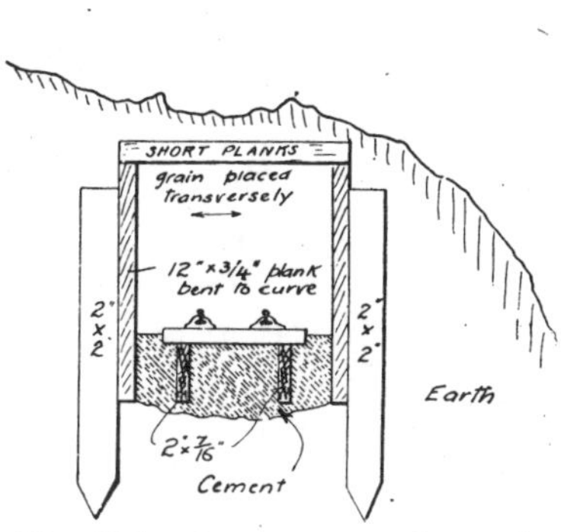

Fig. 736.—Outdoor tunnel, on the cut and cover system

Fig. 738

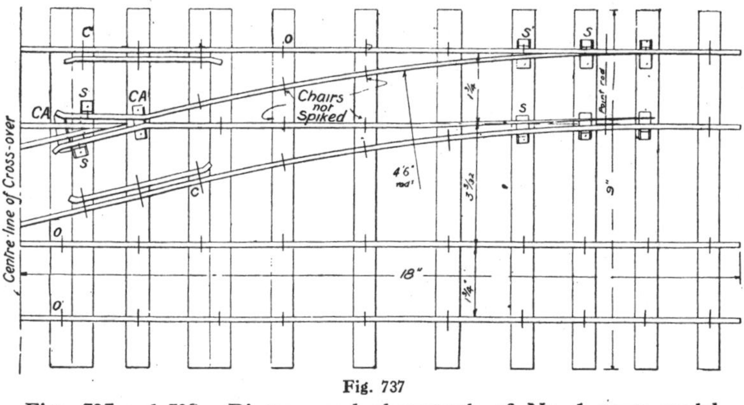

Fig. 737

Figs. 737 and 738.—Diagram and photograph of No. 1 gauge model railway cross-over road laid in "rustless" steel track to points, the work being duplicated in the case of the former.

The total length of a cross-over from point to point depends on the distance between the two sets of rails known in railway parlance as the " six-foot way." These have been fixed for model work as follows :—

Gauge 0 ($1\frac{1}{4}$ in.), six-foot way $2\frac{3}{32}$ in.
Gauge 1 ($1\frac{3}{4}$ in.), six-foot way $3\frac{3}{32}$ in.
Gauge 2 (2 in.), six-foot way $3\frac{1}{4}$ in.
Gauge 3 ($2\frac{1}{2}$ in.), six-foot way $4\frac{1}{8}$ in.

In the drawing (Fig. 737) the ordinary chairs are marked " O," slide chairs " S," and check-rail chairs " C." To hold the frog of the rail " check-rail " or " double " chairs are altered by cutting off one wing. The positions are marked at " C A." The apex of the frog of the rail is formed by filing and butting the rails as indicated in Fig. 739. Slide chairs are used to hold the ends of the wing rails of the frog. The point lever connection may be arranged as shown in Fig. 740, but by using $\frac{3}{32}$ in. wire and thin or lock nuts the scheme shown in Fig. 741 is very good. The forked clip is soldered on to the cross rod, and it is essential to the success of the arrangement that the nuts should fit very tightly on the screwed rod.

Outdoor railways may be cheaply laid with strip iron, Fig. 742 showing various constructions. Rust is the only real drawback, although either of the systems will last a fairly long time. With the square rail the screw-holes impair the surface of the rail. Angle-iron is not at all bad, and is easy to fit up, except perhaps at curves. The use of strip iron (D, Fig. 742) in grooved sleepers is fairly satisfactory where good big sleepers are employed and a fairly deep and heavy rail. Like the bulb-iron system (E, Fig. 742) it is more suitable for a passenger-carrying railway. Fig. 743 shows a chaired and keyed road used in all sizes of model railways. It is perhaps the best, but is the most expensive track.

Fig. 742 shows model railways made up of commercial iron. A, shows square iron drilled and fixed with screws; B, tee-iron fixed with spikes or screws; C, angle-iron drilled and fixed with screws; D, strip iron in slots (with or without wedge); and E, bulb iron with wooden key.

In all outdoor lines the evil effects of the weather must be combated. Therefore, rail, sleepers, and all accessories must be heavier in proportion.

Scenic Effects on Indoor Railways.—Realistic effects in indoor railways can be easily obtained by building up the surface of the "site" or creating depressions which must

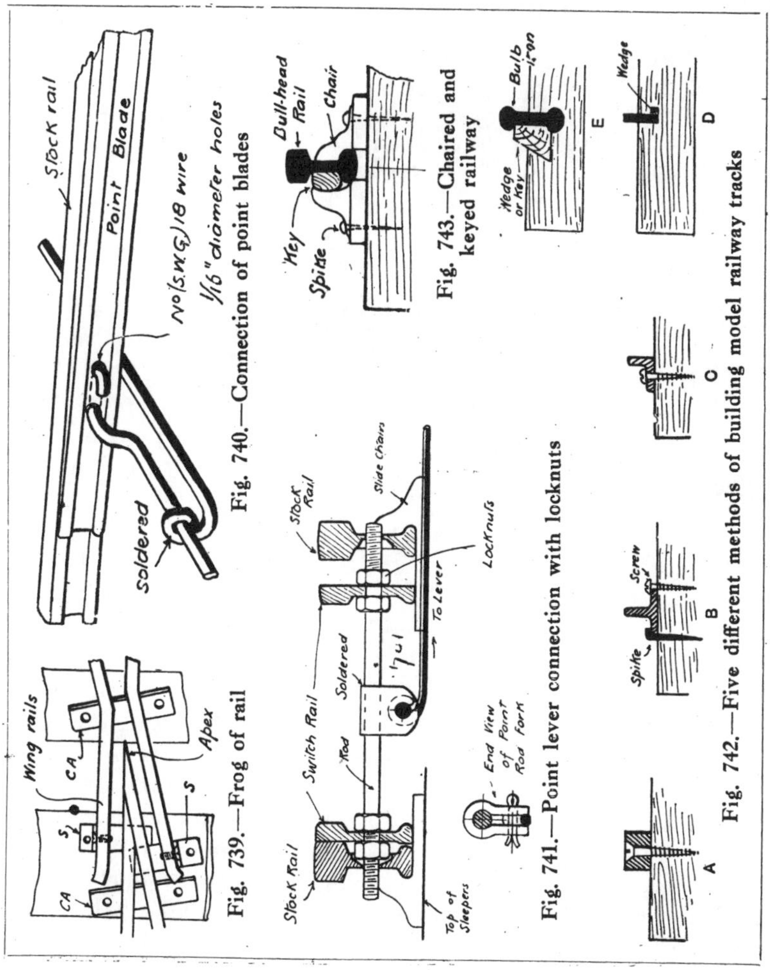

Fig. 739.—Frog of rail

Fig. 740.—Connection of point blades

Fig. 743.—Chaired and keyed railway

Fig. 741.—Point lever connection with locknuts

Fig. 742.—Five different methods of building model railway tracks

be bridged. The accompanying photograph (Fig. 744) shows an entrance to a tunnel, all parts being made in wood, papier-mâché, moss, etc., and painted in natural colours. Distance scenery may be applied to the wall behind the railway, and for those who are not expert with the brush, wall-paper friezes, which are obtainable in 7-in. to 21-in. widths, may be employed. The sketch (Fig. 745) shows the method of building up the cutting leading to the tunnel illustrated in the photograph just referred to. A rough wooden frame is first erected and cardboard nailed to it. Portland cement and sand or other suitable plaster is applied to the cardboard. Station buildings, platforms, signal boxes, may be added to the line according to the spaces available. Fig. 746 shows another view on the same 2-in.-gauge railway, a terminal

Fig. 744.—Scenic effects: a tunnel entrance

station with a bridge, and a wall-paper frieze the background. In Fig. 748 a station of a $1\frac{3}{4}$-in.-gauge line is illustrated in which the background was not at the time of photographing fixed up.

Bridges.—Girder bridges make very realistic models, and in outdoor lines are useful where the line crosses a garden path. Fig. 747 is a photograph of one end of a $1\frac{3}{4}$-in.-gauge

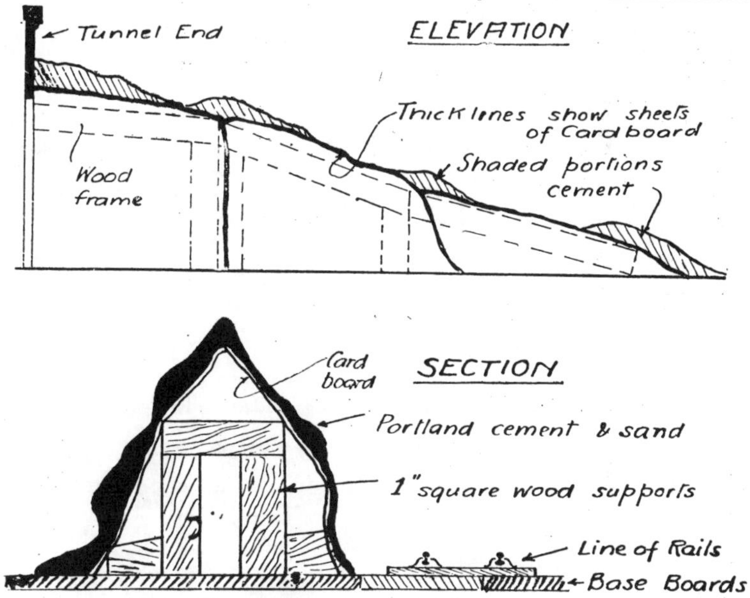

Fig. 745.—Details of model railway "cutting"

bridge made out of T and strip steel. Care must be taken in all such removable bridges to see that the clips or dowels provide for the true alignment of the running rails. Fig. 749 shows how this may be arranged; A is a spring clip (*see also photograph*), and B is fixed to one of the upright supports. In an indoor line the baseboard of the line should be depressed, and a ravine formed which can be bridged, the line of rails remaining quite level. A suitable design for a bridge for a $1\frac{1}{4}$-in.-gauge line is illustrated in Fig. 748A, one or more pairs of trusses cast in brass from a light metal pattern being used. The trusses in this case are for appearance only, a board actually carrying the railway. For larger bridges when used indoors, even in No. 0 gauge, lattice and other girders may be made in wood. If well made without glue, and well painted, wooden lattice girders stand very well out of doors.

Fig. 746.—View on 2-in.-gauge indoor railway

Fig. 747.—Part of 1¾-in.-gauge girder bridge for outdoor railway

Over bridges and tunnels are also much used by model railway engineers. A station with a small road bridge at one end, made by an amateur, is illustrated in Fig. 750.

Model Wagons.—Goods rolling stock is easily built, and where the amateur has a very limited kit of tools he may elect to purchase his locomotives and construct his wagons and carriages. Wheels, axles, bogies, and other turned metal parts are standardised fittings, and are sold by various dealers. The Leeds Model Co., Halton, near Leeds, have an extensive range of No. 0 and No. 1 gauge fittings which

Fig. 748.—Station on a 1¾-in.-gauge railway

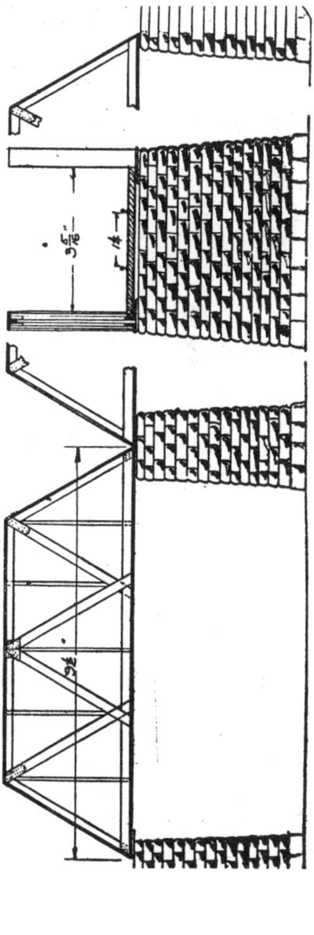

Fig. 748A.—Bridge for 1¼-in.-gauge railway

Fig. 750.—Station and road bridge

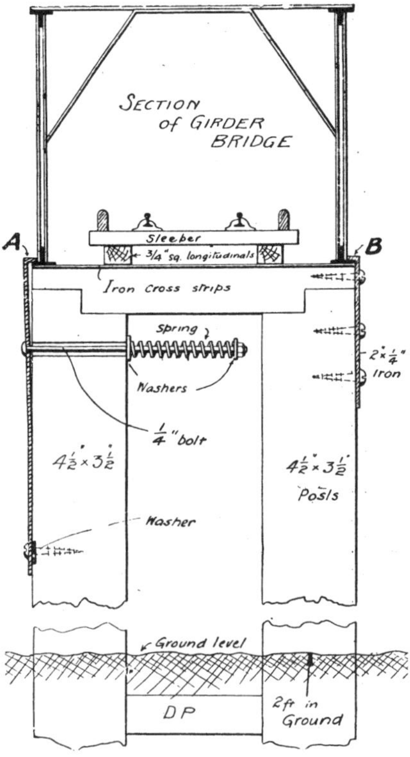

Fig. 749.—Holding removable model girder to permanent part of track

are entirely British made and compete in price with German model fittings of inferior finish.

Fig. 753 shows a model open wagon of simple design. The essential metal fittings are axle guards (that is, the **W** frames attached to the wooden underframes and holding the axle-boxes), wheels and axles, and drawhooks. The drawhooks shown are those supplied by Bond of Euston Road, but the Leeds Model Co.'s fittings may be applied. The latter's drawhooks push into a hole made in the headstock, and are then riveted over at the back.

The wagon illustrated in Fig. 753 is of the "dumb buffered" kind now

Fig. 751.—Model G.N. brake-van

almost obsolete on British railways. Its use in the model is intentional, as on sharp curves models with scale size spring buffers are apt to "buffer lock," whereas with the wide dumb buffers shown in Fig. 753 the vehicles will traverse almost any curve. The detail (Fig. 754) shows models of spring buffers applied. The vehicle with this type of buffer may be made $3\frac{1}{4}$ in. wide instead of $3\frac{3}{8}$ in. To obtain very broad-faced dumb buffers,

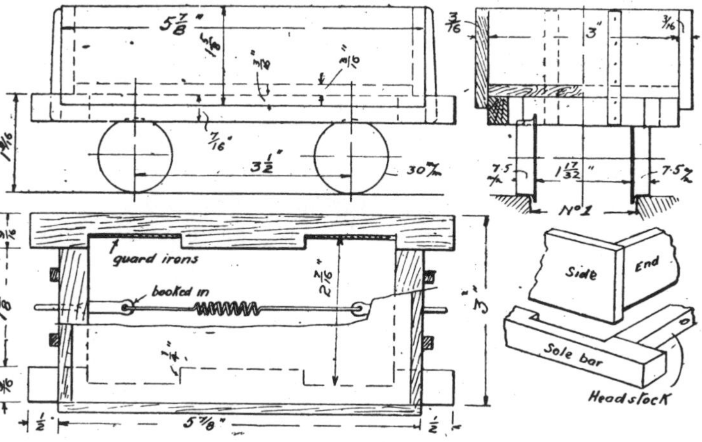

Fig. 753.—Model "dumb-buffered" open wagon

Fig. 752.—Model L. & N.W.R. wagon

the wagon shown in Fig. 753 was made wider than the scale equivalent. In any case, wheels and axle guards should be obtained, as a slight difference in the distance between the notched portions of the solebar may be necessary. In the dumb buffer vehicle the side timber of the underframe (i.e. the solebar) is carried right through. In the spring buffered wagon it stops short at the headstock or buffer plank. The sides of the body overlap the solebars, while the ends are placed on top of and flush with the headstock.

In building, the floor of the wagon is first fixed to the underframe, and then the body, which is nailed together on a square block of wood made to the inside dimensions, is fixed to the underframe, the end battens securing the body in place. The model L. & N.W.R. 10-ton wagon (Fig. 752) is a high-sided wagon intended for coals and general merchandise. Wagons with lower sides are employed for ballast, minerals, &c. Fig. 751 shows a brake-van. Corner plates and strappings in small model wagons may be made of paper. In larger vehicles these parts would be made of thin sheet-metal.

Model Railway Carriages.—The amateur usually attempts to fretwork the sides of a model coach out of a thin piece of suitable wood, and is almost as often disappointed with the results obtained. The most satisfactory method is to build the sides of the body up with properly grooved and tongued pieces. The lathe is fitted up with a saw spindle and table, and sections of wood of suitable thickness and depth, planed up dead to size, are grooved and tenoned with the saw against a fence. These pieces are then built up, pieces of glass fitting in the grooves at the window openings. The results obtained by this method of construction are in every way perfect, as the corners and edges of all openings are quite clean and neat, and, if necessary, sunk panels can be fitted to the upper part of the coach.

The sides, when finished off, are built into the coach, the roof and corridor partitions being arranged as shown in the general drawing opposite. Bogies, wheels and axles, buffers and other metal parts can be purchased from the Leeds Model Co., Ltd., and if the wood parts cannot be made, these can be obtained loose to any size from Messrs. Baldwin and Wills, Watford.

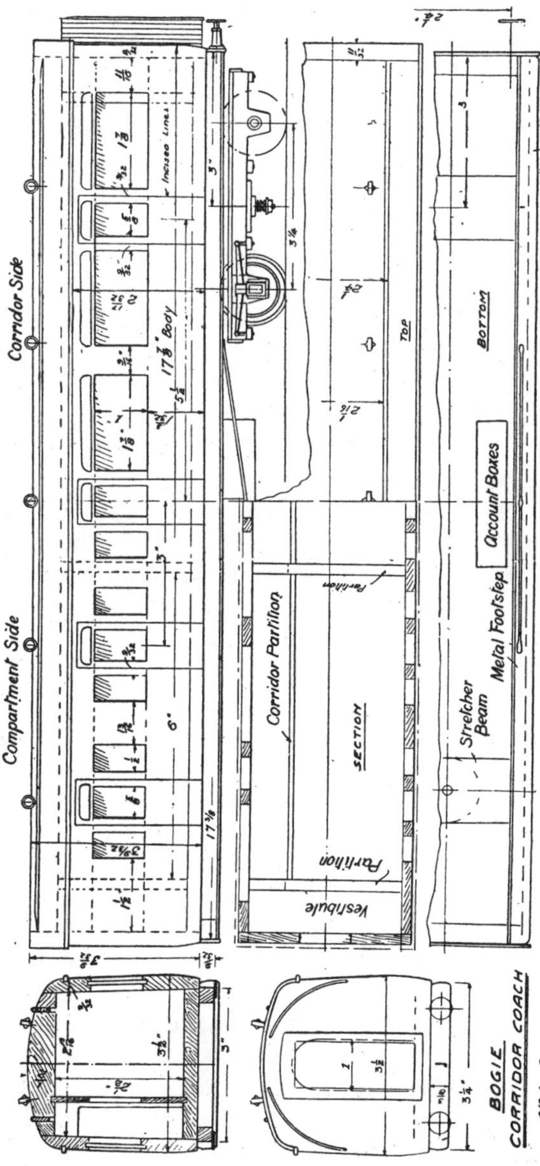

Fig. 754.—Model No. 1 gauge corridor coach

Fig. 754 represents a No. 1 gauge corridor coach measuring $17\frac{7}{8}$ in. over the body and shows the corridor and compartment sides of the coach. Of course, slight differences can be made by cutting down the length of the corridor partitions and reducing the length of the solid "fill-up" panels at the end. The ends of the body are solid, and the top beading is formed by bending strip metal over the top edges of the ends. This is stronger and generally more satisfactory than attempting sharply to bend thin wood, and readers will, in subsequent service, find that the coaches with the metal finish to the top will better withstand any accident due to a derailment or collision. The strips may be bent to shape on a former block. The cant rail strip is, however, made of wood and extends beyond the groove in the side. This is necessary to preserve the continuity. The roof is arranged so that it may be made either removable or may be fixed. The removable roof enables all upholstering, the fitting of electric light, and fixing up of partitions to be done after the body has been built up. Where the removable roof is desired, the rain strip can be fixed to the loose portion of the roof, and its projection will mask the joint. The only drawback to the scheme is that the roof strip is straight instead of curved in plan, but this is a minor objection, as if the strip is rounded off to nothing at each end it looks very well.

The sides of the coach are best built up on the bench, and in fixing the parts together glue should be sparingly used, so that the glass is kept as clean as possible. The most convenient method of clamping is to use what the woodworker terms "folding wedges." These give a parallel pressure, the wedges being of identical inclination, as indicated in Fig. 756 herewith. The glue used should be thin; the work is best done in a warm atmosphere, otherwise the glue congeals before the pieces are firmly fixed together. The end "make-up" panels or the end central panels should be cut out a little longer than the finished size, to allow of an end wedge being used. A hot domestic flat iron is useful in keeping the glue from setting before the rather fiddling work of fitting up the pieces is finished. This operation of ironing the work is practised by joiners in laying veneers.

The bottoms of the coaches may be sawn, with a groove for the corridor partitions. When the sides are finished the solebars and headstocks of the underframes are then fitted on to the underside of the floor, the maximum width of the underframes being 3 in., and the length for the normal coach $17\frac{5}{8}$ in., or $\frac{1}{4}$ in. less than the length of the body. The body, therefore, overhangs on every side, the floor and underframes forming a rebate into which the ends and the sides are fixed. The transom or bogie stretcher beam also serves to stiffen the floor.

The ends are next erected, being glued and pinned to the floor; the specially fine panel pins having no heads are

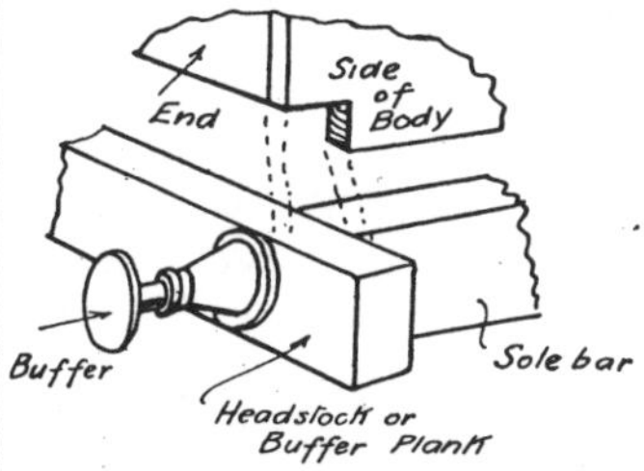

Fig. 755.—Frame and body construction for spring buffers

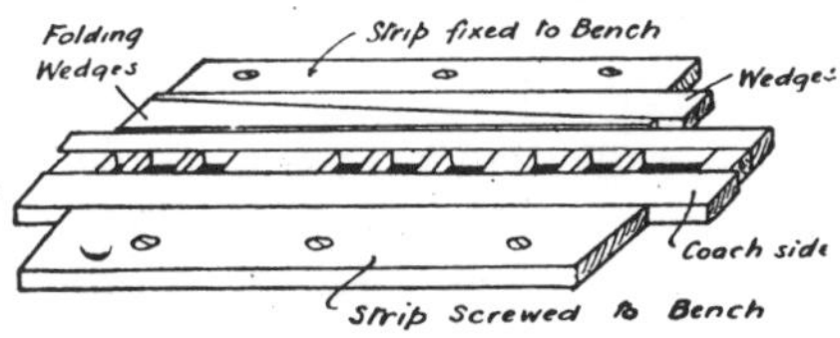

Fig. 756.—The "folding wedge" system of clamping

Fig. 757.—Model L. & N.W.R. corridor coach, built by Mr. H. Jervis

recommended. They do not disfigure the wood, which is a point to remember where the coaches are not painted, but polished or varnished only.

The sides should then be "shot" quite square, and should be fitted with the proper inclinations or "tumble home" between the ends, the $\frac{9}{32}$ in. square strip having been first planted on (glued only) to the top edge, the roof piece, with a rain strip temporarily tacked on, being fitted in place to hold the sides solid and square. With the roof temporarily tacked through the ends, the two cross partitions also being placed inside the coach to keep it firm and at its proper level, the roof and top edge of the sides may then be planed to the correct moulded section—that is, the thickness of the end metal strip higher than the ends, but to the same profile. During this time the rain strip should be placed lower than it will be permanently fixed, and, if necessary, a piece of wood should be placed inside the coach so that the sides will resist the strain of clamping the coach body in the bench vice. The metal edging of the ends may then be applied and the whole roof sandpapered off. Afterwards the rain strip may be lifted up $\frac{1}{8}$ in. above the roof and have its top edge rounded.

The removable roof may then be taken off and the internal partitions fixed. These should be made in a very nicely planed and polished piece of sycamore or satin walnut. The window openings in the partitions must be carefully pierced with a sharp chisel. The finished coaches may be varnished, polished, or painted, according to the colouring scheme of the particular railway company whose coaches are being modelled.

Fig. 757 shows a model L. & N.W.R. latest type corridor coach built by H. Jervis; its remarkable fidelity to the prototype will be noted.

The buffer planks are of $\frac{3}{8}$-in. and $\frac{1}{16}$-in. strip brass. This material is much to be preferred for fixing on metal buffers, the result being in every way most satisfactory in service. The plank may be drilled and then pinned to the headstock. The coupling hooks may be soldered to the plank and further secured to the bottom of the coach. This will relieve the buffer plank of all tractive efforts. Of course, the amateur may add refinements in the way of swivelling coupling hooks with the shanks fitted with springs. Combined laminated and buffing springs may be used in place of the self-contained spring buffers; however, the latter are the cheapest to buy and the simplest to fit.

CHAPTER XX

Miscellaneous Working Models

Model Muzzle-loading Cannon.—The old-fashioned muzzle-loading cannon, with which most readers are familiar, is the simplest working-model gun to make, and can be cast in gunmetal from a wooden pattern. The gun should be short for the bore and outside diameter, the dimensions on Fig. 758 giving the approximate proportions. The gun should be cast solid, as there is danger, if cored, of the core shifting.

A small gun of, say, $\frac{1}{4}$-in. bore may be drilled in the lathe, a straight-fluted drill being used in preference to a twist drill. For drilling, the gun may be held at the back end in the chuck, and then truly centred. The drill may be placed in a chuck in the tailstock or held by a carrier against a hollow centre, and fed up slowly. The drill should be frequently withdrawn to clear the bore of chips and to prevent the drill binding. If the commercially-made drill of the necessary length is not available then a D-bit (Fig. 759) should be made. This type of drill may be made out of a length of silver steel, the shank being turned down and the working end shaped as shown ; it should be hardened to a degree consistent with the material to be bored. In using the drill, it should be frequently withdrawn for clearing purposes.

The trunnions (Fig. 760) are cast on the gun in such a position that the rear end of the gun (the " breech " end) is heavier than the fore part, and in fitting it to the primitive type of carriage shown in Fig. 758, the gun may then be elevated with wedges, or by a simple lifting screw. The trunnions should, if possible, be turned up, one spigot being held in the chuck while the other is being operated on. The size of the lathe is the limiting factor of this job. The gun itself may be turned all over on the outside, except at the trunnions, where the casting must be finished with a file. The gun is fired by a touch hole, a red-hot iron, or a taper igniting the priming powder at this part.

The carriage may be made of wood, and brass bearing plates attached as shown to fit the trunnions. These plates may be made of castings, or they may be hammered out of the sheet, the rounded portions being formed on a piece of steel rod of the right size held in the vice. The wooden wedges, similar to those used in early pieces under the breech end of the gun, are shown in Fig. 758.

Breech-loading Cannon.—While a breech-loading gun will enable the bore to be cored out in the casting, unless cartridges are used there is no great advantage except that the gun can be more effectively cleaned, and also will be more modern in appearance. Fig. 761 shows the end of a brass cannon fitted with a screwed-in breech block, and also screwed with elevating gear. The breech should be a gas or pipe thread, the length of the screwed portion of the breech being equal to the diameter. The breech block is screwed in with two handles, and should meet a gas-tight face at the end of the bore as shown. Fig. 761 shows also a firing device.

The gun is drilled for a little steel hammer and anvil.

The hammer may be removed for cleaning by unscrewing the small gland. After loading and ramming, the breech block may be removed, and an "amorce" cap with the superfluous paper cut off placed between the hammer and the anvil. After fixing the breech a sharp tap on the outer-end hammer will fire the "amorce" cap and ignite the charge. The loading and ramming before inserting the cap is recommended so as to eliminate any ignition of the charge whilst ramming in the powder and wads.

Such guns are, of course, rather dangerous toys, and should be used only when adults are "in command," and even then with due care. Smaller guns, suitable for indoor use and to be handled by juniors, can be made to fire only ordinary "amorce" caps. Such guns may have field carriages or naval mountings as desired.

Model 4·7-in. Gun.—Fig. 762 shows a model of a 4·7-in. naval gun as mounted on a land carriage. The external details of this gun reasonably represent the original, if enamelled in a lead colour. The only casting required is that of the breech end of the gun. The front portion may be made from thick brass tube, and let into the casting. Pad pieces should be cast on the breech end for the trunnion

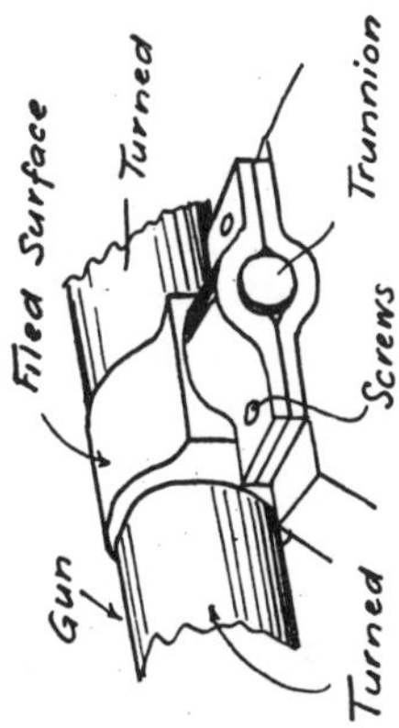

Fig. 760.—Trunnions for model cannon

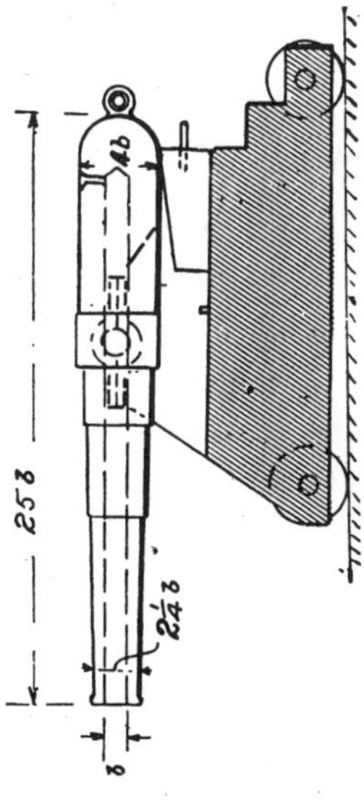

Fig. 758.—Simple model muzzle-loading brass cannon

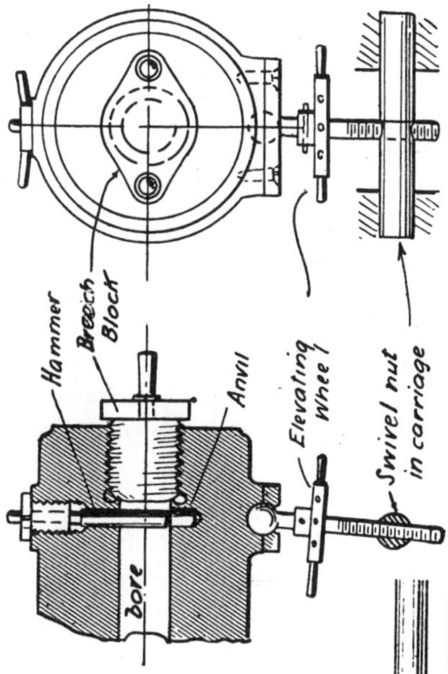

Fig. 761

Fig. 761.—Details of cannon with removable breech

Fig. 759.—Bit for boring model cannon

screws for model telescopic sight, and lugs for the recoil cylinder underneath the gun. This cylinder contains the spiral spring actuating the hammer, and is a piece of thin brass tube blocked up at the breech end. The spindle holding the hammer is fitted into a plug (Fig. 763) made of bright steel rod, and to prevent the spindle revolving this plug is shaped as shown in Fig. 764. The plug, it will be noticed, is also notched to engage the hook end of the trigger. To restrain the plug from turning, a pin or a screw is fitted through the lug and the recoil cylinder as shown in the end view (Fig. 763).

The breech block (Fig. 765) is a screwed cap containing the steel firing pin, and as an anvil for the spring, a steel washer with a conical hole is fitted tightly in the breech end of the bore. To charge the gun, the waste material of the previous " shot " must be removed from the explosion chamber, and one or two fresh " amorce " caps inserted. To keep the chamber cleaner, it is best to remove the superfluous paper round the explosive point of the " amorce " cap. The breech may then be screwed on, and to do this conveniently the hammer should be placed in the " set-to-fire " position. If a projectile is desired, a pea or plug of round wood may be dropped into the muzzle of the gun. To train the gun, the sight tube should be set by the scale (Fig. 766) to the distance of the object, and looking through the tube the gun should be " laid on " the mark, elevating it to the degree required by the scale. The trigger may then be operated. Fig. 767 shows the wheels, and the elevating lock is detailed in Figs. 768 and 769.

Howitzer and Shells.—Very effective but harmless model howitzers may be made to throw model explosive shells. The needful ammunition must, however, be found before the gun is designed. The shell is a kind of squib, which has only a " short life " and explodes well at the end. The gun barrel is very simply made from stout brass tube, and may also be arranged for breech-loading. A section of the gun and shell is given in Fig. 770. The fuse projects through a small hole in the breech of the gun, and is ignited by a red-hot wire, taper, or match. The reaction of the first part

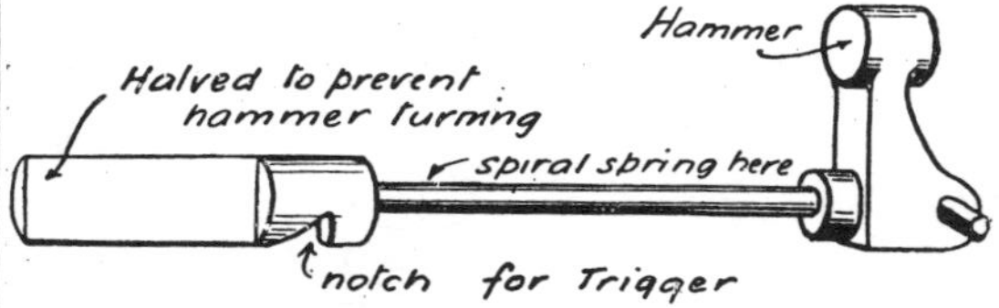

Fig. 764.—Firing hammer

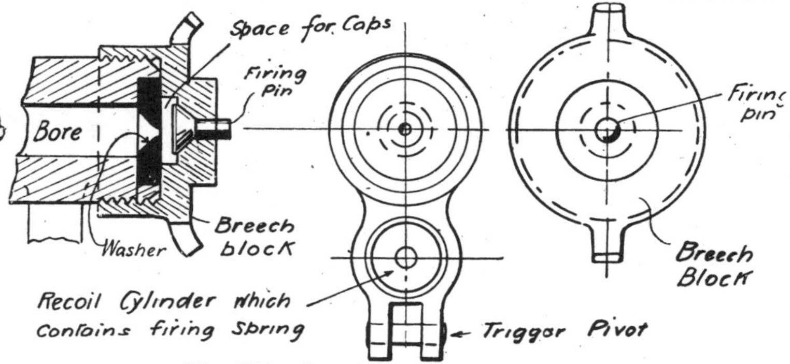

Fig. 765.—Breech end of model 4·7 gun

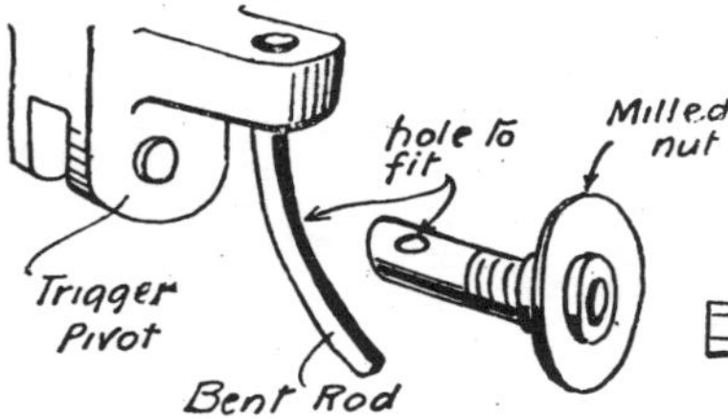

Fig. 766

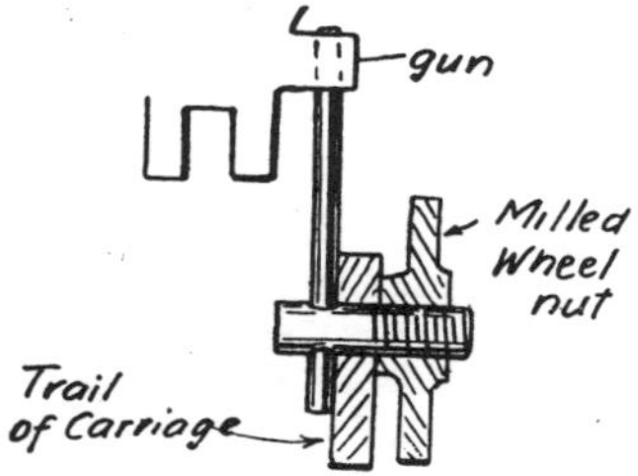

Fig. 767

Figs. 766 and 767.—Elevating lock

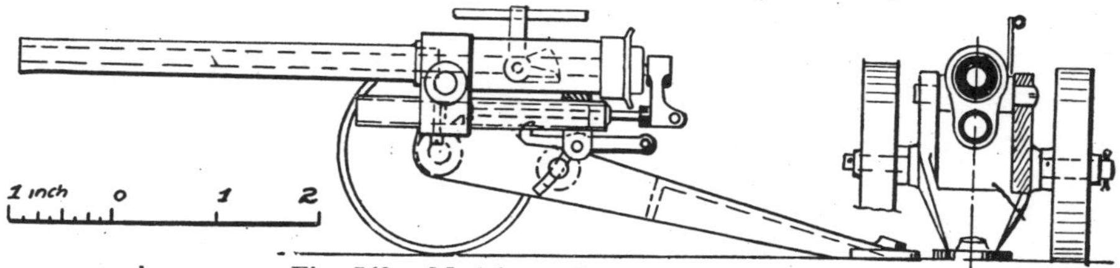

Fig. 762.—Model naval gun on land carriage

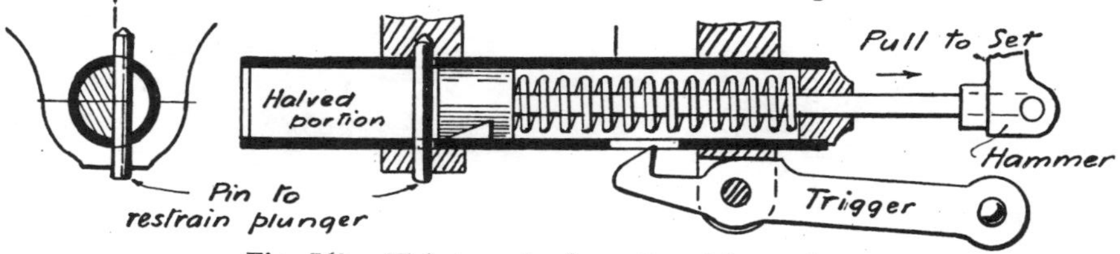

Fig. 763.—Firing mechanism of model naval gun

of the issuing charge, as in a rocket, throws the squib or "shell" out of the gun, and on reaching its objective it should burst. The shell may be made heavier at the nose to give greater accuracy of fire, and it may be fired at masses of wooden ninepins or soldiers. "Shelling the enemy" should prove an exciting amusement.

Scale Model Breech-loading Gun.—Scale model guns may be made to fire standard pin-fire and also rim-fire

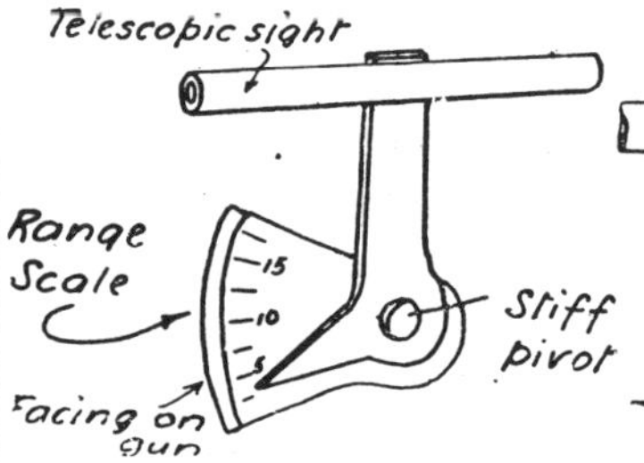

Fig. 768.—Model telescopic sight and range scale

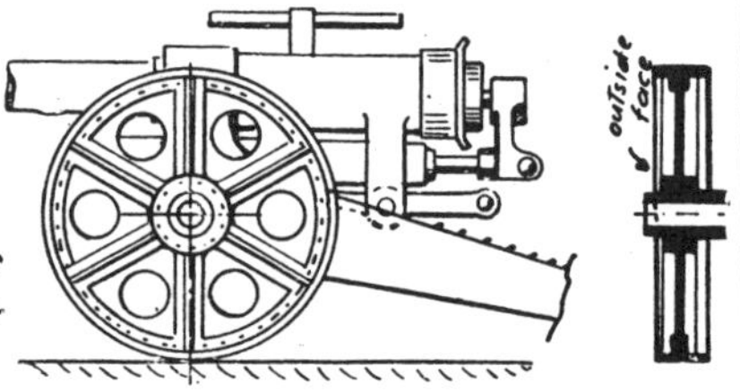

Fig. 769.—Wheel for model 4·7 gun

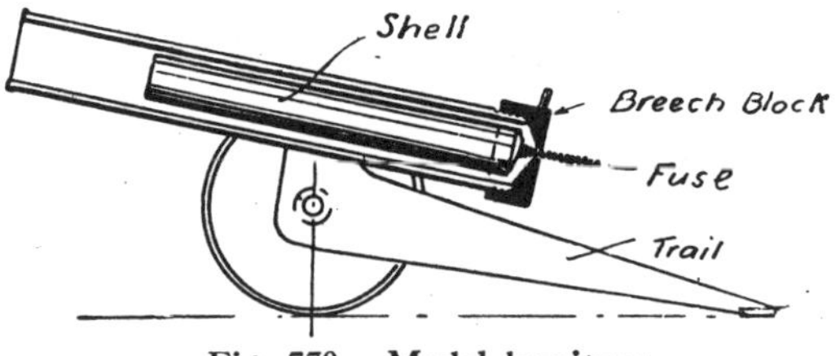

Fig. 770.—Model howitzer

cartridges used in saloon rifles and pistols, and they should have steel barrels and screw-breeches. The firing mechanism is the only difficulty, and the gun must therefore be sufficiently large and long in the breech to contain a spring-loaded firing pin. As rifling is also a difficult process, it is suggested that inner barrels may be made from an old pistol or rifle barrel, if one can be obtained. Figs. 771 to 774 show a model 6-in. naval quickfiring gun made by Mr. J. J. Pike, a London postal official. It has a smooth bore to fit a ·22

Fig. 771.—Photograph of scale model of breech-loading naval quick-firing gun

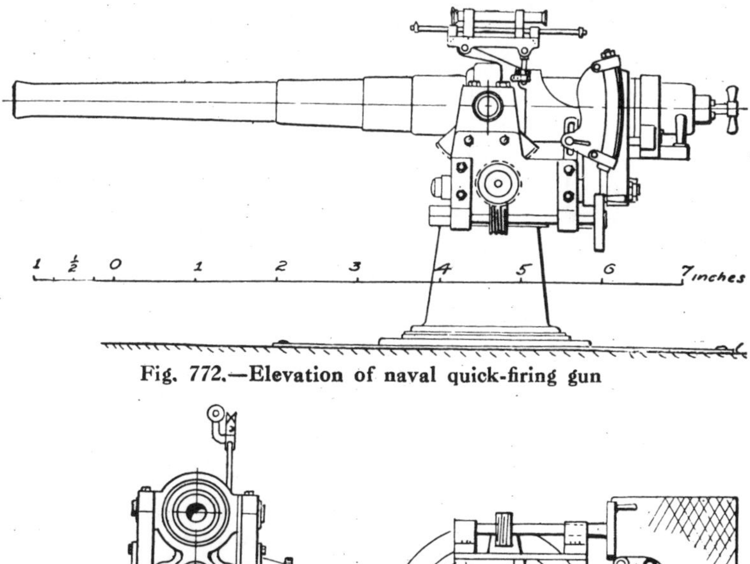

Fig. 772.—Elevation of naval quick-firing gun

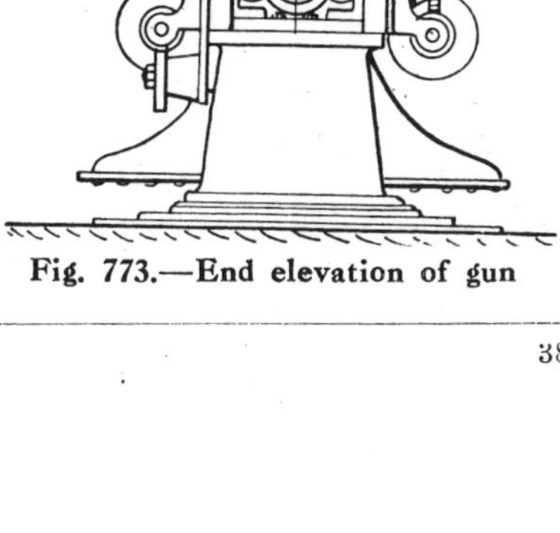

Fig. 773.—End elevation of gun

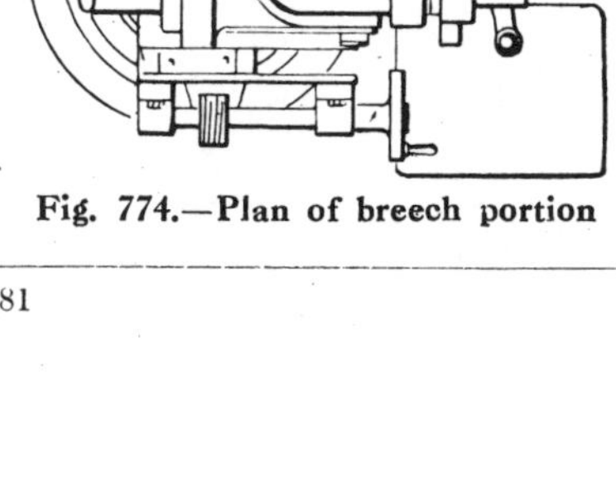

Fig. 774.—Plan of breech portion

cartridge. The breech block is screw $\frac{7}{16}$-in. Whitworth thread, the length of the screw being $\frac{3}{8}$ in. It is divided into six parts, three parts of which are cut away and a corresponding steel bush is fitted to the gun, so that by a single movement of lever and connection rod the breech is closed and turned in a sixth of a revolution. This action locks it securely. This revolving block is bored for spring and firing pin; this pin is $\frac{1}{8}$ in. diameter, and has two flats made with a warding file. A forked-shaped trigger is fitted to engage these two flats; this trigger, on being withdrawn while the spring is compressed, releases the firing pin and explodes the cartridge. The whole breech block turns in a carrier which is hinged to the right-hand side of the gun by means of a brass plate forced up to a shoulder turned on the back of the gun barrel. This plate has three lugs underneath which are drilled for rods carrying pistons and springs in recoil cylinders. On recoiling, the barrel slides in a jacket which is fitted with trunnion ring and plate. Three lugs, in correct alignment with the plate on back of gun, keep the whole from twisting. This jacket also carries the toothed segment on the left which engages with pinion and worm gear, shown in Fig. 771, for raising or lowering the gun by means of the handwheel. The only other fittings this jacket carries are the sights and telescope, which need no further explanation. The other handwheel on the right-hand side is made with worm gear, and by means of mitre gears the gun can be turned through a complete semicircle. This gearing is enclosed in the hollow steel conical mounting which runs in the flanged ring bolted to the steel plate on base. Ball bearings are fitted to make it run quite freely. The two footplates are $\frac{1}{16}$-in. steel plate flanged and bolted to the top of the mounting, which has two lugs fitted for the purpose. The two side plates are split to allow the brass trunnion to swing, and are made from $\frac{3}{16}$-in. steel plate. The two brackets carrying the worm gear are bolted on quite close and firm by means of counterbored screws.

Model Yard Crane.—The design (Fig. 775) may be recommended to those who wish to make a model hand-

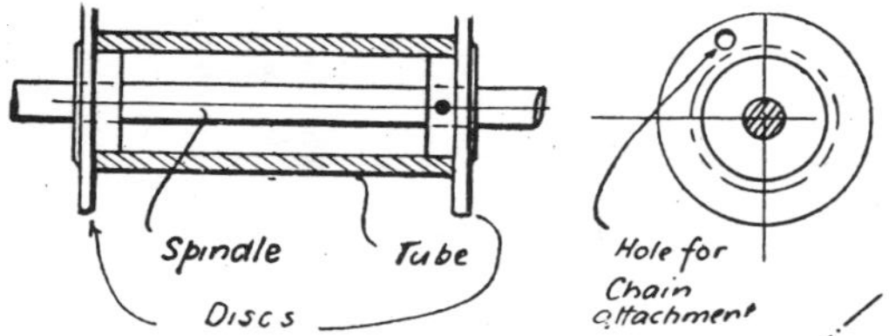

Fig. 779.—Winding drum

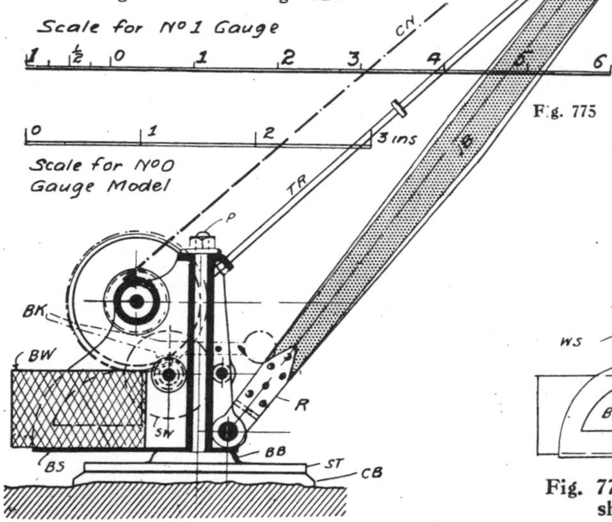

Fig. 775

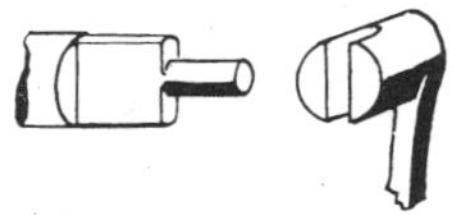

Fig. 778.—Details of loose handle

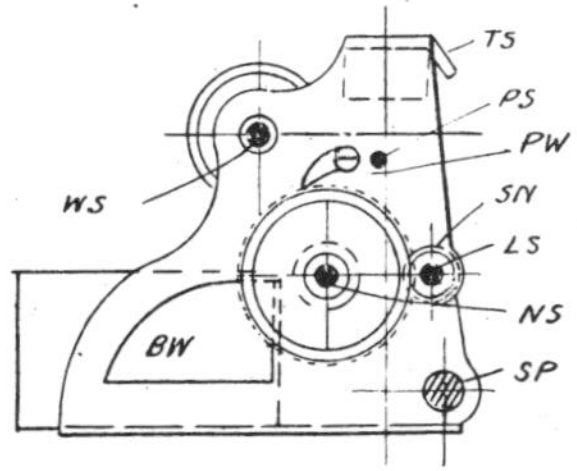

Fig. 777.—Part elevation showing gearing

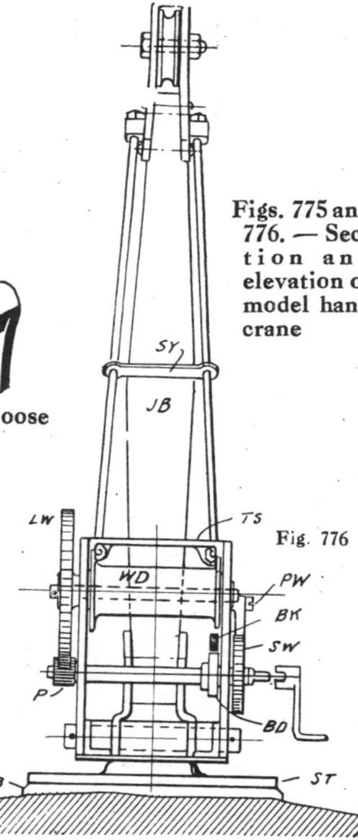

Fig. 776

Figs. 775 and 776. — Section and elevation of model hand crane

crane such as those used in railway goods yards, and scales of inches are included for two sizes of models. As in all model cranes, the initial consideration is the gears. In the illustration there is a large wheel L W for the first speed, gearing into a twelve- or fourteen-tooth pinion, $1\frac{3}{4}$ in. diameter, and a smaller one S W, 1 in. diameter, on the first driving shaft N S, gearing into a similar pinion on the low-speed shaft L S. If wheels of these dimensions cannot be obtained, then the design must be altered to suit wheels of similar character, but slightly larger or smaller, as the case may be. Larger wheels are to be preferred to obtain the required clearances. The crane is double-geared, and the change is effected by simply removing the handle from the normal speed shaft N S to the lower speed shaft L S. The design for the loose handle is shown in the sketch (Fig. 778). In place of the ordinary handle, which fits on a square-ended shaft, an alternative may be adopted by turning down only a part of the spindle end. The other portion is filed flat until its thickness is the same as the smaller diameter of the spindle. A hole is first drilled in the handle, and then it is slotted with a small warding file to fit the flattened portion of the spindle.

The crane has no mechanism for the slewing. It is fitted on a post P of $\frac{3}{16}$-in. diameter steel rod fixed into a boss B B on the square base plate S T. The side frames F are two $\frac{1}{16}$-in. brass plates suitably shaped and fixed by short pieces of angle brass, and soldered to the bottom stretcher plate B S. The leaden balance weight, which is used to counteract the weight of the jib and the load being lifted, may also be used to stiffen up the bottom of the frame by being screwed to the side frames and to the bottom plate B S. The tops of the frames are tied together by means of a strip T S flanged down at the ends and screwed and soldered to the side frames. Both these cross plates may be strengthened by a piece of tube being soldered into a hole drilled beforehand, which tube fits over the main spindle P. The top strip should also provide two small projecting lugs at the extreme ends, which are bent down at an angle to take the lower end of the tie rods.

This completes the main frames of the crane, but before they are fitted together the winding drum should be made. This is built up of a piece of tube of any size under, say, $\frac{1}{2}$ in., fitted to two ends of brass, as shown in the detail Fig. 779. The whole may be pinned and soldered to the winding spindle, and a small hole drilled in the larger flange to provide an attachment for the chain or cord. When completed it may be placed in the main frames, and the latter finally fitted together.

The second- or slow-speed gear is on the right-hand side, and the large gear wheel and its pinion on the left-hand side (*see* Fig. 776). In both cases they are outside. Inside the frames on the spindle N S is pinned and soldered a small disc of metal B D to act as a brake drum. A brake lever B K, which is balanced so that when it is not deliberately pressed down it does not bear on the brake drum, is fitted over this disc. The jib is of square section wood with the edges chamfered. The top and bottom ends are strapped with $\frac{1}{16}$-in. brass plates, those at the bottom being cranked to give as wide a bearing as possible on the swivel pin S P. The plates should be screwed together with long small-diameter screws, say $\frac{1}{16}$ in. or $\frac{3}{32}$ in., the wood being squeezed up between the plates. The top plate is in one piece, bent to form a retainer for the chain, and provided with holes for the pulley pivot bolt. To keep in position, tubular distance pieces will be required on the bottom pin S P outside and between the strap plates. The pulley may be of brass turned with a half-round groove. The weight W, which is used to keep the chain taut, may be of lead, and the hook filed up out of sheet metal pushed through a hole in the weight. To retain the weight on the hook, and also to provide a connection for the chain, the top end may be hammered flat, as shown.

The "chain" may be a suitable cord (fishing line), or, if it can be readily obtained, actual chain may be used. The tie rods for the jib are fixed to the top plate as shown, or in any other convenient manner. The small lugs may be soldered on, or, if desired, can be bent up out of the strap plate. They are fitted with a cross stay S Y near

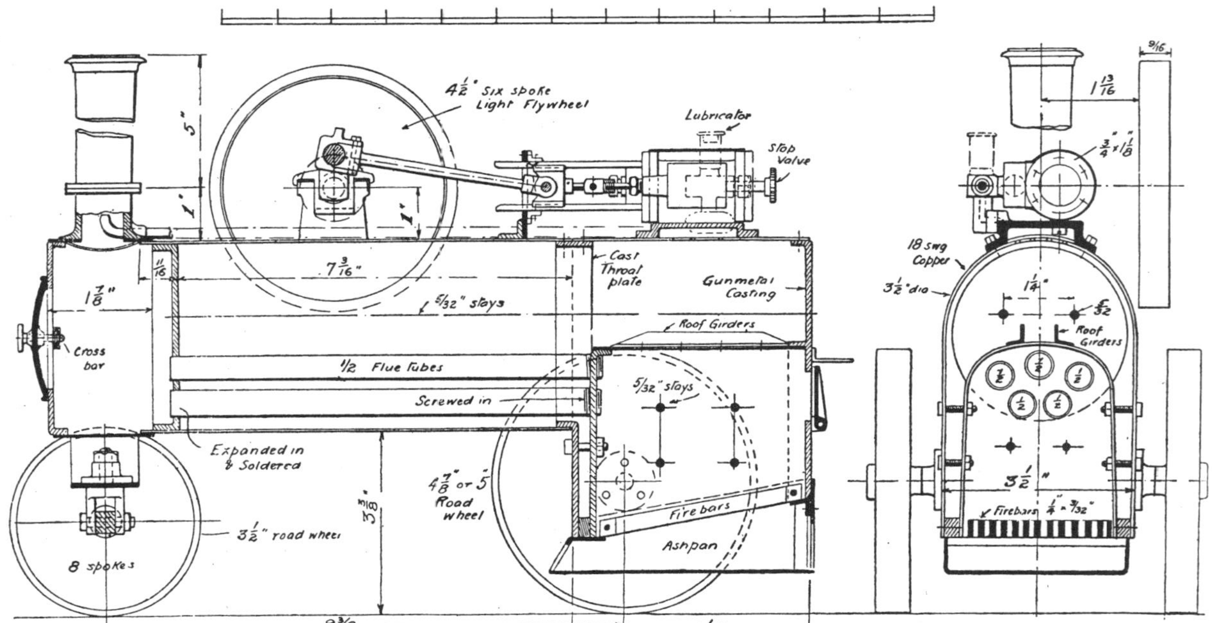

Fig. 780.—Two sectional elevations of model portable engine

the centre. This stay acts as a support for the sagging chain. A pawl is required to prevent the load running back. This is shown in Figs. 776 and 777 at P W, and

Fig. 782.—Plan of machinery of model portable engine

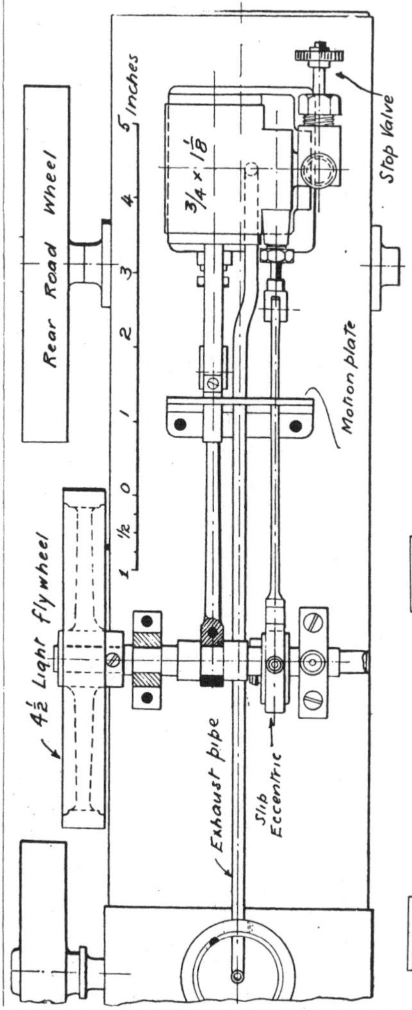

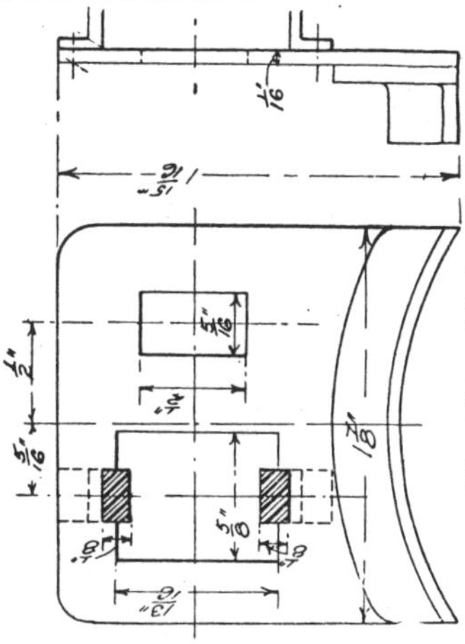

Fig. 783.—Motion plate

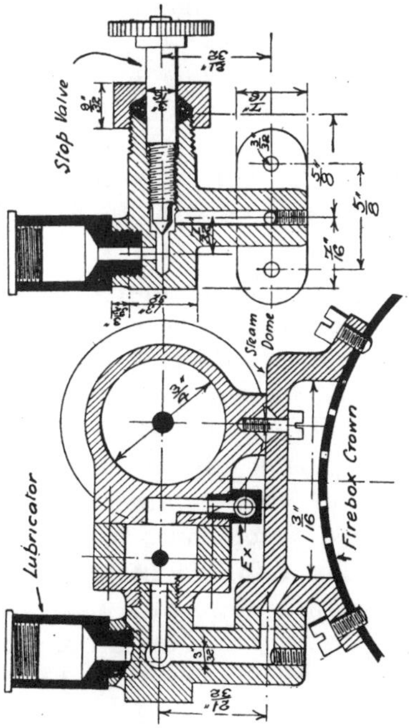

Fig. 781.—Cylinder for model portable engine

when thrown back and out of use will require a stop pin to support it, as at P S.

In Fig. 775, the letter references not yet mentioned are as follow: J B—jib; P L—pulley; H K—hook; R—jib straps; B W—balance weight; C B—concrete base; W D—winding drum; S N—slow speed pinion; W S—winding spindle.

Model Portable Engine.—Both the traction and portable engines are popular prototypes for working models. An example of the former is illustrated in Fig. 780. As in the original, a solid-fuel boiler is fitted to the model, and the cylinder is mounted over the firebox. The boiler barrel is built up of $3\frac{1}{2}$-in. copper tube with a cast tube plate and throatplate, the wrapper being made of No. 18 S.W.G. copper plate. The back-plate is cast, and has no water-space, the construction being similar to that illustrated in the boiler for the model M.R. locomotive described in an earlier chapter. The firebox, however, has straight sides, and also has a flange bracket to support the axle of the rear wheels.

The interesting feature of the design is the attachment of the cylinder (*see* Fig. 781), which may, by the way, be of the ordinary pattern, obtainable finished and ready for steam. A flat "steam dome" casting is screwed to the firebox top, small holes being arranged in the latter to allow the steam to enter. To this is previously screwed the cylinder. A combined stop valve, lubricator, and steam connection conducts the steam from the "dome" to the steam chest, all the passages being formed by drilling. The exhaust is led out, underneath or on top, according to just how the cylinder is made, through an elbow attached to a pipe leading to the chimney base (*see* Figs. 781 and 782). If the cylinder has a longer stroke than $1\frac{1}{8}$ in. a thicker piston must be fitted to reduce it. The connecting rod has a forked little end, and is attached to a two-bar crosshead. The slide bars are supported by a motion plate (Fig. 783) built up of sheet and angle stuff. The road wheels may be built up, the tyre being a cutting off a piece of tube or else a strip of $\frac{5}{8}$-in. by $\frac{5}{64}$-in. stuff bent up, jointed,

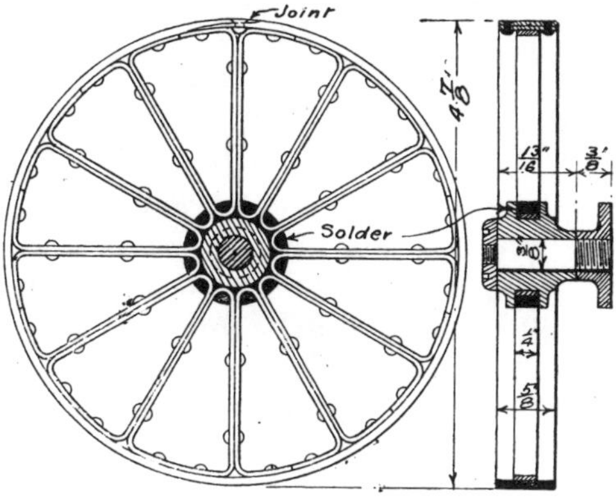

Fig. 784.—Road wheel

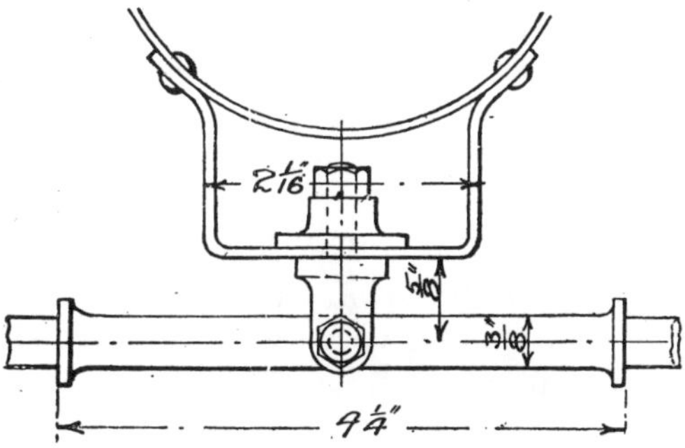
Fig. 785

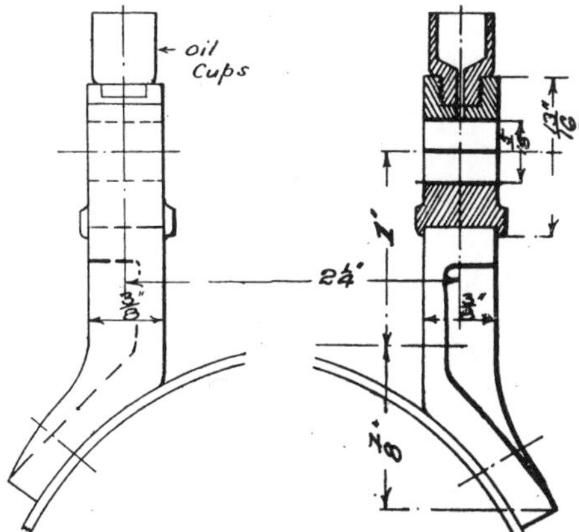

Fig. 788.—Main bearings of crank shaft

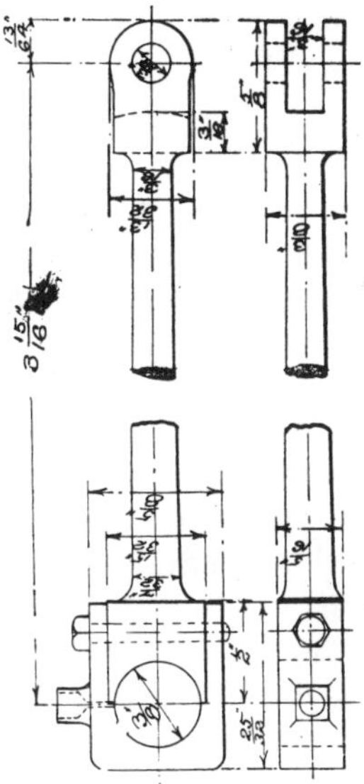
Fig. 787.—Connecting rod of model portable engine

Fig. 785.—Bottom of smokebox, etc.

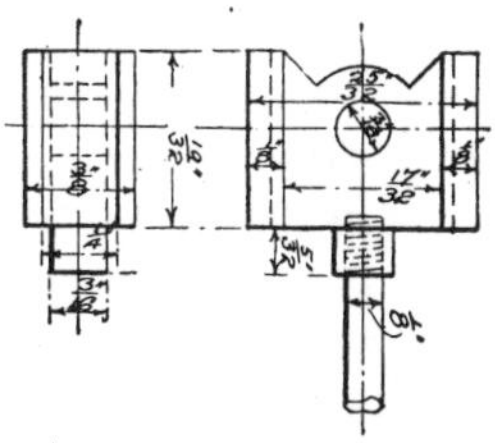
Fig. 786.—Crosshead

and riveted as in Fig. 784. The small wheels are supported on a forked swivelling and pivoted bracket attached by a U plate fixed on the bottom of the smokebox (Fig. 785). The engine, if well made, should work for twenty-five to thirty minutes on one charge of water, and, if desired, the boiler may be supplied with water from a separate tank by means of a hand pump. Figs. 786 to 788 are engine details.

Model Steam Hammers.—While a model steam hammer made on a small scale would hardly be satisfactory as a working model, the amateur may require to build one on exactly the same lines as adopted in real practice. In the earlier steam hammers the steam was used only to lift the piston, the latter falling by gravity for the working stroke. In modern hammers the steam is also arranged to press on the top of the piston, helping its descent and very greatly increasing the force of the blow. For hand working, a hand lever is used at the side of the frame. This lever is attached to a piston valve, working over the usual three-ported valve face. In Fig. 789 opposite a piston valve with internal admission is shown. A lever-operated stop valve S V (Fig. 789) is fitted between the steam supply and valve chest, to enable the hammer-man to vary readily the steam-chest pressure by a lever S L. This is especially necessary in the casc of automatic working. The automatic gear is usually attached to the same valve V as that operated by the handle lever H L, and is controlled by the position of the tup T. A roller R is fixed on the tup, which engages a bell crank lever B L fixed to a convenient part of the frame. This opens the valve V, and alternately admits steam to the upper and lower sides of the piston. In some cases an adjustable gear is also provided in the automatic arrangement, so that the operator can vary the length of the stroke while the hammer is striking. This lever is shown at A L in Fig. 789. In all cases the inertia of the tup, etc., must be considered in designing automatic valve gear. For a model hammer, Fig. 790 provides a design for one which will work by hand or automatically in a less complex manner, the valve being a plain slide valve. The standard is of cast-iron complete with valve chest. The cylinder is bolted on to this standard. The hand gear is directly connected to the valve spindle. The valve is a plain three-ported slide valve. The piston has no packing except two or three

Fig. 789.—Valve gear of steam hammer

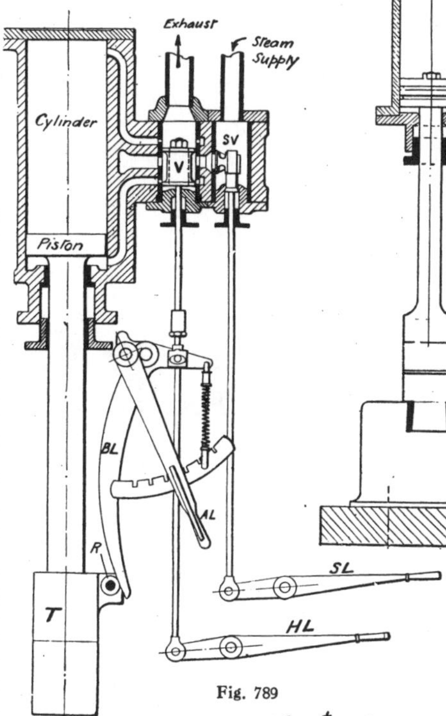

Fig. 789

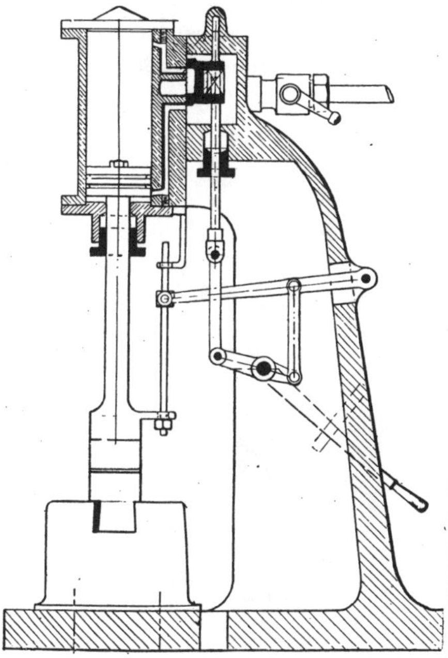

Fig. 790

Fig. 790.—Section through working model steam hammer

1 ½ 0 1 2 3 4 5 inches

grooves. The ports enter the cylinder at an appreciable distance from the cylinder covers. This is to provide for cushioning the piston at each end of the stroke. The automatic valve gear consists of a series of levers connected to a tappet rod. The tappets are actuated by projection on the tup or end of the piston rod. The anvil is separate, to facilitate the casting of the standard without cores or core-boxes. A slide valve with ordinary outside admission is used instead of a piston valve, which would hardly be satisfactory in a working model.

Model Boats.—Model power boats are built by amateurs from two widely differing points of view. On the one hand, the model-maker desires to build a replica of some vessel or type of vessel he favours, and, except for such alterations

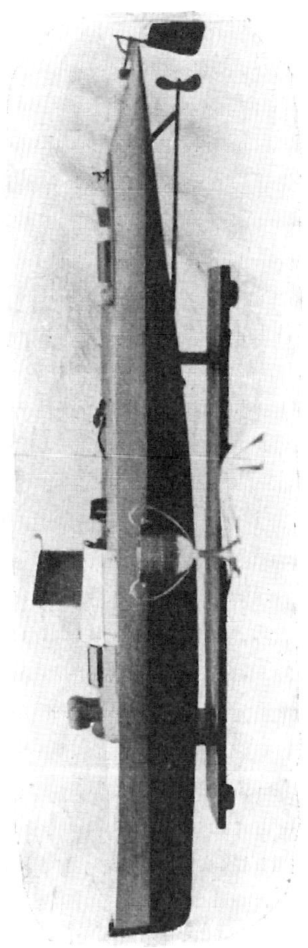

Fig. 791.—Lt.-Col. J. R. Harvey's 6 ft. 6 in. model steam boat "Lalage"

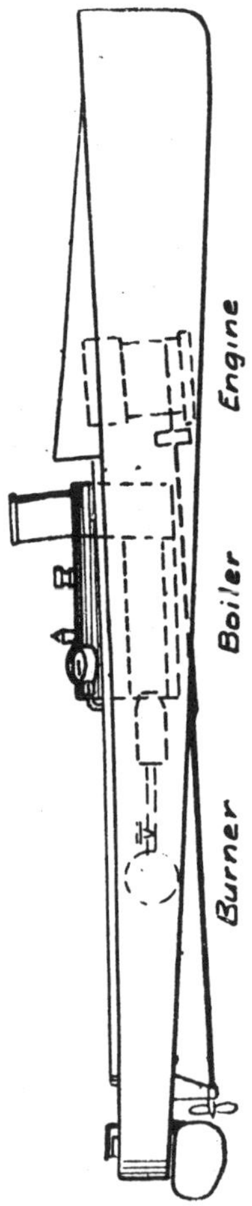

Fig. 792.—Disposition of machinery in model racing boat

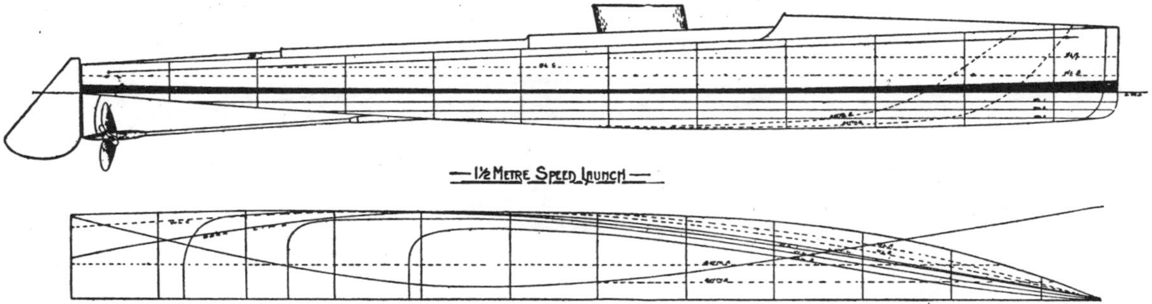

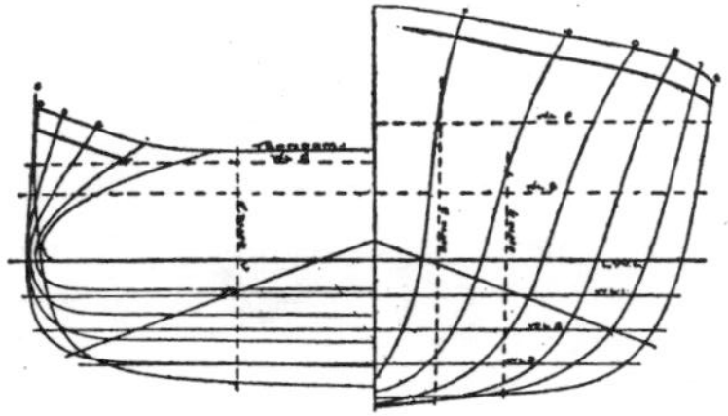

Fig. 793.—1½ metre racing boat, designed by Mr. C. F. Brierley

Fig. 795

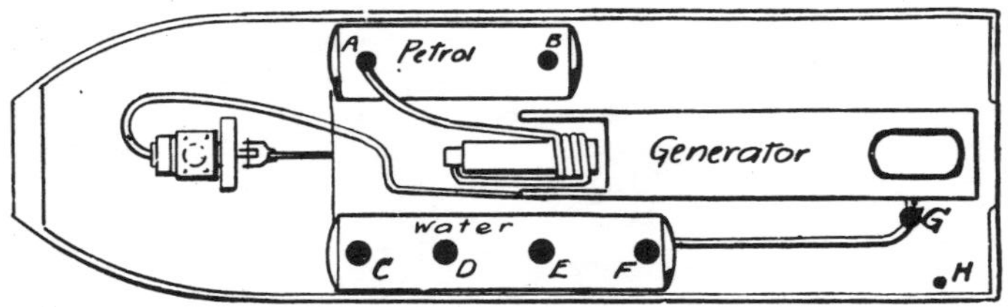

Fig. 794

Figs. 794 and 795.—Model hydroplane with flash boiler

Fig. 797.—Wiring diagram

Fig. 796.—Electrically-driven model torpedo-boat destroyer

as are necessary to make it work, does not deviate from the prototype in any main feature. The other amateur builds a model boat with the sole idea of speed, and the model racing boat has now become a well-known type. Lieut.-Colonel Harvey's 6-ft. 6-in. (two-metre) racer, designed by Mr. C. F. Brierley (Fig. 791), is a typical example. The boiler of the flash type and the 4-to-1 geared force-pump deliver the feed into an air balance tank. In small boats of this type the engine is often placed in front of the boiler, the propeller shaft passing under the boiler (*see* Fig. 792). This allows the shaft to be placed nearer to the truly horizontal line.

Fig. 798.—Electrically-driven model torpedo-boat destroyer

The lines of a $1\frac{1}{2}$-metre (59 in.) racing boat, designed by Mr. C. F. Brierley, are given in Fig. 793. This boat may be built on the "bread and butter" or "layer on layer" principle. The boiler and engine may be arranged as shown in Fig. 792. Another type of model racing boat is the hydroplane. These boats are of square cross section and flat-bottomed, and as stability can be obtained in small sizes they are much favoured by members of racing clubs. The diagrams (Figs. 794 and 795) show a 2-ft. by 7-in. steam-power boat made by Mr. G. D. Noble. The engine is placed near the bow and the funnel near the stern. The hull has a single step; that is, the keelboard is stepped up one-third of the length. The boiler (flash) has a total of **10** ft. of $\frac{3}{16}$-in. by $\frac{1}{4}$-in. steel tube in it, the larger diameter being nearer the engine, which is single-acting with a $\frac{3}{4}$-in. by $\frac{5}{8}$-in. steel cylinder. The boiler is fed on the air-pressure system, as shown, the water container and petrol tank having the following fittings. In Fig. 794, A indicates petrol needle-valve; B, petrol filler and air valve; C, water filler; D, air-pressure valve; E, pressure gauge (200 lb.); F, water supply valve; G, check valve on boiler; H, rudder post. The boat weighs only $6\frac{1}{4}$ lb. in working order, the speed on test was $4\frac{1}{2}$ miles per hour.

Such a craft as just described would, however, be tabooed by many marine model enthusiasts, who believe in modelling well-known types. Figs. 796 to 798 illustrate a model of a torpedo-boat destroyer, which is a favourite prototype among amateurs. This particular boat is driven electrically from an accumulator, a system of propulsion which ensures the least likelihood of damage to deck fittings and also the least possible attention. However, owing to the weight of accumulators, electric boats are seldom very speedy. Fig. 796 shows the electrical connections and also the position of the motor and accumulator. Model torpedo boats, owing to their comparatively small beam, are rather difficult to make stable, for which reason all heavy machinery should be kept well down in the hull and the deck fittings should be as lightly made as possible. Fig. 798 is a photograph of the finished boat made to this design by Mr. G. A. Brown.

CHAPTER XXI

MODEL G.C.R. EXPRESS LOCOMOTIVE

THE Great Central Railway locomotive No. 423, "Sir Sam Fay," is one of the most popular of modern engines, and as a prototype for a small-gauge model it has many favourable points. The boiler is very large; the cylinders are inside the frames, and drive on to the leading coupled wheels. The wheels are six-coupled, and the frames and footplates are raised over the coupling rods, this method saving a good deal of work when it comes to modelling the locomotive. Some illustrations of the locomotive and tender are given by Figs. 799 to 810, and it is regretted that lack of space does not allow of all the details being shown separately.

The gauge for the model is the No. 1 standard, namely, $1\frac{3}{4}$ in. between the rails, and to simplify the mechanism only one double-acting cylinder is used. The boiler is of the water-tube type, the outer shell being no less than $2\frac{1}{2}$ in. in diameter. The inner barrel is $1\frac{3}{4}$ in. in diameter and $10\frac{1}{2}$ in. long over the end plates. This should provide plenty of steam, and the water should enable the locomotive to run for at least twenty minutes with one steaming. The water tubes may either be two $\frac{1}{4}$-in. outside diameter tubes (silver-soldered in) or three $\frac{3}{16}$-in. tubes. The furnace space—due to the particular cylinder and wheel arrangement of the original engine—is very large. Three wick tubes may be employed, two of which are of the rectangular pattern.

The tender is of the six-wheeled type used on all modern Great Central Railway locomotives, and in this model is arranged to carry the spirit tank (on a level of the lamp) and an extra supply above the footplate level. The lower tank can be replenished as required by the small cock shown in the sectional drawing. The steam is superheated—as in modern practice in real locomotives—by passing the steam pipe through the fire and flues.

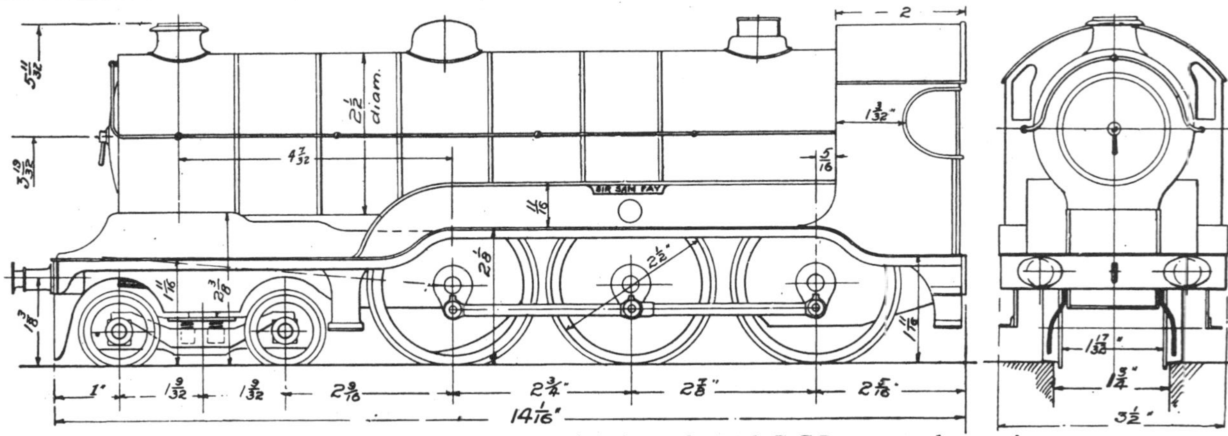

Figs. 799 and 800.—Side and end elevations of model G.C.R. express locomotive

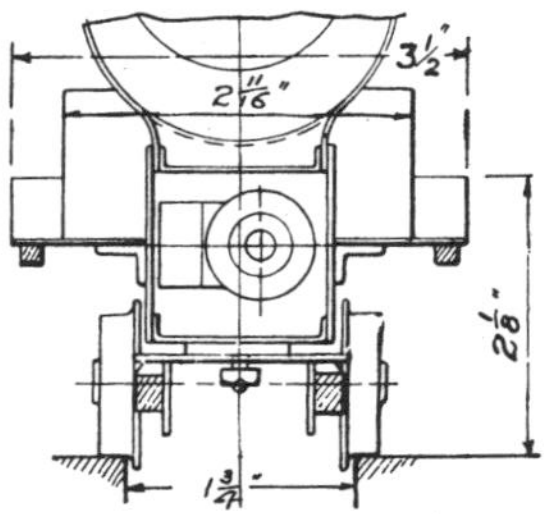

Fig. 801 (to the left).—Cross section at firebox

Fig. 802 (to the right).—General view of model G.C.R. locomotive

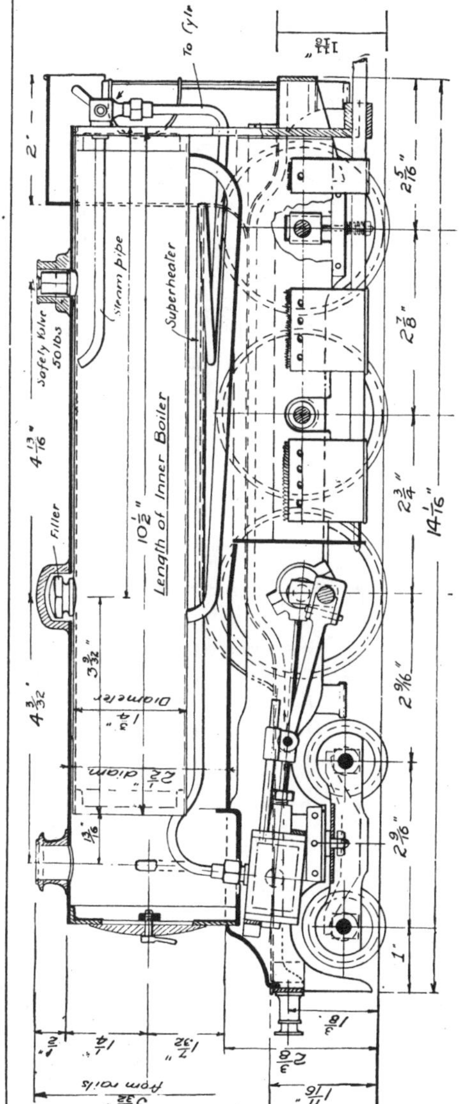

Fig. 803

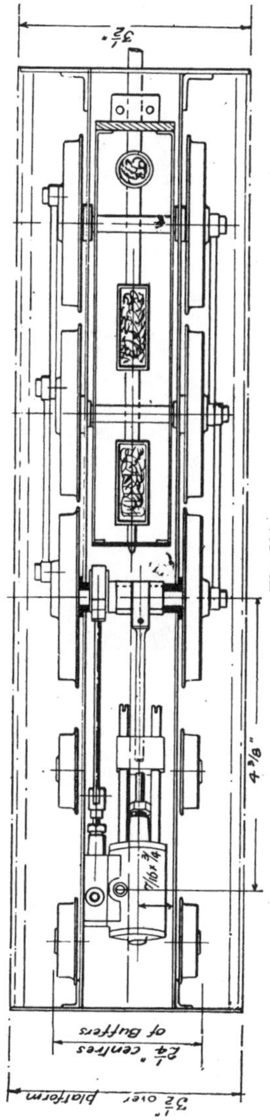

Fig. 804

Figs. 803 and 804.—Vertical section and plan of model G.C.R. express locomotive

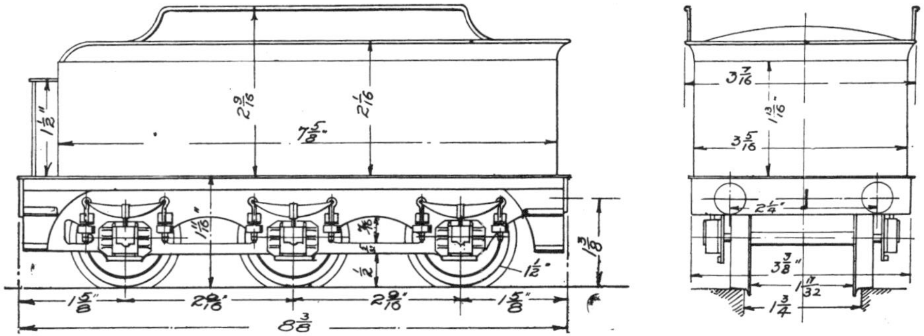

Figs. 805 and 806.—Side and end elevations of tender

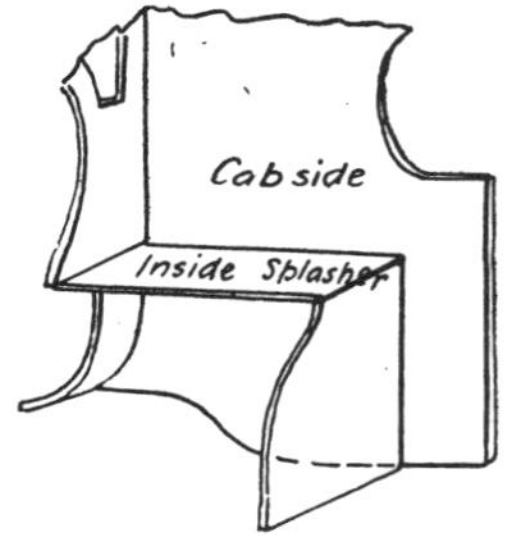

Fig. 810.—Wheel splasher inside cab

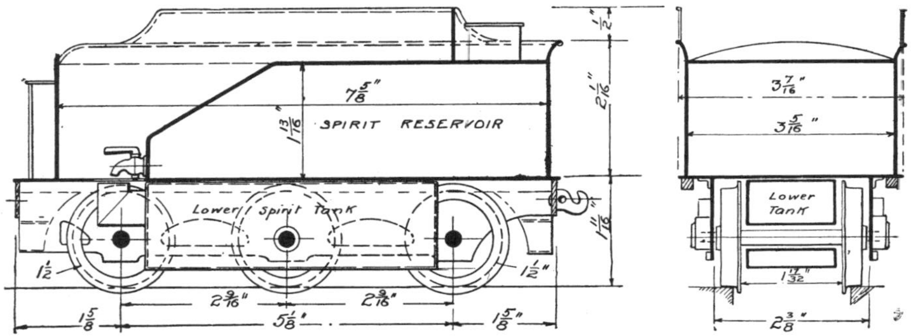

Figs. 807 and 808.—Two vertical sections through tender

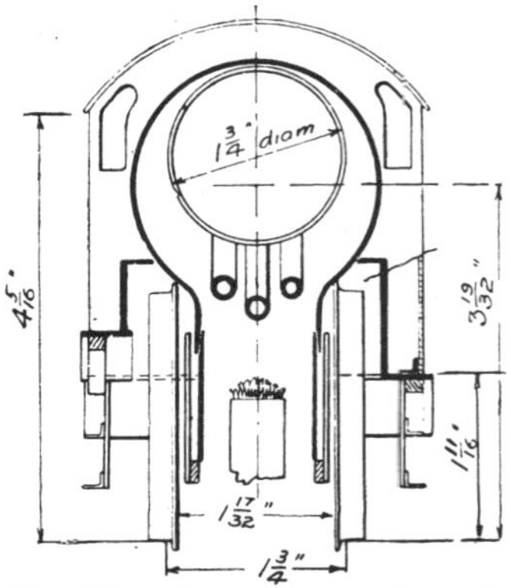

Fig. 809.—Cross section through model locomotive firebox

INDEX